AUTHENTICITY

* * * *

Inimitable Quintessentials

for my Chelsea Arts family

Ben Wright

in this epoch,

Ben
2024

The author has endeavored to observe the legal requirements of previously copyrighted materials and photographs with respect to the rights of the suppliers of the historic documents. The author has attempted to present this information as accurately as possible and expresses regret for any errors or omissions.

All rights reserved. No part of this book may be reproduced or transmitted in any form or by any means, electronic or mechanical, including photocopying, recording, or by any information storage and retrieval system, without permission in writing from the copyright owner.

This book was printed in the United States of America.
Softcover ISBN-13: 978-1502707215

Copyright © 2014 Ben Wright

Mailing address: P. O. Box 382, Hot Springs, Arkansas 71902
E-mail: duendebw@gmail.com

Dedicated To:

Rodman Frates

Saucier Adept

Enhancing Every

Living Moment

For

All

Of

Us

FRONTISPIECE

In 1956, I made a contractual agreement to join NROTC (Naval Reserve Officer Training Corps) at University of Pennsylvania in Philadelphia and was required to attend three classes and one afternoon weekly of Naval Science and military training, the second part being instruction in close-order drill and the sixteen count manual-of-arms with a rifle carried while marching to the orders of our drill instructor, Sergeant-Major Parks, United States Marine Corps, a combat veteran of the fierce fighting at Iwo Jima and Inchon, Korea. This military figure was a formidable and inspiring influence who told these midshipmen (to be commissioned after four years of intensive education and training as Unlimited Line Combat Officers with the rank of Ensign) that contrary to our impression that we might be losing our identities by pledging allegiance and obedience to the naval component of the United States armed forces, especially as we learned to respond automatically to orders delivered on the *grinder* (his slang term for the paved parking lot which had been assigned as our drill field) – we would, each of us, discover our *inimitable self* – that we would come to recognize within us, an identity which only those who have pledged their lives in a higher cause, in defense of their country and their comrades-in-arms, are ever privileged to encounter. to know. to embrace and treasure. When I heard this statement, I reckoned that its author was suffering from "shell-shock" and had no more clarity of cognitive ability than a "punch-drunk" prize-fighter.

However, in the years since that initial military indoctrination, after many career failures, diseases, defeats from drug and alcohol abuse and while serving others in colleges, universities, prisons, and mental institutions to recover from the wounds thereby inflicted to the body, mind and soul, I have come to admit that Sergeant-Major Parks was the sort of Saint Francis in the world of action who would guide my own development and whose inspiring influence would finally deliver to me a *quintessential* understanding of my *inimitable self*. *Quintessential* derives from the word which in Alchemy defines the moment at which transformation from dross material becomes the ethereal and most essential purity [sometimes represented as *golden*] when an elixir is released into the atmosphere and all who ingest or inhale are transformed to a heavenly state [the term, *quark*, in Quantum Physics designates this transfer of material to pure energy; in Spanish culture, the word, *duende*, denotes this crucial event, usually acclaimed with the exclamation of "Ole" in the so-called "moment of truth" in the *faena*, in the bull-fight when the matador and the bull become wedded at this point which can deliver death – and the same exclamation is shouted when the flamenco dancers reach a virtual coital union in their performance [in French poetry there is reference to orgasm as the "little death"]. My self-actualizing experiences which I recount in the following pages will inform the reader as to how I have achieved my *authenticity* and will provide examples of the incidents in my life which have illuminated my awareness of *quintessential inimitable* self and identity.

"Sooner or later … the artifice of entertainment – constant, ceaseless entertainment – will drive most people to seek authenticity. *Authenticity* will be the buzzword of the twenty-first century. And what is authenticity? Anything that is not controlled by corporations. Anything that is not devised and structured to make a profit. Anything that exists for its own sake, that assumes its own shape." *Timeline* (Michael Crichton, *Random House*, 1999, p. 479)

I had wanted to take a slow cruise back to America with one of the Spanish Trans-Mediterranean Company ships which at that time offered cabins for a transit on their line from Algeciras to the Canary Islands to Miami, but Marian insisted that we fly home, and yet did agree to a stop-over in Jamaica and the Virgin Islands and then a weekend in New Orleans as a sort of cultural cushioning for the re-entry to our country. Jamaica became a blur of rum drinks, marijuana, hashish, and a vicarious dabbling in our acquaintance with the new Rastafarian revolutionary rage which had beset the land as the people freed themselves from their yoke of British colonialism and began the process of independent self-rule with a democratic new autonomous republic. Bob Marley's music had provided the Hossanas which proclaimed and worshiped the Ethiopian king, Haile Selassi, as a reincarnation of a true messiah to all the Africans displaced from their original homes and cultural identities by European slave traders to this island paradise. Marian became so enamored by the music and the political movement that I was amazed that her extreme right-wing Republican soul could be so seduced and subverted by Reggae tunes and radical revolutionary rhetoric that accompanied *the beat*. The rum and susurrussing gentle surf and swaying of palm trees in our cabana on the beach there had a complementary affect on her subconscious transference. I was so pleased that she could adapt sympathetically to this radical political movement, and yet I knew that *this honeymoon*, as well as our own, would most likely be over, done with and repressed and rejected, once she reunited with her roots in that mansion on Fremont Place, Los Angeles: the reactionary redoubt of her family's arch-conservatism, the nest whence derived most of her belief system and soul impulses, regardless of her swaying now to the African rhythms of the sheik in dreadlocks, the animistic, atavistic magician of the islands, Bob Marley.

When we tore ourselves away to hop over to the more conventional Virgin Islands, still very much under the rule and influence of their British and Danish colonialist developers, Marian suffered withdrawal reactions [there was no cannabis available on any street corner or even in the dingiest bars in the Virgin Islands] for the first few days whose suffering were curbed only by increased doses of handsful of Valiums and increased quantities of rum and vodka. We learned to snorkel and explored some of the more remote lagoons and bays by driving a jeep four-wheeler through some dense jungled wilderness, until I had the misfortune of stepping on a spiny sea anemone, virtually crippling my entire left foot. The pain of operating the foot pedal clutch was excruciating, driving out of that remote beach, shifting several times up and down to negotiate the terrain before arriving at a clinic where a native nurse tried to extract the spines. Finding them so deeply imbedded they would not emerge, he then recommended that I soak the throbbing foot in heated urine for an hour or more, a method I tried for several days thereafter, but finally went to a proper hospital in Christenstad where an actual trained surgeon extracted the spines with scalpel and tweezers. As the aneasthetic wore off in the days following the surgery, I utilized Marian's remedies of rum and Valium and her Empirin Compound heavy-duty pain-killers which she employed for her heavier cramps during menstruation or those crippling episodes she had with cystitis.

So when we left the Virgin Islands and flew into New Orleans, we both were so heavily intoxicated with alcohol and narcotic pain-killers that we must have appeared to be dangerously under the influence of perhaps illegal chemical substances, that we were invited to leave the Customs Inspection line and were placed in a separate room where several agents of Immigration and those federal authorities for Dangerous Drugs and Firearms began asking us leading questions. This melodramatic scenario, intended to intimidate and terrify us, in actual fact so amused us that we began acting up and giggling in glee – not the best way to return to one's homeland. If this had happened in today's environment of paranoid governmental suspicion and repression of basic human rights, we would have probably both been placed in solitary confinement in Guantanamo Bay, Cuba, and water-boarded – at the very least – for the next few months. What most seemed to confuse and even offend these starchy interrogators were the many large glossy photos they found in our bags. The people with whom we appeared posed or candidly lolling about with, were some of the most famous film actors of that time: Vince Edwards, Jack Palance, George Maharis and others whose images were daily seen in the television programs in which they starred in America and were projected and broadcast around the world. It was Marian's insouciant and virtually patronizing manner and vocal delivery that relieved us of much more harassment. Her Marlborough School and Wellesley College signature accents impressed our antagonists more than I would imagine they would care to admit. Whoever said there is no class system in America? Just as in England, where social strata markers ring from the mouths of all speakers, from the broad Cockney working-class to the *plummy* Royal mumbles, too highly situated in the social scale to ever be bothered with pronouncing words distinctly, as this might be too much like *work* - relegated to the plebeians -or, any of those below the ranks of the peerage and their blood relatives. Marian's accent was amazingly similar to that distinct ring projected by members of the Ruling Class of England, sounding as if she had a pencil slammed back in her mouth between the molars, so that what issued miraculously was richer than gold or any such base substance of mere monetary denomination. Hers was truly a *class act*.

"Really, my Dear Fellows, these photos are indeed of our most intimate friends, taken while we were doing a film in Spain, up in the Guadarama mountains, above Madrid, just last month. But cold. Look at the pull-overs and fleece-lined jackets we were bundled in. See Kate O'Mara there in a period frock, but bundled up under a bomber jacket, with a full sheep's hide around her neck and bodice. And Neville Brand and Vince Edwards in their cowboy costumes - see those long-barreled revolvers in the holsters on their gun-belts - but note that they are also tucked well into heavily padded overcoats. Neville looks rather like that dear old Chinese leader - what is his name - Mao, the one who's always jumping in the Yalu river swimming his laps when he's not strutting around in his flak jacket waving that little red book."

She spoke as if she were addressing a classroom of her own species, forgetting that her references to these movie stars and that political giant (Chairman Mao), one of America's arch enemies at that time, as if they were neighborhood playmates in a playground available to all, and where the rules were to protect the privileged and amuse them in diversion from their other lofty, much more important concerns.

"My husband was their professor. He's returning to University of California, the one in La Jolla [that precious Southern California coastal village which everyone knew boasted the highest income per capita, per square foot, of any community in America, except for perhaps Scarsdale , New York, or Sea Island, Georgia] , where he is teaching Humanities and Philosophy. Jack [Palance] and Neville [Brand] and Vince [Edwards] and George [Maharis] were his little pupils on location. They had to toe the mark and deliver their lines to his satisfaction before the director, that old dear Henry Levin, would allow them to be recorded in his film prints and recordings. And some of them were rather backward, and virtual retards. George [Maharis] has such a strong New York accent that my husband had to keep him after school, as it were, before he could sound like the part written for him - a Missouri farm-boy who served in the Civil War as a Confederate infantry-man, transformed into gunslinger in Quantrill's Raiders."

I protested politely that George Maharis was actually a most willing and talented student, but agreed that the accent had been tricky for him to maintain in every scene throughout the film.

" Well, you know very well, and you confided in me when you came home some days from working wirh George, that without Jack Palance's help in guiding George, you would have been tempted to give up."

"Sure, Jack is a consummate actor and both he and George come from roughly the same region, and had considerable off-broadway theatre experince in common. But Jack is one of the most convincing people I've ever met. One does not argue readily or easily with that man ... ".

As we had begun to natter on about our film pals, the agents decided to usher us out of the office and usher us back on in to our country as approved goods. Not exactly U.S. Prime, but as the saying goes , 'Good enough for government work'.

Were they star-struck, or merely becoming bored? Had we responded to their intended intimidation or inquisition in a manner they had never been trained to deal with? Where was the instruction manual on cases such as ours? There was no practicable frame of reference for them to employ to continue harassing us unless they could find some weapons [when they encountered Marian's hunting knife which I had returned to her on her arrival in Madrid, I told them she used it only for cleaning her fingernails] or prohibited pharmaceutical substances other than the pain-killers and Valiums Marian carried in huge quantities - but accompanied by prescriptions from her physicians. So we continued our banter as we were released on to the streets of that magical city, New Orleans. We found a funky old hotel in the French Quarter that looked like the set for any number of film-noir productions - Sam Spade in the 1930s - and felt delighted with our discovery. I called an old friend of mine from college named Jim Travis, and he met us for dinner, amazed that we should have found ourselves such a place which he told us had a rich history of debauchery and crime which even in this town was extraordinary, rather like that hotel in New York City, the Chelsea.

Jim was an established businessman in town, and so he contacted his travel agency to book our train tickets for the journey we had projected by rail across the lower portion of the country, to eventually deliver us to the famed Union Station in Los Angeles. We decided to leave within the next forty-eight hours, but were still able to saunter about Jackson Square, and then we visited Tennessee Williams' former street of residence, before swaggering up and down Bourbon Street, satisfied with the street performers and not lured into any of the over-priced restaurants or strip joints, but savoring many of the side-walk cafes offerings, especially as we returned to the old wharves and drank the coffee laced with chicory and sampled the pastries there as well.

As I was still drawing on the large roll of bills I had been paid in Madrid, I did not hesitate in buying us a Pullman compartment First Class all the way to Los Angeles. I was comforted to remember that I had left some money in my checking account in San Diego, so even if my cash-roll should soon be exhausted, we could set up our residence in the La Jolla, or even Del Mar area when I returned to my graduate work and the Teaching Assistant's Fellowship I had been promised by Professor Andrew Wright, director of my doctoral program. Curiously, Marian had never offered to contribute financially. I was later to learn that she had always available to her an unlimited amount of money from trust funds, but never did she offer to provide any cash for any expenditure, and this had been true in our travels across Europe hitch-hiking and later on the boat with Sam. Although we had to endure some extreme hardships when I could not pay for lodgings - once we even slept in our tent in the garden of a guest-house which charged merely a minimal fee and allowed us to use their back-door toilet – she had never offered to contribute anything to our communal funding. When I once had asked her why she did not contribute to our mutual living expenses, she answered unequivocally, "A man pays for his woman."

Just how much I would eventually pay for the privilege of marrying Marian, I would not have been prepared to believe if I had been told at this point in our still deeply satisfying honeymoon. Our sexual relationship was not extraordinary. Satisfying, but nothing special. Neither one of us were particularly adept at any of the more extreme variations of basic coupling. Our Kama Sutra manual would number no more than four basic positions, and the passion we expressed was rather that of two middle-aged friends and not the quality of starry-eyed teenagers. We were neither, but I felt comfortable with our union. Our sweetest moments were when we were propped up on pillows together in bed reading and sharing what we found in our preferred texts.

We had begun our entire affair in this fashion, after all, those many years ago when the young Ensign Wright, recent Honors graduate of an Ivy League university had visited the Crawfords at Fremont Place and had chattered endlessly with their precocious daughter about books. I had given her a list of my favorites from the World Literature course, a challenge to any talented and advanced undergraduate, and she had devoured all in a period of weeks, not the three months allotted that particular course term, and she seemed to understand them all. It was only later that I began to suspect an aberration in Marian's intellectual gifts. She probably was a victim of a form of autism which some literary critics also later diagnosed with her own favorite author, Vladimir Nabokov: Asperger's syndrome. She could read at lightning speed, remember virtually everything on a page – a truly photographic memory such as President John F. Kennedy supposedly possessed – but she was hard-pressed to comprehend any congruent comparative relationships between groups of ideas or thematic resonances. Something on the order of Sherlock Holmes's criticism of Dr. Watson: "You see, but you do not observe" – but so yawning a disparity that sometimes her conversations sounded like verbal renditions of Jackson Pollock's splash orchestrated canvasses. Forms and colors appeared in abundance, clusters that begged for interpretation, but they were inchoate; very little was connected, except perhaps in the eye or mind of the beholder. Marian's Senior Honors thesis which she wrote while attending classes at the Sorbonne in Paris was considered by her approving department at Wellesley to be a work of genius. She had stitched together a pastische representation of Nabokov's life-work that served as a re-presentation of his creative genius which only a mind capable of his own bizarre and inimitable metaphoric leaps could have engineered. They were birds of a feather, flighting in a vortex of literary expression that was at once centrifugal and centripetal: linguistic exempla of the astrophysicist Stephen Hawking's discovery of Black Holes being the nether end of galaxies.

But Marian would sometimes burst into tears as she tried to express the frustration she experienced whenever she looked at lines of poetry on a page, or even heard that subject mentioned She just could not understand the basic notion of metaphor, and levels of ambiguity enraged her. She craved specificity. Hard evidential data. I was heart-broken that I could not begin to lead her through this labyrinth, the imagistic archipelago that comprises the essence of the poetic experience. Marian's limited sensibility deficiency extended into the musical realm as well, or rather, did not allow her to enter that realm at all. She did not enjoy listening to music. It was all noise as far as she was concerned. Reminiscent of Muffy Taylor's remarks when she heard classical music playing in my home at University of Pennsylvania: "church music" - that's what Muffy said that it sounded like to her; and it was not something she relished. For Marian it was all just noise. And the lyrics? Poetry! Too much like that literary nonsense for her to abide it for long. Fiction could be bearable because there was a narrative formula, a logical sequential process. But poetry, and therefore, music? This was forbidden territory for us to enter. I must go there alone, but never to expect my bride to accompany me unless blind-folded and deafened by ear-plugs. So how were we to continue our companionship outside any territory where these threatening cultural factors might lurk? Easy enough. I read my own selections to myself, sometimes poetic, and did not discuss them with her, and when I had music playing on a radio, I simply switched it off when my love entered the room.

Our train trip across to Los Angeles was elegant, relaxing, but uneventful. I cherish recalling a sense of feeling eminently self-satisfied as I smoked a cigar and drank Scotch whiskey and looked across the posh First Class compartment at my wife as our coach hurtled through the barren wastelands of the Great American Plains. Were these *the good old days* we would look back on fondly and nudge each other saying, "Do you remember that trip, darling"? We would need many such nostalgic recollections to comfort and console us from the next succeeding months in adjusting to our new home.

Our first encounter in Grand Union Station was with Marian's family, that is Chuck and Madeline ("The girls at Marlborough always just called me Mad, but you can call me Mom" - I demurred and addressed her as Madeline). In place of a porter to assist us with our baggage, they had brought the Iranian house-boy Allie, but as we had only two bags, which I could easily heft alone, I did allow him to carry one, and I swaggered along beside him with the other one.

When we arrived in the circular drive at the Fremont Place mansion and parked, I followed Allie to the front door, but was blocked by Chuck as I stepped over the threshold. He held his hand against my chest and attempted to look menacing and immovable.

"Not so fast there, Mister. No bearded, long-haired hippies are allowed in Fremont Place. I'll go upstairs for my clippers and electric razor, but you'll have to clean up before you come into this house."

So there it was. Our first actual confrontation with the *powers-that-be*. Mr. *Whiteman* Republican challenges the Wild Radical Ravisher of his daughter on the border of his sacred homeland fortress. A new version of "Birth of a Nation", D.W. Griffith's alarm to White America of the growing threat from the unwashed, unclean, low-down, Negroid rapist gangs about to pounce on their fainting white women ... and robbing all their money too. I looked back at Marian, and smiled. I am certain that I startled her when I shrugged and sat down on the doorstoop and agreed to at least have a shave.

"Sure. Bring the clippers and the razor. I meant to visit a barber before we arrived, but we were running short of time. I can do the beard and shave the whole face right out here in nature's own beauty salon, but I would rather go to a proper barber in town for the hair and perhaps some styling."

After I had thus demonstrated my sincere intention to comply with the family's tonsorial ordinances by applying the clippers to remove the beard and mustache, I was invited indoors to utilize the complete bathroom facilities, upstairs, in the master bedroom where Chuck loaned me his own razor and grunted approval as I cleared away all whiskers from my entire facial area. My skin was pink and vulnerable, and I felt as if I had been sorely wounded. I could well imagine the castrated sensations Samson must have experienced when he was shorn of all his hair and felt deprived of his masculine prowess. However, I still had the ample hair on my head which hung almost to my shoulders, and I could see Chuck lurking behind me with a sort of hunger in his eyes as he assayed the remaining hirsute affront.

Germany's World War Two concentration camps shaved the hair of the men and women, ostensibly as a sanitary measures, but the effect was hideously demoralizing to the Orthodox Jews, especially the Hassidim for who the long hair was synonymous with devotion to God and one's distinctive masculine identity. The shower I was invited to take that day, was not the chemical composition offered those unfortunate victims of genocidal pogrom, but I was not as yet comfortable in my new abode, hoping that Marian and I would not be staying longer than a very few days before going to La Jolla to set up residence for my return to studies at U.C.S.D. She had become like a child again, and in fact, she began spending long hours in her old bedroom which bore all the marks of a teenage girl's boudoir. As I settled in there, I felt something like a vicarious child-molester.

There was a declaration of Marian's identity in that physical space which did not allow for the presence of a grown man, especially one who would crawl in to the bed with her and reach out for her body in a most adult carnal manner as I needed to do so more purposefully now, or so it seemed, to assert my sense of masculinity. The next alteration of my sense of identity came the following day when Chuck declared that we would now visit his barber, downtown, so that I would be presentable enough for my first visit to the California Club, the stronghold of all the ancient guardians of the Establishment in that state. Although I had my Brooks Brothers blue blazer and a Glen Plaid suit from that same eminent Eastern Seaboard clothier and a few button-down Oxford cloth shirts and "rep" ties, he suggested we pay a visit to his own tailor some time soon, to put the final stamp on my new image. Would I begin to look like the son he had never had? Would I look like a bastard of Ronald Reagan, or even more terrifying, some of the other more dreadful, close friends of this family: Richard Nixon, and his *hench-people* - Erlichmann and Halderman? Where would all the genes of Eliza Rogers go? Must I even send my love of poetry to the Stepford Wives second-hand rumble sale? I tried to remember if I had seen *any* body hair on Chuck the last time we had been swimming in the family pool in the back garden. Would I be asked to shave under my arms and remove all the hair from my chest ... and my legs? How far did this Republican cleansing obsession reach? Were they all taking a high-colonic every morning?

Fortunately, I suppose, Marian and I left Los Angeles before I could be introduced to Chuck's tailor. Most of the suits he wore appeared to be of the same Hickey Freeman style my father had: wide lapels, ample-waisted and baggy-legged so that very little of the wearer's body was revealed. The general visual effect was that of a wide presence: sturdy and substantial, the signature of a businessman, a pillar of the community, reluctant to back down, intent on forging ahead – all the personality traits of the M*over and Shaker*, the C*aptain of Industry*. And not an image that I was as yet prepared to assume – if ever. When we arrived on campus in La Jolla, many of my doctoral candidate fellows looked at me as if I had betrayed the cause – whatever that was. I certainly did not display my former scruffy features, and most of the faculty in the Literature Department greeted me more warmly than I had expected, and I noticed that we had a striking similarity in our outward features, especially as I had now become clean shaven and wore a virtual military haircut. This was actually the department stamp, following the model of Roy Harvey Pearce, Robert Elliot, and Andrew Wright. Andy, as he demanded he be called, had actually served with the O.S.S as a commando in the Second World War. Robert Elliot had become a naval officer in that conflict and had served aboard combat vessels in the Pacific. So there was a model for this look, and I was now becoming more accepted by those in charge of our academic *discipline*.

After little more than a brief welcome home chat, Andy, director of my doctoral program, informed me that I would be scheduled for the examinations at the end of the first term of courses, in the last week of November. My next shock was to learn that I had been loaned out to the Philosophy Department as a Teaching Instructor to assist the notorious Herbert Marcuse in teaching his version of a Freshman introductory Humanities course. Although I knew of the man from some encounters on campus, notably when he had presided in some debates about Civil Rights Issues and the Viet Nam War that had become rousing public events in the Revelle College plaza, often attracting media coversage from national network crews. Only a few months before, he had joined the radical psychologist R. D. Laing in declaring an international manifesto from the Roundhouse Theatre in

London; and in Paris, that April, students had taken to the street, rioting and arousing world attention under the banner: MAO. MARX, MARCUSE! I had read in *Time* and *Newsweek* while I was still in Madrid, at that same time, that Marcuse was considered the undisputed leader of the new political movement, the New Left, which had seized the hearts and souls of students everywhere. His own doctoral candidate student, Angela Davis, now an instructor at U.C.L.A., was a sort of latter day Boadicea, leading the hordes of his followers, although she had been branded a pawn of Stalinist Russian political ideology as she had admitted to being a member of the Amercian Communist Party [Mort Sahl had quipped that the only dues-paying members of the American Communist Party were undercover F.B.I. agents]. On the day I went to meet my new Humanities professor, on the floor that housed the Philosophy department above the main library, I was first invited to be accepted into that particular fold by the Chair of Philosophy. As I sat down for my briefing, I realized that my appearance was noted by secretary and various graduate students, and I became aware that I might represent the great bourgeoise outsider to these – with the exception of the Chair himself – scruffy, and ragamuffin inhabitants of this academic realm, those dedicated to questioning and confronting the *status quo*, the Establishment. The chief of the department assured me that Marcuse had examined my credentials and that he, himself, as chair of the department was satisfied that I could cope with the curriculum which Marcuse proposed to present in this segment of the Humanities sequence. Popkin then made a rather odd remark. He said that he was most favorably impressed by how I was dressed and groomed, telling me that Marcuse would be particularly pleased by my appearance, as he was definitely an academic of the Old School. I was wearing a Navy blue blazer and charcoal grey trousers with a button-down Oxford cloth shirt and a *rep* tie, thereby broadcasting what was then called the Ivy League or Preppy style.

When I entered Marcuse's office, he did seem pleased to meet me, and as we sat down to discuss the course I would be assisting him in teaching, I felt that he had accepted me and endorsed my qualifications with little more than a few European gestures which I felt reassured by. We even smoked the same small cigarillos, and at that time it was a bonding ritual to join in taking a smoke, as we did that day in his office. I was somewhat surprised when his doctoral candidate, Angela Davis joined us for some idle chat after I had settled in and was just about to bid farewell. Herbert encouraged me to stay so as to become better acquainted wih this formidable lady. We actually knew each other from chance encounters in the library and in the student union cafeteria, but I had never had much chance, nor had I any inclination before, to establish a more personal relationship with her. We discovered that afternoon that we both were preparing to take our doctoral qualifying examinations – both written and oral – at the same time in November. Somehow, I had considered that she was far ahead of me in her candidacy because she was now an instructor at U.C.L.A. However she had completed only one year more than I in graduate work as she had studied one year in Germany before arriving to begin her formal training in Philosophy with Marcuse in California. She had already selected her dissertation topic, and it was to be a fresh investigation of the philosopher Emmanel Kant. I still felt in awe of her academic credentials as she had been an undergraduate at the Philadelphia Main Line college, Swarthmore, and then had studied at the Sorbonne in Paris before going on to Germany. She possessed an easy fluency in both those languages that had always seemed impossible for me to master. And yet we were both from the same part of the country, and as we conversed, we discovered that we both had Cherokee grandparents.

Actually, we could have been distant cousins. She certainly did have several personality traits and signature qualities of character that appeared in my family; especially the stubborn self-reliance and something bordering on arrogance, which I considered a justifiable pridefulness, but others found threatening, and would sometimes confront, or dismiss as insouciance. We actually came to like each other, and Herbert Marcuse was pleased by this. Although we were not to teach with one another, Marcuse on later occasions, in my presence, told her that I was as effective an instructor as she, and then would remark that he had never encountered such good teachers. High praise from Caesar, indeed. Actually, in some of the meetings the professor conducted with the other teaching assistants, I was held up to them as an example of an ideal instructor. My technique was actually dynamic adaptation of the Socratic method. I began by interrogation, then posed rhetorical questions and somehow got students involved in heated debates in my classrooms, without ever really leaving the arena as resource agent and arbiter of the more angry assaults that might fulminate. I rarely lectured for more than a few minutes, and that was merely to explain the ground-rules and insure that certain philosophical definitions were abided by or referred to in the classroom discussions.

What a delight it was to teach for this remarkable man. He thoroughly enjoyed the lectures he delivered to the Freshman students who crowded the auditorium once weekly to hear him present the main lecture material which was then further examined by the teaching assistants who held two seminars as follow-up for discussion and the assignment of essays to insure understanding, comprehension, and to elicit any further inquiries regarding these learning experiences. Marcuse was keenly interested in discovering if any of the students could produce questions in these classes that he could then incorporate into his subsequent lectures in development of the entire course. Although this professor was world-famous for his theory of "repressive tolerance" and had been renowned for his interpretations of Freud, particularly in regard to Marx, in the contemporary moralistic realm, rivaled only by Norman O. Brown, the dynamic Sociology professor at another University of California campus, Marcuse's humility on the podium delivering a lecture to teenaged American students, I found to be incredibly candid, relaxed, relevant, and immediately understandable and palatable. I particularly remember the manner in which he introduced the subject of Freud as we began our study of Freud's, *Civilization and Its Discontents*. Herbert stepped away from the lectern and walked off the main stage to stand on the floor of the lecture hall, and then he casually strode back and forth before the audience, as he chatted about how intimidating a famous lecturer might seem if he were wearing the mantle of office and remained in that authoritarian position when delivering his opinion. He, meanwhile, was opening the jacket of his suit and loosening his tie as he spoke.

"Do we remember the Twentieth Century as the age of Freud or Ford? Was the sexual revolution or the manufacturing assembly line the most essential cultural influence of the past century?" Herbert played with these notions and queried how they impacted on the average person's existence, and then moved effortlessly on to the particulars of the seminal theories of the father of Psychology (Freud). He presented the Freudian paradigm in a most readily understandable form as he cited the first of the components of the Subconscious (the Id):

Thanatos and Eros. When he said the name of the latter, Eros, the creative energy that generated sublimation and all artistic production in human life, he stopped ... and looking about impishly ... presented the following caricature of himself.

Stripping his suit jacket off and flinging it back onto the stage, Marcuse then swept the palms of his hands up through his hair and then brought them down to his chest and mid-section, as if he were scrubbing his body with them, as he began a monologue in a lower pitch, almost crooning.

"The great professor bathes himself, never in his suit or academic gown. Bare and completely naked. As he sits in the tub, reaching down to soap himself, he sees between his legs a small pink object. It is not a toy. It is not a loofa. It is not the rag, for he has that in his hand. This small pink thing, floating there, attached to his lower belly is what he knows to be the representation on his body of that concept which Freud called Eros. It is not a winged cupid flying in the air. It is real. It is attached to his living body. It has feeling ... sensation. This is the real Eros. The creative power. The source of all beauty and art in man's life." He stopped and looked about him, his eyebrows arching in humorous grimace, and he laughed as he picked up his jacket and climbed back on stage toward the lectern.

Most of the students *got it* and were howling with laughter. The *old fart* was talking about his *pecker*. He was describing his penis floating in the bath-water, and the image was unmistakably linked to the concept of the Erotic, that organ of regeneration, the impulse of creativity, Freud's sexual component of the Id in the Subconscious.

Eros in Action.

Afterwards, when some of the teaching assistants were assembled in his office, Herbert was delighted to replay the incident, and that was the first time I heard him pay a compliment to my teaching. As we were praising the professor on his stand-up comic demeanor when he had delivered the dynamite lines about his penis and Cupid and the Id, he rounded on the assembled student teachers and pointed at me saying that I was a model of this sort of attention-grabbing technique. I did recall that one of his graduate students had asked permission to sit in on a few of my classes, and it was that this person had reported to Marcuse some of the more outrageous analogies I, myself, had drawn between the assigned lecture material and real-life experience. I particularly recalled the image that Freud provided of prehistoric Man encountering a smoldering tree trunk which had been struck by lightning and thence was consumed in flame. I had offered a cartoon Flintstones scenario of the males competing with each other in extinguishing some of the smaller flaming portions of wood by arcing their urinary streams on to the tree, and then their women companions, who by nature of their essentially different biology, therefore could not participate, chiding the men, making jokes about their silly game, and convincing them to drag the remaining ignited fragments in to the cave-dwelling to warm them from the frosty weather; and there it was that one of the animals, perhaps an early domesticated canine had been rolled into the embers, roasted, and provided the first cooked meal - an unintentional, but nonetheless, savory *first barbecue* - in history. Civilization, as we know it, was thus born. Man utilizing the elements to improve his standard of living. So, what costs have we had to pay, to bring us to the assembly-line hamburger and automobile and instantaneous world-wide telecommunications: MacDonald's, Ford, and A.T.& T. / N.B.C [this was well before Internet and Micro-Soft]. I then challenged any student to justify why he or she should have to be sitting in a classroom at their age of physical maturity when they would have – in fact – been qualified as hunter-gatherers and breeders for at least the past six to eight years. Why must their full entry into normal human society be postponed till they achieved an undergraduate or graduate degree, which could demand the expenditure of another six to eight years in academic *apprenticeship*. What were the "discontents' of our current "civilization"?

This particular class had become such a turmoil of debate and venting of some, till then, repressed anxieties, that the discussion spilled out on to the plaza where many of us remained during the lunch-hour and then, only reluctantly, did bid farewell, till next class meeting.

"This young man is a teacher. He shows them how to learn, to inquire. The true Socratic method. Do what he does, and the student will become a teacher too, and a responsible, moral citizen."

Thus spake Herr Professor! If I never again receive such praise, I shall forever indeed be satisfied that my professorial vocation was [at least, so it seemed, at that precious moment] truly realized. I had been recognized as a teacher, by one of the greatest ones in history. Ominously, and coincidentally, Marian's parents decided at about this time to officially proclaim their approval of our marriage, to endorse us as *bona fide* members of Los Angeles society. What an irony. What a hoot. What the hell?

I had just been accepted and embraced as a vital member of the inner cadre of this inspiring leader of the international movement called The New Left, and coincidentally, synchronistically, at the same time in my history and in the unfolding contemporary history-in-the-making of the new student revolution, I was to be ushered in to the *sanctum sanctorum* of one of the most arch-conservative segments of American West Coast Fascist families! Contradictory? Potentially explosive? Destined for disaster? How was this happening?

Marian had not revealed to her family what my occupation actually was. She had led them to believe that I was serving as a sort of factotum research assistant and part-time teaching aid to various faculty members at U.C.S.D.'s Revelle College campus. She herself was not aware of the reputation of Marcuse, and because Angela Davis was actually employed at U.C.L.A. at this time, she was not close enough to be a possible "contaminating" influence, as far as Marian reckoned it. I did try to explain the situation to Marian, but she was really quite oblivious to the actuality of the historical moment. She would sometimes refer to these people as my pet projects: "Those pitiful Jews and Negroes you find so diverting; you always will enjoy the plight of the underdog and the unwashed heathens". She really did not credit these people with having any impact on the contemporary world which was still ruled by her family's friends, Richard Nixon and Ronald Reagan, and the Military Industrial Complex. I do remember encountering Haldeman's mother having a chat with Marian's mother in the Fremont Place garden one afternoon. I heard the woman make reference to the morning prayer sessions Billy Grahame held in Nixon's presidential, oval office, and then I thought I heard her say that they would read a passage from *Mein*

Kampf. Surely I did not hear that! I do remember asking her if that was the book she had mentioned (Adolf Hitler's biographical Bible), and the woman said that the entire staff believed that they could learn a great deal from that book. Surely I had only imagined that conversation. It was not till many years later [1980, when I was teaching at University of Miami and living in Coconut Grove], when I had lunch with G. Gordon Liddy in Miami, Florida, where a friend of mine was arranging with him to do a television interview with this member of Nixon's Watergate "Plumber Squad" that I was able to attempt to ascertain if I had indeed understood Mrs. Haldeman correctly. Liddy affirmed and confirmed this. Of course there were readings of Mein Kampf in the oval office with president and staff, he proudly asserted. Liddy himself had loudly sung the Nazi Storm-Trooper's anthem, the Horst Wessel song his entire time in prison to let the Blacks and ethnic minorities resident there know just what his beliefs were. He then said that he would expect me to join in the next Grand Movement to establish the Reich in our own *fatherland,* that my work undermining the Holy Cause would be forgiven as I had the mettle of the kind of soldier who would be necessary to recruit for that final takeover.

I demurred. I told the man that he was truly and certifiably mad to ever imagine I, or any sane person would want to be swept up in his megalomania and Fascist fervor. Yet American foreign and domestic policy today does indeed appear to show me up as the deluded one, and he, now a successful and richly rewarded radio program producer and highly paid public speaker, is realizing the fruits of what then appeared to me to be his demented illusions. However, even in that year when I met Liddy, students throughout America were concerned to know that their government was not enacting harm upon the people of other nations. They had protested the war in Viet Nam and many were alarmed by the violation of Human Rights in South Africa, and only shortly thereafter, with the release of the film 'Cry Freedom' and the album by Peter Gabriel, 'Biko' which decried and condemned the torture and beating to death of the civil rights leader Stephen Biko by police in South Africa had become a rallying cry for the release from prison of Nelson Mandela who then was elected president of that country.   Now there are few if any protests by students or anyone else on behalf of all those civilians being killed in Afghanistan and Iraq whose deaths our political leaders dismiss as meaningless "collateral damage". No wonder that Libby and his ilk are so popular and successful today. There is an impressive building in Washington, D.C. which has been named in honor of one of the most racist, and sexist power-mongers, J. Edgar Hoover.   I am only surprised that no public parks or communal toilet facilities in that area have not been named in honor of his live-in homosexual lover, Clyde. There is still time. There is time.

The reception held at Fremont Place, in the Crawford home for the newly-weds, Ben Wright and their daughter, Marlborough and Wellesley graduate, Marian, whose debutante ball had been a featured event at the Beverly Hills Hotel only five years before, received a full two columns on the *Los Angeles Times* page in the Sunday edition. Fully half of one entire column was occupied by a photo of the couple (Marian and I) sitting by the family swimming pool looking adoringly at one another. I was startled at how military my pose appeared to be, but with a three-piece suit, a "regulation" short haircut and a clean-shaven face, I looked as anonymous and socially acceptable as any palace eunuch could be. Marian glowed. We actually were happy, although she was given to starting her cocktail hours earlier now that we were esconced in the family home. Some days she was already slurring her consonants before lunch-time. It was only two months later when we had returned to La Jolla that my Literature Department office mate, David Burns, asked me politely if Marian had always had a weight problem. I only then noticed that she indeed now waddled and that her hips had become grossly enlarged. She rarely rose from bed before afternoon since we had moved back to La Jolla, and more and more often, she sought excuses to spend days on end at Fremont Place where she could be even more sluggish and bedroom-bound. I remember the party as being large and glittering, but I was disappointed that none of the Hollywood personalities with whom we had worked in Madrid were in attendance. Only somewhat later did I learn that Marian's family thought it better to not mail those invitations which I personally had addressed and signed. There was some off-hand remark made about a cousin who had become head of one of the major film studios, and he was referred to as if he had "come to no good end", whether that was merely *ipso facto* his involvement with the film industry - "show-biz"- or that he was some sort of degenerate, I could never discover. When I asked about him, I was told that there were some subjects not fit for discussion. Subjects considered unsuitable for mention in this household comprised a wide range of topics: from basic Civil Rights; to school integration; to Immigration policies; the war in Southeast Asia, and America's right to exploit whatever country had natural resources which were in short supply domestically; to abortion; to pornography; to just about anything that did not reflect advantageously upon the denizens of Fremont Place and the California Club; the elect, the chosen ... the Crawford family.

Over a hundred people attended the splendidly catered affair. My only *faux pas* was to leap into the swimming pool fully clothed, expecting others to follow. They did not, and I pulled myself out to go change into another regulation dark suit , and then found that 'Zorba, the Greek' was playing on television in one of the rooms just off the main living room. I was rather inebriated on whiskey and champagne, so I was not urged to rejoin the main social interchange until I was told that a friend from my childhood had arrived, a fellow named John Burke who had grown up across the street from me in Crown Heights, Oklahoma City. He had been several years younger and yet we had included him in most of the neighborhood gang's activities from football, to softball to hide-and-seek, and any of the many games we invented to indulge our childish fantasies. Variations of themes from Cowboy movies had been some of our favorite improvisational scenarios and mock enactments. When I was introduced to John, I was impressed by the strength in his handshake and noted that he was a fine athletic specimen of six and a half feet and well over two hundred pounds of trained muscularity. He had been a college athlete whose specialty was swimming and wrestling, his wife reported to us. John was self-effacing and soft-spoken, but he became noticeably disturbed and turned away when his wife went on to tell about our shared childhood experiences of which I had only the faintest recall, especially regarding an incident that ended this conversation and impelled John to walk away from us and disappear into the crowd out in the garden milling about the swimming pool..

"John never did completely recover from the trauma of the hanging. It seems Ben was playing the part of sheriff and stood him on a soap box with a hangman's noose around his neck, that was tied to a clothesline pole, and he kicked the box away to leave John hanging there and strangling. John's mother saw this from the kitchen and ran out to cut him down just in time after Ben and his friends had run away", she had begun babbling after John had bolted away from us. And then she blurted out, losing her immediate audience and the center-piece of her dramatic monologue, as well. "John. Come back here. You said you wanted to tell Ben how that felt. John! Come back here!" She was now shrieking. But he had folded himself in to the crowd, and we did not see him again that evening

I was curious to know what had happened. I do remember playing sheriff and also being on the opposing side, the bandit. And of course, the wild Indian, the lawless savage. I did vaguely recall doing something rather extreme with Johnnie Burton, but I was not sure if it included a hanging. I really wanted to know. I wondered if I could have been so wantonly cruel. Perhaps so. Some of the games we played were life-endangering, at best. Jumping between roof-tops and from these same heights to the ground. Many of our experiments with fires came close to setting our very homes alight. The risks we took with street traffic in running across some of the intersections we traversed to get to the public playgounds we used - any slips and stumbles could have been deadly collisions with the cars and trucks speeding there. One ten year-old named Bobbie Marshall who lived two blocks away used to do a downhill Kami Kazi racing run on his Donald Duck bike through the busiest intersection at Thirty-sixth Street and Shartell Boulevard. He carried a bottle of Beefeater's gin stolen from his parents in his basket which he upended in voracious, gulping swallows before each of these suicide sprints. His only disaster was that he was caught by shocked onlookers and then was sent to mandatory meetings of Alcohoilic Anonymous which were attended by many of his family's drinking friends. He would have a staggeringly impressive sobriety date today if those lessons actually took: "Hi, my name is Bob M. and I'm an alcoholic. My last drink of alcohol was on April the First, 1948 [it could therefore possibly be sixty-three years ago at this present date (actually I know now for certain that he has over thirty years sober, but I am prevented from saying in this text, by the anonymity tradition of Alcoholics Anonymous)], but I am sober just for today."

Marian's family drove south to visit only once, and they insisted on buying living-room furniture for us. This ensemble consisted of only three pieces: a couch and two arm-chairs as "Uncle" Andy Wright had provided us with the *cama matrimonia*, a queen-size mattress with box springs and oak head-board - he claimed that it was the wedding bed he and his wife had been given by his parents some thirty years ago when first married. Our house was indeed small. It was one of the cabins first built by the Scripps family as an indulgence to their artistic daughter who invited her friends of the same aesthetic inclination to come visit her for extended periods on the ranch which covered the entire area now known as the village of La Jolla. This clump of some five rustic dwellings had been called the 'Green Dragon Colony', so named for a book, titled *The Green Dragon*, written by one of these friends of the Scripps' daughter. The tradition since the turn of the century had been that practicing artists were to occupy these houses for a controlled minimal rent. I had been considered qualified as a poet, and had been given the place in a true fluke of good fortune for only one hundred dollars a month when Marian and I had arrived the previous month. I paid rent to the current owner of the properties, a crusty old curmudgeon named Sam Crosby who had made his fortune up in the Klondike of Alaska in the gold and fishery industries. He introduced me to his son, Harry, a local high-school teacher who was then exploring the painted caves of Baja California and writing a book of his discoveries there and also conducting a massive research project chronicling the original Hispanic history of all of California, later published as the major, land-mark work titled *Antigua California*.

Our house was across the street from the tourist attraction, 'The Caves Curio Shop', so called because there was a steep stairway in the souvenir section of the building which led down in to a massive cave which was filled with waters from the La Jolla Cove which we could look out over from our front porch to the La Jolla Beach and Tennis Club. Prime real estate, where today the properties are worth millions of dollars, but in that year, 1968, students could live well in this neighborhood for a minimal income. My salary as a Teaching Assistant at U.C.S.D was just four hundred dollars a month. The man living in the house just behind ours, as a way of coping with the shock from his wife leaving him, had established a small tea and coffee shop on his front porch and living room. This became one of the most successful tourist attractions in town and still is a thriving business – although relocated to the center of the more commercial area since – known as 'The Pannikin". One of the other houses, perched above ours, became a popular restaurant, but even after I left California, I had passed on the fixed rent privilege of our house to a more dedicated artist, my friend Fred Hocks, who made it his live-in studio and occupied it from the age of ninety-two to ninety-six. I kept the house when Marian left to divorce me, at her parents' insistence – they awarded her a check for $30,000 to begin proceedings, and threatened to remove her multi-million dollar trust fund inheritance if she remained married to me. Curiously, I paid for her return trip to Deya, Mallorca, in the summer preceding the actual divorce action in the fall of that year. She was accompanied by a new friend, Robert Stratton, who then became an intimate confidant of Robert Graves and subsequently wrote and published over sixty books: spy thrillers, crime mysteries, formula westerns, and hard-core heterosexual pornography [three of these latter genre featured me as the protagonist, by name: Ben Wright – one of these novels now sells for over $700 on e-bay, as it has become a popular cult piece].

During those last few months with Marian, I had little time and even less inclination for any sexual affairs which might have been construed as becoming the subject of pornography, and certainly nothing very romantic seemed to be contained in my life at this time. Marian was drunk most of the time every day and sometimes could not be bothered to leave the bed to relieve her bladder ... or bowel. I cleaned up after her and still felt a genuine affection for my *demented debutante*. We made love, but on a most infrequent basis, something like twice monthly. My work as a teaching assistant for Marcuse required me to read material with which I was unfamiliar, especially Neitzsche, Hegel, Marx and Engels. Works by writers such as Kafka and Achebe were more enjoyable, but the philosophical materials required my most intense coincentration and undivided attention. In addition to the reading was the grading of essays every other week, and then individual conferences with each student (my class consisted of fifteen) for an hour each week in my office.

I was also cramming for the forthcoming doctoral qualifying examinations in several subjects. I still am unable to fully believe that I had acquired any competency in these fields for which I was to prove myself of an expert level of awareness: all of English literature, from Beowulf to Virgina Wolff as the cute title of that spoof of such a survey declared; a century of Spanish poetry and prose (the nineteenth); all of American literature; a special focus on Medieval and Anglo-Saxon studies, with demonstrated competence in Middle and Old English language; Linguistics, both Structural and Transformational, as developed by Noam Chomski at M.I.T.; and a working knowledge of the History of Ideas, according to the precedents established by Professor Lovejoy of Johns Hopkins University, and a thorough awareness of English Philology, derivative of study of Henry Sweet's early grammars and glossaries of Anglo-Saxon, including the most contemporary work of the M.I.T. Linguists. I was to spend a week writing answers to all the questions composed by the professors most qualified in these fields, and then was to have an entire day devoted to personal examination and interrogation by the entire assembled group. I well remember certain key incidents that occurred in the days just before the official "blood-letting" - a term that had been coined by one of the first candidates to have run this academic gauntlet, and survived, 'bloody, but unbowed'. My mind swirled with references to Ashley Montague's research in the rites of passage in various primitive cultures that required actual physical ritual mutilation, from the tearing of the pectoral muscles pulled by the leather thongs when the victim was made hoist on the Sun-Dance pole, to the variations on circumcisions of both male and females, the most severe being clitorectomies accompanied by the removal the entire *labia majora* with girls in Moslem or African cultures. My sexual activities had ceased entirely in the weeks before these examinations and I remember joking, with a distinct *gallows* flavor, with Uncle Andy (my doctoral director, Professor Wright) that I hoped that I would not be presented with many questions about Jane Austen or other feminine writers, as I had become numbed to all heterosexual desire in these weeks, and that I was now almost estranged from my recent bride, Marian. His response was chilling: "Welcome to the fellowship, my son". However, for many months after I had completed this academic ordeal, my sexual impulses were slow in returning to anything like the normal libidinal drive for a healthy young man.

It was not as a direct result of my less than adequate sexual performance that Marian was induced and bribed into beginning divorce proceedings. There had been one rather ugly incident for which I could not imagine making any sort of apology, or expecting any to be paid me. This had been a attack with intent to kill me which I had repulsed in my own living room one evening having cocktails and idle chat by the fireside with Marian's sister and brother-in-law. Having survived the academic "blood-letting" of the doctoral examinations, with another rather shocking assault from one of my professors, I was beginning to feel constantly battle-ready, pumped up with adrenaline, and wary in just about every social encounter. Since the academic event preceded the familial incident, I shall describe that situation first.

In November, as the time drew near for the actual examinations, I spent every free moment reviewing all my resources for being prepared to answer any question that could have given me in my fields of study. I remembered how I had been able to second-guess the areas of focus the questioners had chosen in that television quiz show, 'The General Electric College Board', in which I had competed when a student at Penn. I had even guessed the first question that had been posed [In the Christmas Carol, 'God Rest Ye Merry Gentlemen, where does the comma appear in the title? After the word *Merry*, because the word was used in that context as an adverb not an adjective modifying *Gentlemen*] winning a bounty of Scotch whiskey from my pals and shocking Allen Luden the Master of Ceremonies who feared that repercussions from such scandals as had occurred with 'The 64,000 Question' could spill over into his arena. Actually, I was aware that each of my professors would indeed ask questions from his own most informed area of expertise; e.g., Uncle Andy was sure to ask about Jane Austen; David Crowne would ask about Chaucer and Beowulf; and both Carlos Blanco and Sandy Sheen had asked me to write my own questions for their sections in Spanish Poetics and Linguistics. I had contrived a truly splendid discussion of Jorge Guillen's poetry and its influence on Federico Garcia Lorca for Carlos; and for Sandy, I fashioned a whimsical interpretive analysis in the prevailing theories of Linguistics for Lewis Carroll's poem, 'Jabberwocky'. Roy Harvey Pearce, as Chairman of the Literature Department, was the supervisor of the entire examination, but I felt certain that Jack Behan, the professor who was framing the American Literature section would choose something from Pearce's realms of greatest publication in that realm: Mark Twain and Herman Melville. Jack would be using this opportunity to show off to Pearce, his boss, just how much he knew of Pearce's published work. Jack had been struggling to rise above his status as Associate Professor for some considerable time, but as a result of the trick he was intending to pull on me, which back-fired on him, he never did achieve the rank of full professor, and retired to take up employment as an automobile mechanic as soon as he had completed twenty years service, just after his wife's suicide.

Jack Behan had been the only professor in my entire graduate school career (San Diego State College, for the programs of Master's at San Diego State and Doctorate at U.C.S.D. and University of Madrid) to ever award me the grade of B for course work. Any student who received such a grade in graduate school was considered to be unworthy of remaining there; however, I was not dismissed, although it had clearly been his intention to orchestrate my exit. He had been heard to complain about my former military service, remarking that I was probably a closet Nazi because I had been an officer in the Recruit Training Command of the Navy. He equally abhorred my office-mate, David Burns, who had served an enlistment in the Marine Corps. Supposedly we had been "housed" together in the department office assignment because we had, both of us, the distinct stink of the extreme masculine: military veterans, and therefore a potentially violent sub-species. David had been expelled at the end of the previous year as a result of a grammatical error that had appeared in the note he had left on the department office doors when he had left late at night to fly home to be at his mother's death-bed in Michigan. When he had returned from her funeral, he was invited to attend a meeting of the doctoral committee who had decided that he was unworthy to continue as a doctoral candidate. Why? In the past two years of study, he had received two grades of B and because the error in the hastily written note had violated some rule of accepted university-level grammar - it was never revealed what this highly offensive flaw was supposed to be - the rumor was that he was considered to be deeply morally afflicted, as evidenced by a grievous grammatical error, and therefore was deemed unacceptable as a student preparing to be eventually awarded a doctoral degree by the purist, pedantic professors of our department.

There was a tenured professor in the Literature department who was an active member of the local United States Navy Reserve Intelligence Division, with the rank of full Commander and was the man who may have organized and directed the F.B.I. spy rings on all of the University of California campuses. This zealot had instructed all his teaching assistants in the Humanities segment which he directed, to punish severely any errors in spelling so that offenders were to submit the misspelled word written out one thousand times to prove they were truly repentant. Any error in spelling he declared to be an indication of a "deep-seated moral flaw" (his very words) ... "that must be expunged!" - [also his words].

David Burns had visited my house on many an evening to quiz me on material from that enormous text (1,673 pages), the veritable Bible of English Literature, *A Literary History of England,* Albert Baugh, *et al,* editors and compilers. Although disqualified from ever again pursuing the D. Lit. degree, Burns was wholeheartedly eager for me to succeed. A true friend and incomparable ally. He was quite amused by what Jack Behan tried to pull off in order to sabotage my examination, and was especially delighted in how I turned that professor's wily deceits around on him in a devastating boomerang response. Jack Behan had been one of the committee members who enacted David's dismissal. Sometimes there is a sweet revenge which treasonous individuals bring upon themselves. The form of the martial arts which I always had found most efficacious and pleasing to employ when engaging violent "physical assaults upon my person" as the textbook might phrase it, was called Aikido, in which the energy and force of the assailant is used upon himself. Although I had studied Shotikan Karate at U.C.S.D. with Nishiama, the man who had trained the Japanese officer corps in World War Two, still I have usually found Aikido to be my favored form of self-defense. There is something pleasing to the karma maintenance chip in my psychic mind-set that thrills to the self-destruction of my most vicious opponents as I reverse energy fields and whip-lash them in to painfully damaging collisions utilizing their own savagely focused forces. The old Aikido master is said to remark to the *raging bull* rushing at him, " How sad that you choose this manner in which to commit suicide."   This is another way of expressing the psychologically disarming, "Sorry you feel that way" to someone hurling abusive insult, but the most profoundly metaphysical verbal defense, with innate and deeply rooted Aikido intent is probably a Master's remark of simply, "So?"   One must recall with relish that devastating refrain employed by Kurt Vonnegut after every crushingly tragic incident in his novel *Slaughterhouse Five* ; 'So it goes'.

Jack Behan approached me only three days before the oral section of my examinations, on the Friday afternoon after I had completed the last of the written examinations. I had stopped by the coffee shop in the Student Union after visiting the Revelle College library on the main plaza and was just sitting down to drink a beverage, when Jack approached and asked if he might join me. He asked how I felt about the examination I had just completed. I told him that I was amazed at how much I had written and was pleased that so far I had remembered most of what I needed to provide as referential evidence in the answers. He then did what I was at first surprised by, but had always suspected he might attempt. He was convinced that I was a much more naive and innocent character than I truly am. The very military training which he was convinced had rendered me somewhat stupid and unworthy of doctoral candidacy, was indeed the very training that had made me so suspicious and virtually paranoid. I well remembered the drills we had called "Beat-the-Devil" as preparation for our roles as Unrestricted Line Combat officers, in which a wildly unpredictable set of circumstances were thrown at us to test our agility in decision-making which could shift the balance between life and death for ourselves and those in our command.

He boldly asked me if there could be any particular author or field of inquiry about which I felt that I was unprepared and would not be able to deal with competently in the forthcoming oral examination. Since Jack's area of literary expertise was American Literature, and he was the expert who would be examining me in this field, I chose to tell him what I hoped would be bait for the trap he intended for me, but that would indeed *hoist* him *on his own petard* when the appropriate moment came. How could I possibly know that this would occur? How could he have been so convinced of my innocence and vulnerability? How did I suspect that he would set about to sabotage me, as indeed he did in the next week? Perhaps Jack could have profited by having had at least an exposure to R.O.T.C. in his undergraduate education, or how had he avoided even the most basic melees in the streets of the city where he grew up? Was he as naive as he was presuming me to be?

"I never could get past the first chapter of *Moby Dick*, and that short story so many of the critics rave about, what is it called, 'Bartleby Scrivener'? Is that the title? Supposed to be grim and depressing - *existentially challenging*, or something like that. Why bother?"

Jack's eyes were alight with a sort of "feeding frenzy', like sharks sniffing blood in the brine. His breathing even sped up as he circled to probe further.

"You mean to tell me that you never really got into Melville? Why, that's the subject of some of Pearce's most acclaimed essays. Wow! Guess we better steer clear of that!"

" I don't want to lean on our friendship, Jack," I mewed. "Do you think I need to worry about Melville?"

"There's only about a dozen other writers that can be brought in to the final orals. Not to worry. I'm in your corner."

I was amused that he should use a metaphor from boxing. I would never have reckoned Jack for a devotee of the pugilistic arts. He was using the term, surely, to put *macho old me* at ease.

He rose to leave the table and as he did so, he smiled wryly and said, "You don't need to know this, but the title of the story is 'Bartleby, *the* Scrivener.' That was his job. He was a scribe, as copyist. That's what the job was called. It was not his family name. Scrivener was not his surname." Jack was choking with amusement and appeared to be full of jubilation at having set the trap for me and enjoyed twisting the knife which he would go home to further sharpen for the final thrust in my gut on Monday. I merely tried to look appropriately chastened, and hoped he did not suspect that I was indeed wise to his scheming. He turned and seemed to skip away without another glance back at me. I feel certain that his weekend was a pleasant time of projecting my forthcoming disembowelment by his Melvillian harpoonier's thrusts when we entered the final oral examination *lists* [to mix metaphors, all gory and mutilating, and most likely, exquisitely toothsome for Jack Behan's dreams of finally bringing me down ... and *out*].

I dressed in my herring-bone Navy blue three-piece Brooks Brothers suit with white button down Oxford cloth shirt and the tie with the Episcopal church seal and small red stripe on dark blue silk which had been designed and produced for my *prep* school, Casady. Marian was actually moderately sober this morning and joined me in a breakfast we ordered at our favorite restaurant on La Jolla Shores near the Beach and Tennis Club. I reveled in the ritualistic preparation for my "moment of truth," as if I were a bullfighter entering the *corrida* to confront a one-ton raging bull. The composite of *the beast* were assembled at the doorway of the seminar room which I was invited to enter first and to take a seat at the head of the table at the farthest end away from the doorway.

Roy Harvey Pearce, Andrew Wright, Carlos Blanco, David Crowne, Sanford Sheen, and Jack Behan, all professors in their fields, experts in their disciplines, my examiners, and perhaps, future colleagues, actually smiled at me, Jack, the most effusively. Pearce conducted the exercise, calling upon each man, in turn, to ask anything he should consider necessary to insure that my answers to the written examination had been satisfactory and to probe my knowledge and understanding of any tangential, peripheral material which would serve to confirm my solid understanding of the required materials. The most amusing exchange occurred with Sandy Sheen who had delighted in my essay comparing Structural and Transformational Linguistics theories in an interpretation of Lewis Carroll's 'Jabberwocky.' Some of the examiners appeared awe-struck as I replied to several of David Crowne's Anglo-Saxon queries in that same language [nobody is sure as to how these words should be pronounced as the last fluent speakers have been dead for over a thousand years - we can only pretend to speak it as it was heard in Hrothgar (Grendel's victim) or Hygelac's (Beowulf's king) mead-halls]]. That was indeed showing off, and David and I exchanged knowing glances in so far as my grammar and vocabulary were grossly incorrect, although I had pronounced the words with assurance, at least according to what the most informed scholars would suppose that dead language to have sounded like.

Jack Behan was my last interrogator. He appeared to relish the initial gambit, selecting his words scrupulously, like a chief surgeon reaching for the scalpel to make the first and deepest incision, leading up to the barb of his first point of inquiry with deliberate measure. He expressed satisfaction with my written examination, but said that he was uncomfortable with what he considered to be an avoidance of one particular writer in my survey review of significant voices in American Literature: Herman Melville. The examination question had been an open-ended one which asked that I discuss what the most influential writers in the history of American Literature had said were the defining characteristics of the American identity. I had cited everyone from Cotton Mather, to Nathaniel Hawthorne, to Mark Twain, Ernest Hemingway, John Steinbeck, even Nelson Algren and John Updike ... but, not Melville.

Behan then made claim that *Moby Dick*, and the short story, 'Bartleby, the Scrivener,' were two of the most quintessential definitions of the American consciousness and identity, that they must be discussed in depth, at this oral examination, or he would not feel convinced that I should be advanced to full doctoral status, and he would consider me unqualified as a candidate for the degree and would declare this examination a failure. He leaned back in his chair and folded his arms over his taut belly with the pleased demeanor of one who has just swallowed a sumptuous meal washed down with a rare and costly vintage wine. The silence in the room became palpable. I removed three index cards from my inside coat pocket, glanced at them just to make sure I could remember page numbers and dates with exactitude - I was allowed note cards by the rules of this examination - but I returned these to my pocket, folded my hands in a steeple prayer *mudra* in front of me and sighted over the inverted V of my joined finger-tips and allowed more time to pass, so that Professor Pearce finally asked that I respond.

I had spent Saturday and Sunday reviewing a lengthy essay I had written for an American Literature course at San Diego State College when I had been enrolled there in the Master's degree program. Professor Glen Sandstrom, my instructor in that course, was editor of the most prestigious literary journal in American Literature and had urged me to publish this piece as he had awarded it the grade of 98, or A+. The subject of that essay had been *Moby Dick*, and it had made particular reference to the *existentially challenged* figure in one of Melville's short stories: 'Bartleby, the Scrivener.' I had compared the quills wielded by that tormented *copyist* soul to the harpoons used by the hunters of the whales in the great sea adventure and allegory of American identity in that monumental novel by Melville. I had made significant reference to the most telling and acclaimed recent essay on this same subject by Professor Roy Harvey Pearce. I had also alluded to the friendship of Melville with Hawthorne and had examined how both men had developed the theme of the *isolato*, the lone wolf, the very embodiment of what Ralph Waldo Emerson [Pearce claimed a virtual familial inheritance from Emerson's ideals in this particular 'history of ideas'] had claimed to the be the essence of the American "consciousness" in his seminal definitive essay, 'Self Reliance.' Again, this theme had been a favorite subject of Pearce's in his major text which examined the Mountain Man and the Western frontiersman personality as it was portrayed in American literature. When I had cited material from this essay of mine in Behan's course in American Literature, at U.C.S.D., he had dismissed my contribution in the seminar discussion as spurious and misinformed. Now, at last, I would have an opportunity to test my understanding and interpretation of Pearce's critical work with the author, himself, and Behar would have to allow me this opportunity, without maligning my interpretation unilaterally. Also, I would now be afforded an opportunity to demonstrate to Pearce my high regard for his scholarly influence in my own study of Amercian Literature. And what a surprise I was now about to spring on Behan, in front of all his colleagues, and especially in the presence of his immediate boss, Professor Roy Harvey Pearce.

"I am indeed prepared to discuss *Moby Dick*, as well as 'Bartleby, the Scrivener,' and with particular focus on the subject of the notion of the American identity," I said. I then began to relate what I had written in that essay which Professor Sandstrom had so enjoyed, and as I cited Pearce's published work which I had referred to in my discussion, with emphasis on his Emersonian principles, I could see the Chair of our department glowing with satisfaction. Carlos Blanco and Andy Wright nodded in acknowledgment of my well proffered complimentary citations from his publications [I had decided to also reference his most highly esteemed texts (*Savagism and Civilization* and *Continuity of American Poetry*)] defining the American identity – I was laying it on rather thick, but I reckoned I was now insuring Pearce's loyalty to my cause as I prepared to throw the gauntlet down before Behan in only a few more minutes]. As I concluded my argument, I could see that I had won the respect and admiration of all present ... with the rather notable exception of Behan.

Since Jack did not look as if he cared to say anything at this juncture, I decided to provide him with a lead-in remark, and I am even now amazed that I had the discretion to not be more confrontational:

"I would be particularly interested to know Professor Behan's reaction to my answer," I offered. "Especially as it was he who asked me on Friday if there were any particular author about whom I felt I was not well enough informed to be able to satisfactorily answer any question in this examination today. Because I suspected that his inquiry was not indeed in my best interests, and having observed some other devious behaviors in this individual when I took a course with him and when I served as his teaching assistant, I decided to provide him with a decoy, to allow him to set about whatever sabotage he had intended to undertake. I told him that I had not even read *Moby Dick* and that I was completely unfamiliar with anything of much importance about the author, Herman Melville, other than the most general information. When he asked if I had read the short story, 'Bartleby. the Scrivener,' I lied and told him that I had never heard of this title. Today, the question which Professor Behan prepared was planned to show up my ignorance and to prove my incompetence in American Literature, so that I would fail this examination. It is my belief that I have proven my competence, my education, and my understanding of this subject to a degree which should satisfy the standards of this doctoral candidacy committee. What I question is the qualifications of such a person as Jack Behan to sit in judgment on any such committee or to even be employed as an instructor by our university. May I now ask that ... "

"Mr Wright, you are excused from this examination. Please leave this room. You may wait in the hallway until you are called," declared Professor Roy Harvey Pearce, and all the men on my side of the seminar table rose to allow me to pass and to make my exit. As I was leaving, David Crowne told me as he closed the door, that he would come get me when it was time. And the *time* seemed endless as I waited to discover what would happen. It was no more than half an hour, but I seriously considered just walking away. How could the faculty condemn one of their own? Surely they would close ranks, and I would be expelled, or worse. What could be worse at this point? I could return to Spain and find immediate employment in films, or I could return to Deya and work for room and board with Bill's archaeological projects and pick up living expenses from tutoring in conversational English classes for the locals who were entering the tourist industry job-market. But American higher education, university and college level, was now my chosen profession. My vocation. My calling. My life.

David Crowne opened the door and invited me back in. Professor Pearce announced that the examiners had unanimously found me to be qualified for advancement to candidacy for the Doctor of Literature degree, and he personally congratulated me. Jack Behan stared down at the table and looked as if he had received a whipping. David whispered to me to leave, and to forestall any more embarrassing scenes, I did so, linking my arm with Marian's and inviting her to a round of drinks at the bar of her choosing. She elected the Del Coronado Beach Hotel which her parents had raved about, but she had never visited - that century-old fairyland construction featured in Billy Wilder's film, 'Some Like It Hot,' which had latterly become known only as 'The Del,' and so we jumped in the car and drove down to San Diego and caught the ferry over to Coronado Beach.

When we arrived on Main Street, driving off the ferry, I stopped to take Marian into the *first* bar, which was always the *last* bar I had entered when I was on the drinking spree that we called on Friday afternoons in 1961, "The Crusade," with members of the nascent Seal Team One, coming up the same street from the Navy barracks which were on the beach just beyond 'The Del'; we stopped in every bar for one drink, punctuated by Maxie's [that Seal Team One Scuba Harrassment Officer] chewing up and swallowing of his glass, after a gin and tonic, and then we quaffed our own last drink before hopping the ferry to *ride and raid* over into San Diego, cruising bars from the city downtown on Market Street to Ocean Beach, South and North Mission Beach, and Pacific Beach, till we finally hauled up, and virtually holed up, in either 'The Pour House' or 'White Whale' (where a teen-aged pianist named Tom Waits wailed the Blues) in Bird Rock or the 'El Sombrero' in downtown La Jolla.

And here we were, Marian and I, doing a reverse swing from La Jolla on that old circuit (bypassing the intermediate beaches), and so, on arrival in Coronado, I felt I had to show Marian that last-stop bar from "The Crusade" of my naval officer days. Passing the doctoral exams was a closing of a circle - one of my Physics academic pals had declared, "Happiness is a filled orbital," referring to that ideal atomic arrangement of elements - and surely, this day, I was feeling that I had come *full-circle* [perhaps through a Black Hole].

Next was the writing of the dissertation, the topic of which I had no clue at that moment, and would never quite come to terms with addressing on a basis which would lead me to the fulfilling of that final and essential requirement for the degree. I had heard of others (referred to as A.B.D. - "All But Dissertation") who never wrote the thesis, and yet, I never expected I would be one of those. Little did I know that I would be awarded another degree, the C. Phil., that is, Candidate in Philosophy, to insure that I would receive credit for all the semester credit course hours (over 120) which I had completed when advanced to full doctoral candidacy after passing the examinations. It was only after another thirty years that I wrote a dissertation which was accepted for a doctorate in Cambridge, England, and was awarded the Ph. D. there from Anglia Polytechnic [now named Ruskin] University in 2004.

It had been less than a decade since I had first been on active duty as an Ensign when my social life was an extended *liberty pass* with my comrades-in-arms, and then, only five years thereafter, I had limited my entertainments to those few leisure hours I had to spend with my wife, Lisa. Ironically, we had also made Coronado one of our special places for renewing the sense of the romantic element in our otherwise banal, pedestrian existence. In 1963, we had attended the wedding of my friend Dan "Dog" Hendrickson at a small chapel here, when he had escorted his bride down the aisle in her body-cast and leg in plaster, with her arm splinted and in a sling - she had passed his requirement for marrying a SEAL [this official title had still not been adopted until 1964, but everyone had begun using this term for the Special Forces Navy unit] by completing the obstacle course on their training base just up the road. Her own father had been a highly decorated submarine commander in World War Two, and she adhered to all the rigorous traditions of *service* with honor, and sacrifice, and obviously, as she hobbled, smiling to the altar, she was willing to pay the highest price in physical suffering to marry one of the Navy's new *supermen* - Dan had also qualified as a Frogman, U.D.T (Underwater Demolition Team), and had just been promoted to Lieutenant, Regular Navy.

Lisa and I had often taken dinner in the grand ballroom of 'The Del' where dance contests were held. We had once even won an event as I could still recall the steps of the Waltz, the Cha Cha, and then was able to project an elegant but sexy coordinated series of dazzling maneuvers through Jitterbug and Swing whirls and spins. Lisa and I were good in bed, too. I think that our style as a couple on the dance-floor probably proclaimed our skill in coupling in the sexual event, as well. Marian and I did not dance together. And we were not so very good in bed either. However, we did share a love of drinking that I have rarely encountered even with my most devoted bar-room pals of the male gender. She has been dead now since her maid found her like that in the kitchen of her home in Pasadena, where she retreated after her fifth husband, and an unrelenting career of alcohol and drug abuse. How sad ... my *demented debutante's* demise.

When Marian a I entered 'The Del,' we did not visit the grand ballroom, but headed straight for the beach bar on the ground floor where we could look out over the Pacific, the flat sand, stretching south toward the SEAL training depot and then on to San Isidro and the border-town of Tijuana. As we sat there, I told Marian about my first time in San Diego, at the age of ten, when my parents had brought me and my sister to stay at the original 'Del,' what was then called 'The Coronado Beach Hotel.' It had been my first time to behold the ocean, and I remember that initial moment on this very beach that spread before us. I had inhaled the air laced with sharp aromas of salt and sea-weed, and it was similar to my first swallow of an alcoholic beverage. I was intoxicated, enthralled, captivated by both *elixirs* - I was delighted to learn in my Medieval studies in graduate school that the word *elixir* refers to that substance which enacts the miraculous transformation of base metal into gold in that *quintessential* step in Alchemy. I could not breath the fragrance of that ocean deeply enough to satisfy myself, and only seven years later I enlisted in the U.S. Navy Reserve Officer Training Corps to further my love of the worlds' seas.

On this special evening with Marian, I had ordered a double 'Johnnie Walker Black Label' on the rocks, and I drank it back with exquisite pleasure as I told my loving mate of my boy-hood delight on this beach. The next greatest discovery had been Marian, I told her. I had not mentioned anything about being here with Lisa, our dance contest, and I chose to repress the memory of my bed-time *boogies* with Lisa, as well. I had passed my doctoral examinations, I was with Marian, and embracing the vista of the whole Pacific, and my future in the university spread before me and grew brighter as I ordered another Scotch Whiskey.

The following week, Marian surprised me by buying stereophonic radio and record player equipment which was supposed to be the latest in the state-of-the-art sound systems . The trademark was K.L.H. I am unable to remember what that acronym stood for, but the sound it delivered was exceptionally fine. I had kept my favorite recordings of classical music on vinyl albums: Mozart. Beethoven, Mahler, Bach, Vivaldi. Marian's taste ran from Henry Mancini to Glen Miller to Elvis Presley and 'The Doors' - as unpredictable and as discordant as her own *persona* was when she swung from her conventional, proper, debutante pose to the erratic, raving, drunk *druggie*. Once in an irrational, drunken, jealous rage, she had destroyed almost all of the weekly essay assignments of my Humanities students. I arrived home one evening to find several ripped pages of these student papers thrown in the shrubbery below our front porch, several fragments blown across the street, or crumpled up in the gutter by our sidewalk. The few that had not made it off the porch were covered with scribbled notes in red ink in which Marian had written that she knew that this or that student was either fucking me or giving me blow-jobs. When she sobered up after this rampage, I convinced her that we should seek marital counseling from the psychologist-in-residence at Revelle College.

Bob Kavanaugh, the brother of James Kavanaugh, the former priest who had been Julie's therapist before she died, had another brother, Phil who was a high-paid and controversial psychiatrist to the super-rich in La Jolla and Rancho Santa Fe. Bob, himself a defrocked priest, had more substantial training in the field of mental health than Jamie, but was not a neurological specialist like Phil. He had served Revelle College as an individual counselor and as an administrator of aptitude and profile skills testing materials and procedures. He had even developed and promoted what became a popular evening non-credit course in the Extension Branch: "The Bright Tomorrow: An Examination of Death and Dying and the Possible Future" [coincidentally, Elizabeth Kubler-Ross was just completing her brilliant study on this subject, *On Death and Dying*, in this same year, 1969, nearby, just a few miles up the coast, in Encinitas]. This class was a waiting-list-only offering till his own death from heart attack later that year. I just happened to be in the office when a secretary answered the telephone to tell the caller that 'The Bright Tomorrow' had been canceled because the instructor had died – blunt reality, but delivered in such a dispassionate manner that Bob would have been highly amused. Death cancels all 'Bright Tomorrows' ... and no refunds.

It was Bob who recommended that Marian and I have a trial separation, and I moved out of our La Jolla Cove cottage to stay in a dreary studio apartment several miles away, in Del Mar. Marian claimed she could not understand how this would be of any benefit to our marriage, and she was right. It served to provide the wedge between us that enabled me to more readily accept that our relationship could not last. However, we had already had the incident of the attack from her brother-in-law in our living room which I had quelled so violently that his arm was torn out of socket and several of his ribs were fractured. He had tried to split my skull with a hatchet. It was shortly thereafter that Marian was given the check by her parents for $30,000 to begin divorce proceedings and was threatened with disinheritance and loss of her substantial trust fund if she did not complete the process. Bob Kavanaugh had delivered his advice that we separate lest someone be killed. He deemed it just lucky that the fracas in our living room had not resulted in a homicide. I agreed, because I well remembered feeling that this final act could indeed have completed my reprisal against this family, my wife included, with a most brutal determination – *with extreme prejudice*, as that term had been employed by Special Forces and Army Intelligence 'down-range' units in combat in the Southeast Asian conflict.

The clash with the brother-in-law who had married Lynn, Marian's younger sister, had come about rather unexpectedly in our living room in the house where we lived above the La Jolla Cove, one of those quaint structures the Scripps family had built for the artistic friends of their grand-daughter at the turn of the century. The in-laws were both graduates of U.S.C. (University of Southern California) where Lynn had been president of her sorority and Glen had played intramural football and been an officer in the Right-Wing student government. He had worked summers for the family business and had aspirations to be made a vice-president and manager in a six-figure income job with this automotive parts distribution company while still in his mid-twenties. He was a smarmy blonde, blue-eyed boy, already with a double-chin and a soft pot-belly whose obsequious, sycophancy had charmed Marian's parents, so that he was constantly held up and praised as the ideal son-in-law; and I was the renegade maverick who had somehow sneaked in the back door [by way of a marriage registry office in Gibralter, in a geographical location that any member of Marian's family would have difficulty in pointing to on a world map] to upset all the elaborate, finely engineered, marital negotiations that Madeline Crawford had so artfully contrived, until then, to place Marian in her proper niche in Los Angeles society. However, I was prepared to indulge Marian's need to be polite to her sister, and so, I had agreed to the visit and had set about early in the day becoming inebriated on Scotch Whiskey on the rocks with a splash of soda, in a connected sequence of at least four large glasses, one after another. I was not slurring my words, but I knew that I had crossed the invisible line where my inhibitions, both verbally and physically had been substantially eliminated. I felt like a caged tiger, and was aware that I was becoming alert for any opportunity to slash out at our Hitler-Jugend manque guests upon the slightest provocation, by the time we had finished our meal and sat around the fire-place quaffing snifters of Napoleon brandy, and I was half-way through one of my favorite cigars, a long black cigarillo from the Canary Islands.

Glen offered me a perfect lead-in for my initial assault, by asking a pointed question about Herbert Marcuse, and the most controversial political issue of the time at U.C.S.D.

"Tell us what it's like teaching for that Commie professor whose student Angela Davis is stirring up all the colored folks in our home town, L.A.? She's still on the faculty of U.C.L.A., that is until someone shoots her, or the F.B.I. slams her in prison where she belongs, or sends her and all the spooks back to Africa," Glen snarled in challenge, a smirk spread over his face, which Lynn imitated as she nodded her assent, and then turned to Marian as if expecting her agreement.

I savored the moment. What a purely racist, moronic remark my brother-in-law had laid out for me to engage with. It was as if his dialogue was formulated to portray him to be what he actually was, or even more repulsive and repugnant. I decided to toy with the material and to lead in to a rejoinder that neither he nor Lynn would have imagined me to contrive.

I related the story about Marcuse's introductory lecture on Sigmund Freud to the Freshman Humanities class in the lecture hall, about how the endearing old curmudgeon had stepped down from the podium and had asked his audience to imagine him taking a bath, and then had described what he saw as he looked down in the water between his legs: a small pink object which he knew held some of his most essential feelings - the penis, which he then compared to the sub-conscious component of the Freudian paradigm: the *Id*. He then discussed the Graeco-Roman character embodied in the name Eros, with an aside to the subject of the erotic, and these implications in the genre of *Romantic* World Literature. But, he maintained, it all still came back to - *or down to* - that pink thing between his legs. His best-selling book at the time, *Eros and Civilization*, discussed this issue in a brilliantly enlightening fashion and had become the most popular text for students of the New Left throughout the world. The bottom-line of the lecture presentation had been, however, that Marcuse told the Freshmen that the little pink object down there between the legs was probably one of the most important things in life. So there!

I had my own *small audience* [pink little things] in my thrall, and as I looked from Marian, to Lynn, to Glen, I took in a deep breath, and then with a deep relish, almost with a lustful gasp, I unleashed my stingers.

"Marcuse maintains that one of the greatest reasons for the intense hatred of Blacks by the White Middle-Class Male Establishment is their deep fear of the average Negro male's penis. In other words: simple *penis-envy*. That most Caucasian males are terrified of the average Black man's genital superiority, and that these frightened little pink-skinned "woozes" are afraid that as soon as their simpering blond bitches find out the truth [that Negro males really do have bigger penises] that they will all want to a have a truly satisfying fucking by these wild *niggers*. Not only do these Buck Bloods have rhythm, and can jump higher than any of us, once they screw our women, these girls will never want our inadequate weenies anywhere near their sweet, twitching pussies again."

I counted a full dramatic pause of ten before carrying on for my now spell-bound, gob-smacked in-laws, but then I offered the not so rhetorical question, with glee, "Don't you agree?"

And then I swiped with a back-handed bitch-slapping, "When was the last time either of you had a really satisfying fuck? Huh?" I paused again, but for only three beats now, as I felt the deck begin to roll under my feet as we entered the Gale ... seas pitching to white caps ... froth and dark waters about to blow across our decks.

"Come on now. We're all family here. Lynn, when was the last time Glen went down on you and sucked your vulva till yours ears rang, and you mouthed his cock till it was at last hard enough to wiggle in to your vagina for at least a few seconds before his premature ejaculation? Huh? As I said, we're all fam ..."

But I could not finish that mock-conjugal appeal before I registered Glen's manic, outraged reaction, a screaming, "I'll show you, you nigger-loving, Commie ... " challenge, as he grabbed the hatchet resting next to the fire-tongs, from beside him at our fireplace, and began to swing it down toward my head. My thighs flexed before I actually thought, and I was propelled upright out of my chair in front of him.

My left arm thrust up as my elbow crooked to form a block to his forearm which held the weapon, and my right hand thrust up behind his upper arm to clasp my left wrist which now I tilted over in a brace to propel his body over my hip which I had thrust in under his side ... and over he went ... and down with a thud, a heaving gasp, and a scream, as I wrenched his wrist away from his torso so that the upper arm was pulled out of the socket and the hatchet fell from the splayed fingers of his hand. I had fallen with him in such a way that my right knee had crashed into his chest, collapsing several of his ribs on that side. The pain registering from that arm torn from its socket, and the shattered ribs, had flown to his consciousness as an all but unbearable horror and physical insult.

I was feeling some anger welling up in my own consciousness, and had thrust my right thumb up under his soft jaw as I grasped his throat and began to gouge into his eye socket, but I stopped ... I was falling forward, as I felt the impact of a full bottle of wine splattered against the base of my skull and I turned automatically to grab the hand of Lynn who had just brained me, to twist away the jagged top of the bottle which she was about to slash my face with.

No sooner had I thrown her away from me, than, still in a half-crouch, I received the crash of one of our dining room chairs which my now frenzied wife, my *demented debutante darling*, Marian, had broken over my shoulders. I grabbed her wrists and slammed her against the wall, almost weeping now as I pleaded, "Why? You are my wife? My love? My God, how can you?" As she spat back: "Fuck you!"

I felt hurt now. I could see the red wine splayed over the white wall in front of where I stood when Lynn had broken the full bottle over my head, into my skull, and as I reached behind, above my neck, I could feel a mushy texture with glass fragments enmeshed in to the flesh ... and bone, there. Lynn was kneeling in the corner, snarling at me like some rabid animal, and Marian was now screaming a stream of curses at me from where she crouched in front of that living-room wall, now aureated with the haggard halo of red wine.

I felt angry then. Some battlefield reaction adrenaline-rush chilled my fascia and hardened my muscles and set my jaw to a clinch as I stomped my heel into the chest of Glen still writhing on the floor in agony beneath me. I actually howled a banshee cry, whooping and snarling, as I then grabbed both women by either hand, and pulled them toward the front door and then flung them out on to our porch.

"If you don't get out of here and away from this house, now, I swear

I am prepared to kill all of you, and as painfully as I can manage", I shouted.

I have no idea how I can be so articulate in moments like this, but it has been a gift, or *curse*, of mine for as long as I can remember. I meant exactly what I was saying, and as I turned to pull Glen from the floor, I said to him in measured tones, "I really hate to let you go. I would have loved to kill you slowly, and with some exquisite pain," I almost complained. Like passing up a truly special dessert after that favorite meal. And only those readers who have tasted the blood of an enemy, at the point of vanquish in a combat, will appreciate how difficult it may be to forgo that inimitable pleasure of the final blows, to a climax as sweet as any sexual orgasm ever known. Therefore, sighing heavily, with some regret, I dragged the man by his other arm to the front door and half-kicked and shoved his twisting, screaming form out on to the porch where his women-folk took charge and helped him down the steep slope to their car parked by the curb; and I presumed that they drove back to Fremont Place.

I did not expect to see Marian again, and at this point, I was no longer so much in love with her that I really cared. I stripped down, showered, had a stiff drink of whiskey, and telephoned the only person I felt I could trust in such a situation, David Burns. After all, that's what Marine Corps *grunts* are trained for: bloody engagements of a combative nature. When he arrived, his sense of humor was intact, and his first remark, after a cursory examination of the broken furniture, shattered bottle, and glass fragments imbedded in the bloody, wine-stained wall, *and the back of my head*, which still was seeping blood into a towel I had soaked in icy cold water, was to ask whether I had eaten all the creatures I had butchered in the front room, or did I have some left-overs I would share with a pal. He was serious, however, when he asked some more particular questions.

What time had all this mayhem occurred? Had I done more than just severely injure my assailants? Had I killed anyone? Would there likely be any criminal charges against me? Were there any witnesses that would testify in my behalf? Was Marian gone, or was she lurking somewhere, armed and potentially dangerous?

I told him that the worst harm I had done was to smash some of my assailant's ribs [hopefully, I mused] and may have pulled my attacker's arm from its socket, and I informed him that mayhem was a felony as it was particularly defined under law as tearing of a piece away from the physical body itself (e.g. ripping an opponent's ear away from the head, or biting the nose off – considered especially heinous if swallowed); otherwise, the offense came under the general category of disfigurement and simple battery. Nor had I drunk any of my brother-in-law's blood. And yes, Marian had gone away with her family members, hopefully for good.

David was most concerned about the time parameters. Our dinner had been at around 7 P.M., and it was now past 10 P.M. He had received my telephone call only fifteen minutes before, at 9:45 P.M. and had leapt in his car and sped the distance of no more than one mile away from us off La Jolla Boulevard where he lived on the opposite side of La Jolla. What had happened between the actual time of the incident, which was anywhere between 7:30 and 8:00 P.M. and the time of my telephone call to him at 9:45 P.M.? What happened to an hour and forty-five minutes, or almost two hours of the evening? Had I been unconscious? Knocked out?

I told him I had taken a shower and changed clothes and then had lain down for a few moments before I called. Later, in the Emergency Room of Scripps Hospital, the presiding physician reckoned that I had received a severe concussion, and after X-rays, discovered a fracture, and that I had lost consciousness during that approximately two hour period before telephoning David ... and he reckoned that I was lucky to be alive. If the blow had been even two inches lower, I would most probably be dead. I made no such hackneyed remark as "A miss is as good as a mile," nor did I care to linger for any longer than it took for the doctor to explain to me what symptoms to watch out for if I were to develop any blood clots inside the skull, and to warn me to come back to the hospital immediately if I experienced periods of double vision and dizziness and nausea. Burns' remark in jest was. "There goes your drinking career," and "That should cut down on the cost of your next drunk."

Although David urged me to come spend that night and even the next few days at his home where he and his wife could look after me, I declined. I actually was rather looking forward to some time on my own in my lovely eyrie perch in that 'Green Dragon' colony above the lovely La Jolla Cove. "And aside from all that, Mrs. Lincoln, how did you enjoy the play?" has always been one of my favorite throw-away lines. I savored the next several days spent in lazy langour – I was between semester terms for another week – we operated on a trimester system: three semester units that fell between September and June, and then there had been a fourth one begun as a summer session, which was not as yet incorporated into the full annual academic package. Many years later, teaching for Community Colleges of the Air Force in Europe for University of Maryland, I taught in a program that offered five semesters annually, each compressed *semester* only for two months of intensive cramming, so that a member of any of the Armed Forces on active duty could achieve the equivalent semester credits for a full four year undergraduate diploma in about two years of class attendance.

I had very little preparation for the coming term as I had been a Teaching Assistant in the entire Humanities Sequences of the full two years in the time before I had taken my "year abroad" in Spain, so I merely opened the notebooks and textbooks from this next term and was ready to walk into classes semi-conscious. So much of the *same-old, same-old.* But I was wondering what might be in store for Marian and me. I did not receive a telephone call from her till several days later, leaving enough time for Glen to have seen a doctor to have his broken ribs attended to and his arm stuck back in socket, and to prepare a medical bill which she said I was expected to pay: several hundred dollars that would devour both my monthly salary, the G.I. Bill tuition subsidy, and the part-time tutoring I did for a few dollars an hour with former students from La Jolla Country Day School. I asked her as politely as I could, how Glen and Lynn would welcome the felony charges of attempted murder and aggravated battery. The silence on her end meant that they were all huddled together discussing this unexpected reply, and when Marian's father was the next voice I heard, he did his best stentorian declamation and told me that he would pay the medical services for my recklessness, but would personally instruct his law firm, the best in California – he was quick to mention – to take all measures at their disposal to wipe me out and expel me from his state if I even so much as dared to whisper, ever again, any such words that should imply criminal charges against members of his beloved family. It would seem that I had effectively gotten his attention and might have provided an irritant to his otherwise placid and soporific residence at Fortress Fremont Place.

Marian did not call again for another couple of days, but when she did, she was all effervescence and cute teasing, with some sexual innuendo included. Primarily, she was promising to arrive the next day with a load of gourmet food and some champagne which would be chilled in a silver ice bucket in the commodious back seat of her mother's aqua-marine green Lincoln Continental convertible, an automobile that only those who were so outrageously rich that Thorstein Veblen's concept of "Conspicuous Consumption" from his land-mark, *Theory of the Leisure Class*, could flagrantly display, flaunting their ghastly lack of artistic taste in unseemly color of automobile as their nose-thumbing to all who observed it noisomely cruise by. I actually adored the car, and yet I had told Marian I abhorred it, thereby guaranteeing that she would find every possible reason to drive it to our residence whenever she could, to needle me ... or so she reckoned. I discovered that I was looking forward to this reconciliation with my wife. Our sexual acitiviy was always best when there had been some conflict, and this incident with Glen and Lynn was the most volatile and grievous to date, so maybe we would move from savage oral sex, to high-geared fucking, to even some anal penetration, with blood and tears (*hers*, I meant to insure). Ooo, la, la!

Of course, I would pay for my concupiscence and romantic indulgence as I should have been expected. Marian and I were able to maintain a relatively amiable interaction for only a matter a a few hours after this newly contrived honeymoon. She felt certain that I would be willing to forgive the life threatening assault and to agree that I was deserving of stern correction of my remarks defending my "Commie, kike professor and his nigger followers," and that Glen and Lynn had every right to *sort me out* and try to show me how to *mind my manners*. I realized that she herself had been subjected recently to disciplinary measures just short of the physical extremes I had endured in that attack, in order to imprint in her consciousness the *extreme prejudice* which was her awareness of *basic right and wrong*. No wonder that expression -*extreme prejudice* - had been employed in ordering the annihilation of entire *villes* and other troublesome political foes - by death - in the war conducted by the leaders of the Republican right wing in Southeast Asia. I decided to go A.W.O.L. before I was invited for the equivalent of an *interrogation/helicopter ride* by my in-laws so that I would never again be caught off guard in the path of their dreadnaught missions of *instruction in adjustment of attitude* to their command doctrine. I moved out of our 'Green Dragon' cottage.

No sooner had I begun asking within the Literature Department for a new residential abode, than I was offered several possible accommodations. The best was to occupy a guest house in the back yard of a newly arrived professor and his wife, Dr. Sacvan Berkovich, a man whose forename had been derived from a combination of Sacco and Vanzetti which his Anarchist mother gave him to commemorate the unjust execution of these men she considered American martyrs.

Moving in to his home was certainly a declaration of my left-wing credentials for anyone to observe, and I relished the idea of announcing this to Marian. I began spending greater portions of my evenings at 'El Sombrero', and often went to bed with a beer-drunk buzz. I also had a one-night dalliance with an undergraduate philosophy major named Jamie, but her confused sexual identity issues would not allow for a really satisfying activity between the sheets. I was offered another live-in arrangement with a fellow Literature doctoral candidate who was a sexual gymnast with newly awakened libidinal hunger who had just recently ended her first marriage and was intent on making up for all the sex she considered that she had been missing by her commitment to matrimony. I lasted at her house just two days and six or eight sexual performances before she told me to leave so that she could really get down to serious serial fucking with a Freshman student of hers from a Humanities section she instructed whom she claimed could double my output and possessed a penis at least two inches longer. He was a timid looking sort, with a full black beard and haunted eyes and hunched shoulders. I rarely encountered him on campus, and when I did, I noticed that he looked like a pursued man, moving across the quadrangle plaza in jerky, spasmodic lurches.

I maintained my residence at Sacvan's for the remainder of that term, and would visit Marian at La Jolla Cove from time to time. I busied myself with teaching a sequence of the Humanities and I also attended classes in Shotokan Karate taught by Nishiama who was reputed to have trained the Japanese officer corps in World War Two. I learned some basic *katas* but never felt more than mildly committed to this form of the martial arts and still believe my early University of

Pennsylvania schooling in Aikido and Judo and what was titled "Unarmed Defense" by a former Army sergeant Korean War veteran who was, on a good day, like a rabid, pit-bull terrier, and taught methods of disfiguring, mutilation and permanent crippling, as a bonus for staying after class on rainy days. This training has probably been of greater benefit to me than any of the more doctrinaire methods of instruction I have had from sane ranking masters in the Asian martial arts..

I was sometimes invited by Marcuse to accompany him to public gatherings, although I no longer taught for him directly. The famous professor had been fond of my company when I was his Teaching Assistant and *factotum* body-guard, and it seemed that he had developed a real liking for me. His manner was always avuncular and teasing, as if I were a part of his own family. I shared this intimacy from time to time with Angela Davis and only one or two of his other students and colleagues. The most memorable evening we spent together was when Eldridge Cleaver arrived on campus to deliver a speech at the basketball court where he then directed a performance by his Black Panthers. Huey Newton, their usual leader, was in prison at his time, and Cleaver had seized leadership [the entire controlling consciousness and dominant philosophy had radically changed since the founding of this organization by Stokeley Carmichael to simply teach children in the deprived ghettos about Black pride]. Dressed in black leather trousers and jackets with black berets jammed down over their foreheads, this marching display reminded me of close-order drill by elite military honor guards, and such a martial tableau was for Marcuse a chilling reminder, he said, of the Brown Shirts, those Nazi political fanatics who began marching in terroristic threat in his student days in Munich, Germany. After this event, the professor and I were invited to attend a small party being given in one of the homes in the La Jolla hills by Superior Court Judge Roger Ruffin and his wife Bee Bee, an event which was actually a staged introduction of Eldridge Cleaver to Angela Davis.

When Marcuse and I were introduced to Cleaver, the professor was polite and respectful and made flattering remarks about the Black leader's best-selling book, *Soul on Ice*. No mention was made by my apparently subdued friend about the startling display of fascist swagger that we had both observed in the basketball court. Was the charm of our hosts what restrained Marcuse from remarking on the shocking similarity to that show with his own experience of the Nazi rallies? I know that I was particularly attracted by Bee Bee's manner and Judge Ruffin's elegance. Some years later, Tom Wolf wrote a narrative piece about a New York high society cocktail party honoring members of the Black Panthers, and the effect was to show up the glaring hypocrisy of such a soiree: the White Establishment who were the target of scorn and hatred by the Black militant movement were, in effect, toadying in sycophantic posturing before their arch-enemies, a charade more than desperately ludicrous.

I was aware that Cleaver might actually be an *agent provocateur* in direct command of J. Edgar Hoover because of my own escape from becoming one of their agents on the U.C.S.D. campus when I was approached and offered such employment just before going to Spain. We may never really know what his role was, whether he was actually paid by the F.B.I., but every incident, from the horror with the

Soledad Brothers, to the unforeseen demise of Haileh Selasie in Ethiopia just after Cleaver's arrival there, mitigates toward suspicion that he was betraying the best interest of his race and perhaps was a tool of the most subversive reactionary elements in the American government. Whatever his allegiance, Angela's attitudes and actions changed radically after this meeting as she became a hard-core Stalinist and at times so extreme in her proposals that she seemed patently demented. It was only shortly after this night, that she rallied a group of Black Panthers to join her at Revelle College plaza and began a short march toward the library, threatening to burn it to the ground because the faculty senate had refused to name the new Third College – just being constructed to the north of the first Revelle campus – Lamumba- Zapata College. She halted her march just at the steps where Professor Herbert Marcuse stood and declared that she must physically walk over him to accomplish her barbaric and destructive purpose. She turned away and called off the fiasco, ordering the Panthers to dismiss.

Bee Bee Rawlins and her brother Robin, a painter, had grown up in Taos, New Mexico, where their parents collaborated in writing children's books. D.H. and Freida Lawrence lived there at that time, and the English novelist's wife became a profound influence on the beautiful blond girl whose adventurous spirit eventuated in a pregnancy by a Ute Indian when both were in their early teens. Freida encouraged the girl to have the baby and the Bright family welcomed the child, especially as by the genetic fluke that played in my own family with the native American heritage, this infant was born with blue eyes and hair the same platinum blond as his mother's. When only in his teens, he went to New York City where he became a favorite model, and then colleague [perhaps mignon / lover] of Andy Warhol and was his assistant director in several films. One of these was about surfers and beach life and was shot on La Jolla Shores where Judge Roger Rawlins played a role in which he appeared totally nude driving a dune buggy and when arrested by the San Diego police for violating some code of decency, there was a huge amount of coverage of the "scandal" in the local press. But there was never much written about Bee Bee, and only a few knew that the reason she stayed in bed most of the time, hardly ever making any public appearance, except at the small parties she hosted in their home, was that she was a heroin addict. How this was never exposed is an enormous credit to her husband who protected this secret till he left his work in San Diego and they moved back to Taos. He was still the most politically radical voice speaking out on behalf of the Black and Hispanic Civil Rights movement, but his own precious treasure, his darling princess, Bee Bee, was never beseiged, nor was her narcotics addiction ever exposed

Bee Bee was a bosom buddy of Angela Davis, and she acted as if she had known Eldridge Cleaver since childhood. Was it her addict insider street smarts or just an incredible depth of understanding that so many Taosenos seem to possess, some magic that radiates from that Pueblo and the mysterious Blue Lake where only a precious few "Anglos" (as the non- Indian, non-Hispanic is called in New Mexico) have ever been allowed to visit by tribal sanction? She was *gifted*, in the best sense of that expression. Frieda Lawrence, as her mentor, had nurtured her sensibilities; and the Great Manitoba of the Native Americans in that Sangre de Cristo mountain range of northern New Mexico had tempered her soul. She seemed to know much about me and welcomed me as Herbert's side-kick as if we had been a "unit" forever. Herbert, himself, appeared hopelessly smitten and enamored of her, and I was startled to discover that he had only met her this evening. We would all be here again on several other occasions in the future, the most notable party being that which the Rawlins hosted to welcome Allen Ginsberg and introduce him to Angela Davis – as he had begged me to arrange. His private audience with Marcuse had been more difficult to orchestrate as Herbert was decidely homophobic and believed that Ginsbeerg was more shameless *showman* than *shaman*. Finally, I had succeeded in arranging a lunch date for these two icons, most ironically at the German Rathskeller in La Jolla Shores across from the La Jolla Beach and Tennis Club, a restaurant notorious for its ownership by haughty refugees from World War Two Germany who were rumored to hold a special party each April in honor of *Der Furher*'s (Hitler) birthday and dressed up in Storm-trooper uniforms; and this neighborhood was notably the richest and most decidedly fascist in San Diego County. Herbert had also insisted that I borrow a Mercedes Benz from one of my rich friends to drive him and the poet to their meal. It was on that day that I overheard some conversation that I wished I had secretly tape-recorded.

Allen told Herbert that he thought the entire war in Vietnam was a business enterprise of the Mafia whom he said owned over fifty per cent of General Dynamics, most of AT & T, Sheraton hotels, several major insurance companies and at least half of the major film companies in Hollywood, all originally acquired through a maneuver by the Crowne Corporation which held title to the Empire State Building, and that this outfit was owned totally by the Mafia. [I was thinking, 'What about that helicopter company owned by Lady-Bird Johnson, L.B.J.'s wife? Charlie Bludorn owned Paramount Pictures through his Gulf and Western conglomerate, and he was Jewish. Then there were the major oil companies. Burmah Oil, owned by the Oberling brothers, Will and Joe, from Oklahoma City, which possessed most of those rich oil reserves in the Burma Sea which had made the Sultan of Brunei the richest man in the world – that was where Vietnam was strategically located']. Although I wanted to join in this conversation, I chose to let the exchange flow between to two until I was truly amazed at Allen's last remark about the Moslems. He had asked Marcuse the question, "As a Jew, how do you feel about what is going on in the Sinai, Palestine, and Jerusalem?" and then launched into expressing his own belief in what would be the only solution, without allowing Herbert to even begin to answer.

"The wisest of the Sanhedrin must consult with the most enlightened of the Sufis. Only on such a level of inspiration can there be achieved any reconciliation. And then there must be trance-dancing in the streets. Dervish spinning and rejoicing and celebration and sublimation – a truly dynamic implementation of the thesis of your book *Eros and Civilization*. Marx, Marcuse, Freud and Hillel howling out the New Age."

Flattered, but not complimented, Herbert made some remark about having to go to a faculty senate appointment and asked me to call for our check. When we attended the party to introduce Allen to Angela, I had already been through a "bit of bother" with the great poet. Upon the arrival of his flight from New York, I had been driven to the airport by some of his more fanatical student fans, and we had been placed under arrest by a virtual S.W.A.T. team of San Diego police. The vehicle which the students had brought to welcome the poet was a sort of beach-boy version of a dopey Cleopatra's barge assemblage on the stripped bed of a pickup truck which held several nappy-haired hippies with their dreadlocks hanging down to their knees accompanied by their girl-friends in varying degrees of undress and body paint; the requisite hound-dogs and at least one billy-goat and a cock-rooster were also stacked on to this Dionysian psychedelic motor-float. Fortunately, there were no drugs found when the police rousted out all the occupants; either they swallowed ... or their goat did. One of the students had a small Super Eight movie camera and was recording the entire scene [this was later shown on San Diego television news and we watched it on the set at the Rawlins' house during the party] while I implored the senior police officer to let us go on our way, which was to a reception in Ginsberg's honor - I thought it politic to avoid saying that it was to introduce him to Angela Davis - at the La Jolla home of Superior Court Judge Roger Rawlins. I asked that he telephone the judge to confirm my story, and as he had one of his subordinates set up this communication loop, I asked him if he was acquainted with Ginsberg's poetry. He smiled and replied that of course he was. He said he was most familiar with 'Howl' and several other of the more scandalous pieces, and I was amazed when he mentioned the most sexually explicit, 'Please, Master', and then he winked conspiratorially. When he spoke on the telephone, he immediately became even more subdued and turned to me with a nod before putting down the receiver and saying that we were free to go and that all charges of creating public disorder were dismissed. As I was leaving, he said to give his best regards to Bee Bee. What a gal!

At the party, after we had seen the news footage and I had passed on the police officer's greetings to Bee Bee, she took Allen and me to one side, and said she had to tell us a few things or else she would consider her party not as successful as could be. She then lowered her head and confronted the poet, almost causing Allen to wilt against a wall as she began to berate him.

" Look here, Allen, it's perfectly obvious that you have spent hardly any time tonight with anybody since we introduced you to Angela. You spoke with her for only a few minutes, and then just turned your attention back to what has seemed to be obsessing you since you arrived, or since you came in our door. And that is my friend, Ben, here." Bee Bee turned and gave me a squeeze and then lopped her fingers into clasping mine and held me close to her as she again addressed Allen.

"Ben has probably made love to just about every woman in this room - with the exception of myself - or will get around to doing so before the year is out, but he will never make love to you. So just get that thought our of your mind. You have been looming about him like some love-lorn moon-calf all evening, and he has not even noticed. He is so beyond any homosexual inclination that I imagine he is surprised even now as I'm telling you both this. So look around for some other target for your romantic yearnings. There are a few men here who would be most flattered by your attentions. But just forget it with our Ben. Okay? He is terminally heterosexual."

And so it was for the rest of that party. I drove Herbert home, and Allen was escorted to another *affair* by one of those men whom Bee Bee had mentioned. I had no more difficulties with the great poet until another time later that year in San Francisco, and when I shared my dilemma with Michael McClure, he told me that he had endured the same sort of nonsense with Allen for some considerable time, as well. So when McClure and I attended an event where we knew we would encounter Allen, we went in holding hands and told him that we were engaged.

Neither of us was bothered by Ginsberg again, at least never with any romantic overtures such as he had made to my English class when he had visited it: "Any man who makes love with me will make a direct connection through my ensymes and DNA to Walt Whitman, the father of all great American Romantic poetry. I have made love with the man who made love with his last young lover, the son of President Chester Arthur." Allen was bragging about his sexual relationship with Neil Cassady who had told him that his own sexual congress with Chester Arthur's son had connected him to that man's love affair consummated with the then elderly Walt Whitman. Allen's sales pitch never worked with McClure or me, but it probably seduced some of the scholarly homosexual students who were obsessed with what is called in graduate literary studies, *Source Work*: the origin of ideas and influences for writers.

By the end of term that year, Marian and I had one of our most touching moments, and one of the last ones, as well. I had come to visit the house at the La Jolla Cove as she had told me that she had something important to discuss. Her parents had demanded that we have an annulment of our marriage and had arranged with their Episcopalian priest to have our union declared a non-consummated arrangement for living together, in a platonic state, which the Registry Office in Gibralter had endorsed merely contracturally. I was expected to sign a sworn affidavit that we had never indulged in sexual intercourse and that our union therefore had never been consummated, so that Marian could regain a *prima facie* virgin status – as far as her church was concerned – and then she could enter into a religiously sanctioned marriage contract with some truly worthy member of California society – to be selected by her parents.

I was actually shocked by all this: the audacity of her parents, their need to cleanse their daughter of my possible spermal contamination, to declare that our marriage had been a charade, and that Marian was a virgin, the purpose being to offer her up in a more profitable marriage marketing scheme as an *unsullied debutante* – as she ostensibly was, before I so defiled [defoliated] her condition, and tarnished the family escutcheon. After I had somewhat recovered from this shocking proposal, I asked if they were willing to pay me some sort of behind-the-scenes non-stud fee for this service as collaborative consenting eunuch. No. Their terms were that no legal punitive measures would be taken against me if I signed and just accepted their terms to never have contact with any member of the family again – and I was then informed that restraining orders against me had already been obtained from the appropriate judges in San Diego and Los Angeles, and that from this very day I would not be allowed within fifty feet of any of that precious family, or Marian especially. If I refused to accept the conditions for an annulment of our marriage, then the divorce proceedings would commence immediately, and I could expect to pay dearly for the *extreme* privilege of having been her husband: hardly nine months at this point.

To provide emphasis for her decisiveness and to demonstrate to me her family's determination to be rid of me as soon as possible, she then showed me the check that her father had presented to her in the amount of $30,000. She waved it at me saying that if she did not cash it, or if she should balk at their legal assistance, she was to be disinherited of a trust fund of three million dollars that was already in place for her from her grand-parents, and that her own family was preparing to excise her from their Last Will and Testament completely, if she were not divorced from me within the year. With tears streaming down her cheeks, her eyes radiant with hurt - *and some perverse delight* - she pleaded for me to finally understand what she was all about, that she would be nothing without her parents' support and money.

I grabbed the check from her hand, and told her that if she kept bawling like this that her tears might wash away the writing on the check. I placed it on our mantle, and she began to laugh, saying, "Couldn't (I) see that it was a certified check and that the numbers could not be erased by water, and that the signature could always be re-imposed. But thanks anyway for always looking out for me," she assured me, as we embraced, laughing and crying now, the both of us, our last moment so close together; and so, of course, we decided to make love, furiously and fervently. And then, in a post-coital stasis, I left her in our bed in our Green Dragon cottage and went to drink beer for the rest of the afternoon at 'El Sombrero.'

I was met there at the bar, only a short time thereafter, by Robert Stratton, whom Marian had called to ask to console me. He and Marian had become closer friends since our separation, and although his reputation was as a compulsive sexual athlete with every woman he encountered, I am assured, even to this day, as we are still close friends, that this relationship with Marian was absolutely platonic. She reminded him of that wife he had left with four children to support, along with her fiendish addiction to codeine (so like Marian's alcoholic and pill excesses) which Robert had supplied by frequent day-trips to Tijuana, buying her gallons of that elixir to maintain her habit. The most startling similarity between Robert and me was our facial features. Although we both were older than most of our colleagues at U.C.S.D., having served in the military and having had jobs in the market place and divorces as well, for some odd genetic reason, we looked like twins from the neck up. Robert was more muscular and about two inches taller, and although he wore his hair down to his shoulders and was clean-shaven, except for long drooping *bandito* mustaches, our basic facial features were those of such close relatives that many thought us to be brothers. He had come to the university as an undergraduate, having served as a private in the U.S. Army and then after working for I.B.M. as a computer programmer in order to support the four children he had engendered with his high-school-sweetheart-addict-spouse, one day he decided to alter his life radically. Carrying a long machete, he confronted his boss, slapping the weapon flat on his desk, declaring that he was losing his mind working for I.B.M and wanted Workman's Compensation for having a nervous breakdown, as he was then obviously demonstrating. He got it, and he then left his wife and children, made a bare living playing eight-ball pool in various beach bars till he had arranged for the G.I. Bill to supplement the Workman's Compensation he received to fund his enrollment as an Anthropology major at U.C.S.D. He still harbored a smoldering sense of repressed outrage with himself for having wasted so much time before finding his vocation as a student, and as we both were dealing with some broiling, volcanic magma in our subconscious personality equations, he guided me to accompany him in beginning Shotokan Karate training with the famed Nishiama. I only participated for a few months, and never even acquired a belt, but in these classes, I met many members of the Black Panthers and some *Chicanos* who called themselves the 'Venceremos [*We Shall Overcome*] Movement'; and I was able to athletically vent much of my resentment against my own *enslavement* to Marian and her family; also, Robert introduced me to several sexually active and willing young undergraduate women with whom I also purged my turbulent libidinal urges.

We were becoming fast friends and redoubtable comrades; and as we drank together that afternoon of Marian's divorce ultimatum, we were waxing virtually conspiratorial. He told me that Marian had invited him to fly to Mallorca with her in a few weeks, paying all expenses for travel and lodging, but not his food and drink, and she had been weaving for him an appealing fantasy, providing fore-tastes of the magical artists' colony in Deya, and had tried to dazzle him with descriptive narratives about the magnetic allure of her *close friend*, the historical novelist and mythographer, Robert Graves. I was amazed and amused and bemused and bewildered by my Marian's proposal. Robert found it most appealing, but was not prepared to encourage her plan any further until he had spoken with me, making it clear that there were no sexual or even limpidly romantic notions at play. I was delighted by the idea, because then perhaps I could get the house back for the summer, and if the divorce were to be moving apace during the summer months, then by the beginning of Fall Term, I could probably keep that jewel of a residence for my own home. More essentially, there would be someone whom I knew and trusted in Marian's company for the next few months, during which time she would be assailed by her family to wreak me as much harm as possible, and I knew that Robert would be her primary confidante and yet still would remain my *shoulder-companion* [that resonant term for Anglo-Saxon warrior comrade] at the onset of the turmoil of divorcing depredations that the family intended to wage against me.

That summer in Deya, Mallorca, did indeed provide a profound awakening for Robert. He not only met Graves, but the two of them became close friends. Robert knew how to massage the knotted upper shoulder muscles of the grizzled old survivor of the World War One trench warfare where he had been so gravely [several puns to be *severely* there] wounded that he was piled in a heap of corpses and an official dispatch was sent to England and his family that he had been killed in action. The welts of scar tissue that decorated his hunched upper back were a formidable challenge for any masseur, and even my friend Robert (with his focused delivery of strength into the tips of his fingers from karate training) told me that the target of his energies was often unyielding and resisted his most determined attack, but Graves averred that my friend was the only person who had ever effected a relaxation of those adamant upper torso sinews knotted by the explosive blasts sustained in the combat experience of his youth in France.

I had sub-let the house on the cove to fellow graduate students in the Literature Department, while I went to work as a sub-editor on the Mark Twain *personal papers* in the Special Collections section of University of California at Berkeley, administered by the editor-in-chief of the Mark Twain University Editions, Frederiick Anderson, editor for the Twain Trust, who took me on as a part-time editorial assistant because I had a letter of reference which I was able to convince Albert Stone to write for me. Professor Stone was the author of the ground-breaking classic literary critical study on Samuel Clemens, *The Innocent Eye.* Albert Stone had left Casady School where he had been my Eighth Grade English teacher, almost twenty years before, and had written his doctoral dissertation at Yale which was published as that book, and he had then become a professor at Auburn University in Georgia. He remembered me as a relatively gifted boy, and it was his recommendation which secured me my summer job at Berkeley.

I found Marilee Maury, divorced wife of one of my friends, Jacques Maury, Parisian French and Turkish varsity wrestler from Penn and then U.D.T officer in the Navy. She and I had been lovers before she met Jacques; I had actually introduced them. She invited me to stay at her apartment in the Mission district, whence I rode a bus daily back and forth to Berkeley. On July 14th, Bastille Day, I was unable to return across the bridge because as I was leaving the main library, I was thrown in to the shrubbery by the tackle of a girl who saw that I was unaware that students were being fired upon with rubber bullets and tear gas canisters by police, sheriff's deputies and National Guard troops, ordered to do so after surrounding the campus, by Governor Ronald Reagan who had been convinced by his advisers that the Berkeley students would most likely stage a protest or launch a riot of some kind as a celebration of the revolutionary historic Bastille Day in Paris on this date – so he had decided to anticipate whatever the students might try to do to upset his calm, peaceful school; and he ordered this armed assault. One student was blinded and several were severely injured that day. Many were toxically infected by the Agent Orange tear-gas [a common-place weapon used in Viet Nam – although outlawed by the Geneva Convention]. My new-found *comrade-in-arms* [we were still locked in one another's *arms* where we lay after falling together in our 'modified paratrooper roll' evading the potentially deadly rifle and tear-gas grenade launcher firing of Reagan's militia] introduced herself as Karen Kerne [I did not tell her of my date with Heather Bethel at Penn whom I asked out only once, immediately adoring the tingling resonance of this alliterative name, but also in order to have the pleasure of introducing her at a sedate cocktail party and listen to whether people tried to repeat her name, or could even begin to do so without giggling] and Karen asked me why I had not dived for cover when I heard the gun-shots. I assured her that I thought this was merely another pursuit of some criminals on campus by the police and that it would have nothing to do with me, a mere scholarly drudge from the inner sanctum of the library. She tugged at my hair which actually had begun to grow rather long and the beard I had allowed to cover my face for the past months.

"You look like a hippy, a radical, and therefore a perfect target for the pigs out there shooting at us - even if your clothes are rather non-descript". [I was wearing old fatigue khakis from the Navy and a faded blue military enlisted man's work-shirt - not exactly preppie or collegiate, either]. She escorted me back to her room in a large boarding house behind the campus when the siege had subsided somewhat, and there, we proceeded to perform the ritual so many students considered as necessary to psychic well-being - a sort of *spiritual dialysis* - as ordinary as brushing one's teeth after most meals: we rolled up some marijuana, smoked it, and then made easy-flowing, soul-calming [Missionary position - mutual orgasm] love, and fell asleep.

I rang Marilee to tell her that I had been caught in a melee at Berkeley and had not been able to get back across the bridge, but would be home the next evening. She did not even ask where I was staying, preserving the understanding that we had agreed upon to allow each other total freedom without any need for pretensions or lies. I wanted to tell her that I had been rescued by a damsel *from* distress, but felt that her feelings might be injured if I mentioned what had actually transpired: a lovely sexual interlude with a complete stranger. Yet I knew that Marilee would be unconditionally accepting of my sexual indulgence. She and I had been sleeping together since the first night of my arrival, and our sexual intimacy had been virtually of a matrimonial nature. We made love easily and well -.like good friends should - if possible. But there was not the passionate intensity to our coupling that we might have experienced if we had just met - as I had just done with Karen.

When I did first meet Marilee and dated her and had sex with her, she had told me that I had taken her virginity, but as we became better acquainted, she admitted that when she was only fourteen, that she had been deflowered by the manager of a hotel in Cairo, Egypt, where she had gone on a holiday, courtesy of her father, who owned the Beverly Hills Hotel. This first lover had been a long-time associate of her father who had mentored this man in the hotel business in various parts of the United States, and later, in some of the Arab Emirates. He claimed that he felt like like a son to her father, whose only child was Marilee, so in a way this loss of her virginity was clouded over in her mind by a sense of almost incestuous guilt. The most ironic feature of Marilee's subsequent relationship with her father was that he told her to never try to make contact with him after she had married Jacques Maury. This famous Hollywood businessman, the owner of the flagship hotel of Beverly Hills, the oasis of the film industry - especially its famed 'Jockey Club' bar where so many agents, actors, directors and producers *schmoozed*, and forged profitable movie deals - this man was an Anti-Semite with a savage hatred of the Jews to whom he really owed so much of his success. So I was sensitive to Marilee's feelings, and when I arrived in her home the next day, I allowed her to rave about how lucky I was to have not been shot or severely beaten, as so many of the students trapped in the Bastille Day punishment had been. I told her that some *students* [the anonymous third person plural: *they*] had taken me to *their* residence and given me a couch to sleep on. I was really touched by her great concern for my physical well-being. My own Marian had not exactly been a doting mate or a nurturing companion.

I did not try to make contact with Karen until I was just about to return to San Diego, as I did not know if she would want to see me again, and I definitely did not want to do anything that might hurt Marilee. Probably my relationship with Marilee was one of the healthiest, *and shortest*, I have ever had. We attended public picnics in Mission Park, Golden Gate Park, and we were usually mildly high on Marijuana and wine, indoors and outdoors. We attended the premier showing of 'Easy Rider' in the Castro neighborhood [an area whose residents were flamboyantly celebrating Gay Identity], and the entire film showing became a Happening with all the Haight Ashbury hippies and the street people from the Tenderloin, Mission and Castro whooping up every epiphantic moment of this filmic, psychedelic symphony.

I did invite Marilee to move back to La Jolla with me, but she said that since her mother still resided there and because she had so many unhappy childhood memories from that town, that she would have to mull this proposition over for awhile. One of her friends had been another shy, but attractive girl, who later became known as the film star, Raquel Welch, the two of them having been close competitors in the annual 'Rough Water Swim Meet,' a race from La Jolla Sores Beach, a free-style swimming event across the Cove to the caves where I now had my home, and back to the Shores. Neither had ever won, but they consoled each other in the showers and the locker-room - she and Marilee were both rather flat-chested and therefore exceedingly shy, then, about their nakedness. Raquel's fuller figure which had become so famous for one photo of her in a clinging wet bathing suit, prominently displaying her breasts, had been a successful surgical implantation paid for by her Hollywood agent. I had once suggested that we look up her old swimming mate, but

Marilee said that would involve going to Hollywood, another place where she had nothing but sad memories; and so did I, if I considered the closest neighborhood, just off Wilshire Boulevard, Marian's, Fremont Place.

In the Special Collections at Berkeley, I had been investigating the formative years of Samuel Clemens, which I had decided to focus upon for my doctoral dissertation. I intended to start writing this thesis in the fall with Professor Roy Harvey Pearce, the pre-eminent Mark Twain scholar at UCSD, whose last learned journal article, 'Post-Script, Huck Finn', was still considered one of the most insightful interpretations of *Huckleberry Finn*. Although I had told my boss, Frederick Anderson of my desire to delve only in the area of Clemens' youth as a river-boat pilot, aged twenty-three, just before the Civil War (1858), he had placed me in a huge stack of correspondence sent to the writer dated some thirty years later and until the author's death in 1910. I had been startled to find one letter from Warsaw, Missouri, which spoke of the writer's visit there when he had been a river-boat pilot just before the war, when he was courting the daughter of the most prominent man in town, Judge Joseph Pelletier Wright, who subsequently became commander of Confederate forces in the region in the Civil War, with the rank of colonel. The daughter of the judge, Laura Mark Wright, then just fifteen years old, had become acquainted with Clemens on a steam-boat trip the family had made just a few weeks before. According to the author of this letter, the young suitor, although a qualified Mississippi steam-boat pilot, was still not considered of a suitable social class for presentation to this prominent family, and he had been treated rudely, and then was literally driven away from the town in a shameless fashion. The informant wanted Samuel Clemens, now a famed author, to know that he, the humble author of this letter, had been ashamed of the Wrights' behavior and knew that Laura and that young man Sam Clemens were most fond of each other; however, at this date, 1878, the author of this particular letter wanted Clemens to know that this same woman now lived in Dallas, Texas, where she was a school-teacher known by her married name, Laura Dake.

I then discovered, after asking Frederick Anderson if there had ever been any mention of a woman named Laura Dake; and that is how I became aware of an extensive correspondence by Clemens with a school child in Dallas, Texas, named Wattie Bowser, beginning about this time. *Coincidentally,* the boy's teacher was Laura Dake. In these letters, Clemens recalled the most beautiful moments of his own youth as having been when he was an apprentice river-boat pilot on the Mississippi, and the particular moments in the voyages he remembered best was in that portion of the river where he had first met young Laura Wright on-board his vessel [I was able to find evidence of that meeting with Clemens' comments about the section of river and the date when that occurred in other sources], but Clemens made no specific references in these letters to Bowser of his acquaintance with the school-teacher, Mrs. Dake. She must have found this most amusing, and deeply moving at the same time.

As I continued my research in this dark corner of the young Sam Clemens' life, I was later startled to discover that all of the successive editors of the Twain private papers had scrupulously erased most notes regarding Laura [*Mark Wright*] Dake. Frederick Anderson, the current editor and my boss, became cagey when I mentioned having found this letter and yet he did admit that many scholars would agree that an ephemeral piece written by Twain toward the end of his life, entitled, 'My Dream Sweetheart,' probably was referring to some girl he had met during his river-boat piloting days, and might be a portrait of this girl, but any other evidence of Laura's importance was dismissed by Anderson. With the help of one of the other editorial assistants who became my friend at our lunch-breaks, Ralph Dickey, told me that he would show me the original holograph copy of 'My Dream Sweetheart' and that I would be startled to see how the first editor of the Twain estate papers, Van Wyck Brooks, had excised all those lines written by Clemens that could have possibly revealed the identity of this secret lover. When I saw the typescript that was taken from the hand-written Twain holograph manuscript, I was heart-broken to consider that almost a quarter of the entire work had been ruthlessly chopped away, thereby obliterating the tender tribute which Clemens had meant to pay his secret love. The lines that were crossed out by Brooks clearly belonged in reference to a young woman who could be nobody but Laura Mark Wright, projecting a portrait which was a virtual holographic [Samuel Clemens' handwritten manuscript] photograph of this young woman.

In another coincidental occurrence – Carl Jung calls these incidents "synchronicity" – I have come to regard them as God-being-anonymous, and my friends, the Quantum Physicists such as Fred Wolf, maintain that it is merely a function of leaks between the membranes of parallel universes – I found a deeply poignant note written by Samuel Clemens at a most critical point in his life, literally in the first conscious moments on the morning after he had seriously considered committing suicide in Angel Camp, California. He had hidden out in this remote place after fleeing from threats made against his life in San Francisco where his passionate journalistic defense of the Chinese workers imported as slave labor had gained him the hatred of many of those who were ruthlessly exploiting these often unwilling immigrants *Shanghaied* from their homes in China [clearly an ironic reverse of that term which normally referred to sailors impressed/enlisted against their will on board vessels bound for *that oriental destination*: China, and such involuntary servitude having since become a synonymous term for such forceful, press-gang labor]. On the night before, he tells in his notebook, that he had held a cocked and loaded pistol to his head after drinking most of a bottle of whiskey; then he had put down the weapon and wandered in a semi-trance state out onto the dark hillside where his tent was pitched. For some unknown reason, his footsteps stopped, just at the rim of a precipice, over which, if he had taken one more step, he would have fallen into a ravine, a sheer drop of over a hundred feet to the jagged rocks below. He considered that his life had been providentially spared. He went back to the tent, and upon arising in the morning, he wrote the following lines.

"Saw Laura this morning. Sing matin, matin. Laura Mark Wright." Then in bold capital letters: "**WRITE!**" and , "The Twain shall meet where the Woodbine Twines."

The last line was scrawled directly under the first entry so that the word *Twain* posited directly below Laura's middle name *Mark*. I could not believe what I was seeing. Could this indeed be the derivation of that tediously long - and usually incorrectly debated subject - of Clemens' choice of a pen-name, a *nome de plume which* became world famous. Instead of designating two fathoms [twelve feet] of water for safe passage over a body of water required for the hulls of most Mississippi river steam-boats, or the more desperate attempt at explanation as being the shouted order for two drinks or two shots of alcoholic beverage at a bar: "Make that twain, barkeep!"

'Where the Woodbine Twines' was a popular song of the 1860s which promised that lovers would be united where the woodbine twines; *matin* is the first morning prayer service held in French Catholic churches, and it was significant to discover that Laura introduced young Sam to a rudimentary practice of a few French phrases while she was a passenger on-board his river steam-boat. Ironically, the writer Mark Twain, in his later years, held the French language in scorn and glorified the German idiom. However, one of his novels (which he considered one of his most seroius works) was written about Joan of Arc. Perhaps his sensibilities were forever afflicted by his treatment by the male members [brothers and father] of the Pelletier family, particularly the judge, later a colonel of Confederate armed forces in Missouri. As I continued to investigate the case, I discovered letters from a medical doctor residing in St Louis who claimed to have letters from Twain to Laura [Mark Wright] Dake, and from her to Twain, written at the turn of the century. The only one I was ever able to see was an entreaty from Laura on behalf of a young man whom she says is richly deserving of a scholarship to further his education so that he may become a medical doctor. Twain's response was to send her a check in the mail for $10,000. This would be comparable today to twenty times this sum and was an extraordinarily generous offering. Who was the young man? Why was Twain so lavish? Did the *twain* again *twine* (in the *woodbine* of their epistolary reunion)?

Laura Dake resided in San Diego in her middle age and till her death. Twain's only surviving child, his daughter Clara Samasoud, married to a professional gambler, also chose to live in San Diego, and died there in 1960, just after I had arrived to begin my active military duty at United States Naval Training Center. Ironically, someone who knew of my interest in Twain had offered to introduce me to her, and only two weeks later, she died, without our ever meeting. Laura Dake had falsified her age in application to the San Diego School Board and so taught far beyond the normal age of retirement, and reportedly was adored by her students, some of whom I encountered to interview. The house where she lived was in the neighborhood near San Diego State University, and for some curious, apocryphal reason, which nobody could explain to me, it had always been called "the Mark Twain place," and there was even a rumor that he had visited there. However, Twain was such a public figure from the turn of the century till his death in 1910, that his high profile would have triggered journalistic notice, and his movements from Connecticut to California would certainly have been remarked upon by press on both coasts, if he had indeed come to visit Laura in San Diego

All of the other letters which Laura received from Twain, she is reported to have destroyed at the request of the editor of the Twain estate papers, Van Wyck Brooks. Therefore, the evidence I had from the St. Louis doctor was truly valuable. Every other scrap of material connecting Laura and Sam was scrupulously eliminated, hidden or destroyed. I attempted to carry my investigation farther, but Professor Roy Harvey Pearce, a staunch supporter of the Twain Establishment, and deeply suspicious of whatever *anomalous* evidence I had found, and especially that which implicated any of the highly respected editors of the Twain estate papers such as Brooks, advised me to drop it. His advice was such that he refused to continue as director of my dissertation if I insisted on continuing in this inquiry. I asked for another director to be appointed, and I was told by Andy Wright that only Edwin Fussel would take me one. Already I was being considered to be a *maverick,* or a *loose cannon,* and no faculty member wanted to incur Pearce's displeasure. I myself gave up on the project as I was then blocked by Anderson from viewing the papers again and as I was experiencing some shocking alterations in my personal and professional life at this point. I gave up on the investigative sleuthing and just became a drinking partner for Ed Fussell who enjoyed alcohol and inebriation even more than I, as we pretended to be preparing another topic for a doctoral dissertation, and I received graduate credit hours for the time we spent getting loaded and feeling sorry for ourselves as we were both going through divorces simultaneously.

Ten years later while on a visit to Dallas, Texas, I telephoned Professor Pascal Covici, Jr. [son of John Steinbeck's amanuensis and editor] who held his tenured position with the English Department at S.M.U. (Southern Methodist University) primarily because of a book he had written about the relationship of Mark Twain with the Dallas schoolboy, Wattie Bowser, Laura's pupil. He invited me to visit his home when I told him briefly about the nature of what I had discovered about Laura. In all his most thorough-going academic research, he had not known of the special connection of Bowser's teacher to Samuel Clemens. As he generously and most graciously responded, "This material would invalidate most of my book and would make many of the most senior Twain scholars in this country look like fools. No wonder Professor Pearce refused to continue directing your graduate research. And Frederick Anderson, as well as all the editors preceding him, has a vested interest to protect. This information could upset the very foundation of the Mark Twain Trust, worth conservatively estimated to be worth several million dollars. *There could even be an heir lurking behind all this.* What if there were to be a *direct lineal descendant* of Clemens [Laura and Sam's child] still living?

All of these possibilities had occurred to me, and I had even considered that my own grandfather might be the illegitimate son of Laura Mark Wright and Samuel Langhorn Clemens. In my later investigations over the years after I left my graduate work at U.C.S.D.

with a conditional degree, the Candidate in Philosophy (C. Phil.), I had visited the home of the deceased St Louis doctor and seen the letters which Laura had written regarding the money Clemens sent her to aid the young man she was helping to continue his education; I also went to Warsaw, Missouri, but all that was left of the Joseph Pelletier Wright family was one male descendant who worked as a truck-driver living in a trailer, who said that there had been some old photos of the family from the time of the Civil War, but that his children had broken into the trunk where they were stored and tore them all to pieces. Most of the official records stored in county court houses had also been devastated by the ravages of that war, but I did locate the Wright family burial plots in nearby St. Joseph, Missouri, where the judge and his wife and two generations of family were buried. Most curiously, I found some records indicating that Laura Mark Wright had been sent to stay with relatives in 1863, only shortly after Sam Clemens' visit to Warsaw.

Her return home was coincidentally accompanied by the announcement of the birth of a child to the elderly Judge Wright and his wife; the child was named William Stage Wright. In the Wright plots at the St. Joseph cemetery, I found a small stone with the name Willy and the date 1889.

My own grandfather, William Stage Wright, became acquainted with Eliza Rogers when they encountered each other at the starting line for the opening of the Cherokee Strip, the Oklahoma Indian Territory Run for Homestead Land in April, 1889. He married this mixed-blood woman who claimed that a piece of land had already been staked out for her deep in the *Territory* (overlooking where Oklahoma City is now situated) by her cousin, an Indian Scout for the U.S. Army. Wright married her that afternoon, and the next morning, they took a leisurely honeymoon ride (rather than a *singular run*) in his wagon, to settle on (homestead deed declares this as Southeast Quarter of Section 9, on Township 12, North of Range 2, West on Indian Meridian in Oklahoma Territory) and occupy a few days later, what became known after 1904 statehood as the Wright Farm on Northeast 63rd Street, between Sooner Road and Air Depot Road, Oklahoma City, also the site of the Wright Cemetery (bestowed as a small land-grant gift on this community of early settlers by my grandfather). Grandpa Wright revealed to some people – though he was normally a taciturn and deeply private individual – that he had discovered when he was a young man, that the person whom he had supposed to be his father *was not*, and so he considered himself a bastard and therefore left home to go establish his own family in the Indian Territory.

If my grandfather, William Stage Wright, born at about the same time as that late edition to the Joseph Pelletier family had *arrived*, coincidentally, when Laura Mark Wright had returned from her *extended hiatus* in St. Louis – that is, if he had been her illegitimate son, whom the family then claimed to be a very late addition to a large family already reared by the middle-aged judge and his wife, who was most likely beyond child-bearing age, then was this child perhaps the offspring of that presumptuous young river-boat apprentice pilot, Sam Clemens, who had come courting Laura uninvited and was driven away when it became obvious that he and Laura were greatly enamored and may have actually consummated their love affair? Was my grandfather Mark Twain's son? The child who was supposed to be the youngest son of Joseph Wright was named William Stage Wright, the same name that my grandfather bore, and he had told people in the Oklahoma Indian Territory where he arrived to homestead with his wife, Eliza Rogers, that he had discovered that the man he had believed to be his father was actually his grandfather and that since it was not revealed to him who his actual father might be, that he considered himself a bastard and therefore was not certain that he was legally entitled to the surname Wright, which was his grandfather's ... and ironically, that same name of most of his Negro neighbors (who had probably belonged as slaves to his grandfather before the recent Civil War – and the senior member of that Black family, Fred Wright, looked like a coffee-colored version of himself, with striking blue eyes and a commanding physical presence) in this Northeast section of what became known as Oklahoma City

I did not continue in my research for long after returning to La Jolla, because after Pearce refused to continue supervising my dissertation project, the divorce by Marian's family pushed me into a financial corner – I was court-ordered to pay her legal fees and costs, and I had to borrow the money as a National Endowment student loan – and then I unexpectantly lost my job as a teaching assistant at U.C.S.D. – under most peculiar circumstances.

I had taught only one class of my Humanities section and on the second meeting of that first week when I arrived in my assigned room, I found that another graduate student had been sent to teach my course. I immediately went to Andy Wright's office to tell him about the error. He was the chairman of the department as well as director of my doctoral program, and I had assumed *until now*, that he was my closest friend on that faculty. He had written and signed the letter which I had assumed to be the effectual legal contract for teaching this course.

"Someone is in my classroom, and he says he is assigned to teach my course," I announced as I stood at his doorway. I was not invited in, and his reply struck me like a hard fist implanted in my solar plexus.

"What course? *Your course?* I was not aware that you were employed by this university any longer," and he turned from his desk to arrange a book on the shelf behind him, his hunched shoulders signaling my dismissal.

"Andy. I have a letter which you wrote and signed, offering me this job as a teaching assistant. Your signature confirms the contract."

"Have you studied law as well as literature? Oh, I almost forgot about your military courts-martial work. Good heavens, how amazing!"

I actually reminded Andy that he was in charge of my ongoing doctoral program and that I needed a salaried job to be able to continue writing my dissertation. He told me that I could go and talk to Dean York who might be needing a research assistant, but that he was unaware of any teaching assistanceship employment available for me at this time in Revelle College at U.C.S.D. When I reminded him that I had a letter signed by him offering me this job for this very semester, he shrugged and implied that I must be deluded.

I took that very letter to the local office of the American Civil Liberties Union and was told that I could do nothing about this because as an non-tenured faculty member that I had no *vested interest* at U.C.S.D. and therefore no contractual rights to challenge legally what had been done to me in such a high-handed, cavalier, and patently illegal manner. I am ashamed to say that I backed down. I was so afraid of Andy's power, that he might then have me dismissed as a doctoral candidate and erased from the university transcript rolls in some Kafkaesque punishment for daring to confront his precious power base. Instead, I telephoned my favorite former professor, from my first graduate course at San Diego State College, Professor Leonard Frey, who now, coincidentally had been promoted to chair the department of English there. Within one week, I was offered the position of Assistant Professor, teaching two upper division courses: Introduction to Theatre, and the Romantic Period of American Literature at San Diego State College The salary was substantial enough for me to pay some outstanding bills, but I was unable to re-purchase the most precious of my belongings which I had sold in the past month to pay the rent and buy food. The Martin guitar I had owned since my mother's death, which I had carried with me and strummed for those past fifteen years, was the last of these treasures to go, and it was gone for good. I have never purchased another guitar since then, and do not play one even now, if afforded the opportunity. My sense of that loss is final – rather consonant with the anecdote I once heard about Arthur Wellesley (later to become renowned as the *Iron Duke* Wellington, victor of the Napoleonic Wars and foremost general of his century, who smashed and burned his violin when he decided to forsake his childish pursuits and enter Sandhurst Military Academy. So it goes.

Fred Hocks once shared a vignette from his past in which he recounted his financial reversals, and his attitude bespoke the indomitable spirit that the true artist maintains regardless of the adversity and losses. While I was driving him one afternoon in the central part of San Diego, Mission Hills, one of the most thickly populated areas of the city, he made a strange remark. He told me with a sweep of his hand that once this entire area had belonged to him, that it had been his ranch, where he had owned a home and had been actively producing his art work, in the company of a loving wife. However, he had traveled up the coast to stay for some time in Santa Barbara with a group of artists whom he believed could help him to learn more about in the technique and practice of his craft as a painter. While he was away from his San Diego land, the taxes had come due, and he had not paid them, so that his wife was evicted and all his paintings which had been in this home were lost, *as was his wife*, who swore to never cohabit with him again. When I asked how he felt about such a major loss, he merely shrugged and told me that his talent as an artist had been enormously improved by what he learned about himself and his technique from his colleagues in Santa Barbara, and that he had never enjoyed maintaining a large ranch anyway. With a deep belly laugh, he again swept his hand about the horizon and declared that this portion of San Diego was the ugliest place in the entire county, and thus, he had avoided having ever to feel responsible for such a cultural blight. When I remarked that he could have become a millionaire, many times over if he had held on to this property and sold all the acreage as city lots, he looked at me as if I were insane, and told me how this would have most certainly have destroyed his soul as an artist, that no price could ever be fixed on such a treasure as the talent which he possessed and had refined – that so many people he had known, did sell out, for money and fame, and their lives were therefore worthless – and shameful.

The only other story which Fred told me about his early days after arriving in America was when he had experienced the San Francisco earth-quake and had taken the uniform of a dead soldier who was there to maintian martial law, and how he had then traveled the beleaguered city and received royal treatment as a member of law enforcement at that crucial moment, and there was one other rather apocryphal tale about his time in his *own uniform* as a young Army cadet attending *gimnasium* [European equivalent educational level of our American high-school and junior college] in his birthplace of Aachen, Germany, where he had become the favorite of a rich, titled uncle's young wife. We sat closely together on a bench in his studio one day as he held an old sepia photograph in our laps and pointed to the lady - his aunt by marriage - sitting in a canopied swing in her full late nineteenth century skirts and prim lace collar, spread over her ample bosom. He snickered gleefully as he told me how he had sat next to her on that swing - sometime in 1898 when he was just sixteen - as she discreetly unbuttoned his military tunic, reached for his genitals and then sedately bowed her head to perform *fellatio* on him, with all the rest of her family seated inside the house, blithely unaware of the intense sexual congress taking place only a few feet beneath their windows. The family was gathered behind the French doors above these shrubbed gardens and carried on with their orderly social affairs and never suspected that the two people in that swing were experiencing exquisite orgasmic delights. I could never get him to validate one other rumor been told by his art student, Ellis Jacobsen, about a gun-fight Fred supposedly had in a bar-room brawl in Arizona where it was said that a sort of bench-warrant was still in effect for his arrest for shooting a man. The most important lesson I learned from Fred was to relish every moment and to dedicate life's experiences into sublimation as an artistic expression in one's chosen medium. Material possessions must be subsumed to the greater calling, one's vocation as an artist, and money is to be used to maintain one's sustenance in order to be totally free to create, unburdened by allegiance to any master but one's own higher consciousness and inspiration. Fred, who lived to practice his art till he died at ninety-eight, said that ten years in the artist's mind can pass as quickly as a moment, and therefore one must seize the day: *carpe diem*. "Live every moment as if it is your last, and one day you will be right," could well describe the vigorous assault Fred made on each instant as the artist who placed every intense sensation on canvas as blazing coloristic representations of abstract expressionism.

It had been in 'Studio Seven' in San Francisco which Fred shared with the poet and literary critic, Kenneth Rexroth, that Allen Ginsberg had publicly delivered the poem 'Howl' for the first time to an audience of a gathering other than just close friends. The event was proclaimed as a monumental moment in such occasions because the subject was so blatantly homosexual and revealing about the world of heavy drug use among the young, the so-called Beatniks, for whom Ginsberg was considered to be a founding member, along with his closest associates from New York and California, Jack Kerouac, author of *On the Road* ,and Neal Cassidy, the model for the protagonist of that novel. In 1965, while I was in my first year of graduate school at U.C.S.D., Rexroth had received an appointment as a sort of poet-in-residence and honorary professor, paid the highest academic salary, and now resided on a more or less permanent tenured basis, at University of California, Santa Barbara. Fred asked me to drive him there for a long overdue visit; the two men had not seen each other since being roommates at that San Francisco studio many years before. I had encountered Rexroth after first meeting him at Penn in 1959 only the following year when he and Lawrence Ferlinghetti gave a performance of poetry accompanied by jazz at 'The Pour House,' the *artsy* bar in the 'Bird Rock' area of La Jolla, in 1960. Fred was delighted that I was acquainted with his friend, and so we arranged a trip up north to have an afternoon and then take an evening meal at Rexroth's home.

I borrowed a reel-to-reel tape-recorder from U.C.S.D. Literature Department attempt to memorialize the conversation between these two. My technical skills were so inferior that only small portions of their chat are intelligible, but I do remember specific details that I wish now I could corroborate from that garbled tape recording. Rexroth maintained that Ronald Reagan, had been zealous and dedicated in his efforts to win substantial pay increases on behalf of the Screen Actors guild in Hollywood - Labor Union activity that one would later hardly believe possible for such an ultra-conservative member of the Republican party - but that such activity had really been perfectly in character for him, at that time, for this man who was later elected Governor of California, and then became President of the United States. Rexroth claimed to have worked intimately with Reagan in several activities on behalf of the Communist Party and therefore found it amusing that his old *comrade* had swung so drastically to the Extreme Right. Although Fred Hocks had never been an actual Communist Party member, he supported many of their activities and fearlessly aligned himself with many of their protests. In downtown San Diego, in 1963, just after his eightieth birthday, he had led a march on Market Street, protesting against the Viet Nam war, chanting, "Ho, Ho … Ho Chi Min."

The two men chattered on about so many former and current friends whom I had not heard of that I just listened to the musical rhapsody of their concerted voices. Benny Bufano, whose statue of Saint Francis stands outside the San Francisco airport, I was aware of this monument, and I found it most amusing that both men considered him an opportunist and not a truly first class artist - or even a skilled *artisan* - Rexroth made the snide remark that Bufano never really learned how "to do hands" - and Fred nodded in agreement.

Later, over dinner, Fred remarked that Rexroth was becoming too complacent and that he must pay some attention to his diet and take more exercise. He pointed to our host's expansive waist-line and then pounded his own firm mid-section which had not an ounce of excess flesh - his pectorals, also, were still firm in his chest, lifting above his rib-cage in the form of a physically fit man, many years younger. Rexroth was not amused, and he became agitated when Fred turned down his offer of a Havana cigar after dinner, but was relieved that a snifter of fine reserve brandy was accepted wholeheartedly, by both of us. I wondered if I should try to finagle that precious cigar, but decided to demur. We were not invited to stay over as house-guests for that night - perhaps Fred's criticism of Rexroth's bloated appearance rankled with our host, or it just may have been that so much of *nostalgia* can so easily become *neuralgia.* When I returned to La Jolla, I was sorely disappointed to hear that the greater portion of this recording was muffled and so weak that even at fullest volume, it was virtually inaudible. Perhaps modern technology will enable me to salvage this artifact - I still have the tape - but I have not tried to listen to it recently.

On the drive home, Fred mentioned reading an article in the newspaper about a poetry conference to be held in San Diego in the next week and told me that Robert Creeley, Edward Dorn, Richard Brautigan, and Michael McClure were some of the guest speakers. Perhaps I could convince the local news media to sponsor me as their correspondent as a sort of *ad hoc stringer* for the event and pick up some cash for my effort and also have the opportunity to hob-nob with some of the most dynamic writers in Amerca. I telephone Ed Self, publisher of *San Diego Magazine* and he agreed to endorse me as his representative, but would pay me only when a finished article was ready for publication; however, I knew I would be too distracted by the events to pay much attention to journalism. I wanted to be in the event and could not afford the entry fee, and would hope that there would be enough snacks provided so I could be fed during the next week. Also, I had just been offered the job at San Diego State College, but would not begin work for two weeks and would receive no pay for at least a month. So I could present myself to the conference as an Assistant Professor in Theatre and Literature from State College, as well as a staff journalist from *San Diego Magazine*. It worked.

I was warmly received by the English Department of Point Loma College who had attracted this unusual assemblage of some of the most popular poets, as well as a controversial Rock and Roll star who esteemed one of the participnats, Michael McClure, to be his mentor in Poetics. Aside from learning more about the craft of poetry, this star of 'The Doors,' Jim Morrison, was scheduled to show a film he had directed and produced while a student at U.C.L.A. Many other film-makers and musicians who were not officially listed in the conference catalogue visited and contributed their works to the events in this forum which was becoming like a *Happening*, those occurrences that had first sprung from concerts in the Filmore Auditorium off Market Street, and spilled out on to the streets of the Mission, Castro, Haight-Ashbury and Golden Gate Park in the San Francisco Bay area, and then transplanted like high-velocity, wind-borne, psychic, viral spoors throughout the country to Chicago, Houston, Memphis, New York City, and over to London, Amsterdam and Paris ... and even to the Soviet Union.

One of the most historically significant such *Happenings* was spawning as we began our Southern Californian anomaly. In Woodstock, New York, a farmer's land was becoming the *genius loci*, the most monumental musical concert in recent history [Paul Krassner, former editor of *The Realist* magazine, Abbie Hofmann, and Wavy Gravy, scion of 'Ant Farm' , were some of the seminal, initial leaders of this event] which would be imitated, but never again equaled, in Glastonbury and on the Isle of Wight in England. It was the singer and poet-*manque*, Jim Morrison, who first announced this phenomenon on the second day of our conference in a seminar being chaired by Robert Creeley, who was telling his audience about the establishment of the Black Mountain School by Charles Olson, himself and Robert Duncan, Edward Dorn and a most select and inspired group of other poets and scholars.

"Something's happening on a small farm back in New York, right now. A place called Woodstock. Bands from all over are coming together there, and they are about to hold the most awesome concert ever," Jim Morrison proclaimed just after Creeley had declared that nothing quite like Black Mountain had ever spontaneously occurred in America, a conjunction of some of the most brilliant creative energies of this century, drawn together to share and learn and generate a renaissance of poetics like never before, and probably never to be replicated.

The entire room looked at Morrison; and only one person spoke up. It was Bob Creeley who responded by saying that he had heard some rumors at the University of New York at Buffalo just before he flew out to this San Diego conference, but he thought that an event of this magnitude would take months to coordinate, so he figured that if and when it happened, that he would be back in New York, so that he could attend.

The rest of us were incredulous and reckoned that Morrison was just buzzing on some of the chemicals he was reputed to ingest in overdose quantities. However, in the following days, when news of Woodstock had flooded television screens and radio wave-bands and had received front page newspaper coverage, some of the participants, especially those natives of the Eastern Seaboard were talking about leaving our specialized literary event and traveling back to participate in what was becoming the most massive mega-concert and *Happening* of the century.

Diane Waikowski, from New York City, was one of the most anxious to leave, but Bobby Creeley, Bob Creeley's wife, talked her into staying for this one week. I was pleased that she did stay, as I had come to fancy her, and if I had not already accepted the job at San Diego State College, I would have accompanied her on the cross-country drive to her home, as she had invited me to do. The few times that she and I had planned an evening together, something had always occurred to interfere with our plans, usually some heavy drinking soiree with Richard Brautigan and Michael McClure who had become fast friends from the moment we first met. Richard and Michael had bonded as a result of a street fight gone wrong in San Francisco two years before.

Someone had threatened Michael, and as Brautigan was taking off his glasses to defend his friend, one of the assailants rounded on him and shattered his jaw. The McClures had taken Richard into their home for the first weeks of his convalescence, and Michael's wife, Joanne, had fed him soup and nursed him, aided by teenage daughter Jane, who, some years later, graduated from medical school and became a pediatrician practicing in Marin County. Richard presented Jane with his famous ten-gallon hat - the one he wore in the photo on the cover of his first best-seller, *Troutfishing in America.* When Jim Morrison was residing in the McClure's guest room, Jane snagged several of his shirts and other articles of clothing; she could have become rich by selling these memorabilia of these Amercan Pop cultural heroes, Brautigan and Morrison, but I would imagine that all these mementos are in some closet or have been worn by her children in that humble suburban home she now occupies in Marin.

Morrison had come to McClure's notice as a result of his daughter's raving admiration of the musician, and when the two men encountered each other in London, they became better acquainted, and it was in England that Morrison asked McClure to become his mentor and guide in transforming his lyrics to actual poetry. As a student at U.C.L.A., although Morrison had been primarily studying film, he had also become enraptured by the English Romantic poets, all of whom he could recite accurately and dramatically; Keats, Coleridge, Shelley, and Byron were his favorites, but it was with a special intensive reverence that he spoke any of the lines of the great master, William Blake, especially from that epic, *The Marriage of Heaven and Hell,* whence he derived the name of his group 'The Doors,' from Blake's line about the "... the doors of perception," following Aldous Huxley's lead from his novel by that title, concerning that English novelist's experience of L.S.D. at the Menninger

Foundation in Topeka, Kansas with the resident psychiatrist, Dr. Robert Lynch, who first introduced him to the use of mescaline and psylocibin.

In one of the first seminars, Brautigan had noticed that my vocal delivery bore an uncanny resemblance to that of his best friend, Michael McClure. Our voices registered in the exact same octave and our mellifluous flow of language and musicality was virtually identical. The only explanation for this could have been that we were both from the same region of the country (Oklahoma and Kansas), but also it was more derivative of our being of similar literary persuasions or inclinations, and therefore we delivered our words with identical reverent care and precise punctuation. When I came to first stay with the McClures on Downey Street in Haight-Ashbury, Joanna commented that we even walked the same way and had the similar manners of affectation in our postures and gestures. She found this *doppelganger* effect hilarious, as did Jane, his teenage daughter. The two women sometimes did imitations of us, and I was amazed at how grandiose I must appear when I am first observed by others. I do affect a kind of theatrical pose and have a tendency to make flamboyant sweeping gestures with my hands and arms.

My own daughter, Marina Wright Muelas, who grew up separately from me (having seen me only at age four and ten and eighteen) has the same mannerisms. I had noticed this posture and movement in all my father's brothers, and had considered it to be the Indian way, as I have also noticed this bearing in other male Native Americans whom I have known in Oklahoma. But Michael is Irish and was reared by his mother, a nurse who worked and lived in Wichita, Kansas. Perhaps, my *twin* speech and similar physical demeanor with

Michael McClure was a projection of our poetic ideation and derived from shared fantasies of our ideal self-images. Once when Michael was being interviewed for the introduction to an anthology of poetry and a tape recorder was used for the job, I was present and inserted some comments while the recording was being made, and later, the interviewer had to ask Micheal and me to sort out whose voice was making which remark, so that only McClure's would properly appear in the printed version.

From the first days of the conference, Brautigan and McClure and I teamed up after the official sessions were finished to go out in to town to visit the sights which most tourists never encounter. We spent most of our time in La Jolla and Del Mar, and both poets particularly liked my Green Dragon cottage, overlooking the Cove. In the following year, Richard asked to come down to celebrate full moon by preparing his special Stonehenge Stroganoff, a sumptuous feast [I still have that secret recipe (and a photograph of Richard and me stirring the broth) for this offering; a tantalizing tidbit for his many admirers and fans], for all our friends. Michael also found any excuse he could to come stay with me in my home. However, the one person who never quite seemed to fit in was Jim Morrison. He always wanted to be with Michael McClure, but his social skills were so clumsy that he often would only stay with us for spurts and then would abruptly leave, usually in a huff about some imagined affront.

One night, at the Point Loma poetry conference, Michael asked me for some money to buy a bottle of wine so that he and a couple of girls could spend the night in a sexual romp in their dormitory room at the host college. I had only ten dollars and some change I needed for gasoline to get me home and back for the next day's conference, but I gave him the ten. He paid me back the next morning, and I was amused to think that the two men had sneaked in to a women's dormitory at a fundamentalist Christian college to have a sexual encounter. It must have been cramped and *conventually* unappealing, but then it was also probably exciting in the risk factor and the thrill of possible discovery by campus guards or dormitory matrons. When I saw the two girls who had breakfast with Michael and Jim that morning, I hoped that the wine had provided some romantic gloss, because the two students looked like puppies of indeterminate breed, with much baby fat and no expression of any sensual appeal whatsoever. They were in a state of ecstatic delight, having spent the night with such a famous Rock and Roll star and the dashing poet-laureate of the Hells Angels. Later that day, when we were having coffee with one of Brautigan's close friends, John Carpenter, (whose last novel *Hard Rain Falling* was currently selling well), he was sharing with us how he always had a medical doctor (a close friend) give him a large dose of penicillin after all these literary conferences, because every time he attended one and had sex with any of the *groupies,* he always could be sure of catching some venereal disease, especially gonorrhea. Leon Russell's song about these admirers of the celebrities - "Let me sit in your lap and give you the clap" - came to mind, and I sang this line, to everyone's amusement, except Michael McClure's. He looked decidedly uncomfortable, and I recalled that he was one of the very few poets who actually had a live-in partner. The other exceptions were Bob Creeley and Ed Dorn, and their wives were accompanying them at the conference. I had met Ed Dorn while hitch-hiking with Marian in 1966, when he held a Fulbright scholarship teaching at University of East Anglia in Colchester, with his first wife. Marian and I had just met Anselm Hollo, the Finnish poet in London and became friends over several pints of bitter in a pub there. If Michael developed symptoms in those days immediately after the conference, there was that great danger of infecting his wife. Actually there would be enough time - over the forty-eight hour span usually required for developing the first ticklish indications of infection of the urethra -

before the end of the conference and his return to San Francisco. But McClure still looked nervous.

I was pleased that Ed Dorn remembered me from my visit to his residence in Colchester, England. He said he was sorry to hear that Marian had left me, but then he, himself, was also with a new wife, and they had a small baby as well. He told me that his dream was to become a tenured professor at some university – later his wish was fulfilled – because his greatest pleasure was in delivering a prepared lecture to a hall filled with attentive students. I found this surprising as I had imagined that most poets would want only to read their work or discuss ideas with informal assemblies of like-minded talents, such as were to be found at this conference. Dorn presented his latest work in progress, *Gunslinger*, an extended poetic caricature of Howard Hughes and megalomaniacs of his ilk in the American archetypal stamp, delivering his reading in a small auditorium at the college, and I was impressed by his lecture and then his skilled reading of the work. He would indeed make a splendid university professor, I thought at that moment, although he projected himself in the *persona* of a literary "gunslinger" whose ammunition was poetry. Curiously, when my critical biography of Roger McGough was published by Mellen Press and the poet's photo appeared on the front cover with mine on the back, McGough wrote a letter to me to say that he thought that he looked like the professor, but that I looked like a *gunslinger*.

I had always imagined a poet to be a bandit of sorts, like the wandering minstrel, called *picaro in the* Spanish classical mode of the *picaresque*: the prototype of Kerouac's narrator in his novel, *On the Road*. The notion of outlaw artist is is in character with the protagonist of Tom Robbins' *Still Life with Woodpecker*, a free-lance demolition expert (bomber) who blows up buildings as purely provocative acts. Robbins explains that true art is an expression for itself, with no intentional goal in the mind of the artist ... perpetrator, or, *bomber*, in this case. The wandering *scop* - the Irish bard in William Butler Yeats' apocryphal story, 'Crucifixion of the Outcast,' who is publicly executed on a cross by order of the abbot of the monastery where he had complained too loudly about the inferior bed and miserable food he had been given for the night before, when he had just wandered in and asked for a sleeping accommodation. The *Wound and the Bow*, Edmund Wilson's discussion of the artist as having to live outside the conventional social realm, afflicted by a noisome wound of that extraordinary talent of a genius (Wilson chooses the persona from Homer's, *Iliad,* of the archer, Philoctetes, afflicted with a stinking sore from a snake-bite), yet this man is needed above all others to send the arrow to its bulls-eye (this wounded warrior's inimitable gift in superior marksmanship from his mentor, Hercules; to let fly at the best target on that wall of Troy), so that the majority of mankind must hold their noses to bear the artist's presence and willingly bear his company only as long as is necessary to achieve desired ends, for the benefit of all.

When Robert Duncan arrived at our conference one evening from his home in San Francisco, to deliver his poetry, he literally somersaulted on to the stage, and then sat on the apron of that stage to comment on his bizarre entry, remarking that poets have been so long considered as clowns or jesters, by the general public, that he declared that he would juggle, if he were so skilled, to play in to that mind-set, and was willing to do whatever would arrest his audience's attention so that they would then listen to his words. He commented that for so long he had been treated like an outsider by the established academic world, that now when his works were published with such success and high critical acclaim, that the University of California invited him to be a visiting professor, that he was inclined to decline out of resentful spite for all the disappointment he had experienced in the years before, when he had applied for any menial position there, and been rejected as merely an unpublished *avant garde* poet – an *outcast.* His audience this night consisted of many of his colleagues from those years before, and there were aspiring poets who attended this conference hoping to learn survival strategies from artists like Duncan who most definitely could be sympathetic to the arduous struggle for recognition – or merely publishing – in this field.

That same evening, after Duncan's reading, we were invited to a showing of the film Jim Morrison had produced as his graduation project when a student at U.C.L.A. His career as a performing musician, lead singer in his group, 'The Doors,' had coincided with the last years of his undergraduate work and had projected him from the nightclubs on the Sunset Strip to venues in large stadiums throughout the West Coast of America, so that much of the film footage was of this experience of a band on stage and on the road: wild parties, groupies, and the raucous bedlam associated with such chaotic *crusades* or *pilgrimages* of the popular musical productions of that genre in the 1960s. Many members of the audience who were already fans of 'The Doors' – the greater proportion of the undergraduates present – applauded loudly at the end of the film. However, when Jim Morrison took the microphone on center stage and asked for comments from some of the older and more professionally qualified artists in attendance, a few of whom were film-makers and screen-writers, he was offended by their critical remarks (some were acerbic and dismissive), and with an explosive reaction to one comment in particular, he flung the microphone to the ground and stomped off the stage, cursing and swinging his fist at the audience. He leapt in to his rented car parked just outside the building, laid rubber on the pavement there, and then drove on to the lawn in front of the administration building where he revved the engine and swerved the car in circles, plowing up the grass in ugly gouged muddy disfigurement till there was hardly any lawn left, and then he wheeled his vehicle on to the street outside the entry gate and roared off into the night. So much for *his* learning experience, at the conference! Curiously, he was in attendance the next morning, and his agent arrived to make a substantial payment to the college to repair his vandalism from the night before.

After all the classes that day, which was coincidentally the closing of the conference, Michael asked that I accompany him and Brautigan and a few other close friends to have a few drinks with Morrison. We gathered in a garden at the bottom of the main college lawns - or what was left of them, after Morrison's uprooting and devastation of the theretofore smooth grass expanse there - and cushioned our bottoms on the soft carpet of grass that furnished this small enclosure surrounded by branches of bougainvillea and other flowering vines and shrubs. Michael seemed very concerned about consoling Morrison over his hurt feelings from the night before. Brautigan and I agreed that this was an over-reaction to criticism that was not meant to be altogether malicious, albeit, it had sounded somewhat harsh. However, we set about quaffing from the few bottles of whiskey that were passed around the circle of some six or seven serious drinkers. Morrison had brought along a scruffy, young fellow whom he called by the name of Angel, a sort of "step-and-fetch-it" *factotum* who was supposedly a *minder* (body guard). Angel claimed to have ridden his motorcycle with some chapter of the Hells Angels, but was never accepted for membership in any particular group. According to the stringent standards of Free-Wheeling Frank Reynolds of the San Francisco club, a man had to display *real class*, to prove himself worthy of acceptance by the fierce outlaws who comprised this elite cadre. If this lad, named Angel, had any *class*, it certainly was not of the mettle or distinction required by any chapter of Hells Angels I had ever known or even heard of. Richard Brautigan had shared with me some apocryphal *insider* lore: that when Hells Angels met, they French-kissed each other, and when they bid farewell, they simulated *dry-humping* (anal intercourse) each other's rears, and that the origin of the Red Wing's badge worn by some, was to signify that a member had performed cunnilingus on a fellow Angel's "Momma" (a wife, girl-friend or accepted female *groupie*) when she was at the height of a menstrual cycle, when her flowing blood from her vulva would soak his mustaches to resemble Red Wings. This particular young fellow, Morrison's *hench-person*, was a Southern California caricature of a Quasimodo or Igor character-type, cast to assist a mad professor in his demonic laboratory experiments and perhaps collect body parts from recently dug graves. As we finished almost all the liquor in the bottles, Angel was grovelling before Morrison, begging to be of some assistance to his *master*.

"What can I do, Jim? What do you want? What can I get for you?" Angel pleaded soulfully.

"Yeah, you can do something for me, Angel. You can amuse me," Morrison snarled as he swiped an empty bottle across the boy's forehead, which then spurted blood which ran down over his brows into his eyes. "Go buy us some more whiskey, and stop that ugly bleeding. You know how I hate the sight of blood. Ugggh!"

Both Brautigan and I rose at the same instant. Michael remained seated beside Morrison, shaking his head, and then giving us a look to indicate that we could just shove off, that he would handle matters here. We were both on our way to my car as Angel bolted past us to Morrison's vehicle holding his tee-shirt up on to his brow, tying it into an improvised head-dress tourniquet as he ran to fetch more booze for his idol.

So much for *the lives of the rich and famous*, or words to that effect, both Brautigan and I exchanged the same dismissive remarks as we made our way to the El Sombrero in La Jolla and then to my place to sleep it all off.

"Michael thinks he's worth it," Brautigan later remarked, but would make no further comment.

Michael McClure was Brautigan's best friend at that time, and if Michael considered Jim Morrison worthy of his companionship and loyal nurturing, then Brautigan was prepared to defend McClure's opinion. Yet Morrison's gratuitously, nasty assault this evening, and other similar petulant vicious behaviors that he was reported to have inflicted upon other helpless victims, deserved serious psychiatric attention if not the pressing of criminal charges and observational confinement in a sanitarium, or perhaps even such an extreme remedy as a lobotomy – if not reprisal in like form and degree of violence. So far, Jim Morrison had escaped any punishment for his haughty rampages worthy of a Caligula or Nero in their psychotic flamboyance.

By spending much of his time with McClure, Jim always would be provided the protective company of members of the Hells Angels whose code of conduct would allow for many of Morrison's excesses – as long as these were never enacted against any of that brotherhood. Bullies like Jim Morrison rarely leveled abuses against those who were capable of self-defense. His minion, Angel, was paid to be a whipping boy, and like some dutiful puppy, he adored his cruel and vicious master.

My college classes began the week following the conference, and although I made some attempt to organize my voluminous notes into a presentable article for *San Diego Magazine*, I knew that I would probably never do so. My preparation for my first class required some extensive reading – the old formula of seven hours preparation for each hour of lecture time, often really does equate (when a lecturer is serious in his dedication) – and I wanted to justify Professor Leonard Frey's decision to place me in an upper division course as a neophyte assistant professor. I intended for my initial lecture to be monumental and dazzling ... and *academically sound.*

It was! I have always had a vibrant stage-presence and with all the ammunition I had acquired from some of our country's leading poets at the recent conference, and with my need to prove myself a star in the university literary sphere, I was literally strobing and radiating sparklers when I stood before that first class: "The Romantic Period in American Literature" was the course title in the college catalogue. My gambit was simple and arresting. Because I had come to wear the costume of the stage-hippy of that epoch – bell-bottom broad-striped trousers, full sleeved peasant blouse with necklaces, and my long, reddish blonde, sun-streaked hair tied with a bandanna over my forehead and knotted behind – looking like so many of the students in my class – I declared, when I assumed the podium and grasped the lectern, as if I were wresting control of this class for those of us who had paid our tuition and were NOT ready to assume the passive role of instructees for this semester, "Where in the hell is this professor? Does anyone know what this geek looks like? Who is he? He's already late, and if he doesn't show up soon, I'm going to the Registrar and demand my money back."

I stood there watching the shocked assemblage, many of whom appeared highly amused and perhaps inclined to follow my lead to the Registrar's office. I remained at the lectern for another five minutes, and at ten minutes past the hour, I announced that I would teach the class, if no one else stepped forward with better qualifications. Then I introduced myself as the Ben Wright who had been appointed to direct this course, whose name actually was affixed to their printed course schedules and appeared in the catalogue as a member of State College faculty. I cited my academic credentials, my completed doctoral courses and examinations from U.C.S.D., but I also added that I was a hippy, an outcast, a poet, and a complete fraud, and that San Diego State had just performed one more huge fuck-up at the expense of the tax-payer and those students who were indeed serious about acquiring an education. I stopped and waited a full ten beats before going on to say that any students who wished to go to the Registrar's office now, to demand their tuition money back, were free to do so, with my blessing. However, I did want them to know, that when it came to being an expert in the concept of the Romantic, and especially as it pertained to the American notion of such an idea, then I was most likely the best qualified to present material in this field – that I had failed in most of what were considered primary achievements of the American Dream, having walked away from high-paying prestigious employment, disqualifying myself for membership in any Chamber of Commerce, Rotary Club, or more especially, any Country Club, and was especially unwelcome at the La Jolla Beach and Tennis Club – that I was the sort of young-man-on-his-way-down that most Middle-Class mothers warned their daughters to stay away from – that my last wife, a Los Angeles debutante, had been paid enormously to divorce me – and therefore, I had taken refuge in the only alternative to money and fame, and that was to become an academic *expert* in Romantic ideation and hopeless dreaming, that I indulged in the mental masturbatory exercises of writing poetry, short stories, screen-plays, and even a novel or two. I could probably present an ideal example of what not to do in order to avoid any material success or respect in the community, be it San Diego, or any substantial metropolis from New York to California - that I, so very like Henry Thoreau, author of *Walden*, or *On Civil Disobedience*, would be able to inspire as many of my colleagues to turn away from their expected career goals and humble strivings for contributing to the public good, as defined by those most concerned with maintaining the stability of the status quo. My dedicated intention was to serve as a subversive, a character like Socrates' gadfly, to sting the rump of the body politic, to disrupt, to question, to provoke, to unceasingly ask why all my dreams could not come true, why I could not make love, sing, dance, play and carry on long past time when I might be told to come home, clean up my room, do my homework, the dishes, wash the car, mow the lawn - need I go on?

I would represent the hopeless adolescent, the pilgrim seeking the Holy Grail, the Fool on the Hill, the Sirens' call, the aching yearning for the improbable, but *oh-so-desirable* ... in a word: the Romantic. I could only guarantee one reward from this course. Every student, at the end of this semester, would be awarded his or her *virginity*.... that pure, innocent, quintessential virtue of belief in the impossible would be renewed - absolutely. Seeing that only a few stumbled to escape my continuing blather, I then focused my first lecture on one of the required texts which I had ordered for this course: *A Bibliography on Amercan Literature for Ed Dorn*, by Charles Olson, founder and first *rector* of the Black Mountain School. As I had just been in the company of Dorn and several other alumni of Black Mountain, only a day or so before, I had truly *hot news* from that front. I decided not to mention being in the company of Jim Morrison, although the mention of his name and his group, 'The Doors,' would have certainly roused my audience. I still felt not only ambivalent about this person, but had been deeply disgusted and offended by his antics.

My class was deemed a success. The Registrar's office telephoned me to report that not only had more than ten withdrawn after my first meeting, but that now some twenty-five were begging to be allowed late entrance; I must give my permission, as the normal course limit was forty and this would swell the size to fifty-five. There was seating for only sixty, and so the Fire Marshall must approve the increase. Leonard Frey also called to tell me that he was pleased with rumors he was hearing about my class. He reminded me that by giving me this upper division course, that he had offended some of the more senior faculty who felt they deserved such desirable assignments, but that now he was sure that his decision had been correct, and that everyone would benefit from my contribution. I felt deeply satisfied [praise from Caesar, indeed] and wanted to continue to bring credit to my mentor, my very first instructor in graduate school who had terrified his class by declaring that any flaw in spelling, grammar, or even typographical error in our first required essay would constitute a failure of the entire assignment. I was one of the very few to receive the grade of A in his course, and I had become one of his most favored students from then on. I had been teaching secondary school English Composition for two years at that time, so I, myself, had become a ferocious editor of student essays and was able to scrutinize my own work with an intense attention to the slightest anomaly in any mechanical flaw. I well remember poring over some papers I was correcting, while I was attending his classes - I had driven straight from work at La Jolla Country Day School where I was instructing English - during the fifteen minute break we were allowed during his three hour evening course. Professor Frey approached me as I was bent to my editorial labor on my own students' writing and said something I shall never forget: "Our type become either Special Investigators with federal law enforcement agencies like the F. B. I., or long distance runners." He then directed my attention to two gold figures that dangled from the watch-fob between pockets in his waistcoat. One was the Phi Beta Kappa key, and the other was a running shoe. He told me one was awarded at his undergraduate university for academic excellence, and the other by the A.A.U. for his long distance running championships. I told this vignette many years later to my friend Alan Silitoe. His most famous book (later a popular film), *The Loneliness of the Long Distance Runner*, a revealing and enlightened analysis of this personality type (the outsider, the outcast ... the *artist?*). Was this a portraiture of Alan Silitoe, Leonard Frey, or ... me?

I had indeed attempted to become a federal special investigator of sorts, when I tried to change my naval officer's career designator to Intelligence from Line Combat. This had been when Lisa and I first returned from Oklahoma to settle in to San Diego and I had joined the naval reserve unit at my old command, U.S. Naval Training Center, at Point Loma. I had attended two months of Naval Intelligence meetings there, and when I requested to be officially transferred to a Naval Intelligence designation, I encountered difficulties that I could not have expected. I was already somewhat bored with the nature of the work, as Intelligence gathering was indeed rather a romanticized excuse for pursuing mundane accountancy procedures, and the mentality of all the other Intelligence officers appeared to be that of shop-keepers or bookkeepers - drones and drudges who just filed away reports from agents in the field. I suppose I had imagined the work to be that of the agents who were out in the field doing the reconnoitering and spying. Also, I had discovered that the abiding personality of the officers at this particular base was rather of a vulgar and petty-minded stamp. Our commanding officer was an overweight motorcycle buff who rode his huge Harley-Davidson Gold Eagle from El Centro, some fifty miles east of the city to our weekly meetings. He had the rank of full commander and swaggered about as if he were an admiral. He made so many sexist, racist, and anti-Semitic remarks, also reveling in telling jokes that belittled homosexuals and aggrandized bullies, so that I once asked him why he had chosen a particular topic for his humor, and I was met with an outraged reaction which should have warned me to back off or apologize.

So I really should not have been surprised that when I had my official interview, requisite for the transfer of my designator, attended by a couple of officers of equal rank to this commanding officer, that I was asked questions which by their very nature were meant to disqualify me for work in any classified security field. The questions were of the sort we had been taught to use when attempting to impeach all testimony of a witness in cross-examination in courts martial: "When did you stop beating your wife?" Mine was thrown out as a sneering opener by the C.O. (commanding officer). "We understand that you teach poetry and *other-world* ideas in our schools. Do you ever coach football? Did you ever play *ball* [meaning *football*]?"

The question was meant to imply that I was a sissy, and an "other-world" one at that [one of those Americans who actually considers that there may be other "worlds"; that is, other nationalities with rights to their opinions, and who might be listened to if their views did not collide with America's foreign policy – in other words, was I a potential turn-coat and traitor?]. That I did not coach football at the secondary school where I taught and that I might somehow have avoided playing that hallowed American sport which idolizes bullying and violent aggressive expression was the real cutting edge of his question. For a moment, only, did I consider attempting to answer the question as if it were not already an Anti-Personnel Claymore type mine triggered to explode no matter which way I moved. I decided to take the most offensive stance and to attempt to blow away my antagonistic commanding officer, hoping that his colleagues were not as benighted and demented as he.

"I did play football at my own secondary school, until my senior year, when I was tackled and sustained an injury to my knee which I needed to heal before the Spring tennis season when I captained our conference-winning team. But the main reason I decided not to play football any longer was because of the homo-erotic games being conducted in the locker-room showers by so many of my team-*mates* - pardon that expression. [as I had emphasized the word, *mates*]. I can imagine that you delighted in all this post-game hoopla, sir, but that was never the source of my pleasure. I was ... "

He did not allow me to continue, interrupting with a fierce blast. "Are you calling me some kind of cock-sucking, little fairy? You low-down son-of a- ... "

But he was also interrupted in mid-insult by one of the visiting officers who actually grabbed his sleeve and held him back from what looked like a round-house punch coming in my direction, and this man muttered words meant to calm him and attempt to return this interview to a proper official level.

"Let's just calm down, Gentlemen. We are all officers here, and I feel certain we can return to our interview with some decorum." And then this particular man, a commander who was not overweight or of any particularly dissolute demeanor, carefully opened a manila folder and turned some pages which he peered down at before raising his eyes to address me.

"Lieutenant Wright, we have evidence that you have been in the care of a psychologist in the past few years. We must ask you if you are still receiving treatment for some mental disorder, and if so, what is the degree of the severity of your mental incapacity? This is certainly not a condition which this board could agree to waive or approve ... or condone ... in considering your candidacy for entering the Intelligence branch of our naval forces."

Yikes! Talk about cross-examination techniques for impeaching a witness, or declaring a mistrial, or preparing charges for an entire Inquisition with only an *auto da fe* as a possible consequence? Was this man's name Torquemada, the Spanish Grand Inquisitor, himself? I looked at his name plate badge: Moore, it read. For the Spaniard, in his consciousness of a mythical history, and actual historical past as tyrannic rulers, the bogey men are the evil Moros, the savage North Africans threatening to reclaim his ancient homeland. My present *bogey man* was a Mr. Whitebread (albeit, one of a family of *Moores*). This character looked like the sort who waters his petunias in his small suburban garden from a spray nozzle while dressed in golfing green Bermuda shorts with a faded Madras cotton shirt. Yet his delivery of this question had cut me off at the knees, just above tennis shorts' line. The Claymore had spoken, and I felt deafened and was hard-put to reply. But I did; and thus ended my career in the United States Naval Reserve, although at this particular moment, I did not realize that I was singing my swan song as a member of the United States Navy.

Already, members of this board had ruled out any possibility for me to be considered for reclassification as a Naval Intelligence officer. I had begun to entertain the idea of applying for the new high-speed torpedo-attack boat forces, like those P.T. boats that John F. Kennedy had served in during World War Two. Only a few of these models had actually been put into commission at this point in 1963, but I knew of them because of my friends in the SEALs who had been active in Viet Nam since 1960 and because of some of the briefings I had been privy to while still in training with Naval Intelligence. These vessels were being designed as river patrol craft, later to become famous as the vessel used by Martin Sheen starring in Coppola's film, 'Apocalypse Now,' forging upstream to the stronghold of the Green Beret Colonel Kurtz (Marlon Brando) *gone native*, and therefore, to be handled with *extreme prejudice* - assassinated by the dedicated young Green Beret captain played by Sheen. And then of course, there was the real-life U.S. Navy Lieutenant John Kerry [later Massachusetts senator and then presidential candidate], but he was not to be heard from till he began his anti-war protests some time later.

I actually admitted to having had some psychological counseling which had been recommended by my last commanding officer, and had been referred to a civilian associate of the medical department from my former command. I had developed pre-ulcer stomach disorders which were considered a possible result of the stress I was experiencing as Recruit Personnel Officer at that time. I explained that I had availed myself of this treatment for the few weeks necessary to relieve the symptoms and would highly recommend this as an alternative to prescription drugs for similar stress disorders with any other person, civilian or military. I knew that this could be the only possible record in my file of such an unusual occurrence in a junior officer's career - psychotherapy was considered to be as extraordinary as visiting a witch-doctor or voodoo practitioner, at this time in the American Armed Forces. So I did not mention that I had continued to see Morris Price for weekly sessions of psychological counseling for the past two years. However, the few weeks which were indisputably on record for my "treatment" for what was interpreted by these board members as a "mental disorder" constituted a screaming admission of my instability, and therefore, proof of my unreliability in any position considered to be of a security risk to the military.

"However," Commander Moore offered calmly, "If you will submit to some psychiatric examinations from the staff at the Navy Hospital at Balboa Park, and we are satisfied with the psychological profile we receive from such an appraisal, we will re-convene this board at a later date for your re-application for transfer to the Naval Intelligence dsignator, but let me assure you now, that your performance this evening has led my fellow officers to not be well disposed toward such a procedure. And I strongly, personally, advise you to get some immediate psychiatric treatment, no matter what. That is all." And folding his hands over my file which he closed with that conclusive gesture, he rose and ordered the other officers dismissed.

I discussed this experience with Morris Price only a few days later, and he howled with amusement. If I were psychologically well-suited to continue service in the Navy, then all the work we had done to unsnarl my most knotty neurotic problems would have been for naught, he remarked. He found my P.T. boat illusion the most hilarious of any of my more flamboyant fantasies to date. I had long ago given up on the idea of joining the SEALs, but only after some deep probings into my most disturbed memories of child-hood abuses by my parents did I understand that I need not continue to seek out such soul-endangering punishments to serve as verification [or *authentification*] of my identity. Then I discussed my sense of deepest trauma, however, my sense of Langston Hughes' poem 'Harlem', the lines about what happens to a "dream deferred" - does it dry up and wither like a raisin in the sun or does is finally burst from its putrescent, implosive turmoil and explode? I was feeling that constantly growing sense of a churning within me from my sense of aching for an advance in my education and seeking my place somewhere in the world of higher education. Morris nudged me along to enroll at summer school and then night classes to begin graduate work in literature at San Diego State College and then to apply for the doctoral program which had just been established at U.C.S.D in La Jolla; and I did, at last, find myself teaching my own university courses as an assistant professor at San Diego State, just five years later.

I completed that first teaching semester to the satisfaction of Leonard Frey and had become one of the most popular professors on campus. Only Jerry Farber had more of an ardent student following. His best-selling book, *The Student as Nigger*, had brought him national attention as a spokesman for the student and any second-class citizen of color. I adapted his book to the curriculum of my next course entitled, "Introduction to Literature," along with *The Teachings of Don Juan*, *Black Elk Speaks*, and *Another Roadside Attraction* [the only novel so far written by Tom Robbins, Richard Brautigan's pal whose first book had at this time sold only a few hundred copies]; and I even included such bizarre novels as Ishmael Reid's, *Yellow-Back Radio Broke Down*. Of course, Richard's own *Troutfishing in America*, *Confederate General from Big Sur*, and *In Watermelon Sugar* were all required reading. The only mainstream texts I included were Thoreau's, *Walden*, Melville's, *Moby Dick*, Faulkner's, *Sanctuary*, William Burroughs,' *Naked Lunch*, Jack Kerouac's, *On the Road*, and Albert Camus's, *Stranger* and *The Myth of Sisyphus*.

Juan Goytisolo, who at this time was my dinner partner almost every evening, as Carlos Blanco had convinced him that I was the only person whom he would find *simpatico* at U.C.S.D. where he was currently Regent's Professor of Literature, advised me to include his pal the renegade convict (Saint – some called him) Jean Genet, and some other politically radical North African writers like Achebe on my list. If I could have found a decent translation of his close friend, the Cuban, Guillermo Cabrera Infante's novel *Tres Tristes Tigres*, I would have gladly included that. As it was, my course was modeled on Farber's central theme from *Student as Nigger*, that being the notion of *provo*, as defined as being a provocative act by students, or artists, or any radical individuals, which is so outrageous – *provocative* – that it arrests attention, but with no particular political or social comment or remark implicit in this act or event. Tom Robbins, in his subsequent novel, *Still-Life with Woodpecker*, had created his protagonist, named Woodpecker, as just such a provo artist, who bombed buildings, any selected public structures, just to get attention, as what Robbins conceived to be the purely poetic act worthy of the social outcast who could thus be deemed to be a true artist. To launch my course in such a *provocative* mode, I announced on the first day that all students enrolled would automatically receive the grade of A for their attendance at lectures, which I then intended to transform into co-creative, participatory learning experiences.   Attendance would be taken, and only two excused absences were allowed to justify the final grade of A. The desks, which were described as "student stations" in the inventory of the school's Supplies Department, were to be removed, and would be replaced by bean bags, sleeping bags, carpets, throw pillows, and whatever other comfortable and comforting interior decorations and furnishings we as a group decided were appropriate to our unfettered search for the meaning of Literature, the study of the fine art of written expression and better understanding of our selves and our place in the contemporary world.

My class was completely enrolled, with a waiting list, and not all because of the guaranteed grade of A. My fame, or infamy, was growing. During that fall, I had made frequent visits to San Francisco, staying in Haight-Ashbury with the McClures and even *crashing* in Brautigan's spartan residence [the expression to *crash* at someone's *pad* being most appropriate in Richard's case as he had one bed only and I had to curl up in a sleeping-bag on the floor of his other room, normally used only as an office], and both poets had come to stay with me in La Jolla, several times, as well. Richard and Michael visited my classes. My students were eager to ask about their associates and artistic colleagues such as Jim Morrison, Bob Dylan, Jack Kerouac, and Free-Wheeling Frank Reynolds of the Hell's Angels with Michael, and Janice Joplin, Richard's ex-girlfriend. My classes had become "free-wheeling" affairs in which students would sometimes perform impromptu skits with musical accompaniments to poetry which they read and danced to. There was one student who had been in my English class at La Jolla Country Day School who sat in the back of the classroom playing a guitar in what sounded like the Classical or even Flamenco style, depending on his mood. He claimed that he was running riffs on my delivery and providing the musical counter-point of whatever the students contributed to my declarations.

What I had initially proposed as a co-creative experience in the discovery of the search for the meaning of literature had become a unique art form in itself. However, I still followed a format that derived from my eclectic selected book list, delivering lectures that at times must have seemed like dramatic monologues, and perhaps even appeared to be trance invoked evangelical rants with *vatic* supernatural resonances. I would open a class meeting with a snippet or verse from a poem, a novel, or a play, or a currently popular movie or song – from the Doors' "Baby, let me light your fire ... Break on through to the other side," or Albert Camus's statement from *Myth of Sisyphus* that the only essential question for any philosopher is whether or not to commit suicide, or the chapter from Brautigan's *Confederate General from Big* Sur which provides a catalogue listing of the number of punctuation marks in the book of 'Ecclesiastes' in the *Holy Bible*, or Kerouac's description of that sense of a writer's rage to know, to consume, to live, to travel, to see, which surges out of the *persona* of his protagonist, Dean Moriarty, from *On the Road*, to Thoreau's apocryphal statement from *Walden* that the majority of people lead lives of quiet desperation, to which I would append my own tag-line, "And go even to the grave with their song still unsung – so what is your song? Have you sung it? Have you ever even heard it? Do you know the beat? The beat? The beat?" ... and I would repeat and repeat and repeat ... this line, or one similar to it, till someone in my audience would respond, or even ask where we were going with this. The theme of the course became like that of my life: *Anything Sometimes*. One idea would lead to another.

As Michael McClure had remarked that he had begun practicing Tai Chi as a method for gathering and focusing energy in order to develop a new poetic form, so I discussed my own instruction in Shotokan Karate and the recent work of a U.C.S.D. Physics doctoral candidate named Lester Kirby who had established a foundation for the study of mental focus and its relation to the martial arts. I invited Robert

Stratton, who had his black belt in Shotokan, to show the basics of the movements in my class, and in demonstrating a blow to the face, he slipped on the floor and broke my nose. He then delivered a skilled para-medical re-setting of the damaged nose, with my tearful consent, in the next few minutes. That was a truly dramatic presentation, which everyone enjoyed ... more than I. There were other *dramatic* moments in my classes, but this was a time of great upheavals in the universities and colleges in protests against the war in Viet Nam, and students began to realize their power to change and even determine academic policies and to register their influence in the general public consciousness.

Our first campus-wide shut-down at San Diego State College was in protest over the firing of a faculty member, and it was Jerry Farber who led and orchestrated the strike which then moved on to an occupation of administrative offices and a closing of the college for several days. I joined the group who were occupying the main building and was amazed at the festive atmosphere. It was like street theatre and an ongoing performance of music and ranting speeches on behalf of this particular professor and in dedication to the general idea of re-investing power to the people, that was providing students with a stronger voice in decision-making for all college policies. Many from my class were in attendance and formed impromptu seminar sessions with Farber, that radical author of those ideals in the *provo*. I did not facilitate or lead any discussion groups as I did not want to politicize my ideas beyond that level of definition, but I wholeheartedly did urge many of my students to gather around Farber and solicit his comments on this very event which we were all participating in.

I had not brought a sleeping bag, and was not eager to spend the night on the ground nestled in some of the blankets thrown down in the quadrangle, and when an attractive red-head, a more mature student – not one of mine; she claimed to be a Physical Education major – who was wearing a loose fitting tee shirt, no bra, and skimpy shorts that just covered only half of her well-turned full hips, suggested that we go back to my place where she promised to make dinner and relax us both, I readily agreed. Her tastes were simple. We stopped at the first supermarket and bought a bag of mixed salad and a large steak. Her skills in the kitchen were even simpler, and we both agreed that the singed meat was better with the flesh still raw within, and after enduring only a few desperate chews, we were in to my bed and I was nibbling her breasts and had begun engorging a more luscious repast between her readily spread legs. We performed like old friends, and then I slept till dawn, when I realized that I was alone in bed and that my friend, whom I vaguely remembered telling me her name was Teresa – or was it Tess – was not in bed with me. I heard a strange commotion coming from my living room, and when I walked in, I found her kneeling in front of the empty fire-place, chanting what sounded like some sort of dirge.

I had supposed this woman to be a "mature" student, but in her present state, she looked not only well into middle age, but also definitely decrepit. Her hair hung down like the knotted tresses on my sister's Raggedy Anne doll after a thorough chewing by our dog; her eyes were glazed and seemed sunken in above dark pouches in their sockets; and her moans sounded like a mumbling gibber of a sort of Catholic rosary. I distinctly made out the Our Lady, and Hail Mary, jammed in to the repetitions. There was definitely some Latin phrasing in what sounded like tag-ends of Gregorian chants.

I went to the kitchen, passing carefully behind her so as not to interrupt her concentration, and returned with a glass of cold orange juice from the refrigerator. When I knelt beside her and offered it, she slapped me away and snarled like a feral animal.

"I was the bride of Christ and you fucked me! Jesus and Mary, forgive me, for I have sinned. How could you? How could I? How? How?" she raved. Then began the chanting and sobbing, subsiding in heaving gasps. So I just sat down on the couch by the window and looked out toward the Cove and wondered what an apocalypse I had brought in to my humble home.

I remembered Bob Kavanaugh's brother, James, the former priest who had also become a psycho-therapist and helped me with Julie. I went in to my bedroom and telephoned him. Fortunately, he was awake and not expected at his office for a couple of hours. I described what was appearing to be a religious psychosis unfolding in my living room, and he told me to ask my guest to have a few words with him. When I boldly offered the telephone to the woman, telling her the name of my friend who would speak with her, it was as if I had dashed cold water over her face. She reached for the receiver and began talking rapid-fire, sobbing, gulping, yelping ... and at last, laughing. After only a few minutes, her hair appeared to have returned to its natural luster and body as she ran her fingers through it and massaged her neck and upper shoulder. She tossed back her head, and rising from the floor with dignity, handed the telephone to me, saying that *Father Kavanaugh* would speak to me. She walked out of the living-room and in to the kitchen as I took the line.

"*Father James?*" I asked my friend, the *ex*-priest. "What is this all about?"

The scolding I might have received if we had not been acquainted for some time before, and especially bonded by our heart-breaking association with Julie Aschmann [he had treated her till her suicide], came as a soft reproach and a proposal of action which James would enact within the next quarter hour, the time it would take for him to drive to my place. He would take *Sister Teresa* to a *special* (church) clinic where she would receive some prescribed sedation and counseling from men and women like herself, and I was to keep this incident to myself and hopefully never have to experience it again. The wild red-head whom I had just *deflowered* - she had complained that she was just at the end of her period, and that was why we had such a flow of blood during and after our sexual intercourse - was in actuality a nun, who, until only two days before, had spent the last twenty years (since the age of sixteen) in a convent. She had gone to James Kavanaugh for counseling when her spiritual crisis had occurred. After only one visit with this renegade ex-priest, she had bought a change of clothes and scored some *street* L.S.D. and Marijuana which she had imbibed in virtual over-kill amounts. She had then taken a taxi to San Diego State College where the student sit-in was in full swing, where she reckoned she would find her *new spiritual guide* and be awakened to her intended new identity. I was her choice of *ad hoc guru*, and my bedroom became her psychedelic *sanctum sanctorum* into sexual awakening - and that new spiritual awareness which had frightened the living *Bejesus* out of her. So much for my Casanova credentials. I have never claimed to be that *Mr. Right* in bed, whom many women claim to be seeking.

She was officially listed as A.W.O.L. from her convent, and if she wished, James could arrange for her to be considered for re-entry after a sort of ecclesiastical debriefing by the Mother Superior, the Abbess, who was still a close friend of his. It would seem that there were processes already in place for re-educating and re-sanctifying such errant young women and men who breached their vows, and especially now that there were such models of radical withdrawal from clerical orders as my friends the Kavanaugh brothers, James and Bob, both ex-priests, working as psychotherapists in association with their truly radical brother Philip, the notorious psychiatrist to the rich and famous of La Jolla and Rancho Santa Fe, who encouraged his clients to such sexual and sensual excesses that to call him their *lay-*brother would have been to belabor and beleaguer the art of punning.

When I mentioned that she had certainly acted erratically in bed, and cried out "Jesus Christ" in the most alarming fashion when I had assumed certain positions and showed her a few of my favorite moves, he remarked with a fiendish chuckle that I was indeed lucky that I had not urged her to perform *fellatio* because she might have bitten off, and swallowed whole, my member, as it might have seemed to have been the Eucharistic host representing the body of the *Christ* with Whom she *was* at last performing her consummation of marriage, and then she could have quaffed the blood of my wine till I, myself, had perhaps been welcomed to a new spiritual dimension – Death – and received last rites in my own little degenerate chapel on the Cove. I asked him to just lay off the jesuitical jibes and get over to my place as quickly as he could, to recover his lapsed, but now sated, *sister,* to be *transported* from my now (for her) gloomy regions of contemplative asceticism.

As I put down the telephone, Teresa came out of the kitchen with a plate of scrambled eggs, toast, and two cups of coffee. I thanked her graciously and mentioned that there was a half melon in the bottom of the refrigerator, but she merely smiled, nodded a conspiratorial assent, and turned to go back in to fetch us slices of that luscious delight which she had already placed on a plate, and she then brought back in on her return. We were just finishing our breakfast when James walked in the front door and reached out to enfold his new charge in his arms. What an impressive parochial manner he still radiated.

You can defrock the priest but you never can remove that loving Christian glow of caring. Perhaps it is even more sincere and unconditionally loving with those who have been defrocked. Was I defrocked? The archbishop of Los Angeles never allowed me to "turn the collar," to be ordained, so I had no *frock* to lose, no *habit* to cast off. I am sure there is a lovely pun in that remark, the *frock* being a synonym for *habit,* or vestment worn by a priest, and disrobing being required, in most instances, for performing a sexual act of coupling with another person, in the most satisfying manner, although some rogues brag about keeping their boots on - both male and female - while engaging in this act. There were many of the devout who never acknowledged Rome's decision to expel James Kavanaugh, and so, when Sister Teresa called him Father, she was not being ingenuous, or intentionally ironic ... or even dishonest.

That next week, I received a call from Bob Kavanaugh, thanking me for being in contact with his brother and assuring me that Teresa had been welcomed back to her convent with no great fan-fare *apropos* of the return of a prodigal. He teased me about my evangelical stripe and reminded me that it was never too late for me to consider the seminary and prep again for ordination, maybe this time in his church. There was an order of Saint Francis that had become active working with the most marginal of the population, the "street people," the drug addicts and prostitutes and the indigent, the outcasts and the cast-offs. I had met one or two of this men who had at first appeared to me to be themselves members of this lowest socio-economic stratum, and I had been startled to learn that they were actually monks, who although their clothing was ragged and dirty, that underneath, they each wore a special girdle of their order of Saint Francis. One of these individuals I even supposed to be a drug dealer, a pusher, because he was living with addicts, and yet he seemed to be in control, calm, and so cool, I figured he must be heavily armed as well. He was "holding" all right, but it was not a side-arm weapon, but rather the Holy Spirit in the most vital and meaningful sense.

I had actually discussed this alternative life-style with Bob, but could not accept some of the tenets of his faith, and most particularly, I was not at this point ready to be smitten celibate, by whatever means, for any cause, or vocation, my recent misadventure with *Sister Teresa*, notwithstanding. Nor, in her particular case, would I have much fancied becoming the actual Eucharistic supper – 'This is my body. This is my blood. Eat. Drink. In memory of me!' Yikes! What a model! Dionysius's *maenads* tearing madly through the streets of Athens in their drunken religious frenzy, raping, and then tearing the flesh from their sexually assaulted victims and savoring that fresh red meat and quenching their thirst with that hot blood, as flavorful and *nutritious* to them, then, as their wine god's own bodily nectar. And then there was Isis, or was it Osiris, or whatever Egyptian or Mesopotamian god required sacrificing, to then be ritually consumed by his or her lip-smacking omniverous devotees. Ah, religion. Moveable Feasts which I could forgo, especially now, in my present state, providentially released from Sister Teresa's fond, but Praying Mantis *mudra* embrace.

Bob Kavanaugh then declared that James would like to become one of my students, to audit my 'Introduction to Literature' class at San Diego State. James was beginning to feel supremely challenged by his new vocation as a psychotherapist. At this time, the state of California required very few qualifications for anyone to set up as a Counselor who then used the title of psychotherapist. James had no training for this work other than his experience as a shepherd for his congregation-flock in religious matters. The Confessional might be construed as the original Freudian couch for the uncovering and healing of deep-seated neurotic traumas, but the blessings and assignments of redemptive repetitions of the rosary and other such ecclesiastical bromides were hardly to be compared with the intensive personal inventories taken in the rigors of psychoanalysis ... and then, there were the pharmaceutical alternatives that psychiatrists - trained and licensed medical practitioners – were able to offer in place of prayer and meditation. Before the age of anti-depressants, there was a broad spectrum of tranquilizers and other soporifics that the medical doctor practicing psychiatry could prescribe, which the priest could not access.

Like my Julie, many of James clients had died while in his care; suicide or other misadventure resulting from their own experimentation with pharmaceutical remedies available, often more readily, from the local drug pusher - this occupation on many college campuses, now replacing the more menial jobs formerly offered the average college scholarship student.   Many a pre-med undergraduate was also a lay-pharmacist who could supply anything from Californian home-grown Marijuana, to Maui Wowie, to Colombian Five Star, to Thai Sticks, and even Afghani Black or Morrocan Gold hashish [all cannabis derivatives]; and then there was Crystal Methamphetamine, Cocaine, L.S.D. and Angel Dust [that criminally dangerous over-stimulant derived from animal tranquilizers; used routinely by veterinarians, and therefore available to drug dealers, if stolen] - but curiously, the sale of heroin and morphine was still in the control of the hardened criminal elements, but many of us knew members of The Hells Angels and could score any amounts from these representatives of the world of Organized Crime. Ironically, however, these "outlaw bikers," had become the protectors and *guardian angels* of the student protest movement and particularly the anti-war faction, ever since being turned on to the use of L.S.D by Allen Ginsberg at a party in the Ken Kesey commune. Free-Wheeling Frank Reynolds was one of the first to be converted, and he had thenceforward become a student of the poetry of John Milton and William Blake. His autobiography had been written by Michael McClure when this poet was being initiated into the motorcycle club as their Poet Laureate. There was even a member of the San Diego chapter of this coven of psychopaths who attended my class regularly [*auditing*, as he would never have deigned to lower himself to enroll in any such socially approved activities as an educational institution], and I was loath to refuse him the privilege [albeit *illegal* - the only currency of value to any member of that club, being the very term *illegal*] as he had contributed some poetry which did have marginal artistic merit ... and his services as my body-guard were offered as his tuition fees. There was even in our class a senior member of the San Diego police, who, in his off-duty life, was becoming a sympathizer to the alternative life-style which in his working day he was encouraged to repress and punish. So, why not welcome America's most famous defrocked priest to our *pride*? Like lions we roared and roamed our literary savannahs. To call ourselves a *flock* diminished our sense of animal power. We were certainly not *sheeple*. So, neither were we a flock nor a herd. Ironically, in this context, the first poem James offered as his introduction to join the class [our *pack*] was entitled, 'There Are Men Too Gentle to Live Among Wolves.'

Many students recognized our new member, as his story had been featured in *Look* magazine when the Catholic Church had excommunicated him for his best-selling book, *A Modern Priest Looks at an Out-Dated Church*. He and his new wife had appeared in the front-cover photo, walking hand-in-hand, on a California beach. Curiously, two students decided to drop the course because they feared punishment by their parish priests for attending a class with this virtual Anti-Christ figure, and these were a young man and woman who visually proclaimed themselves as the most radical of hippies: she wearing clothing and jewelry that declared their departure from the *status quo* - diaphanous blouse with no brassiere, and necklaces and bracelets and ear-rings that would have lumbered a Gypsy, encumbering both him and her, and their hair hung down to the waist in ringlets decorated with multi-colored beads; however, they had both re-affirmed their dedication to Jesus Christ in their last intense L.S.D. trip, which for so many had been a spiritual questing and chemical pilgrimage. They bid us farewell with Christian love, and even told James that they would pray for his redemption ... or, notwithstanding, Indulgence, from a few centuries in Hell and agonizing torment for his Cardinal sins.

James did not return to the priesthood, but he did remain in my class and wrote several other poems which derived from the thematic thrust of this first poem which declared a poetic consciousness that must survive and proclaim itself, like a latter-day Saint Francis, even in this contemporary world where predatory and ravishing human sensibilities prevailed - *wolves*- and even reigned and ruled, as did the American political leaders who had placed our young men in the 'killing fields' of the Viet Nam conflict. The class appreciated his contributions and helped him to edit and refine what became a series of substantial corroborative resonances to his plaintive poetic polemic. When he told me that his agent had a contract to publish this collection and wanted him to participate in a series of television talk-shows appearances, James invited me to accompany him in this promotional campaign and offered me half the royalties from the first year's sales if I would consent to do so. I declined the offer. I was not that enamored with his writing - I found it too politically flavored to satisfy my definition of pure poetry - and I did not feel like aligning myself with James in an endeavor that was his personal crusade. His voice was not mine, albeit I agreed with everything he said. I had also written a few purely political poems focused on the horror of the war in Viet Nam as well. If I had accepted his offer, I would have been much richer for it. The royalties from that first year were in the amount of over $500, 000. And James published several other books of poetry thereafter. He had found his true calling, his *metier*, and he never had to return to practicing psychotherapy after these publications, and his *actual ministry* to his flock was probably much better served, not only in California, but to multitudes of soul-searching readers throughout the world.

One of my own anti-war poems became widely distributed. It dealt with the heart-breaking visits I made to the U. S. Navy hospital in Balboa Park where some of my former students - both from UCSD and La Jolla Country Day School - were in rehabilitation from their injuries in Viet Nam. This particular tract supposedly had been used as a deterrent in reporting for Basic Training and an inspiration for claiming Conscientious Objection exemption, or even for justification in fleeing from the United States to Canada, Mexico or Sweden to escape the Universal Military Draft. I was informed that the poem was reproduced in thousands of copies and had brought me infamy as a veteran who declared this war to be a farce and a fraud, and that I was considered a major threat to the work of those patriotic *hawks* who promoted this debacle in Southeast Asia.

When I was invited to deliver my poem as the keynote feature for a candle-light anti-war protest rally, to be held at the La Jolla Cove Park, something happened that made me aware of how effective my polemic writing had perhaps become. One afternoon, about two weeks before the event, a portly, well-dressed man with crew-cut blond hair arrived at my front door to deliver me with a threat on behalf of his para-military group, the Minute Men - their volunteers consisted of many American veterans with extreme Right Wing political convictions who gathered in such remote areas as the

Borrego Springs desert for military combat training in preparation for the *Wars of the Race* (White Aryan against all those people of Color) which they fervently believed to be coming soon, and they were claiming that they were dedicated to serve in defense of our country as the original Minute Men militia did in the American Revolutionary War. Their enemy was not a foreign invader, but rather the communist sympathizers, and racial equality leaders of the Civil Rights movement whom they believed would mongrelize the Amercian population and oppose the white supremists who rightfully should be ruling the United States. Their membership was a more zealously, militant version of the Ku Klux Klan, John Birch Society, and some confused former followers of the American Bund (Nazi Party).

As I approached the door and opened the screen, I saw that my visitor was Bruce Riggins, my former room-mate from West Point Loma Boulevard in San Diego, from that time when I was a U. S. Navy Lieutenant Junior Grade, serving on active duty at U.S.N.T.C. We had parted most acrimoniously, as I had effectually placed Bruce *on report* (under arrest) – virtually filing criminal charges against him – for his excessive cruelty in the administration of his command of the 4013 Retraining Battalion in the Recruit Training Center.

At that time, I remember having remarked to Bruce that I had witnessed the testimony of one of his colleagues who had testified in a court-martial investigative hearing which resulted from the crippling and possible blinding of a young recruit who had been subjected to both a "blanket and scrub party" by his fellow recruits for supposedly shaming them with his lax hygiene regimen. Because this man had not achieved the required standards in his personal appearance during inspection by the battalion commander (a lieutenant j.g.), the drill instructor (a senior chief petty officer) for this group of eighty recruits, had *suggested* a blanket be thrown over him and he be beaten severely by all ("blanket party"), and then to be scrubbed down, over his entire body, with stiff floor brushes and lye soap, by this group of seventy-nine bullies, the entire company.

His skin had been stripped off, his vision impaired, many bones were broken, and there were several internal injuries, from these monstrous punishments. When he was admitted to the Balboa Navy Hospital for Intensive Care, someone with a conscience had demanded to know who had ordered and implemented such a barbaric measure, and thus, there was a court-martial investigative hearing at the Administrative Command at U.S.N.T.C.

As director of Recruit Personnel, at that time, I had attended the hearing and was shocked to hear one battalion commander (a lieutenant j.g.) testify that these *instructive measures* were unusual only in that they had been somewhat extreme ... and *had been found out.* Then with a smirk and a chuckle, this junior officer said that some of the measures he knew to be employed were even worse. When I narrated this incident to Bruce, he guffawed and said that if I ever wanted to visit his special re-training unit, 4013 Battalion, that he would show me what this friend of his meant, but had never been able to put into effect, as well as Bruce did. The recruits who were not meeting the standards in the regular battalions, who were deemed to need more intensive *instruction,* were sent to 4013, where there was a ratio of one D.I. (senior petty officer drill instructor) to every ten men, rather than the normal balance of one to eighty. Normally, a battalion consisted of ten companies – eight hundred total, commanded by a junior officer of at least the rank of lieutenant, junior grade. When I returned to active duty for the summer of 1963, a year after my original release, I held the rank of lieutenant, and commanded 1,200 recruits, as, at that time, company size had been augmented to 100, because of a war-like crisis impending then, and my battalion consisted of twelve companies.

I had decided to visit 4013 one afternoon after lunch with Bruce. On the ground floor of his unit, intensive instruction was being conducted in primary laundering operations by chief petty officers glowering over the humping shoulders of recruits bent to the job of hand-washing clothes on scrub-boards suspended above soapy, watery sinks. The petty officers were barking cadences for the hand-sweeps on the boards so loudly that I had to cover my ears as we passed them on our way up the *ladder* (Navy parlance for stairway) to the upper *deck* (floor) to Bruce's office where he promised that we would have our coffee. In the main *passage-way* (hallway) on that upper floor, several young men were standing with their backs to us, their faces pressed against the *bulkheads* (walls); they were leaning against with their full weight held by their foreheads and bridges of their noses. As we passed behind them, Bruce fiendishly shouted, "Good afternoon, you Pukes. Daddy's back home now to teach you manners!" and he slammed his crooked elbow into the back of the head of every man, crushing faces into the wall and breaking their noses as he did so. Most screamed with the pain and fell to their knees sobbing. Bruce ordered his petty officers to jerk them up and ready them for entry to his office for their next *instructive procedure*.

"Have to soften them up and get their attention, so when they come in for their next increment of enlightenment, they will never forget my words of wisdom", he said, chuckling with self-satisfaction.

Two men were at the opposite end of his office being drilled in calisthenics by a petty officer. They were raising and lowering rifles above their heads, down to their chests, then to their shoulders – except that in the rapid repetition of the sequence, they both were so exhausted that sometimes the rifles struck their heads as they lowered them – and as they continued in more accelerated cadences, the rifles did not clear their heads each time, and they were sustaining more damage to themselves, bashing their skulls with the heavy weapons' metal bolt assembly.

"Can't blame me or my petty officers if these worms can't follow the drill properly, but they'll have to answer with more punishment for the damage they do with their thick skulls to government property – those fine M-1 rifles." Bruce guffawed, as he vocally picked up and echoed the drill instructor's cadence, and thereby succeeded in increasing the speed and rate of cranial mishap, striding across the room to stand over each of the victims and shouting into their faces, spittle flying from his mouth which had become distended in sadistic delight, only inches from their now blood-soaked heads.

I could have declared that I was placing Bruce and this particular drill instructor *on report* at that very moment, but I wanted all the *instructors* at the 4013 unit to be placed under arrest – to stop this insane cruelty as soon as possible. I well remembered my experience as a midshipman on the *U.S.S. Midway* when I had confronted that Marine Corps captain, the Officer-in-Charge of the brig on that ship who had been effectually disfiguring and mutilating his prisoners. My actions then had proven to be futile. I did not, at that time, have the rank or experience to deal with such arrant disregard for human rights practiced aboard a U. S. Navy ship at that juncture. My rank now, however, was at least equal to that of the offending party – who also was my room-mate and friend – and I knew and trusted some of the power structure at this command.

So I merely told Bruce that I had an appointment, and glancing at my wrist-watch, I turned and left the building and walked directly to confer with the most sane man at the command, whose office was just across the drill field from the recruit barracks. Captain Justin Brown, M.D., was the chief psychiatrist in charge of all psychological testing and evaluation for the Recruit Training Command and had become one of my closest friends from my first week on active duty. Since then, we had met each morning for breakfast, and often shared lunch, as well. It was he who had delivered a startling report regarding my psychological fitness to Captain Larry Cook, commanding officer of U.S.N.T.C. when I was ordered to undergo a psychiatric examination to decide if I were indeed qualified to continue serving as an officer on active duty in the Navy. Cook had fumed and flown off the handle in our welcome interview, and had called his adjutant to remove me from his office – on my first day on active duty when I reported aboard his base. He had then had a request made to the Bureau of Naval Personnel that I have a psychiatric evaluation, so that I might be medically processed out of the Navy and be dismissed from active duty.

All I had done to incur Captain Cook's towering rage was to remain calm and cool as he had read the report about my *misconduct* as a midshipman, a full year before, on the *U.S.S. Midway* [when I had dared to place that Marine captain on report for his cruelty], warning me that such insubordinate behavior would never be countenanced in his command, and then when he stumbled over one of the words used by my N.R.O.T.C. program commander, Colonel Gentleman, U.S.M.C., to describe my attitude – *insouciant* – I had attempted to politely explain the meaning of the word for my new commander, whose education had been limited to only Naval Science courses at Annapolis. He exploded when his literacy was thus maligned, but I was quick to then tell him that I was really most impressed with his war record, that I had read with fervor what he had done in his last combat engagement against superior Japanese forces, and then I cited almost *verbatim* the scripts of the justification for his awards of the Silver Star and the Navy Cross. I was just beginning to wax rhapsodic regarding his special relationship to his Destroyer Squadron commander, who was riding Cook's ship on that fateful day in the Pacific on Leyte Gulf in World War Two, Commodore Ruthven B. Libby, whom I had met in the very incident cited aboard the *U.S.S. Midway* – interpreted as my *misconduct in placing a Marine captain on report* - when that senior officer was then Commander-in-Chief of the Pacific Fleet with the rank of Vice-Admiral - and it was he who had decided to turn me over to the Marine Corps staff aboard that ship for disciplinary *instruction*. I was attempting to be chatty in a *bon-vivant* style, trying to achieve some sort of bond by referring to the irony of our mutual acquaintance with the famed Admiral Libby, and to strike a resonance with the deep valence notion *of we-are-all-comrades-in-arms* ... when the captain rose to his full height behind his desk, slamming both fists down with a resounding explosion and bellowed for his adjutant to come expel me from his presence.

Captain Brown's subsequent appraisal of my fitness for military duty and for leadership roles, particularly as a Line Combat junior officer must have threatened Cook with a life-endangering outrage of temper, perhaps even a mild heart-attack or aneurism. Dr. Brown wrote that seldom in his over twenty-four years of military experience, with considerable study of the history of war-fare and the personalities of great leaders, from Alexander the Great, to Napoleon, to the Duke of Wellington, to Washington, to Robert E. Lee and Ulysses Grant, had he encountered anyone more suited to command and leadership positions than that of the personality and character he had examined and evaluated with Ensign Ben Allen Wright, U.S.N.R., whom he was proud to serve with as a fellow officer in the same command and whose presence in any military establishment was to be considered a treasure beyond compare ... And the report built to a crescendo of such apotheosis and aggrandizement of my leadership profile that it would have seemed to any cynical reader perhaps contrived to drive whoever [Captain Larry B. Cook] had ever questioned the capability of Ensign Wright, to be dim-witted ... or perhaps even childishly vindictive. Captain Brown did make a passing remark to that effect, that anyone who might question Wright's leadership, might be well-advised to review the basics of the standards of military and social norms, and be assured that Ensign Wright was indeed an exemplary model, the very epitome, of the ideal officer in any branch of the armed forces of the United States of America..

Captain Cook made it known that he was displeased with me, and orders were issued that I should not be allowed to reside in the Bachelor Officers' Quarters; and I became aware that many officers avoided my company when I had any meals at the Admiral Kidd Officers' Club. However, Captain Brown often invited me to meet for lunch with him and members of his staff, several highly skilled psychotherapists who then became some of my closest friends. Dr. Brown warned our small assembly the first time we met, at a table of our own, well removed from officers seated in the rest of the dining room, "Beware of the pariah of N.T.C. This otherwise harmless appearing young officer has been deemed virtually untouchable by our righteous commanding officer as it is strongly suspected that he listens to classical music and may even write poetry. I, myself, have distinctly sniffed the stink of intellectual in his manner and mein, so be warned, all of you."

After I left Bruce Riggins at 4013 Unit, that day when I had witnessed his cruelties, I announced myself to Dr. Brown's receptionist and was ushered in to his office within a few moments. Although I rushed the delivery of my report, and only sat down when ordered to do so and to take some slow, calming, deep breaths, the psychiatrist acted as if he already knew what I had narrated to him.

"We have received several reports from highly reliable sources that Riggins has been stepping well beyond the accepted parameters of what is considered appropriate to the accomplishment of his specified duties. What was to be an intensification of the military training, it would seem, has become an excuse for Lieutenant Riggins to indulging in some very unhealthy sadistic behaviors. If you will just tell us what you have observed – and you need not make an official written report – or we will be forced to submit all of this to the the legal department, and that might provide grounds for a court martial. I would rather just eliminate the problem here and now and replace the current management, the officer-in-charge and all of the current staff at 4013."

I agreed to cooperate and to provide an exact legal deposition of what I had just seen, and told the captain that I would also tell Bruce that he was no longer welcome to stay in the house where he paid one third of the rent. The lease was in my name, and therefore, I was able to give him notice to leave at any time. He would perhaps make a scene and might even threaten me, but I was unwilling to abide the presence of such a monstrous personality in my home. I would most likely tell him that I had made this report to Captain Brown and was not averse to taking appropriate legal measures if necessary. I knew the exact Articles of *The Uniform Code of Military Justice* and the pertinent citations of the Geneva Convention which he had been so flagrantly violating. I would never forget my encounter with that Marine Corps captain in charge of the brig aboard *U.S.S. Midway*.

"Riggins will know the author of his expulsion, and he will be made aware that some punitive measures may be enacted against him, but if we merely resolve the major issues from my office, then he will merely be transferred to another command or to a position where he can do the least harm within this command," Dr. Brown replied. "I will suggest a letter of reprimand be placed in his file after an office visit with Recruit Training Command's, Captain Goepner and N.T.C.'s Captain Cook. I will be present for this disciplinary discussion and a transcript copy of all this will be sent on to Com Eleven (Commandant Eleventh Naval District).

Bruce Riggins was fortunate indeed to have been allowed to complete his term of active duty with no further disciplinary measures taken against him. He was transferred within the command to the job of assistant to the Public Information Officer, his duties being to arrange dinner parties and cocktail lunches for the officers' wives and to greet visiting dignitaries and escort them about the base and to take them on tours of the San Diego tourist attractions, from Balboa Park to Dana Point, the Torrey Pines Golf course, to the famed La Jolla Beach and Tennis Club and the Coronado Beach Hotel. As his first two years as a junior officer had been spent onthe staff officer of Commander of the Sixth Fleet in the Mediterranean, doing basically the same sort of social chairman's job, I was told that he reveled in his *promotion* to this sweet billet as a way to wind down his next few months of active duty. That evening, when he returned to our house, he went straight to his room and was packed within an hour. As he drove away he saluted me smartly, and we did not encounter one another except in passing in our cars on the base in those last few months of his active duty there.

So, now, over eight years later, when I found him standing on my porch at my house on the cove, I was amazed to notice how he had changed in the past decade. The once rosy cheeks were now florid with many broken capillaries accentuating the purplish hue beneath his eyes, which now, instead of radiating a bright blue fire, appeared to sizzle in limpid depths. His mouth which once smirkd in jesting was now twisted in loathing grimace, and his body was as if inflated, his bulging waist spilled over his belt, and the buttons on his shirt strained to hold the material in place. He looked like Tweedle-Dee with a bad hang-over and an acute problem with constipation. When he spoke, I was amazed at the hoarseness deep in his throat that reverberated with bronchial tissue assaulted by chain-smoking or some equally distressing self-inflicted abuse. What he had to tell me was appropriately accompanied by this harsh resonance.

He told me that his cadre of the San Diego chapter of the only true Americans who remained to defend the heritage of our White Christian founders, the latter-day patriots called the Minute Men, had targeted me as one of the most dangerous foes of freedom alive in this part of Southern California. As an enemy of freedom, democracy, the United States Constitution, and all human dignity and decency, it had been decided that I must be eliminated. I could, however, leave the area permanently, he told me, especially if I decided to do so before the La Jolla Cove Candlelight anti-war gathering next week, and thus, I would be able to save my life, for the time being. But if I chose to present my *filthy* poem, as planned, at this *unholy* and *evil* gathering of America's *traitors* to our dedicated men sacrificing their lives in Southeast Asia, then there was to be a judgment carried out against me that would render me hopelessly crippled for life, and helpless from the neck down. My spine would be broken in such a way as to leave me conscious, but unable to move any of my limbs, and to be incontinent of bowel and bladder till the Minute Men should decide to deliver me finally to the sweeter alternative of death itself.

Bruce had retained that flamboyant eloquence and facility of descriptive detail which had made him that much more feared as the swaggering 4013 Battalion commander. He spoke of my threatened mutilation with a relish which virtually caused him to salivate and forced him to wipe the spittle from the edges of his mouth with the back of his hand. I was tempted to ask him how long it had been since breakfast, as he did truly seem to be working up a ferocious appetite. After he had finished his spiel, he looked winded and almost dizzy. I was inclined to invite him inside to calm down and have a drink of water, but here was a man who had just offered me either flight from a formidable punishment or a torturous handicapping for life. I had to recall that except for his hasty packing and leave-taking at West Point Loma Boulevard, that the last time I had seen this individual, I was to witness his sadistic assault on the helpless recruits in his command in Navy boot camp, with spittle flying from his mouth in the same hungry frenzy as he had just enacted for me, on my front porch, overlooking the calm waters of La Jolla Cove. I considered telling him to go fuck himself, but I had always considered that insult to be almost a blessing – to go have sexual intercourse with oneself had never seemed to me to be an undesirable condition, so I said what probably hurt Bruce more than anything I could have threatened physically.

"I barely recognized you, Bruce. You have not aged well, and you could lose about fifty pounds. You'll never be able to have those burst veins in your face removed, though. I would enroll in Alcoholics Anonymous, Weight Watchers, and I have a good friend who is a psychotherapist who can help you with Anger Management. Just some advice to an old comrade-in-arms," I offered, and then turning to close the screen door, I said, "Now I am going to telephone the police to tell them to come and listen to your clumsy death threats."

His vanity was such that the cheeks blushed a deeper shade of purple, his neck swelled with rage and his upper body shook with barely restrained impulse to strike out at me, the door, the house itself. I was surprised that he did not begin stomping in furor. Bruce had always considered himself a dashing, handsome figure, as indeed he had been when physically fit, some ten years younger, and in the sleek Navy blue uniform with a gold stripe and a half circling his sleeve. He had been the very model of a Hitler-jugend promoted to Stormtrooper officer status ... and he would have been much happier with this fate than the alternative dealt him by his post World War Two American identity, which he still made the best of by qualifying as a Line Combat officer in the United States Navy. Now he had become a pudgy, alcoholic, hate-filled member of a clump of white-trash, neo-Nazi, para-military clowns who dreamed of discovering some authentic identity in their pretensions to defending a Constitution that by its essential integrity would outlaw any and all of their activities and purposes. The suffering neurotic knows he is sick, but the psychopath knows he is right. Bruce had crossed the line from mentally disturbed to dangerously mad. No Twelve Step Recovery program could help him now, and very few of the best forensic psychiatrists would be able to treat him, except in a controlled environment, such as a lock-up ward in a sanitarium. As I stepped inside, I reached for the hatchet by my fire-place and as I turned to go back to my front door, I saw that Bruce was scrambling down the stairs toward the street.

I presented the reading of that poem at the La Jolla Cove Park Candlelight Anti-War gathering. I climbed up on to a stage where I provided an easy target for any marksman; however, old Fred Hocks wanted to stand up there beside me to be a possible buffer to any incoming ordnance when he learned of my threat from the Minute Men. My Hells Angel student and also the guitar-playing virtuoso who shadowed my every move also wanted to be there with me, along with several other self-appointed body guards who suddenly appeared to surround and protect me from harm. I had told only my friend, C.C. Neber, about my visit from Bruce, and only because she was familiar with my past military career in San Diego. Against my warning to keep this matter to ourselves, she had confided in Fred and had asked my students to watch out for me on that night. I chose to stand alone on that open stage. There were no rifle shots or any other kind of attacks against me or any of the several hundred participants who held lighted candles in the soft twilight and applauded my reading with murmurs of assent and support.

After my reading, another man climbed up on stage. He was the main speaker, an active member of the local Friends Meeting, a Quaker who along with many of his dedicated congregation was willing to make the same ultimate gesture Thoreau had, by refusing to pay federal taxes - which were used to finance the military machine - *and going to prison.* "When there are unjust laws, the only place for just men is in prison" from *On Civil Disobedience* was quoted by Martin Luther King when he was thrown into Birmingham jail after his civil rights protest. These true believers, many who were prominent and comfortably, well-to-do, local residents, were stripped of their property (in lieu of taxes due) and were sentenced to terms in prisons where the prisoners gang-raped them and systematically tortured them in righteous patriotic fervor to show their support of the Viet Nam war and their hatred of any traitors to America's commitment there - these cruelties were enacted by convicted criminals, self-righteously assured that they were promoting and endorsing the United States' foreign policy in Southeast Asia!

Although many friends congratulated me on presenting my poem in the face of the Minute Men threat, I praised the more substantive courage of these humble Quaker heroes who were willing to sacrifice so vitally to demonstrate their *conscientious objection* to violence. Many people active in the ant-war movement of that period had noted that Richard Nixon claimed to be a Quaker. What protest had he ever made to violence? It was rather like Hitler's extreme form of vegetarianism – *vegan* - and the example of his turning away with horror from a fish once served him for dinner, saying, "Did that die for my sake?" - this Nazi monster who was the author of the Ultimate Solution for Jews by wholesale extermination during the Holocaust. And Richard Nixon was ordering the bombing of Cambodia and the proliferation of over three million anti-personnel mines there, who when queried as to whether this had been approved by Congress, answered simply, " I'm president, and I'll do anything I want."

I survived that minor dramatic incident with Bruce Riggins, only to receive a letter in the mail on the following Saturday which made another death threat, but for no apparent political reason. As I opened the letter, enclosed in an envelope advertising a motel in Arizona - brown sandy paper, appealing perhaps to those seeking solace in the wind-blown desert climate of that state - the first words that *hailed,* and arrested my attention, were the lines which Walt Whitman employed as the title of his poem dedicated to Abraham Lincoln, his presdident and commander-in-chief of Union Armed Forces at that time of America's Civil War: 'O Captain, My Captain!' Several lines below this bold greeting was written in a tight black ink cursive, "Dear Ben," followed by one of the most startling statements I had ever read:

"I just made love to my girl-friend – 'my favorite squeeze,' 'my old lady,' to use a couple of the currently popular terms for the primary heterosexual relationship that we encounter in modern popular fictional writing – I avoid the expression, 'my better half,' or 'soul-mate,' as I recall, with gleeful amusement, your explanation of the derivation of those terms from Plato's notion that every man is born with another half somewhere in the world, and that the romantic Greek ideal was to encounter that missing portion of oneself and bond with 'him' to achieve perfect sexual fulfillment, but that the idea was purely homosexual – a man finding his other same-sex, missing-half. So when modern couples talk of the 'soul-mate,' or, 'better half,' there is an underlying irony that contradicts the usually accepted heterosexual quotient and equation for the ideal marriage of man and woman. I have also drunk most of a bottle of tequila and feel just about drunk enough to do what I came to this flea-bitten motel in Mexicali, intending to do. I am holding a straight-edge razor to my throat and am preparing to slash, as I look deeply into my eyes reflecting from this stained mirror. But the eyes I see are not mine any longer. They are blue, intense, somewhat mad. Yours! The reddish brown beard encircling the lower face is wreathed around a laughing mouth, and I can hear what you are telling me to do.

"So I must slash your throat, not mine. I even feel the tumescent tug in my penis, telling me to go back and fuck my lady again, and rest up to drive back to San Diego, to be ready for your class on Monday, when the eyes you will see, the last face that you will behold, will be mine, as I take your life, delivering the greatest gift one can ever receive: Death. I do this because I love you, and I could hear you pleading with me just now to not take my own life. So when you see me – for the last time – on Monday, it will be with my passion and deepest regard that I join us to this most primary purpose. You could not possibly know who I am, as I never participate in class discussions, and in that enormous lecture hall, there are at least a hundred of us arrayed before you. However, at some point, during your lecture, this Monday, I shall become the most important person in your life, and the very last acquaintance in it. Till then, My Captain."

Whoever this student was, he had been paying attention to my lecture material. The reference to Plato had always amused the ones who claimed to be coupled with a loved one. The allusion to Walt Whitman's esteem for Lincoln and his soldierly regard for that great president was not a footnote that most students would readily recall; so. this had to be one of the more seriously attentive members of my audience. *Serious* was probably the most appropriate term to apply to this character, but *disturbed, demented, dangerous* were the very next words that then occurred to me. I could not dismiss the threat. This man was declaring his intention to kill me. But why had he sent the letter? Why did he want me to know what he intended to do? What was he daring me to do? I could easily go immediately to the police. However, the local law enforcement agencies had not been kindly disposed toward students whom they considered to be trouble-making, anti-war, drug addicts, little better than blatant criminals protected by their privileged status on the campuses which were like islands of anarchy floating in the lagoons of complacent supporters of Nixon's militant national and international imperialist policies. San Diego had always been described as 'A Dirty Old Government Town' as the title of one of Mason Williams' popular songs declared. Only members of the United States Armed Forces, particularly the U.S. Navy, could expect to be on friendly terms with the local police, or

Highway Patrol, for that matter, as well. I still carried identification as a member of the Navy Reserve, with my rank of Lieutenant, and I also had a membership card with the Young Republicans tucked in one of the plastic windows of my wallet, but I only resorted to this ruse when the police braced me and harassed me on those occasions when I drove with the top down on my MGB and my (*radical*) long hair declared my suspicious identity and they pulled me over for questioning and a rough, invasive personal *search*.

I could also appeal to one of the crew of Hells Angels who followed me about, claiming to be my body-guards, but they might over-react and slaughter or maim many innocent students and bystanders to prove their devotion to this duty. My *pen-pal* acquaintance from the Mexicali motel was daring me to be bold and abide by the covenant I had declared for our classroom: autonomy and freedom of intellectual expression, even to the most radical level – in this instance, at the possible price of my life. Many years later, in 1985, when I decided to explore the possibility of employment once again in the American academic field, Professor Wai Lim Yip, the Taoist Chinese who was Chair of the Department of Literature at UCSD, a man who had barely escaped Mao's death-dealing Red Purges of dissenting intellectuals in the Peoples' Republic of China, wrote a letter of recommendation for me that stated that "Ben Wright, would readily offer his life [*lay down his life, gladly die for*] in dedication to his principles and ideals, if any such challenge were to be presented him". What a bizarre letter of reference for academic employment in the United States? What was I now demanding of myself in "dedication to … principles"? Was it worth it? Would I survive this ordeal? Shouldn't I just call in sick and cancel class on account of imminent disaster, and thereby heed my personal survivalist instinct?

Instead, I decided to prepare a lecture on Death and the notion of finality in the American literary concept of this most intensely

Romantic concept. How many times, indeed, had I teased my classes with the quote by the Swami Coomeraswami: "When death comes, let me not be unannihilate, but rather let me celebrate this moment as my greatest, my last," or the other jingle, "Live every day as if it were your last, and one day, you'll be right"? I actually wove these phrasings into the opening of my introduction, on this, what might be my *final lecture*, and then quoted Albert Camus's startling challenge from *The Myth of Sisyphus* in which he states that the only essential challenge for any philosopher is to answer the question, "Why not commit suicide now?"

I then rolled over into a definition of suicide differing from homicide only in the direction in which one pointed the gun. I moved this along to the German Romantic movement, referencing Goethe's, *The Sorrows of Young Werther,* which supposedly inspired the suicides of thousands of young nihilistic readers of this book in late nineteenth century Germany, and I then retold the anecdotal plot of *Axel's Castle in* which the courageous young knight who vanquishes the evil uncle and all his defending monsters to rescue the princess and heiress of the Castle, and then, when this exquisitely beautiful couple - the triumphant consort-to-be and glorious princess - in their pre-nuptial union, assay all the treasure of this kingdom and begin then to consider the rich and loving plentiful years before them, then decide that the only way to insure that there never be any disappointment, that they commit suicide together at that very moment to preserve the Romantic ideal. And they do kill themselves together, dying within moments of one another. Romeo and Juliet with truly Teutonic resolve. I then made the remark that Cinderella was driven to join an all-girls motorcycle club when her Prince began cross-dressing and brought home one of his *pages* , named Bruce, and declared that he was coming out of the closet at last and that his Bruce would also live "happily-ever-after" in their castle and that the crystal slippers could also fit the tiny feet of his darling *page* who would thenceforward be their constant and most intimate companion. I then went on to say that the lost version of *Beowulf* told of a blood-bath mutual suicide of that hero with Grendel and *its* mother , and that one of the original versions of the Camelot legend was that King Arthur, Guinevere, and Lancelot were locked in a frenzied bedroom *menage a trois* resulting in the death of all three, and that Mordred, Arthur's natural son by his incestuous sexual coupling with his half-sister, Morgana la Fey, arrived to witness this, then grabbed Excalibur and disemboweled himself with that mighty sword in a Middle English version of the Hari Kari Samurai ceremony and his mother, Morgana, beheaded him as he completed the agonizing drill; and then she carted the entire heap of *royal* bodies on a Fairy barge to the Isle of Avalon with the Lady of the Lake, who later was to establish the dyke motorcycle gang that Cinderella joined ... and besides, there was a rumor that Pocahontas. ... and then I just giggled and virtually collapsed on my desk and said that story-time was over, and so I might be *departing*, in a very short time ... depending ....

A husky young man with shoulder-length hair, wearing a tie-dyed tee-shirt with cut-off sleeves, then rose from his seat in the middle of the third row and applauded. Several other students, all similarly clad, females as well as males, also began to rise and clap their hands. Before more than a dozen had begun to deliver this ovation, he snapped out the order to stop.

"Sit down. Shut up. You have no idea what's coming down," he barked viciously, and the room was stilled.

"You have time to go on," he said to me. "Tell us more stories, or do whatever you like. I drank that whole bottle of tequila, fucked my *own lady of the lake* - in her case, the Salton Sea, out near Borrego

Springs in the desert – and slept the rest of the weekend. I want to have a coffee with you after class. Oh, yeah, you are spared. Rave on, Captain, My Captain."

Thus, I was *reprieved* by Gordon Carter, who met me at the Student Union later and told me that he wanted to apologize for any anxiety he may have occasioned with his death threat. He admitted that he had been intending to kill himself in that motel after coitus with his love-mate because he was in a state of shock from having found his father's body, just the week before, hanging by the neck, a suicide, in the hall-closet in the house which the two shared in El Cajon. Gordon's father had reared him as a single parent since the mother's death in an automobile accident ten years ago. Gordon claimed that I had become a father-figure for him from the time he had joined our class, and as he had become aware of his own father losing his grip on reality – he had intuited some imminent disaster for about the past two years. That I should have then become a substitute for Gordon's own death wish, a sacrificial offering to relieve him of his own *execution*, Gordon wanted to explain to me in more time than we had then, so we planned a meeting to which I invited my friend and, psychological counselor, James Kavanaugh – with Gordon's approval and agreement. This meeting proved to be most beneficial for both parties, as James agreed to become a mentor in self-awareness as well as in poetic craftsmanship for Gordon, who later decided to establish a poetry workshop and publish a magazine for other aspiring writers. When I encountered Gordon eight years later, he was married and the owner of a thriving landscape gardening company and still served as the editor-in-chief of the poetry magazine which was recognized as one of the most valuable editions of its kind in California.

Kavanaugh, as most know, had become a hugely successful published author with many bestselling books to his credit.

I had survived and still derive some satisfaction in knowing that I have enabled many other aspiring writers to prevail and succeed. However, during that term I taught at San Diego State College, there were other challenges and adventures. Some of the coeds provided me some deeply satisfying sexual experiences, but they also attempted to blackmail me by revealing that I had broken the unspoken law against professors bedding their students. In my own version of the Duke of Wellington's, "publish-and-be- damned," response to a similar threat, I simply announced to the entire assembled class that several of their members who had been having sex with me were intending to expose my sin, and so I would admit this *quasi-criminal concupiscence* to all and sundry and invited any other lusty young co-eds to come bestow their sexual favors whenever they wished, and I would be grateful and unashamed in my acceptance of these venal gifts. Some women boycotted class for a few weeks, but then dropped by my house to climb into bed once more, cursing me and causing me to sustain a virtual whip-lash injury to my neck as I granted cunnilingual sexual performance, their athletic thighs nearly crushing me breathless in multiple orgasms, rageful and wanton , and *unforgettable*. One of them was a country-club swimming instructor and competitor on San Diego State's varsity swim team, and her dolphin kick had developed thighs that were like the sheet-steel sheaves that support the suspension system on an eighteen wheel trans-continental truck. I am lucky to have survived such passion - more difficult to endure than any attempted blackmail.

Even when I was trying to avoid dangerous campus encounters, I seemed to find myself in virtual minefields I had never imagined to be life-threatening. My favorite check-out clerk at the local supermarket provide one of the most surprising examples of this sort of well-camouflaged booby-trap. With her hair tied behind her head, in a *sensible bun*, Dana Jordan appeared to be the epitome of conventional and wholesome Southern California woman-hood. We had begun our conversations when she had noticed some of the Native American texts - *Black Elk Speaks*, and *The Teachings of Don Juan* - that I sometimes had sticking out of the pockets of my sports jackets as I delivered my shopping to her conveyor belt cash register checkout station. She told me that she was completing a Master's Degree in Anthropology at San Diego State College and asked if we might meet sometime to discuss our reference sources and compare notes regarding Social- Anthropology. It sounded benign and promising. She looked so demure and harmless. Her hair tied back in a *sensible* ... [beware of clichés; they can disguise the greatest deeply hidden dangers].

Dana Point is at the juncture of Mission Bay and Ocean Beach and Pacific Beach in San Diego, named for Richard Henry Dana, Jr., author of *Two Years Before the Mast*, the epic narrative of a young Harvard undergraduate who signed on as an ordinary seaman aboard one of the old square-rigged sailing ships in the early nineteenth century (1834). His description of the California coast and its seaports at that time are some of the mos accurate historical accounts we have of the state when it was still emerging from early Spanish colonial rule. The Dana I was visiting had told me that her family had named several members of their family, both genders, for many generations, in honor of this maritime adventurer. She lived not far from Dana Point, on a quiet suburban street of conventional bungalows in the center of

Pacific Beach. I assured myself that at last I was to find peaceful and relaxing, non-threatening company with this young lady - away from all the radical political and drug-crazed loonies that I was usually involved with. From outlaw bikers to Zen Buddhist acrobats and macro-biotic Maoists, to acid-head Tantric chanters running naked in the Cove Park on skate-boards and pogo-sticks, I had at last found that essential sanctuary where I might actually touch and taste serenity and sanity. As I was welcomed and offered a cup of Lipton Orange Pekoe tea, from a bag in a plastic cup on a formica coffee table in front of a motel style hide-a-bed couch, I believed that I could relax and let down my guard. I actually gave a most audible sigh of relief as Dana corroborated my intention by telling me to relax while she went into the next room - I had to presume was her bedroom, as the only other rooms had to be the kitchen, which I could see connecting in back, and a bathroom I presumed to be adjoining her sleeping quarters. She had said she wanted to get into *something more comfortable.* Another cliché, not unlike that of the *sensible bun.* I fully expected for her to play some Muzak background music by Lawrence Welk, or Perry Como.

She had been attired in her super-market uniform with thick cushioned soles on saddle-oxford shoes. I expected she wanted to don some jeans and flip-flops or sneakers. Just as I had sipped almost my entire cup of tea, she came back into the living-room and sat down so close to me on the couch that I was first shocked by the cloud of perfume sweeping from her body - *Chanel Number Five*, was it? Marilyn Monroe said that was all she ever slept in - and then I registered what Dana was wearing in addition to that formidable chemical covering. The fabric was black, but so sheer, that is to say, diaphanous, that I could see the color of her skin and the bright aureales of her nipples on her full perky breasts which were only partially covered by the long honey blonde tresses which now fell to her waist and the small of her back. She was pressing against me with a purring insistence and pushed my tea cup and saucer away to place a brown paper bag in the center of the table.

"I have waited so long for this moment," she virtually moaned. "At last I have you with me, the only person who will really understand what I am doing. I knew it the first time you checked out with me. You had a copy of *The Tibetan Book of the Dead* in one pocket, and in the other, Rider Haggard's, *She*. You mumbled something about Robert Graves', *White Goddess*, and then, Malinowski's South Pacific study of matriarchal sexual mores, *Sex Among the Natives*, and I knew you were the one I could share this with."

She took my hand at the wrist and thrust it into the open paper bag before us. She then turned her now heavily mascaraed eyes up to my face and pursed her fully, lustrously, reddened lips in a beseeching, open plea, her tongue pointing suggestively to the center of that lifted upper lip.

"Grab one. Reach in the bag. Take it out. Tell me what you think. What you feel," she implored. She pressed my hand deeper into the bag.

I could feel several baseball shaped objects and grasped one which felt like a shriveled apple or potato. As I pulled this out of the bag, my mind did not care to register what my eyes were actually beholding. I held what appeared to be a shrunken human head. The lips were stitched closed and the features were deeply wrinkled. The texture was like old leather, a deep brown in color, but the hair which tangled in my fingers was reddish and blonde. I had seen reproductions in plastic of such grotesque objects in some of the more bizarre novelty shops in Tijuana, Mexico, but this was definitely not plastic. It was like leather or some sort of tanned hide.

"This is not plastic," I said. "What is it? Where did you ever find ... ?"

Dana's hand grasped my knee and her grip tightened as her fingers pressed into my thigh. "It's real. This one was a blonde girl. Can't you see her hair. Her eyes were blue, but they're shut now."

I dropped the *horror*, and it rolled off the table on to the carpet, but Dana had turned the bag on its side and was spreading an array of some five other heads out, to display them for me. Her fingers lovingly turned each one up so that the face was looking directly at me, and she smoothed back the hair of each, so that I could see a variety of colors and even distinctly differing features in each physiognomy.

"I told you I am doing my Master's in Anthropology. Last summer, I went to visit my uncle who used to be a missionary in the deep regions of the South American rain forest where he was adopted by one of the tribes and became the first white man to ever be instructed in the art of head-hunting and sacramental shrinking. You might notice that there is a representative selection of racial and ethnic types in this collection. My uncle's work, but two are mine. Some of these examples had also been missionaries ... *who were not accepted into the tribe* ... as you can see. Except in this fashion. I mean ... Well, you know what I mean.

"I was accepted, and initiated, and have proven my craftsmanship and am now the first white woman to achieve this honor and practice this art. My Master's degree will ... " Just then, the telephone on the wall of the the entry to her kitchen rang, and she rose to go answer it. Her conversation grew animated, and she seemed alarmed. When she turned to walk back, her manner was anxious, and she appeared to be making an effort to regain her composure.

"Bad news," I asked. "Shall I go? You look as if you might want to take care of some other business."

"No, it's all right. I'm not going to let that bother me. I've waited too long to share this all with you. Please don't be upset."

"Why should I be upset? I mean, I can see that you're serious in your anthropological field research, and I'm truly impressed with your handicraft, but, well, I don't think I can stay much longer. You see, I was only dropping by for a cup of tea and ... "

"You overheard my conversation, didn't you?" she blurted, with a flush of red blush, rising in her bare shoulders and throat. "They say he only broke out early this morning. He can't possibly reach San Diego county before this afternoon."

"Who broke out? Of where? And why?" I exclaimed, and rose so abruptly that I tipped over the coffee table and sent all the heads tumbling out over the floor like that first break in the opening of a snooker pool game.

Dana rushed to embrace me, and as she did so, the left top of her upper garment fell away, and my hand reaching up to her, grasped her exposed, full breast. I pulled away as if burned and tried to twist out of her envelopment. Her arms were now around my neck and she was pleading with me tearfully.

"My husband. Yes. He did escape again, but they know he'll be coming directly here like he did last time, and so they have already sent a team to intercept him before he kills anyone else. He doesn't know we've been seeing each other, and he doesn't know where you live anyway."

Her assurances were only serving to send increasingly terrifying messages to my survival instincts. I had made my way to the front door, half dragging my would-be seductress, head-huntress, ex-check-out-clerk, over the scattered anthropological artifacts beneath our feet, one of which I stepped on, and I was almost thrown off balance by it, as I reached for the door-knob. With some degree of abhorrence, I kicked at the shriveled, small knob that had effectually tripped me up, and twisted the metal knob in my hand, but found that the door had been locked ... and would not open.

"Please don't leave me. Maybe he'll listen to you. The last man, the one he killed, was actually in bed with me at the time. You're fully dressed ... and you're a professor."

"Just unlock the door and let me go," I demanded. "I am not exactly wearing academic robes, and you are dressed for an orgy, so I don't think we can make any assumptions about what your husband will think, other than that we are together alone in your home, and you look as if you are having anything but counseling from me regarding your scholastic career. Please unlock this door. If you don't let me go right now, I promise you, I will never want to see you again."

Somehow that worked. And I never did see her again. I easily changed my shopping to another supermarket, and Dana made no effort to locate me and come visit me where I lived, although I was an easy target for just about anyone who cared to find me. Although parking was at times difficult to encounter near my doorstep, I was on one of the most frequented streets in La Jolla, and that was why the remark, "I was in the neighborhood and thought I would just drop by to see if you were home," was used often to catch me in my lair.

That was the line used by the hairdresser who dropped by one afternoon to ask if she could cut my hair ... *naked!*. That was her second opening line, and I had already invited her over the threshold and so had to negotiate *that ploy* with hospitable courtesy.

"I've seen you walk past our shop so often, just up on the street behind here, and I have had this dream of cutting your hair, *naked*. I don't mean that you have to strip, or anything. I just would like to do my magic for you completely nude, right here in your living room, with that incredible view of the La Jolla Cove below us. Nothing sexy, except for me, in my own fantasy. Okay? How about it. No charge. My gift to you for the pleasure of fulfilling a dream of mine."

And I never saw her again, after that tonsorial exercise. She was quite beautiful: slender and well-formed, the proverbial perky breasts and a tight bum, sleek loins and a well-trimmed mound of Venus, black and richly glistening like the hair she let down over her shoulders as she undressed and sat me in a chair with a large beach towel around my upper body. She merely trimmed my hair, which I preferred to wear almost shoulder length, and her chatter as she worked, hardly allowed me to respond, except when she asked for my reaction to one of her remarks, or asked me one or two direct questions.

It never occurred to me to reach out and slip my hand up between those lovely legs and pivot that pudendum on my wrist and upper arm and pull her over on to my lap to *couple*.

Perhaps she had reckoned that her comments about her husband and his work would excite me in some way; however, this was anything but the case. She told me that they had bought a house inland in one of those planned communities which were rumored to be owned by the Mafia, and she said that her husband, a man who was easily aroused to jealousy, was a henchman for one of the Italian developers, but because he was Irish, he could never expect to rise in the organization [be *made* or *mobbed up*], unless he could prove himself as a *soldier* as ruthless as one of the *boys* from the old country (Sicily, presumably) of his boss's origin. As she chattered blithely on about the parties she had to attend on her weekend days off, I began to envision a life-style peopled with character actors in the mold of De Niro and Pacino, and again considered how lucky I had been to escape Dana's courtship and I then began to recall certain unsavory details of the mating ritual of the Praying Mantis.

So when my hair-cut was finished and my visitor asked if I might offer her a drink for her services, making no effort to clothe herself, but actually sprawling with her legs open and her arms outstretched on my only easy chair, I felt anxious to find a way to dismiss her and usher her back out my door. I did pour her a stiff brandy from one of my Spanish selections that I had found on one of my forays in Mexico, a formidable herbal brand called 'Fernet Branca,' a sip of which usually stops a fully grown man in his tracks. She quaffed it as if it were 'Creme de Menthe,' and as if she were the plantation owner's wife just settling in for early evening cocktail hour on the front porch swing. Her elegance and *savoir faire* challenged Truman Capote or Tennessee Williams to provide a refined portraiture of this sort of stereotype. I was amazed that she asked for a refill, and then another, and I was aware that her limbs were becoming vitalized and energized, as color rose in her skin and ripened at the surface. I was feeling my own body beginning to respond, and aching to tangle in a copulative embrace or waltz her into my bedroom or just hammer away at that inviting nubile body right there on the overstuffed chair and tumble her on to the carpet for a final fall and thrusting finish to a non-A.A.U. approved wrestling triumph. For some providential good fortune, or not, two females arrived on the porch just then, and opening the unlatched screen door, boldly walked right in.

Winke Self and Becky Yianalos stood in front of the doorway, hands on hips, virtually challenging my reclining guest, as if they held territorial rights here. My hair-dresser pulled the towel we had used for my haircut from the floor, draped it around her and fled into the bedroom where she set about dressing in the clothing she had flung in there when she had arrived. I smugly crossed my arms and smiled with some satisfaction, deciding to provide them with a truly far-fetched explanation, to which they were not entitled, anyway.

"You're late, as usual," I scolded, hoping my visitor in the bedroom could hear me, and reckon that she had overstayed her welcome in any case. "My friend was helping me to decide whether or not I want to enroll in those Life-Drawing classes the University Extension will be offering next month. I was just about to attempt some charcoal sketches of her as you came in. I guess I had forgotten our appointment time, and I was dawdling about, just trying to get myself in the right frame of mind to do a few strokes with her. It's been so long since I put pencil to pad, or even attempted to reproduce the human form ... you know what I mean. I just can't seem to explain myself, and anyway, I think my friend was embarrassed with your coming in like this. She was just getting comfortable ... and ... "

A tightly wrapped, fuming, feminine package in black hair and glowering facial features with clamped jaw and clenched fists, charged past all three of us, straight to the door and out onto the porch, before I could continue with my nattering nonsense. Becky was just rearing back to deliver one of her guffaws, and Winke was curtseying with an exaggerated aplomb, as I tried to reach out to stop the excited egress of my bellicose barber. When she was well down the stairs and out on to the street, I turned to my most recent guests and offered to open a bottle of white wine I had chilling in my kitchen refrigerator.

As we sat back and enjoyed our cool drinks, I told my friends what had actually been going on. Unfolded newspapers were still cradling snatches of my shorn air below the legs of the easy chair used in the recent trimming, and the actual event was not much more unusual than many other La Jolla enterprises, except that usually naked men and women did consummate their union in some heterosexual resolution, which in the instance today, had been on the order of *coitus interruptis* ... before I could even unbuckle my belt.

Becky's own sister, Dierdre, a gorgeous creature who never left their home, had refused to attend school and spent her time nurturing birds and animals, was rumored to ride a horse, bare-back and naked on certain moon-lit nights down on the shore alongside the La Jolla Beach and Tennis Club, or so legend and local hearsay whispered. I had begged Becky to inform me of her sister's next nightly outing, but finally had given up waiting and had actually made a date with Dierdre, who visited me in my home, with her cockatoo and favorite raccoon, and allowed me to disrobe her and taste her reputed physical delights in my own domain. She was, indeed, a creature of unusual features: something half-wild, feral, smelling of the deep forest and responding to the sexual act as if it were the most essential element in human behavior. She was probably the most exciting, *and frightening* fuck I have ever experienced. Her love bites went deep and drew blood, and her orgasms closed her vaginal walls so severely, I felt that my penis might be pulled out by the root. The smells she exuded I have never been able to identify or encounter again, like a scent of humus and emerald liquid in levels of the earth only fathomed in excavations far below those depths reached by the most special burrowing animals: moles, newts ... and dragons.

Becky suspected that Dierdre and I had been together, but nothing had been discussed regarding this engagement. I suspected that Becky would have been delighted to share my bed as well, and her manner of implying this was sometimes almost embarrassing, to both of us, or anyone who happened to be present when she attempted to express her feelings for me. Winke was particularly unsettled when her best friend seemed to be intent on making a play for me, usually expressed in an awkward clumsy fashion, like making some insulting remark or aggressive physical contact which I had to rebuff, sometimes emphatically, to our mutual discomfiture. Winke and I had been lovers on one occasion only, and we had been avoiding any other encounters ever since. I had felt particularly restrained because Ed Self, her father had been a drinking pal of mine since my first arrival as a Navy ensign in 1960 when I had discovered 'El Sombrero' bar in the back streets of La Jolla. Ed's wife, Jan had been the best friend of Nancy Stork, the wife of the president of the P.T.A. at La Jolla Country Day School, and she had been one of the first people Nancy confided in when the two of us began our sexual liaison when I was the teacher of her two daughters and son. Intimate sexual involvements in this small town were a Byzantine intertwining whose schematic outline would befuddle anyone. One of the jokes at La Jolla Country Day School was that the most confusing event of the year at the school was Father's Day.

Once when I had delivered Winke to her home, her parents had taken me aside after she had gone to her room and asked me if I could advise them regarding her apparent promiscuity and how to curtail it. As I had been a trusted instructor at Country Day School and now was an assistant professor at her college, San Diego State College, I was, for them, a most reputable authority to consult in their anxiety for their teen-aged child's apparent meandering from the straight and narrow moral path. They told me that they suspected her closest friend, Becky Yianalos, of introducing her to drugs and encouraging her sexual licentiousness. I told them that I considered Becky to be an unwholesome influence, and that they should discourage any further contact with the Yianalos girl. I told them this primarily to engineer a process for detaching Becky as an unwanted chaperone from Winke so that I could have an unobstructed opportunity for more sexual flings with her, myself.

Winkle was infuriated when she learned of this particular perverse maneuver with her folks. Curiously, although she and I never again were intimate, she did invite me to spend an early morning snuggle in bed with the two of them (she and Becky) at Winke's beach cottage in North Mission Beach. I had arrived at the place at about midnight, and Winke had said that they both felt so non-threatened and comfortable with me, that they would enjoy my sharing the king-sized bed with them to sleep till late morning and then have a brunch on the beach together. I cherish the memory of occupying the center of that bed with each of my female friend's heads on either of my outstretched arms, and we actually slept, although our thighs did rub together, and I felt my erect penis rub against one, and then the other girl's side and back, several times, but with no connecting or relief, and I actually fell asleep without any ejaculatory resolution. We had a hearty breakfast and even some Bloody Mary cocktails accompanied by some Thai sticks rolled to stout joints which we smoked as well, and I felt that somehow we had consummated a familial, perhaps even filial, bond, that sexual intercourse might never have accomplished for us. Our friendship endured many more years beyond that night. I heard that Dierdre, whom I never saw again, never did leave her room and had become enormously fat (*morbidly obese*), weighing in at over three hundred pounds. Winke took over as editor-in-chief of her father's *San Diego Magazine*, and Becky managed the family toy store in La Jolla till it was sold.

Only once did I see Winke in the next few months. She asked if I would allow her to bring a new boy-friend by my house to play Crosby, Stills and Nash's track from their album entitled, 'Marakesh Express', so that I could tell them both what it was like to take the actual railway route that the music so romanticized. She acted as if I were some *guru* and worldly-wise traveler whose tales of Morocco would somehow enlighten them and provide a special blessing to their enjoyment of the recording. I mentioned Paul Bowles and especially his book, *A Hundred Camels in the Courtyard*, and I recommended smoking *kiff*, that is, hashish, and dining on *couscous* with lamb and sultanas, and then I just looked intently into Winke's eyes and tried to understand why she had requested this visit. I saw nothing in her response to indicate that she had wanted anything other than my testimony and travelogue commentary. When I politely asked if they were planning a trip to North Africa, she protested on his behalf that he was enrolled in law school at U.S.C. (University of Southern California, in Los Angeles) and that she was too committed to editorial work with her father's magazine and could not begin to consider doing such a frivolous thing. My Winke had become nothing more than another young American voyeur. And what was I, to be feeding the fantasies of these two conventional and respectable young yuppies? To what purpose? Would I ever lure her into bed again? And if so, what possible pleasure other than the most mechanical biological charade could be served? The last time I ever met Winke was in the editor-in-chief's office of *San Deigo Magazine*. I purchased some toys at Christmas, one year, a decade later from the Yianalos shop; I think it was Becky who served me, but it was hard to tell who that La Jolla matron behind the counter was. "Spring too long gongala," reads Ezra Pound's poem regarding youthful yearnings and nostalgia ... fading ... away.

I was able to buy some *kiff* (hashish), from Barry Lanes, our oldest U.C.S.D. resident drug-dealer. Not for Winke and her companion, but for Juan Goytisolo, the most recent Regents Professor, the Revelle College equivalent of a poet-in-residence. Juan was a novelist whose spirit of extremes in prose style and poetics had been compared to the Marquis de Sade, the philosopher whom this Catalan maverick writer worshiped. Carlos Blanco had asked me to be an escort and friend to this most unstable and highly strung artist whose English language skills were as limited as my Spanish fluency, but whose temperament Carlos reckoned was consonant with mine ... not exactly a compliment, but acutely perceptive and intuitively accurate. The first night when I picked him up at his suite at the La Jolla Beach and Tennis Club, I noticed that he kept a fully packed suitcase with the lid open, propped at the end of his bed ... he explained that he was always prepared to travel in a moment's time. My own mode of travel has been described by one of my life-long friends, as that of a fugitive-from-the-law. I myself kept a bag packed and ready in the house I the occupied over the Cove. Juan agreed heartily on my choice of the 'Rancherito,' the only authentic Mexican restaurant in town. He asked our waiter several questions over and over, just to hear the man's accent, which to a Spaniard's ear was like a comic routine.

However, Juan provided the most sublime joke when the chicken we had ordered was placed before him by our waiter. Juan had appeared to have been enjoying the corn tortillas dipped in Guacamole and pungent, picante salsa, by way of our first course, but now he pushed away from the table as he gasped in horror at the quartered poultry on his plate. He exclaimed that he could not participate or collaborate with such an indecency. This chicken was obviously a suicide, he announced. We all were stunned. How can one respond to such a pronouncement? The waiter, a Mexican, and therefore one of those ethnic models from whose world Gabriel

Marques had created the notion of "Magical Realism", merely offered to go and kill the next chicken so that the gentleman could be assured that his meal would be *kosher*, so to speak. Juan was delighted by the man's aplomb and slapped him on the arm and called him brother. We resolved the dilemma by my taking this ill-fated chicken, and I shoved my plate of *enchiladas* and *chili rellenos* in front of Goytisolo.

Robert Stratton invited himself to many of our evening meals, and Juan found his company amusing, as Robert was also a fan of De Sade, and was an aspiring writer. The Shotokan Karate classes that both Robert and I attended, taught by Nishiama, the man who had instructed the Japanese officer corps in World War Two, were also of interest to Juan because several of our fellow students in this martial art were active members of the Black Panthers. Juan claimed that his close friend, the ex-convict writer, Jean Genet, had founded an organization named the White Panthers. Their activities were equally, if not more, illegal and always at odds with the prevailing government of both America and France. Many years later, when Robert visited Juan in Paris, he discovered that Goytisolo was an active agent of the Algerian Resistance movement and had supplied enormous sums of money in support of their revolutionary activities. Juan's involvement was so dangerous that he could have been sentenced to life in prison or murdered by extremists of the prevailing French colonial government. Today, Juan lives in North Africa, and is one of the more revered foreign residents there, and he is considered by the Spanish intellectual world to be the most important living writer that Spain has produced in the past century.

That Juan was acutely aware of international affairs was corroborated by his identifying several visiting German, French and African *scholars* who appeared at some of the university and Jonas Salk Foundation functions we happened to attend together. I was not surprised to see that several of these people were often in the company of that dean of Financial Aid and Foreign Students whom I was certain was C.I.A. However, Juan's perverse sense of humor sometimes threatened to stir up these factors in a surreal fashion. A particular example of his delight in what might be considered psychopathic was his fascination with Tijuana's seamy night-life. Once after a dinner at my favorite restaurant, near the Jai Alai fronton, owned by a Basque family whose sons were all *pelota* players of considerable renown, Juan insisted that we find the sleaziest dime-a-dance bar and brothel in town, one that would be frequented by only the poorest and least cultivated Mexican *peons*. I was pleased to discover that particularly potent liquor refined from the peyote cactus plant was served alongside tequila and beer in the place we found. The music was a deranged version of Mariachi and some Cuban and Caribbean [most likely Jamaican/Haitian] strains, but there might even had been elements of Hawaiian and Cajun flavors, as well. Loud and throbbing and as physically stimulating as a Hell's Angels' *Bar Mitzvah.*, the floor was clotted with bodies embracing and virtually copulating as they swayed and bumped into arms and legs flashing and thrusting with what would otherwise have been crippling speed and intention.

I stood at the end of the bar where I sipped my tequila, and licked at lemon and salt washed down with chilled "Dos Equis" beer. I could hear Juan laughing and shouting into the ear of one of the toughest looking cowboys who leaned on the bar beside him. Juan was pointing at Robert who stood in front of both of them, and occasionaly would reach out to squeeze my friend's impressive biceps. I thought I heard him say "*gobierno, agente, policia*" repeatedly, laughing and raising his open hand in front of the cowboy's face, which remained rigid and severe and so lacking in expression that he seemed even more formidably fierce. The man finally shrugged and moved away to grab one of the small women who had just been released by her partner on the dance-floor. Robert motioned to me to leave as he took Juan by the arm and led us all out into the clear, clean, night air where we hailed a taxi and headed back to the border crossing at San Ysidro. It was only after we arrived back at my place in La Jolla that the entire incident was explained. Robert said that Juan had been telling several men in the bar that he and I were C.I.A. and F.B.I. and members of an elite secret police who preyed upon illegal immigrants and drug dealers and the white slave traffickers who worked in such bars as we we were in that night. When I confronted Juan with his perfidious deeds, he merely shrugged and said that all Americans were C.I.A. and F.B.I and there would be no such agencies if we had not created and supported them. I rather too swiftly replied that he and all Spaniards must then take full responsibility for creating Francisco Franco and the Falangists and the Spanish Foreign Legion. He smiled and agreed. Trying to debate with this man was like throwing a round-house punch at an Aikido master; I just would just wear myself out and end up damaging myself more than my opponent.

One of Robert's anthropology colleagues, Jamie Winston, began to spend considerable time with us. Juan was particularly fond of her because of her masculine name which corresponded to that of his poet brother, Jaime, who lived in Barcelona, but also because the two of them were both still toying with their own gender identities. I had spent a night with Jamie, sort of a ritual enactment of a twentieth century *comitatus* by means of sexual intercourse, and I consider having sex with her to be one of the most easily forgotten physical encounters of my life. I believe we discussed Kierkegaard as we attempted to bring each other to orgasm, which as I recall, was as unsuccessful as our understanding of this philosopher's own desperate leap of faith when logic failed. I do recall, that when she played a Beatles album at dawn, the track, "Here comes the Sun," had then, a most special appeal for me, and I savored the instant coffee she brewed, probably more than our *aubade* moment as newly arisen once-upon-a-time and nevermore-again non-lovers. We did become fast friends, thereafter, and I was delighted to observe Juan taking an interest in an American other than myself, whom I did not consider to be representative of my country's identity for any foreigner to consider as an appropriate model of our national mindset. Also, this was the first, and thereafter proved to be, the *only* female, Juan found in the least attractive in all of San Diego at that time.

They shared a perverse sense of humor that I think was best displayed by Juan giving Jamie copies of his book which his students and admirers had purchased and brought to him for his signature. He told Jamie to make an appropriate gratuitous remark which he would translate into Spanish for her, and then she would forge a most unconvincing flourish of his signature. As there were no examples of Juan's signature available to use in comparison, all of these forgeries went undetected. However, I wondered if any of these students should ever attempt to sell their copies to rare book dealers with the supposed signature of the author, what would have been the result?

Michael McClure told me once that many of the poverty-stricken San Francisco poets of the Beatnik epoch would often hold parties at his home and sign copies of each other's collections of verse which they then sold to rare book-dealers to meet monthly living expenses. Ruthven Todd told me that when he and Dylan Thomas were approached by the first librarian from the University of New York at Buffalo who set up their collection of holographic manuscripts of modern poets, that he and Dylan were dashing off verse after verse on empty unfolded cigarette packets which they sold to this aggressive American collector for Five Pounds Sterling apiece, enough at that time, to pay a week's rent in London a*nd* buy a bottle of whiskey. I well remember Laurie Lee, selling copies of his book, *As I Walked Out One id-summer Morning*, which had been the best-selling paperback novel in Penguin's history of publishing. Laurie would carry a few copies of the book with him to the Queen's Elm pub, just a block from his flat, and he would inscribe the book to whoever would buy him a bottle of his favorite Irish whiskey from the publican, his best friend, Sean Treacy.

There was one other woman whom Juan could tolerate, but he never expressed a strong preference for her company; perhaps, this was because she was conscientiously attempting to become a lesbian, but people like me kept interfering with her intentions. Rhonda was a close fiend of the Rawlins and also of one of my few female pals, other than Lynda Brent, the person we all referred to simply as Brent, who hardly ever allowed her first name, Lynda, to be used. Rhonda was married, but separated from a former professor of Biology from San Diego State College, who now was a window-cleaner who called himself Butt-Man and would sing anthems to himself as he performed the most daring window-cleaning on swinging scaffolding at elevated heights on the few multi-storied office buildings in La Jolla. Refusing to wear any safety harness, and reputedly usually out of his mind on various psychedelic drugs, the least of which was L.S.D., Butt-Man also carried a tape-recorder which could be heard loudly proclaiming the skills and wonders of this demi-god known by the common folk of San Diego county as the Butt-Man. These monologues were so upsetting to some of his clients in the mundane, and otherwise conventional and tranquil office spaces that he served from the other side of the glass, that he had lost several high-paying clients.

Rhonda had become one of my friends as Herbert Marcuse delighted in hearing her narrative of adventures with Andy Warhol in some of his film projects and how she bedazzled and subverted many men in the local chapter of the John Birch Society whose Junior League member wives she had seduced, and in some instances, had converted to hard-core lesbian roles. Perversely, Rhonda and I became sexually intimate when I told her I had a dose of clap (gonorrhea) and had not as yet visited a doctor to effect a cure. She wanted to be infected so that she could pass this most contemptible of social diseases on to one of the John Birch husbands whose wife she could not seduce, but could then have contaminated in a more street-nasty sense. I was more than willing to participate in this twisted act of social protest and gesture of political *provo* [that Dutch term for protest with no exact definition ot purpose - the subject of one of my favorite San Diego State College class projects - remember?]. Rhonda was good in bed - that is, she possessed all the sexual skills that a diligent and compliant house-wife of the many years of her theretofore ordinary southern California marriage [long live the *Stepford* Sisters] would be expected to have, with the scornful bitterness and cache of resentment which added just that twist of spiteful spice and vigor that provided her orgasms with a vituperative and curse-filled invective. Like fucking a top-dollar Las Vegas whore with a scorpion-tail clitoris and the vaginal spasms of an epileptic in *gran mal* seizure! I so enjoyed our initial bout that I invited one of my female students to join us the next afternoon in my bedroom. This sweet co-ed had confided to me her fantasies about becoming a lesbian, and was needing just a nudge to leave her varsity football player lover, and the Methodist Youth Fellowship in which she had been active since puberty. After only a few caresses and deep kisses with Rhonda, I left the two women locked in a throbbing purposeful embracing and only returned to the house when Rhonda answered the telephone there a few hours later and said that her new girl-friend needed for me to come and drive her back home. Rhonda and I actually spent several frolicsome nights together, and it was she who introduced me to one of her lovers, the famous Dr. Jonas Salk, Nobel Prize Laureate, inventor of the Polio vaccine,whose foundation offices next to the Scripps Oceanographic Institute was receiving great acclaim with such luminaries as Jacob Bronowski, Michael Crichton, and John Hunt sharing directorships and providing publicity of their bold new experiments and discoveries on an international scale. She had been his lover *after* my doctors had cleared away *that* John Birch Society bound dose of clap.

I was pleased to become acquainted with Dr. Salk, and did call on him once for a chat in his office to enlist his support of an environmental group who were blocking the real estate development of Torrey Pines Park. I had been asked to write the script for one of our major protest presentations and to invite as many powerful public figures to attend our *Town Hall* meeting at the auditorium of the Scripps Oceanographic Aquarium. I invited some of the high-ranking generals and admirals I had known when married to my first wife, Lisa Cook, and many of Judge Roger Rawlins's high-profile friends from San Diego government. That gathering was a huge success; we blocked the greedy developers from destroying one of the finest public wilderness areas in Southern California. The entire landscape adjoining that park where it rejoins the old Highway 101 entering Del Mar, is now spattered with housing and covered in asphalt, and defaced and disfigured for eternity.

Rhonda and I had parted company shortly before this when I had introduced her to Richard Brautigan on one of his visits to La Jolla from San Francisco. I did not suggest that she have sex with him, but somehow they did reach that juncture, and according to her report, he was savage and totally mad in his bedroom behavior. She said that once he climbed up on her dressing table and crouched there while howling like a coyote and jerking on his penis like some demented simian sub-species. Whatever happened spelled the end of our relationship – Rhonda's and mine – even as casual visits in such public places as restaurant or in an open-air sidewalk bistro. She had developed a repulsion for me thenceforward and would leave any venue I joined – "flinging away with high disdain" as the phrase was turned by the eighteenth century novelist Henry Fielding. When I asked Richard what had happened, he refused to comment. He had a distinct penchant for anal intercourse, what he called "farmer fucking," or "corn-holing," but I can not imagine that he had attempted to subject Rhonda to that indignity ... unless, of course, she had wanted such a deviation. There was something else that had occurred, which I am meant never to know, and do not need to. But I do regret the loss of her friendship. I have had only a few other sexual relationships with women who preferred lesbian partners, and I had always found such encounters a very special delight and have thereby been instructed in amorous practices that I would not have otherwise learned.

My other friend of inchoate gender, Jamie, who still did visit me, I was convinced, more to encounter Juan Goytisolo than to be in my company, brought by some zealous friends of hers in the Anti-War Movement and asked me to provide them a particular favor. My advice was needed *particularly* because of my former *service* in the Armed Forces of the United States. Jamie's friends were providing the final escape segment out of the United States on the "underground railroad" which was transporting young men who were unwilling to respond to their draft induction notices. Some were being sent to Mexico and then places like Costa Rica which held no extradition agreements with our country. Others were going to Canada, and some even to Sweden. What Jamie's friends needed was someone like me to screen the escapees in the final stage of their progress, to insure that there were no *agents provocateurs* (infiltrating American government agents implanted to destroy this network). As I had been not only Recruit Personnel Officer but also a battalion commander in the actual boot camp at the United States Naval Training Center, San Diego, in addition to having been a courts-martial officer familiar with practices in the Recruit Training Command punishment divisions, and the actual Navy and Marine Corps brigs, my experience made me an expert in matters relating to this project. My *particular service* probably did indeed save our entire enterprise in the very first days of my participation. It also revealed some rather astounding machinations by the United States government and the Republican party whose reverberations reached all the way to the oval office in the White House.

There was a young man, named Howard Clark, whom we were screening before final arrangements for his flight to Canada, the extra funding for this escape being deemed necessary to effect as soon as possible as he was claiming to be a recent escapee from the brig at the United States Marine Corps Recruit Depot in San Diego. When I met and interviewed him, I decided to shift my approach to interrogation. As I bore down on him, I discovered one flaw after another in what I began to call his *cover*. I had found his hair-cut suspicious when we were introduced. There was at least a half-inch of hair on his skull. "Brig-birds" had their heads shaved, and if he had escaped from Marine Corps confinement only days before, his hair would not have reached even an eighth of an inch in length. Also, as I *went on the muscle*, that is, increased my level and degree of intensity and oppositional questioning, he did not assume the recruit's virtually automatic verbal responses with the "Sir" after every reply. When I shifted gears and then became *good-cop*, he relaxed all too readily so that I would never believe he had even been nominally or partially institutionalized by even a few days in boot-camp or brig.

I called in Robert Stratton to assist me. His background had been Army infantry enlisted, but his current methods of confrontation were more derivative of street-life survival and Shotokan Karate's intensified focus of combative attack. Robert actually used his hands and firm grip to extract the truth from our Marine *manque*. The only uniform Howard Clark had ever worn was in the Cub Scouts at his elementary school in El Cajon., California. However, he had indeed been *enlisted* to serve in another *armed forces* whose membership became our journalistic material for a block-busting newspaper article which was first printed in the *Los Angles Free Press* , then the *Los Anglees Times*, and finally appeared as features in both *Time* and *Newsweek* magazines.

This young man had been employed by the F.B.I. to infiltrate our "Underground Railroad," and by a stroke of luck and my expertise, accompanied by Robert's pragmatic savagery, we had plucked him from our midst and discovered his perfidy; however, in our follow-up interrogation which Robert delighted in supervising, we had discovered Howard Clark's other more shocking affiliation. He, along with several other young men and women, had been recruited by members of the Republican Party to be trained as *hippy activists* at the Republican National Convention which was to be held in Los Angeles in three months times. Howard had attended meetings at which he had seen as many as one hundred other young people like himself being indoctrinated and trained in the criminal, vandalistic behaviors they we being paid to exhibit when they would be delivered to the arena of the Republican Convention and introduced there to make their aggressive entry which was to then be repelled and subdued by law enforcement; and then martial law was supposed to be declared by the mayor of Los Angeles. Then, after subsequent minor riots were occurring throughout California and other key cities in the United States, staged by similar trained *hire-a-hippy* vandal bands, martial law was to be declared, along with a National State of Emergency, to be proclaimed by President Nixon. In such a dire condition of violent turmoil, and with a state of martial law prevailing, it was planned that the presidential election for that year could be canceled, and the Nixon Republican *Reich* thereby be established to retain the presiding president and mandate that his oligarchy remain in power from *then on*, for many years into the future, in United States history.

Insane? Incredible? Impossible? But was this any more psychotic than some of Nixon's current foreign policy? His response to mass protests over the bombing of neutral Laos, the *commander-in-chief's* response had been, "I am president of the United States, and I will order the bombing of anybody I want to bomb."

The entire idea for enacting a state of National Emergency so grave as to require the institution of martial law – and therefore probable suspension of *habeas corpus* rights - throughout America, seemed preposterous to those of us who heard Howard's story, but as he relaxed and expanded by telling us the extent of the planning and training sessions which he and over a hundred of his California *colleagues* attended, we began to realize that some Rasputin had sold Czar Richard Nixon on a monumental scheme for enslaving the entire American population and in establishing a tyrannical dynasty to be ruled by W.A.S.P. *military-industrial-complex*, probably the cream of the graduating classes of that ethnic stamp from U.S.C and Stanford, and then those greater intellectual elite who could be weaned away from pinko professors at the major ivy league universities. Howard was from a White, upper middle-class family; his father's lower-rung executive status had forced him to reside in the less than desirable suburb of El Cajon where he was in middle management of a factory there which employed over two hundred Latinos and Oriental unskilled workers. Howard had been sold an idealized future of becoming one of the select *storm-troopers*, like those S.S whose loyalty had been to Hitler himself, to serve the dream vision of the new Fuhrer, Commandant Nixon, flanked by Ehrlichman and Haldeman, his prize *Hitler-jugend*.

G. Gordon Liddy, who, after the Watergate scandal, served a five year term in prison rather than reveal the actual criminal activities in the White House. As a former F.B.I. Special Agent and close confidante of Nixon, the boss himself, Liddy considered himself to be one of the chosen, the elect, the honor guard and a leader in the special forces troops of the new *Reich* which he believed would indeed someday be established in America. When I had lunch with Liddy, an icident I mentioned earlier in this book, in Miami, Florida, twelve years later, he had told me that he wanted me to serve with him in this elite band. He was especially eager to have me join after I told him of the revelation we had made upon discovery of this *hire-a-hippy* strategy that had been planned in California to trigger the declaration of martial law and the subsequent wild-fire riots to be staged throughout America at that same time, in order to justify the declaration of martial law *everywhere* and the cancellation of the presidential elections ... from then on!

The media relished the news release of this hot story: *foiled-hire-a-hippy-vandal-invasion-plot.* Nixon was forced to cancel all his plans for staging his national nominating convention in California where his Mafia associates had promised him elaborate assistance and reinforcements for his ideological zealots. Instead, he had to rely on the Southern *family* scion, Beebee Rebosso in Miami to set up the convention there. The only example of a near riot was the forcible expulsion of former Marine Corps Captain Bobbie Muller who was literally flung out over the restraining bannisters leading into the convention hall, wheel-chair and all, as he led a group of other wounded combat veterans protesting the Viet Nam war. The most atrocious police brutality scenes were enacted upon protesters at the Democratic Convention in Chicago, and these were not staged by any special interest groups such as the republicans had employed in California … it had become merely more middle-class ordinary citizens outraged by ineffectual political response to anti-war sentiment in the majority of the voting public in the United States.

Shortly after the story of Howard Clark and his disenfranchised horde of would-be convention invaders was published, some of us began to believe that there might be a light at the end of the tunnel. The glimmerings of the discoveries by the courageous journalistic team of Bernstein and Woodward of other nefarious activities by Nixon and his disciples promised that there might be an arousal of outrage by the average American citizen, and that the current Republican regime might be about to tumble, and the shameful conflict in Southeast Asia might come to an end.

A considerable amount of time had to pass before all this did occur. The Watergate spying scandal was published and was presumed to have been engineered by the president, himself, but was never to be tested in court, as Nixon tendered his resignation and placed in office Gerald Ford, and this ploy assured that no follow-up investigation was ever made. Slowly, but eventually, the potential threat of a tyrannical take-over of America was averted. The Atttorney General, Mitchell, was sentenced to prison for obstructing justice, and the *master plumber* of the Watergate subversion, G, Gordon Liddy, also was convicted and served a substantive term behind bars. Ehrlichmann claimed that he found Jesus and was awarded a publishing contract and high-paying speaking tours after his release from prison, and many of the other hench-*people* [to use the politically correct non-gender specific term for Nixon's inner circle] also found ripe rewards in publishing their laundered memoirs. Democracy prevailed and we began to believe again that truth conquers all. We even left Viet Nam ... and only slid into imperialist posture a few times thereafter in Central and South America in the following decades.

In the weeks following the Clark incident and leading up to the awakening of the news industry - first the *Los Angeles Times* picked up the story we sent that city's Free Press, and then the major magazines, *Time* and *Newsweek* - somehow, Jamie's friends' version of the action Robert Stratton and I had *resorted* to in winnowing out the testimony from Howard Clark had provided me and my pal with some notoriety. Some versions probably had it that we had stopped short only of employing methods invented by the Spanish Inquisition to interrogate our *client*. I was becoming amazed, as well, at the fantasmagoric splendor that the narrative mosaic of my European exploits had bestowed upon me. The mantle of myth which these experiences had thereby attributed to me would have taken most mortals at least twenty years to accomplish, and then, only with a chunk of Superman's fabled *Crypton* in their pocket. I listened to some of the *reportage* with relish, especially when my identity in the audience of which I was a member, incognito, was not apparent to that tall tale-teller, wherever and whenever that happened to occur.

So I was not so startled as I might otherwise have been, when a beaming platinum blonde sidled up to me outside the Revelle College library and addressed me: "You must be Ben Wright, the Errol flynn of the Literature Department. I've been wanting to meet you. Let's go to dinner tonight. My treat. I know you only frequent Mexican restaurants, so let's go to your favorite. Here's my address in Pacific Beach. See you at seven. I'm Kathy."

And as she *beamed*, and then turned to walk away, she cast a naughty wiggle and twist to her supple rear. I looked at the address, and knowing it would be easy to find, I put the note in my pocket and hoped I would remember when the time came.

I did not forget, and when I pulled up to the curb leading up the cement walk to the door with her number, she was already coming down the steps, carrying a large leather suitcase. I was just getting out of my side of the car, as she swung the case on to the metal luggage rack on the flat trunk top of my MG sports car. She asked for some rope to tie it down and explained that she would not be bringing it home after dinner, because if her instinct was correct – and it always was, she assured me – that we would decide to live together, and so she would just come back to move in with me tonight and be mine for evermore, or at least until we decided to split up.

"I forgot to tell you my credentials," she tossed over to me as she slid into the passenger seat after executing some impressive maritime knots to secure the case to that frame. "I was elected president of Women's Liberation at San Diego State College before I transferred to U.C.S.D. And I am just establishing a chapter here and will be president till we elect someone who is as strong to lead as I am."

Kathy Woodward moved in to my home that very night and remained there for several months until she was awarded a Fulbright scholarship to go to Paris to study at the Sorbonne for the next academic year. We adapted to one another readily, and she told me that I was one of the least chauvinistic men she had ever met. "Imperialism begins in the kitchen," was the line she quoted, which meant that tasks assigned as gender-specific in household chores, such as washing dishes and mopping floors, formerly considered insulting to masculine dignity and only fit for "girls," when magnified, was the basis for the oppression of all the ethnic and racial groups, ruthlessly exploited by the empires deriving from British and American foreign policies. There were those Cecil Rhodes (Rhodesia, Africa) tyrants who spoke of the "white man's burden" to educate and elevate the dark-skinned peoples indigenous to the regions these colonialists conquered. And according to Kathy, all this repressive and exploitative wrong-doing began in the kitchen with the simple tasks assigned to children. She was startled to see me on the business end of broom and mop and washing dishes as each one was used in preparation or completion of any meal. She delighted when Richard Brautigan came to visit us on a full moon to prepare his special feast, "Stonehenge Stroganoff," the recipe for which I have today [He mentions this meal in one of his novels, but only I have the actual list of ingredients and the blue-print for their assembly. I also have a photo of the two of us leaning over the cauldron sipping the first spoonful of the concoction]. As we two men took over the kitchen and wrought our culinary magic, or wizardry, Kathy and her colleagues in the nascent U.C.S.D. Women's Liberation chapter crowed their approval and had to admit that some men were not imperialist *manques*.

Kathy told me that she had actually planned to snare me when she heard about the Howard Clark incident. It was a gambit not unlike the one her estranged husband, Bob Woodward, was involving himself with at the *Washington Post*. I spoke with him on the telephone when Kathy and he were in contact, and I was enormously impressed by his courage in pursuing the publication of this investigation of the Watergate criminal activities of Richard Nixon's gang. Bob had also been an officer in the Navy, having served in a Communications department on a line-combat vessel in the Viet Nam conflict. He well knew the power of government agencies, and I was amazed that he carried on his investigation when it would have been so easy for the power elite/elect to have crushed him like a bug and removed even the stink and stain from everyone's awareness. When Nixon was about to finally resign in 1974, in an interview with the British television presenter David Frost, upon being asked if a president could commit an illegal act, Nixon had glibly replied that anything a president of the United States did, could not be deemed illegal, because if the president did it, then it was, *by definition*, legal. This was the madness of that moment, the prevailing insanity that read like Chapter Twelve of *Mein Kampf* in which Hitler declares that if a lie is told repeatedly by those in power, it thereby becomes the truth, and that is the power and result of effective propaganda, and the Machiavellian means of ruling the Reich or Republic [Plato made the same statement in the Twelfth Ion of his *Republic*].

I did not have Kathy's company for more than a short period of a few months, as she became more engaged in her preparations for the scholarship in France and was on several transits to the libraries of the University of California in Los Angeles and in Berkeley. Our love affair was not intense, and as I spent more time visiting Michael McClure and Richard Brautigan in San Francisco – and she did not find their company congenial – we grew more and more apart, so that we were passing one another – one might say, like "ships in the night" – except that we rarely spent even an evening together, and so, we barely took time to be intimate, except for an afternoon or two of clumsy cuddling and awkward coital groping. One afternoon, when she arrived from the U.C.S.D. library and we attempted a quick coupling, and I had only a half hour before bid a fond farewell to Dierdre Yianalos, who had unexpectedly dropped by for some intense rutting, I was hard put to explain why there was still a warm, sticky stain in the center of the sheets which had spilled from my passionate encounter that very afternoon before Kathy's dive into our bedroom. It was not long after that unfortunate coincidence that Kathy found that she needed to spend most of her time away from our common ground. She had moved out within a week of that embarrassment of Dierdre's lingering spoor which I had not tried to explain away with any convincing excuses.

The more time I spent with my poet friends, Michael and Richard, the less I really cared to maintain any sustained intimacies with any particular women. I actually felt quite satisfied to go drinking and reveling with them and was not inclined to seek out any one steady female companion. I do not recall going for any length of time without sexual satisfaction, however. Whenever I was with either Richard or Michael, there were always an abundance of women who made themselves available to us for whatever time we could make available to them for sexual jousting. I suppose these women were literary groupies. I do recall one of them arriving with a bag filled with copies of books by my friends, imploring them to sign some personal notation in return for whatever sensual favor my friends should care to sample from her. Decadence, or merely another twist on consumerism and shopping?

It was when Richard was staying at my house one weekend that I received the telephone call that informed me that my father was near death. The general manager of his companies told me that a ticket was waiting for me at an air-line counter at San Diego airport, and that he would meet me at Will Rogers Field, Oklahoma City, when I landed and that he would drive me to the hospital. I had not seen my father for several months, and that was only after an even longer period before, as our visits were justifiably constrained by his having officially disinherited me seven years before. Oddly enough, he had invited me to visit him – paying for my round-trip flight – earlier in that year so that he could tell me that he was dying and had attempted a bizarre sort of farewell conference with me. I had arrived at his residence at that time and been brought into his bedroom in the new house he had bought (having sold my childhood home in Crown Heights a few years before) where he kept a live-in nurse who was attending to his more dire needs twenty-four hours a day. He was propped up in bed and appeared to be in relatively chipper spirits as he listed all the malfunctions of his physical being and laughed as he told me how unreliable his body had become. Aside from being incontinent of bladder and bowel, and long ago having given up any notions of sexual activity, having been impotent for several years after the radical surgery that had been performed upon him for prostate cancer – he had bragged to his closest associates then that he could, as a result of the surgeon's skill, "Fart through my pecker." Now, he complained most bitterly, that he could not even abide his favorite meditational indulgence: Chivas Regal (Scotch Whiskey), on the rocks. The ice caused his asthmatic bronchitis to virtually strangle him, and then the liquor shot through his body "like a dose of salts', he complained, making him "shit like a goose" and humiliate himself with no more control over his sphincter than a month-old babe. Then he laughed, and boasted, "But I still have all my own teeth!"

He spread wide his mouth and pointed to the orange-colored stubs (he still smoked three packs of cigarettes a day, even though emphysema had virtually destroyed his ability to use his lungs in any healthy manner to deliver oxygen to his blood-stream) that were indeed all intact, but worn down to the bare serviceable minimum needed for chewing. This display he often enacted upon his lady friends, the women whom he dated, and took dancing (he had achieved a polished degree of skill in ballroom dancing) at least twice a week before his entire body began to sabotage all his romantic intentions and fantasized heterosexual adventures. His body was a testimony to the triumph of mind over matter. Aside from the jagged knife scar stretching from his right wrist up along his forearm and across the biceps and over the shoulder on to the still firm pectoral muscle of his chest above the nipple which I remember him showing me to denigrate the use of or even the carrying of such implements as a pocket-knife, especially with combative motive, there were the massive wounds to his arms and legs and spine received in more than one drunken collision with concrete abutments on highways where he had fallen asleep intoxicated driving well above the speed limit. The first time I had been roused by telephone calls from hospital Emergency wards to come to rescue him was when I was only fifteen, a year after my mother's death, and I had ignored the requirement for a legal driver's license to jump in one of our cars to race to help him either to be treated for his damage, or check him in to a hospital room, or, as more often happened, to drive him from whatever site he had landed in, cursing and complaining, so that he could self-medicate with more whiskey and then set about beating me senseless for merely being young and undamaged ... so far. Often these sessions would twist into his condemnation of my very birth as the cause of his wife's death - that my delivery had so torn her womb that he was convinced that this trauma had implanted the cancer which later consumed her entire body. Not logical, nor sane, but enough manic motive for his demented orchestration of a reason for revenging himself on me. And that I looked so much like her, and possessed so many of her features of character as well, would all combine to serve to exacerbate and exaggerate his rageful assaults in these moments.

There was the radical prostate cancer surgery which he endured just before her death which had crippled him in so many other ways: incontinent of bowel and bladder and impotent – these were the initial effects, as well as the incipient effeminacy engendered by the estrogen hormone treatments which caused his breasts to become almost identical to those of a pubescent female. Somehow, through his study of some new alternative holistic, naturopathic and lunatic fringe-health alternative herbs and exercises, and particularly, his reading of a book entitled, *Psycho-Cybernetics*, he began to regain his strength, and virility, and was walking miles every night, riding a horse most weekends on his farm, and he had enrolled in and completed many months of instruction in ballroom dancing: from the waltz, to the mambo, the rumba, the cha-chaa-cha, and I suspect, even the tango and swing/jitter-bug. Along with his love of European cuisine – his favorite restaurant became 'Jacque's International' – he had collected a bevy of widows and divorcees who adored being invited by him to dine and dance twice weekly. He had continued at this frantic race to re-capture his youthful vigor, but his tobacco smoking habits, and his continued gobbling of handsful of barbiturates and amphetamines along with the heavy consumption of wine, whiskey and cognac, had finally incapacitated him and brought him to a confinement in this bed at home with a nurse in attendance twenty-four hours a day. Nevertheless, he had enjoyed himself more than most men who might have endured similar afflictions: disease and injuries that could lay low many a less resolute spirit.

"I paid for your plane ticket to come here to see me before I die," he announced, without much preliminary frosting. "I don't reckon I've got much longer, and sometimes I think I might as well just use my pistol and get it over with. Can't screw, or drink, or even walk more than a short distance before I have to go shit myself. But I've got some questions I want to ask you. Set my mind at ease."

"It's your nickel," I assured him. "What do you want?" and I chuckled in imitating that manner of his when he answered the telephone with the gruff challenge, "What do you want?" - never a more civil, "Hello, what can I do for you?"

We joined in a shared relish of this gambit which would surely seem offensive to more well-mannered folks. This was the Ben Wright, 'Bull-of-the-Woods' trademark. The word *curmudgeon* barely begins to describe his brutally brusque, yet beguiling, demeanor. I settled myself down in the easy chair at the far corner of his room and waited for his questions.

"Who is this man, Marcoose? Some federal agents have come to see me to tell me that he's trouble and that you are in with him on some business that might get you both killed. Why is the F.B.I. so riled that they come visit me and your sister to find out more about you. What are you two up to?"

I didn't try to correct his pronunciation of Herbert's surname, but I did assure him that we were engaged in causing the F.B.I. as much trouble as we believed they had caused the average American citizen with their attempts to intimidate and cripple the rights to free speech and freedom of choice in political activities, especially in regard to those people who declared themselves to be of the New Left, of which Professor Herbert Marcuse was considered the leader throughout the world. I admitted that I was indeed engaged in activities which the federal government would deem illegal, especially those which were designed to transport Conscientious Objectors against the Viet Nam war out of the United States into neutral countries where they could remain till the war was finished. I said that I had been a teaching assistant and had served as a body-guard for Marcuse, who was a professor of Philosophy and a devout disciple of Karl Marx, a small copy of whose works had belonged to my own father when he was also a devoted follower of that doctrine when he was a member of the I.W.W. (Industrial Workers of the World) before becoming disillusioned by the misinterpretation of these beliefs by the Communist take-over of the Russian Revolution, when even Trotsky had to flee to escape the insanity of this perversion of a pure, socialist ideology. I had never before been so outspoken about these matters in front of my father, and I watched a bemused expression on his rugged face then ease from grimace into a smile of benign acceptance and even amusement, verging on conspiratorial bonding.

"You say that you're his body-guard? So you gave your word to this man? You would give your life to protect him? Are you a Marxist, too? I sure hope you're not a Communist?"

"I gave my word, and so I must stand by him. Yes. I may agree with some of Marx and Engels' ideas, but frankly, I don't think they readily apply to modern economic issues. Communist? They are as banal, boring, and pig-headed as most of the Southern Baptist fundamentalist Christians I've known, and in the long list of those pledged to assassinate Marcuse, Joseph Stalin stands most prominently as one of the first in line, eager to wipe the man out - Marcuse's too pure a Marxist for heavy-handed bullies like Stalin and his gang."

"You read my old high-school notebook on Socialism, eh? I wondered what ever happened to that piece of trash." He waxed whimsical, and looked bemused and even younger as he recalled, "That teacher of mine, he had me all wound up. We were going to free the workers of the world, fight for the pure, new order ... and then he fell in love with one of the richest girls in town. Her sister, Henrietta Ames, was in my high-school Latin class at Central.

"Their old man founded the Texas Oil Corporation: Texaco. That spoiled gal led my teacher on. Hearts and flowers. Moony madness. He fell head over heels ... Yep. That's how I found him. Stretched out there in his room at the boarding house. Blew the top of his head off with a Colt's .44 six-shooter. So much for the Revolution, too. Bunch of Jew-boy intellectuals ... that Lenin and those fuzzy-heads ... put together that Communist Party sham ... Trotsky had to run. Marxism shot all to Hell. Like my teacher. Fell for that rich bitch ... sold out ... shot all to Hell."

"Well, we haven't been shot at yet," I said. "But plenty have offered to shoot Marcuse. Every time I stand up on a stage with him, I look out into the crowd, trying to spot that metallic glint of a barrel. I was only shot at once in the past few years, and that was on Bastille Day, at University of California, Berkeley, up by San Francisco. Ronald Reagan, the state's governor, was expecting the students to riot, so he sent in the National Guard and the Bay Area police to shoot rubber bullets and tear-gas at anyone on the campus who looked like a student. I was there and looked enough like a student to be a target. I was tear-gassed, but not shot. I heard that one student was blinded by that barrage, but that story never made the papers."

"Sounds like you been having fun," he smirked, and then laughed so hard he had to rear out of bed and make his way to the bathroom where I heard him evacuating noisily on the toilet. When he returned, he waved his arm in the air and then pointed toward the telephone on his bedside table.

"Go in the other room there, the guest-room. Wait till you here me tell you ... and then pick up the phone in there. I want you to listen in to a conversation I'm going to have."

When I heard his shout, I picked up the receiver on the end table there, and I heard my sister's voice asking why my father was calling. He told her that he wanted to know if any more of the federal agents, "Those F.B.I. special investigators," had been to see her. He asked if they were they still wanting information about her brother?

She seemed delighted by his query and sounded enormously pleased with her report of how she had just that morning hosted two of these agents in her home, serving them cinnamon rolls, and had given them many more details about her errant, possibly *terrorist* brother, whom they assured her they intended to either lock up in a penitentiary for the next several years or perhaps take care of "*with extreme prejudice*" – and did Daddy know what that meant? It was what they said in Viet Nam when they removed the enemy, leaving no trace, just eliminating them. Did Daddy know that? – she asked eagerly.

She was almost giggling with delight. She was being such a good girl. Daddy's little girl. A real patriot. The perfect American mother. The sister who ...

He interrupted her to say, " I think you might be interested to know that someone is on the other line here at the house. And he has heard every word."

"Hello, Dear Sister. It is I... the Big Bad Wolf, or so your G-men folks would lead you to believe," I offered. "But really it's just the same old onnery little brother that you used to tattle on at school, and at home, and just about any place you could, and get rewarded or admired for being such a Goody Two Shoes. What has the F.B. I. offered you? Once upon a time they also tried to ply me with gifts and treasures and favors ... and then they just resorted to threats."

"I didn't get anything," she shot back. I'm an American patriot and you ... you're a subversive and an enemy and dedicated to tearing down our Constitution, the Christian Church, the family ... "

"The family? Have I been the one who turned a member of the family over to the prosecution of federal agents to enforce laws that are employed to repress the basic freedoms of our people?"

"Okay, you two. Cut it out," Daddy interrupted. "This is becoming a debate and I'm getting bored. This is my dime my you're talking on, and ... "

"But Daddy, he's a Communist and immoral and ... "

"A Communist he most certainly is not, but immoral? If he's anything like his old man, if he'd been born a girl, he'd be the wildest whore in town. Now do either of you have anything decent to say to each other? If not this call is finished. I just wanted your brother to know what you've been doing with those F.B.I. fellas. I sent 'em packing, myself. Self-righteous, mealy-mouthed pricks!"

"Let me say this to my sister," I asked, and then said, "Phyllis, I know you believe you are doing the right thing. They probably told you they'll send me to prison where I could learn a decent trade and be rehabilitated as a humble, Christian citizen - albeit with no right to vote, as a convicted felon - but I want you to know that probably those agents you've been talking to really want me dead, and there are many ways they can arrange that just as soon as they have me in custody. I know too much for them to allow me to remain alive ... and vocal. After all this is over ... some say, 'After the Revolution' ... but I merely hope that after Nixon is out of the White House and our young men are out of Southeast Asia as a military presence, that you and I can once again be able to embrace and call each other family."

Her scream and string of curses, most unlady-like, and certainly not what her Sunday School classes could have ever imagined her spewing, was again interrupted by our father.

"So long, Sweetheart. Love to all the kiddies," he added.

As I came back into my father's bedroom, he was propped up in bed, his arms folded over his chest, and his facial features wreathed in a serene repose. His eyes sparkled, and his appearance was most like that of the drinking order of Jesters of his Masonic Temple where he was a thirty-second degree Mason, rather than the more ascetic, detached Buddha. Apparently *transformed* by the telephone exchange with my sister, he was inviting me to comment on what had just transpired.

I was not forthcoming, so he tossed me a lead-in: "A decent trade? Rehabilitated? A humble Christian citizen? How about that?"

"I could probably help my fellow inmates get their G.E.D. - that is the high-school equivalency diploma. I could still help you get yours, you know. But you know I'd flub Auto Mechanics - your own decent trade - just like I did when I was trying to learn that craft by working in your shops. The Christian thing, I could also fake, just like you have. I really think she means well, but you and I both know, she's always been a few sandwiches short of a picnic. Hate to say that about my own next of kin, but ..."

"Next of Kin? Brothers and sisters are the closest biological match there is ...I read that in *The Reader's Digest*. She's your closest blood relative. So maybe you could loan her a sandwich or two. You're full of baloney and you got the vinegar, never short of piss, neither," he jibed, as if he was winding up for one of his comical commentaries, and I always relished his wit, even when I was the butt of his humor.

"Kin is one of the things I was meaning to talk to you about. You do remember that I disinherited you some time back."

"Six years ago. When I began teaching at Casady," I said, feeling still somewhat injured and resentful of his decision. "You said, at the time, that you thought all teachers were Socialists and just didn't have the guts to admit they were really Communists. But I always figured that was just your way of avoiding admitting that I was crowding your life-style and you were afraid that I intended to have you committed to a sanitarium or mental asylum for observation after one of your most criminal drunk binges when ... "

"Well, I know now you're not a Commie," he hooted with glee. "Pure Marxist. Isn't that something Ready to die for your convictions or be convicted for your ... "

"Pretty good try, but the loop won't twirl", I interjected - making reference to Will Rogers' stage gambit when his lariat wouldn't spin, but his story would, and he would say maybe that was the point of missing the trick throw, so he could twirl out one of his yarns. We both loved what we shared as common knowledge of that cowboy humorist whom Grandma Eliza *Rogers* Wright called "Cousin Will."

"Be convicted to life with no parole, or sent up so the feds can put me down with 'extreme prejudice' ... before I ever try to learn a decent trade."

"But you are willing to risk your life to protect this Marxist professor? What's his name?"

And there seemed to be a quality of something like envy in his tone of voice. Was that because he envied the unfaltering Marxist dedication of Marcuse, his influence over so many young people, or was it something like a twinge of jealousy for the charismatic power this professor had exerted on my mind and will, replacing the *father-figure* that he had wanted to actually be in my life? I had indeed found a person *in loco parentis,* yet here I was, sitting with my own biological parent who had renounced his legal fatherhood and executed legal documents to deconsecrate and annul our familial bond. Our biological connection was undenial. My personality was a replication of his rigorous self-discipline and fierce moral courage, but because I was so identical to him in my rigid personality, our basic differences had proven, indeed, to be irreconcilable.

"You are my blood. You have my spirit. There's no denying we are ... " He began to falter, but then recharged his rhetoric with a heave of his chest and a virtual primeval growl from the depths of his heart. "I disinherited you. Cut you out of my will. Legally, you're no son of mine ... anymore."

He stopped speaking, and looked long ... maybe even *longingly,* at me, and when he spoke again, his voice was soft and benign, almost blessing. And what he then said was a sort of benediction I shall never forget.

"Ben Allen," he intoned my full name as only he and my mother, and then those elementary school teachers who had likewise been instructed to call me. "I almost called you, *Son*. That would have been in violation of the documents I signed and certified ... relieving you of that title."

"Just call me Ben. No one will mistake us for the same person. As you used to tell people who asked why you had not named me Ben Junior, that if they were too stupid to tell the difference between the two of us, then they weren't worth talking to in the first place," I reminded him, and we both had a chuckle, substantially lightening the mood.

"Okay, Ben. I'll get down to why I wanted you here ... aside from that conference telephone call with your sister." He again assumed the severe mein, and his tone became measured and exact. "I'm dying. I will probably be dead in the next month or two, according to all my doctors, and I can afford the best ... and the most honest.

"I really have been curious to know what you've been up. Especially whatever has got the F.B.I. so riled," he paused and began to smile impishly. "They don't know whether to shit or go blind." He stopped as he savored one of his favorite expressions. We shared the salty phrase like a bone with luscious barbecued meat we passed between us and both gnawed at with gusto.

"They been here many times and telling me you're some kind of subversive scaliwag, real thorn in old J. Edgar's side. They tell me he throws your name around his office in a frenzy like a cat-o-nine, whipping his boys up to smash you or lock you away where the sun don't shine," he cocked his head to one side, and squinted his eyes at me as if he were taking a bead along his rifle's barrel.

"What in God's name have you been up to?" He paused long, and then with a lip-licking relish, challenged,
"Whatever it is. Keep it up. Give 'em Hell. Throw more commotion at 'em than a jackass in a tin barn ... and then some. Don't cut 'em any slack." He paused to catch his breath, his face now beaming with a glee and excitement, "Give 'em Hell for me and that onnery old reprobate Karl Marx and Trotsky ... and Eugene Debs. I just wish I could be around to see the finish of them sister-mishap eatin' yellow dogs."

It had been a long time since I had heard him allude to the lowest life-form he ever employed in such a surrealistically descriptive, colorful down-home phrase from my father's early youth on the homestead in the late nineteenth century Indian Territory. His term, *yellow dog*, was synonymous with coward; but when joined to *sister-mishap eatin'* was called up *only* when truly riled: *sister-mishap eatin' yellow dogs*. How that image could ever have been *engendered* - and perhaps that verb is ill-chosen - would truly challenge the best Transformational Grammar Linguist from Chomski's inner cadre at M.I.T. Those meta-language specialists who can track to origin a deep valence meaning for this *-mishap eatin'* - could construe only to refer to a person who would eat the miscarriage, that is, the foetal remains (placenta) of a miscarried child-birth of one's feminine sibling. How could this be? *The Horror! The Horror!* Something to stop Joseph Conrad's Mr. Kurtz (*Heart of* Darkness) dead in his tracks, and insure that if such aboriginal outrage be mentioned, that novella would have been banned or burned and never read in the Western world ... and then of course, John Milius could never have convinced Gray Federickson to produce his rendition of it as a film called 'Apocalypse Now,' in extrapolation as one of the most repulsive representations of incidents of unspeakable horror from the Viet Nam war (America's most shameful *miscarriage*).

"To Hell with 'em. Keep it up. Give 'em Hell." He was in the habit of repeating himself when at his most vehement, and Hell was the worst fate he could invite his enemies to endure, including those even so low-down as to relish eating their own sisters' placenta, or worse. He was enormously pleased with his outrageous out-pouring. Clinical psychologists referred to such expletive expression as *venting*. I was happy that this reunion of ours had provided him with such a diversion from his physical suffering. Sick-bed was not his appropriate milieu. *Patient* was not a word that would ever describe his temperament nor his condition in medical definition. "Roar, roar at that good night," were words I recall reading in Dylan Thomas's poetic treatment of his own father's unwilling demise. This man, my biological and genetic source was not willing to give up easily this life he had so abundantly imbibed and savored.

"I can't call you Son, anymore, but I will tell you that you are probably the finest man I have ever known. To Hell with it. Not *probably*," he choked up as he struggled to say what even to this very moment of my life, which now is almost the length his stretched to then, "You are the finest man I know. Any man would be proud to call you Son."

Notice. He did not actually call me, *Son*. But that compliment from such a man, was to receive the highest form of recognition as a man among men – whatever that construes to mean. It is the greatest inheritance I can imagine ever receiving, and even after what actually transpired upon the event of his death, I have ever since that moment held as being greater than any treasures I have ever known.

"Give me a kiss and say goodbye," he ordered, opening his arms and reaching out to me.

We kissed on the lips as men in his family did – was that an Indian custom? As we had always done. I do not think it is a practice of many other families. We never hugged. That gesture would have been considered inappropriate among men, maybe even regarded as *sissy*.

As we stood apart then, looking each other squarely in the eye – two equal men – he gave a huff of amusement and reached into his bedside table drawer to draw out some paper money – one bill.

"Here's a fifty. Go buy you some pussy. A gift from me. Maybe my last," he snorted and almost choked with glee.

"I don't have to pay for pussy. It comes to me free, but I will buy some good whiskey and toast you with it when I go to bed tonight," I replied, lifting my hand as if holding an imaginary glass.

I flew to Denver, Colorado, that night, checked in to the Brown Hotel where the Modern Language Association was holding a conference – the annual employment hustle where colleges and universities interviewed and hired hungry young doctoral candidates and even those errant floating professors dissatisfied with their current positions. I had accepted the invitation from the Career Counseling office at UCSD, and was curious to sample what might be on offer to a maverick like me. I had my temporary job as Assistant Professor at San Diego State College, but I was willing to inquire about other positions in American academic institutions. Reed College, the most exceptionally "alternative" school and some other experimental places in New England had reputations that sounded appealing, challenging, intriguing.

I attended only a few of the erudite offerings by scholars who had impressed the editors of P.M.L.A. (Publications of the Modern Language Association), that most exclusivist of learned journals in the field of literary studies. One of our U.C.S.D. professors had a scheduled appearance. This was one of my favorite instructors, Dr. Robert Elliot, the eminent Eighteenth Century Enlightenment expert and one of the world's foremost authorities on the subject of Satire, who held an hour's lecture focused on the cartoon character created by the cartoonist Walt Kelly, a lovable opossum named Pogo whose name became the title of this comic strip. It had been in this satiric medium that Kelly had dared to spoof the insane and vicious actions of Senator Joseph McCarthy and his House Committee on Un-American Activities in the 1950s and to make the general public aware of the huge injustices wrought by this legislator and his witch-hunt which had destroyed the careers of so many of our finest writers in the film and theatre world at that time who had been accused of Communist and subversive activities. After the lecture, I congratulated Elliot on his offering, and he made the odd remark, "If you really wanted a substantial position in our field, all you would have to do is ask me. But you never have." He then turned and walked away from me as if I had done something to offend him.

It was Elliot who had been most sympathetic about Julie Aschmann's death -- that supposed *suicide* with her drug-using lover - "It is always the best, it seems, that we lose," he had said to me as we both bowed our heads and mourned her loss, together in the privacy of his office. It was also he and his wife who had visited me when I was doing graduate work (University of Madrid, with Dr. Carlos Blanco) in 1967 in my apartment on Calle Lope de Vega, in Madrid. This middle-aged couple had gone to the Hostal Casanova next door, by mistake, while looking for my residence. They had been greeted warmly by the girls there, all prostitutes whom David, my roommate and I had bonded with over many after-hours drinking sessions in their quarters. The Elliots told me that the girls all seemed to have romantic passions for me and David. I told them that we had been tutoring them in English as Casanova was a boarding school for waitresses applying for jobs in American and English hotels. Robert Elliot appeared to believe me, but his wife grinned broadly and gave me a conspiratorial wink as I delivered my whopping lie.

I attended one other session at this M.L.A. Conference that caught my interest. An hour's discussion of the history of the semi-colon, a punctuation mark that had not been used until after Chaucer's time, but was still a device credited to the Middle English period. As a teacher of English Composition, I have always been alarmed at how often students use this punctuation mark in the place of a comma and then could be charged with writing what is called a Fragment Sentence. Thomas Jefferson painted broadly with it in his opening lines of *The Declaration of Independence*, but Kurt Vonnegut, the popular twentieth century novelist claims to have so abhorred the semi-colon that he never used it in any of his voluminous written works. I was delighted to sit and listen to a scholar from a small back-water southern university – perhaps it was Sewanee – hold forth rhapsodically on this iconic symbol for an entire hour. These were only two of the arcane and esoteric delights which I savored at the M.L.A. Conference that year in Denver.

With that gift of the fifty-dollar bill from *Daddy*, I had purchased a bottle of twenty-one year old malt whiskey. After attending these two performances and ducking in and out of a few others, I retired to my room where I drank my fine booze with only ice and a splash of water. Feeling a glow of benevolence toward all my fellow pseudo-intellects, I sauntered down the winding staircase to the lobby where I plumped myself down in an overstuffed easy-chair, a emblematic survivor of the Golden Age of this hotel's origins, and was just beginning to subtract one hundred years from my consciousness of my surroundings when I became aware of the approach of a stunning beauty within only moments of settling in for my solitary appraisal of the milling crowd. She stood by the side of my chair, one hip cocked as she looked me over, and I could almost hear her purring with satisfaction in approval of what she had found, before she uttered her first enigmatic remark.

"I'm a Tangerine, and I stopped in to have a drink in this bar which is supposed to be of some special historical note, but even with several double whiskeys, I still don't feel particularly satisfied."

"Did you say tangerine? I think a twist of lemon is what's recommended with most whiskey cocktails," I retorted, as I turned my head to see that this was a gorgeous hunk of woman-flesh, perhaps even nudging the ideal of voluptuity to its limits, a more classic Titian model of the full feminine form than was currently popular in most American fashion magazines. Her eyes-lids were deeply mascaraed, and her long eyelashes brooded over emerald green eyes that seemed to be pools inviting plunges that might obliterate all memories thenceforward. She was alluring, and foreboding, and magnetically vibrant. She appeared to be enwrapped in velvets and exotic furs, and her neck and ears sparkled with jewelry that was complemented by a dazzling diamond ring which flashed at me as she held out her hand in introduction, and I was impelled then to rise and tell her my name and that I too, had not found much solace in several draughts of whiskey, but had not as yet visited this famous bar. I asked her if she had any suggestion as to what we might do. She actually led me by the elbow to the main entrance and told me she was taking me home with her. A sleek B.M.W. coupe, her "ride," was parked in front of the front door.

When we arrived at her own doorstep in a snow-clotted street of Boulder, Colorado, we had been chatting happily for over an hour, and I had discovered her to be an altogether charming and intriguing person. She was indeed a *Tangerine*, that is to say that she had been born in Tangiers, Morocco, of French colonial parents, but had been sent to school later in France and then England where she had "read history" at one of the better known colleges of Oxford University. That was where she had met and fallen in love with the actor, Peter Sellers, who had asked her to marry him and had bought that extraordinarily outrageous diamond ring she had flashed in my face while I was still at a relative disadvantage, seated in the lobby of the Brown Hotel. Had she hypnotized me with it? Perhaps, or was it the beguiling perfume that now filled my senses with arousal as we stopped the car and the first fresh mountain air rushed in to invite us out and up the steps to her home where we frolicked and laughed and promised to never part – until only a day later – she told me she had to catch a plane to Costa Rica, but that she would drive me back to my hotel and that within the next week she would probably land on my doorstep in La Jolla.

"Wham Bam, Thank You, Ma'm," was an expression that young men of my generation had used to describe such encounters. However, it was the male who was most ordinarily the author of the brevity and superficiality of such light-hearted emotional engagements. Had I been used merely for her delight? Probably. Did she respect me afterwards? Who cares? I had a magnificent time and had drunk most of her booze in her well-appointed, luxurious home; and there was still a half-bottle of fine whiskey left in my Brown Hotel room. I checked out the next morning, and, never saw her again after she dropped me at the curb of the hotel that chilly day.

When I returned to California, I was beset with the task of catching up with my course lectures, which I actually did plan, although my method of delivery would have appeared to be an anarchistic and spontaneous game of literary, poetic, and musical hop-scotch, to more orthodox members of the academic establishment. I was attempting to keep up appearances with discussions of my doctorate with the professor who had been assigned me by Roy Harvey Pearce, a charming poet and respected critic of contemporary issues in literature, Edwin Fussell. Unfortunately, every time we met, as he was a chronic acute alcoholic and I was never averse to drinking, we managed to become so intoxicated on the beverages he kept on hand in his home, that I never even began to write an outline for my thesis. Also, the students on campuses throughout the country continued to shut down various schools, and San Diego State College was rendered inactive at least every other month - or so it seemed - that spring semester.

It was also at this time that several events occurred simultaneously that might have catapulted me on a sabbatical from all my activities and commitments to my life as a student, teacher, or even a resident of the United States. However, I had become so enured to surreal events and threatening incidents by this time, that I merely reeled from the shock, and took a few days leave in the Haight Ashbury home of my friend Michael McClure, and at that time, with Richard Brautigan, and assorted hangers-on from Lawrence Ferlinghetti's, City Lights Bookstore, and Enrico's restaurant in North Beach. We still browsed about all of the San Francisco area in a relish of theatrical and poetic events that were constantly generating a sense of renewal of spirit and hope among our generation. As we visited several bars and drank ourselves into to euphoric states - what Brautigan called "qualifying for the Nobel prize", as so many of America's literary laureates had been hopeless drunks - one could forget almost any dreadful matter, and even cavort sexually with women one would never recognize if ever encountered again.

What propelled me to fly to The Bay Area almost as soon as I had returned from visiting my father and meeting my Tangerine, was a dinner I enjoyed in Del Mar with Fanya Jordan and Sam, her husband. I had been one of several to partake of a huge offering of spaghetti in the rented home of Fanya, U.C.S.D. philosophy undergraduate and the sister of Angela Davis, and Sam Jordan, who was studying pre-medical courses, hoping to be admitted to medical school the following year. He was on parole from a conviction he had received for some street violence in his home town of Detroit, having served only a little over a year of actual prison time. His academic record, also at U.C.S.D., had been outstanding, and he and his wife expected to continue graduate work in the San Diego area, most likely at the same university, when they received their Bachelors' degrees. The dinner ended pleasantly, with all of us helping to wash up and tidy the couple's small residence. It was the next morning when I arrived at Revelle College and walked on to the plaza, that I learned of the after-dinner *festivities*. However, just as I entered the plaza, I was overwhelmed by noxious odors and a grisly stench which I would have at first associated with a barbecue of the fatty spare-ribs so popular as home-cooking in my Southern background.

Meat had, indeed, been burned ... but it was not pork or beef. The cannibals of the South Pacific regions refer to this meat as *long-pig*; that is, human flesh. A teaching assistant in the History Department, Tom Rayford – he had just had a discussion, we later learned, regarding his opposition to the Viet Nam conflict an hour before, with his doctoral director, one of the world's foremost authorities on the Spanish Civil War – he had left that office, walked on to Revelle College plaza and squatted on the paving, and then poured gasoline over his head (he must have left the full jerry-can sitting beside the building before his conference with his professor– the action having been conscientiously premeditated), and in imitation of so many Buddhist monks in Southeast Asia, had self-immolated as a protest of the War. There was a small piece of cardboard lying there beside him, with the words, "Stop the Killing in Viet Nam." It had been scrawled in an almost infantile script - perhaps his nervous condition had impaired his artistic focus.

His burning body had been covered by blankets wrapped around him by some students who had rushed from their dormitory rooms adjacent to the plaza. An ambulance had arrived in minutes after the call, but it took a full three days of agonizing suffering for him to finally die in La Jolla"s Scripps Hospital, attended by his family, his father a major in the Air Force just returned from service in Viet Nam and probably Laos, as our primary Air Force base at Udon Thani in northern Thailand allowed our facile entry and exit across those borders where we were aggressively dumping enormous loads of bombs and anti-personnel land mines at that time. I was standing on the apron of the plaza paving, stunned by the acrid smell, and what I had been told by students who had assisted in the rescue, some of whom were busily attempting to scrub away the sticky fatty pieces of burnt flesh imbedded in the flag-stone tiles. I was just turning to leave when I spied a hulking form standing beneath the arches of the library, who seemed to be waving a bandaged arm at me and calling out my name. I cautiously approached and was not certain of the person's identity till I was almost beneath the arch myself. It was Sam Jordan. His head wrapped in a blood-soaked bandage, and his arm was in a sling, looking as if it had been set in plaster. There was so much white gauze wrapping about him that his black skin was just barely visible peeking out at certain folds, but his eyes were fierce, and his mouth told me harshly to come in out of the direct sun-light and join him there.

As soon as I was standing alongside of him, I asked him what had happened. I had left him and Fanya only a few hours ago at their home in Del Mar. He told me that he was waiting here while Barry Schwarz, a teaching assistant friend of ours from Philosophy was consulting with Herbert Marcuse upstairs in his third floor office in the library. As soon as Barry left Marcuse, he was coming down to drive Sam to a "safe-house" where he could be hidden and protected till a legal defense campaign could be launched on his behalf.

"For what?" I almost shouted at my injured friend. Then he began to tell me what had transpired in the hours since I had last seen him. The virtual burning alive of another fellow graduate student would not pale in comparison with what Sam told me, but the two experiences were harrowing and equally horrifying.

The night before, in Del Mar, just after the last guest, coincidentally, that being Barry Schwarz, had left Fanya and Sam, a couple of deputy sheriffs knocked on the door, and when Sam opened it, they slammed him across the room and on to the floor. They then grabbed Fanya and began pistol whipping her, calling her a "Commie Nigger Bitch" and used the same terms to refer to her sister, Angela Davis, and then they told her and Sam, who was still on the floor, that they could not live in such a decent community as Del Mar and that they were moving out that night. As Fanya resisted physically, and broke away from her tormentor, the lawman fired a shot from his pistol which struck her in the side and threw her to the floor with Sam. Her husband, at this point, feeling that the situation had become life-threatening, crawled back into the bedroom where he kept a loaded pistol under the bed and then returned to exchange gun-fire with the officers who were then kicking and molesting his wounded wife. After Sam hit one of the deputies in the arm with a shot from his pistol, the two men fled. Barry Schwarz had heard the gunfire as he drove down the hill from the house, and he raced back to find Sam and Fanya, both wounded by their attackers' assault. Sam had been hit twice and Fanya only once, but both bullet wounds required immediate attention. Somehow, Barry was able to get them both Emergency medical attention and treatment before the "all-points" bulletin was sent out to apprehend them on charges of criminal assault with deadly weapons, and attempted murder of police officers.

Fanya had received only a flesh wound, but she was so shaken by the incident that she had stayed in safe-keeping with Barry's wife who was driving them in her car around town till a secure hide-out could be located. Sam had been hit twice, once in the arm, with the other bullet striking him in the upper chest, but he was already recovered sufficiently to be ambulatory. Angela had been contacted, but perversely refused to call in any assistance which her position of leadership in the Black community provided her access to. She had been disgusted with Sam's refusal to join the Black Panthers and enraged by Fanya's support of her husband's decision. He could not possibly have done so, as it would have been a *prima facie* violation of the conditions of his parole; however, possession of the fire-arm with which he had defended himself and his wife would probably be cited as a violation of the parole, along with a number of other felonious actions that the criminal justice system would pile on in prosecuting the case of attempted murder of police. He told me that he had already spoken by telephone with Judge Roger Rawlins, who had begun to pull together a group to join in gathering money for the defense fund. Jane Fonda had even been contacted, and the Hollywood radical Left were are alerted as to the urgent need to rally behind Sam and his wife, notwithstanding Angela having forsaken them. Ah, politics. Where would it all lead? Eventually to the resignation of a president of the United States and even the criminal conviction of the Attorney General of our country for obstructing justice. More importantly, we would leave Viet Nam.

It was then that Sam delivered the knock-out punch of information over-load.

"Haven't you heard what's happening at Kent State? It's on all the radio and television broadcasts," he asked, in a virtually whispered tone. "The National Guard are shooting and killing students there. It's not even certain if they were assembled for an anti-war protest. It may be like what happened at Berkeley with Bastille Day. The *Man* decided to *off* more students."

I must have appeared to be reeling with shock, because Sam grabbed me and held me upright and spoke softly, "Go home, Man. You can walk down the street and not get shot. You're white. And free. Go while you can."

And I did. I found my car, drove to my house, packed my bag and called Michael McClure's place in Haight-Ashbury. Joanne, his wife answered, and was quick to agree to welcome me to stay that weekend, or for however long I needed. I just told her that many shocking things had been happening and that I needed to take a break.

The McClures did not own a television, but we purchased many newspapers and found that the best coverage of the slaughter of the students at Kent State was by the *Christian Science Monitor*. They appeared to present the most fair-minded and clear picture of what had happened. Students were killed, but the commander of the National Guard unit could not answer the most crucial question. Were these soldiers ordered to shoot to defend themselves, and if so, against what? There had been no active student protest of any sort to repel, nor had there been any aggressive act by any group, student or even "outside agitators," as was so often cited in such incidents. Who had provided the troops with live ammunition? Were we not told that usually these were merely rubber bullets, harmless but painful when delivered at high velocity against a human body mass?

None of these questions has ever been answered to the satisfaction of the families of those who were killed that day. A meager amount of money was delivered to pay compensation to the victims' families, but this would in no way provide any recompense for their loss. We also read about the death of my fellow graduate student at U.C.S.D. His agony had been prolonged by attempts to save his life, but his burns were so severe that he finally succumbed after three days, during which his family were assembled at his hospital bedside to witness his demise. His father had arrived, so one journalist reported, in his uniform as a major in the United States Air Force. How many bombs had he collaborated in dropping on innocent Southeast Asian civilians; how many had been burned as horribly by napalm, wantonly thrown down over these helpless people beneath the airplanes in our wholesale bombardments of millions in Viet Nam, Laos, and Cambodia. Yet this young man, the major's son, lay writhing in desperate death throes, hoping to send a signal from the privileged intellectual elite of our Southern California campus where some of us did feel compassion, and could participate in expressing the utmost grief for those whom our armed forces so nonchalantly slaughtered.

I returned to the U.C.S.D. campus only a week later, not exactly restored and recovered from the traumatic events of those few days, but I was resolute in my determination to assist my friends Fanya and Sam Jordan in any way I could. Barry Samons and Roger Rawlins - what an odd couple they made: a bearded, long-haired, Jewish political activist whose street savvy derived from an impoverished, but "red-diaper," childhood in the Bronx, and the patrician, elegant Rawlins, who looked like an *Esquire* magazine advertisement for the most up-market clothing and accessories to be worn while riding in a Rolls Royce or Bentley automobile, but whose political fervor was dedicated to the Black Civil Rights movement in its most extreme expression with the Black Panthers, and also pledged to the *chicano* Hispanic community with Venceremos, whose leadership many suspected of being Maoist - these men had organized a gathering to collect a defense fund at the home of the co-director, with Jacob Bronowski, of the Jonas Salk Institute. Most of the prominent Nobel laureate scientists in our part of California would be present, and Jane Fonda had also promised to attend, bringing all the Hollywood New Left activists in her train. I was surprised that Juan Goytisolo wanted to attend this event with me. He said that he had been telling his pal, Jean Genet about the latest *outrages* on our coast, and that *Saint* Jean sent his blessings and the best wishes of his White Panthers from Paris - whether or not such a group ever existed will always and ever be a well-kept secret between these two eccentric writers: Genet and Goytisolo.

I had only to walk a few blocks to the gathering as it was held in a house leased by the Hunts only a short distance along the cliff-side overlooking La Jolla Cove. John Hunt had become a friend of mine when we had encountered one another in bookstores and somehow discovered that we shared the same Oklahoma background from our youth. However, John's childhood had been spent on Native American Reservations as his father had been an official with the Bureau of Indian Affairs, an administrator on some of our state's tribal settlements. John had been in the Army at the close of World War Two, and had used the G.I. Bill to finance his studies in Paris, France, where he had attended the Sorbonne. I had heard from a mutual friend that John's doctoral dissertation at that prestigious university had been rejected, and he had not, therefore, received any credit for all the years of study spent there as a student. However, he had met and married a beautiful woman who was a member of the aristocracy, and rumor also had it, that John had served as a front for some of the C.I.A.'s financing for *avant garde* Amercian publications and theatrical productions in France and elsewhere in post-War Europe. He was now co-director of the Jonas Salk Foundation with Dr. Jacob Bronowski, that Renaissance-man from Britain who held doctorates in both Biology and English Literature, who had been a close friend of Robert Graves and had stayed in one of that family's guest-houses in Deya when he was an undergraduate at Cambridge University in England, and then he continued to be a frequent visitor to Mallorca for many years thereafter.

Juan Goytisolo joined me to attend the party, and he was anxious to point out to me, as we had only arrived and were ordering our drinks from the bar, just how many agents of the C.I.A. from Europe were also in attendance. His giddy chattering (although all in Spanish, it was ighly likely that the many bilingual guests probably understood his remarks) in reporting all this to me, became so extreme that I had to ask him to control himself so that we were not suddenly considered to be a threat to these otherwise "undercover" individuals and removed from the party with *extreme prejudice.* He just swelled with extravagant bravado, and walked straight up to several of these men and introduced himself in Spanish, French and English as the newly appointed leader of the White Panthers and offered to put these agents in touch with his confederate and comrade-in-arms, Jean Genet. John Hunt came to my rescue at this juncture and told me he wanted me to meet a close friend of his wife. This was a strikingly beautiful French woman he now steered me toward. Her name was Francoise Gilot, and she was the former mistress of Pablo Picasso. She had only recently broken away from her intense relationship with the megalo-maniacal painter, and John told me that she was exploring the possibility of now residing in our somewhat sophisticated village of La Jolla. He also asked that after I chatted with her for a few moments, that I take her across the room to introduce her to Dr. Jonas Salk, whom he knew I was effectively enough acquainted with in order to be able to present her to the eminent scientist.

I was enamored of Francoise from the instant she received my hand and held it as if I were the most important person in the room ... No, the most fascinating man she had ever met ... knowing that we had spent all our lives preparing for just this magic moment. Her inimitable gift was to project a sensation that enclosed, embraced, enthralled whoever came within her personal space in what felt like a radiant sphere of vibrant, glowing energy. The words used to describe what a wizard might cast as a spell to enchant, bewitch, beguile, only nudged at the notion of what happened when one met Francoise. I was not at a loss for words to tell her how delighted we would be in our humble community, were she to decide to reside among us. I was blathering blithely on about what special people and places we could offer to allure her, to convince her to decide to live in La Jolla, and it seemed then to be the most natural gesture for me to guide her over to Jonas Salk to whom I then introduced her and felt that I had actually brought about a perfect match. I had. Two weeks later they were married and remained husband and wife till death *did them part*, many years after this first encounter at a fund-raising event held on behalf of Fanya and Sam Jordan in the home of John Hunt.

Jane Fonda did not arrive, and I am still waiting to meet her and ask if she appreciated that bouquet of a dozen yellow roses I sent to her dressing room on opening night of 'There Was a Little Girl,' adapted from Christopher Davis's novel, *Lost Summer*, on premiere opening night of that play directed by Elia Kazin in Philadelphia which I attended with Chris in 1960. I lost track of Sam and Fanya Jordan after this fund-raising party, but the criminal charges against them were dropped, and the money raised was given to them as a sort of *ad hoc* scholarship supplement. Angela had refused to attend and had denied extending any assistance to her sister and brother-in-law, stating that since Fanya would not join the Communist Party and Sam refused to become a Black Panther, that they were unworthy of her esteem and aid. I could hear J. Edgar Hoover's connivance in this decision which perhaps may have been dictated to her by her new comrade-in-arms, Eldridge Cleaver, who was still operating as chief of the Black Panthers, as long as Huey Newton remained in a California prison. So may activists shared this fate, along with the infamous Soledad Brothers whose cause Angela was wholeheartedly and vehemently supporting, *unto the death*, as it later turned out in the court-room shoot-out that ended that dreadful case. The Chicano and Native American activist, Tijerina, who had been protesting the Treaty of Guadalupe, which had ceded former tribal lands promised to New Mexico Indians and given over instead to the Kit Carson National Forest territory, had been charged with murder and then manslaughter of an F.B.I. Special Agent in a fracas involving his defense of his wife in a brawl with that federal investigator. He had been sentenced to life in prison and all efforts to appeal the conviction had been denied and his cause had become only a memory for many in the Venceremos Latino movement (today he is living a free man in Mexico). Most people has forgotten this man and his cause. Why have I remembered? He and I had spoken together in front of the Revelle College library on the day he visited our campus, only a week before he entered prison to begin his interminable sentence. I told him something sentimental, like, "I will keep you in my thoughts." I have

BOOK TWO

Oklahoma, and some – "Way Back Yonder in the Injun Nation" – with many reservations

I was summoned to fly to Oklahoma City by a telephone call from Jim Peck to my house in La Jolla when Richard Brautigan was staying that day with me. Richard had taken the call and was solemn as he handed the receiver to me. He said that it sounded like something tragic; some tone in Peck's voice rang dolorous. My father was dying. There was a ticket to Oklahoma City, awaiting me at American Airlines' counter, Lindbergh Field, San Diego Airport. Richard was psychically highly sensitive. So am I. Death resonates with us.

As I flew home, I hoped I would arrive before *Daddy* died. As it was, when I entered his hospital suite, he had just been declared dead by his personal physician. He and the other *hench-people* in my father's employ, all except Jim Peck, his General Manager, who had telephoned and had sent me the air-plane ticket, appeared shocked to see me – some even seemed frightened. My sister was enraged and babbled about calling the police to arrest *that Commie terrorist ...* and she screamed at me to get out of that room and to leave her with *her* father. I returned her bombast with some more withering invective of my own, and the others escorted her out and left me alone in there. I jammed furniture against all the doors and returned to the bed where I tore away all the now useless life-support tubes and devices. I swept the upper body, tat barrel chest of Ben Wright's bullish form into my embrace, and squeezed ... watching his rugged face react in a deathly grimace; and I began to chant the incantatory Native American choral strains that he and I had so often intoned with his mother, Eliza Rogers Wright.

My *ad hoc requiem* ceremony was interrupted by the breaking in of a team of security guards which my sister had summoned, and as she was demanding that I be placed under arrest for criminal trespass, Phil Daugherty, my father's best friend and attorney, held up his hand to quell any further uproar, and made a proclamation that changed all of our lives dramatically from that moment forward. He declared that everyone present, particularly those who were immediate family and direct heirs of the deceased, Ben Eugene Wright, and he indicated that the people who were then present in this room, were indeed these aforementioned, needed to know that according to the most recently executed Last Will and Testament of Ben Eugene Wright, that his only son, Ben Allen Wright, had been named as the beneficiary of the majority of the stock in the corporations heretofore owned by the deceased: American Electric Ignition Company, of Oklahoma City, Oklahoma, and Amarillo, Texas, and Ben Wright Incorporated, a holding company owning all the real estate and the Soil Booster Corporation, the organic fertilizer manufacturing concern, and the Ben Wright Farms. There would be a hearing in the next week of the more exact particulars of this latest Will which had been dictated to Phil Daugherty, the sole executor of the estate, only a few weeks before now. However, Phil had deemed it necessary to declare the new ownership particulars at this moment because there was dire need for some appropriate actions to be taken as soon as possible in so far as the corporations were at this moment in enormous debt and the banks who held notes on the loans which were in excess of well over half a million dollars, might be deciding to demand of these loans, immediately, and thereby force the companies into receivership as bankrupts.

Phyllis looked as if she might have a heart attack or a stroke, so enraged and so stricken did she appear at learning that she was not the heir to her father's entire fortune and the majority of the stock owned by his corporations. I was now named the owner of the majority of the holdings, and was to be the heir entrusted to make the crucial decisions regarding the future of these companies which employed over seventy people, many of whom had been loyal and dedicated members of these family corporations for over fifty years. Their lives, and those of their families, I considered to be intimately involved in the decisions that I would be making in the next hours ... and from now on.

I looked directly into Phil Daugherty's eyes and said, "If this be so - and I have every reason to believe you, Phil - I want to hold a meeting of the board of directors of the companies owned by Ben Wright in his office on Seventh and Robinson in downtown Oklahoma City within the next hour. Can this be arranged?"

With a confident smile and a firm handshake, Phil's response was in the definite affirmative. He then turned to announce to all present, who were members of that board of directors, that we would be holding that meeting as soon as we could arrive at the office, a mere half hour drive from the hospital. He then turned back to me and said, "My closest friend in this world, from the time I was sixteen years old and in high-school, has been Ben Wright, and from this moment on, I shall consider this Ben Wright [me] to be my closest friend, and I hereby pledge that same loyalty as I did to the first Ben Wright, to whom I pledged my friendship, then."

It was almost an avowal worthy of the Knights Templar, or any other such order of a dedicated chivalric brotherhood and service to a higher humanistic purpose. Phil would indeed be an invaluable ally in the days and years ahead, although I knew that his personal beliefs and principles were of a tenor that would have made us enemies to the death in any other circumstances. He had been a member of the Ku Klux Klan, as had so many leading citizens of our community, my father included, and this inner core was impenetrable and deadly; however, he was my sworn friend and advocate, both in the legal and the fiscal sense, now and thenceforward; and it was with his help that we began to clear away the wreckage of Ben Eugene Wright's past decisions of disastrous financial consequences. Phyllis said that she just wanted to put all the stock, merchandise, and real estate on the auction block and then split up whatever cash was left over from such a sale. The nature of our business was that we were a central distributor for over fifty major automotive and industrial parts manufacturers, and our contracts assured us a substantial 65%, or better, discount on all the supplies we held in our warehouses; well over two million dollars worth of goods which would only yield, at best, a fraction of that amount, if sold at auction. Our best policy would be to maintain the sales force and programs already in place and attempt to cut costs, and thereby realize a substantial profit to pay off all the indebtedness and meet our weighty payroll obligations to the employees.

This was basically the policy we decided to adopt after a brief meeting of the board of directors, and then I met with Jim Peck to decide upon the firing of all employees who had been hired within the past year and who were not as yet vital members of our operating staff. We were able to trim away some fifteen people and to thereby decrease that next month's payroll obligation by an appreciable amount. I then set about installing a profit-sharing process for most of the rest of the employees so that we could all participate in cutting costs and increasing sales *in house* and *out* in our marketing territories with 4,000 customers on all distribution sales levels, which encompassed not only Oklahoma, but half of Texas, New Mexico and Arkansas.

Although I had told Jim Peck that I felt we should fire all the most recent employees, there were a few people that I believed were anything but an asset to our organization, and these were some of our more senior people whom I believed my father had retained because he was so sympathetic to their major character defects, mostly deriving from acute abuse of alcohol, which he was loath to condemn without confronting his own problem with that substance and admitting that he would be the "pot-calling-the-kettle-black," were he to so assail them. Several of our best salesmen had been alcoholics or severe abusers of that chemical substance, and I knew this well, as I had indulged in beverage over-indulgence with them on company time and using corporate funds, padding expense accounts to pay for these dalliances. Joe Whitehead, a red- faced, virtually, full-blood Choctaw had been the worst alcoholic, but Peck informed me that he had died only a few months earlier. There was also a man named Rube Goodgin, Whitehead's closest pal and drinking companion, who had formerly owned a hamburger stand on the corner adjacent to our offices, whose flamboyance at the griddle and in selling his foodstuff to the sidewalk traffic had so impressed my father, that he had been lured into our employee and had become one of our premiere salesmen, and I was told that he had joined Alcoholics Anonymous and was an officer in their meetings that were held by Jack Lanier, our director of Magneto repairs in that specialist shop which was attached to our main service department on the downtown office premises. The other most outrageous and colorful drinking companion from my days as a young man with the company was named Quentin Brown, whose nickname, "Cooter Brown," was part of a clichéd reference to hopeless drunks in the *patois* of Oklahoma boozers: as "drunk as Cooter Brown" was a nickname for one who would be as desperately inebriated as one could strive to be – synonymous with being "drunk as eight kinds of owl shit," another expression for this blasted state that I have heard only in Oklahoma and have encountered in slang spoken no other region of the United States.

"Cooter" was thrilled that I was to now directing the companies and particularly the home office of American Electric Ignition for whom he was the Oklahoma City sales representative. We had never sent him out into any of our territories away from the city, as his behaviors were so erratic that we needed to keep him near, in order to be subject to direct, virtually daily supervision by our Sales Manager and General Manager. I could not help recalling the incident in Shakespeare's, *Henry the Seventh*, when Prince Hal is named as heir to his recently deceased father, and his old partner in wenching and wining and other degenerate pastimes, the rollicking Falstaff, races out of a crowd during an official procession and attempts to embrace his former partner in vice, and is arrested and subdued, and the newly crowned King Henry, formerly his *dear Prince Hal*, tells the household staff to rid him of that obnoxious person, acting as if he has never in this life seen the dear old dypsomaniacal friend.

I was polite and warm in my greeting of "Cooter," but as he waxed rhapsodic in recalling some of our mutual misbehaviors, I remained silent, and I patiently waited for him to finally wind down, and he did, indeed, appear *winded* by a *tour de force* performance that could have challenged any actor bold enough to take on the soliloquy-ridden roles of a Hamlet, or a King Lear ... or, both. I looked gravely into the beaming, florid face of my former partner in dissolute endeavors and told him gently that his services were no longer required by the company, that his draw-account, which had surpassed any two months of normal commissions (he had become quite a financial burden as few customers cared to buy from him or even allow him on their premises), would be absorbed by our bad debts accounts ledger and that a check in the amount of a normally fruitful month of sales would be issued. I offered my handshake in gratitude for all that he had taught me when he had awarded me the rather audacious nickname of "Flash" when I had been active with our sales teams in my late teens and early twenties.

When the board next met to decide how to consolidate and rebuild toward achieving a profitable income from the operation of the parent company, American Electric Ignition, my sister, Phyllis began to see the benefits of continuing business, and she became enthusiastic. However, she was most aroused when we opened the private safe which our father had kept in his office and then surveyed the special lock-box in which he had squirreled away our mother's jewelry and his own collection of diamonds and pieces of platinum which he had winkled out of old magnetos that had passed through our oil-field ignition specialty shops over the years. There were several thousand dollars' worth of trinkets, and I offered her all but his thirty-second degree Masonic ring which held a four carat diamond as I offered this to Jim Peck, his closest business associate, a fellow high-ranking Mason, and our combined companies' General Manager. She was almost swooning with delight at my generosity. I was happy to have *Daddy's* first straight-edged razor and a harmonica - which he had never learned to play - also in this private treasure trove.

My next act of generosity, which I now blame on jet-lag and general goofiness, was to give away his entire herd of polled Hereford cattle, including the ponderously "hung" Rockefeller bull that sired most of that herd. I endowed our farm manager, Alvin Fisher with this trophy and the rest of the cattle, when I drove out to see the old farm spread the next afternoon after a busy morning at the offices in town. When I accepted Fisher's condolences and then listened to his craven plea for what he claimed my father had offered to leave him upon his demise, the sort of thing my father would neve had done - "Ben, your daddy told me that when he passed on that I was to have that semi-automatic Remington shotgun and my pick of the herd. Yep, he told me I could pick out any cow and would get that there gun." And although I knew Fisher to be a conniving, lying, nasty sort of down-home vermin, I declared that not only would he receive that gun, and my father's pig-skin hunting jacket and game-bag, but that he could have the entire herd of cattle, some seventy fat, lazy animals that roamed the rich pastures on our hundred and twenty acre farmland. His inheritance was worth such an enormous amount that I cringe to even begin to calculate its dollar value now.

I walked the farm that first afternoon I was back home, after so many years, and as I sauntered over the fields, I remembered that my last time doing this had been with my father when I had just returned from active duty in the U.S. Navy. He had been quite physically fit then, having become accustomed to walking several miles every night after work and riding one of his horses over the land on weekends. When his body had finally been declared no longer alive, only two days before, in that hospital, his chest still measured fifty inches and his waist was no more than thirty-two - phenomenal proportions for a man his age, seventy-five, but he had been called the *Lumber-Jack*, *Bull-of-the-Woods*, and the *Iron Man* by his contemporaries and all who knew him. I myself have always maintained at least the twelve inch difference between waist and chest, and even now at that same age of seventy-five, measure thirty-six inches at the middle and forty-eight around the chest.

The expression, *to saunter,* from the observation of peasants in France watching the first Crusaders marching off to Jerusalem, on their way to the *San Terre* - the sacred land, that was, according to a vignette to that effect written by Thoreau, in *Walden.* I felt as if I were covering sacred ground as I trudged my old terrain; however, I was disappointed when I reached the West Forty, the rolling pasture that contained so many buffalo wallows, where I could look out over the entire expanse of Oklahoma City which was indeed the beginning of the great American plains, spilled down below our moderately jagged stone outcroppings of our farm called the Crossed Timbers region, the very end of the rippled Ozark mountains flowing down to us from Missouri and Arkansas. I was saddened to look out over what had been also our land, another eighty acres which my father had sold for only $20,000 just before his death, this land which originally he had pledged to me to build my home where I would have been able to look out over the city beneath our old homestead estate.

Yet, I still did relish meandering through some of the outcroppings of the bared teeth of ancient stones that were crested by thick groves of stunted black-jacks, groves where cattle would often enter to give birth or to hunker down in to die. My father had told me that these were places that his mother, Eliza had deemed sacred energy centers, saying that the most powerful forces from within the earth's wrinkled crust were articulated out of these suppurated flinty lesions out on to our verdant surface where these dwarfed trees wreathed that gift for living creatures to be attracted into for healing and any other special revelations required, where they would decide to lie down within one of these sanctuaries. And as I stretched out within the enfolded bower, I rested my head on one moss-covered stoney extrusion and let my mind caroom over the past decades of my life as I closed my eyes and floated deep into that ancient *genius loci*. I did chant the old Native American mantra and found tears rolling down my cheeks, and my face tingled as a breeze evaporated the moisture, and I felt psychically awash, and bathed myself in the enchantments of my grandmother's healing spells. It was almost as if I were making a eucharistic communion with my roots, the tendrils binding me to this land were caressing my spirit and welcoming it home to its deepest valences. I chanted, and throbbed and melted in to my origins.

I later rolled the car down the tree-canopied graveled road to the red-rock pillar at the corner of our exit on to Northeast 63rd Street and turned left to look out over the ridge at Oklahoma City. My view was bordered by the Wright Cemetery, a two acre plot of land given to this early Indian Territory community of homesteader neighbors by my grandfather, William Stage Wright. I stopped to look at some of the more intriguing tombstones, some forty of which were inscribed with poetic remembrances by the survivors for their deceased. The Myers family had many members buried here, and Ruth Myers Lincoln, who resided in a nursing home in Little Rock, Arkansas, and who lived to be a vigorous 111 years of age, told me that she wished to be interred here, near her Oklahoma kin, when she should finally succumb and expire (her family in Arkansas buried her in that state). One plinth marker, an obelisk with four wide sides on its vertical marble surfaces, held engraved verses for each of the four wives buried beneath, none of whom had survived past the age of thirty. I looked about to find the last one of these wives, but could only find the husband's grave alongside these four. Had his last wife buried him and then moved on? I could find no other memorial for this family. Only one of my own father's family were buried here. We had arranged for Ben Eugene Wright to be sealed away in the Rosehill Mausoleum next to his wife, my mother, in this Nichols Hills suburb of Oklahoma City, at the intersection of this same road, Northeast 63rd and Western Boulevard. I have elected to request my privilege of burial at sea, as a former United States Navy officer and have so stipulated this wish in my Last Will and Testament. However, this vista on the last ridge of the Crossed Timbers overlooking the spread of Oklahoma City, before the Great American Plain was a tempting offering for an eternal home for one's remains. Someone in the neighborhood had maintained the grave-yard, keeping the grass mowed and the tombstones clean and unspoiled by mossy blemish. I sat down in the grass, and as I leaned back on my elbows, a long black snake slithered across the ground not more than a few feet away. A bull snake, non-poisonous, and unafraid of me. It was as if I had been greeted by the earth (the serpent is supposedly the familiar of the Mother Goddess, Oestra/Oethra) itself, and I knew I had been welcomed home.

I lay there for almost an hour more, listening to the rustling of leaves in the trees surrounding that side bordering my entry road, and after standing to urinate behind one of the larger stones, imagining my amino acids and liquid essences filtering down in to the loamy reservoir of these early settlers of this same landscape, I walked back to my car and headed west to the Four Corners gasoline station which was also a local general store. In the parking lot, stood the only telephone booth for many miles, and I noticed that I was the only White person in the immediate vicinity, but I reckoned that was just because this entire area was a Black neighborhood, except for our farm, and a couple of other Caucasians residing farther east toward the towns of Spencer and Jones. The large school-house farther north on Sooner Road, toward the Kickapoo Reservation, was the Frederick Wright School, named for the father of one of my father's playmates at the turn of the century. However, as I came in the store, I felt myself to be an intruder in a completely alien scene. I actually felt a chill, and sensed a threat from the several people, all Negro, who stopped what they were doing and became silent as I entered. I opened the cooler to select a soft drink, the ubiquitous Coca Cola - *a color-blind beverage* - and just as I pulled it out and made for the cash register, I became aware of the presence of a large man who had just emerged from the room in the back He was equal to me in height, over six foot three, and his physical strength was announced by a boxer's poise and the grace of a natural athlete. His hair was a curly iron gray, and the icy blue eyes that fixed me with confrontational fierceness were a reflection of mine ... and my father's: an undeniable family feature, a genetic marker. Was this an African American cousin of ours? There were many Wrights living in this part of town, and they had all arrived in the Sooner land-rush days, the Oklahoma Run, in the opening of the Cherokee Strip for homesteading in 1889. Those who had accompanied my own grandfather had most likely been formerly slaves owned by our own progenitors named Wright. They had their own cemetery, just a half mile down Northeast 63rd to the west. The segregationist policy of "separate-but-equal," that *apologist,* Booker T. Washington's, explanation for racial division, had remained in effect throughout Oklahoma for most social interactions, except the public schools which had dutifully integrated during the late 1950s. I now felt myself to be out of my appropriate "turf," and I was then bluntly told this fact, by the man who stood before me, hands on hips, positioned like a drill instructor directly before me.

"You can pay for that coke and leave, Boy. You should know you don't belong here," he proclaimed, emphatically using that term *Boy*, which racist Whites employed to denigrate Black men.

I was alarmed and amused ... and delighted ... to find an opponent equal to my own sense of upset and outrage from events of the past few days .... and the social inequities deriving from American history. Perhaps it was real grief for my father's death, or the shock at the financial disaster looming over all his affairs, or my memory of all the social injustice I had observed as a young man growing up in Oklahoma and my activities in the Civil Rights Movement and my alliance with the New Left as Marcuse's assistant and body-guard, or perhaps it was just the incredible irony that a Black man who was probably a close relative whose biology was so similar to mine through no fault of his forebears who were enslaved and literally *fucked over* by my own ancestors was now standing in front of me - "in my face" - defiantly telling me that I *did not belong here*. But I felt as if I was about to shout out who I am, and so I said *just that*, as calmly and stridently and proudly as I was able:

"My name is Ben Wright and I own that farm just across the road. My family homesteaded that property in 1889 and gave the piece of land to the community that is called the Wright Cemetery and the cemetery given by the other Wright family, the African Amercian one, most likely my own Black cousins, is just a mile west down the road from this intersection. So, I do belong, and I will pay for my coke and drink it wherever I choose to stand."

The man looked at me with anger flashing in his eyes and *squared his jaw* to retort, "There is only one Ben Wright, and he is my best boyhood friend, and he owns that farm, not you, young man," he had altered the term of address to a less insulting term.

I *squared my shoulders* and locked his fiery gaze with an equally igneous response, saying, "I have to agree with you. There is only one Ben Wright, and you are looking at him now. Your boyhood friend, my father, the man for whom I am named, died yesterday in Baptist Memorial Hospital. So now I am the only Ben Wright that lives. And I am here to become your friend as well."

I held out my hand with an open palm and watched him as he registered what had just been delivered. His face transformed from that of a steeled fighter to a stunned, but feeling person. I saw years of regret and sorrow and resentment and grief pass over his wounded, yet stalwart mien like storm clouds driven before a summer squall over inland waters in a seaside cove. His eyes remained fixed on mine, and I detected tears forming at their corners. When he spoke, it was with a voice at once embracing and compassionate and welcoming and reassuring.

He nodded his head toward that back room, inviting me to follow him, "I see him in you. No denying it. Come in back with me. We need a drink of the strong stuff."

He had some moonshine corn whiskey in a jug, sitting on the table in his back room office *cum* library, but there was a bottle of Jack Daniels up on the top shelf of the back wall bookcase which he reached up and brought down after first offering a pull on the heavy stone jug, laughing at the rude gesture as if we were old pals who held the same attitude for such banal indulgences of our *lessers*, knowing that the moonshine was only for emergencies ... or hangovers. This was a most special event. This was too special an event for such *dross* stuff. We were to toast our new bond of friendship and wash away the tears for our lost one in the next moments. We both had that unique respect for *occasion* that all *Wrights* savor and excel at celebrating. We sat across the table from one another as the glasses were filled to their brims and then touched them together and quaffed the *elixir*, all this performed silently, as if long ago orchestrated by a masterful Director.

My host's eyes were as wet as my own, and we let the tears flow down our cheeks without saying a word. His features then burst into a frolicsome grimace as he laughed and told me the following:

"We always let your Grandma pass for white. Don't ever forget that," he chortled. She and my Ma were the mid-wives ... and sometimes, folks called them witches. They healed ... but they could cast a mean spell if roused to do so. And they were sometimes called on to do some harm to those who would harm us and our'n".

The last rustic pronunciation of the possessive of the third person plural was the only lapse he had made in otherwise proper English. The public school up the road was, after all, named for his father, and his own education had been more advanced – high-school and two years of Teacher's College, I was to learn later – greater than my father's, which had not been past the Eleventh Grade. What I wanted to know, of course, was what my own father had been like as the boy whom this man was telling me had been his best friend. How had that boy become the racist, closed-minded monster that I had come to despise and confront on these very issues of racial prejudice, and worse? So, I told Fred, as I came to call him, as one of my own closest friends from then on, about the conflicts between myself and Ben Eugene Wright. I did not, however, reveal the membership card that I had found in the wallet of my father which declared him as a knight of the Klu Klux Klan. When I told Fred of my association with Angela Davis and Marcuse and the New Left and even with certain members of the Black Panthers, he was as taken aback, as most anyone of the White Middle Class who read only the establishment controlled newspapers and magazines would be. He allowed me to explain what was behind all that apparent anti-American activity, on behalf of my California colleagues. I was able to access his finer instincts in such matters by referencing Ralph Ellison and that writer's monumental novel, *Invisible Man*, which had its opening chapter in Oklahoma City's prestige hotel, The Skirvin Tower, in that horrifying scene from the part entitled, "Battle Royal." It was to be our neighbor who lived only a half mile back up Northeast 63rd, directly across from the Wright Cemetery, Hannah Atlkins, the first Black woman Lieutenant Governor of Oklahoma, who would establish the new main Oklahoma City Library, to be named, The Ralph Ellison Memorial Library, on Northeast 23rd Street, which was the only enticement to ever bring that embittered man back to our hometown for the inauguration event, so bitter had been his memory of racial oppression when he was a student attending the all Black Douglass High-School.

When I left the Four Corners store that day, I knew I had made a friend, and this was one of the few former associates of my father's who was not of the Right Wing, fascist mind-set. When I met with Jim and Phil later and asked them what they knew about Fred Wright, I was told a story about my father that at first startled me and then pleased me immensely. Neither man offered any opinion regarding this particular incident, but I could tell that they both had been shocked by what had happened. In my last year at Penn, 1960, when I was home on Easter holiday from Philadelphia, I remember some of the particulars about this event, which had not made much sense to me at the time, and which my father had explained to me in only the most evasive terms. Fred had called my father at his office, to report to him that some members of the Ku Klux Klan had attacked the home of a man named Tye who rented the old farm house which stood on the west forty acres of our Ben Wright Farm property, with an entrance at Sooner Road, just a half mile south of Four Corners store. Tye, an old Native American *Indian* whom Fred and my father had known as children, had been allowed to rent the house as a virtual maintenance fee of twenty dollars a month. He had lived there for as long as anyone could remember with a white woman, and they were considered to be a common-law married couple, in clear violation of the old community mores against the coupling of Whites and Indians. Consequently, some hot-heads in the Ku Klux Klan had decided to make an example of this breach of their White Supremist beliefs, and a gang of men had arrived one night at the farmhouse with the intention of killing the couple living there. Tye had been alert enough to take his wife down into the tornado shelter, as bullets tore through the house and even slammed into the door of the underground dugout. Satisfied that their prey had been murdered, the men drove away, and Tye and his wife waited a considerable amount of time before coming out of hiding and then going to report their narrow escape to Fred who had the only telephone in the area. No report was made to local law enforcement agencies as they most likely would have not been sympathetic to Tye. As soon as my father had been informed of this incident, he swung into action. He told Fred to spread the word throughout our area that Tye had outsmarted the Klan and was still residing comfortably in his home. My father then prepared a surprise for the gang that he knew would return to finish their *execution* job on Tye and his wife.

I remember my father dressing that evening in his old fringed leather hunting jacket, and I recall him cleaning and loading his .32 caliber pistol which he had once told me belonged to someone who had been in the Spanish Civil War (I was later honored to become a close friend of Milton Wolff, Commandant of the Lincoln Battalion, International

Brigade, of that war). He refused to tell me where he was going, and I was so involved with Carolyn Coe and focused only on having sex with her every night, that I did not insist on accompanying him to whatever nefarious activity he was about to involve himself in. I should have noticed that he had brought a pickup truck home from the office, and if I had looked in the flat-bed, I would have seen that he had rigged several spot-lights and a huge police siren to a series of car batteries. It was with this equipment that he lay in wait that night for the Klan to return to Tye's home, and when they approached the house, he flipped his switches and flooded them with light and terrified them with the screaming siren as he fired off several rounds from his .32 caliber pistol. These three men withered under his assault and he placed them all under "citizens arrest," and he then ordered them to crawl into the back of his pickup, and he ushered them in their subdued, smitten state down the road to the office of the Spencer's local sheriff. The article that appeared the next morning in the *Daily Oklahoman* did not provide his name, but it made this single vigilante sound like some character out of a John Wayne, or Rambo film.

I heard the story in a roundabout, second-hand fashion, as I came in the offices that morning and encountered Ed Stroh (the new owner of the Auto-Lite ignition parts manufacturer, the heir to the Detroit Stroh Beer fortune who had married one of Henry Ford's grand-daughters) as he was being escorted out of our building for his ride to the airport. He was commenting to Jim Peck who was accompanying him out to our garages that my father had canceled their appointment the afternoon before when he received a telephone call and had rushed to his separate inner offices and returned dressed in leather hunting clothes, with a pistol belt slung over his shoulder saying that he had to take care of some family business before he could discuss any more automotive sales proposals with Stroh who had flown to meet us to launch a massive sales campaign. However, it would appear that

Stroh was more than satisfied by my father's arrival at his hotel for an early morning breakfast conference to assure the Auto-Lite owner that we would commit totally to the proposed sales incentive package that would guarantee the sale of at least one million of their spark plugs and a considerable amount of accessory ignition products in the coming year. He had brought Stroh to the office to meet with Jim to sign all the contractual materials, but had then dashed off before answering the Detroit man's burning question: "Was Ben Wright the wild vigilante portrayed in the front page of the newspaper he had read this morning at the hotel?"

Stroh was asking Jim this question, and receiving no apparently satisfactory answer. I did hear Jim say that whatever the boss did when he dressed in his fighting gear was anybody's guess, but that there would for sure be "more commotion than a jackass in a tin barn" when the Bull of the Woods went on the warpath. Stroh just smiled and shrugged and said it was always a pleasure doing business with us and that our territory was his favorite ... to visit, and the way he emphasized the word *visit*, anyone could tell that he would never want to spend more time than was required here than for just a *visit*. It was an accepted truth that all our major manufacturers, the companies back East for whom we were central distributors such as Auto-Lite, Carter Carburetor, and Briggs and Stratton, would send their prospective top-flight managers to our region to insure that they were truly fit for top leadership roles, if they could pass the acid-test of survival in Ben Wright's, American Electric Ignition Company's far-flung *Wild West* sales territory which reached from Little Rock, Arkansas across all of Oklahoma to Amarillo, Texas and into New Mexico as far as Albuquerque and on down into Texas as far as Dallas, with over four thousand customers who all possessed a loyalty to Ben Wright as fierce and familial as any *mafioso* owed to his *godfather*.

When I asked Jim what the true story was, he just laughed and said it was a hell of a lot better than some of the old man's drinking binges. I read the newspaper article again and saw that the man who had been saved from an attack by three men presumed to be "night-riders" with the Ku Klux Klan was a Native American known as Tie, whose home was on Sooner Road in Northeast Oklahoma City. I did ask my father at dinner what had happened, and he did say that he had learned of some people who had harassed his friend Tie and that he had gone out to speak with them and asked them not to ever try to come on his farm again or he would charge them with criminal trespass. When I showed him the newspaper article, he just laughed and said that was some nonsense those fellows wrote to sell papers. I did not press him to deliver the full particulars of this incident, and now, all these years later, I was truly delighted to discover what had really happened. At the time when it occurred, I had been too besotted with my current girl-friend and more intent on satisfying my own sensual appetites than caring to ferret out the real story of my father's shoot-out defending Tie from the Klan "night-riders." Now when I got Phil Daugherty and Jim Peck to relate for me the true version and to tell me about Fred Wright whom I had not met until this encounter at Four Corners, I began to consider my father to be a much more complex and admirable man than I had imagined before.

I encountered more of his friends and associates during this time immediately after his death, preparing for the funeral which my sister hoped to *produce* as some major event of stately splendor, and I would have preferred to have a cremation followed by tossing his ashes out on the prairie into the Crossed-Timbers cluster of dwarfed black-jack grove at our farm. However, there were many who would have it otherwise. Some of the notable figures in our community and one man in particular who was of national prominence, Federal Court Judge Alfred "Fish" Murrah, requested to be the feature speaker to deliver his eulogy and this rather surprised me. Phil, and his brother,

Fred, former commanding general of the Oklahoma Forty-Fifth Division of the United States Army, whom John F. Kennedy had appointed as a Federal Judge, as well, both urged me to elect "Fish" Murrah to the honored task of delivering the last words over my father lying virtually *in state* at the Hahn-Cook funeral home across from the Rose Hill cemetery and mausoleum where he was to be interred. Phil let me know that not only was "Fish" a fellow deacon at the Crown Heights Methodist Church but also a member of the Jesters, a select and elite Masonic Order, and, Phil also implied, but would deny in direct questioning, that "Fish" was also a brother knight of the now discreetly unmentionable Klan. I sincerely hope this was a false allegation and believe it to be.

I was perversely amused by Leelah Hahn, the most prestigious funeral director in Oklahoma, whose undertaking business had been the final repository for every person of any wealth or social standing since the establishment of Oklahoma as a state. She had been a close friend of my own mother, and the two women had both suffered with the abusive antics of alcoholic husbands whose binges had been periodic and therefore easier to conceal from general notice. Her husband, "Cookie," had even been one of my father's bottle buddies and the two had become notorious for some of their more difficult-to-cover-up escapades. So I was bemused and surprised by her consternation and worry, telling me that her beauticians and cosmetic aestheticians [even in Oklahoma such euphemistic titles were now being applied to basic morticians who attempted to work the dead meat into a smiling "natural" appearance for the ever popular open-casket ceremonies] were encountering difficult challenges with my father's facial features. His mouth turned down in a fierce grimace – that same feature he wore when he grabbed a ringing telephone with the growled affront, "What do ya want?" – was proving almost impossible to mold into a benign *Mona Lisa* mien.

I relieved her anguish to some degree by reminding her that with all the surgery he had undergone in the past ten years for skin cancers deeply embedded in his face, that there was little natural muscle tone to re-sculpture, and that if anyone who knew my father even casually, would consider any expression of pleasure on his face to derive from his intention to inflict extreme physical harm in a most formidable physical assault, and the effect of implanting any such facial expression on his corpse might wreak havoc among those who chose to pass before the casket and saw such a dangerously menacing demeanor on the Iron Man's visage. "Leave the scowl on," I told her, and, I thought to myself, 'thereby avoid a possible riot in the otherwise quiet cloister of her funeral home'.

I decided to indulge in an ironic touch to the public viewing which I was told had attracted hundreds of visitors over the few days we set aside before the actual funeral ceremony. There were an abundance of floral sprays and wreathes and bouquets arranged in the main chapel where the body had been placed, the usual "slumber rooms" not having nearly the capacity for such a grand event as this was becoming. I decided to place a special floral display on the casket itself. As the official flower of Oklahoma was the *red-bud*, which only blossomed at this time of the year, and it was prohibited by law, with punishment by imposition of heavy fines, to pick or display this flowery wreath of bright red petals, I made a tour of all the neighborhoods of the very rich, from Nichols Hills, to Cashion Place, to Quail Creek, collecting bunches of these now blossoming *red-bud*, and when the back seat and trunk of the car was filled, I took them to place as a benedictory shower of illegal homage on the casket, and I placed a note in bold, black letters on a large piece of white cardboard : "To: Ben Wright ... From His Greatest Admirer, Ben Wright."

The floral display lasted for more than a day before Lelah herself had the gumption to remove it, along with the surrealistic eulogistic inscription. Both my sister and myself were amazed by the large number of people who arrived to pass by the casket and offer their condolences. Many farmer folk along with the best dressed ladies and gentlemen of our city and from many other locations throughout our state and across its adjoining borders, signed in to the guest book at the entrance foyer. I was coming to realize that the old man did indeed have an impact on a multitude of others. His advice to me was to always leave an impression, a lasting memory, that you never knew when you would pass a certain way again, and you would want people to remember you and perhaps even welcome your return. His abiding attitude was the salesman's creed, a twist with an Okie twang on Willie Loman's "smile and a shoeshine" that the playwright, Arthur Miller ascribed to his unforgettable, albeit lamentable, protagonist in *Death of a Salesman.'*

Judge Murrah stopped after only a few moments in his speech to brush tears from his wrinkled cheek, and many in his audience were similarly moved, some even howling audibly from the back row which was standing room only. Murrah referred to many of the men my father had established in their own businesses, providing cost-free stock for their initial automotive parts inventories and free training with our company's education department in repairs and even basic bookkeeping, so that they could launch "going concerns" which no one else would have deemed possible for these uneducated, and sometimes, truly marginalized individuals, some of whom had spent time serving sentences in jail and prison. My dad's favorite offer, "How about a clean white shirt every day, your own car and home, and something to leave your wife and kids?" This sounded better from Murrah at the lectern than the old man's cynical remark that for some folks, "A clean white shirt, three meals a day and a good fuck, might just kill 'em", intending to mean that some people just can not bear the good life, and so maybe should never be offered it. I was beginning to agree with Murrah, however, that my father had been a remarkable person who had helped many in need. He always donated generously to the Salvation Army, saying that they believed as he did that a man could be *down*, but never *out*. I also then recalled the half-starved Bollar family whom he delivered to work our farm in the 1940s who arrived so hungry that their two boys, Mickey and Pete had leapt in to the barn storage bins where we kept lumps of fodder for the young calves, and ate them hungrily, saying that these cow biscuits were good for people as well as the live-stock because they contained dried sorghum molasses with the oats and other grains. When I told my father about the boys' behavior, he just put his hand on my shoulder and said solemnly that these folks had known hunger like we would never have to experience, and that was why he had brought them from their destitute community down in Texas to live and work on our farm. He thought it an educational experience for me to stay for some weeks with the family, working with them and getting to know what it meant to be a farm-boy. I enjoyed those days, but I did not consider the rustic life anything I would want to have for myself. Waking before dawn to milk cows, by hand, and to collect eggs from the chicken-house, and to spend long hours weeding the rows of vegetables was not what I considered a desirable holiday routine. For diversion, the boys ran foot-races down to the largest pond and then stripped naked to dive into the muddy water; evenings were spent sitting by the radio listening to country music and ranting preachers, and I could not convince them that the comedy programs of Jack Benny or George Burns and Gracie Allen were more worthwhile entertainment; there were some subtleties in the gag-lines that whizzed past my friends without any recognition; our frames of reference were light-years apart, and I was considerably dismayed and embarrassed when Mrs. Bollar asked me to teach her how to read. She had a grade-school primer which she was attempting to master, and as I was still having difficulty myself with the rigors of this discipline - I am dyslexic and did not learn to read with any competency till I was over ten years old – and this was at a time when I was still just nine … and functionally illiterate.

I was not only embarrassed by Mrs. Bollar's appeal to me, whom she presumed would be as smart as all other "city folk," especially my own parents and sister who indeed could read and write … and I clearly could not, and was as illiterate as she, but I was also feeling inadequate in so far as I was unable to extend an invitation to my farm-boy pals to come and stay with me in our home in Crown Heights. My mother had made it clear, declaring this in front of my father before I was packed up for my indoctrination on the farm. There was to be no reciprocity, no presumption of social equality in this transaction, and that when I left the farm, although I might visit there again overnight on certain occasions, that there was to never be any presumption of social equality with Mickey or Pete – they were our employees and their socio-economic status was thereby clearly defined as such: our vassals. I tried once to explain to Mickey that I was not at liberty to invite him to come stay with me in the city, but he was unperturbed by this, and assured me that he had no desire to leave his beloved farm and to be adrift on sidewalks and asphalt roads where cars whizzed about and ran down folks from the country. His illusion was one shared by other farmer folk, and I was amazed at the sense of division held by the grown-ups as well. Mrs Bollar presumed that everyone in the city was a walking "spelling-bee" who might rush up and assault her with questions from an almanac or dictionary or even an encyclopedia while she might just be trying to find her way through the down-town street enclosed by all those sky-scraper monstrosities that for her were like what she imagined embodied the Behemoth that her preacher had referred to from the pulpit of her pentecostal congregation, equating the ways of the urban populace to those of Babylon and Sodom and Gomorrah. She was mightily relieved that there would be no plans for transporting her innocent young boys to our foreboding streets … and alleys.

Nevertheless, the Bollars considered my father their savior in a purely economic sense. He had removed them from their miserably poor share-cropper farm in Texas and planted them in a lush, productive homestead which produced enough milk and butter, vegetables and eggs, and even beef, from the ample herd of Hereford cattle so that they had plenty to eat and were entitled to share the profits from the excess commodities that were sold in town from Mr. Bollar's conscientious stewardship of the farm. They were thriving and able to even set aside some money now from these profits and the salary paid, in addition to that. So again, as Murrah had proclaimed in his eulogy, my father had indeed shared his resources and wealth with his fellow man.

Several years later, in 2005, when I was visiting Oklahoma City and decided to take the official tour of the Murrah Memorial, I was approached by Paul Murrah, the son of that same famous judge for whom the demoilished building had been named, which was bombed and became famous for such a heinous crime and deep tragedy enacted by a terrorist of the extreme Right, who was inspired by a group of neo-Nazis of the self-appointed militias of Minutemen, like that man convicted and executed, McVeigh, who was only a single member of the widespread virus and cancerous political affliction in America. Paul Murrah told me that he was deeply delighted to see me in Oklahoma City and that my father had been one of his father's ideals and that he, himself, considered himself fortunate to know me, as well, and to call me a friend. Such tributes are difficult to abide, except with merely a spoken "Thank you," which I gave him then. I do not enjoy considering the horrible irony that the Murrah Federal Buidling attack by bombers was perpetrated by people who were of the White Supremist ideology that was derivative of identically kindred hatred engendered by the Ku Klux Klan, and that perhaps the esteemed judge himself belonged to that cult would have provided some credence for the remark by Malcolm X (a devoted member of the Black Muslims at that time) when John F. Kennedy was shot, that the "chickens had come home to roost," meaning perhaps that a deadly retributive karma was enacted with that assassination, and thus was it perhaps so, as well, with this bombing in Oklahoma City. When the identity of "Deep Throat," the key informant who enabled Bob Woodward to validate and corroborate evidence in the Watergate case against President Richard Nixon was revealed to be the high-ranking F.B.I. member, Mark Feldt, three decades after the president resigned from office rather than face criminal charges. There was a peculiar irony revealed about this man who provided the information that unseated Nixon. Feldt himself was charged and proven guilt of unlawful surveillance and spying in the case of the members of Weatherman who had been waging what Feldt called a "Civil War" in America with their terrorist bombings. He was guilty of the very acts of law-breaking which he enabled Woodward and Bernstein to expose in their *Washington Post* investigative journalistic expose to end the reign of fear that Nixon, with the help of the F.B.I. [notably the expertise of F.B.I. Special Agent, G. Gordon Libby and others of his fanatical fervor, was essential in engineering the work of spying by the Watergate "plumbers"] had imposed in the virtual tyrannical, totalitarian political climate at that time.

So all the events and the history behind such figures as Murrah and other Oklahoma figures of power and influence had contrived to create me, the son of a mixed-race, "rags-to-riches," successful, capitalist entrepreneur who had attempted to share his wealth by enabling others like him to become independent businessmen, but who had disinherited that son [me] because he [I] , appeared to be too intent on sharing his wealth and that of other members of his merchant class [following ideals established by the founder of the Industrial Workers of the World, Eugene Debs], I seeming to be a young man who might become a truly radical Marxist revolutionary, and yet was re-inherited because that father when he had recalled his original early idealism in the son's pledged loyalty to the leader [Herbert Marcuse] of what was then called The New Left, and now this son was entrusted with the Herculean task of saving the father's businesses from bankruptcy so as to maintain the salaries and retirement programs of the employees of the father's foundering enterprises. The son was gearing up to do just that, and would use the skills he had learned as an outcast from this very system, in order to make a "going concern" [that lovely term from accounting and finance meta-language to designate a business which becomes profitable and thrives] of the wreckage inherited from this man of many tempers and strengths and wiles, the father of this Ben Wright, himself called Ben Wright [any irony to his middle name being *Eugene* ... Debs' first name?].

Jim Peck and Phil Daugherty were my primary team for reconstructing the home company, 'American Electric Ignition,' from the economic wreckage which my father's last years of alcoholic megalomania had wrought. Mark Harris, who held the title of Credit Manager for all the companies, had been the man who had placed my mother in her first job as a secretary to the president of the First National Bank in Oklahoma City in 1916, just months before she joined my father's small firm, after she was fired for appearing to be too intelligent and cagey for her boss at that bank to feel comfortable with ... or so she told us. My father found her to be too outspoken and assertive, and fired her after only a few weeks, and yet he had fallen in love with her, as well. She and her mother moved away to Kansas City, Missouri, from the boarding house residence of Mark Harris and his family. My father then discovered himself so stricken by this unexpected sense of desire and aching need for this particular woman, that he followed her to Missouri and begged her to marry him. She agreed to return to work with him as a partner, and then she became that person whom many considered the guiding wisdom of what blossomed into a thriving enterprise, a profitable and successful business that eventually employed over seventy loyal and dedicated people.

I had grown up in the business, and I knew every aspect of it, having been behind a broom sweeping out all the interior spaces from the warranty garages and shops, to all the warehouse floors and the office spaces in between. A large majority of the men and women in the main buildings in the city had known me since my childhood. Miss Timmens, a Victorian stereotype of what had been called a stenographer, who still dressed in outfits like those which Popeye's sweetheart, Olive Oil was depicted as wearing in that famous comic strip. Her hem-lines reached the floor, and she may have even been wearing hightopped shoes if one could ever have glimpsed an ankle in her demure attire. She enjoyed telling about how my mother had stood me on one of the desks at the front of the main office to sing Christmas carols and Negro Spiritual/Gospel songs that I had learned from our "colored" housekeepers.

I do not remember these incidents, but I have blocked many memories from the age of four or five. There was a distinct sense of family in our company, and I called on this special energy to rebuild from the wreckage sewn by my father's last few years which had virtually destroyed our ability to continue in business. I was amazed to see that many of our executive personnel and sales force were willing to pitch in and assist in unloading shipments of engines and boxes of heavy machinery parts on our loading docks, and many of the personnel cross-trained to assist in sections of the building when others slowed down, so that there was no dead-time slack in any of the processes that pulsed through our company in the delivery of orders to our far-flung customers. I had Robert Stratton flown in to make a financial consultant's appraisal [his years as an I.B.M. Executive were deeply ingrained and not forgotten] and he implanted some state-of the-art computerized programs to expedite our own antiquated systems and to eliminate waste motion and expenses in operations. After only a few months, the banks that held our major indebtedness were willing to allow us time to prove our worth and our ability to repay all that we owed them. And we did ... within two years time.

During this initial period, I had returned to California to complete the courses I was teaching at San Diego State College, and I was unwilling to contest the latest notice of dismissal from that English faculty even though such loyal friends as Professor Leonard Frey had offered to help me and to attempt to promote my rehiring. I had decided to devote myself to rebuilding my father's main company, American Electric Ignition, which had a subsidiary in Amarillo, Texas, and this was also the holding company for the organic fertilizer enterprise called Soil Booster. This particular undertaking, the fertilizer plant, had cost millions of dollars over the years since its founding in 1948. My father made a contract with Oklahoma City for the exclusive rights for one hundred years to retrieve all the sewage sludge which was delivered into the city's main treatment plant lagoons located on East Reno Boulevard which lay southeast of the Oklahoma County fairgrounds and Douglass High-School. Our plant for treating this dried sludge, heaped up on the Soil Booster property, was just next door, and so our trucks had only a few city blocks to drive to collect and then deliver these massive loads for processing at our plant. My father's design for the treatment under high drying temperatures in enormpus rolling drums and the mixture of certain chemicals to then package this martertial to become fifty pounds sacks of the most organcally pure fertilizer in America, was imitated and marketed successfully as the product named, *Milorganite*, produced by the city of Milwaukee, Wisconsin, who replicated our process exactly, as their own. Our particular procedure was hampered, snarled, and finally destroyed by the large amounts of plastic fibers which had begun to accummulate in all waste materials entering the city sewer pipes' effluents in the early 1950s, when clothing became manufactured with increasing amounts of plastic. We were never able to effectually filter out these damaging insoluble agents; our machinery ground to a halt when assaulted by these substances. Also, the only markets sophisticated enough to buy our product, derivative of human feces, were in the states of California and New York; our shipping costs [rail and truck] then became prohibitive, and so my father had to finally shut down his dream-child, after over twenty years of futile struggle, and millions spent in research and development. I probably could today collect and sell the sludge from those lagoons, which is perfectly effective as fertilizer, as all the toxicity has been removed by its slumber in the holding tanks and lagoons of the city for only a few weeks, but I have never attempted to undertake this Herculean challenge.

When I felt assured that my actual presence was not required in the reconstruction of my father's financial affairs, I left for travel in Europe, not realizing that this life of travel was to last for most of the remainder of my life, with returns to America in the first five years to complete the consolidation of that project and to sell the company to Jim Peck. Thereafter, I have lived in several places at once in a nomadic style that has focused on Mallorca, England and the United States – with sorties into the Pacific and Southeast Asia [Hawaiian Island of Maui; Bangkok and Chiang Mai, and Nong Khai, Thailand; Bali, Indonesia; Oolongapo. Subic Bay and Manila, Philippine Islands; and Southeast Asia] – in criss-crossing patterns that can be explained only in terms of the projects most derivative of those locales and my needs for sustenance both physical and psychic and spiritual. My recovery from active alcoholism began in Mallorca where I remained for the greater part of three years when I b egan attending Alcoholics Anonymous meetings in Palma, and then I discovered that England provided the most nourishing program of interactive therapies in the form self-help twelve step groups and actual psychotherapists' guidance in that country for the subsequent eighteen years. The first five years in Mallorca and England were spent attempting to discover my appropriate metier in written expression with one more dabble as an actor in a feature film ['Nicholas and Alexandra,' Columbia Pictures, 1971] while creating a Summerhill style school in San Agustin, a suburb of Palma, Mallorca, for children of foreign residents , and establishing a Not-for-Profit Foundation with the help of Sam Coffing in Coconut Grove, Florida, for the study of Mythography ['The American Institute of Mythographic Studies'].

When I first returned to Mallorca, a few months after leaving my house on the La Jolla Cove which I sub-let to old (then ninety) Fred Hocks - I left all my clothing and "traps" for him to use [we wore the same size sports jacket; and luckily, all my trousers and shirts fit him, as well] and he remained in that idyllic artist's redoubt across from the Caves Curio shop above the Cove, till the owners, Tyrolean Rental Company properties was sold - most of the original Green Dragon Colony which the Scripps family had originally built in this location, and Fred relocated to a simple studio apartment in Mission Hills, San Diego where his own ranch spread had lain over half the century before.

On one of my rambles in London, I had met a buxom blond from Oklahoma, a graduate of Oklahoma State University, like my sister, but unlike Phyllis, she, Patty Ward, had found employment in San Francisco as a physical therapist - I was later to learn that, in reality, she had been employed as a massage therapist, who would deliver a "Happy Ending," and any other sensual delights, in between, above, below ... or beyond. It was not until we had been together for a few months and I had developed some venereal warts accompanied by genital herpes that she revealed to me what her *actual* occupation had been. We consulted some of the finest medical specialists in

Spain, England and the United States before our condition improved, and it was during this ordeal that she tearfully confessed her past to me and the doctors. I was treated by a doctor who described himself as a "Syphlologist," a practitioner whose life had been devoted to studying the various disguises that were worn by the disease know as Syphilis, which could lie dormant for years and then appear in the guise of any number of ailments in the secondary stage before erupting in tertiary form with full-blown chancres which herald the incipient deterioration of the spinal cord and the central nervous system. It was he who finally effected a cure for my warts which had covered my penis and threatened to enter the urethral tract where they could substantively block urination and would eventually require a surgical removal of the penis itself, if allowed to continue to spread into that region. The several burns of my penis were like so many perforations in a garden hose used for sprinkling a flower-bed, and when I told my woeful condition to Richard Brautigan, he made this the controlling metaphor for his tragic love-story *cum* [no pun intended] killing-spree, entitled *Willard and His Bowling Trophies*. In this novel, Richard endows his male protagonist with the agony of venereal warts *inside* the uretheral tract, and his girl-friend's warts are implanted only on the walls of her vagina, and therefore her condition *can* be cured by freeze-burning them away, and thus, she is thereby freed to go on to have another love affair, whereas her stricken mate must endure the only remedy – *penectomy* (surgical removal of the entire penis) which will allow him to urinate, but never again, to be able to entertain any normal physical process whereby he may *procreate*, or enjoy any normal male sexual performance.

During this period of recuperation, I detached myself from Patty, who chose to live with her former commune located on the street in Haight-Ashbury parallel to Downey, where the McClures lived, and so that I would not be tempted to become sexually active with her, I avoided that neighborhood, the McClures, and even Richard Brautigan for several weeks. I found converted a garage in Oakland, and somehow was contacted by Kathy Houting, a devoted and sensible woman who had traveled with me in Spain in the year before this, in the summer when she was finishing her studies in English at University of Wisconsin. It was in that situation, esconced with Kathy in a dreary Oakland garage, that I wrote my first poem in a new style, which became my signature mode for the next few years, and was the title, *What Next: What Next*, of the first book to be published, the following year. I was so distracted by Kathy, Oakland, and my increased drinking of alcohol, that I was fearful that I had somehow plagiarized a poem of Brautigan's, and therefore made contact with him again, and he assured me that I had not stolen anything from him, that our manner of expression was similar, and he reminded me that many people could not tell the difference between my vocal delivery and that of our mutual friend, Michael McClure. I was becoming deeply disturbed by what I was imagining to be a decided *chameleon* tendency in my personality, that I might be actually losing my identity by imitating these poets I so admired. Nevertheless, I began, once again, spending time in North Beach at 'Enrico's' restaurant and our favorite bars in that locale, and was virtually abandoning Kathy Howe and our residence in Oakland.

Soon I was planning to return to Spain with Robert Stratton who had found a house I could rent in Galilea for a minimal rent. I announced this decision to Kathy who became distraught and bitterly rancorous and accused me of leading her on in the belief that I was in love with her and had intended to live with her indefinitely. With functional psychopathic aplomb, I dismissed her pleadings and told her to "get a life". This was a phrase which had not as yet become over-used, so the sting for her was particularly poignant. I left her and never saw or heard from Kathy Howe again. I spent my last night in a motel with a female groupie who had besieged Brautigan and McClure to sign copies of their books at 'Enrico's', and since I had no book to sign, she had asked that I impregnate her with a child as her time of ovulation was appropriate for my last night before flying out of San Francisco [I often wonder if that insemination was successful If so, may the child and mother please let this author and *father* know].

Richard took me shopping that afternoon and we found a denim suit made in Romania which the tailor had ready for me to wear in a few hours. On that flight to Amsterdam, I sat next to a recent California college graduate, Anne Zeff, who spent the first night in Holland with me and declared that she had awarded me her virginity and would travel with me from then on. She and I moved into the large Galilea, Mallorca home of Nora Constens, whose complex of houses became known as 'S'Esbart' (the Mallorquin word for "nest"). Nora spent here winters in Germany and wanted someone to keep the houses operative till her return in summer, and therefore I paid low rent and allowed Robert Stratton and his girl-friend to live with us. He wrote his first novel, and I revised and edited my first book of poetry which Ruthven Todd and Anne Zeff guided to completion, so that I delivered my first public reading of it for J. R.Witt's 'Contemporary Arts Foundation in Oklahoma City, Oklahoma

When I had been living with Patty Ward in Mallorca, the previous year, for our first months together, I had found an upstairs floor of one of the finest examples of roccoco architecture in the Terreno section of Palma. I had adapted two of our six bedrooms to a studio for Patty's sculpting in clay which she claimed was her artistic training from college. I spent most days a couple of miles up the Paseo Maritimo in the section named San Agustin, developing the experimental school established by Dr Stanley Amdurer with another associate, Larry Watts, a Californian who claimed to have been part of the Wolf-Man Jack *persona* who had become a legend as a late-night disk jockey on radio in America: "The Wolf-Man sees you when you're naked" had become his sizzling trade-mark for the popular radio offering. Stanley and Larry had invited me to be part of the school we named simply, American Community School.

Our first few students lived in the pension we had leased, and as we grew larger, expanding to offer all grades - elementary through high-school, only the core student body lived on the premises. I was startled and pleased by how quickly our enrollment expanded. There were other schools like ours which catered to the foreign residents' children in Mallorca; however, none of them had our dynamic "listen-to-the-student" governing philosophy which we derived from our appreciation of the principles of Summerhill in England where a student did not have to attend any classes, and could spend the entire curriculum from elementary through to graduation from secondary school, and still remain illiterate ... but emotionally stable and happy ... and hopefully not neurotic. We required attendance in classes and provided all the most essential courses in reading, writing, mathematics and science; biology and chemistry were not offered until we had built laboratory facilities. I stayed with the school only for the formative years, but always as a consultant, although I did teach some classes in History and English to the students - ages fifteen through seventeen - for a few months.

I had also landed a small speaking part in the film, 'Nicholas and Alexandra,' which Sam Spiegel was producing in Madrid with Columbia Pictures. I was the Aide to Czar Nicholas, who informs him that the people are rioting in Moscow. What a line to deliver! "*They are rioting in Moscow!*" Probably one of the most poignantly, meaningful lines in modern history. My agent, who had placed me with the director, Henry Levine in 'The Mauraders,' as an actor and Dialogue Coach under a fictitious Spanish name so that the producers would not have to register me with the Screen Actors Guild (S.A.G.), and therefore could pay me less, and this agent introduced me to

Spiegel who told me that he himself had been a Teaching Assistant at one time at the University of California, and he hired me personally, without informing his director, Franklin Schaffner, who did not want any speaking roles played by Americans. Spiegel told me that I was the first actor he had himself hired since Peter O'Toole in 'Lawrence of Arabia.' I mentioned my friendship with Robert Graves, T. E. Lawrence's former roommate at Oxford University and author of the first biography which the swashbuckling war hero had authorized and endorsed. I did not mention that Graves had decided that I was the actual reincarnation of Lawrence, but I had bonded with Sam Spiegel, immediately, anyway.

As I was not needed till the Second Unit filming in the north of Spain during the snowy winter scene when my role is to stop the Czar's train, supposedly in western Russia, and leap aboard his private car to announce the dire news of the Revolution, I was able to return to Mallorca and carry on teaching till I was called to be on hand, for that all-action, no-dialogue scene. My report delivered in the railroad car to my commander-in-chief, Czar Nicholas, would take place on a sound stage in Madrid where the interior of the Czar's coach was constructed. It was while preparing in Make-Up for this action scene that I first met John Box, the Second Unit director, who decided that I must shave my face and leave only a mustache - otherwise, with my full beard, I looked like an identical twin to the actor, Michael Jayston who was playing Czar Nicholas - I thereby took on the appearance of a young Joseph Stalin for a close-up that Box wanted for the opening of my action: I was then to be seen standing in the middle of the train-tracks, and then, I was to run, and leap over the cattle-guard of the locomotive which was skidding to a thunderous stop in a blizzard. I was to perform this action in the full dress uniform of a Russian general officer: with ceremonial sword; and heavy overcoat; and high black leather boots; sprinting over railroad *sleepers* (*ties*, in the American idiom).

When I attempted this action scene, we filmed at least eight *takes* before Box decided we had a possible *print*. I was not high enough ranking as an actor to be invited to be present for those rushes in the evening after each day of *shooting*, but I was informed that Box decided to use the take in which I had inadvertently caught my ceremonial sword between my legs in the run to jump over the trench in which the camera was placed for my subsequent leap on to the train [this entry into the Czar's coach is to be imagined in the viewer's mind, as my next appearance on screen was my opening the door into the czar's private coach bed-chamber on the sound stage in Madrid several months later]. Box chose this shot because agony from the pain of the slapping into my groin of that sword was just the grimace that looked best for that scene, according to Box's opinion of what the Aide to the Czar should show in the expression on his face at that moment. This was later corroborated by Schaffner's approval of the print. That's "show biz." I was not needed for filming again until later that spring, and although I telephoned the Madrid offices of Columbia Pictures every week, and I had a telephone where I was residing in Mallorca, it was not until the most awkward moment that I was told to report for my page of dialogue and interactive *Interior shoot* with Czar Nicholas.

At Easter holiday, when 'American Community School' was closed for two weeks, Patty and I decided to take a short trip to North Africa, to visit Morocco, riding on the Marrakesh Express and savoring the exotic delights of Casablanca. It was in this magic city that I discovered a restaurant which had just opened in a deconsecrated mosque. Patty and I were possibly their first customers, and the premier celebration offered us was probably the most exquisite and elaborate ever presented there. The two of us were esconced in huge silken pillows and were fed sumptuous delights, many courses of fragrant, spicy, hot and cold dishes – so many different courses, that I stopped counting, and would have been unable to do so anyway, as we were offered the hookah pipes, the hubba-bubba stationary cylindrical hydrant with hoses which were proffered us by the gorgeous dancing girls whose sleek, writhing bodies were barely covered by flimsy veils, their tattooed faces wreathed in sensual smiling entreaty to suck in more ... deeper ... and deeper ... as they bowed, dipped, twisted and swayed away and around us, weaving their musical renditions from the Haute Atlas mountains, dancing feverishly to the rhythms from the cradle of Hamilcar Barca, Hannibal's father, and all the tribal Berber nomads that had inhabited this mysterious country for many centuries. We may have made love right there between courses. I was in a miasma of myriad emotions and physical sensations and delectations. I do remember the lamb in cous-cous, but I do not remember any interruptions or anything other than one sustained orgasmic sense of delightful flowing of peak pleasure not unlike the pleasure of a grand ejaculation in the sexual *moment of truth*. So perhaps we did not actually copulate at this banquet, but the pleasure we both experienced was so similar in its intensity, that we seriously questioned one another after we were taxied home to our hotel, and found ourselves still chortling with delight, enwrapped in naked embrace in our bed there. We did not make love then, but slept like babes, till I was awakened in the afternoon as we lay sprawled out trying to recover from our over-indulgence of food, drink, hashish, and sensual intensities, by a telephone call from Madrid's Columbia Pictures office which had been directed to the hotel by Stanley Amdurer whose office at our school, in the pension where he actually lived, had forwarded the urgent message to this hotel which he himself had recommended we stay in. I was scheduled to perform, *the very next day*, in Madrid ... at 1200 Noon.

I had the concierge arrange tickets for us on the Rapide Marrakesh Express Train with connections to the Tangiers -Algiceras ferry, and then I could not find any airplane connection from that first place in Spain or Cadiz or even the British-held Gibralter, to fly me to Madrid. The nearest flight was from Malaga, and I reckoned that if we disembarked from our Tangiers crossing before noon that a taxi could race us to a plane that would land in Madrid in the early afternoon. I telephoned Columbia Pictures' office and told them my proposed itinerary, and they assured me that my Make-Up call was for noon, but that the shooting of my scene was not scheduled till after 3 P.M. that day. Whoof! What a charge it was going to be to race up the coast of North Africa, leap on to the ferry and roll out in to a taxi and speed up the southern coast of Spain to the Malaga airport ... *and we did.*

I had not regrown my beard since the Second Unit scene that winter, and my mustache needed only a slight trim, as did my hair. The Make-Up session lasted less than a half hour, and I was ready for my call to the sound stage well before 3 o'clock that day. Patty was a most able running mate. She not only kept up with me, but was like the ideal personal assistant/secretary any executive could ever desire, and she hefted her own baggage on the trot without any stumbling. She even helped me to assist some of the sea-sick Arabs whom we held as they heaved their vomit over the side of the ferry during the crossing from Tangiers. Curiously, there was another man who was doing the same, and I thought perhaps he was on the way to Madrid to the same sort of job. His features were so familiar, and I was amazed, when we went in to the bar to have a coffee, that he introduced himself by the name of an actor that anyone of my generation knew as a famous star: Basil Rathbone, Jr. It was his father who had played the role of Sherlock Holmes in almost all the films made of that famous detective, and starred in many other well-known British films, besides. He gave me his card which I kept for many years thereafter. He was a former R.A.F (Royal Air Force) F-4 Phantom jet pilot who was on loan to the Saudi Arabian Air Force instructing their young flight officers. His

Arabic had been most fluent when we were playing nurse-maid to the sick Moroccans and that explained his ease with our work on the decks. When I told him where I was going that day, he asked that I give my regards to Sam Spiegel, an old family friend.

When I arrived at the studio, I was in the Make-Up Artist's chair for only a few minutes to barber my mustache and hair and to apply powder to my face and slightly darken my eye-brows. I slipped into the Russian Army uniform, and left the overcoat and sword to put on later, as the set was moderately warm and these were clothes designed for Siberian winter, where I had last been recorded by the camera stopping Czar Nicholas's train in a freezing blizzard. I slumped into a canvas deck chair and as I reviewed my lines, waiting for my call to the set, I was approached by the Dialogue Director who wanted to know if I needed any assistance. Since I had still not revealed my actual nationality, as Frank Shaffner, the director, was so opposed to any but British or European actors being in his film, I decided to play a game with this man. I mentioned to him that I had been a university student at one time, had "read" [this being the colloquial term used by British university students for our American expression "study"] Anglo-Saxon and Medieval Literature, and had encountered much of the authoritative research in those fields by the University of Oxford linguistic scholar Henry Sweet who had been the role model for the fictional character, Henry Higgins, in George Bernard Shaw's, 'Pygmalion,' later adapted to become the hit musical comedy, 'My Fair Lady.' Professor Henry Higgins, like Henry Sweet, had been such an adept speech pathologist, that he could identify the socio-economic and geographical background of anyone he met after listening to them speak for only a matter of minutes. I challenged this Dialogue Director to tell me my background. I then delivered for him the lines I was to exchange in the forthcoming scene with Michael Jayston, who was playing the role of Czar Nicholas, and then related to him, in a less theatrical manner, more in a conversational tone, the narrative of my race to arrive in Madrid on time from Casablanca that day.

He stroked his chin, stepped back and paced for a moment and shrugged his shoulders before turning to make his judgment. His eyes twinkled as he presented his assay and opinion, which he believed to be authoritative and undeniable. His pose appeared to me to be that of a pedantic prig.

"It is obvious that you are an actor, a man with a very acute ear for accent and manner, with a finely tuned ability to imitate an emulate those whom you choose to mimic. Because of that quality, able to disguise your working-class family background, I would say, from the region of County Cork, so that when you entered Trinity College, Dublin, and consorted with many of the Irish title-holding English undergraduates there, that you were accepted as a person of some status well above that of your birth and actual pedigree, perhaps even assuming the mantle of the landed gentry of that country, what would be called in England, *county*, a veritable squire, in a word, a *Gentleman*, an identity you could only pretend to aspire to, but for social purposes, in the academic and theatrical world, enough to keep you afloat in the superficial swim of things," he declared, and then pulling back and folding his arms, with his head bent forward and his eyes looking up from under his brow, he said, "Sorry if I struck so deep, dear fellow, but only an expert would see through that veneer, or should I say, only someone such as I would recognize the true timbre in the ring of your bell, and I promise, I'll keep your secret."

It was all I could do to keep from bursting into laughter at this pretentious ponce; however, being an *actor*, and feeling pleased that my pose had been so successful, I pretended to be rather offended and injured, and expressed my gracious gratitude for his pledge that he would not unmask my supposedly snobbish affectations. Our encounter was interrupted by a call to rehearsal for the *shooting* of my scene. I climbed up on to the sound stage which was a cutaway of the interior of the Czar's bed-chamber in the private train-car. Czar Nicholas was to throw off the covers of his bed as I entered from a door in the rear of the room. I then was to approach my ruler with humble dignity, bow, and present my line reporting the people *rioting in Moscow*.

Somehow, whenever we did the lines, Michael found it enormously amusing and would answer with a bizarre *ad lib*, something like, "Well, did you ever, Darling?" which he delivered with an exaggerated imitation of a camp *diva*, flinging his bedclothes over his shoulder, and striking an obscene pose. Shaffner allowed this playfulness only once, and scolded him sternly, so that the next time we tried, I just got his pursed lips and batting eye-lids, miming the same sort of response, and I had difficulty in completing my statement. Finally, after only a few more rehearsals, we both appeared to have become more serious about the scene. Shaffner was satisfied and was ready to shoot. I was instructed to stand on the balcony which adjoined the door entrance, behind the sound stage, till I heard the call to *begin*, and then was to enter, swinging the door inward ... and speak...

Because my last appearance on camera had been with Second Unit, when I stopped the train, leapt over the cattle-guard and climbed the ladder to the Czar's private car, I thought that I should work up something of a sweat and at least get my cheeks naturally flushed from the exertion, so I began performing the most basic *kata* I had learned in Shotokan Karate. I did not kick, but I thrust my left arm out in front with bent elbow to block and then slammed my clenched fist forward to an imagined target directly ahead and let go the explosion of the twist and expulsion of full body energy ... doing this from right to left, in articulated focus, several times ... *and I did not hear the call to begin.*

Suddenly I had before me, an actual physical target with which I connected with fully focused explosive force. Frank Shaffner's huge Havana cigar, disintegrated and crushed into the director's mouth as my fist slammed it backward, propelling his body to crash on to the sound stage whence he had rushed from his cat-bird seat by camera. He had just then jerked open the door to try to find out what had been rocking the entire stage built high above the floor on huge springs to simulate the private railway sleeping compartment of the Czar of Russia. I had not realized that my shifting body weight, jerking back and forth in the tight explosive *kata* sequence had transmitted such energy in to the entire elevated set so that it was actually bouncing about like a bucking bronco, albeit this was a construction of wooden planks so that such a rodeo simile would be more appropriate to an analogy with the Trojan Horse on amphetamines with a stinging burr up its ass, and Odysseus and his combat squad inside having a rollicking sexual gang-bang before they launched their surprise assault that night in Priam's city. Whatever the havoc wreaked on the camera crew, lighting team, sound recordists and gaffers surrounding the director that afternoon, the effect was to render Shaffner gasping for air, sick to the point of convulsive thrashing about, before he could be given some water to stop his gagging on that smashed cigar, the location doctor rushing him away to a local hospital for further trauma examination; nevertheless, the entire set was *struck* for that day, and we were all told to go home and be ready for an early morning *shoot* of this scene the next day.

As Michael Jayston was leaving that day, he brushed by me and said, "Nice job. We all have wanted to take a whack at that prick since we started this turkey." I came to understand that even the highest paid actors and staff on that film company felt the same. Shaffner had not endeared himself to anyone, and yet he was truly democratic in treating everyone the same ... as if we were all his lowly servants, or more appropriately, his serfs, and that it was an enormous effort on his behalf to even have to deal directly with any of us. As a matter of fact, any instructions he delivered were transferred through assistant directors, and these underlings were so poisoned by his manner, that often the orders delivered were punctuated by threats or abusive language which we were led to believe originated with our exalted leader and lord, His Majesty Franklin Shaffner. So it was extraordinary that he had been impelled to leap from his seat by the camera and to cross the stage to tear open that door so that my *karate* punch landed perfectly on target on his mid-facial region, the bulls-eye being that Havana stuck in his mouth. Several pages of his rolled copy of the *Wall Street Journal* which had been held under his elbow against the side of his body were also strewn out over the floor of the stage. What a statement had been made there. Director flattened, Havana smashed, *Wall Street Journal,* spattered. Filming - Cut!

I picked up Patty at a hair-dresser's salon that was only a few doors away from the cafeteria where all the news stringers for U.P.I., Reuters and A.P. gathered during the early evening, and I had a chance to chat with my former roommate, David Cemlyn-Jones, who had already heard about the fracas on the set and was attempting to sell the story to Loren Jenkins [this Pulitzer prize-winning journalist, later becoming International Director of National Public Radio in Washington D.C.], who was still U.P.I.'s man in Madrid, but to no avail. David, in his Marxist fervor, loved the images of the cigar and the financial newspaper - both shattered and splattered - as representative of symbolic weapons of the film world's field-marshal fallen in the capitalistic money-mongering fray, Hollywood's holocaust on Franco's fascist free-hold being bartered for American gold and privilege. Neither Loren nor I could stomach the exaggerated attempts at political propaganda by our pal David, regardless of his alliterative lyricism, so we bought him several more drinks, and told him that *come the revolution,* he really would love strawberries. A badly clichéd joke, but our most effective means for staunching our pal, David's, putrefying polemics, especially when we doused him with his favorite brand of double whiskeys on the rocks,

Patty and I decided to stay over that night in the Victoria Hotel in Plaza Santanna. I awarded us V.I.P. status with a suite whose enclosed French windowed terrace overlooked the center of the square. This was the hotel that Hemingway loved to stay in, especially during the very special week of San Ysisdro, in Semana Santa, the Holy Week, when the few selected *novilleros* are honored with their *alternativas* (the blessed rites-of-passage ceremony to becoming thenceforward, full *matadors*, recognized throughout the world of taurine spectacle as masters of that vocation). The young noviates would be accompanied by their impresarios, cape-handlers, and even close family members. I had once been privileged to be in the rooms of a certain *novillero* as he ceremoniously dressed in his "suit of lights" and then bowed in prayer before the altar that had been installed just for that specific ritual in his suite, to religiously dedicate himself and his performance in the ring that day, before being driven in a limousine to the bull-ring on the other side of town for the most meaningful *corrida* of his life, the one in which he would become *knighted,* as it were, acclaimed from that day forward: *matador.*

Before arriving at the hotel, I took Patty to the favorite bar of all *aficionados* on Plaza Santana, the 'Cerveceria Alemania,' where Hemingway had hob-nobbed with all the bull-fight crowd, and where I had composed and written that poem of mine, 'Madrid,' which was later published in my first book of collected poems. We *tapa-hopped* then in various other bars before choosing a restaurant on Calle Echegary, the street famed for food as well as for *bordellos* in this quarter. We then returned by way of 'Las Gabrielas,' the Flamenco *tablao* where *chotas* (shots) of rich, red wine were offered for only a few pesetas, and 'El Canon' (the cannon), a famous Flamenco *cante jondo* singer with a thundering *basso profundo* delivery was vocally blasting the echoing painted ceramic walls of what had been in the time of the Republic, one of the most infamous whore-houses, before all happiness and frivolous sex or any radical behavior, thenceforth had been prohibited by Generalissimo Franco and his Nationalist Falange armed forces in 1936.

When we finally arrived at the hotel, well after midnight, Patty and I had begun arguing about some petty issue, and in order to quell our spat and to wrest some sleep out of the disappearing night, so that I might be somewhat more alert for the final filming on the morrow, I attempted to strip her clothes off in order to wrestle her in to bed to settle our differences in copulative combat and coital resolution. She would have it otherwise, however! She somehow eluded my grasp and tore out of our rooms into the hallway, screaming and declaring her possible rape and injury, to all who could hear her. A few bell-boys did, and we all raced after her voluptuous form with long blonde tresses flying like a cape behind her till she was cornered on the mezzanine just on the ramp connecting to the dimly lit bar there where many of the bull-fight crowd were gathered to discuss that day's *corridas* and the ones to come. I fully expected some cape-handler to rush forth to sweep her up in his *veronica*, but it was actually one of the more conscientious bellboys who tore a tablecloth off and enwrapped the now unresisting buxom beauty in its protecting folds. She followed me demurely back to our rooms, and we enacted a sedative copulative ritual to slide then into the arms of Morpheus and thus be refreshed for the coming day of my final filming at the studios.

We returned to Palma merely for me to finish the courses in American History and Creative Writing which I had been conducting at the American Community School, and then we planned to book a flight back to the States in June. We traveled up through Andorra to buy some duty-free goods, then went into France, and I wanted to take a side-trip to visit Luxembourg, to investigate the special banking services available there. I was amazed to discover in the bar attached to our hotel that Jim Morrison's music, especially his newest release, "Riders on the Storm," which he had revealed to me was his interpretation of the last lines of T.S. Eliot's, 'The Love Song of J. Alfred Prufrock,' just before the most heart-breaking lines telling that the "... mermaids do not sing to me," was a recording which kept playing again and again on the juke-box there. I looked forward to telling Jim about this when I arrived in San Francisco, and I was sure to encounter him at Michael McClure's. 'The Doors' was on the hit-parade in Luxembourg. What a special treat. I reckoned he would enjoy knowing that.

As it was, I did not see Jim when I arrived there, but I did talk to him on the telephone from Michael's home where I spent more and more time separated from Patty who preferred to reside in the commune household where she had lived before, on just the next street over, and parallel to the McClure's Downing Street residence, there in the Haight-Ashbury section of San Francisco. I was never comfortable in Patty's former home as there were more people than I could keep track of, and it seemed that it was a sort of drop-in center for many "street-people" of questionable integrity. Michael and Joan, his wife, and Jane, the daughter, all seemed eager for me to occupy the spare guest-room on the second floor where Jane had her bedroom, as well. Jim Morrison and Rip Torn, the actor who had played the lead role as Billy the Kid, in Michael's shocking play, 'The Beard,' were regular guests occupying this room. Jane loved being in co-habitation with such stars; only two years before, Richard Brautigan had lived here while recuperating from the broken jaw he received attempting to defend Michael in a clumsy street fight with some bikers who resented Michael's specially crafted "hog" (motorcycle) designed by the

Hell's Angels' best mechanics and artists to award him the title as their Poet Laureate, as he had been so designated by his best friend, Free-Wheeling Frank Reynolds. Richard Brautigan had given Jane the famous ten-gallon hat that he was photographed wearing on the covers of his novels, *Troutfishing in America* and *Confederate General from Big Sur*, his reward for her nursing care during that convalescent period.

I was still in close touch with Richard, but he and Michael were "at swords' points" as a result of Richard's refusal to attend protest meetings to defend the whales and other such environmental issues which Michael regarded as essential to the humanistic concern of anyone who declared himself to be a poet in America. Michael had accused Richard of being little more than a dilettante and a virtual "lounge lizard," McClure's term for such an all too dedicated, or dissipated, frequenter of bars and coffee shops. Michael had ceased drinking alcohol at this time, as had Jim Morrison. I do not know if either had joined Alcoholics Anonymous, but they were both certainly off the booze. I found it a healthy release from the avid wine guzzling and pot-smoking I found so prevalent in Patty's company of friends, but I was surprised that Joan offered me her hidden "stash," as she called it, of stale burgundy, corked and secreted under the sink, when I admitted I could indeed use a bracer on some evenings. When Jim did visit at Downing Street, he now seemed a different man entirely. I had remembered him as a pudgy and pouting creature who often sat in the corner of the living room, grumpy and self-absorbed, with his own bottle of whiskey and an 'Incredible Hulk' comic book. He would only join in any gathering of guests or visitors if Michael pulled him out of his sulks and literally guided him into a conversation. This *revised* version of Jim Morrison, who had sometimes been virtually antagonistic with me, and who had usually been accompanied by his body-guard, an ineffectual hanger-on named Angel, a lumbering, fleshy youth who claimed to have been a member of the Hell's Angels [highly unlikely]. This Jim was sober and might as well have been a reincarnation replacing the one I had formerly known ... and had, therefore, avoided whenever possible.

In certain circumstances, Jim and I had been placed in confined spaces together, as had occurred when Michael had arranged an early morning fishing trip from the Embarcadero in San Francisco a couple of years before when Jim was at the height of his most abusive use of drugs and alcohol. As the small fishing vessel tossed about in the bay, Jim was *tossing* [vomiting] his last full meal over the side, and when he did return amidships to try to regain his equilibrium, he seated himself, or rather, slumped his retching body on the deck next to where I sat, as I carried out the work of smashing the heads of the fish we had caught with a marlinspike to render them immobile ... and dead. As Jim registered what I was doing, he howled with outrage and accused me of being a murderous psycho. My hands were covered with blood – as a matter of fact, I was bloody up to my elbows, as we had caught over a dozen fair-sized fish so far – some gore had even splattered my face and had clotted in my beard, so I probably did appear maniacal and frenzied with blood-lust. I responded by tossing one of the still living fish into Jim's lap, and as it flounced about at his mid-section, I told him that I was just trying to prevent any further erratic behavior on behalf of our wild and resistant catch, and therefore I was rendering them insensate in the most humane manner I could contrive, bludgeoning them into the deepest sleep: Death.

Perhaps it was my cool, detached manner of explanation for my fierce activity, and that I was using language of a formalistic tenor and cavalier tone, but his reaction was to rush to Michael and beg protection of his mentor and to demand that we turn back to port immediately – *if not sooner.* Michael attempted to calm him and explained that as I was a highly experienced "blue water sailor" –

Michael had relished the tales I had told him of my exploits aboard the yacht, *Nachen II*, in the English Channel, North Sea, Kiel Canal and Baltic - but added to the very factor in my maritime pedigree that Jim considered most repulsive and dreadful, was that I had been a Line Combat officer in the U.S. Navy, and this last piece of information, which Michael considered would assuage any of Jim's fears and reassure him of my competence and trustworthiness was the very feature which gouged the most plaintive cry from Jim - that I should be restrained forcibly, and he told Michael that my body should be weighted with lead and thrown overboard, before I could wreak any further harm. His own father at that very time held the rank of Vice Admiral. Jim had grown up in a strictly regimented discipline and knew the heavy hand of military rule ... and punishment. Most of his rebellious nature was in reaction to this early childhood mind-set in an attempt to escape the father-figure in authority, the fascist embodiment of all that he most loathed ... and feared. Were we now to enact the Freudian primal cave scene, so long postponed in Jim's development as he vicariously later portrayed and enacted in abreal narration in one of his more chilling songs. Need he now confront and kill *Daddy*, so he could fuck *Mommy*? Fortunately, we now were just at the farthest point outside San Francisco Bay, and the captain had made his turn to take us back to the dock, so that Jim did not panic anymore, and we arrived at dock-side without any further incident, and split our catch with the others in our party and proceeded back to The Haight to get some rest and sleep off the exhaustion of our adventure on the roiling sea. Jim was careful in the future to always bring along his protector, Angel, if he knew I were to be present.

The new, alcohol and drug-fee Jim Morrison no longer employed Angel and he appeared to have become confident in his own being, 'comfortable in his own skin', enjoying that state of psychic well-being that the New Age healers and members of Alcoholics

Anonymous promised seekers of enlightenment and serenity. He welcomed me back home from my European ventures, and when I told him that he was on the Luxembourg "hit-parade," he was pleased and amused. It was after a casual lunch served by Joan and Jane out on the deck which Michael had commissioned to be built since I had been gone, that Jim approached the subject of his new poetic endeavors. He was aware of the work I had done in editing the last few collections of Michael's works of poetry, and he asked if I would consider having a look at his latest writing and perhaps guide him editorially, as I had done with Michael. There was no formal contractual agreement, as I had offered my services in friendship in the same manner to Michael, and I was prepared to do the same for Jim. I wish now that I had been more sanguine and focused on business and profits and royalties, but I had never known there to be any such stink to the matters of artistic creativity among poets whom I knew. Michael wrote the introductory poem to my own first published book, *What Next, What Next* with no request for sharing of profits or royalties from sale of the work. He told me that he had written personal tributes of this sort for only Jack Kerouac, Sam Shepherd, and Bob Dylan. Did this poem now elevate me to be one of that august pantheon?

This humble Jim Morrison, who implored my poetic mentorship on this day, was a far cry from that wild youth who had burst in to a poetry seminar at the San Diego, Point Loma college conference of writers and film-makers in September 1971 announcing that spectacular event in the history of American music was happening that day in a place called Woodstock in New York where Rickie Havens had led performances that were now being joined by Arlo Guthrie, Ravi Shankar, 'The Who,' Joan Baez, 'Sweetwater,' 'The Incredible String Band,' 'Country Joe and the Fish,' 'Sly and the Family Stone,' Jimi Hendrix, Janis Joplin, 'The Grateful Dead,' and so many more headliners in Pop music that it left Jim gasping to carry on in his delivery of this news to our startled assemblage of writers and performers and academics and publishers.

Ken Kesey had bussed in a legion of his Merry Pranksters, Wavy Gravy had set up the infra-structure of food supply and basic hygiene with his commune 'Hog Farm' for an encampment that was growing from a thousands to perhaps half a million [the final estimate for the entire attendance was roughly 450,000]. Abbie Hoffman and his Yippies were assisted by Paul Krassner, former publisher of *The Realist*, delivering politically biased press releases. There had been "Happenings" as impromptu Street Theatre events throughout the world prior to this concert at Woodstock, but never anything of this colossal size. Thousands of music-loving hippies were gathered to throb for days in a celebration of love and communal expression of their erotic and artistic beliefs and dedication. Jim appeared to be in that state of *exstasis* which Dionysian *maenads* claimed to experience in their total abandonment to wine and sexual indulgence; this being that special Jim Morrison signature that he delivered in his most popular hits, 'Break On Through To The Other Side,' and 'Baby, Let Me Light Your Fire,' which were the derivative of his own understanding of William Blake's epic poem, *The Marriage of Heaven and Hell*, whence he had derived the name of his group 'The Doors' from the line containing the key phrase "... the doors of perception." Aldous Huxley had also chosen this phrase as his novel's title, *The Doors of Perception*, in representation of his first hallucinogenic experience with mescaline and L.S.D. at the Menninger Foundation Clinic in Topeka, Kansas, under the direction of Dr. Robert Lynch (later, in 1965, on the staff of the Salk Foundation) in whose La Jolla, California home he died after writing *The Island* in which Lynch is the character called "Doctor."

On that day, and for subsequent days at the conference in San Diego, Morrison had carried on in a zealous revel for his fellow musical *vatics* on the other side of the continent, and I had considered him such a self-indulgent exhibitionist, so childish and self-centered that I did not care to know much more about him, although Michael McClure, whose poetry I enormously respected and whom I had just met, spent most of his free time at the conference in Jim's company. The one evening I spent in their combined company was so disgusting that I tried to avoid Jim Morrison from then on, but could not do so as he continued to cleave to Michael as his guru in poetry.

So this new, *reincarnated* Jim Morrison, the one not soaked in alcohol or seething with some insane pharmaceutical mixtures from cocaine, to meth-amphetamine by way of barbiturates and hallucinogenic tranquilizer tablets, was actually a personable and charming individual who spoke informatively about the history of ideas and the practice of poetics in articulating the hopes and dreams of all artists in what we call Western Civilization. I now readily agreed to offer my perspectives and opinions regarding the development of Jim's writing of poetry. It was some time not long thereafter, when I awoke some mornings at Downing Street and spoke from the McClure telephone to Jim in his apartment in Paris, France. This was on the last day (22 July 1971) of Jim's life, and I had been discussing with him, some of his writing, and then, afterward, I decided to drive down the coast to stay overnight with a friend of mine, a medical practitioner, Dr. Miller, in residence at the commune of the 'Grateful Dead' in Big Sur.

When I returned to the McClures and Haight-Ashbury the next afternoon, I could feel the chill of some tragic cloud that enveloped the house, even as I mounted the stairway up to the top floor where the family resided. It was JoAnne who guided me to the dining table to sit down across from Michael who had not as yet greeted me. I had begun to say something about regretting if I had forgotten some appointment, or that I might be interrupting some special family business, when Michael waved his arm in a broad sweep before him and said simply, "He's dead."

JoAnne added, "Jim. His wife [Pamela Courson, with whom Jim had applied for a certificate of common-law marriage in the state of Colorado some time before] found him in the bath-tub. He said that his chest and stomach hurt, and then he went to sit in hot water. He did not come back to bed. When she went in after some time, she found him there, dead ... in the tub. She called us ... and then a doctor. The funeral and burial will be in Paris (Pere Lachaise Cemetery)."

I have heard that the cemetery where he is interred has been visited every day since then, for almost forty years, now. His music is still popular and echoes in the consciousness of so many young and now the older, who heard in his verses and his plaintive intonations, the poetics that he and I and Michael discussed and tried to place in print. He died clean and sober. He was not stricken by an over-dose of some drugs or by alcoholic poisoning, and I am quick to point out to anyone who remarks to this effect in my presence - regardless of the *Rolling Stones'* printed testimony of Ray Manzarek, his key-board player, who was not there at the time, that Jim had been injected with heroin by his wife - that I spoke to him on the telephone on the last day of his life [June 22, 1971] and that he was clear, cogent and insightful; and, that the McClure family told me that his wife, Pam, reported to them that he was not indulging in any mind-altering chemical substances during that day, and in that last evening, when the pain took him while he sought relief from the pure hot water in his own home bath-tub.

Many of those poets and performers of that epoch who were considered super-stars in their field have now faded from public awareness. Richard Brautigan, Michael McClure and even Lawrence Ferlinghetti, himself, whose 'City Lights Bookstore' publications launched so many of the original Beatnik greats and these other iconic American poetic voices, have faded in popularity since the vibrant 1960s, but the music of 'The Doors' [the name of that group so appropriately derived from Blake's poetic line: "If the *doors of perception* [italics mine] were cleaned, everything would appear to man as it is, infinite."] and their *vatic,* prophetic lead-singer and composer, Jim Morrison, still throbs and reverberates in the consciousness of millions throughout the world. Michael McClure continued delivering poetry readings, performing sometimes with accompaniment by Jim's keyboard player, Ray Manzarek, intoning the opening lines of Geoffrey Chaucer's *Canterbury Tales*, beginning with that proposition in those particular lines that April is the cruellest month. Yes, it is, as it stirs ancient longings of our youth and our clearest notions of the *inifinite*, as did Jim in his echoes of Blake's gleanings from his discoveries in the *Marriage of Heaven and Hell.* Ezra Pound's cryptic line, "Spring too long gongala," resonates, but without Jim's plaintive, deep-throated scream.

Although we still hear echoes of Richard Brautigan's influence in the album by Janis Joplin when she quotes lines from his poem, 'Love's Not the Way to Treat a Friend,' when she launches into one of her heart-wrenching love ballads - perhaps it was 'Take Another Little Piece of My Heart' - his novels are now collectors' items, and his volumes of poetry are mostly out of print, as well. However, when Helen Brand was his agent, as well as the promoter of Kurt Vonnegut, then Brautigan's surrealistic novel, *The Hawkline Monster*, which I edited on a whirlwind trip to visit him in , Florida, was on the American Book of the Month Club list and definitely a best-seller. Richard had made his move to Montana at that time, and had bought a ranch there, as well as almost an entire abandoned mining ghost-town. His pals had become such *glitterati* as the film-makers, Francis Coppola and Roman Polanski, and the actors, Jack Nicholson and Peter Fonda, and the writers Jim Harrison and Tom McGuane, and even the musical star Jimmy Buffet. Several of these elements were gathered in Key West when I arrived to stay with Richard there in September 1973. I was met at the airport by the wives of Tom McGuane and Peter Fonda, who told me that Richard was so involved with the filming that was going on that we would have to wait till evening to even see him or any of the Montana Gang as they referred to those who were enacting a documentary homage to Ernest Hemingway with a French film crew who had convinced this bunch of artists (all who had taken up Montana residence in a sort of loose-knit commune of like-minded creative personalities) that they should inter-act in a late Twentieth Century re-enactment of the effects of Hemingway's influence on their inspiration to contribute to America's culture. Certainly, this latter-day Chaucerian pilgrimage in one of the former homes of that infamous Nobel laureate novelist was conducive to the excesses in alcoholic consumption that eventually killed that writer of *The Old Man and the Sea*, which many literary critics consider to be nothing greater than the last senile gasp of a once brilliant craftsman.

I was perfectly content to wait with these wives, who so resembled each other that they might have been sisters. I was deposited at the motel where I was entertained by some nubile young woman who was occupying Richard's sprawling suite of rooms. My jet-lag was not severe, although I had just flown in from Mallorca. Like any of the countless, mindless groupies I had encountered when in the company of the super magnetic poets, Brautigan and McClure, this eager girl had undressed me and assisted in my shower, and then performed the ritual of fellatio and spread her long, tanned legs to hump me gracefully to my slumber, saying that she would do so again later, if I wished, since Richard was too fatigued by his heavy drinking bouts to require much sexual performance.

I did not actually avail myself of her offer during my week's visit, as Richard had a screaming row with her when he did arrive, and she was flung out, leaving behind only her sweet memory, and the most severe case of herpes simplex genitalis I have ever contracted, which lasted for the next thirty years in my body [many years after Brautigan's actual demise], reminding me not so much of her, as of Richard, the *author* of her affliction, who himself came to suffer so extremely from this disease that when he visited me last in Mallorca, in 1984, ten years later, just before his suicide in Bolinas, California, he was unable to have anything like normal sexual relations with anyone. I have not, by grace of the great medical skill of my doctors in England, Spain, and America suffered from any recurrence of this scathing, painful, suppurating rash on the penis for several years now, but I shall never forget Richard, in any case.

Even more ironic events of literary osmosis occurred between Richard and me in the years to follow, especially with his portrayal of a man whose sense of time dimension is radically altered by a head injury and concussion which I had described to Richard just after I had my own skull fracture with concussion in Mallorca which necessitated the reconstruction of my eye socket and the plastic surgery for the entire right side of my face in Moorefield Eye Clinic and Kings College Hospital in London. My first novel [still unpublished, although written in 1977], *Ghost Dance*, is narrated in the first person voice of a man recovering from just such a severe skull fracture and concussion. I had remained in close contact with Richard, with frequent long distance telephone conversations between us, even when he was residing in Japan [I was in Mallorca, England, and the United States], during my recuperation from this accident. I described to him, in painstaking detail, the enormous challenges I confronted in the ordeal of recovering my cognitive functions during that period from 1973 to 1977 when, at last, I deemed myself capable of writing cogently once more.

However, during my visit with Richard and while editing *The*

Hawkline Monster took place during that frenzied re-enactment of the Hemingway-*experience* re-creation for the French film crew in Key West, was when I met Jim Harrison and Tom McGuane. Close friends of Richard's, they were both residents of the new artists' colony springing up in Montana. Tom had a home in Key West as well as in Montana. I was in his studio behind his Key West house when he received a telephone call from the location where his novel *Missouri Breaks* was being directed at that very moment as a film by Sam Peckinpah. Tom was invited to take over direction of this film because Peckinpah had continued in a drunken binge from the first days of shooting and was considered completely unreliable to continue to work on the project. Tom accepted this dream-job of every writer who has sold a film to Hollywood. Although he did not receive the "final cut' privilege at the end of filming, reserved by the producers, and was not awarded the title of director, he did have such enormous artistic license that he was able to extracted from Marlon Brando one of his most deeply moving and individualistic roles since 'Last Tango in Paris'. I met Jim Harrison at the same time, and although we were the same age, he appeared older, more grizzled and actually, downright degenerate, as he had only one eye and was often unshaven – not a designer-cut fashion statement – and he was usually drunker than anyone in the crowd. Richard told me that his nickname was "Mexican Sheriff" because he looked like a caricature of that sort of *persona* – on a good day. I was most impressed by the title of his first published fictional work, *Letters to Ysenin*, a fantasy about that mad Russian poet who had been married to Isadora Duncan and who had written his suicide note in his own blood from his slashed wrists, and as he had not then expired, had then hammered away at a piano to get the blood to flow all the way out, but then had to resort to hanging himself, a *last-gasp* effort to complete the job – a man who did nothing halfway. His wife had asphyxiated herself by wearing an over-long scarf that caught in the spoked wheels of her sports cars which she drove away and succeeded in strangling herself and dragging her *expiring* body some distance farther down the road: a couple I had always wished I could have met ... *before* their demise. Jim's subsequent novel, *Wolf,* had been produced as a film in which Jack Nicholson played the part of the protagonist who assumes the character of a wolf in order to cope with his own deep personality disorder, but finds that he is still hopelessly maladjusted and unable to fit in with normal human society. Nicholson had first encountered Jim and read this book in Montana where he had decided to insure that a film was indeed produced [he had personally partially funded the pre-production costs] from Harrison's own personal nightmare.

Something of this sort of event had transpired with my own personal trauma and tragic experience with the skull fracture and grave injury in that accident in Mallorca that required the major surgery to my head and face in London. As I recovered from the severe brain damage and came to cope with the disfigurement to my face that the surgery initially provided – it took two years more before the scars had faded and I regained control of the facial muscles – I had let my hair grow so long that it fell over that ugly side of my physiognomy and I would only sweep the hair away to shock people who had not expected to behold such grisly damage. However, the real challenge was in recovering my sense of balance in social skills and particularly in writing coherently once more. When I began the novel which I entitled *Ghost Dance,* as I already mentioned, I conversed with Richard Brautigan often by telephone as I struggled in writing through the sanative pathways of declarative prose, attempting to realign the neural circuits and thereby regain my mental balance and stability. I believed that once I completed this endeavor, that I could be assured that I was recovered from my near-death experience with the injury. I had reconstructed myself just as I would repair a mechanical product. My first reading after leaving the hospital had been *Zen and the Art of Motorcycle Maintenance.* I decided that this book would become the master-plan for my newly super-charging sublimation of my crippled psychic, creative magma, a cognitive regeneration. As the protagonist of that book recovers from his "nervous breakdown" by learning basic motorcycle mechanics, in like manner, I decided to reconstruct myself. I also re-read Carl Jung's. *Memories, Dreams and Reflections.* This autobiographical recollection of the psycho-analyst's reconstruction of his psyche and personality in the location of his favorite childhood vacation retreat, Bollingen, also became a model for the rebuilding of my own sense of self: psyche and personality..

As a further amplification of the actual physical activity I had designed to re-educate my mind to logical, mechanical processes in a tactile and actual sense, I had bought a boat that had been abandoned after the death of its alcoholic owner, Commander Robert Luker, a former U.S. Navy missile designer who had drunk himself to death in Mallorca after arriving with his yacht, *Tsunami,* which was a mad-scientist's conglomeration of cutting-edge mechanical and electronic equipment which had then lain untouched and forsaken at the Real Club Nautico, [The Royal Yacht Club] in Palma harbor. The boat which had cost over $100,000 to custom-build in Port Hamble, Isle of Wight, England, was sold to me by his widow, Patricia Luker, for only $15,000, but there were enormous problems with the papers entitling her to sell any of his property – his estate had not been probated, and there was a holographic Last Will and Testament written to bequeath all his belongings to his lover, a woman who owned the Bar Hawaii, on Paseo Maritimo, where he had died of a heart seizure, stricken as he attempted to have his last bowel movement on the toilet, on her premises there. Not only was it unclear as to Patricia's entitlement to sell his boat, but the taxes and permission fees for the boat to remain in Palma harbor, *or even in Spain,* were anything but legally patent and secure.

I rebuilt the boat and adapted myself to it, cruising from Mallorca to the main-land of Spain, then to Cap D'Agde, France and from there, transported it by truck to England [by international maritime law, any boat which passes through three different Customs inspections and is deemed to be owned by whomsoever possesses it in that process, becomes the legally owned property of that individual - I had thereby become the *de facto* legal owner of *Tsunami* regardless of any probate decisions regarding Commander Luker's estate], where I was so fortunate as to acquire one of the only two moorings at the Madingley Club, in Twickenham, just below the Richmond Bridge on the Thames River flowing into London. I had begun writing the novel about my experience of emerging from a brain damaged state of shock, to recover my wits and sanity, and Richard Brautigan had encouraged me to send this to his agent, Helen Brand, in New York City. I did not realize that he himself had published a novel only a few months before I later arrived in the United States, having shipped my boat to Canada, crossed the Great Lakes and cruised down the Hudson River to New York City from Buffalo to tie up at 79th Street Pier on the river side of the city where I went to call on his literary agent in her offices. I was greeted by a guard at the door and treated like an intruder and when I telephoned, I was informed that Ms. Brand would have nothing to do with me, that she considered me presumptuous to think I could even approach her. I telephoned Richard and he did not answer for some considerable time - more than a few weeks; and when the telephone was then answered, it was by a young woman who said that she was his private secretary and that Mr. Brautigan had gone to Brazil and would not return for several months. I thought I could hear his snickering laughter in the background. What a reversal of the former bond of close friendship with this devious individual. I felt deeply injured and betrayed.

I did not see Richard again for another seven years until he appeared in Bar Bosch in Palma, Mallorca, just a few months before he returned to California and killed himself. In the meantime, I had read the novel he had produced during the period I was writing mine, and telephoning him to discuss the problems of trying to think clearly as I was recovering from the effects of my severe concussion and brain damage. His novel was the portrayal of a man who sustains a concussion and severe brain damage and imagines himself to be transported in time to live in Babylon. Obviously, Richard believed that he had stolen my autobiographical material, and feeling guilty, had attempted to completely dismiss me from his life. However, in 1984, when he arrived Palma in amorous pursuit of a young Korean woman, daughter of Mallorca's first symphony orchestra conductor, my former drinking pal was suffering from the most debilitating effects of herpes genitalis and what had become acute chronic alcoholism. He acted as if he was deeply grateful to encounter me, one of his oldest and most sincere friends.

I was myself, in the early stages of recovery from the ravages of alcoholism, having enrolled in a Twelve-Step program and had not allowed myself drink or drugs for over two years, and as a primary tenet in recovery, which required the practice of absolute honesty in all my affairs, but would not allow any rancor or resentment, I sat down at a table on the forecourt of the Bar Bosch, on Plaza Pio Doce, Palma, Mallorca, and revealed that I knew all about the novel, *Dreaming of Babylon* [the book Brautigan had written about the brain-injured man who suffers from lapses of consciousness and imagines himself in Babylon], and I assured him that I understood perfectly how he might have supposed that I would consider his use of my personal experience a theft of basic material, and that he had, therefore, sabotaged me with his agent, Helen Brand, in order to protect himself, but that I was now must forgive him, as a basic requirement of my program of recovery from an alcoholic mind-set and attitude. Because Richard had known only the personality which was vengeful and violent in that pal he called Ben [the poem he had published by this title simply, 'Ben,' was about his inability to connect with this friend by a telephone which rang unanswered in a trailer on a frog-pond on my farm in Oklahoma in 1972], he was reluctant to believe what I was telling him. Immediately he protested his innocence, but pledged to give me all the film rights to *The Hawkline Monster,* and he crowed with delight to tell me that his book was still a best-seller throughout the world and had been translated into fifteen languages besides English. I told him that I would be better pleased if he were to just accompany me to one of my Twelve-Step alcoholic recovery program meetings, and I asked him to try to not have another drink for the rest of this particular day. I reassured him that I did not want anything of a material nature from him, and I tore up the page of paper on which he had written out a holographic entitlement to his novel's film rights and threw this shredded waste into an ash-tray. Curiously, and ironically, only two months before this, I had rejected an offer of 50,000 Pounds Sterling from my literary agent in London for the rights to my own *Beowulf* film treatment, to be produced as a three part mini-series for A.B.C. (American Broadcasting Company); I had considered the producer, a man named Brown to be a greedy moron, and I was too prideful to accept his largesse, just as now, I felt only repulsion for Brautigan's offering. I was, however, willing to proffer my notion of how to recovery from the crippling effects of alcohol abuse to this one-time drinking pal.

I was never able to convince Richard that he might have a problem with his drinking and that he also could accomplish what I had – abstaining from drink – by attending meetings with others who also shared this allergy to alcohol and were able to live without this chemical as part of their daily diet. I offered him a spare bedroom in my house in Puigpunyent, with the only condition being that he not be drunk when he came to stay with me. During the entire month he stayed in Palma, supposedly to *court* his Korean girl-friend in the San Augustin section of Palma, I am unsure where he spent his nights, because I usually received some incoherent ranting messages on the answer machine of my home telephone, and when he did reach me to talk directly on the line, he was gibbering in inarticulate rebukes against his girlfriend or some bar owner who had thrown him out, and I could only presume that he spent his nights wandering the street looking for all-night bars where he could slump and "cry in his beer." I agreed to drive him to the airport when he at last decided to return to America, and perhaps I would have taken photos of his farewell, if I had then known that I would never see him alive again. Oddly enough, he told me then that he had recently posed for a photograph by a Japanese cemetery in Lahaina, on the Hawaiian island of Maui, holding a chicken in his arms. I have since visited that same cemetery when vacationing there and have taken several photos of my own, but never with a chicken, nor was there a sepulchral poet named Richard Brautigan hovering in the foreground.

It was only a few months later that he ended his life, with a bullet from one of his many hand-guns, shot through the head in his house in Bolinas, California where I had once visited him, having driven all the way from Oklahoma City with Sylvia James, probably the sexiest, most alluring –and promiscuously, unfaithful woman – I ever cohabited with. Richard had been house-proud and had acted thrilled to play host to us in the only residence other than an apartment I had ever known him to occupy. I remember one gesture that particularly startled me, however. He grabbed the television set from its stand in the living room and brought it to Sharon, kneeling with it in his arms as if offering it to her, and said it was hers, if she would pledge never to cuckold me, his good friend, Ben. She nodded in acquiescence, and he then returned the set to its stand. I never asked either of them what had inspired this scene, and could only assume that Sylvia had made a seductive, presumptive move on Richard, and that he wanted me to know that there was nothing of a sexual nature happening between them. I later discovered that there actually had been sexual intimacies between Sylvia and mos of my male friends or associates.

I hold no resentments regarding her infidelities, as I myself, had sexual liaisons outside our relationship. as well. However, I was sometimes reminded of this demonstration of Richard's regard for his male friends. The first question he usually asked men whom he was considering for close friendship was, "How did you deal with your last cuckolding by the woman you loved?" The short story, 'Pacific Radio Fire,' is reminiscent of this theme, in which a man consoling his pal in such a romantic misadventure, watches as the rejected one sets fire to his portable radio as they sit together on a San Francisco hill-side and listen then to the top love songs drop in the combustion from high ranks on the hit-parade to the lowest depths in the conflagration. But I felt decidedly uneasy about Richard's gaff, which I wanted to dismiss as just a cutesy bonding with Sylvia, but had she already made a sexual move on Richard when I was in another room or out in town visiting one of my favorite bars, "Smileys" or "Snarleys"? I retold the anecdote about how Richard had purchased his first television set to play all the re-runs of 'I Love Lucy' for the poltergeist who had inhabited his spare room in the apartment he used to rent in San Francisco. He said that a psychic friend had told him that the teen-age girl who had manifested as his noisy ghostly roommate had died when the series had just begun showing in America, and that the only way to soothe her rages was to play this televison program for her. Sylvia would not believe the story, but I knew to be true, as I had spent nights at Richard's place and was not allowed to occupy that spare room, but had to toss a pallet on the floor in the living room when I stayed the night.

Over ten years after our visit, Richard's body was found in this Bolinas home, only about six weeks had passed after his suicide, and there was only one message on the telephone answering machine, and that was a wrong number. He had last been seen at his favorite restaurant,

Enrico's, in North Beach, San Francisco. It was reported by one of the waiters that he had left hastily after seeing an Oriental woman at the bar who reminded him of his last girl-friend. Perhaps this apocryphal tale is true. Perhaps not. Richard was in an acute alcoholic depression during the entire time he was in Mallorca when I last saw him, in 1984, and suicide was probably the only reasonable *career decision* for him, as Gore Vidal said of Truman Capote's untimely death: "Good career choice, Truman."

I could imagine such dark drunken states as I well remembered our "tooth-countin' mornings," a phrase Richard favored to describe our desperately, fragile, hung-over condition when we drank together over ten years before and roamed the San Francisco streets all night, and I would pass out inebriated to sleep it off at his tiny apartment. We counted the teeth left in our mouths and checked to see if there were any lodged in our knuckles from others we might have encountered the night before in "fist-city" altercations, although neither of us were actually combative nor aggressive ... unless provoked. Most of those mornings, however, Richard set to work as soon as he rose, locking himself in his office, to "pay his dues," as he called it, demanding of himself at least one complete poem before he would consider drinking that first cup of coffee, or if suffering from the severest hang-over – "the whips and the jingles" – he called this miserable state. Then we would drink a beer, instead.

It was on one such dawning that I believe that I inspired one of the poems which he said would keep the critics busy trying to analyze and decode it – *and thus was it so*. This was in the age before pop-top cans – there really was such a time which sorely challenged all thirsty men – and I was in the grips of the "mother-and-father" of all crushing withdrawal symptoms from my hang-over and desperately felt that I needed a beer to assuage my tremors, and I was searching every inch of Richard's kitchen for a can opener – "church-key," as we sometimes reverently called it – and finally I was yowling in despair and was just about to slam the business end of a hunting knife into the top of the beer can to release the healing foam for my parched, juddering lips, when Richard walked out of his office, drove past me to the drawer of his night-stand and pulled out the blessed instrument of this very exact functional purpose which he handed me with that beneficent remark of the usual invitation which had become our mutual launch for our alcoholic indulgences, "Have a drinkee-winkee, drunkee-wunkee!" On other occasions, Richard would make this same remark when we set out to indulge in an evening or weekend of heavy drinking. "Let's go and qualify ourselves for the Nobel Prize," meaning that no American literary laureate in memory had not been an alcoholic. Richard was intent on continuing his writing every day, no matter how steeped in alcohol his body became, and his own literary output was prodigious and prolific; that is, until I last saw him in Mallorca when he was unable to string together even two sentences which were not absolute gibberish. Perhaps the poem he presented to me on that morning at his apartment when I was in need of the beer was a precursor of the decline in his talent.

"Here's the poem of the day. This should give the literary critics something to chew on, trying to figure out what it means," he sniped.

CRITICAL CAN OPENER

There's something wrong

With this poem

Can you

Find it?

However, he *was* correct in his surmise that literary critics *would* chew over the words of that *iconette* of our mutual late morning San Francisco hangover and would attempt to find poetic depth of meaning and assay its value to place it within the canon of American literary tradition. What mattered most to me then was that Richard found the goddamned "church-key," and I was able to slake my thirst and calm my rattled nerves and aneasthesize my exploding hair follicles. We took little time then to decide on a ramble down into town to find a cheap diner for brunch and a bar to begin our qualification calisthenics for the Nobel Prize award. We ended up at Vesuvio's in North Beach, and as Lawrence Ferlinghetti was already there surrounded by some of his bookstore hench-people and various writers and poetic wannabe's, it soon became one of those days which later faded into a blur of giddy gabble and wandering from bar to bar. I do remember asking at the time whatever had happened to Paul Krassner, and the fellow sitting next to me told me that he *was* Paul Krassner. He might have been. I thanked him for *The Realist,* and also for his contribution to launching the Woodstock festival and for slaking my anti-social, rebellious appetites till the last publication (1975) of this journal in which the center-fold cartoon depicted all the Walt Disney cartoon characters in a sexual orgy [Snow-White *running a train* (fucking) with all Seven Dwarves and Goofy *shagging* Minnie Mouse] long before he took on the mantle of editor-in-chief of *Hustler.*

The other extraordinary personality I had met in Ferlinghetti's company had been the poet Gregory Corso in the apartment above City Lights Bookstore. Corso had taken apart the telephone and was poking about inside it and laying the pieces out on the floor where he crawled and gibbered threats at the disabled contraption - on a paranoid acid (L.S.D.) trip that Ferlinghetti assured me would do him no harm, and might even improve the working of his telephone, once it had been reassembled. I did not stay to see the results. I had rather hoped for a conversation about some of the poet's work which I had admired and wanted to discuss. I had first been introduced to Ferlinghetti in 1960 at 'The Pour House' bar in the Bird Rock section of La Jolla where he was performing a presentation of jazz and poetry with Kenneth Rexroth, whose introduction of me to Ferlinghetti must have impressed that poet and publisher, because he always thereafter treated me with respect as a virtual colleague. Tom Waites had been playing piano in that same bar, but generally was the house musician across the road at 'The White Whale'. He was only twenty years old at the time and had not as yet affected the gravelly, bluesy, vocal *persona* with which he later delivered his songs such as 'Short-Change Charlie Got Wasted By His Own Thirty-Eight,' and he was a long way from becoming Francis Coppola's darling in such films as 'Cotton Club' and 'One From The Heart.' I did not see Tom again till he was acting in those films, in 1983, but somehow he remembered me, although I had changed my appearance considerably from the clean-cut young naval lieutenant he had known in the 1960s in San Diego. I have been so fortunate to have met many of the people who have become cultural icons of twentieth century America. Curious and ironic paradox, that, because I have so often been considered an *icono*-clast and those I most admire have had the same revolutionary, radical mind-set. Our fragmentary beings co-constellate a psychic and cerebral mosaic which some can observe as a higher consciousness, a supra-real *geistgeschicte*. We all radiate and broadcast a stink and dangerous high-voltage charge of what Erasmus (*In Praise of Folly*) called "benevolent madness" and others acclaim as something akin to Dionysian dervish dynamism.

I remember meeting, quite by chance, in the lobby of a movie theatre, Stewart Brand, one of the primary editors, along with Kevin Kelly, of

The Whole Earth Catalogue, and I told him the same thing: "Thanks." However, I was more effusive in my expression of gratitude when Michael McClure took me to a private screening of a film made by Clay Wilson whose cartoons, explosive and also iconoclastic as R. Crumb's, 'Fritz the Cat,' had become favorites of mine. Wilson's portrayals of clashes between the Hell's Angels and his cartoon creations, 'Big Bertha and her Dike Motorcycle Gang' in which male and female genitalia – penises, scrotums and breasts – were sliced off bodies and flung about the page in a dazzling dance of death, delighted me as nothing I had consumed since first encountering certain equally delicious passages of Baudelaire's, *Fleurs du Mal*, or Comte de Lautreamont's *Maldoror*.

Wilson's film was a tongue-in-cheek, mock documentary portraying a professional percussionist named "Bongo" Wolf (his preferred instrument being the bongo drum which he carried with him everywhere in a special hamper). With a sort of suburban magical realistic touch worthy of Peter Bogdonavich, the opening scenes were in the home kitchen of Bongo where his frumpy mother fed him a peanut-butter sandwich with a large tumbler of milk, asking politely when he could be expected home from work, to be answered that he was to play an all-night session *again* in Oakland. He was warned in a maternally appealing manner that he was to be sure to have a good supper and try to have some milk at hand on the band-stand by his station. Bongo assured Mom that he would take good care of himself and would not become fatigued or malnourished; he showed her that he had a pocket full of Reese peanut-butter candy bars and some Tootsie Rolls.

We then observe him walking out the front door on to a sidewalk and strolling along well-manicured suburban lawns to the covered bus stop on the corner. Then from our P.O.V. [screen-writer's abbreviation for Point Of View] we cut then to him sauntering along a littered and menacing side-walk in a city. He rings the bell at one of the storefronts and enters. There are a few people in the rooms we observe [Interior Shot] but there are posters on the walls which proclaim that this is the headquarters for the 'Vampire Society of America.' Bongo reaches in the side pocket of his crumpled and ill-fitting sports jacket, pulls out what we then can see are a set of false teeth with prominent canines that appear to be fangs, and his upper lip does not quite cover their protrusion as he stuffs them into his mouth. He speaks to the secretary whose back has been to our P.O.V. (Point Of View), and as she turns from her typewriter, we are shown that she also has a set of protruding fangs. As Bongo enters a larger room, which is furnished with easy chairs and a couch-sofa, we observe other normally dressed, ordinary-looking people, but all wear the fangs of the "undead" vampire breed. This Establishing Shot then Segues into Bongo leaving the building, boarding another bus - *sans* fangs - and we then watch him exiting his transportation and walking across an empty parking lot and up a wide loading dock which approaches stairs leading into a huge warehouse. An Interior Shot shows us a stage with sound equipment and theatrical Kleig lighting which Bongo approaches, climbs up onto, and then seats himself at a station which appears to be so familiar to him that he seems to be absorbed by it and appears in a state of complete relaxation. He removes a set of bongo drums from the hamper that he had slung over his shoulder, and attaches them to some other drums and percussion equipment that is fixed to stands which are easily within reach of his extended arms as he is seated in this *station* surrounded by other *stations* which have musical instruments attached. A saxophone rests leaning against one chair while guitars stand at attention alongside another.

Bongo again slips his hand into his jacket pocket, and lifts the dentures to his mouth which is wreathed in a broad smile as he allows the fangs to project his glowering smile to the still otherwise darkened and empty warehouse auditorium. His hands reach out as a lover would to his lady's projected breasts, and as his fingers begin a rapturous tapping on the bongos. His entire body appears to become filled with a new muscularity and an energy that expands and builds to what then becomes a frenzied, ecstatic engagement with his instruments, his art, his orgasmic, musical fulfillment. His head tosses up and down, then twists in rhythmic resonance, and we can see that the veins in his neck are standing out like knotted sinews, as are several across his forehead. His mouth grimaces as if in a bestial feeding frenzy, and the fangs flash out with menacing ferocity. Bongo has become Wolf, a lycanthropic transformation, a transcendence to a metaphysical plane, a *persona* unlike some of the bigger-than-life fearsome characters and caricatures for which Clay Wilson has gained so much fame and notoriety as a cartoonist who portrays the altered states of mind derivative of the psychedelic new world of San Francisco's 1960s.

Michael McClure was welcome at all the most *avant-garde* performances, exhibitions, and screenings in the Bay area, his fame lasting long after his first performances of 'The Beard' at John Lion's Magic Theatre in Berkeley in 1967, that shocking dramatic presentation of the encounter of Billy the Kid with Jean Harlow in Hell in which the serial killer psychopathic teenage outlaw legend played by Rip Torn, enacts a performance of cunnilingus on stage to seductively subdue the platinum blond former Hollywood mega-star. This block-buster of a theatrical enactment of such a sexual practice, coincided with Mario Savio's Free Speech Movement notoriety on the campus of the University of California, just a few blocks down the street. Not since the Third Century in Athens, when the Dionysian rites of phallus worship and indulgence in excessive carnality were the epitome of theatrical presentation had such sexual license been delivered to audiences. McClure was considered then to be the savage young Turk of American theatre. John Lion's venue in Berkeley had derived its name from Hermann Hesse's work in which there is an advertisement: "Anarchist Evening at the *Magic Theatre*, for Madmen Only. Price of Admission - Your Mind."

Sam Shepard had also been one of the earliest playwrights to contribute to Magic Theatre, but Michael McClure's works were the best known and became a virtual signature of the attitude of the productions: 'The Cherub,' 'Meat Poem,' 'The Charbroiled Chinchilla,' 'The Pansy,' 'The Brutal Brontosaurus: The Shell,' 'The Authentic Life of Bruce Connor and Snout Burbler,' 'Spider Rabbit,' 'The Pussy,' 'The Feather,' 'The Growl,' and a few others that were part of a series entitled 'The Gargoyle Cartoons.' Lion's first production had been a play by Ionesco and he followed McClure and other California writers into the realm of some of the new, visual realities of Clay Wilson and R. Crumb.

I was becoming alarmed with the notion that my own life was being confabulated beyond my comprehension, and it was after another mini-sabbatical in Mallorca, residing in Galilea in order to be near the poet and William Blake scholar, Ruthven Todd, that I assembled and edited my first collection of poems, *What Next: What Next*, and I returned only to visit San Francisco once more, only to then discover that I might be dying with some exotic liver disorder. I had not felt extraordinarily ill, but I noticed that sometimes I was overly tired and occasionally nauseous. The first medical doctor, who noticed my altered state, was a general practitioner, who did laboratory tests of my blood and then sent me to a specialist, a hemotologist. Then the two concurred that I was suffering from some liver disorder that could prove fatal if I did not stop drinking immediately. My liver was acutely damaged, and my physical condition was degenerating daily. I bid farewell to McClure and Brautigan, saying that I had to return to Oklahoma to attend more closely to consolidating and paying off the debts of my father's estate. I told Anne Zinn, my girl-friend who had spent the winter with me in Mallorca and who had designed the cover of my book, and who was probably the most sexually satisfying women I have ever known, that I no longer loved her and that I had decided to make this farewell final. She accepted my decision, but protested that she would always love me. She probably does. I did not want her to linger and languish and try to be my attendant as I lay dying, for the doctors had told me that I could not expect to live for more than a few months. Stark. Dark. Bleak. And not much more to look forward to. But I could not bear the idea of anyone, especially a loving and steadfastly, loyal comrade, such as Anne Zinn, having to endure the death throes or any of the last agonies I knew must be part of the *casting off of this mortal coil.* I decided to settle back in on the farm where I had spent so many happy moments when a young boy. I would prepare for my demise. I even idled some time in the Wright Cemetery. I found that one of the neighbors had been attending to its upkeep. The grass was mowed, and there were no brambles or bushes cluttering the plots. There were still spaces available for a grave, and my remains would be surrounded by those of at least twenty of the earliest settlers in this region from 1889, the official opening of the Cherokee Strip.

I bought a fifty foot long house trailer and moved it onto a plot I had cleared next to the largest pond on that farm, one that was next to a huge stand of trees that was the property of our nearest neighbor who had not resided in the area for over ten years. Alvin Fisher, the resident farmer, helped me to dig a pipeline of almost a half mile in length from his well at the old main house down to my trailer site. I had used a Ditch-Witch to dig the lengthy pipe-line, riding the machine and goring out a hole over three feet deep, feeling like a monster-mole or some clay-chewing omnivore, and was able to share the experience, riding that apparatus with Edward Ruscha, the artist, whose works were beginning to make him world-famous. His painting of the huge Hollywood sign had been purchased by Dennis Hopper, and many others were grabbed up by actors like Arnold Schwartzenegger, and since that time, his prices per canvas have risen to $500,000 to a million each. Ed was in Oklahoma City at this time visiting family said that he loved riding the pitching machine, and I am still expecting to see some of his artistic work to be inspired by this experience. Once when I was about to travel to Los Angeles, Ruscha had asked me to scrape up at least a pound of dirt from around home-plate on the baseball diamond at his former elementary school, Putnam Heights, and to also purchase and bring with me six packets of 'Redman' brand chewing tobacco. Later, I learned that he had used both substances, to paint canvasses, as tribute to some of the particular elements that had been part of his youthful developmental menu. The dirt from the baseball diamond embedded in his skin and clothing from his childhood baseball games and the chewing tobacco, one of his first experiments with adult substance abuse – we all tried a *chaw* or two, to emulate the behavior of many of our favorite baseball players of that time.

During this last visit to California [perhaps forever], I had made contact with two of my favorite former students from La Jolla Country Day School: Larry Ness and Kent Trent. Larry was living with a woman who had divorced her film producer husband who was responsible for many of the mindless 'Gidget' surfing films of that period – "itsie-bitsie-teeny-weeny-yellow-polka-dot-bikini" bimbos of the beach being the main allure of these formula soft-core porn picture shows. Larry could do little more than carpentry at this time, suffering what then became fashionably known as Post-Traumatic Stress Disorder, but he was eventually diagnosed by the V.A. (Veterans Administration) Hospital as suffering from a Clinical Depression, resulting from his several years U.S. Army active duty in the Viet Nam war. His girl-friend was most sympathetic; she loved him deeply. His carpentry did not provide anything like a substantial income. He would craft custom-design pieces for the few who knew him and special ordered his work. Larry was not approachable on any comfortable level any longer. I had risked violating several laws changing money orders for him to transfer in to gold to provide for the family of his Vietnamese wife, May, who remained in that country when Larry returned after the war.

Ben 1947

Briggs Mechanic Guy

Magneto Man 1914

Wright Family

Gibraltar Straits

50 cal. Ben

Captain

Poet

Perico & Ben

Rex & Ben

Sir Roddie

Bob Close

Janet

Francois & Pablo

Maya

Anna

Married Couples

Saskia's Birthday

Maya in *Merddin*

Commandant Wolff

Brautigan

Morrison

Dr. Villaescusa

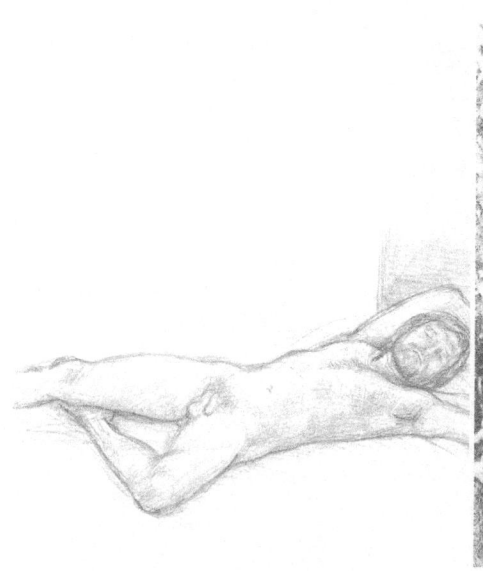

Charcoal Life Drawing
by Saskia Deboer

Funeral Pyre

Sarong

Bull Sarcophagus

Picador   BB & C

Sketch   in Madrid   Alemana

Boogie Street

Aide to The Czar

Jay Bernstein & Ben

Beckett & Cluchey

I do not know if they ever divorced, but I was told that their child had died in infancy. Larry did not care to discuss any of this. I learned it mostly from his best friend, Kent Trent, who had been able to avoid the Army draft with a valid Conscientious Objector certification, but then he had *wounded* and virtually *crippled* himself with some misguided experimentation with L.S.D., as had so many other young people of this epoch. Kent had subsequently traveled abroad, and by the utmost happenstance, had encountered a friend of his family's Christian Science community who had become a successful feature film-maker in London. Michael Laughlin, an heir to a few million dollars, who was a close friend of many of the few members of the Christian Science congregation in Rancho Santa Fe where Kent's family resided, had begun producing films in England and South Africa, but had recently returned to Hollywood since his marriage to Leslie Caron, the star of 'Gigi' and co-star, with Gene Kelly, of "An American in Paris.' She was also an ex-wife of Warren Beatty and had borne two of his off-spring. Kent wanted me to meet this couple and was anxious for me to work for Laughlin on a film he was currently producing. Unfortunately, when we did meet, I found the young producer to be a pretentious bore, and I did not like him, but I was fascinated by his wife, that lovely French dancer, Leslie Caron, whom he had taken away from Warren Beatty. On the afternoon we met, Laughlin was shooting a film, directed by some young Hungarian whose name I have long since forgotten. However, he was keen on the idea of filming actors as they improvised their lines and created corresponding interaction, and I was invited to play opposite Leslie Caron in a scene which was to occur in a movie theatre while we sat together and discussed what we were seeing onscreen. The film was the adaptation of Kurt Vonnegut's, *Slaughterhouse Five*, one of my favorite novels.

I had no trouble making conversation with my *co-star* as we sat next to one another. I told her how the novelist, Vonnegut, had waited many long years before he felt he was able to write his own version of what happened in the Second World War, that he, like the protagonist, was a teenaged boy who had been captured at Bastogne by the German Army when he was serving as a Private in the United States Army. He had been captured as a Prisoner of War and was interned in Dresden, Germany, where he was incarcerated in a subterranean meat locker (thus the title, *slaughterhouse*) deep below the streets of this ill-fated city which was fire-bombed, killing in one murderous air-raid as many people as were later exterminated in the bombing of Hiroshima by the atomic bomb. Vonnegut had, at first, wanted to write an adventurous epic fictionalizing his experience, assigning himself a swash-buckling heroic role, but finally he decided to attempt to tell the horrific truth of his grim experience when he and his fellow prisoners were brought up above ground, to the incinerated city, and were put to work packing the charred human remains into body bags, or in many instances, just plowing them under into the earth in mass burial sites. Vonnegut had compared the senseless waging of war by ground infantry troops to the Children's Crusade in the Middle Ages in which children from all over Europe were incited to march off to the Holy Land, many of whom were to be sold into slavery to North Africans who met their boats from Marseilles at their ports in Algiers or Tangiers. All rather ugly facts from seven hundred years ago to the present, concerning the disposal of superfluous unemployed youngsters in the martial machinery always available to gobble the disenfranchised and hopeless. I was blithely yakking away, and Leslie had to tug at my sleeve to allow her to participate. She was, after all, the star, and I was merely a wandering minstrel who just happened to be introduced by Kent Trent as a rather bizarre character who might liven up this particular shot.

At dinner, to which Laughlin, Caron and Truog invited me, I felt that my brain was being picked by the two film people. They were interested in the time I had spent in Mallorca and told me that they had been negotiating with the French government to develop part of the coast-line of Sardinia as a more culturally representative plan than had been done by greedy touristic promoters in so many other parts of the Mediterranean. They asked me who I thought would be an ideal architectural supervisor for them to use as a consultant. I recommended the team that had planned the Salk Institute in La Jolla and gave them the name of the husband of a former University of Pennsylvania sweetheart. I knew that this architect had been brought from Philadelphia specifically to be connected with the designing of the institute and had been intimately involved in the final building, for the past several years. When I subsequently returned to Oklahoma to begin my preparation for what I had then to presume would be my demise, I received a telephone call from Kent Trent who told me that my suggested design consultant idea had been partially fulfilled, that Leslie and Michael had met the Salk project team and had offered them the job, and that I was to be granted the position as a consultant with the title of Poet-in-Residence, at a salary which I was free to name. I demurred, of course, most reluctantly. I could not begin to say, "Sorry, I am busy with dying. Some other time, perhaps?"

What does one say? I spoke with Anne Zinn on the telephone a few times, trying to comfort her for the ultimatum I had laid down regarding the impossibility of our ever being together again. She was pleading to join me in Oklahoma where she had accompanied me in my first public reading of my poetry a few months before at the Contemporary Arts Foundation, directed by J.R. Witt. She had become close friends with J. R. but she had also crossed swords with Alfred Golding, the multi-millionaire heir to the fortune his father acquired by registering the patent for the grocery cart, which he had purchased for a few hundred dollars from an employee whom he the fired [so many fabulous fortunes based on deceit and fraud – the Hoover and Singer sagas are similar]. As they were both Jewish, she could slam his pretentiousness in ways I had never seen any other woman dare, or *succeed* in delivering. When we first entered his "bachelor pad" apartment which occupied the entire rear portion of a motel in the city alongside thay famous American highway known as Route 66, she remarked on his conscientious affectations of what was supposed to be the *Playboy* magazine's Hugh Hefner architectural ideal: "How unique! Authentic Jewish Renaissance!" she crowed derisively.

Our host, Golding, was not pleased by her humorous barb. He reacted by telling her all about the Henry J. Kaiser estate that he and his brother, Montgomery, were negotiating to purchase on Waikiki Beach, in Honolulu, Hawaii. He then carried on bragging about how they had bought a DC-10 to ferry their polo ponies from an airstrip near this new island home to any part of the world, so that they could compete in polo matches with crowned heads of many kingdoms and empires and sheikdoms. She responded by remarking on his coiffure, saying that his latest attempt at straightening out his kinky curls had failed miserably, and thus, we were invited to leave. I had not bothered to try to heal this rift since returning to Oklahoma City, and when Anne asked me if I had seen any of our fiends, Al's name was not mentioned. When I said that I was told by other friends of mine, that Al was now managing to hold an Oklahoma City version of orgies in his "pad", we began to reminisce about our own experience of this popular phenomenon of social interaction, or more appropriately, *intercourse*, in Mallorca.

I had known Bill Matthews who was the editor-in-chief of the pornographic novel industry when he had arrived in Terreno when I was involved with establishing the American Community School, and when Robert Stratton arrived in Galilea, needing room and board and desperately in search of employment, I introduced him to Matthews who had taken up residence in one of the palaces built by the Archduke Salvatore along the coast-line between Valldemossa and Deya. Bill was offering contracts to write hard-core pronographic novels, which would pay a few thosand dollars upon completion and acceptance by the publishers who were owned by the Mafia, or some equally sinister branch of International Organized Crime. Robert found that he could crank out a novel in about a months time and became quite proficient at the craft. He offered some piece-work to Patrick Meade who was living with his wife in their home,'Can Cid', in Galilea; however, this proved later to stir up trouble within the Meade's household, as Patrick's wife suspected that his visits to the palace in Deya were more than merely instructional in the editorial sense - Patrick had begun to attend the orgies that Bill Matthews considered essential, not only in the training of his writing staff members, but as an enhancement for his own decadent voluptuary proclivities.

Bill was an ex-convict who had served time at San Quentin and other similar institutions (California Men's and Chino) for drug-dealing in California, and he was a man who wanted to catch up on all the sensual delights he had been deprived of by the draconian, criminal-justice system. When Patrick's wife discovered her husband's infidelity, and flagrant sexual indulgences, she brought legal action against Stratton, for leading Patrick astray, and against me, for being Stratton's mentor. She denounced us both to the Guardia Civil. In the time of Franco, a *denuncio* could be most damaging. Under

Napoleonic law, which was the basis of the militaristic totalitarian rule of the Fascist State in which we were then living, one was *guilty until proven innocent*. Therefore, Robert and I decided to leave Mallorca, as our pleadings with Patrick's wife were of no avail in staunching her venomous resentment for our having introduced her husband to the orgies, even though his wind-fall work with the pornographic machine was now paying for their sustenance and more. I have heard it said more than once, "No good deed goes unpunished." We had pulled Patrick out of a desperate financial crisis and then were denounced as whore-mongers and degenerates. Some few years later, the marriage dissolved and Patrick found another woman, Stephanie, one with money and a magnificent home, who lived in Deya, and he settled in there ... to work no more. They pursued their mutual hobby of musical performance – Patrick claimed to have attended Juliard School in New York, but then, every word he spoke was questionable, and his brain had become so jangled by daily smoking of hashish, that it was remarkable that he could contrive even this creditable credential for himself, or would feel a need to, as all his worldly needs where thenceforward provided for by a woman who adored him, and eventually bequeathed him [she died of cancer a few years after they met] a most valuable home in Deya to sell

However, before Anne and I pulled up stakes and departed for America, I decided to accept the offer to attend one of the orgies held at the Marivent Palace on the road from Valdemossa, just outside Deya. The only requirement for any man's attendance was to be accompanied by a female, and Anne was eager to see what could possibly be so intriguing about such a lecherous event. The path-way in to the grounds of the estate were protected by a huge wrought iron gate which was guarded by one of the servants that Bill had retained to maintain the huge gardens and to attend to the upkeep of this grand stone pile which was said to contain over twenty bedrooms, in addition to a huge dining room ... and even a ballroom. There was an enormous cellar in which stood a sarcophagus surmounted by an ornately carved marble statue of a young man – supposedly modeled on the ideal of Alexander the Great, astride a rearing horse meant to represent Pegasus – and it was said that within this ornate statuary crypt lay the body of the Archduke's last *amanuensis*, secretarial and personal confidante, a young man, still in his teens, who was said to have also been the lover of Salvatore, although the nobleman was usually of a decidedly heterosexual *bent*, and had also sired a considerable flock of illegitimate off-spring among the local female peasants in his feverish sexual licentiousness; so many residents of these Mallorcan coastline villages are blondes, whose lower lips bulge petulantly in the inimitable Bourbon genetic signature which belonged to Archduke Salvatore's pedigree stamp. The enormous cost and extensive artistic craftsmanship required to enshrine this young man's remains bespoke a regard of immense esteem from his employer and master, a greater memorial than for just a valued servant, obviously the deep and caring expression of a severely bereaved benefactor.

When Anne and I arrived, I asked Bill if we might go directly to view this special feature of the palace, and he was more than glad to take us past the ballroom and down the stone steps leading in to the region below the main floor. We glanced inside the large main arena (a space rather like a ballroom [one avoids a pun]), already filled with bouncing naked bodies whose squeals and shrieks declared that the orgy was already in full swing. Bill then left us, so that he could return to attend to his frolicsome crowd, and so, after paying our respects to the entombed deceased lover of the Archduke, we climbed from this sombre region back to the large kitchen and then followed stairs up another two floors to select a suite which we decided to make our eyrie bolt-hole sanctuary which we hoped was so far distant from all the riotous activities on the ground floor and in the area just one floor below ours, that we could enjoy ourselves, and perhaps even fall soundly asleep that night, without becoming embroiled in the rampaging rapine of the orgy itself. During the afternoon we slept, the quiet dreaming of two innocent babes, and then as the sun dipped over that calm Mediterranean sea, Anne nudged me and said, "What the *fuck* are we doing here? Let's go see an orgy! I can't imagine any of my U.S.C. (University of Southern California) sorority sisters have ever had such an opportunity ... or ever will."

So we *descended* - a most appropriate term - for indeed it was a *descent* into something that I have only witnessed one other time, several years later, when I was breaking away from the gravitational field of my last marriage in San Diego, and I remember feeling completely out of my depth, although, at the California orgy, I was standing in the shallow end of the outdoor backyard swimming pool, shortly after arriving, observing a couple performing what even the *Kama Sutra* might be challenged to describe, on and over and around the diving board, and I exclaimed my astonishment to the petite girl standing waist-deep next to me, when suddenly my penis was grabbed and *pulled,* and looking at her upturned gloating face, I yelped my protest, as she just calmly reminded me, "You are at an orgy, after all. What did you expect? If you want me to go down on you and suck you off, we'll have to climb out of the pool. I can't hold my breath so long."

So, that day in Mallorca, when Anne and I entered the central room of the palace, which was most likely designed as a ballroom or banquet hall for large numbers of more socially polite guests, we were taken aback at the dog-pile of bodies, writhing in a rugby scrum that appeared to be an orgasm/organism unto itself. We did recognize a few of the entwined forms: Annie Truxell and her long-time lover, Jakov Lind; Larry Watts, my former colleague in the American Community School; some Terreno, Deya, Soller, bar-flies; and even a couple from as far away as Puerto Andraitx. The remarkable feature was that any one or two of these people were attractive individually, but piled and ensnarled in this throbbing heap, they looked no more appealing than sausages piled in coils or gutted chicken carcasses bunched in the butcher's glassed market show-case. I did not know whether to politely nod to those I knew, whose faces were blank with sexual efforts, and what appeared to be strain, almost pain. Anne and I turned away together and headed for the kitchen where there were some *tapas* laid out on a large table, and we both grabbed large drinking glasses filled with what proved to be Sangria, laced heavily with brandy floaters. I was offered some dope in a pipe, and when I drew it deep in to my lungs, I could feel the power of the concoction rushing to my central nervous system, after only the first few hits. The man who handed the pipe to me said, "Only a few snorts are all you need. This is ripe Moroccan *culado* [meaning it had been smuggled in from North Africa in someone's *culo* (ass-hole, or colon)] laced with Black Afghani hashish, some speed (amphetamines) stirred in, and spiked with something to stiffen your rod: Strychnine."

When Anne and I had returned to our bed upstairs, my head was spinning like a *gargoyle ferris-wheel* [e.e. cummings's poetic phrase which I had not till that moment truly appreciated], and my visual perception of the room was a kaleidoscopic miasma, and Anne had become, for me, the most devastatingly luscious sexual vamp I could imagine – sinking my aching penis into her, and driving, driving, driving, then shifting into high-geared fucking, into a desperate place where I could not believe I could dive any deeper. I could not ejaculate, and as I pulled out, my dear friend Anne sucked and pulled my cock, massaged my balls, and stuck her fingers far up my rectum to chide my prostate to release my load. So this was Strychnine? Some men have reported being bent so far backwards with that penile frenzy that seems to refuse release, that they almost shatter vertebrae in the spine. I felt that I was being broken on a Medieval rack and that my limbs were tearing asunder; nevertheless and notwithstanding, my comrade-in-arms, my stalwart fuck-buddy, Anne, finally relieved my agony, and the orgasm I experienced was a flood that would have daunted Noah or Captain Nemo. We slept; but at dawn, we left that palace of degenerate delightning and drove back to the welcoming and familial embrace of the mountains of Bauza and Galatzo, in our sweet shepherd's sanctuary of Galilea.

So it was with many fond memories of Ann Zinn, and some deep regrets, that I settled into the trailer I had anchored with steel cables to the bank of the pond at the southern end of my farm just outside Oklahoma City where I fully expected to die within a few months. Oklahoma has been called "Tornado Alley," and I had pointed the front end of my fifty-foot Airstream design rig in a Southeasterly direction, whence blew these devil storms, and I had taken the extra precaution of tying down each corner into a "dead-man" anchor, a cemented hole with braided steel cables to hold my home to earth when the winds should gust mightily. I painted the outer aluminum shell a pale blue, with black trim surrounding it, just as if it were the cover of my book of poems, *What Next*, black and blue, in the same layout. I told people the book cover was my life in retrospect: black and blue, bruised and battered ... *but unbowed* [an obvious play on that redoubtable poem 'Invictus' (Nelson Mandela's favorite, as well)]. Who could ever forget that refrain, [my] "head is bloodied but unbowed"? Therefore, to tell Anne again by telephone that she was never welcome in Oklahoma City, especially not ever to come in to my bed or receive my embrace ... this sexy, passionate playmate of my last gambol in Galilea, and that orgy!

After Bill and his crew evenjtually vacated that palace, a year later, there was a woman who moved in with her drug-crazed son, who stabbed her to death - something like thirty-nine times. Why do they record such exact measures of frenzied assaults? Why do we want to remember the exact numbers? After this incident, in combination with the reputation this mansion, as a center of the Mafia's European production of pornographic literature and as the scene of many extravagant orgies, the price for rental of the palace, with its vast gardens and with the gardeners' maintenance work included, was no more than a pitiful few hundred dollars (I heard it rented, with gardeners and utilities included for $425 per month). Patricia Luker, the widow of the U.S. Navy commander who had died of a heart attack on the toilet in "Bar Hawaii' (Paseo Maritimo, Palma, Mallorca), leased the place. Patricia had pretended that her daughter, Diandra, was supposedly the illegitimate off-spring of Joan Miro, or, at other times, that the father had been Don Juan Carlos, the King of Spain, or Robert Graves; the sire was whomever seemed most impressive in whatever situation Patricia Luker occupied at that time she was attempting to impress someone with her braggadocio. She took Diandra to the Presidential Inauguration ball of Jimmie Carter where she introduced the dim-witted child as being a Spanish princess, and the daughter more than made up for her ignorance and minimal I.Q. by performing as a pathological liar almost as adept as her mother. The two women currently were residing in the Marivent Palace of Valdemossa, Mallorca, and Michael Douglas, who was attending this event in Washington D.C. with his best drug-using buddy, Jack Nicholson, fell for the scam so totally, that he married Diandra within the next few weeks, and then spent a small fortune in fabricating a pedigree in Spain to prove to the world that he had, indeed, married a *royal.* She bore him a son, Cameron [later sentenced to a prison term for manufacture and sale of illegal drugs], and then Diandra ravished Douglas in a divorce suit to win over thirty million dollars, and she then settled in to a palace built with his Hollywood millions, near the original ill-fated edifice of the Archduke Salvatore on that same Valdemossa coast. Bill Matthieson, after he had vacated the palace, had bought my automobile, a flaming orange Fiat sports coupe which he ran head-on into a bus coming up from Palma at seventy miles an hour, killing himself, and crippling and disfiguring his girlfriend, Diana, eldest daughter of Carl Gay, Robert Graves' amanuensis.

When I had almost completed digging the half-mile long pipe-line on my farm, connecting the house trailer with the main farm-house water well, I remember turning the last spadesful of red clay in the trench over the PVC pipe three feet below, my body aching, not just with the foot-pounds of labor involved, but with the extra arthritic pain I had been experiencing throughout every joint of connective tissue. I had been consulting with the McBride Clinic in town where the doctors had prescribed a drug called Qualude to relieve the pains I had been able to barely endure with many long hot showers each day and handsful of Empirin Compound in doses women usually employed with severe menstrual cramps. I tried the new drug, and found that I felt so dopey - like my experience with Valium - so clumsy, that I continually was dropping things or bumping into walls, and the pain was merely muted, but still ranging through my entire body, and my cerebral cortex was aware that all systems were snarled. I told the doctor at McBride that I could not bear this prescription, and only later did I learn that I could have sold my dosage for enormous amounts of money to the drug-dealers on the streets, as this was becoming a favorite entertainment elixir of those who had used barbiturates and sleeping tablets mixed with amphetamines to achieve the effects of a relaxant with shrieking, hallucinogenic over-tones. I was satisfied with a daily smoke of some Marijuana which we called "Texas Tops," the best buds of cannabis plants from our neighbor state. So pain in every movement had become my daily fare. Although I no longer had to drive the shovel in to the ground; however, merely the minimal effort of lifting and tossing the clay clods lining the trench was a menu of self-inflicted torture.

Just as the air cooled one afternoon, when the sun approached the horizon and its leave-taking was about to usher in that dusky glow which the Spanish word *crepuscula*. Henry James tried using it once in declaring the *crepuscular*'s arrival – inadequately, and ineffectively – and the word stood out from the text of his novel like a putrescent sore [not a sore thumb (although Tom Robbins employed those manual appendages to startling symphonic effect with Sissy Hankshaw, that hitch-hiking diva, his protagonist in *Even Cowgirls Get the Blues;* that word would not be repulsive or painful enough) and the image does not render itself to analogic transposition. *Crepuscula(r)?* "It just doesn't sound right, Henry."

I rose (painfully) from my labor, held on to the shovel handle's tip, leaning against it like a crutch, and then I gazed up over the Blackjacks by the pond, toward the dam, behind which I could see the tall full crown of the old oak that stood higher than any other tree in the immediate landscape, and for some reason, I began to chant the sort of sad keening that I associated with Indians gathering in Pow Wow, and more particularly the peculiarly reassuring over-tonal resonances sung for me by my grandmother, Eliza Rogers Wright, when she had combed out her long black pig-tailed hair into torrents of cascading tresses flowing over my five year-old frame which she had encircled and enthralled with her witch-woman spell. I then thought words that I did not speak. 'Am I going to die? Will it be here on our land? Be it your will, that it be so, that it comes to pass ....' or thoughts to that entreaty and purpose. Essentially I was asking ... 'Will I die soon? Do I need to die?'

This reverie was shattered by an explosion. Like a crack of thunder, I heard it. But the sky was clear. Then I saw what must have made that thunder-clap explosion report. The top of the old oak was no longer visible. I knew, without seeing it yet, what had happened, but I ran to the top of the dam, and looked down on the shattered tree. The entire trunk had been split in two, *to'shivered*, as the expression was written in Medieval texts, for a spear shattered in the lists of a tourney in combat-of-arms between lance-bearing, jousting knights. The tree's fully leaved branches lay onto either side of the split, open, raw trunk. There was a sepulchral hush in the lot which had held this massive tree at its center. A phenomenon had occurred for which I could think of no natural cause. The sky was blue and clear, though the chill of dusk was now falling. But there had been no cloud containing lightning – yet a bolt from the blue had torn this mighty oak down.

I walked back to the trench and picked up the shovel. That would be all the work for that day. I felt that I had been answered. Had the tree died for me? Was this my redemption? Had my grandmother spoken?

I think so. I am alive today, and from that day on, my health regenerated and returned. The pains in my joints began to subside. The hematologist asked me what I was taking that had reversed my condition, that was indicating on all his laboratory tests of my blood that I was in remission of whatever had been killing me. I could not answer to his satisfaction, or really, to my own. I had been able to recall my grandmother combing her long black hair as a blessing shower over me as a small boy. I could remember the chant she intoned as she did so, and I had, on that particular afternoon, offered that same chant as my father and I had done so often together. But, for the life of me – and this clichéd phrase was most appropriate, given these particular circumstances – I could not begin to understand what had happened that afternoon by the pond when the giant oak had bifurcated, exploding with its self-demolition, as a signal report to me from Eliza Rogers Wright that it was not meant for me to die soon – I *think*. I do not *know*. Yet I do *believe*, now, that what happened was a sign that I was going to live many more years; and I have, for an additional four decades, or I would not be writing these words now, in my seventies. However, I can not explain any of this. But I hold on to it *for dear life* – another clichéd phrase that seems most appropriate, under the circumstances.

I had kept in close touch with J. R. Witt, director of a remarkably courageous project, the Contemporary Arts Foundation, a theatre, art gallery, and center, *genius loci*, for all the most *avant garde* artistic projects in Oklahoma City at that time. I had presented my first public reading of my collection of poetry in this venue, and I had arranged for Michael McClure to come to deliver a poetry reading there as well, this endeavor financed by Robert Franks, as so many of the more original and distinctive artistic projects of this epoch were. Robert was able to vicariously indulge in all the most radical activities by financing them, usually secretly, as his public *persona* as president of a major investment banking firm. Robert served as an officer on the board of directors on several other corporate bodies in the Southwest. He was one of the most effective fund-raisers for the Republican Party. I once heard him boast that he had raised $250,000 in a single afternoon for the visit of Vice-President Spiro Agnew, whose reputation was smeared some time before the Watergate scandal of his boss, Richard Nixon. J. R. Witt was on good terms with both sides of the political spectrum as he actively solicited funding for his foundation from all who would deign to support him. The National Endowment for the Humanities and Arts in Washington, D.C. has begun a project entitled Poets-in-the-Schools, and Talmadge Stands was the director for this program in Oklahoma. J. R. had recommended me to her, and she hired me to begin work with this experiment. Published poets who also demonstrated some teaching ability were paid $100 per day to visit in the public school system throughout the state. On a day's visit, the poet was to visit classes and then perform a short reading of selected poetry, often his or her own, for the entire assembled student body. The pay of $100 a day was most substantial at this time when the average wage of a school-teacher was little more than $5,000 a year.

My first job was to visit the state penitentiary at McAlester, because I had told Talmadge of work I had done previously in California in prisons and with the San Diego based Sinanon half-way house project begun by my friend Superior Court Judge Norbert Ehrenfreund. Sinanon was focused on those ex-convicts who had self-identified as alcoholics and/or drug addicts while incarcerated, who needed special therapy and required virtually monastic living accommodations when released and were still "at-risk" of relapse and recidivist behaviors. I was to be the pilot program director for Oklahoma prisons for the Poet-in-the-Schools project. I felt a bond with the incarcerated men who were in my class which we decided to call Creative Writing; it sounded more elegant than Basic Composition. Several of the inmates had brought their journals which were already full of reminiscences and their solitary attempts at narrative and poetry. I left these first sessions knowing that we would have a productive and exciting time ahead of us in discovering and refining some creative skills and developing mastery of written expression. When I reported to Talmadege in her home, I sensed a chill in her response. She thanked me for my report and then informed me that I would no longer be working for Poet-in-the-Schools, nor would I be invited to return to the prison unless I was willing to abide by some strict dress codes. I was startled, as I had worn a Brooks Brothers blue blazer and white Oxford button-down shirt complemented by a regimental striped tie: Ivy league university, or prep school uniform. She placed her heavily ringed hand to her chin and widened her mascaraed eyes and blinked as she said: "The beard. It has to come off. We have only clean-cut poets representing the National Endowment in American schools," she hesitated and then smiled archly, "Or in any institutions of instruction or rehabilitation paid for by our decent and clean-cut taxpayers."

I was shocked and amazed. My beard was relatively short, not shaggy. I maintained it at an overall length of a quarter inch with electric clippers, and my neck was clean-shaven. I protested that

Walt Whitman and many other great American poets had worn beards, and I even referred to Abraham Lincoln's decision while in office as president to cease shaving.. Talmadge just shook her head, would not respond, and escorted me to her front door. That was the last time I ever saw this woman.

I did not shave my beard and I began making inquiries about other unspoken strictures within this progam. I discovered that there were no women employed, nor were there any Native Americans or Blacks although these minorities were a substantial proportion of the general population of our state, Oklahoma, whose name translates as "home of the Redman' and is 40% Native American; and the Black/African American population is half that number. How had Talmadge Stands contrived to overlook this statistic – probably too absorbed in her other obsessions. I drafted a letter to the Oklahoma legislature and our representatives in Congress and the Senate in Washington as a protest of this exclusion of the appropriate proportions of minorities for Poet-in-the-Schools and began collecting signatures on a petition which had grown to a few thousand in the next few months. In the meantime, J. R. Witt had been approached by a couple of ex-convicts from McAlester who had heard about my visit from some of the inmates in the Creative Writing class. I had made a strong impression, and I was being invited to join the editorial board of an proposed underground newspaper, to be named 'Home Cooking,' which was being established by the ex-convicts. The editor-in-chief, and the actual publisher factotum, was a brilliant man who was called "Teach". He had taken up residence in a one room converted garage on Classen Boulevard, three blocks north of Northwest 23rd Street. When we met, I felt I was renewing a long-term friendship. We connected. We found ourselves laughing and hooting with glee at the notion of any newspaper that would challenge the dreadnought publishing and broadcasting monster owned by the E. K. Gaylord monopoly: The Daily Oklahoman; The Oklahoma Times; WKY- AM and FM and their NBC affiliate television station. The owners of the 'Kansas City Star' had once attempted to establish a competitive newspaper in the state, but they had been financially destroyed by Gaylord's ruthless entrepreneurial tactics verging on urban guerrilla warfare. No other newspaper had ever again dared confront the giant monolith still controlled by E. K. Gaylord, the original owner of Oklahoma Publishing Company, who at the age of 104 years still arrived at 7 A.M. every day in his offices in his multi-storied building at Northwest Fourth Street and Broadway in downtown Oklahoma City. We pledged ourselves to fell this dragon, or at the very least, inflict some wounds which would make him wince and maybe even whine

As I was still laboring under the assumption that I had only finite time left to me on earth, at best, a few months, and, as I had been proscribed from working any longer as a Poet-in-the Schools unless I sheared my beard, I decided to join forces with these men, and I became truly enthusiastic about tilting at the formidable nuclear-powered windmill of the Gaylord news-service monopoly. I was living on my farm in the trailer with a woman named Cynthia Newton whom I had met in the Canary Islands when I had stopped over there to visit with Larry Walters who had become attached to her in a *platonic* relationship - *so he told me at the time* - and in staying in touch with her by postal correspondence, I had learned about a disease she had developed which a doctor in the Canaries diagnosed as Brucellosis, otherwise known as Gibralter fever, or simply, undulant fever Cynthia had become seriously ill and destitute, and in desperation, she had she had gone to stay with a girl-hood friend who lived in Bermuda. I decided to meet her there.

When we met at her friend's home, we seemed to ed immediately and became passionate lovers, moving into a bungalow for the next week and rarely left the bedroom there. I brought her back to live with me on the farm, which was probably the most acute and severe alteration in life-style she had ever endured. Cynthia claimed to be a New York city debutante, to have trained in ballet with Balenchine, and subsequently to have become an instructor in Art History at Marymount College. She said that her father was a Wall Street stock broker and that her mother was a disillusioned, displaced member of the Russian aristocracy who lamented her social displacement in solitude with large doses of codeine and gin and refused to have contact with either her daughter or her divorced husband, Cynthia's father, who, himself, also refused to see his daughter and had cut off any financial support to her for a number of years before.

I fell in love. What a mission of mercy for me to devote myself to as I confronted my own impending terminal illness tragedy. Cynthia's disease called Brucelosis, named for the Scottish veterinarian who had discovered it and died from its devastating effects which attacked the central nervous system, and rendered its victims blind and paralyzed in the terminal stages. In the initial stages, there was constant dizziness and nausea and lassitude and exhaustion, all of which Cynthia began manifesting soon after we arrived in Oklahoma. Unpasteurized milk from infected cows was the usual manner by which people were infected with this disease, and Cynthia had lived on a primitive subsistence farm commune with some drug addicted hippies for several months upon her arrival in the Canary Islands. Curiously, the first doctor to diagnose and discover her ailment was a physician living in Las Palmas who had been famous as the indestructible medical practitioner who survived the Bridge on the River Kwai Japanese concentration camp which became well known as the film, 'Bridge on the River Kwai.' He had also become her lover, she later admitted to me, as if that were something she should be ashamed of. I considered her fortunate to have known such a man, and an even greater privilege that she had known him so intimately.

As a synchronistic surprise, at the same time as Cynthia and I had become cohabitants of the trailer on that frog pond, I received a telephone call from Edward Ruscha telling me that our pal from high-school, Mason Williams, needed my help. Mason had become so famous in Hollywood for his music – 'Classical Gas' is still heard on radios throughout the world, and several albums of his songs were produced and marketed with enormous success – and he had been the key writer of the hit comedy television show, 'The Smothers Brothers'. I had recently read an article in *Time*, stating that his yearly income from royalties on his music was over half a million dollars.

Why would Mason need my help?" I asked Ed. If anything, I might want to ask him for a boost in my career as a writer in the Hollywood gold-mine, and he could certainly take me out to dinner when he was next in town, at 'Christopher's,' Oklahoma City's exclusive *Cordon Bleu* restaurant where Ed's gay brother, Paul, worked as a waiter, and where no meal cost less than a small fortune.

Money was the problem, Ed told me, and Mason could not even afford to stay in a motel, much less buy a meal in a restaurant, not even at our Oklahoma fast-food, favorite, 'Beverly's', where "Chicken -in -the-Rough" (fried chicken with French fries served in a basket, cost only a few dollars). When I protested that I had just read in last month's *Time* that Mason was yielding over $500,000 every year from his musical royalties, Ed then told me an apocryphal tale which left me stunned, amused, and more than anxious to immediately provide succor for our devious, and benighted partner and pal who used to be expelled from high-school almost as often as I had been, when we were in our teens, usually for some brilliantly provocative behavior or performance, so like my own devious delinquencies, so that we had bonded as spiritually artistic soul-mates, when Ed had introduced us at that time.

Mason was flat broke. His accountants were working over-time in Los Angeles to remedy a huge rift he had recently torn in his fiscal fabric. He had just about bankrupted himself, and even with the royalties flowing in, the monthly payments allotted for his high-profile life-style in his Belaire home and his monthly accounts payable from spending sprees in Sunset Strip night-clubs and restaurants had just about toppled him from his prominent peak of affluent well-being. Here is what had happened, and because of the profligate perversity of my friend, I came to love him even more, and could truly call him brother.

Some weeks after the television program , 'The Smothers Brothers Show,' had been banned from broadcasting by an F. C. C. (Federal Communications Commision) ruling that their material was unfit for consumption by decent American households because of the radical political slant and implied sexual innuendo and salaciously suggestive implications of the scripts, and although Mason had flown to Washington D. C. to present a "Talking Blues" protest before the United States House of Representatives [he later confided in me that he had ridden First Class on an airplane, and was seated next to our boyhood, cowboy, film star, Roy Rogers], there seemed to be no way that this hilariously amusing program would ever be allowed to be broadcast on television again.

Mason suggested to Tommy Smothers an idea for what he deemed to be a karma repair-kit solution to their disappointment. Mason said that perhaps they had all become too financially secure, virtually, that they had become "stinking rich," and therefore could not claim to be dedicated and honorable artists. He reminded Tommy that their great poetic hero, Dylan Thomas, had always been poor and had died in penury.

Mason proclaimed his belief that they were therefore compelled to take extreme measures to recover their artistic integrity. They must become poor.

So the two "wannabe" poets, Mason and Tommy, drew out all their money out of their banks, in cash, which between them, amounted to about three million dollars. They packed this cache in denominations of hundreds, fifties, twenties, tens and fives, in the trunk of Mason's automobile, leaving a few boxes of the booty stacked on one side of the back-seat so that there was still room for a rider to occupy that area. The plan was to pick up hitch-hikers as they drove across the United States, offering whoever climbed into the car for a ride, to dip in to the treasure trove, to take with them whatever they could carry, often, many thousands of dollars. Their crusade did not even last till they reached New York City. Somewhere around Akron, Ohio, they had depleted their treasure so severely that Tommy caught a plane back to Los Angeles, using a credit card, and Mason spent some of the last hundreds to buy a pickup truck with a camper bed attached and set aside the rest for gasoline and food to carry him and one of the hitch-hikers whom he had not had any money left to endow, a girl named Peggy Jean, from a truck-stop cafe outside Canton, Ohio.

They arrived at my farm, and we had to take everything they brought in that forlorn vehicle two miles down 63rd and across the North Canadian River to the laundromat in the nearest township, Spencer, named unfortunately for one of the early settlers in the area who had proven to spawn an endless succession of degenerates and no-count swindlers. The other nearest townships were Witcher, with a population of three, that being a family that died out the very next year, and Jones, where a barbecue restaurant fronted for a notorious *hot-mattress-house* where only the most desperate would arrive for anything but the spare-ribs and beer served in the front parlor. We took Mason and his Peggy Jean on a short tour of these other towns while the wash-cycle ran and then returned to set the driers while we treated ourselves to the minimal offerings at the local Dairy Queen. Cynthia was still mildly startled by rural America, and Mason was reveling in reverie for his boy-hood spent in this rusticity. Peggy Jean was non-plussed and seemed to possess the attention span of a four year-old. Actually, it soon became apparent that Mason could have committed some federal violations (the violation of the Mann Act being the least of his offenses) and might be subject to any variety of prosecutions for his alliance with her, as it came to light that she was barely fifteen years old and was not even of an intelligence that would have belonged to a normal ten year old child. Cynthia was not as horrified as I might have supposed because she considered my pal Mason, himself, to be substantially sub-normal and a prototype of the Okie stereotype she had considered as type-cast for the television program, 'Beverly Hillbillies,' a portion of which she had seen once on our television set, and then demanded that it be removed from her sight, and the song 'Classical Gas' and 'The Smothers Brothers', both of Mason's authorship, were features as alien to her as a reference she once made in conversation - learning to *go on point* under the instruction of the famed ballet dancer, Balanchine - and therefore, as Cynthia performed some of her balletic exercises on the dam of the pond, speaking of her actual time *on the boards* as a dancer, she habitually baffled Peggy Jean, whose only notion of ballet might have been triggered by the sight of toe-shoes, which she might then suppose to be some punishing surgical dressing for ingrown toe-nails. Who knows?

Our time of living all together, lasted only for a week, after a a series of conversational gamuts that might provide the impression of comedic gag-lines with no lead-ins, or vice versa. Mason and I had a delicious time recalling our last few years and catching up on gossip about teenage associates. Cynthia spent her time posing and prancing in those dance gymnastics on the top of the dam while Peggy Jean occupied herself in chasing after cotton-tail rabbits and the butterflies and meadow larks that visited the wild-flowers in our pastures. Mason often sat on one end of the pond under the largest willows, with his guitar and a notebook, in which he sketched out new songs. One afternoon, he presented me with a copy of a song he said he had written some time before but had only now felt satisfied and now considered to be finished. It was a ballad about Oklahoma roads, the dusty meandering sort that lend themselves to sentimental rhapsodizing and heart-rending home-sick refrains. He offered it to me as a gift to my new pet project, the underground newspaper, 'Home Cooking,' and declared this to be his contribution to complement the artistic impulses of the ex-convicts from McAlester State Pernitentiary where, he then revealed to me, his own father had spent considerable time – that explained why Mason had lived only with his mother, a neurotic hair-dresser who had then flung him out at the age of thirteen, so that he had elected to move in to live till graduation from high-school, with our mutual pal, Edward Ruscha and his family.

Mason's fame was so enormous, and the song so lyrically appealing, that as a front-page feature for the first issue of 'Home Cooking,' every copy of an initial publication run of two thousand was sold by our long-haired street vendors who profited ten cents on each newspaper which we offered for only a quarter of a dollar. We were a "going concern" as the accountants would deem a self-supporting enterprise, and I was grateful to Mason for his e*ndowment.* Therefore, it was difficult for me to confront him shortly thereafter about an issue that Cynthia had brought to my attention, a health threat which we could not disregard. Peggy Jean had complained to Cynthia about a genital condition which Mason had assured her was a concomitant of her puberty, just a "growing pain," he had told her. The irritating speckles that had appeared along the hair-line above her pubic area, rising toward her navel, and seemed to be spreading, had itched so much that she was reaching in to the crotch of her jeans and scratching herself almost constantly. Having shown this condition to Cynthia with the ingenuous confidence of a girl trusting a mature sophisticated woman of the world, had not remedied her blight, and when Cynthia discovered some irritations appearing on her own lower belly, and told me about this mutual discovery, I immediately checked my own pubic bone region and realized that we had all probably been afflicted with the *crabs*.. Yep! Those nasty creatures that are usually transmitted by sexual contact with another who is a carrier of these insidious parasites which burrow in below the epidermis in the body areas covered by pubic hair. The treatment can be as extreme as shaving off all body hair and covering the skin with a tinctured ointment and then washing all clothing and bed linen and towels in boiling water. Every surface in bathrooms must be disinfected, and even then, there may be a chance that the hardy monsters will survive and re-infect. Peggy Jean told Cynthia that she had been suffering from this "growing pain" when she first met Mason in Ohio, but that he had assured her that it was something she would have to get used to and that it would be gone by the time she reached her sixteenth birthday which was still several months away.

I telephoned Edward Ruscha in Los Angeles and told him about what had happened, and he burst into laughter and told me that Mason always seemed to have a case of the crabs, and that once when they were room-mates, and he had discovered himself infected by this pestilence of Mason's, that he had taken all their linen and underwear, soaked it in boiling water, drained off the crabs and made a soup which he left on the stove, and when Mason came home and hungrily slurped up the deadly broth, Edward had the pleasure of telling him that he was gobbling up their pubic crabs. I doubt if the story was true, for it sounded .like one of Mason's own surreal narrative inventions, but I told Ed that I was unable to continue my hospitality with such contagiously infected house-guests and that I was going to give Mason his marching orders that very evening when he came in from town.

There were no histrionics, nor any recriminations, as I presented the ultimatum to Mason. He and Peggy Jean left quietly the next morning after stripping all their bedclothes off the fold-a-bed couch they had occupied in the front living room. I considered burning the infected linen but reckoned that I would place everything in the same boiling disinfected process at the local laudromat. I remembered my pal, Del Negro, the actor [the mad monk in Werner Herzog's 'Aguiira, Wrath of God'] once remarking about a friend of ours in Mallorca, being so filthy and so socially repulsive that he was rejected by the local laundromat. Cautioned thereby, I decided to visit the facility in Spencer *at twilight*

Mason was magnanimous and effusive in his expression of gratitude for my hospitality at the farm, and he presented me with a collection of all his albums and swore that he intended to repay me some day for my generosity and said that he was especially grateful that we had not made Peggy Jean feel shame for the discomfort she had innocently brought in to our home. I do not know if he explained to her exactly what her unfortunate condition was, and the two of them probably may have carried on with their mutual infestation and affliction well after her sixteenth birthday. However, I knew I would miss the company of my talented friend, but Cynthia later proclaimed that she was intending to demand his dismissal for continually calling her Cindy, a nickname she considered highly disrespectful and rude. Yet it was not long, thereafter, before she would desert me anyway - and I have never heard from her again - nor do I know where she went, other than to New York City. The Salvation Army contacted me several months later with an appeal from her mother, who had reported her daughter to be a Missing Person, and as I was the last known contact for her, I was requested to provide information as to her whereabouts. She had left me no trace or clue as to her next location. I hope she is still alive and well. *So it goes*!

Cynthia and I had not been exactly blissful before Mason's exodus, and I should have paid more attention to the signs that clearly signaled her dissatisfaction and desire to escape Oklahoma ... and me. Her condition with fevers and dizziness and depression resulting from her Brucilosis was exacerbated when we discovered that she was pregnant, as well. We arranged an abortion for us in San Diego, California. Cynthia said that she wanted to take this drastic measure, because even though she said that she loved me and that for many years she had been a practicing Roman Catholic, especially when she had served as an instructor at the Christian college, Marymount, she feared that the foetus would be irreparably harmed by her disease. There was no doctor who could convince her otherwise.

I tried reading to her from Brautigan's novel, *The Abortion*, before and after the event, but there is nothing that will amuse a lapsed Catholic about the murder of an unborn infant. Our love-making ceased after we returned from the critical surgical event in California. So when the executives of American Electric Ignition Company provided me an opportunity to leave for a week, I asked her if she would be bothered by my absence and she was enthusiastic in encouraging me to do so. The company had received a special award from the Auto-Lite corporation for selling over a million spark plugs that year, and the prize was an all-expenses paid trip by airplane to - ironically enough, Las Palmas, Canary Islands, where I had first met Cynthia - and the Sales Manager and Executive Vice-President were both pleading that I accompany this group to act as an interpreter and guide for the group consisting of all of our salesmen, both in-house and those on the road in our far-flung territory from Mid-Arkansas to the Arizona border, along with our best and most loyal customers who had purchased this gigantic hoard of automotive parts. These would be the warehouse distributors, clients whose association with American Electric Ignition stretched back to the original contracts my father had landed as Central Distributor of Auto-Lite in the 1920s when the owner of that stock was a professional gambler who had once been the pay-master for Pancho Villa in that Mexican revolution, a mercurial man who had won the controlling stock in a poker game, and was one of my father's favorite card-playing and drinking pals since that nefarious beginning as a corporate head of the major after-market manufacturer of ignition parts for Ford Motor Company. Johnnie Halliburton had also been a poker crony of Daddy, who said that the Texas oilman was the only man he ever met who was more ruthless and dangerous than himself. So there was the thrust of history demanding that I accompany our clients and employees receiving this bonus bounty, and frankly, I was growing weary of Cynthia's guilt-ridden mopery since that surgical procedure in San Diego. As I said before, there is no way to liven up or amuse a lapsed Catholic who has consented to and participated in an abortion, regardless of the grade of psychedelic drug or vintage of the wine offered after the blood-letting and flushing away of the infant's shredded body parts.

On the next to last day in Las Palmas, when I tried to reach Cynthia by telephone, as I had each day we had been in Spain, she did not answer my call. When I returned to Oklahoma and arrived at the farm, I was prepared to scold her for her lassitude, and then when I came in the door of the trailer, I knew she was no longer there. She did not even leave a note bidding me farewell. It was some days later that I received a telephone call from a man in New York who purported to be her companion. He actually attempted to blast me for her pitiful physical condition, accusing me of being to blame for her wretched health. I did not even attempt to argue. I merely stated that I still loved Cynthia and asked what I could do to help her, and I did request that she call me herself, if for no other reason that to allow me to bid her my fond adieu. This man told me that the best thing I could do was to send her entire wardrobe to an address he gave me and to send at least a few thousand dollars to pay the costs of her return trip and re-established residence in New York.

I did return the entire wardrobe (over fifty pounds in total weight) by U. P. S. and I sent a check for several hundred dollars, payable to Cynthia Newton. I never heard from her directly again, but two years later I received that inquiry from the Salvation Army asking for any information I might possess regarding her last known whereabouts, on behalf of her mother who had filed a Missing Persons report on her daughter. I felt somewhat lost and certainly abandoned for the next several weeks, and then Sylvia James arrived at my doorstep to tell me that she had fallen in love with me and was leaving her husband to move in with me and that there was a mystical certainty about this destiny because she was my poetic Muse and I was hers as well – so there!

I had also recently received a telephone call from California asking if I would not be delighted to have an exquisite dinner with fine Marques de Riscal rioja wine [Hemingway's favorite, as well as mine] followed by Napoleon brandy and a wild all night sexual romp with the one person who would always love me no matter what: Marian. She then went on to tell me that her live-in lover, a young film producer in Hollywood, had just dropped dead that morning, and after that, all she could think about was how I had always aroused her most lustful longings; and so she had decided to call and make a date for that very evening.

When I was certain that Marian was indeed serious about the death of her lover – and probably had indeed considered that the most reasonable solution to her present dilemma would be to rush to grab the one man she had always relied upon in any dire circumstances, and it had always been that in the most dreadful situations, that her champion, Ben Wright, that latter-day knight-errant, lance-for-hire, eternal soul-mate, would be steadfast and true, and on-call when needed. However, I was now reluctant to be her life-net, even with the inducement of the rich meal - whose accompanying wine and brandy I was no longer allowed to imbibe - and although I had pleasant enough memories of her as a sexual partner, nevertheless, I asked her to crank back to discussing the crisis that had triggered her reaching out to me. *Had her lover actually died?* Was it only that day? What had been the apparent cause of death? Where was the body of the deceased now?

As a practicing sociopath, a border-line psychotic, and pragmatist of fine acuity, Marian told me simply that they both had indulged in snorting many lines of cocaine and drinking much liquor the night before, and that when they had gained consciousness this morning that he had immediately begun the same doses of coke and booze before breakfast and then drank some eye-opening coffee. After he had snorted several lines and splashed several fingers of brandy in a snifter and quaffed this like a medicinal draught, he suddenly grabbed his chest, rolled back his eyes and keeled over, spilling most of this last loving-cup over the bed-clothes as he fell across Marian on her propped-up pillows, with a grunt and a gasp ... and then stopped breathing. He was definitely dead, and this had occurred only about a half hour before she telephoned me, catching me at early lunch-time, which was only about 10 A.M. in California.

I decided to take the adult parental role in this situation as I always had for my darling, demented, debutant, ex-wife. I instructed her in how to contact the police and coroner, to enlist the services of a local funeral home and to then proceed to provide for burial or cremation according to whatever his family and attorney had been instructed by her lover to do in such an unlikely event. She promised to follow my advice to the letter, and only a few hours later, she telephoned to report that she had carried out my instructions. In the next week, she called to let me know how mindful she had been of my counsel and that she was arranging for a celebratory wake to be held in their shared home after the funeral and interment. I did not hear from Marian for some time thereafter, and could only presume that all went according to plan.

However, it was not more than two months later that she telephoned again and began by screaming, "You rotten bastard. It's all your fault. I should have never listened to you. I'm pregnant now, and you're going to pay for the abortion!"

According to Marian, she was pregnant because I had advised her to hold the remembrance wake for her lover, and she had gotten herself so wasted on drugs and booze and had had sex with so many of her lover's friends during that event that when she discovered that she was pregnant she had no idea who had actually inseminated her, and so, as far as she was concerned, it was all my fault for proposing the idea of a memorial in the first place. In Marian's world, once a person's worth was used up, one merely dismissed the awareness of that person and carried on with pleasure-seeking and self-preservation. I reminded her that she still owed me that special dinner she had originally called to invite me to. That was as sociopathically attuned to her mind-set, as any other response I could come up with at that moment, and she began fumbling to argue that point rather than pursuing the demand for money to pay for an abortion, until I blathered on by telling her that I had some friends in Tijuana who were specialists in that particular surgical procedure, and as I began to describe where their clinic was located and how to go about reaching them, I then heard her go into retch reaction, and I knew that my darling debutante would not care to continue our conversation. Actually, I did not hear from her again till her next marriage, and then the two others, following that one, so that I lost track of her entirely, until many years later when I telephoned one of her aunts and was told that Marian had been found dead in her Pasadena home by the housekeeper in 1994. "I remember hearing your name", Aunty said, "You were one of the early ones."

One of the *early ones*? Did the aunt really refer to me, Marian's first husband, as one of the *early ones*? I suppose that was to be my place in the family memory bank. So be it. I have missed my fonder memories of Marian. By my bedside, I still keep a photograph of the two of us, posed in the cockpit of *Nacken II*, with Sam Coffing, when we were moored in that yacht harbor, Cowes, Isle of Wight, that summer in 1966. She and Sam are both dead now, yet at that moment they were the two most important human beings in my galaxy: Sam, my best friend and blood-brother; and Marian, my soul-mate and lover. Yet I have been fortunate to have many other close relationships, and as I was recuperating from Cynthia's most recent flight and abandonment, I received a telephone call from Susie Smith, that U.C.S.D. undergraduate who had accompanied me on my first trip to Mallorca, who had then left me for some Southern California surfer whom she met in Palma. Susie told me, now, that she had been living out of doors, following some John Muir ideals she had encountered in his writings about the grandeur and inspiration of the wilderness, and she was trying to discover herself by living in a tent and becoming one with Nature. She said that she was *centered*. I replied that I had heard that being *centered* was a desirable state of mind and spirit, and then found that I was having difficulty not yawning as she elaborated on her pilgrimage in order to attain this stable sense of identity. I often will flee any discussions of psycho-therapy or analysis of dreams, unless I could be enticed by some special stimulant into enduring such dreary and boring soliloquies. Susie was only worthy of such attentive listening when she was naked and actually in bed with me performing the sexual act with her horse-woman's sleek, sinewy body. She did not "give good phone" as some cynical people would refer to what was coming down the line to me. I did not ask her address or invite her to come visit, and I must have sounded as dismissive as I actually felt - so that I have never heard from her again; however, the next call I received was from another undergraduate woman, whose company I had enjoyed in Madrid a year ago and with whom I came close to being killed with, in rather dramatic circumstances, on an 'Air France' flight to New York City at Christmas.

Linda Paul had been on a Junior Year Abroad program with Eckerd College of Saint Petersburg, Florida when I met her in the company of Tom Entwistle at the night-club, 'Cuevas Sesamo,' just off Plaza Santana on Calle Principe. She had been playing some Hungarian rhapsodies on the bar piano in this nightclub situated in the cavernous basement one level below this street there, where many of the more politically radical and imaginative students met and caroused till early in the mornings. She claimed to be a Hungarian Gypsy, and as we seemed to have established an intense attraction, and Tom remarked that it was lamentable that we could not consummate our passionate inclinations in this oppressive fascist state under the oppressive rule of the still living ruling tyrant, Franco, I took this as a dare and asked Linda if she would come up to the street level so we could find a hotel where we could go have an hour of love-making. I bet Tom a thousand pesetas (equivalent of $20 in that year) that we could breach the moral restraints and pledged that we would return in an hour, to announce our triumph. We *did* find a receptionist in a nearby pension who accepted the fifty peseta (one dollar!) bribe I pressed on him and allowed us to check into a room where we made love twice in the hour, and then we returned to flaunt our flagrant promiscuity and collect the thousand pesetas.

Linda and I spent the next few days together and purchased tickets on the same economy charter flight back to the States: Madrid to New

York with Air France. We shared seats near each other, but I was placed in a position that proved to be most significant on that flight and was therefore the only passenger to be privy to knowledge of the disabled landing gear which would be cause for our plane to make a virtual crash-landing upon our arrival after crossing the Atlantic and spending the over six hours that the crew and officers devoted to a frenzied but surreptitious effort to lower the gear that had become stuck upon our take-off from Madrid's Barrajas airport. At first, I readily complied with the request that I move away with my seat-mate to allow the engineer to pull up the floor-board plates behind a screen erected to occlude any view by other passengers of the work at hand, but as I forced my way between the busy bodies around this site and saw what was going on, I told the engineer what I suspected was happening and he urgently bade me keep this matter a secret as he then informed me that we were planning to execute a controlled crash-landing when we arrived, but that our risk would be enormously increased if any more of the passengers - mostly youthful students who were blissfully unaware of anything but the impending Christmas holidays to be celebrated with their families in the United States - were to become aware of the imminent danger which we must confront in landing with only one landing gear intact upon a field that would be prepared with foam and rescue vehicles long before we set down. I pledged that I would keep the grim secret, and when Linda joined me in the new seat I was assigned farther toward the front, I told her only that my chair had become stuck, and as I could not adjust the recliner, that I was occupying this more comfortable position till arrival.

However, as we began circling Kennedy Airport some hours later and looked down on the field, now white with foam, which the festive passengers cheered, believing it to be a blanket of snow, and we observed many multi-colored lights around the runway - actually the alarm signals adorning all of the various rescue vehicles assembled to pull the injured from the probable wreckage – the delighted congregation of my fellow travelers roared their appreciation for the holiday spirits displayed in a brilliant mosaic spread below us, as we began our final descent into Kennedy, having purged all extra fuel above the sea. I had scribbled a short poem which I had wrapped in tin-foil from chocolate wrappers, and had pressed it to my chest beneath my tee-shirt under my dress shirt and had buttoned a vest over this to possibly preserve my last words if my body should be incinerated in the ultimate conflagration of an explosive holocaust crash-landing. This poem I included as the last entry in the collection of poems published the year after: *Runey Tunes*: "My last words / Were so angry / I could not hear / My last words."

Had I been able to employ rice paper and a brush with heavy black ink, this would have seemed more like the final verse which a Samurai *executes* in his last battle; I considered this a significant gesture, and a close approximation of such a sacramental act.

Having thus attended to my poetic *last rites*, I then approached the chief steward, a flushed-cheeked, *bon vivant* whom I informed of my cognizance of our impending fate and requested that we each hold a bottle of his best cognac, crooking our arms, intertwined, and imbibe in hearty gulps as we touched down [hopefully not an altogether euphemistic metaphor for our impending meeting of the runway with our disabled landing gear]. In the rushed next few moments as we rapidly descended, we did bound ourselves together in our mutual toast, and as the plane slid on to the runway ... and that wing with damaged landing gear dropped and dragged and shattered and ignited and sputtered in the dampening foam; and then the aircraft spun about several times before coming to a skidding halt, my French comrade-in-grog and I had swallowed almost a half bottle each, which, when we jolted to our stop, we both spat in a spray over each others shoulders. We were rolling about on the deck laughing and snorting, our limbs entangled in a ludicrous embrace which buffeted our bodies from the bulkheads against which we slammed back and forth before we finally could untangle and rise to survey our newly granted life-scape.

The aisles were strewn with debris, tumbled from the overhead racks, sprung by the jolting arrival, and the heads of the passengers were only beginning to peek upward from their *foetal positions forward-leaning crash-protective* crouches. I walked back to Linda's seat before anyone had unbuckled and risen to block my way, reaching over to plant a kiss on her cheeks which were stained with tears.

"Life in the fast-lane. Worth every ounce of adrenaline and even soiled undies. *La vida es un Tango. Tenga que bailarla*". (Old Spanish saying, "Life is a Tango. One must dance it"), I chided playfully. "Would you like to retreat to the toilet compartment for a celebratory shag here at Ground Zero?"

She nodded her head and suggested we wait till we disembarked and could find a hotel room ... which we did, as quickly as we possibly could clear out of the jumbled compartment. The staff were assembled at the exits to thank us for flying 'Air France' and expressing their desire that we join them again soon for another journey together. What *savoir faire*! What *elan*! What Gallic style! Viva la France!

We did indeed locate a hotel room with an adequate double bed, and so my last night with Linda was one of passionate excess, and I delighted in telling her how I had restrained myself, over our entire Atlantic transit, from revealing what I had known of that incredible impending landing, although I had become aware of the possible disaster soon after take-off in Madrid. I considered myself tremendously courageous and cool beyond any definitions of the heroic ... and also perhaps completely moronic to even consider such inane notions as these.

I did not hear from Linda again, for several months until I had settled in to the routine of the farm and my recovery from my supposedly fatal blood disease and liver malfunction and the relationship with Cynthia and the production of the underground newspaper, 'Home Cooking,' and my battle against the National Endowment for the Arts and the Humanities "Poet-in-the-Schools" program. I was delighted to have contact with her again and was surprised that she considered me her *one-true-love* after some eighteen months with no contact. She had written to the American Electric Ignition Company post office box address, and so I was delighted that we were again in communication. She had wanted me to come teach at her college, Southeastern Florida Presbyterian which had just recently been enormously endowed by the Eckerd Drug Company so that the name of the school would henceforward be Eckerd College of St. Petersburgh, Florida. The English Department chair-person was scheduled to take a sabbatical leave in the next semester, and so there was to be a temporary job opening as his replacement which would include the honorific and well-paid position of Poet-in-Residence, as well. She was convinced that I should have this appointment. The only other contender in serious bidding was an old friend, Diane Wakowski, whose published poetry was far superior to mine; however, my academic status was much more formidable than hers; my Candidate in Philosophy degree, the all-but-dissertation doctorate in Comparative Literature from U.C.S.D. far out-ranked her mere Bachelor's Degree from N.Y.U.

After Cynthia's departure, Sylvia James, a sexually extravagant and egotistical local woman, had left her husband of ten years, to move in with me and had convinced me that she also was dying of a rare blood disorder. Actually, Sylvia was so permanently zonked on combinations of L.S.D. and amphetamines which she had scored from a variety of former lovers, some of whom had medical and veterinary prescription writing privileges, so reality was only an occasional visitor to our new household. Sylvia was also an aspiring poet and had just published her collection of bromidic jingles which she was convinced were profound poetic inscriptions: *Heist Your Own Petards*. Regardless of her intellectual pretensions, her sexual performances were more than enough to satisfy my libidinal longings, and she also proved to be a formidable ally in the ongoing campaign against the National Endowment's flawed Poet-in-the-Schools programs [I learned, only a few years after this incident, that the director for the National endowment for the Humanity and Arts, with an annual salary of $250,000, was Professor Reynard ("The Fox," his own sobriquet, contrived from the Medieval legends, with that animal as the ideal of craftiness) Bormann, who may have helped engineer the spy ring for the F.B.I. in the University of California campuses which had destroyed so many academic careers (including my own) in the late 1960s] and we actively solicited many hundreds of signatures on the printed protests we had sent to the Oklahoma State legislature and to the United States Congress and Senate, which eventually did elicit the alarm of those in power [Bormann, in particular] ... and Talmadge Stands was told to resign as Oklahoma director for Poets-in-the Schools, and she was censured for what was finally deemed racially biased policies of hers by prohibiting African Americans and Native Americans employment as poets to visit schools in Oklahoma.

I was actually offered her job, but demurred, as Eckerd College had simultaneously invited me to take the lucrative post that Diane Wakowski turned down, which Linda Paul had so skilfully contrived to make available for me in St. Petersburg. In one whirlwind airplane trip, in which Sylvia accompanied me to raise awareness of the National Endowment struggle and the latest scoop news story which

'Home Cooking' had just delivered – a young woman had been mysteriously killed after she had begun protesting working conditions in Crescent, Oklahoma where the Kerr McGee uranium and thorium plant had been discovered to be poisoning employees. Karen Silkwood had been run off the highway by a hit-and-run driver, coincidentally as she had just gained national attention for her revelations about the murderous contamination of fellow employees by radioactive materials in her work place. A young professor, at a junior college in Edmond, Oklahoma, had Silkwood's partner as a student in his Creative Writing class, and he was able to help this woman carry her version of the possible assassination to New York City, where Mike Nichols was contacted and decided to produce this story as the film starring Meryl Streep as Karen Silkwood, and Cher, as that partner 'Home Cooking' had tried to get Associated Press, Reuters, and United Press International to cover the story but they dismissed our reportage. I had contacted Simon Winchester in England, and during a lay-over in the airport in New York, Sylvia and I had encountered Pete Seeger, who sat down with us and took out a guitar to play 'Osceola,' the lament of the Native American chieftain who had been cruelly imprisoned and died in confinement at protesting oppression of his people.

When I arrived in London to seek out someone to assist us in broadcasting the Silkwood story to the world, before I had located Simon Winchester – he had recently won Journalist of the Year" for his courageous coverage of the Belfast riots and the perfidy of the British authorities in their oppression of the Irish cause for freedom from the centuries-long dictatorship of these third-class citizens of the United Kingdom – I located Michael Horowitz who had come through Oklahoma on one of his American poetry reading tours. Michael had organized the first International Olympiad poetry festival at Albert Hall only shortly before, and his contacts in all realms of the public information world were formidable. I had organized a poetry reading for him at the Center Movie Theater in Oklahoma City as part of the midnight movie series which attracted all the street people of that epoch, and he had just minutes to deliver some of his poems before the feature film, 'King Kong,' covered the screen, and he was dancing about shouting his limericks on the dark furry belly of the cinematic idol monster, to the taunts and cheers of a stoned and drunk crowd of Oklahoma's alternative cultural assemblage. Michael stayed with Sylvia and me at the farm only for one night and then was provided a bedroom in the home of Paul Ruscha whose telephone Michael abused by calling all over the United States arranging more poetry reading gigs. When I encountered Michael in London, I took him to task severely for this devious deed which had cost Paul more than he could afford on his salary as a waiter. In courtly recompense, Michael invited me to a swank drinks party in the London neighborhood of Chelsea in what I was to discover later was the home of the grand-daughter of the famed symphonic composer, Gustav Mahler. I spent the night in bed with my hostess after she ushered all her other guests out the door, and I became a resident of her salon for the next two weeks and even for the week after that, while she was in Vienna, Rome and Paris. The name she used at that time was Marina Fistoulari-Glass (her biological father was the Russian composer and conductor, Anatole Fistoulari, and her former husband was the American musical genius, Philip Glass with whom she had lived for a few years in Poland). I only learned her relation to Mahler after meeting her mother, Anna, who lived in the Belgravia section of London with her husband Albrecht, once the *amanuensis* of the Nobel laureatewriter, Thomas Mann. What an irony that was! There has long been the rumor that Mann seduced Mahler and had sex with him on a Pullman coach traveling from Berlin to Vienna and that he had based his novelette, *Death in Venice,* on his memory of that homosexual interlude. Who knows? Who cares? Never let the truth get in the way of a good story, Ruthven Todd would have suggested snidely.

Michael Horovitz informed me that Rick Cluchey was hosting performances of the San Quentin 'Cage' in London (Hampstead's 'Roundhouse Theatre'), and I had attended a production of this all-convict theatrical work in La Jolla as a Sinanon project when I had been involved in that organization with Superior Court Judge Norbert Ehrenfreund when I had just begun doctoral work in 1965 at U.C.S.D. I had bonded with Rick from the moment we met as I had smuggled some beer back-stage to the performers. Therefore, I reckoned I could readily call on my old criminal pal and ask his advice about my nefarious underground newspaper project back in the States. I was both amazed and enormously pleased to discover the great good fortune that had befallen Rick and his theater company which consisted of convicted felons whose sentences had been presumably for life-terms, as many had, like Rick, committed murder. Only the most hard-core inmates of San Quentin had qualified for Rick's first stage-call tryouts. Rick claimed to have performed Samuel Beckett's soliloquy *tour-de-force* 'Krapp's Last Tape' for himself each day as he awaited execution on Death Row. When he received reprieve of his death sentence, he wrote the play, 'The Cage, 'a syncretism of the works of Jean Genet and Samuel Beckett which he then was allowed to perform before the entire prison population, to such acclaim and approval by the warden that the governor of the state of California, Pat Brown, was invited to attend a repeat performance of this play. Governor Brown was so positively impressed that he recommended that Rick's production company tour all prisons and correctional facilities in the state, and that is how I happened to first attend its performance for Sinanon in San Diego in 1965. 'The Cage' was then invited to be presented in prisons throughout the United States; and subsequently, it was performed in cities throughout the world: Paris, Rome, London, and in many other major metropolises, even in the Soviet Union. Eventually the proposal was made and approved that Rick and all members of his company be granted life-time paroles, contingent upon their continued involvement in the theater; and later, any theatrical occupation was considered an appropriate qualification for allowing these paroles to remain in effect

I encountered Rick at the Roundhouse Theater in Hampstead, London, and after the show, called on him in the dressing room where I was greeted as if I were a life-long friend ... all because I had sneaked some beer to these rascals back in 1965 when they were still under strict surveillance and in custody and still doing "hard time" at San Quentin. When I told Rick about 'Home Cooking' and our struggle to reveal the injustices oppressing inmates in the state penitentiary at McAlester, Oklahoma, and then related the incident of the untimely death – probably murder – of Karen Silkwood, and our inability to receive any attention or even notice from the news agencies of the Establishment. Rick pledged to lend his full support to our endeavors. Ironically, one of the young volunteers working backstage with Rick's group, was a student from the Webber-Douglass School of Dramatic Art, in Fulham, near my Chelsea Arts Club, who was a Junior-Year-Abroad under-graduate from University of California, Santa Barbara. This was Holly Palance, the daughter of my former acting pal, Jack Palance. When we went to a nearby pub for drinks after the show, Rick regaled us with a chilling tale of how he had almost been instrumental in the killing of Holly's father when Jack had been working in a film being shot in one of the prisons where Rick was incarcerated, before his ultimate tenure at San Quentin. Rick had planned with his cell-mate to grab the actor as he passed near them, and to hold a knife at his throat to effect their release and escape, and they fully intended to cut Palance's throat rather than risk his fierce resistance if he should have chosen not comply with their demands. The night before their intended attempt at kidnapping Palance, there was an arbitrary shake-down of all cells in their block, and the *shank* – Rick's slang for the knife-like murder weapon – was discovered and confiscated.

"So buy the rounds of drinks, Holly," Rick proclaimed gleefully. "Your old man narrowly escaped my evil *clutches*. The great beast Cluchey doth declare it so!"

Some years later, Holly appeared on television performing with her father, but by that time I was no longer in contact with the Palance family, so I do not know if she ever passed on that chilling apocryphal tale to her father. Rick and I worked out a strategy for attracting international news media attention to the dire prison conditions in Oklahoma, and it was Simon Winchester who actually arrived at McAlester State Penitentiary, and he also put the spotlight on the Karen Silkwood story, and it was only a year later that her family received a settlement out of court from Kerr-McGee in the amount of several million dollars for the unlawful taking of her life, and then the governor of the state was prosecuted for several of his illegal practices which had triggered the riots in the state prison which had resulted in the deaths of several inmates and guards. He was sentenced to serve many years in the new prison that was constructed there. This was indeed poetic justice, but too late to really alleviate the suffering that had been endured by so many convicts who had been inhumanly punished and died already.

Another form of justice was to soon be enacted, as Rick was only shortly thereafter to be *discovered* and *rewarded* by his great idol, Samuel Beckett, who attended a performance of 'The Cage' at the Roundhouse Theatre and then went backstage to meet Rick who had never expected to have such a miracle occur in this life-time. In the conversation between the two men, the story of Rick's eschatological swan-song performances of 'Krapp's Last Tape' on Death Row was so fascinating for Beckett that the Nobel laureate playwright asked him to deliver a private audition of this piece in the darkened auditorium of the theatre. Beckett had been obsessively curious about such lugubrious matters since he had pleaded to have the man released to his custody who viciously assaulted him and left him for dead in the Paris Metro some years before; the simple-minded homicidal criminal had no recollection of the event as he had been in alcoholic black-out when he attacked Beckett, and he spent the last years of his life working as a janitor for his mentor, Beckett.

When Rick delivered his 'Krapp' for Beckett, the creator of this *persona* applauded the rendition, declaring that henceforward, there would be only one actor in the the entire world who would receive his endorsement as privileged to play this role. Also, Beckett demanded that Rick leave whatever else was occupying him and come to Berlin to direct all Becket's theatrical productions from that moment on ... and for evermore. And thus were the destinies of these two men fulfilled. A Detroit , Michigan, Polish high-school drop-out turned semi-professional hit-man, ex-special forces United States Marine Corps private, who found himself on San Quentin Death Row reciting a soliloquy written by an Irish genius, had been wed by an artistic bond that would have to seem so extraordinary that I am surprised if anyone reading this narrative can begin to believe it. I do, and you have to take my word for it.

My next few months were also to prove so bizarre that I am hesitant to report what I *think* actually happened. Did I receive word of a contract on my life? Was it canceled by the intervention of a man whom I only knew in the most unusual manner and am not sure if my description of him can possibly be credited as reliably near to truth. Was there ever a contract paid to an Oklahoma City criminal family to have me murdered or shot so brutally that I would thenceforward be a quadriplegic basket-case and no longer a threat to whomsoever I had so offended that it was deemed necessary to move me off the playing board?

Dolores, a cocktail waitress and former high-priced call-girl who had been the female dominant presence as manager and hostess of the Night-Hawk private club in the Black Hotel, later, a semi-respectable cocktail lounge and supper club, which until the reprieve of Alcoholic Prohibition laws in Oklahoma in 1960, had been a "speak-easy" drinks lounge and front for the sex trade in the center of the downtown city. This formidable lady had been the confidante of lawmen, gangsters, legislators, judges, and anyone who decided what would happen and where anything would go in the state and even in the entire political network that was now controlled by the likes of the heirs to Louisiana's Huey Long machine, or the oil industry's heavy hitters, Johnnie Haliburton, Robert S. Kerr and Lyndon B. Johnson. So when I received a discreet telephone call from her asking that I meet her in the parking garage of the Black Hotel at mid-night one Saturday, I was scrupulously punctual and pulled in to the darkened drive, off the street, just at the stroke of that hour. I paid the attendant to hold my car as I approached the door at the side which connected to the exit from the club. Dolores was pushing the door open as I walked up. She motioned for me to take her to my car which we then drove back into the quiet city street.

Dolores told me that she could not reveal her source, but that it was indeed reliable, and actually was what she had overhead in hushed tones being discussed between two men at the bar as she was refreshing their drinks. My name was clear to her, and the reference was to a job contracted to a notorious Lebanese *family* who had arrived in our state after World War Two who had carved out a part of the gambling, bootlegging, and prostitution trade which they had wrested viciously from the Dixie Mafia who held territories in the Southwest, which the Detroit and New York Sicilians had never been able to grab away from local criminals. However, the Levantine cunning and relentless grappling for any scraps on the board, had enabled this family to now maintain an effective criminal business syndicate, and their work as contractors in killing and crippling were infamous for clumsy but hideous results. They were the cut-rate specialists in the field, doing jobs for half the price of the regular *mechanics*.

I was startled, shocked, and really offended that I should have been slated as a target for these grim thugs. I had known one of the sons at elementary school, and he was the nastiest bully on the playground, one who bit and kicked from behind, and once I had humiliated him in front of a targeted youngster he was attempting to subjugate. I had made this young member of that Lebanese family wet his pants as he yowled and bawled in front of the entire Fifth Grade there on the basketball court as I rebuked him and delivered retribution for his cruelty. Was this *boy* to be given the job, I wondered? What a small world!

I thanked Dolores and did not ask if I could give her any money for her courageous and compassionate gesture. She had known me since I first began frequenting her lounge back in the speak-easy days in the 1950s when I had often to drag my father out of his various venal entrapments with whores he had taken in to the hotel catacombs, and it was Dolores who many times assisted me in extricating him from some potentially dangerous situations with formidable pimps and outraged or damaged call-girls. We had bonded in a virtually familial manner, as I was then just fifteen, had not achieved my full masculine growth – this was shortly after my mother's death when I was still in the throes of awakening to my father's beastliness, and I was an innocent and callow adolescent – and Dolores had been like a big sister, or surrogate mother, and I think she felt a strong affection for me in the most filial sense, although her profession mitigated against any such involvements. She was truly worried that I might become a victim of this gang, and I assured her that I would take measures to protect myself.

There was only one person I knew to whom I could go for advice in such a matter. That was Jim Holly. There were so many tales about this man that his aura approached the mythic in splendiferous radiance, and if true, would be adequate warning to any sane person to avoid such an individual, unless accompanied by a U.S. Navy SEAL Combat Assault Team with additional special training by the best criminal forensic psychiatrists available. I had only once felt uncomfortable in the company of my pals on the original SEAL Team One in Coronado - however, I did squirm once when Max, the SCUBA Harassment instructor, after ordering a gin and tonic in our favorite Coronado Beach cocktail lounge, chewed up his cocktail glass, and then swallowed the bloody mess with a leering grin at those of us standing with him in that bar-room - and Rick Cluchey only caused me a shiver or two when he told of his tactical *enforcement* to achieve his position as *Bull* (that convict in command of all others at a penitentiary) in San Quentin, so I was slightly nervous as I rang the door-bell to Jim Holly's home in the most expensive real estate division of Nichols Hills, which was known as the Holly Development which was just below the Rose Hill Cemetery, that *final* residence of only the very rich in Oklahoma City, also a Holly property. The real estate and oil fields owned by Jim had been inherited from his mother, who was reputed to have been the mistress of Huey Long, the Louisiana governor whose populist political machine could have landed hm in the White House, and whose battles against the reigning old oil magnates on behalf of his downtrodden constituents, had made him one of the richest men in the South. Cemeteries were a prime real estate treasure, many of which Jim owned throughout the states of Oklahoma, Louisiana and Texas, along with vast tracts of city lots in all major cities of those states which were providing housing for the richest people in those areas.

Jim had also bought a hotel in Acapulco, Mexico, before such investments had become popular. He had developed this resort as a device to lure his Hollywood drinking buddy, Errol Flynn and his room-mate, David Niven from their dissolute lair in Malibu, California: "Cirrhossis by the Sea." In one of the more out of control binges these men indulged in, Jim had shot a Mexican National in the forehead with a .45 caliber pistol, and Phil Daugherty had to personally arrive in Acapulco to post bail and pay off the judge and police. Since that grim incident, Jim had to amuse himself by remaining in the United States. He was reluctant to travel in Europe, allegedly because he was still chary of some indictments that had spun out of the Nuremberg War Crimes Trials regarding his machine-gunning of Italian personnel – during world War Two when this country was still allied with the Germans as Axis armed forces – surviving sailors afloat in the sea off their coast-line subsequent to the sinking of their combat vessel by American aircraft, one of which had been piloted by Jim when he was a captain in the United States Army Air Corps. So, not only had Jim been "blooded" in the war, but he had also wreaked deadly havoc thereafter; and I had been told by Phil Daugherty that Jim employed the most lethal hit-man in the Southwest – Billie Joe Briggs – on a hefty monetary retainer, to do any jobs he deemed necessary in the conduct of his business affairs. Billie Joe's fame was as an intrepid enforcer of policy who fearlessly appeared with a sawed-off shotgun to either persuade or eliminate opposition to whomsoever had employed him for a contract. Thus-far, no charges had ever been brought against this killer, as his actions were swift, smooth, and efficient, and he left no evidence, or *witnesses* at any scene of the crime.

Jim greeted me warmly and reminded me that he had offered me an open invitation to his home and hospitality which included everything , except his current live-in favorite sweetheart, Carole Sue, a former high-priced Dallas call-girl, who claimed to have once performed as a stripper with the famed exotic Texas dancer – also allegedly a prostitute – Candy Barr. Carole Sue and I had become friends over a dinner hosted by Jim at the Petroleum Club some months before when she had asked me for a list of books I considered appropriate for any college student to read and know. I had written the titles of some twenty from the Harvard 'One Hundred' and University of Chicago's 'Great Books' series ... and she had read most of them and called me by telephone to ask questions about subjects that were challenging to her and about which she felt ignorant. She really wanted to learn; she had earned a high-school diploma before entering her current *profession* Jim had offered to pay her out-of-state tuition at Central State College in Edmond, Oklahoma, the fine Liberal Arts institution just north of the city. So I did feel welcome, and Carole Sue immediately rushed to bring our her dog-earred texts to pick my university English Literature instructor's mind, as Jim poured me a non-alcoholic drink, remembering that I was still nursing a feeble liver. Before Carole Sue could set about rolling a joint, to settle down to "party mode," I decided to present my rather dreary request. I spoke directly to my grave concern, telling Jim that I had received notice from a most reliable source, that someone had placed a contract on my life with the Lebanese *family.*

Jim did not even blink, nor did he question the source of my discovery, but he picked up his telephone and rang Billie Joe. I heard Jim's specific instructions to pay a visit to the *family,* inquire about any contract on the life of Jim's close friend, Ben Wright, and to cancel that contract, by *any means necessary.*

Carole Sue had just prepared a mixed green salad and was setting about the grilling of some Cajun basted chicken breasts when Billie Joe telephoned his report to Jim, who was howling with laughter as he finally set down the receiver. He was sputtering as he described Billie Joe's rendition of the interview which was conducted with his shotgun's barrels jammed down the throat of the eldest member of the Lebanese *family* in the living room of his home where all the male members unfortunately had been all been assembled for that elder dean's [*don's*] birthday celebration. Unlucky happen-stance for him. Rather delightful coincidence, for Billie Joe played best to a crowd, . It seems that the old man, who was probably not altogether continent of bowel and bladder at his advanced age, had lost control of his urine and colonic contents and this had lent more dramatic effect to the demand that Billie Joe made of the entire family to insure that no harm whatsoever should come to one young man named Ben Wright, and reminiscent of the warning Jack Palance had made so many years before in Madrid to Charles Stalnaker, if I were to even contract a cold or mayhap stub my toe in the foreseeable future, that the barrels of Bille Joe's shotgun would be discharged in the orifices, facial, anal. and even some to be newly bestowed – and thereby *excavated* – of all members of the *family*, regardless of gender or age. Billie Joe had waxed gleefully descriptive of the wholesale havoc he intended to wreak if any harm should ever befall one of his dearest friends: Ben Wright.

I had never had the dubious privilege of meeting Billie Joe, so I was most impressed by the passionate regard he espoused for me, all on behalf of his primary benefactor, Jim Holly. He did come by the house within the next hour, and I was surprised to find him a most disarmingly shy sort of person, humble in the presence of those whom he considered his social betters, and he expressed excessive regard for my university professorial identity and had been told by Carole Sue of my efforts to assist her in her academic yearnings. The two of them were like brother and sister, and I felt that indeed I had been gifted with a friend for life, a most staunch and steadfast advocate – what the Anglo Saxons would have regarded as a *shoulder-companion*; that is, a warrior's comrade-in-arms, in the truest sense. Somewhat scary, but sincerely touching. I have been most fortunate to have had several such friends and acquaintances, from members of the first SEAL Team, to Jack Palance, to Rick Cluchey, to several convicts such as Teach with 'Home Cooking,' as well as John Clark, editor of the McAlester Oklahoma State Penitentiary literary gazette, to members of California's Sinanon, to others in prisons from the British penal institutions known as Wandsworth and Wormwood Scrubs, to even my pal in Alcoholics Anonymous, called "Scrap-Iron" Charlie Wilson, with whom I worked in Arkansas correctional facilities where he had served some thirty-six years of *hard time* as an inmate. Is there some criminal stink that they smell on my mantle? Do I exude the mad-dog, atavistic pheromones that they immediately identify as the true, bad-blood, wild strain? "Free-Wheeling" Frank Reynolds, leader of the San Francisco Hell's Angels referred to the character designator which his gang called "class," sometimes codified by the *comitatus* rites-of-passage ceremony required for winning the Red Wings badge, proudly displayed on the waistcoat or jacket – that requirement being to perform oral sex, cunnilingus, on any gang member's woman when she was at the peak of her menstruation, to soak one's mustaches in her red blood: *Red Wings rampant*! Frank granted me recognition as a man of "class" from our initial meeting in Michael McClure's home in Haight-Ashbury in 1970.

Thus was I released from an Oklahoma, *home-town*, contract on my life ... I think. So many events were coinciding in this latter part of 1973 that I was often confused and befuddled, but generally, my career appeared to have taken a great leap in the academic realm. At the same time as the National Endowment directors decided to fire Talamadge Stands and to admit to any charges of discriminatory practices in disallowing Native Americans and Blacks employment in the Poet-in-the-Schools program, they offered me the directorship position for Oklahoma. And simultaneously, I was flown to Eckerd College and allowed an interview before the entire assembled student body. I was posed a question by the chair of the English department, whose job I would be filling, along with the position described as Poet-in-Residence: What were my *poetics*?

My Poetics? How would I express my philosophy of poetry, my belief in my craft as a writer? I answered simply that my greatest literary hero, and philosophical influence, since my childhood and well into my mature years had always been Winnie the Pooh, and that his obsession with the only matter worthy of poetic or philosophical consideration had always been the substance known as honey. The search for, the pursuit of, and the consumption of that elixir, that nectar of the gods, was, and would continue to always be the quintessential of my personal poetics. Honey. Yummy. Yummy. And I then performed a deep bow from the waist, before my audience, who rose to applaud my honest revelation. I got the job. Diane Waikowski had turned it down the week before. My C. Phil. (Candidate in Philosophy) degree in Comparative Literature from U.C.S.D. and the confidential letters in my file written by Andrew Wright and Roy Harvey Pearce which these two former mentors had intended to damn me and deny me employment in any respectable American academic post, on the contrary, had impressed the department Chair and his colleagues most favorably. As Professor Wright had warned that my *insouciance* would most likely offend fellow faculty members, and Pearce had predicted that my mind-set as a *maverick* would always upset other academics, were the very factors which determined my assurance that the job was to be mine in the next year. During the few days that I remained in St. Petersburg for confirming my contract, I saw a house for sale at the ridiculously low price of $4,000; I bought it and then I returned to Oklahoma to celebrate with Sylvia before beginning my new job at Eckerd College.

I was already suspecting Sylvia of extra-curricular sexual promiscuity, but this was finally revealed after I had taken up residence in my new home in St Petersburg. It was within the first month of my stay, when I had arranged for Sylvia to move in with me, that she finally admitted what had been a fact of life which I had been unable to comprehend for several months before. She admitted, over the telephone, in one of the three hour conversations that had become my *drug-of-choice* since arriving at Eckerd College – one of the benefits had been unlimited use of my office telephone at no cost – that she had been intimate with friends of mine: her euphemism for actually fucking like a crazed rabbit at every opportunity. She maintained that her excessive sexual activity was derivative of her sure knowledge that she would be dead within the year, that probably she had only seven months more and that she appreciated all that I had done for her in these, her *last moments on earth*. What could I say? I would not want a frail young poet, such as her, to suffer any more than necessary to satisfy my own carnal desires. Now, could I? Even today, when Sylvia and I discuss this period, we are careful to avoid any mention of this actual betrayal.

So I had continued to disregard the most obvious clues and hints regarding Sylvia's promiscuity till it was irrefutable. She made a clean confession and apology for having led me on for so long, but then, she claimed that she made her decision to spend the remaining few months of her life with the man she truly loved (whoever that was, I did not want to know). I also was now well away from all that messy intrigue and had begun to dabble in a heavy-petting relationship with one of my students at Eckerd, a truly gorgeous nineteen year-old whose mother sent me a death threat when were had only become acquainted ... long before the sexual fore-play that often resulted in our mutual orgasms from intimate masturbatory caressing at my home. I was never scolded by any of my fellow faculty members for such dalliance, but I did catch the chair of the Philosophy department leaving my office one day when he had been snooping in my desk and book-shelves. He had become obsessed with the notion that I was a Satanist, and he was certain he could find evidence of my allegiance to Beelzebub somewhere in my personal effects in that office. It also transpired, that recordings had been made of my lengthy telephone conversations with Richard Brautigan on the same pretext, but this was only revealed as I called the police in to investigate possible theft by this misguided philosophy professor, who coincidentally was also an active Presbyterian minister to a local fanatical congregation whom he had incited to believe that the Devil lurked in every dark corner ... and also that the *Rapture* was truly at hand, probably to arrive in a few months. I was alarmed and amused at this degree of paranoia in the surveillance measures that had been ordered on my behalf, deriving from the fear among most of the devout Christian members of the faculty that I might possibly be of a diabolic persuasion and commitment. The deep-seated fears of most residents of Southern states has not changed appreciably in the past forty years since I have lived outside of the United States. Certainly, in Arkansas where I have now resided when not traveling since 2004, I have encountered much the same degree of fundamentalist Christian fear and loathing of anything or anyone who is even slightly eccentric. I myself, since I came to teach and reside in Arkansas, have been branded a virtual Ant-Christ on several occasions. I have even been banned from attendance at certain Alcoholics Anonymous meetings and am barred from entering the premises to attend similar meetings in the high-priced and prestigious drug and alcohol treatment center (Quapaw) in Hot Springs. Members of the local Unitarian Church have even asked that I not attend services as I am suspected of having dangerously radical notions of *free-thinking*. How did Bill Clinton ever survive his childhood in this city?

My further employment at Eckerd College would have been impossible, however, given the zealous fundametalist fervor of the majority of the faculty and staff. Intellectual freedom could never have co-existed in such a repressive religious climate. Paul Eckerd, the man who endowed the college and demanded it be named for him would never allow any magazines such as *Playboy*, or for that matter, any product, printed or otherwise, which displayed any part of the human form naked. These were banned for sale in any of his stores. So I was relieved to be going to England and thence to India with Marina Fistoulari Glass on a tour which we had planned with Rom Gopal, the famed Temple dancer. I decided to do this after Marina came to visit me, just after her mother mailed me a Sacher Tort chocolate cake, which arrived by Special Delivery post in a wooden box on my thirty-fifth birthday. The cake was from the famed chef at the Sacher Hotel in Vienna, where Gustav Mahler had conducted the symphony orchestra till his death in 1910. Marina's arrival was punctuated by a life-endangering event which occurred in my lovely ginger-bread house in St. Petersburg.

As I built a fire in the pot-bellied stove in my living room and placed a vinyl disk on my phonograph turn-table to play a movement from a Mahler symphony entitled, "Allegro con Fuoco," the roof caught fire from sparks floating out the stove-pipe chimney. At first, I thought that some nasty static had come in over my sound system, and I began fiddling with dials and attempting to seek the purer instrumental orchestration, but then I realized that the noise was issuing from outside my stereo player and that the roof was crackling, on fire, above my head. I ran outside and saw flames dancing on the roof-top, and I grabbed the garden hose and pointed up on to the growing wall of burning wood. My neighbors had rushed over into my yard and told me that they had called the fire department. Marina was standing beside me in her night-gown, as she had already gone in to crawl in to bed, as I had arranged the musical treat for us to wrap ourselves around as we cuddled in to our night-time drowse. I was in my pajamas and dressing gown. She was quite alarmed, and as she tugged on my sleeve, she told me that she had taken off her jewelry and had left it all on the bedside table. The ring which her grandfather, Gustav Mahler, had given his young bride, Alma, on their engagement, was one of the items still inside the house which was now becoming totally consumed in the conflagration.

Without a second thought, I raced back over the porch steps and burst in to the bedroom and swept my hand over the table scooping up all the jewelry there and then bolted back outside just as the first fire-engine roared into the yard. My hair was scorched and my face had been blackened in the heavy smoke. I realized that I had been holding my breath during this dare-devil feat, and I found myself panting as I handed the treasures to Marina, and then leaned over to rest my elbows on my knees as I crouched down and gazed at the *ginger-bread* ... now become *burnt toast*. Miraculously, the high-pressure hoses quenched most of the demolishing inferno, and a scorched remnant of the basic structure survived. In the following weeks, insurance coverage rebuilt the entire house, and it was lovelier than before, because I had a personal involvement in all the design and decorating reconstruction.

When I left St Petersburg at the end of term to join Marina in England, I leased it to a loving young couple from my Creative Writing class at Eckerd who subsequently broke up, and the theretofore *sweet dear girl* then wrote a letter to tell me that she was trashing the house because she reckoned that I was a Satanist and that my diabolic karma had infected her relationship and poisoned her true love, so she intended to punish me and to have the house exorcised and had called on the chair of the Philosophy department (also the minister at her church) at Eckerd to supervise the spiritual cleansing. Her father was a deacon in that man's Presbyterian congregation. The house was virtually demolished, and when I returned to town and repaired all the damage, I found a single mother who was thankful to have such a decent place for her and her teenage son, so I gave it to her for what the British call a 'peppercorn rent"; that is, I charged her the most minimal amount, and five years later, I sold it to her for a price well below the market value ... but still, considerably more than the original price of $4,000.

BOOK THREE

Return to International Consciousness

Only a week after the last day of classes at Eckerd College, I flew from Miami to England. Marina Mahler met me at the airport in London and told me as we rode in a taxi to Hounslow, the suburb nearest Heathrow, that she had met the man of her dreams only the week before, and was intending to marry him, so she was placing me in the home of a friend of hers whom Marina asserted was the illegitimate daughter of Modigliani [this information did not in any degree assuage the deep hurt that her decision inflicted, but Marina seemed to believe that placing me with such a notable person, albeit of bastard pedigree, might somehow provide me solace]. Nicole, her friend, Modigliani's whelp, did indeed look like one of those elongated figures with which that painter decorated so many of his canvasses. During our first long talk, in her small flat, where I occupied a virtual closet which she designated as a guest room, this sad, and deeply troubled *gamin-gone-wrong*, told me that when she met Pablo Picasso that he told her that she was the spitting image of her father, whom he called "that broke-back sailor." She spun the yarn of her life, equal to any sea-story of the genre which mariners have for millenia told one another to pass that endless time tossing through monotonous hours voyaging the waters of the globe. I was amazed that she had been able to endure the economic and physical disasters she claimed she and her mother had been subjected to. Their national identity was somewhere between Hungarian, Moldavian and Yugoslavian, and I even heard a hint of Albanian and Bulgarian in some of the episodes when they had been pursued by agents she claimed were aligned with the international conspiracy to eliminate them for their original Romanoff royal Russian blood-line. The only tragic chord that might perhaps be based on truth was her revelation that she was afflicted with terminal cancer, and had been having to undergo a course of radiation that was wearing her resistance down so that she rarely left her residence except to replenish food in the cupboard. That she was delusional was obvious, but she was well-intentioned, and had pledged her friend to sequester me here in Hounslow, rather than allow me to invade Marinas luxurious Chelsea residence, now occupied by the latest matrimonial candidate and *true love*. I took a taxi to Earl's Court after only one night with Nicole, and rented a suite of rooms in a pension which also provided simple over-night Bed-and-Breakfast accommodation in virtually the same price range I would later pay for a furnished two bedroom ground-floor flat in the more salubrious nearby neighborhood of Kensington. This was at a period when an overnight stay in London cost less than a small meal in a cafe ... with several bottle of beer. Prices were even lower in Spain.

I made contact with all my former drinking pals from 'Finch's' and 'The Queen's Elm' pubs on Fulham Road, and the Chelsea Arts Club, where I net-worked through Bernard Stone, owner of 'Turret Books,' still located just off High Street Kensington. Stone's book store was on the ground floor of the building where Ezra Pound had resided during his British residence just before World War Two. The American poet then left to reside in Italy where he proclaimed his adoration of Mussolini and all things Fascist and then launched his vitriolic, anti-Semitic and anti-American radio broadcasts, transcripts of which later provided *prima facie* evidence for the government of the United States to bring charges of High Treason against him. Professor Robert Spiller of his former university and mine as well, University of Pennsylvania, and Senator Jacob Javits, convinced his prosecutors that

Pound was legally insane and had him committed to Saint Elizabeths Hospital from 1947 to 1958 when he returned to reside in Rapallo, Italy till his death in Venice in 1972. Ruthven Todd presented his daughter with a poem [the lines told that the cats of Rapallo -"Ask only that our tribute to Ezra be recorded."] in homage, in 1973, which she said was the most poignant of all the tributes paid her father, who had always roamed streets at night, feeding the hungry stray cats, in whatever country where he lived.. I always enjoyed browsing in 'Turret Books' and felt some blessed poetic energies in Pound's former abode [he was another lad from the far West (Idaho) who came to study at the College, University of Pennsylvania, where I was an Honors English major, and had studied some of his poetry [not just 'The Cantos'] and even translations from the extant Anglo Saxon corpus of ancient sea-farer's verse], and so I decided then that I wanted to become part of the London literary scene once more.

I petitioned the National Poetry Society to host for me another one-man show in presentation of my latest published collection of poems, *Runey Tunes*, my creative experiment with the ancient Anglo-Saxon form of poetics known as *gnomics* [the sayings of gnomes and elves and any of the many *eotenisc* creatures originally residing East of Eden who survived the Great Flood because they were amphibian and possessed preternatural survival strengths like Grendel and his mother and other such monsters as Tolkein discussed in his most notable Anglo Saxonist essay, 'Beowulf: the Beasts and the Critics.'] Christopher "Kit" Wright was the active secretary of this prestigious establishment, and he promoted my project so that I then set about doing radio broadcasts and interviews with *Time Out*, so that when the event took place, we had a sell-out crowd and live coverage by 'Capitol Radio.' I combined my reading with musical accompaniment of Rag -Time piano and a surprise ending I fiendishly devised with one of my most demented students from Eckerd College who had followed me to London. Hillary McCormack, the only living male heir to the Chicago McCormack Reaper fortune, who had spent most of his mature years in and out of rehabilitation centers struggling with his addiction to alcohol and mind-altering drugs, ranging from the psychedelic to the deadly opiads and even some courtship with that animal tranquilizer P.C.P. - also called "Angel Dust." His current live-in lover, was unable to follow him across the Atlantic as no American passport is issued to convicted felons, and this man was a scarred and psychopathic Black ex-convict who called himself, 'The Devil.' This youth, who had grown up in the Florida penal system, bragged openly about all those he had killed or mutilated - he constantly promised to "do" anybody I should choose for a target, as a gift to show his high regard for me, as I was the poetic mentor - a virtual father figure, as far as 'The Devil' could conceive of this notion - of his lover, and protector, and keeper, Hillary. When this wild character had once driven me to the airport in a top-down Cadillac convertible which was one of the toys Hillary had given him, I was surprised that no police had stopped us, and deeply relieved that they had not, as 'The Devil' was wearing only a skin-tight 'Speedo' bright, red bikini, into the crotch of which he had jammed a .45 caliber automatic pistol which his hand continually reached for, and caressed, as if it were truly an extension of his ample penis which rode just below the heavy barrel of that gun.

My planned surprise ending for this *Runey Tunes* presentation was that Hillary should stride up the center aisle of the main assembly room where I was delivering my reading of a poem from a lectern. He was to throw the lectern aside and scatter the remaining pages of poetry to fall in disarray to the floor. He was then to grab the piano player and shove him off his stool, and return to take center stage as he began to disrobe and shout his own poem which was intended to sound like a more outrageous version of "Howl" than Allen Ginsberg could ever have composed.

Hillary performed these maneuvers. and as he stood before the audience, he ranted and raved, and tore away his clothing and soon stood completely nude, as I slunk into the front row and acted as if I had no intention of attempting to interrupt this flamboyant outburst which might be the act of a truly dangerous maniac. No one else made any move and as Hillary finished his delivery, he stomped down the main aisle and made his retreat out the entrance before anyone tried to stop him. I rose and walked to center stage, bowed to the stunned and silent audience and I expressed my thanks for their attendance and appreciation of my poetry, the Rag-Time piano accompaniment, and for this bizarre finale, delivered, which I then informed them, had been delivered by one of my more promising students from Eckerd College in Florida. There was no applause. Mumbling discord wafted through the retreating assemblage, and I sat down to consider when would be best for me to make my retreat.

A florid faced man approached me then and sat down beside me. He reached out and placed his hand on my shoulder, saying, "That was rather extraordinary. Perhaps too much for a British audience, especially in these hallowed halls. We met once in Mallorca, but you may not remember me. It was at my friend Ruthven Todd's home there in Galilea. I also have a house there, at the top of the village, and I am offering it to you if you would like to go there and have some solitude for your writing."

Alastair Reid, former amanuensis to Robert Grave, translator of Pablo Neruda and Gabriel Marques, poetry editor of *The New Yorker* magazine, whose poem, 'Curiosity,' I had taught in secondary school and university and which had influenced me to take some of the most significant risks of my life ... this great poet was offering me his sacred eyrie, the highest house in the highest village (Galilea) on my beloved island of Mallorca. What a reward for perhaps the last performance I would probably ever be invited to present at the

National Poetry Society!

It had been Alastair who had placed Ruthven Todd into his last treatment program for acute chronic alcoholism which was the 'sleep cure' in which the patient was chemically sedated for several days while the body supposedly detoxified from the physical addiction to alcohol, and upon awakening, there were strong suggestions from a team of psychological counselors that were intended to divert the person from drinking any alcohol ever again. Alastair had then transferred Ruthven to the 'Pension Eolo,' the one room village boarding facility owned by Manolo, the mayor, and his wife, in Galilea, and then had arranged for the lease of Can Bielo just below that building in a prominent position at the very center of town, next door to the shoemaker and postmaster. Ruthven never imbibed spirits again, but he drank gallons of the local wine which was delivered to him in five liter basket bottles from the *bodega* which was located in Margarita's food market and telephone center higher up the hill on the path leading to Alastair's house. When I first had arrived in that village, visiting Ruthven in his home, I had been advised by Ellis Jacobsen to rent one of the houses belonging to Nora Constenz, a rich German woman who told everyone that she had been an actress who had once danced for Hitler, but had been thoroughly *de-Nazified* after World War Two. Therefore, I came to know the village well, and was more than eager to accept Alastair's invitation .

I was deeply complimented that Alastair Reid should want to help me. Perhaps he would publish some of my poems in *The New Yorker*? He was at that time, however, in a controversial situation as it had recently been revealed – *exposed*, perhaps would be the more appropriate term – that the young rustic poet from El Salvador whom he had translated and promoted first in his magazine and later in publications of these collected poems, that this Central American genius was, in actual fact, an invention of Alastair's, a sort of

Lieutenant Kije, the officer created *on paper* supposedly a member of the Russian army, who was promoted all the way to general before the farce was discovered and *exposed*. A student writing a doctoral dissertation on the work of this young poet whom Alastair was mentoring, had actually traveled to El Salvador and attempted to search out the writer in his village, and after following up many a false lead had been able to confront his translator, Alastair Reid, who finally admitted that he had created this poetic *persona*, and that the brilliant youth had only ever existed, *on paper,* in the fertile imagination of the Reid.

It had also been Alastair who really was the actual, activating genius behind the publication of the first issue of *The Black Mountain Review,* which Robert Creeley had assembled after he arrived in Mallorca. This American poet had arrived on the island, hoping to be mentored by Robert Graves, but because Graves considered Creeley's physical appearance repulsive – one eye was missing, and Creeley rarely wore a patch to cover this disfigurement – the grand old man of Deya had told his *amanuensis* at that time, Alastair Reid, to remove him from the village. Alastair had taken Creeley to Banyalbufar, where Creeley settled in for the long winter, writing the only novel of his career, *Island,* and then commuted to the city of Palma where Alastair had introduced him to the printer who produced the first edition of that poetry review (*Black Mountain Review*) which changed the history of mid-century American poetics under the influence of Charles Olson, *rector* of Black Mountain College. Shortly thereafter, there was the discovery of the sexual relationship which Alastair had been carrying on with Margo Nichols [married later to Mike Nichols, the film director], one of the first so-called *White Goddesses* of Robert Graves, who had been employing his interpretations of these contemporary embodiments of his ideals of his Muse (The Goddess) to conduct his extra-marital affairs without overly offending his wife, Beryl. The last of Graves' *Goddesses* was a teenaged ballet dancer named Julie, with whom he openly had a love affair until he was stricken with debilitating dementia in his late seventies. Alastair and Margo left the island and bought an old mill in France where they cohabited for only a short while thereafter. Robert placed one of is most formidable curses on Alastair, declaring him a veritable incarnation of Satan and the Grand Satyr and demanded that all his publishers, particularly Doubleday in America, refuse to ever allow any of Reid's work into print ... *for eternity.*

All the notoriety of this poet (Reid) made him one of my greatest idols. He was raunchy, wild, unpredictable; and his poem , 'Curiosity,' spoke to my *heart of hearts,* the very core of my darkest, most atavistic, primeval soul. The ideal being, that cat who lives out his lives, risking death and unbearable pain, to experience every new dream to the depths of the all possible extreme. "A cat – minority of one / is all that can be counted on / to tell the truth. And what cats have to tell / on each return from hell / is this: that dying is what the living do, / that dying is what the loving do". Alastair Reid was my ideal, as a self-actuated, individuated *being* and therefore, when he offered me that house in Galilea, I immediately accepted and told him that I would be there the very next week, without even thinking of consulting the woman I had recently begun living with. Janet Nichols was a lanky blond from California who had a two year-old son whom she had named Alaric [Robert Graves adored this robust child and used to burst into one of his favorite songs about Alaric the Hun, the man who ravished Europe as fiercely as Attila, but never had such effective popular appeal, but was considered as savage and ruthless as Genghis Khan himself]. Janet had give the child the surname of Michaels, because that was his father's name, a man who had disappeared shortly after the child's conception when the couple were working as croupiers in a Las Vegas casino.

I introduced Janet to Alastair, and told her as I made them acquainted, that we would be going to live in his house the following week. I never for a moment would have considered any objection she might have made regarding any inconvenience that might deter us from such a move. She appeared to be completely in agreement as she was, at this time, absolutely obedient to any of my desires or whims. I have never had such a loyal and committed partner in co-habitation or any other enterprise since then. Janet had only the vaguest idea where the island of Mallorca was located, and to her mind, Spain was roughly equivalent to Mexico, which she adored because of the *mariachis* and bull-fights which she had sampled in Tijuana. She was an ordinary California girl who was willing to leap into any scene and would savor whatever appealed to her senses and might provide her another adventure to tell when and if she ever returned home, which, for her, was Orange County, where her father had become rich by purchasing and managing a string of Hallmark greeting card stores in several strip malls throughout the state. He had then had an affair with his wife's younger sister, had abandoned and then divorced his wife, scandalizing the entire family, and leaving Janet with no money to continue in the community college where she had been only superficially engaged in pursuing an education. Her skills were as a member of the fencing team, and she had also developed a talent for playing Blackjack poker in her forays into Nevada and the gambling casinos there, where, consequently, she was trained as a croupier.

She had become close friends with the wife of my best drinking pal, the sculptor Michael Kenny, as their youngest daughter, Camila, was exactly Alaric's age, and the two toddlers had bonded like brother-and-sister playmates. After I purchased a set of toy pistols, sheep-wool chaps, a cowboy hat and a leather waist-coat with a sheriff's badge attached, Alaric was more than ready to travel to Spain, notwithstanding the howling protestations of his girl-friend, Camila. Michael and his wife Rose-Marie scolded me for tearing this cuddly couple apart, and wondered how I could just fold tent and take off for a destination which sounded not only foreign, but even dangerous, to their British sensibilities; albeit that Michael was originally working-class Irish from Liverpool, his election to the Royal Academy as their youngest member had rather filled his head with some presumptions which we both found laughable when he would admit to his upward mobility in the supposedly classless designation of an artist as Declasse. I think he was just lamenting losing his most stalwart drinking pal [me], and Rose-Marie had found a young mother-pal in Janet. Notwithstanding, we departed and as soon as we arrived in Palma, I bought a sturdy Seat 600 Berliner which was called "the tank" by all those who owned this rugged vehicle It could climb any hill and navigate the roughest, rocky roads carved into the limestone mountains of Mallorca. However, we had to leave it parked at the foot of the hill upon which Alastair's house was perched, on a promontory that few of the villagers of Galilea had ever visited, above a small gathering of some four or five crumbling ruins that had constituted a separate sub-division [*pueblecito*] to Galilea at the turn of the century.

The last hundred yards steep climb to the house was only made difficult when I had to carry a *butano* metal bottle [liquid butane gas] weighing seventy pounds, to fire the stove used for cooking in the house. There was no toilet or shower. Washing up was accomplished in buckets drawn from the well which I dropped a large slab of lime into, in order to purge all the bacteria from runoff water from the roof which fed this deposit, and to kill any contaminants from dead rats or other vermin, or even from any revengeful neighbors who might have come and dumped their fecal matter in there as a nasty trick to abuse the *extranjero/forestero* [foreigner -Alastair] - I had lived in Mallorca long enough to know that many of the local residents harbored vicious animosity and hatred for any of us from across the sea, and that included Spaniards from the peninsula, even fellow Catalans from Barcelona, which was across a body of water, as well.

To provide a toilet facility, I dug a few small repositories in the woods behind the house, some twenty yards away, and carefully stacked a mound of earth by each to cover over any bowel movements dropped into the hole. An entrenching tool and a roll of toilet paper stood on a table by the kitchen back door, and Janet was willing to abide by the rudimentary regimen. Alaric, was another matter. Once he actually, squatted down outside the doorway and dumped a full evacuation of fecal matter there. Janet took to placing him over a shallow plastic bowl and utilizing this as a sort of make-shift chamber-pot which she then carried out and disposed of in the woods. Our shower baths consisted of filling a tin bucket with water, allowing it to heat in the midday sun and then dumping this over our soaped bodies. I found a spigot attachment for a bucket in a *ferreteria* [iron-monger; hardware store] and this then served as a shower which could be suspended on the outside wall and tugged to allow short spurts of water to douse our lathered bodies. Once a neighbor happened to come by unannounced and found the three of us cavorting in this exercise at bathing ourselves all together and was startled and dismayed and probably shocked at what might have seemed a lascivious and erotic activity: a healthful familial frolic.

We had little to do with any of our neighbors. There were none close by, except for one old farmer and his wife. He was named Sebastian, and I had been told that he held some grudge against Alastair for not paying him enough money for some job over three years before, and in revenge, he had shit in the well on several occasions. I heard this from Nora Constens, the German woman who had come calling our first week, and who doted on Alaric - his name and Nordic features (platinum blond hair and ice blue eyes) must have elicited some ancient Teutonic racial-subconscious memory for her, though she said often that she had be de-Nazified by the occupying Allied forces who conquered her nation in 1945. She had invited us often to her home where she fed us grandly, and we indulged ourselves in her steaming hot showers and baths. I decided to make no jokes about Nora's *showers* [references to the S.S. death camps of the Holocaust] before the bonfires that often were lit on cool evenings on her huge terrace overlooking all the village below. Her home and the guest houses, some twelve in all, had been designed and built to resemble what her commissioned Russian architect could remember of the Native American habitations in Taos, New Mexico. There was a large swimming pool that was at the center of all this gathering of residences, and Nora claimed that she planned to have a commune of spiritually enlightened people come and live here, when she could decide between some Zen Buddhists left over from Alan Watts's Esalen groupies in Big Sur, California, and some break-aways from the Findhorn Center-of-Light in Scotland. I had known many of the floating gurus from the communes in California to New Mexico and even the founder of Findhorn, Peter Caddy, his wife, and their spiritual father-figure, McElvy Crombie who claimed a close speaking acquaintance with Pan himself; and of course there was Robert Graves who claimed to have been initiated on the Isle of Mann by the coven of *wicas* embedded there. That I knew so many of these *luminaries* seemed to delight Nora, and of course, she embraced Janet as her soul-mate, especially as she had mothered the radiant Alaric. Ruthven Todd was away from Galilea (in New York) when we arrived. He had snagged a post as Poet-in-Residence at the university located in Buffalo where Carl Gay, the last *amanuensis for* Robert Graves had been made head librarian, in charge of the Special Collection of prominent twentieth century poets' holographic manuscripts, the best collection of such works till University of Texas, in Austin, began to outbid everyone in this field in the competitive auctions of such material.

The only other encounters we had with people in the village, occurred when we bought our food at Margarita's shop and on our visits to the

'Pension Eolo' bar and restaurant which consisted of two tables, serving full meals on the weekends only. The view from the balcony at this establishment was priceless, and some claimed to see Ibiza out across the water on clear days. This was actually physically impossible - Galilea was at an altitude of 1,500 feet and Ibiza lay some 35 miles due West. This was the sort of remark one would hear from the few foreign tourists who might sometimes wander in, but our village was not on the usual tourist itinerary. Our most frequent encounters with people was with the local residents, and our conversations were limited to observances about the weather, and little else. However, there was one *domestic* incident which derived from a comical linguistic misunderstanding which brought three housewives running up the steep path to our very threshold, carrying pitchforks and cudgels. This was when I was suffering from a bout of flu and had a high fever, and Janet had run down into the fringe of town, to the nearest house to plead for some medical assistance. She could not remember the word *Aspirina* and could only gibber to the alarmed house-wife whom she first found at home, "Ayudame. Mi hombre *es* malo!" She thought she was saying "Help me. My husband is sick" What she had told them was that she needed help because her husband *was evil!* The verb should have been *estar* and NOT *ser*. Her manner had broadcast fear and alarm, and so this Mallorquin woman ran next door and marshaled her two neighbors to take up arms and rush out to subdue "the evil one" who might be about to assault this frightened blonde foreign visitor. When they ran in the house and found me lying in bed with Alaric by my side, looking altogether content and unmolested, I was able to tell them that I had a case of the *grippe* and had been bed-ridden for the past several hours and that I would appreciate some *Aspirina* or any other medication or home remedies they could recommend. I had them laughing in only a matter of moments as I explained that my *wife's* small understanding of the language was the cause for this mistaken emergency mission of theirs, and that she would sometimes tell people that she was *embarasada*, which meant pregnant, when she meant to say the Spanish equivalent of *embarrassed*. This was a well-known *amigo falso* (Spanish for "false friend' which appears with seemingly similar cognate words) gaff which non-Spanish speaking foreigners made, and the *ladies* - no longer warrior women - left the house laughing, apparently relieved to not have to engage themselves further in any of the confusing affairs of this not altogether welcome family of *extranjero* (foreign) interlopers in their tranquil village milieu.

Otherwise, our stay in this house was altogether healthy and peaceful. We had decided to clear away all the heavy growth of grass that had grown up between the stone flooring of the terrace in front of the house so that we could sit there and look out over the long valley below, where once had nestled an entire small community, named La Fuente (the fountain), around a deep well which still remained. Far over the next mountain, Bauza, loomed the city lights of Palma, which glowed against the horizon at night. However, we were remote and hidden from any other social intrusions, and we treasured this blessed hiatus in our lives as the most precious time we should ever know.

I had been browsing though Alastair's small collection of books, and was delighted that he had one of the more seminal works of Carl Jung, *Mysterium Coniunctionis*, Volume 14 of the Bollingen Foundation Collectiion translated by R. C. Hull, as well as the autobiography of that same enlightened psychologist, *Memories, Dreams, Reflections*. I had read only some extracts of Jung in research I had undertaken on several essays in literary criticism at U.C.S.D. during my doctoral studies, and had found these useful in shoring up some of my more penetrating, interpretive investigations of character development by my favorite authors. Now I was reading to discover something about my own character development. Was I developing? What sort of character could I determine myself becoming?

Jung had begun his child-like reconstructive self- discovery, the basic material treated in his autobiography, at the age of fifty. He had left his successful medical and psychiatric practice, a tenured professorship, and a comfortable domestic residence and now in middle age, had returned to that idyllic site, Bollingen, the place where his family had all visited for their holidays, and he had now decided to encamp there, constructing a habitat with the barest necessities of comfort and sustenance, in order to construct his mind's *habitation*, each living space, a separate room of consciousness, building one *arena* at a time, adapting to his *living spaces / living rooms*, as he explored his growing awareness of his ability to awaken to his inner vision of his identity - this ego identity corresponding and coinciding with the actual physical compartments he was constructing and construing as the *persona* named Carl Gustav Jung. He admitted that any rational person might deem his undertaking to be mad, insane, the exercise of a mentally defective man. He compared this work to that of a small child building a sand castle, except that his edifice was of sturdier material.

I discussed my reading with Janet, who said that she understood, and agreed that we were also living in a radically rustic milieu, that we had contrived to place ourselves in the most rudimentary living condition and that perhaps we could discover something essential about our inner being, our identity, our character components, but she really did enjoy visits to Nora's where she and Alaric could have long, languishing soaks in the bath-tub in hot, soapy water. She was becoming lean and wiry, and her ribs showed against a virtual *washboard* muscular belly. Her breasts were like ripe melons and did not sag even one degree from her chest. Her long blond hair was becoming like a wreath above her strong shoulders, and the only unattractive feature that she was developing were a myriad of freckles on her upper torso and arms and legs. Our sex had never been so intense before. We were putting Alaric to bed in Alastair's study – he had protested only for the first few days, sleeping separately form his mother – so that our copulative cavorting and noisy exclamations in the several orgasms we delivered to one another, were more extravagant than we had ever shared until this time. If this time could have lasted, I would be devoutly married and devoted to Janet to this day, but, alas, all good things must come to ... and avoiding the rest of that cliché, I will simply state that we all must awake from even our fondest dreams. *So it goes.*

I had read Jung's discussion of the notion of the *key dream,* and one night, I had a visual experience that I was able to recall almost perfectly in its entirety the next morning, and I transcribed it on to several pages of foolscap, so that I could better attempt to understand and interpret it. I had been writing down episodes from several snatches of dreams I had been having, believing that I could thereby delve into my sub-conscious and discover the factors that Jung had written about which reveal that self which we keep subdued and may never acquaint ourselves with ... unless we utilize his methods for recording and then interpreting these repressed quintessential elements of our psyche, according to his model.

In this dream, I had found myself at the gates of a castle, or palace, a redoubt of high stone walls, and as I reached what appeared to be the main entry path, also paved in stone, I found that I was looking over a low wall into a shallow pool of clear water which was bordered by rich green ferns. I could see the raised portcullis of the main gate ahead, and a bright court-yard within, but I was fascinated by what I saw just below the water's surface in the pond, or abbreviated moat, alongside the wall of the ramp leading in to the vaulted walls of this fortress. I leaned over the wall and reached in beneath the surface of the water, trying to make contact with an array of brightly colored stones, or large jewels like rubies, emeralds, and lapis lazuli. Just as I saw that my fingers were about to touch each stone, it whirled away and re-settled in to what became a brightly swirling kaleidoscopic display of a mandala mosaic within the shallow pool of water. As I withdrew my hand and then just gazed at the display, it settled and remained in that same arranged outlay, but the moment I even stuck my finger in to the water, all the stones swirled about in a brightly re-arranging alignment. I then became aware of another person standing nearby me. It was a girl about fifteen years of age, who had the body of a woman, but the manner of a child, and she was throwing her hands up into the air and laughing at my attempts to grasp any one of the stones from the pool. I asked her why she was laughing - and I wish I had asked her how she got into my dream - but she was already telling me that I must know that I could not reach any of the stones, that the treasure would continue to evade me until I learned what I was eventually destined to discover, many more years from now, and that then, the stones, which were indeed precious jewels would all be mine, and when I had reached this state of awareness, that I would not even try to touch them or remove them from that pool. I asked her how she knew this, and how she could know anything about me, or my future, but she just replied with a taunting, lilting, musical peel of laughter as she glided away up through the gate into the courtyard ... and then, as I started after her, I awoke.

I told Janet that I had experienced what I thought was probably a Jungian *key dream*. I did not want to tell her about it and even though she asked to read what I had wriiten immediately upon awakening, I would not share this with her, fearing that somehow I might lose its distinct components and my individual ownership rights to this fantasy. I told her that I planned sit out on our terrace all that day, and I felt certain that somehow the mystery of this nocturnal revelation would unfold for me there. I have no idea what I could possibly have meant, but I chose to eat only a small lunch of raw vegetables – *crudite*, as the French designate such a repast – and then I placed myself in several meditational trances in an attempt to trigger whatever was to manifest the explanation I expected to receive for this seminal development in my incipient Jungian psychic awakening process. The sun passed across the sky, and nothing untoward had happened, and as the sky began to color with a reddening sunset over the sea, I was about to despair of ever being instructed or enlightened further. Was it a *key dream*? Was I to be guided or taught anything ... and by whom, or what? And then, at this critical moment at the crepuscular closing of the day, something *untoward* did occur.

She climbed up over the ridge behind the house, the bright sunlight of the late afternoon, the waning rays playing in the strawberry blond hair she wore in a cascading abundance, unkempt, but somehow arranged by Nature to crown her head like an Anglo-Saxon version of the Afro hair style now so popular among rebellious youth in the world, especially where radical New Left political ideals were sacred. With no hesitation, she walked directly to where I was sitting in my canvas campaign chair and began speaking, with no attempt at any sort of formalized introduction.

"I wanted to speak with Alastair. He always knows what to do. And especially now." She paused, and after looking me over for no more than a few seconds, she went on. "You must be a close friend, someone he truly trusts. No one but his son, Jasper, ever stays in this house. So, you will know what to do.

" My name is Ben. I am a poet and Alastair's friend. I will help you if I can. What can I do for you?"

"My English is not so good. I am learning. Maybe you can teach me more." She faltered, and then, biting her lower lip, and looking somewhat frightened, she stammered slightly, and said, "My father is in a deep depressive state, and he says he wants to die. I love my father. I do not want him to die, even if that is what he says he wants. Perhaps I am selfish, but I do not want my father to die. Can you help me?"

"Who are you? I told you my name. What is yours?"

She laughed, appearing to feel more comfortable then, and replied, "My name is Renee. My mother's name is Barb, and my brother is Don. My father is Richard. Richard Hull. He and my family are all old friends of Alastair. Can you help me ... us?"

The name rang like a clarion ... a trumpet ... a screaming siren. Richard Hull. R.C. Hull. Could it be? Was her father the Bollingen translator of Carl Jung? Was this girl, so like the teasing teenager in my dream – Ruth could not be more than fifteen – and she was such a natural beauty, she had to be a dream-girl – was she the real-life, contemporary manifestation of the nymph who had taunted and allured and enthralled me in that *key dream*?

My first inquiry was of a more prosaic, pragmatic, even pedestrian nature. I asked where Renee lived, and she told me that it was in the next village, Establiments, some six kilometers away, and she had begun walking here after lunch and had taken a path known only to shepherds and the old *contrabandistas* (smugglers), which had brought her up the steep cliffs that hung over the valleys *behind* Alastair's house. I then told her that I could be her tutor in English as I was a professor of English and Literature from university and also secondary school and that I would appreciate her exchanging lessons in Spanish which I presumed was her first language, although she then told me it was Mallorquin, but that she was indeed fluent in Spanish, as well. She said that her mother was Danish, her father British, and that both she and her brother had been born on the island and had never traveled abroad.

When I dared to ask if her father was the translator of Carl Jung, she said that he had been, but was so depressed, that he had been unable to do any work for several months. She told me that her mother said that his work was very important, vital to the study of psychology, and that he was even more wrenched by anguish because he felt that he was shirking his great responsibility in this essential work. I wholeheartedly agreed, but said only that I would take Ruth home, that we could arrange to begin her lessons in English, and that I would speak with her father, and that I felt sure that I could help.

I was so excited about meeting this *key* in decoding my dream, this man who had been such an intimate colleague of Carl Jung, that I was beside myself with exultation. I told Janet that I must take a friend's daughter home, that she had come here, hoping to see Alastair, had been somewhat disappointed to not find him, and that it was not far for me to drive her to her village just down the road. I promised to pick up some more fresh vegetables and fruit in the market there, and be home before dinner in the next two hours. Ruth and I walked down the steep path to where my car was parked a hundred yards away, and I drove to her home in less than half an hour.

We were greeted by her mother, Barb, and her hyper-active brother, Don. Renee told Barb that I would help her father, and Barb told me that if I were Alastair's house-guest that he must trust me and that she could trust me as well. She then blathered that she and her husband had been friends with Alastair and Ruthven Todd since they had arrived in Mallorca, first invited here by the translator and novelist,

Tony Berrigan. She seemed quite distressed and although her outward appearance was stoic and calm, she revealed something that one only shares with intimate friends – and not newly introduced acquaintances. She said that she and her husband had taken L.S.D. with Alastair, and she wanted to know if I had done so as well. With Alastair? Or had I taken the drug? This was unclear, so I answered truthfully, just as if we were old friends, that Alan Watts and Dr. Robert Lynch who had introduced Aldous Huxley to L.S.D. [when he was a practicing psychiatrist at the Menninger Foundation in Topeka, Kansas] had both warned me against taking the substance, as they considered that I might be border-line pyschotic, and then I recalled to her how Dr. Carl Jung had refused to examine certain patients whom he considered might be of that temperament, as they could possibly segue into psychosis and not be able to return from their schizophrenic fugue. I could see that she appreciated my immediate candor and that a huge emotional glacial displacement had moved us toward the subject of her husband's plight, and indeed we were at that moment, physically moving through the drawing room from the *entrada,* to be standing before the doorway that opened into a working library just beyond the dining room table.

There was a man huddled in a wheel-chair, a blanket flung about his shoulders, and he raised his head as I entered his sanctuary, his living and working domain. I spoke first and told him my name and my relationship to Alastair Reid, and I got right to the point. I have never been adept at any kind of diplomacy. I am too impatient to abide the politic or polite. Many have accused me of being a man who knows no boundaries.

"Your daughter came to Galilea to find Alastair Reid, so he could help you with your depression. It is preventing you from working and could be placing you in a suicidal frame of mind. Your work and your life are of the utmost importance to your family, and your job as the translator of Carl Jung is one of the greatest achievements of modern scholarship and medical science. I am here to help you. I know certain methods for reversing negative mind-sets and for transforming *Thanatos* to *Eros*, effecting a creative, pro-active sublimation of these energies, directly accessing the subconscious mind, without resorting to chemical or mechanical alternative practices. Conscious control of vitalizing sublimation is the critical process.

"I know something of autogenics and guided visualization and self-hypnosis techniques, having studied and used its healing for the past several years, and I have been a colleague in the project of Alan Watts and Dr. Robert Lynch of the Jonas Salk Foundation to treat the depressive states of men dying of cancer at the Scripps Memorial Hospital, in La Jolla, California.. I have myself recovered from what medical practitioners diagnosed as crippling rheumatoid arthritis and a hepatatoxic viral affliction, and I have been counseled by many skilled psychotherapists and psychiatrists for more than a decade, and I have also worked for the same period in American penitentiaries with convicts deemed to be criminally insane. I have read much of Dr. Jung's work, and I believe I have a substantial intuitive understanding of his method and purpose. I also am a close friend of Ruthven Todd, and Robert Graves believes I am a reincarnation of not only his deceased friend and Oxford university classmate, T.E. Lawrence, but also declares that we served as warrior companions with Hercules. I could tell you about my grandmother, a Native American woman who practiced witch-craft and holistic healing, but perhaps I should just begin by giving you her song ... "

This was before I had learned Mongolian and Tibetan over-tone chanting, so I just delivered what Eliza Rogers Wright used to croon over my head as she combed out her long black tresses. All of this would have been outrageously inappropriate in any other company or environment ... or country. But this was Mallorca, and I was with people who had arrived in this sort of place for the same reasons I had been originally propelled here ... and had felt at home, and centered at the level of our innermost sense of self, from the moment we had arrived on this *sureallistic pillow*, in this "open psycho ward," as Mark McShane had described Plaza Gomila in Terreno when I had found my first residence on the island. Robert Graves had once hypothesized that the mountains that embraced so many of the valleys wherein the people lived and passed their days – that these huge masses of stone, were actually composed of a substance like the metal of iron [perhaps they were indeed mostly ferrous oxide; iron ore], and that these large blocks of metal were like the plus and minus poles of a magnet which would cause the magnetic poles of every person to spin when within the opposing electrical field and therefore, that everyone's consciousness would constantly be in a state of reversal and realignment, whirling constantly, so that confusion would be the rule, rather than an exception. Hence, all artists, whose true muse is Athena, whose "muddy eyes' – Homer's description of the phenomenon that as the color is perceived in her eyes, the perception shifts to the next color, so that the palette is smeared to become *muddy*, and never any one clearly distinct hue – this becomes the accepted mode of perception of all reality – ever-changing – a permanently kaleidoscopic show – these individuals, *artists*, will feel *at home*, for the first time anywhere, and will make this island their habitation; whereas, normal humans, will always feel in a state of dis-equilibration, unsettled, confused, and even crazed.

So my performance, the chanting, to which I then added some shuffling of my feet to the rhythm as if in a modified Pow Wow stomp dance, was picked up first by Don, the twelve year-old brother who would in his mature years become director and producer of the 'Teatro Sanz,' the theatre company he would establish in Palma to teach acting skills to children throughout the island – who probably would have been so drugged into stupor if he had grown up in American schools where his personality would have been diagnosed as Acute Attention Disorder, and Don Hull would have never been enabled to develop his theatrical talents and become the rich source of education in that realm for all the young of Mallorca. Don began to dance to my beat, and then, a smile wiping away much of the anguish which had motivated her to make her trek up those steep shepherd's and smugglers' paths to Galilea, his sister, Renee, also swayed and rocked to the invocative plaint. I then saw the stern demeanor on Barb's face melt, as she too, joined us, and, as we moved in unison, even Richard lifted his head and rocked back and forth in a reassured manner in his wheel-chair.

"In his autobiography, *Memories, Dreams, Reflections*, when Dr. Jung mentions that when he visited the Ute Indians at their Pueblo at Taos, New Mexico, and observed them celebrating one of their sacred rites, he said that the deeper resonances of their chanting had captivated his inner consciousness like nothing other that he had ever known except for some Berbers' musical performances he had encountered in North Africa some years before. He said that had he not been Swiss and was not then a practicing physician in his own country, that he would have given up all and joined them for the rest of his life, so enthralling was the experience of this communal deep valence timbre," I commented, after I finally brought my own Native American recital to a close.

Richard Hull's face was now alight with new vitality, and I felt assured that my offering had been gratefully accepted by the family and that I would be welcome to come and go as a treasured member from that day on. A glass of wine taken together then, and I made an appointment to return to begin Renee's English lessons, and I asked Richard if I could perhaps assist him in some manner in the work he must once again take up in the translation of 'The Seminars,' the last piece to be fit in to the Bollingen edition currently being published by the Mellon Foundation, whose editor-in-chief was the husband of the last woman to have been visiting at Can Bielo in Galilea with Ruthven Todd. She was a woman whom I had driven to the airport to remove her drunken influence on my friend, at his insistence. She had been his lover, but was so thoroughly intoxicated, that she became incontinent of bladder *and* bowel, in their *cama matrimonia*. [This is another example of the curious interweaving of the tapestry which I can only regard as *flamenco fugues*. I subsequently learned that in the year that Ruthven died, 1978, that the two Maguire sons established the 'Narcotics Anonymous' chapter in Barcelona and that their mother, a person everyone had considered as a hopelessly acute chronic alcoholic, stopped drinking and remained sober for the rest of her life with an active membership in 'Alcoholics Anonymous']. I did not find such a blessing for myself (recovery from active alcoholism) till 1982, in Palma . Mallorca, where I had, what I hope will be my last drink at 'Mam's Bar,' in Terreno, which claimed to be the oldest Amercian owned bar in Spain. Today, the area of Terreno around Plaza Gomila, which was once the hub of all the wildest social activity, is deserted, with only an internet and telephone center and a very few bar cafes scattered throughput on the otherwise desolate streets of that once vibrant neighborhood..

My friendship with the Hull family has continued. But Richard died only a few months after that first meeting, in 1973, when I had continued to visit and tutor Ruth while assisting Richard in his translating work. I had been on a short trip of less than a month to the United States, and when I returned and drove directly to Establiments from the airport on my way to my new home in Fornalutx, I had not telephoned first, reckoning that at that time of day, the early afternoon, that everyone would be taking siesta and a coffee or tea, and I could join them for a languid *post-prandial* snack. I loved having an opportunity to use this term, *prandial*, which referred to any meal, but had derived from the Latin for "late breakfast,' as everyone in the Hull family cherished refined vocabulary. This was the only place I ever heard anyone refer to the *crepuscular* time of day, an expression I had only encountered in one of Henry James novels, and thought it to be so rare, but it was Renee, who later became a professor of Linguistics, who told me that *crepuscula* occurs in ordinary manner of speech in Spanish for referring to the late afternoon, those moments just before what is usually called *dusk* in colloquial conversational English.

So when Barb greeted me at the door with a more than usual dour expression on her face, she told me simply what had happened: Richard was dead. I am often irritated in my American homeland, now, when someone tells me that a person *has passed* or *passed on*. I am then tempted to tell the rude joke about the cannibal who "*passed* a missionary in the jungle," meaning that he had a bowel movement in which the digested body of that Christian do-gooder was contained, but that meaning of the expression, *pass*, most likely would not be understood by the average American whose education renders him or her, semi-literate at best. Where I now reside, in Arkansas, the average Intelligence Quotient (Stanford Benet Scale) is not much higher than 80, twenty points below the Normal average score, and has been designated as Moron in the conventional educational realm.

At that moment, my mental processes ceased, and it was as if my own I. Q. dropped far lower than the average Arkansan's. I was literally *dumbstruck*. I asked permission to enter the *entrada* and sit down. And as I came to my senses, seeing that the library was empty, although the wheel-chair sat in the center of that room, Bea began to tell me what had happened. Her manner was matter-of-fact, and perhaps that is what made the story sound so horrifying.

Renee, whose body at fifteen was as full and sensually appealing as that of a fully developed mature woman, had been gang-raped by young men – who may or may not have been from the village. Even if she had been able to identify her assailants, the local police and the Guardia Civil would not conduct any criminal investigation of the case as she was the product of a union between two unmarried foreigners who definitely were not Christians. In Franco's Spain, only Roman Catholics had any actual legal rights, and it was presumed that all foreigners were not of the true faith. If one did not speak fluent Spanish, whatever the foreign tongue was one's first language, this aberrant idiom was referred to as *polaco* (Polish) in the vernacular idiom. So the "polack heathen" family of Ruth Hull, during the reign of Franco, was not protected by the law, that would be in effect for any Christian Spaniard. Renee would be referred to by most residents of Mallorca by their slang term, *sueca* (Swedish girl) which was synonymous with the English word *slut* – a young woman of no sexual morality.

Renee's family had flown her to London when it was discovered that Renee was pregnant, and Richard had become so severely depressed when the abortion was performed that he had sustained what was diagnosed as a complete nervous break-down. Ironically, and perhaps tragically, a son of his by a former marriage, who had become a psychiatrist, had ordered electro-shock therapy for his estranged father at the Jungian hospital, the Tavistock Clinic, where he was senior resident psychiatrist, and Richard had died of a heart attack during the treatment. Having suffered from poliomyelitis [that disease finally eradicated by Dr. Jonas Salk's discovery of a vaccine; that dreaded *polio* had loomed like a shadow of the Black Plague for me in my child-hood in Oklahoma, where several of my friends were stricken and paralyzed; it was sometimes called by the alternate, more terrifying name: *infantile paralysis*] which had crippled him and virtually immobilized the entire right side of his body twenty-five years before. The severe traumatic effect of the electro-shock procedure – an induced epileptic seizure – had killed him.

I could not forget the next to last finger on Richard's now dead (and decomposing or cremated) left hand which was tattooed with the symbol for *yin* and *yang*. I had imagined a spiritual guide of mine for the two years before meeting him with that identical marking in the same physical position, and I had wondered what I would do now to create a new spiritual guide. I did seek one out, and Richard's virtually Druidic eminence in my psychic realm was replaced by a figure dressed in tweed, whose entire demeanor screamed *county*, the sort of person referred to in England as a *squire*, whose title would be Esquire and his station, that of gentleman; he would have been a squire or page, attendant to a knight, in training to be ennobled once his apprenticeship as shield and sword -bearer and valet and footman and what would be later called at Eton, by the term, *fag* (the understudy and attendant to an older boy, charged with providing *faggots* of wood, kindling, for his fire-place and trusted to heat his morning bath-water and to provide virtually wifely comforts of the flesh – therefore, the term, *fag*, synonymous with homosexual partner in the feminine role) , Eton, College of Kings, located on the Thames alongside Windsor Castle. This replacement spiritual guide for me guide is named Clive, whom I have to this day still called upon for psychic counsel along with his feminine counter-part, a Creole, a girl named Ruby. I received these spirits in my initial training with Paul Fransella in Miami, Florida, in the Silva Mind Control, autogenics, guided visualization training I received there in 1972 when my body was transformed and assumed the new weight of 175 pounds, dropping from the 210 which I regained since I quit smoking in 1993 [at my present age, I maintain a trim 185 pounds]. I would no more tell my secret *mantra* word which I share with these psychic beings, than would students of the Mahareshi divulge their special password given in Trancendental Meditation; nor would Alastair Reid allow his finger or toe-nail clippings or cut hair to be taken by anyone, rather than be disposed of secretly and ritualistically by himself alone ('From "Notes from a Spanish Village" ,' *OASES: poems and prose*, Canongate Books Ltd., Edinburgh, p 216).

After the tragedy of Richard Hull's death *and* Ruth's massive *violation* - in Spanish, the word for *rape* is *violar* - I returned to my new home in Fornalutx where I stumbled about in a psychologically wounded state. I was reaching out for some way of coping with the loss of my literary, intellectual, and spiritual friend, Richard Hull. It was in only a few weeks. before I had the accident which sent me to King's College Hospital, Denmark Hill, London to have the right side of my face and head reconstructed by their skilled surgeons.

However, I was only some weeks away from the near-death experience with Alastair Reid, as he had returned to Galilea and was in the process of writing that essay, 'Notes from a Spanish Village,' for *The New Yorker*, where he had been a poetry editor for many years. Upon his arrival from the Dominican Republic and New York City, Alastair was enthusiastic and ebullient, and we had spent many long hours regaling one another with vignettes from our lives and with spicy snippets from our adventures. He even wrote out in a fine cursively printed long-hand a copy of my favorite poem, 'Curiosity', and dedicated it to me, thus: "Inscribed for Ben Wright, in his inimitable cat-incarnation, with warm Galilean wishings --- AR" [jammed together as one large cursive capital in which the letter *R* - the most prominent - overlaying the *A*].

He shared with us the first version of a poem written about our village, titled 'Galilea,' which I would not see in print for many years:

Bleached white, bedazzled
by the bright light falling,
the hilltop holds me up.

Below, the coastline bares in
Winded, burned to the bone, between
stony green of
the grey grimace of stone,
I look dazedly down.
How to come to rest
in this raw, whittled landscape
where earth, air, fire, water
bluntly demand obeisance?
Perhaps to fix one place
in a shifting world where time
talks and where too many selves
criss-cross and demand
enactment and re-enactment.
somewhere decent to die in,
somewhere which could become
landscape and vocabulary,
equilibrium, home.

(*OASES: poems and prose*, Canongate Books Ltd., 1997, p. 143)

Janet and I were then provided the special treat of hearing Alastair read the first page of the essay which became so famous in its publication in *The New Yorker*: 'Notes from a Spanish Village.' We sat on the terrace as the afternoon waned and the glow of that special Spanish dusk that wreathes high places such as ours gathered about our privileged selves, and Alastair delivered the following lines to us in his mellifluous voice, with now only a slight flavor of his Scot's burr, layered over by his European and South American and

Manhattan wanderings and residences. Trans-Atlantic was an inexact approximation of his vocal stamp; he was an original, like Cary Grant or Edward R. Murrow or David Niven or even Errol Flynn, an *inimitable persona* ... Alastair Reid..

> We are used to being surprised by the place [Galilea] – by the way each house looks out on the village, a different -shaped mountain. The mountains set the atmosphere – grey rocky crests hazy in the heat, with a fringe of pines on the tree line and, on the lower slopes, olive groves and long rows of darker-green almond trees. We climb steadily up, with the slow, bent-kneed plod that the villagers use, turning to look down over the village, a patchwork of ochre roofs and green terraces, and then we walk over the crest onto a small, fertile plateau, on the far corner of which stands our house, and, beside it, a little ilex forest, which falls steeply away to the next valley, far below.
> From the house, there is no trace of the village, and no sound other than the jangle of goat bells, or the bark of the dog on the adjoining farm. Sitting on the stone terrace, I can hear insects rustling in the wheat, the whirr of birds' wings, the stirring of leaves. Sounds of our rattling chain, the thud and plunge of the bucket, the creak of the wheel – loom loud in the attention. Over the village hangs the same towering silence. The hollows form acoustical traps, so conversations across the valley will float into hearing, the words just indistinguishable but the tune clear. The sound of an occasional car does not break the silence so much as puncture it slightly, thus under-lining it. On still afternoons, we can hear the children singing in the forest, shepherded by the nuns. The silence is such that we are careful about breaking it. (*OASES*, 192)

And it was so. We were there in the sanctuary of that place, the *genius loci*, or was it rather, a *sanctum sanctorum*? I have rarely felt so particularly delighted with being at one with all about me, with my companions, my *family*, for such was this coven of Janet, Alastair and I – Alaric, the cherubic child, was sleeping soundly in his bed inside the house, as the last glow of sunlight glimmered and then slid down away into the sea over the horizon toward Ibiza and the peninsula. I could only say, "Thank You," as did Janet; and Alastair merely smiled and nodded his acceptance.

And then something began to sour. Perhaps it had to do with Janet's jealousy of our male bonding and our high-flown literary and intellectual exchanges. But then, I realized that there was something deeply disturbing Alastair. One morning he was in an virtual hysterical state because he could not find his nail parings, which he had set aside the day before to perform some ritual disposal – he considered that if anyone got hold of these or clippings from his hair, that Black Magic – Voodoo – or some other form of Dark Art could be performed, and great harm would be done to him, physically and spiritually... so he informed us.

But there was some other concern he had that was tormenting him, and I subsequently learned that Janet had told him that I was the rich heir to an automotive parts company in Oklahoma. When he asked me directly if I were indeed a rich man, I had to deny this, although I drew a small monthly salary from the company, as a member of the board of directors as we settled the probate of my father's Last Will and Testament and attempted to consolidate all his indebtedness and to maintain a "going concern" – to use the specific accountancy designation for the effort to "stay in the black" – that is "out of the red" – to employ the slang terms of financial experts for such a business meeting its monthly payroll and not being forced to file for bankruptcy, as had been suggested, when my sister and I had first met with the board of directors for American Electric Ignition Company and Ben Wright Incorporated, upon the day of my father's death. As I tried to explain my fiscal profile for Alastair, he appeared to be building to an explosive brink of rage. He accused me of deceiving him regarding my status as a struggling poet. He claimed that I had led him to believe that I was desperate to find a place to live and work in order to continue in my chosen career as a writer. I reminded him that it was he who had presumed that I was poverty-stricken, but that I had never attempted to provide that impression. Indeed, I had invited him to our two bedroom furnished flat in Kensington, and had picked him up in my car from where he had been staying with his agent in Hampstead – this was not what anyone would expect of a starving artist, which I had never pretended to be, and I was really rather offended that he claimed his offer of residence in his home in Galilea had been precedented on his assumption that I was poor. I had presumed that he was offering the residence to a colleague, to someone he considered of an artistic talent worthy of his tutelage and mentor-ship – and I told him this.

He then announced that Janet and I were to vacate his home and find accommodation elsewhere, and this was to take effect immediately. He grumbled that if he had rented the place at the going rate (in the 1970s, this would have been less than $100 per month, at best), that he could have bought a bicycle for his son, who was living that summer in New York City and commuted some fifty city blocks back and forth to work. I laid a hundred dollar bill, Ben Franklin's face beaming, on the kitchen table and told Alastair that there were many more where that came from, but that without a contract, I would pay no more. He did not grab the bill and tear it in two, or even sweep it off the table in disdain. He rose, and began walking toward the stairway which led to the upper floor, his studio and library. As he grasped the rope that served as a hand-rail looped through upright steel posts that positioned on the upward incline, he gave a yelp and fell backward, over the rope, and on to the floor, after taking only three steps up. He lay there moaning, and his face was swollen in a reddened grimace. Both Janet and I rushed to help him sit upright, and to place cushions from the couch alongside and about his body so he could be comforted. Tears were running down his cheeks, and he cursed and bleated a demand that we bring him some water, iced, with lemon juice.

When we had gven him the drink of cold water with at least two lemons squeezed in, he begged for some aspirin or any strong pain-killer analgesics. I had some Paracetamol with Codeine I had brought from the chemist in London, and after swallowing several of these, he asked that we make a pallet for him on the floor where he now lay propped up against the stairway. Alaric was dozing soundly in his corner, and so Janet and I complied with Alastair's instructions, and then retreated to *our corner*, where we shared our double bed, and after turning out the main light, we crawled in under our sheet, where we whispered a word or two, and then we fell asleep.

We were awakened only a few hours later, by Alastair's screams. We rushed to console him, and it was then that I told Janet to dress quickly and set out across the ridge to Nora's house to ask her to use her telephone to contact a doctor, as the situation was looking dire, and perhaps serious and grave. Alaric was still sound asleep, exhausted by his day's over-active play in the hot sun. I sat by Alastair and tried to engage him in conversation. I asked when the pains had begun, if he had ever experienced anything like this before, and I told him that I had sent for a doctor.

He told me that he had eaten some shell-fish in a local restaurant in Santo Domingo the night before his flight to Spain and that perhaps he had food poisoning, but he had no nausea and his bowel was not loose. He just felt very feverish and dizzy and said he was still angry with me and considered me a fraud and a shit. Although he said he felt no nausea, it was as he spit out the last insults that I noticed his breath was rank and putrid. His eyes were rheumy and watery and his entire face appeared bloated and virtually blistered, as if hives from an allergic reaction were besieging his system. His breath smelled like something had died and decayed in some deep recess within him. I did not speak or answer any of Alastair's comments or complaints. I could only sit there and look at his distended facial features and wonder at what toxic entity or malevolence could possibly have possessed the otherwise gentle and prophetic poet I had heretofore considered him to be.

Perhaps some local *bruja* (witch or enchantress) had indeed scuttled off with those missing nail filings he was so distraught about having misplaced, and she was, even now, casting his soul into torments of her pre-Christian Balearic equivalent locale of Hades. These islands had been inhabited by Hamilcar Barca and ruled by his son, the formidable African general, Hannibal, and before that, there had been countless strange and now unknown civilizations that had thrived here. When I was with Bill Waldren, we had made preliminary digs at an overhang beneath the cliffs of Bauza, the mountain that stood at the end of the long valley below the village of Galilea, where we had found human artifacts which were later carbon-dated at 7,000 B.C. I was entertaining such wild speculations when an apparently demonic presence burst in the front door, accompanied by a flurry of blonde chatter I recognized as Janet.

Doctor Pedro (Perico) Villaescusa Garcia, reminded me of one of the only Hispanic - *chicano* - people I had ever known who qualified for membership in the Hell's Angels of San Francisco by Free-wheeling Frank Reynolds who had set the strict requirements for entry into acceptance in that outlaw motorcycle club: *Class.* Perico would become one of my life's most intimate and trusted friends, but at this moment, I was startled by his physical appearance. He was my height, of a definite athletic build – I discovered later that he had been a champion competitive swimmer – and his hair was a wild tangle of black curls that hung to his shoulders. His beard was not as full as he would have desired it to become, yet strikingly similar to that of "Che" Guevara, and I would also learn that his personal dedication to the medical profession had been precedented on the model of that Cuban revolutionary doctor, who had declared, " After receiving my degree I began to travel through Latin America. In the way I traveled, first as a student [see *The Motorcycle Diaries: Notes on a Latin American Journey* (Ocean Press, New York: 2004) – on his motorcycle "La Poderosa II" – in 1951] and afterward as a doctor, I began to come into close contact with poverty and hunger, with disease, with the inability to cure a child because of lack of resources ... And I began to see there was something that, at that time, seemed to me almost as important as being a famous researcher or making some substantial contribution to medical science, and this was helping people (from appendix: "A Child of my Environment," 1960).

But we had no time to waste with formal introductions. Perico strode to Alastair's pallet and squatted down before him, smiling in a mischievous manner, a teasing, virtually taunting grin on his face, and asked if he should speak English or Spanish. Alastair answered in a brusque street idiom of the Spanish –*cotidiano* – and was answered by an expletive from Perico in the same nasty slang that would have withered any proper rules for the conduct of conversation in any language. They bonded on a level probably only possible in this idiom, which I understood as that spoken by my neighbors in the *barrio* of my street, Calle Lope de Vega, in Madrid, where my first conversations were with whores, beggars and criminals. The loving but offensive – if translated literally – terms of address, referred to one's illegitimacy and perverse sexual inclinations, as in some terms in English such as calling another male, *bitch* or *bastard*, however, in the Spanish *patois*, the words *cuño* (cunt) and *tio* (uncle – almost impossible to explain as a disrespectful appellation), was repeatedly voiced by both men. Nevertheless, when Alasatair said that his own mother was a doctor, he was stating a fact, and he did not mean to imply anything about Perico's mother, as would have been the case if such a strategy from "doing the dozens" as in American slum-land slanging matches were employed. Alastair was merely stating that he was familiar with many medical facts, and that he was unable to diagnose his own condition, but he did not believe he had anything more serious than a case of food poisoning. It was then that I observed Perico's practical skills as a diagnostician and a general practitioner of medicine. He pressed his hand in to my friend's lower belly in such a way that Alastair let out a scream which became a string of curses which *did indeed* insult Perico's mother and many other members of his family, and a few revered personalities sacred to the history of Spain ... *and the entire human race.* He then attempted a round-house swing with his fist aimed squarely at the at the doctor's head, which the man lithely parried, and returned with a blow to the poet's lower jaw, so powerful that Alastair was knocked unconscious and crumpled in a heap on the floor.

Perico ordered me to help him pick up and carry the patient form the house, and in no time we had him swung between us and were dragging him down the path to where a sturdy old French Deux Chevaux (Citroen 2CV), the doctor's car, was parked. As we rushed toward the vehicle, he explained to me that Alastair was probably suffering from a ruptured appendix and that we would stop at the main village shop where he could telephone [forty years ago we never dreamed of cell or mobile telephones] to the Cruz Roja [Red Cross] hospital and schedule emergency surgery with the best resident there, Dr. Aguila. I was amazed that all was so skilfully arranged in such short order, and I was becoming aware now that my friend might be actually dying. I asked the young Spaniard if he thought my friend might be in real danger, and his answer was one of those proverbs that only beg the question of mortality, but he laughed and told me that we were on the very edge of life and death, and I was feeling closer to that inevitability as he pressed down the accelerator and drove around the mountain curves in race-car skids that almost took us over the edges above sheer ravines with drops of several hundred meters ... more than once.

When we arrived in Palma and pulled in to the entrance to the hospital, a gurney was wheeled out, as Perico blew his horn full blast in the doorway. I scampered to keep up with the transport of my friend who was beginning to regain consciousness only now, and was being restrained as his body was unceremoniously shot in to the operating theatre where a glowering man was already suited up and ready to begin cutting. I was asked to leave only in order to sign a document which identified me as next of kin and therefore legally empowered to grant permission for what might be a life-endangering procedure. I had no qualms about doing so (perjury was preferable to my friend's demise), and then hurried back inside where I saw the surgeon now extract a greenish, slimy object from the stomach cavity which he held aloft, and laughing, asked if anyone would like to add this delicious morsel to their late lunch *paella*. Perico nudged me and grinned as he told me that this ugly wad of putrefied flesh was the septicemic ruptured appendix – an object resembling a squashed tennis ball left to mold and rankle under some stump – and that the poison in my friend's body would take several days to siphon off, while his immune system would strive to regain some regenerative equilibrium.

As the doctor completed his work, closed up the incision, and the nurses wheeled Alastair off to an Intensive Care unit, Doctor Villaescusa introduced me to Doctor Aguila, the surgeon, and chief of staff at Cruz Roja Hospital. Aguila was aware of my friend's identity and knew of Alastair's former relationship as *amanuensis* to Robert

Graves who had been a friend of Aguila's for over twenty years. Small island. Enormous respect for the arts. Because I was introduced as a fellow poet and colleague, the surgeon was enormously respectful of me and assured me that we had acted in the very nick of time and that, Alastair Reid, this formidable translator of Pablo Neruda and Gabriel Marques, would indeed recover and be once again able to carry on his vital service in the highest of literary art: poetry. I am ever reminded that in Spain, and particularly in Catalonia, and most especially in the Balearic Islands, the artist is esteemed above all others as a virtual prophet ... who is *not without honor* there ... albeit such talented persons as these luminaries, are often considered degenerates and outcasts in America.

When I inquired about the costs for all that had been done for Alastair - the surgery, the Intensive Care, all the supplies and equipment that usually provide a dreadnaught debt in American medical centers - I was told by Perico not to worry, that we could arrange for the payment with the emergency funds which were used for such life-and-death situations, considered part of the service of the International Red Cross, for which the hospital was a sort of subsidiary, and that since Alastair was a British subject, that his National Health program would pay for all the hospitalization and surgical expenses. I was amazed, and enormously relieved.

The more important matter at hand, announced Perico's wife, Vicen, who had just arrived, having ordered a taxi to bring her from the village, was to find a decent place for lunch, to celebrate the successful operation and convalescence of our friend, a *poet*, and to consecrate the new friendship that had thus been established between me and Perico ... and his wife, Vicen. She was a sturdy peasant woman whose home was in the north of Spain, Zaragossa, where she had studied to become a nurse, and had then met Perico there at the end of his studies in the hospital where he had served as an intern.

She was skeptical that any good could come from a bonding between me, an American of obviously privileged background, who had elected to become an artist and had allied with the New Left movement led by Herbert Marcuse, my former mentor, and spearheaded by the fiery and enormously popular, and notorious, Angela Davis, who had become an intimate colleague of mine. Vicen was of the opinion that Perico and I were perhaps all too similar and therefore a potentially dangerous combination. We were both traitors to our class. *Young Turks. Black Sheep. Tear-Aways. Mavericks.* We both possessed an uncanny ability to wrest failure and disaster from the very jaws of success. We fed on chaos and loved swimming in the maelstrom of madness ... she said. Vicen was astute and insightful ... and wise ... and so often right!

What I was to learn, as Perico and I became friends, was that the family name, Villaescusa, belonged to Perico's uncle, one of the most feared and renowned members of Generalissimo Franco's government. He was General Villaescusa, the chief of the entire legal system, head of the Military Court system, the highest ranking officer in martial law in the land, and later was named captain of all Madrid. Perico had been reared by this man, a bachelor, who considered this boy to be virtually his only son. Although the boy had excelled as an athlete, and shone as a scholar at university, involvement with the not only forbidden, but patently illegal, Leftist political activities had sorely tried the patience of this doting surrogate father, who had on many occasions had to bend the very law of which he was the Draconian figurehead and chief, to snatch his nephew from the clutches of not only the dreaded political branch of the Guardia Civil (the Spanish equivalent of Hitler's Gestapo), but also from the avenging dark Inquisitorial demons of the Opus Dei, the deadly ecclesiastical enforcers of Franco's iron rule and crippling Fascist control of all opposition. Vicen feared that each of us might attempt to outdo the other in our *revolutionary* strutting and that we both would end up in prison ... or worse. As it was, we came to argue and to actually physically fight with one another on some occasions, once rolling about in the gravel verge of the roadside at the turn into the final ascent into the village of Galilea at about 5 A.M. one morning after carousing most of the night in the *Barrio Chino* (the Spanish slang term for the red-light [brothel and drug den] district in Palma – literally translating as *China Town*, although there was no Chinese population anywhere on the island). Mike Syson, who had accompanied us on one of our all-night benders and had pulled Perico off my chest as he was about to smash me once more in the face after an extended fist-fight we had been conducting after skidding to a stop just as we reached the village and had wrestled one another out of the car, was shocked by Perico's cavalier remark, "It's allright. If I break his nose this time, I can fix it. I am a doctor, after all!".

For the next week or so, after Alastair's hospitalization, Janet and I stayed with Grahame Duffield and his wife on the other end of the island, in their luxurious home on the beach just outside of the ancient city of Alcudia. I would daily transit the length of the island ((roughly forty kilometers) and back, two hours of hard driving, to check on Alastair, as he was placed in one of Cruz Roja's few private rooms, and appeared to be recovering from the severe septicemia infection from the burst appendix which had virtually poisoned his entire body   He was not conscious the first few visits, and I was alarmed on my second visit by the work of a male nurse who had missed placement of the intravenous glucose drip – the cretin had merely stuck it in the patient's upper arm which had then swollen horribly before we could remedy the situation and place the needle in the vein where it was meant to be. When Alastair did regain consciousness, his first remarks were to again remind me that I was no longer a welcome guest in his home. I assured him that we had moved out and then asked if there was anything he might need from his office there, and I asked if he wanted me to contact Jasper or any other members of his family. He told me that he had already used the hospital telephone and that he was arranging for transfer to a hospital for further treatment in the United Kingdom. I find it surprising even now after so many years have passed, that Alastair never thanked me for my help ... timely and vital assistance which had saved his life.

So I was not completely startled, a week later, when I encountered the person whom Alastair had subsequently appointed as his caretaker, virtually *in loco parentis*, with power of attorney and all rights of a next-of-kin: Gloria Meade, the former wife of Patrick Meade, who had now moved in with another woman (Stephanie, whom he later married and inherited her substantial estate) in Deya, abandoning his Galilea wife and new-born daughter. This was that wife, Gloria Meade, who had threatened to denounce me and Robert Stratton to the Guardia Civil for introducing her husband to the pornography consortium operating out of the orgy palace, "Mar i Vent," on the Valldemossa road outside Deya. It was her dangerous *denuncio* which she had said she would make to the Guardia Civil which had convinced me to flee the island only a couple of years before. This formidable harridan met me at the bedside of my poet friend, and declared that she was now in charge, that none of my services were any longer needed, and that I had been nothing but a nuisance and a burden for her dear Alastair to bear, and he nodded in agreement and added succinctly that I was to leave and to never dare approach him again for any reason whatsoever. She reminded me that she was still capable of bringing charges against me for my involvement with the *criminals* who had seduced her dear husband and had corrupted his effete writing skills and impelled him to abandon his wife and child ... and ... I took my leave, and bade this newly bonded loving couple, Alastair and Gloria, both prosperity and good health, and I returned to my loved ones, Janet and Alaric, in Alcudia, where I was not recriminated with such punishment for my good intentions.

When I told Janet about encountering this woman, she recalled meeting a person who fit the description, and then told me about Alastair's visits to a house he had called The Sid, which she had imagined to be one of his perverse jokes. The Meades did own a home called 'Can Cid,' named for the Spanish epic hero, El Cid (Rodrigo Diaz de Vivar: 1043-1099). When I related the history of my relationship with Patrick and his wife, and how I had decided to leave the island when threatened with a *denuncio*, Janet was outraged and was ready to "take up cudgels," as the British sometimes say, and go show this woman *what for*. I was rather amused, but pleased, that my woman should want to "enter the lists" on my behalf [how many more such medieval expressions for armed conflict I can not now imagine appropriate to this occasion]; nevertheless, I reckoned that our moving to Deya, or Soller, or even farther, would dampen this witch's ire, and especially if she were committed to nursing her new lover, Alastair, through the period of his convalescence, she would be loath to bring any vindictive action against me with the local law enforcement authorities. Her relationship with Alastair would immediately disqualify her for making a *denuncio* as he had already been deemed less than politically acceptable in Spain, for his book about Mallorca (*La Isla Azul*) was banned throughout the country, and he had been reprimanded severely for some of the articles critical of Franco he had published in the international press. He was lucky to be allowed to stay on the island, as he was considered to be of the Marxist persuasion, and not a friend to the current regime.

I was deeply hurt by my friend's change of heart, which really was a betrayal of our comradeship, and a violation of the bond I believed was sacred to all poets, but then he had also betrayed his mentor, Robert Graves, by stealing that great poet's mistress, Margo Callas (later Margo Nichols when she married the American film director,

Mike Nichols) when she was fulfilling Graves' fantasy of her being the living embodiment of the White Goddess, with Graves's wife Beryl's acquiescence and approval. At that time, some ten years before this, Graves had cursed his *amanuensis* and surrogate son, Alastair, and had demanded that all publishers refuse to allow Reid to appear in print ever again. I too felt that I had been cast out of Eden, into the Land of Nod, and as Janet and I searched for suitable housing to rent, I felt more than a twinge of resentment, and could not equate how and why I should be punished for helping Patrick Meade and saving Alastair Reid's life. I did not actually encounter Alastair for another twenty-five years. I was delivering the same speech I had given on behalf of the Robert Graves Trust at St. John's College, Oxford University, at the Municipal Auditorium in Palma, Mallorca, invited as a guest speaker by the British Council, in 1995. I noticed him sitting in the middle of the audience. As I concluded my presentation, which was the last of that evening's speeches. I walked away from the stage down the center aisle, and as I had reached where he was seated, Alastair called out to me and offered to meet me in the mezzanine bar for a drink.

I was charmed, as always, by his elegant *savoir faire* and *elan*. I broached the subject of asking why he should now deem it appropriate to wish to once again befriend me. He stated simply that as I had saved his life, that he felt I might call upon him to do me a favor and that he would have been obligated to comply with any of my wishes and frankly he just did not want to be of service to me. So there. The blunt truth. We had a drink together and then shared my rental car to drive to Deya to visit Beryl , Tomas, Joan, and Lucia Graves at the family home, now the official Graves museum, property of the Spanish government. We then visited some other writers and artists still in residence in the village. George Sheridan, the painter, shocked Alastair by declaring when we met that I had saved his - Sheridan's - life. George often claimed that I was instrumental in curing his cancer because I had come to his house while visiting Deya in 1990, when he was undergoing radiation treatment for a malignant tumor in his throat, and I had instructed him in basic autogenics, a simple regimen of guided visualization using self-hypnosis techniques which I had employed in healing my own crippling rheumatoid arthritis, as well as the injuries to my head and face when it was reconstructed by plastic surgery and ophthalmic and dental surgeries as well, in 1973, at King's College Hospital, London. I was delighted to watch Alastair's reaction to a fellow artist who was so deeply grateful and generously appreciative - fearing I might ask for a favor in return, would never have occurred to George, and he would have given me anything I asked for anyway - for what I had done to help him in his darkest hour. He did present me with a painting of the Buddha as a gift.

During this period of Alastair's hospital confinement in Palma (1972), Janet and I stayed only another week with the Duffields before finding a suitable house in Fornalutx to rent from the former publisher of tourist language textbooks in Canada, Leonard Harrop. I had begun looking for a suitable boat which could accommodate us and which I might use to go exploring for the Corporation Not For Profit foundation I was then establishing with Sam Coffing. The American Institute for Mythographic Studies' was registered in Florida, where I now declared my legal United States residence to be, as I had given Sam my power-of-attorney in virtually all my financial affairs, and this was his home and the site of his company, "International Resources Management, Incorporated.' I was planning to include David Dow on my first voyage back into Scandinavian waters, where we had first sailed as shipmates on Sam's yacht, *Nachen II*, in 1966, when Marian and I had also been aboard, voyaging up the English Channel, into the North Sea, and then into the Baltic. Unfortunately, David was sentenced to ten years in federal prison for his practical joke in stealing government uranium from a nuclear plant in North

Carolina, and then attempting to extort a multi-million dollar ransom for its return. His idea was to use this money to buy a small island in the Caribbean where he intended to establish himself as dictator and declare war on the United States, then surrender gracefully and request money to rebuild his "war-torn" nation. He had pledged to name me as Minster of Culture – and fortunately, I had declined his gracious largesse. The entire fantasy had derived from combinations of David's intake of alcohol, cocaine and L.S.D. Sam and I devoted the next several years to winning his release from confinement. He served over five years in approximately ten different federal prisons, one of which, he claimed was where a psychiatrist from the Soviet Union, who had specialized in breaking the spirit of enemies of the U.S.S.R. in their cruel political *gulags*, had been exchanged when he defected in return for his enacting the same harsh measures on our own American political dissidents – David was considered a politically deviant individual for this latest escapade and therefore became a victim of this exceedingly sadistic warden. David had, after all, been discharged from the United States Army for declaring himself a Conscientious Objector after completing Green Beret Training at Fort Benning where he was then confined to the stockade to serve three years at *hard labor*, after which he had been sentenced to two years on a chain-gang for resisting the assault on some Freedom Riders with whom he had hitched a ride back to Florida ... before he had been sufficiently indoctrinated in their policy of *passive resistance*. So, David had been considered a definite political agitator and radical, although his primary motivation was usually to just have the most amusing time possible ... which unfortunately, was interpreted by law enforcement agencies as making him the epitome of a dedicated Left-Wing, radical, provocateur identity profile. He recounted his "brain-washing" by the Soviet zealot warden as one of the most hilarious examples of bullying that would have made some of the slap-stick, swat-matching episodes of 'The Three Stooges' seem benign and harmless. However, his own "Merry Prankster" Weltanschauung had been severely battered and virtually eliminated by that skilled Soviet psychiatrist.

However, when I was shopping for boats, none of this had as yet transpired, David was still a free man, and it was only shortly after I purchased *Tsunami*, from the widow of its owner and designer, Commander Robert Luker, United States Navy, Retired, that David was removed from my ship's company billet as he had been sentenced to ten years in prison. Janet had befriended Bob Luker's ex-wife when we had been in Deya and Palma. I was always flattered by Patricia Luker who said that I was the handsomest man in the entire foreign community in Mallorca. She had a young man in tow, named Martin, who she told everyone was a sculptor, but in actual fact he was a former *international routier* truck driver from Germany who had played some semi-professional football, and then had learned a new trade as a *gigolo* when he arrived on the island. Patricia was at least thirty years his senior. He seemed to enjoy being her escort and lived wherever Patricia and her daughter, Diandra abode. I had first met this mother and daughter on the archeological expedition to Venta Carteia with Bill Waldren when I first arrived in Spain in 1967, and at that time, Diandra was only nine years old, but already she was showing signs of becoming the skilled pathological liar and poseur she developed into in order to snare Michael Douglas as a husband, having been presented at Jimmie Carter's Inaugural Ball in Washington, D.C., in 1975, pretending to be a titled Spanish princess whose palatial residence in Valldemossa was 'Mar i Vent,' that monument to one of his lovers built by the Archduke Salvatore, that same gothic mansion where all the pornography orgies of Bill Matthews had been held, and after his tragic death, where the brutal murder of a mother by her son (stabbed over thirty times) had made this palace most unattractive for leasing, so that Patricia Luker had been able to snag the place for less than four hundred dollars a month, with the groundskeepers' salaries included.

As a child playing on the beach in the Cala of Deya, Mallorca, with other children, Diandra would refuse to rough-house and scrupulously avoided any physical contact with other youngsters lest her *jewelry* be damaged; she claimed to be wearing priceless heirlooms – costume bric-a-brac as necklaces and ear-rings, which she insisted were the real item. The other children played along with this pretentiousness, only up to a certain point, and then they would grab the valuables and toss them into the surf or bushes, wherever the activities were taking place. Diandra would scream in horror and rush to her mother, demanding that the police, or Guardia Civil, be called to arrest the miscreants who had stolen these treasures. Patricia would console her with some new fantasy and usually find a way to excuse them both and then "fling away with high disdain" from these low-life commoners she had somehow had the ill fortune to have encountered. Patricia Luker also fabricated and confabulated a delusionary script for Diandra's paternity, making mystifying references to Joan Miro, Robert Graves, and the father of the Prince Don Juan Carlos, the last actual king of Spain. Although, when he had been in the money, and was bribing Patricia for some periods of visitation privileges with his daughter, and could bestow enormous amounts of money on the two regal ladies –his divorced wife and daughter – it was admitted that *perhaps* Commander Luker was the biological father of Diandra ... as well. When Janet and I encountered Pat Luker, her husband had died of a heart attack using the toilet in the 'Bar Hawaii,' Paseo Maritimo, Palma, owned by his lover at that time whom he had left Pat to live with in his final alcoholic binge. Pat would not admit readily to most that this had indeed been his fate, but she did pretend that there was no holographic will deeding all his property to his bar-owner girl-friend – a yacht and a grand mansion in Beniaraitx, the village next to Fornalutx – and I believed the document she had fabricated by her lawyer, Antonio Ferrer, an associate of the American Consul for Mallorca, a man named ironically, Bestard, who would agree to any legal contract generated by his pal the lawyer, Ferrer, whose office was next door to his at this upmarket address on Jaimie Tercero, just off the Borne Boulevard, in Palma, near the central Post Office.

For any Confidence Man to succeed, there must already exist in his target for the trick or scam, such a vulnerable weakness as an element of the fraudulent. I have a strain of the deceitful and conniving in my own character, and therefore am a prime target for the scam-artist. I was more or less aware that Pat Luker did not hold *bona fide* clear legal ownership of the boat, but she had been able to wrangle some documents from the lawyer, Ferrer, with impressive appearing stamps and official notary endorsements, so that it seemed that she was the actual, final heir to all the property of the deceased ex-spouse, Commander Robert Luker, U.S.N. – Retired. Although his last lover, the owner of the "Bar Hawaii" actually visited me on the yacht, after I had paid $15,000 to Pat Luker for all the documents, as well as the remainder of Bob Luker's membership at Real Club Nautico, and his entitlement to several months in a privileged slip on their docks, I told Commander Luker's lover that she would have to contend with the American Consul, Bestard, and his Spanish lawyer pal, Ferrer. and even then, she would probably have to travel to California, to Santa Barbara, where Captain Luker, the octogenarian father of Bob Luker, resided, in order to participate in the probating of the inheritance, of which she was really entitled to receive the major portion, *if* the California courts would recognize the holographic Last Will and Testament, handwritten by Bob Luker only weeks before his ugly demise of heart failure while on the toilet at the back of her bar.

I was sympathetic, but I also realized that this woman was as miserably weak a chronic acute alcoholic as Bob Luker, and that she probably would never be able to marshal the strength or confidence to organize her campaign to make any demand effectual in capturing what legally belonged to her ... *and she never did.* Pat Luker pranced blithely about her presumed business as Bob Luker's heiress, selling his Palma apartment and the mansion in Beniaraitx, and nobody ever dared challenge her right to do so. She transferred all the money out of Spain to America and elsewhere, and she was then able to wheedle her way into the good graces of Paul Marriott, original owner of the famed hotel chain, and was staying with him in the U.S.A in 1975 when she then presented her daughter, Diandra, as Princess of Valldemossa, at the Presidential Inaugural Ball of Jimmie Carter, where, Michael Douglass in attendance with his drug-using buddy, Jack Nicholson, became instantly infatuated by this eighteen year-old lovely virgin Spanish *princess* whom he married only weeks later ... and then had to set about establishing a pedigree to fit his fantasy, engineered by some of the most clever and corruptible aristocrats in the city of Palma, Mallorca. One of my closest friends, Tony Juncosa, a top-flight archotect whose patrician family had built the famed Soller/Palma narrow-gauge railway, and had been a sometime beaux of the teenaged Diandra, told me that he had actually seen and held in his hand, many of the fabricated (be-ribboned and officially stamped) pedigree documents manufactured for Diandra by her new husband's hired agents, which claimed she was a part of the most aristocratic Mallorquin family: *Moray.*

In order to avoid any further involvement with the owner of 'Bar Hawaii,' and to remove the yacht from daily public notice and enquiry, I moved her to the 'Alcudia Yacht Club,' as soon as I had repaired its major disabling flaws. *Tsunami* had been custom-built in the Port Hamble shipyard, Isle of Wight, England, under the scrupulous and painstaking supervision of Commander Robert Luker, who had been a skilled guided-missile designer for the U.S. Navy before retiring - unable to receive promotion, regardless of his ability and talent, because of his sad problem with addiction to alcohol and suspicion that he was also experimenting with smoking Marijuana and using L.S.D. He had inherited substantial amounts of money from his parents, retired in Santa Barbara, California, but they had been so distressed by the extravagance and vulgar pretensions of his Australian wife, Patricia, that they had given her an outright gift of $100,000 in return for her promise that she would not contest the divorce he was determined to win before his untimely death in 1973.

Tsunami's hull was of specially steel reinforced fiberglass, manufactured in Norway as a sea-going rescue vessel - actually it was what is referred to as a *planing hull* - meant to be lifted up onto the planing surfaces running the length of the hull by a sufficiently powerful thrust of engines and thereby to increase its speed enormously. However, the gross weight of the craft with all engines and auxiliary installations topped 10,000 pounds. The twin Perkins diesel six-cylinder engines were attached to inboard /outboard Z-drives which could be raised and lowered to increase the pitch and thrust of the power-train, but the hull could never be driven so fast as to lift out of the water onto the planing surfaces; the maximum speed attainable was only about twelve knots (nautical miles per hour), and the boat had been rigged, as well, to carry sail on a main-mast planted in the center of the craft. The generic description of the vessel was motor-sailor, but it was more an hermaphrodite with James Bond illusions - there was a salt-water conversion unit attached to the exhaust manifold designed to distill pure water for extended survival; the port-holes were all bullet proof plexiglass; there was a food disposal and dishwasher which served also as a clothes washer; there was even a wood-burning steel fireplace assemblage that was meant to resemble a New England stove. Everything was over-stated, and crammed into a water-line length overall of not more than twenty-eight feet (the bowsprit, however, did extend another four feet forward) with an eight foot beam, and the ample overhead in the main saloon, for a man my size to stand upright (therefore over six feet three inches in height). With a skilled crew of marine mechanics, I directed that the boat be stripped down to bare necessities for travel which I decided must occur soon, as there were no paid taxes or approved official permissions in effect for the boat to remain in Spain as Luker had never bothered to comply with local regulations, and there could be heavy fines pending if the boat were ever discovered to not possess such acceptable paperwork. Also, by a stroke of providential good fortune, I had learned that by international maritime law, that once I had cleared the vessel through a minimum of at least two other port's custom authorities, that the boat would be forevermore in my absolute ownership. Because Patricia Luker was not pressing the settlement of the probating of her husband's estate in California, and the ex-girl-friend who possessed the Holograph Will was probably going to remain sitting inactively and passively intoxicated in her Palma bar till her own demise, I would have to insure that this boat, which I was intending to become my home, would remain in my possession, *legally*.

Tsunami had been used only a few times before Luker had begun his final drinking binge. After spending well over $150,000 in its customized construction, the entire boat had been loaded aboard a ship and transported to Palma. The first time it had been out of the dry-dock at the ship yard where it was built, was when it had been placed in a slip at the Real Club Nautico. When Luker took her out into the bay and motored about for a few hours, he returned to find his bilges awash with sea-water. There was a leak somewhere aboard this luxurious yacht. The vessel was pulled up out of the water, placed on blocks, and every inch - *or almost every inch* - was examined ... but to no avail. The Z-drives were detached and the flanges where they attached to the drive shafts of the diesels were minutely inspected. No flaws could be found, so they were reconnected and another cruise was made. Upon return to port, the bilges were again filled with water. The boat was considered by many a mariner in Palma harbor to be cursed, and as rumors will spread throughout the superstitious world of sailors, *Tsunami* was deemed a devil ship, cursed, and unsalvageable. For this reason, no one in the boating community of Mallorca was in the least interested in considering this boat for purchase, and I was able to buy it for the price I offered: $15,000

As most people in the boating world know, a yacht in good condition, even a few years old, will sell for anywhere from $1,000 dollars, per foot of water-line length. *Tsunami* was twenty-eight feet, only a few months old, and should have begun at an offered price of about $30,000, at the very least. I had a *steal*. However, there was that problem of the *phantom leak*. I had my mechanics dismount the Z-drives manufactured by Volvo and carefully inspect the seals when we re-connected them. They were patently sound. No water leaked into the boat in this fashion, even when subjected to great pressure and as much stress as we could exert upon the units and their union with the Perkins diesel engines. The only other portions of the hull with penetration through the fiber-glass occurred at the position of the mounting for the depth-sounder and the single interior shaft which served to provide sea-water for the toilet and its exhaust valve. And it was at this *intimate* connection juncture that we found the single point of entry. A fitting attached to the shaft where water was pumped up into the toilet to purge its waste, was missing one screw ... a single screw had not been connected to one place on a plate fixed to the shaft, and through this small hole, what had rushed in, especially when the hull was moving through the exterior water and providing a constant wash below in the bilges, which of course were then pumped continuously by the bilge pumps when the boat was underway - but when this movement ceased, then the water poured into the bilges. Once we placed that screw in its proper mount, and sealed it in, the *phantom leak* disappeared and the bilges remained forever dry thenceforth, and empty of intruding water.

Why had nobody been as thorough-going as I had been? Everyone had presumed that the water leakage problem derived from connections to power-drive units, and the toilet had never been examined with any focused attention. Probably because I was not of the local yachting community, and I readily admitted to anyone that I did not know very much about boats, I therefore had to approach every situation with an innocent eye, with no preconceptions, and thus I could *see* things that others just presumed were not there. That is why I moved the boat to the less salubrious docks at Arenal, a portion of Mallorca that was usually visited only by the lower classes of bargain holiday-makers. The sophisticated inhabitants of the island pretended that this area just did not exist, as it appeared to be little better than a tawdry imitation of an American highway array of low-cost motels and bars, and honky-tonks - discos and strip joints predominating the scene, patronized by lurching *lager louts* from the United Kingdom and Scandinavia who had only the vaguest idea that they were in Spain and not Blackpool, Stavanger, or Stockholm. Anyone concerned with investigating the legal status of *Tsunami* would hesitate before diving into the ugly and noisome territory of Arenal. This section of Palma, where the international airport had been positioned and then skirted by the city of Palma's sewage disposal plants, before outraged tourists had discovered that the city fathers had just pumped that effluent fecal waste into the sea, on the city's *back-side*. It was then buffered by the encampments of Gypsies who were not allowed to live within the walls of any city in Spain under Franco's rule, and then the beach [*arena,* the Spanish word for *sand*] stretched South-west of the cathedral and Palma's port, several miles in a flat beach to the cape, Cabo Brava, and this was the area called Arenal. At the very end of this stretch of sand was a small dock with weekend pleasure craft which then presumed to call itself the 'Arenal Yacht Club.' There was a bar which served food and yet was never geared up enough to provide anything more sumptuous than sandwiches and *tapas,* so could not be named restaurant. It was an ideal hide-out for me, and for this reason, I planned to make my move on to *Tsunami* as my primary residence.

Janet was preferring to spend more of her time in Soller where she had placed Alaric in a Church *colegio* [a general term for *school,* which, in this case, was a most educational variety of play-school, without any of the religious curriculum of the actual elementary classes which he would be eligible to enroll in within a couple more years]. He was a sociable creature, and everyone loved his Nordic coloration: a mop of platinum blonde hair and bright blue eyes. He could hold his own with any of the swaggering little, macho, Mallorquin lads, and the girls all adored him. Although he was required to wear the bib which was the top garment of girls and boys alike, when he arrived some days, before changing into this uniform, he would be in the cowboy attire which I had given him, complete with wooly chaps and pistol belt, his vest with the sheriff's brass star pinned to his sturdy chest – he broadcast a virtual Hollywood presence in that sombre Roman Catholic schoolyard.

I had taken advantage of the separation from Janet to carry on some flirtations with an American photographer for *Vogue* named Roberta Booth [she was strikingly beautiful, as well, having once been the face of 'Princess L'Oreal' cosmetics] and also I had begun meeting with a German divorcee named Karin who lived in a village near Palma, called Esporles, but she worked as a general *dogs-body,* handy-man around the boatyards in Palma. Both casual flirtations accelerated into full-blown sexual relationships rather rapidly. Roberta had a small *porche* (simple workman's hut used for storing tools and at times provided a shelter for a sheep or two – it was about twelve by sixteen feet square, but she had begun to make it a livable camp-out) a quarter of a mile up the cemetery road from the center of Fornalutx. She had purchased this simple shelter from Sonny, a man well-known for his dealing in imported goods from India, Turkey, and Bali, as well as notorious for his trafficking the hush-hush hashish,and even some home-grown Marijuana. Sonny was the epitome of the British expression, *spiv*, one of those fringe characters who hover around the edges of every British enclave, who always will arrange to find you a special deal in any commodity – for a fee. Sonny had been in prison once, and swore he would never be incarcerated again. As it was, he tricked Eric Flakoll [this redoubtable lad, had earned a Black Belt in Shotokan Karate, was devoted to the ideals of Che Guevarra, served as a soldier in Nicaragua and became the body-guard of the president and eventually was commander-in-chief of the entire armed forces of that country ... after his release from a British incarceration] the son of the poet Claribelle Alegria into taking a "fall" for him in a British jail, some five years later. I only once visited Roberta in her place where she had another girl, a model for one of her photo-shoots on special assignment from *Playboy,* staying with her. Most of our dalliance was carried on in the boat either in Palma, or later, in Arenal.

Karin, however, was a much more involved *affair*. Once she actually appeared in the 'Bellavista' restaurant in Fornalutx where I took many of my meals and did my drinking. She walked in, and passed right by the table I occupied with Janet and Alaric, and then hovered outside on the patio, sitting at a table by herself, so that Janet finally remarked on the odd behavior of this woman who seemed to be constantly staring in our direction. She was about to go over and confront Karin, when, as if psychically warned, Karin rose, and swiftly left the premises. I telephoned her from the *cabina* (public pay telephone booth) in the town square later that evening, and told her if she ever pulled such a stunt again, that our relationship was ended. She simply said that she was passionately in love with me and that merely to see me, even in the company of another woman, was a small but intense satisfaction for her deep desire.

Roberta made no such demands. She was completely absorbed in her photographic assignment, a series of shots posed in the cork forest region on the road between Soller and Pollensa. Her model, a person of perfect proportions, and an almost angelic demeanor, with long, lank, platinum blond hair that hung below her waist, must have appeared other-worldly against the jagged stone landscape, that some called a moonscape, it seemed so sheerly stark and empty ... and challenging, in its barren harshness. Later that same year, Roberta told me that *Playboy's* editor had rejected the entire lay-out because there was such beauty in all the presentation, that there could be no erotic flavor or spice to any of the photographs, which would probably only be acceptable in a gallery exhibition of the images as fine art. Neither of the women was offended, as both had plenty of work for which each was paid handsomely. I saw the model on the cover of a major magazine and later as the sole image on a fine calendar. Roberta always had plenty of work for *Vogue,* and her residual commissions from her years as Princess L'Oreal. Her face was distinctively beautiful; only her body had suffered from the ravages of child-birth – she was grossly fat in the middle, and her hips were enormous (she always wore full smocks so that these were not immediately perceived). Also, her boyfriend in London, Bruce Dexter, was the original producer of such major events as the Glastonbury and Isle of Wight musical festivals. He had introduced Jimmi Hendrix to the British rock concert stage, and later had represented 'America,' whose "Horse with No Name" had become a number one hit. His funds of money were enough to enable Roberta to commute to Hollywood, New York, Rio, Caracas, Bali, Bangkok, or wherever her whims would flight her. She had been one of the original discoveries of the famed New York photographer John Avedon and when in that city always stayed at the 'Chelsea Hotel.'

Our relationship was a bond of almost filial affection. As her great-grandfather had been Sam Houston, we boasted of blood ties – his wife had been the Cherokee, Pricess Talehina Rogers, my grandmother's great-aunt (Eliza Rogers), and so we goofed about, telling everyone that we were distant cousins – slightly more than "kissing" cousins – more like "bonking brethren" or whatever alliterative, sexual, or silly term we could light on as the mood struck us. We actually only made love two times as I recall, and it was not particularly special, but it was amusing – we always were stricken with the giggles and probably never needed to nibble any sort of physical orgasmic finale. It didn't really seem to matter. Roberta was like the sister I had always imagined possible to have, and I believe she felt the same about me. I had always yearned for a character like Scout in the Harper Lee novel, *To Kill a Mockingbird*, and Roberta came close to being this *persona*. It was on her Vespa motor-scooter that I had my accident. She had left it in my care when she traveled to America, and I decided to ride it into Soller one night, but the rain caught me after I left a bar in the town square. The winding road back up to our house was slick; I veered, and drove off the shoulder, taking a dive over the ledge and dropped down about twelve feet onto a pile of rocks, shattering the entire upper right side of my head.

My last thoughts before this occurred was that I needed to stay close to the wall opposite the ledge, and in aiming to lean into it, I miscalculated and rammed the rocky side and was bounced away, across the slick asphalted surface, and saw myself heading straight for the shoulder, over which I pitched and shot out into space before falling the height of that terrace, before landing at the base of a tree, surrounded by shrubbery ... and a pile of jagged stones. The Vespa was unharmed. There was not even a scratch on any of the painted surfaces. My speed had not been excessive – perhaps 25 miles per hour. My body was propelled over the handle-bars, and my head and upper torso slammed into a boulder and a heap of stones.

I knew I had done some damage to my face, and had bruised my shoulders and chest, but I had no notion of the amount of time I had lain in that mountain ravine in the softly falling warm rain. We calculated later that I was probably knocked unconscious, and my concussion had put me to sleep for over an hour. When I came to, I was able to stand up, and was strong enough to wrestle the motor-scooter out of the brush. I then pulled and pushed till I had its wheels back on the road. Rather than attempt to ride it to the top of the hill where we were living, I pushed it, in neutral, all the way home, another half a mile.

I did not glance at myself in the rear-view mirror on the handle-bar, or I might not have been so surprised by Janet's reaction when she answered my knock on our heavy oak front door. Her scream was ear-splitting. I laughed and told her I had been trying to get such a reaction from her since we met. Then she threw her arms around me and began sobbing as we stumbled into the front hall. I entered the half-bath there and saw in the well-lighted mirror what had so upset her. My hair was matted with clotted blood. My entire face looked like a huge hamburger patty. The right side was still oozing blood, and my eye was closed over in a sort of exaggerated blood-blister. I told her that I would try to wash off and then go lie down. The pain was not excessive - I have learned over many years and with several other severe injuries that the adrenaline charge from these kinds of traumatic accidents is such that the immediate anesthetization occurs - one of our prehistoric built-in survival mechanisms - and so I calmly set about re-setting the bones of my smashed nose to the original alignment, and even today, the only indication of that last break to my nose forms a ridge that can be felt with finger-tip at the bridge just up between my eyes.

Janet insisted that we call the ambulance from Soller and be driven to an Emergency Room in Palma (there being no hospital or clinic nearer) for immediate treatment. She ran up the stairs to go knock on the door that connected our house to our landlord, Leonard Harrop, on the second landing. I heard them discussing me, and he then appeared in the hallway as I was bent over the wash basin attempting to clear away some of my gory mask. When I turned to speak to him, he also screamed, and then disappeared back up the stairs muttering that he was telephoning the 'Red Cross' rescue unit in Soller.

By the time the ambulance arrived, I had downed several stiff drinks of 'Fernet Branca,' a herbal liqueur that was about 180 proof, and I was beginning to feel the pain which had only just begun to set in, as it numbed before my alcoholic ministrations. I was also attempting to make merry of the situation that seemed to me no more serious than a sprained ankle. I had merely bruised and cut my face. These sort of injuries always appear worse to the observer, and my battle-field reaction response with a huge adrenaline rush had already rendered bearable the greater part of any excessive pain. I was also using the "Hand-Glove Anesthesia" technique I had been trained to employ by Paul Fransella in the Silva Mind Control course I had attended for the past few years. I tried to argue Janet out of the ambulance ride to the nearest hospital, which ironically happened to be the Cruz Roja in Palma where we had taken Alastair shortly before. The ride in the back of that ambulance was daunting as this was many years before the tunnel road to Palma from Soller, and there were twenty-six switch-back, hair-pin turns ascending and descending the Teix mountain. I tried to stay awake, but passed out with the pain now sweeping over me, somewhere down that circuit of winding highway.

When we reached the 'Cruz Roja Emergency' entrance, I awoke and walked from the ambulance in to the Surgery and told the young doctor on duty that I needed no anesthetic, not even Novocaine, nor any other pain-killers for him to sew up the cuts on my face. I had actually straightened the broken nose myself, when we were in the Fornalutx house, aligning it and setting the shattered bones in what appeared to be the center of my mangled face. I remember only the first few stitches, after the daubing out of the dirt and clots, and cleansing of the surfaces for suturing. I had held on to the sides of the table where I lay and found myself involuntarily spasming and lurching in reaction to the procedures. I lost consciousness again, and it was not till morning that I awoke, to find myself still prone, but in a comfortable hospital bed with sunshine streaming in with a refreshing breeze wafting in through an open window.

To my immediate left - *politically his preferred position* - also stretched out full length on another bed, but fully clothed, in combat fatigues, and muddy hiking boots, affecting the costume and languid leopard slouch of his most admired hero, Che Guevarra, was Doctor Perico Villaescusa. As the breeze played over my bed, it delivered to me the acrid sweet aroma of the substance he was smoking - the illegal cannabis contained in Moroccan hashish mixed with the tobacco of a cigarette. As soon as he saw my left eye open - my right eye was heavily bandaged, as was my entire head and jaw - his arm extended the *joint* to me as he whispered, "Smoke the magic weed. It will heal you. I am your best doctor."

I inhaled a puff and held it in my lungs and felt myself almost immediately affected. I remarked that either this was some phenomenally powerful hash, or I must be jacked up on some morphine or another caressing pain-killer. He told me that he had tried to get me some heroin prescribed, but as Dr. Aguila was the supervising surgeon, and recognized us as possibly a couple of drug-crazed hippies, that it was difficult to score anything more powerful that the standard opiates I was on for the time being. How ironic that Aguila was in charge of my case. Perico told me that this surgeon had considered the X-rays indicated no very serious injuries and that as soon as I felt better, that I could be released.. I later learned that either the X-rays were done incorrectly, or Aguila was incompetent, for my condition was indeed very grave, and the injuries were potentially life-threatening.

I discharged myself later that day, and Perico drove me to join Janet in Fornalutx. When I arrived, she had assembled all our bags and belongings out in the drive-way. I was still dazed by my concussion and barely able to comprehend what was transpiring. However, this event was enormously cruel and insulting. The owner of our rented house, the homosexual Leonard Harrop, who lived in his side of the building with his Greek lover, cum house-boy, had told Janet that the shock of my injury, the ugliness of the damage to my face, had so horrified him that he was unable to allow me to remain on his premises. He had returned to Janet the money which we had already paid for the remainder of that month, and then he told her that we must vacate his property immediately, or he would denounce us to the Guardia Civil for immorality and possible Communist attitudes and for insulting Franco [a standard addition to any *denuncio* which was intended to provide an extra sting for certain and harsh punishment].

I demanded to talk to him, and did so. He brazenly told me what Janet had reported. He was not the least ashamed to declare that he could not bear to look on a man's face that was so disfigured as mine now appeared to be and that he would take any legal measures necessary to remove this horror from his home [an extreme variation of Oscar Wilde's quirk of paying ugly people to remove themselves from his observation and physical company]. He refused to look at me as we spoke, and delivered this judgment with his face turned away from me. I was enraged, but I also was so weak and befuddled by my injuries and medication that I could only say that I would never forget this outrage, but I agreed to leave, as Perico was waiting for us and had already been apprised of the situation, and so he drove us to his home in Galilea. After the first night in the Villaescusa household , Janet and I begged one of the two bed-room villas Nora had built about her nest, *'S'Esbart,'* which literally translated in Mallorquin as a word for aviary, or collection of birds - the ten villas she had constructed surrounding her main house on the highest plot of land in the village was intended to be a *Center of Light,* a retreat and a commune and a *genius loci* for spiritual pilgrims seeking *New Age* enlightenment. Findhorn in Northern Scotland had become such a *New Age* center, and many of the vagrant souls that had wandered from commune to commune from Big Sur to Santa Fe to Key West to Bali and Glastonbury were beginning to trickle in to Galilea, having heard of Nora's collection of houses and willingness to support those who pleaded for her indulgence ... but that was the crux of the problem. Nora expected people to *beg,* to *bow down,* to literally *kowtow* [the Chinese word which means to bow low with head on the ground before one's over-lord].

There was considerable animosity between Nora and Perico, because of his efforts to fulfill her stated desire for the creation of a creative commune at *'S'Esbart,'* Earlier that year, he had transplanted an entire family of Gypsies from the slum called Molinar, outside Palma, to encamp on her grounds, and these displaced refugees had used the swimming pool and her toilets and showers in the *cabanas* attached there. Additionally, they had begun digging up all her flower gardens on the many terraces and had planted staple food seeds from corn, to cabbage, to carrots, and the land had come alive with their constant singing and dancing and celebration of the consecration of their newfound homeland. This was not exactly what Nora had in mind. She had envisioned some meek and mild simpering and soulful pilgrims who would grovel at her doorstep and thank her for her beneficence and then probably sing Gregorian chants or Plainsong in muffled reverent under-tones. Not these wildly dressed animals that leaped about her former gardens and had built bonfires to consume in black smoke her lovely rose bushes and geraniums, oleander shrubs, and bougainvillea.

At this time, Nora had beseeched me to reason with Perico, to persuade him to remove this micro-diaspora from her property, and to terminate this *Freedom Garden* [in the late 1960s, the vacant parking lots in San Francisco had been transformed into vegetable plots by the hippies and named *Freedom Gardens*] project, or, as she raged, she would denounce Perico and his friends to the Guardia Civil as revolutionary Communist agitators and white-slavers and drug dealers – which they actually were – no problem in gathering hard *prima facie* evidence for such charges against Spanish Gypsies. I had been successful in effecting a shut down of the *Freedom Garden*, but had then resided in Perico's home during a gala farewell party which had lasted over forty-eight hours – a most intense frolic with his Gypsy friends. I had adapted two of my favorite Jimmy Rogers songs, 'Blue Ridge Mountain Blues' and 'Your Love's Like a Faucet, You Just Turn It Off and On,' to a Flamenco *saeta* [ancient sung prayer , originally meaning an *arrow*, of *passion*] on guitar with two of the more soulful singers of the clan on that particular occasion.

I did not stay here long, as I had already booked a week's return charter flight (non-refundable even for medical reasons) to London which I had previously scheduled for buying some essential repair parts for *Tsunami*. As both the doctors, Aguila and Villaescusa, had assured me that my injuries were not serious, although the bleeding kept oozing up through the bandages wrapped around my head, I decided to leave on the day after Janet and Alaric were comfortably settled at Nora's. I must have looked somewhat incapacitated, but not so much so as to be disqualified for flying on a charter airplane, but as I walked across the tarmac to board my airplane at Palma airport, I was stopped by the Guardia Civil who demanded to know *where the shotgun was that had blown away half my forehead.* I wore a brightly patterned large, red, silk bandanna encircling the right side of my head as a bandage, so that I looked like a manque pirate; but this must have appeared as a *muleta* [that cape used in the final passes of the bullfight, the *faena*] for the Guardia Civil who suddenly blocked my path with his sub-machine gun jammed into my mid-section, ordering me to halt. I dropped my carry-on bag to the ground and automatically raised my hands in surrender, as he posed a most remarkable question.

"Donde esta la escopeta?" he demanded to know. "Where is the shotgun [English translation]?"

I was dumbstruck. My mind was still befuddled by the drink and drugs from the night before , and I was in a post-concussive, mental modality, and I could not begin to imagine why this member of Franco's branch of Stormtrooper Gestapos was asking me about a shotgun. I bent to open my bag, but just as I pulled on the zipper, he laughed raucously and pressed the barrel of his weapon to my chest and ordered me to rise. He then pointed the barrel straight up as he crooked the the butt against his bicep and with his other hand, slapped his hard flat belly, now roaring with gleeful merriment, before saying what explained the entire situation. He wanted to know where the shotgun was that had blown away the side of my head. He was making a joke. So much for Spanish humor! He then allowed me to board the plane after having an enormous laugh, at my expense.

Upon arrival in London, I checked into a Bed and Breakfast in Earl's Court and made my way directly to my favorite haunt, 'The Queen's Elm' pub at the corner of Fulham Road and Old Church Street, only a hundred yards away from the Chelsea Arts Club. *The National Geographic* mentioned this public house owned by Sean Tracey, who had then published his autobiographical novel, *The Smell of Broken Glass*. His establishment had been a 'watering hole" for Dylan Thomas, Brendan Behan, Julie Christie (she rented a top floor flat just across the road which she used as her *pied a terre* when in town), and Augustus John, one of whose sons, the gardener, became a drinking pal of mine before he committed suicide – one of the other sons became Lord High Admiral of the British Navy, he being the person whom Ruthven Todd claimed granted him official permission to wear the gold ear-ring [this simple piece of jewelry was stolen from Ruthven's body by a Scot woman resident of Galilea at his burial – it had been promised to me as my only inheritance from my dear friend, Ruthven] in his pierced left ear, a privilege normally reserved for only those *blue -water* sailors who had rounded the Cape of Good Hope in a square-rigged ship. Many other notable writers, painters, actors, film and television producers and directors gathered in Tracey's pub. I had been frequenting this establishment since I first arrived in London as a student in 1966. So this was my home turf by now, and I had made two close friends whom I could be certain would arrive early evening and stay till closing at 11 P.M. on a daily basis: Michael Kenny and David MacSweeney. I learned that both men were extremely prominent in their individual professions [sculpture and psychiatry, respectively], but what mattered most to us was our staying power at the bar, and willingness to pay for that "next round," which at this time, was not so expensive as now. An evening of normal drinking never cost more than a couple of Pounds Sterling, then equivalent to not much more than three U.S. dollars. A Bed and Breakfast nightly accommodation was the same price, and sometimes less.

Michael Kenny had been the youngest artist ever to be elected to the Royal Academy of Art. His sculptures were considered by some to rival the work of Henry Moore, and yet he still humbly worked as an instructor at Goldsmiths College, where he was chair of the department of Fine Arts; his salary was as low, however, as the lowest pay scale assistant professor in any American state university. His sculptures, when sold, were beginning to fetch substantial figures. When he died in 2001, his work was so prized that he was becoming a millionaire, and he was regarded as one of the greatest living sculptors in the world.

Dr. David MacSweeney, would have been an enormously wealthy man in any country except England where he devoted his entire life to serving in the public health sector, and never did he have a private practice in any of his chosen fields of expertise. Not only was he a member of the Royal College of Psychiatrists, but he was considered to be an outstanding Neurological and Ophthalmic surgeon, and he was also a highly trained Pediatrician. He had been professor of psychiatry and Neurosurgery at the prestigious Middlesex Hospital, London, and later took over the directorship of Leytonstone Psychiatric Hospital. He was also considered to be one of the finest rugby players and had captained not only the Cambridge University team but also the Irish National squad. Richard Harris, when he starred in the film 'Sporting Life,' had made David his model for that rough and tumble character whose role in this film made him famous. With three novels and a book of poetry, *So Why do You Kill Me?*, the cover illustrated by Ralph Steadman, who also illuminated Hunter Thompson's *Fear and Loathing in Las Vegas*, a book of MacSweeney's collected verse which I published, printed by Lawrence Brough of Dawes Press, in 1978 [Seamis Heany had acclaimed it as a very fine work], David was the epitome of what some refer to as a "Renaissance Man."

When I arrived in the 'Queen's Elm,' just off the charter flight from Palma, my head bound up with the bandanna covering the bandaged cuts which still seeped dark red gore, my two best drinking pals were alarmed. David took me into the Gents toilet and peeled back the soggy wraps and sternly declared that I was more severely afflicted than I had been told in Mallorca. He calmly remarked that I might be losing my eye, and could have some damage to my brain. He carefully wrote down the address of 'Moorefield's Eye Clinic' and made me pledge to go there the next morning. Nevertheless, I wanted to drink till closing hour, and did so, buying a pint of Scotch whiskey to take to bed for a night-cap. A young woman, whom I had been "chatting up" at the bar, said she was from Memphis, Tennessee, and invited me to accompany her and her boyfriend back to the flat round the corner which they had rented while their band was performing in London. She told me that her boyfriend played the keyboard for this group, 'The Who.' Peter Townsend, their lead guitarist and singer, was becoming notorious for his outrageous stage antics, and he composed the Rock opera, 'Tommy.' When we arrived at the third floor sprawling floor of rooms, a party was in full swing, but the compassionate American girl insisted on cleansing my still throbbing and bleeding injuries before we snorted some lines of cocaine and smoked Thai sticks, a strong mixture of rare Southeast Asian marijuana laced with hashish. She then offered to perform *fellatio*, as a special favor for a suffering fellow Colonial, but I demurred. When I left an hour or so later, a taxi was called to pick me up and deliver me to my Bed and Breakfast.

The next morning, I was able to consume the entire English breakfast of cereal, eggs, bacon, tomatoes and toast, with strong black tea, before cheerfully striding out onto Earl's Court Road and hailing a taxi to drive me directly to Moorefield Eye Clinic. The first taxi, when he pulled up to me, took a close look at my head and nasty bandages, and then hauled away without allowing me to enter his vehicle. Perhaps I was looking somewhat worse for the wear than I had presumed. At 'Moorefield's,' when I walked to the Main Reception and politely told the nurse that I had been referred by Dr. MacSweeney for an examination, I was not kept waiting more than a few minutes. I was ushered into the examining room ahead of all the people who were sitting on the long bench in this entry hall, to be consulted by first, one, then two, then several doctors, one of whom was called professor. David had not contacted them, but they did not seem to need his second opinion. They concluded that my condition was dire, that I would require immediate attention, definitely surgery, and I was then informed of the actual gravity of the injury I had sustained in my fall in Fornalutx.

There were two doctors in the consultation who asked me if I would consent to signing myself into their care. They told me that if I had sustained this damage to my head in the United Kingdom, that I would have been charged with personal endangerment from recklessness and flaunting the law requiring the wearing of a protective helmet whilst (British idiom – English law) riding a motor cycle or scooter, and that I would have had to pay a steep fine. The blow to my head had actually exploded the diameter of my eye-socket to three times its normal size, and fragments of the splintered bones were virtually at the point of penetrating my brain. The excessive trauma to my eye might mean that I would lose it, and if I did not undergo surgery immediately, I might even die from the damage to my brain from the concussion and possible hemorrhage within my cranial area and the probable puncture of the brain by the splintered bones from my shattered skull. I did not argue the fine points of the proposition, but when one of the doctors told me that my chances of surviving surgery were only fifty percent and that I could expect to be horribly disfigured for the remainder of my life from the scars and the severing of nerves so that my face on one side would be frozen immobile, I had to make some stupid joke asking if an American surgeon could be brought in to join the team in order to better the odds and perhaps save my former *leading man,* movie-actor, facial features.

My humorous gibe was not appreciated, and one doctor actually said that I should just be left as I was and that I could not blame the National Health Service ... from the *grave* [burial or cremation was provided free by Her Majesty's government], unless my embassy considered me valuable enough to ship home for interment. I was startled by the flinty candor of these men, and I made an apology, whereupon, I was literally whisked out the back door and placed in an ambulance which sped me across London to Denmark Hill and the premises of King's College Hospital where a team of surgeons was being assembled to tackle my project. I was placed in 'Twining Ward,' the charity unit in this institution, which was part of a teaching hospital. I was informed later that my case was accepted primarily because I would provide a challenging teaching tool, a unique classroom example, for several of the hospital's medical specialties: cranial and ophthalmic, dental, and plastic cosmetic surgery. The doctor who would supervise and perform most of the dental reconstruction of my upper jaw was a professor of dental surgery, the ophthalmic eye specialist was also outstanding in his field of practice and an academic authority; but the real prize-winner was Mr. Pocock, professor emeritus of several faculties and preeminent plastic surgeon who had reconstructed the faces of many of the most grievously burned and shattered heads of pilots from World War Two and many of the other combat zones in England's post-war colonial conflicts throughout her world-wide empire. I was amused to learn his name, which was the Medieval word for *peacock.* So I was to have three specialists and a general surgeon on my team. The anesthesiologist came to my bedside and interviewed me that day just after lunch, which I was irritated to discover did not include wine or beer, or even a cognac or brandy with coffee after-wards. I informed him that I was used to consuming at least two bottles of wine with every meal, as I had done the very day before. I then told him what I had drunk at the 'Queen's Elm,' - at least eight pints of Holstein lager which boasted the highest alcoholic content legally sold in pubs, and then, later, three Napoleon brandies at the Chelsea Arts Club where I also purchased a half-pint of whiskey for my pocket take-home night-cap, then smoking a pipe of Black Afghani hashish and snorting a few lines of cocaine, before proceeding back to my Bed and Breakfast to drink the half-pint of whiskey and finally go to bed. The young doctor seemed bemused, and told me that he reckoned that the best method for putting me to sleep during my operation would be to merely hit me over the head several times with a hammer. I think he was joking. However, he said that my skull was already the site of many other bashes. The supervising surgeon had told him that X-rays of my head showed at least four other severe fracture lines from previous injuries. *Four previous fractures?* Where was I when all this was taking place? How did I happen to not particularly notice? I do remember losing consciousness when thrown from my horse, Nellie, at age five, when I was riding bare-back with my Choctaw Indian pal, Phil Perkins. My father had made me remount right away and ride again, but a severe headache had lasted for several days afterward. I also recalled having a full bottle of red wine smashed across the back of my head by my wife, Marian's, sister, the blow so forceful that ruby-stained fragments of glass were imbedded in the white wooden wall panels in front of which I had been standing that night in my living room in La Jolla, California. But the other two? One fist fight with a fraternity brother at Penn had knocked me out cold

… and I vaguely remember other bar-room brawls in the Navy and when I traveled in Europe and Scandinavia, in the years following. Actually, I'm surprised there were *only four* previous fractures!

The chaplain's visit was also amusing. He was requesting that I instruct him regarding what religious rites should accompany my demise and how my remains were to be disposed of. It would have been so simple to tell him that I was an American Episcopalian, our ecclesiastic equivalent to his Church of England, which he served as a vicar, and to assure him that the Anglican processes for burial or cremation would suffice to handle my case. However, I was in a perverse state of mind, especially having been informed that my chances for surviving the operation were, at best, merely fifty per cent. The last time I had been told that I might be dying was only two years before, by Dr. Neber in La Jolla, who first noticed what appeared then to be irreversible damage to my liver, later confirmed by Dr. Woodward, my father's internist and also by a hematology specialist to whom Neber had referred me, for confirmation of his opinion that I had no more than a few months to live with the severe cirrhosis of the liver which seemed to be progressing at an alarming rate. Whatever it was, that *terminal disease,* had then reversed itself some few months later and never recurred. I had become so convinced of my imminent demise, at that time, that I had cultivated a plot in the small Wright Cemetery on Northeast Sixty-Third Street, adjoining our family farm in Oklahoma City, and I had planned on being planted there, either embalmed and casketed, or incinerated and sprinkled about that historic hallowed ground.

In this interview with the chaplain of 'King's College Hospital,' I pointed outside the window by my bed in the ward, and I told this conscientious priest that I would be delighted to become some of the actual fertilizer feeding the growth of the sapling that was planted in the small patch of turf next to the pavement of the roadway. I declared myself a pantheist, and when he shook his head indicating confusion, I said that I believed in all deities, all spiritual rituals and whatever religions existed throughout the world, and had reverence for only the power of Nature, a sort of animistic, Shinto, shamanistic eclecticism. I would appreciate prolonged howling and laughter at a wake accompanied by distilled spirits shared by all who might come to bid my remains farewell, and then I would wish for my body to be ground up to mulch, serving as fertilizer to nurture the tree below my window in 'Twining Ward' of 'Kings College Hospital,' Denmark Hill. I did have to sign the document that made explicit my request and did spell out the choice of my religious belief in capital letters: P.A.G.A.N. The well-meaning cleric made some other notes on his clipboard, offering a hasty "God Bless" ... and went away.

There was a large, one-eyed Jamaican man, black-skinned, and so fat that he appeared to be spilling out of the bed next to mine, and had been eaves-dropping. He told me that he would be praying to Jesus for me while I was in the operating theatre. I told him that he could tell Jesus for me that I did not need his help and would certainly not accept it on any Christian terms. The man shook his head in disbelief and crossed himself fervently. I considered letting loose a tirade at this man which MacSweeney and many of his *theatrical Irish* pub cohorts would have claimed to be a Gaelic *flyting* - the art and practice of public insults refined over centuries by Celtic tribes. I had been invited to attend a *flyting* performance in a pub venue next door to the British Museum in London, held in celebration of the re-publication of Robert Graves' first book ever published, *Lars Porsena: The Lost Art of Cursing.* It chronicled the rhetorical skill taught in the Golden age of Greece, later known in Rome as the Latin, *ad hominem* strategy, an attack against *the person.* In modern political contest, this is called called "mud-slinging," but consists of substances flung at opponents, which are often much more virulent and repulsive. "Doing the Dozens" is a term familiar in modern American ghetto neighborhoods; yet, the same practice occurs in the Islamic world and is most refined today in Saudi Arabia as a weapon of verbal assault. I swallowed my bile and focused upon calming myself for my entry into the surgical lists in the operating theatre within the next few hours.

I had two visitors before this *main event*. Michael Syson arrived with packets of British coins carefully wrapped for me to use in the candy and snack machines and pay telephone. Roberta Booth brought me passion and cuddles and even suggested a surreptitious blow-job, but the sheets which we hung about the bed were not sufficient to occlude the snooping -albeit monocular and beclouded visual acuity - of that swarthy, fanatical West Indian disciple of Jesus in the bed beside us. So much for the amenities of a charity ward. There was no privacy, and I had been informed that if I did survive m the imminent *bloodletting*, that I would be expected to help sweep up and deliver meals to my fellow patients on this floor.

That evening I was given a sedative and the next thing I knew, I was awakened sometime before dawn and wheeled down a main hall. The anesthesiologist did not meet me with a ball-peen hammer or even a cudgel, but injected a substance in the vein on my hand and told me to count backwards from one hundred. I got as far as ninety-eight, and then I awoke in a bright lighted arena surrounded by noisy bustling forms - nurses and surgeons. I realized later when I did regain consciousness sufficiently after the entire operation to understand that

I had regained consciousness *in the middle of the operation* and had to be sedated rather quickly all over again, as I had roused and risen at the least practical moment for those still cutting and stitching and probing and maneuvering in my cranial cavity. I distinctly remember the sharp acrid smell of cocaine which had been used to freeze my eyeball and ever since that moment, I have never again enjoyed ingesting that substance as a recreational drug. .On that deepest level of consciousness, I must have recalled the sensation of my frozen eyeball. The anesthesiologist did later inform me of my traumatic awakening during the operation and his speedy response to put me back under, but that my hallucinatory memory vision of my eye-ball suspended and enveloped with surgical cocaine... was indeed correct. Sounds poetic, but the acute pharmaceutical stink of that drug still causes me to as some grave concern about my psychological state, that as there was brain damage and that when the X-rays were more thoroughly studied, with at least those four other severe skull fractures in my life-time, the deep scar tissue fissures indicating that each had been life-threatening, and that I was lucky to be alive. I have come to now understand that there was sufficient damage to my skull to have provided me with brain damage which would explain my erratic mood swings and decidedly anti-social behaviors and virtually psychopathic, homicidally flavored, manners. I was to be kept under close observation and not released from clinical care till more brain-scans and deliberation by the forensic neuro-psychiatric consultants agreed that I was not an actual, definite dangerous threat to society at large, somehow. I asked as diplomatically as possible if it would not be a good idea to provide me a private room, to protect the other patients. My request was considered, and declined ... for economic reasons

My first visitors were Michael Kenny and his ten year-old son, Dominic, who begged to become my blood-brother, so that he could brag to his school-mates that he was part *Red Indian* [the British choice of terminology for Native American]. Michael dissuaded him from pressing this issue while I was still mending from surgery, but I swore to him that we would consummate our *comitatus* ceremony as soon as I was back on my feet. Una, daughter of Jakov Lind [Jewish writer and Holocaust survivor who posed as a Nazi when his other family members were arrested and sent to die in the concentration camps; he served in the Wehrmacht and later wrote his autobiographical memoirs (*Counting My Steps* and *Soul of Wood*) about this life-saving charade], and Eric, son of Bud Flakoll and Claribelle Alegria, the El Salvador poet [it was she who had later written the novel which was placed in Deya, *Pueblo de Dioses y Mandingos* (Village of Gods and Warlocks – rough translation, in English, later published by Curbstone press under the title, *Family Album*, with, 'Village of God and the Devil' as a chapter), in which she had modeled the major villain, an *ugly American*, on my example, as the person who stole the sacred bones from the inner chamber of the high priests in the 'Cave of the Dead', who was punished by the several skull fractures nearly causing death, until he returned those desecrated bones with appropriate atonement to the burial site – in other words, the very story of what actually happened in my life and had catapulted me to Kings College surgical theatre]. Curiously, Eric had decided to join the Sandinista revolutionary soldiers in Nicaragua, and Claribelle begged me to argue him out of this resolve [as I had so influenced him originally to study Shotokan Karate (he took is Black Belt in a London *dojo*) and he considered me as a role model in

Radical political ideals] but he went to that country, served as a soldier, then became the body-guard of the president, and when I last encountered him in Mallorca, he told me that he had become the commander-in-chief of all that country's armed forces. Both of these young residents of Deya, Mallorca, who were like my own children, I was most delighted to have come to wish me well.

When Michael Syson visited , it was to inform me that Janet had telephoned him from Austria where she had traveled with a Deya millionaire dilettante, Fred Grunfeld [she had been in a panic, reckoning that I might never come back to her as she had feared that my injury was grave and also she was thinking that I had used up all the money I had before the accident, as Sam Coffing had telephoned us in Fornalutx to inform me that my affairs had gone badly and that my cash flow was virtually dried up]. Grunfeld was a egoistic, fickle individual who had then abandoned her and Alaric when he found her sexual favors had not been as exciting as he had somehow imagined they would be. Michael had wired her money to buy return fares to Mallorca, and I pledged to reimburse him as soon as I was released from the hospital and could get to a bank. I did have money, although not as much as I had before.

I attempted in the first days I could stand unassisted and walk without toppling over, to comply with the requirements for being a "charity" patient on Twining Ward. I wheeled around the dinner gurney, but was unable to serve more than a couple of my ward fellows. The third one shrieked in horror when he saw my Frankenstein features - the stitched gashes over my nose and upper jaw, and the other sutures joining the patchwork handiwork, still deeply bruised and swollen in a grotesque misshapen mask, were unsettling, and for some, downright horrifying. The disfigurement lasted for so many months, that I allowed my hair to grow long, down to my shoulders, sloping over the right side of my face, obscuring the ugliest aspect of my recent, welting surgical scars. However, in bars, when I wanted someone to buy me a drink, I would fling the hair back and offer to drop the curtain back down ONLY if my favorite beverage were ordered and paid for – *immediately!*

So, my Twining Ward compensatory *services* were thereby diminished to nothing more than sweeping up with a long-handled push-broom, which again, some people complained I did too noisily, as my only foot-wear had been my knee length cowboy boots which made a clatter and commotion that some of the more delicate convalescents found distressing. I tried to hasten my release from that ward by endeavoring to be friendly and polite, which some found sinister and threatening, but, at last, I was allowed to take an afternoon and evening out – I decided to stay in one of my favorite Chelsea Bed and Breakfasts, and to have a drinking spree at the 'Queen's Elm.' I was enormously excited about returning to my hallowed haunt, and I was shouting savagely at the taxi driver to take a short-cut off Kings Road, and in so doing, he became so distracted that he collided with a car just pulling out of a side street. I leapt from the back-seat, flinging a One Pound note at the stricken man and hailed another cab to drive the remaining few blocks to my pub. I was still a public health hazard, notwithstanding my recuperative processing at Twing Ward.

One of my drinking mates that afternoon and night, a former semi-professional boxer, declared that he would be serving as my body-guard, but he was later invited outside by Harry the Hack at the Chelsea Arts Club, and when I began to miss him, I stepped out the front door to find him crumpled in a heap there, having been beaten to semi-consciousness, by Harry, who only admitted this assault a year or so later, mumbling that it had to do with a welched-on gambling debt. I took my friend by taxi to the nearest Hospital Emergency Room for immediate succor for his broken nose and bruised, but not broken, jaws. I counted myself lucky not to have been included in the mishap, and yet, the very next morning, when I arrived at Denmark Hill and was being driven in another taxi on to the forecourt of the hospital grounds, I was amazed that this driver, whom I had also been assisting by shouting my instructions for maneuvering his vehicle, knocked down one of the interns who was about to mount the front steps at the main entrance. Was I carrying an aura of hazard and calamity around with me? Collisions of automobiles and humans were in highest density in my personal space within the last very few hours. However, I had been spared any more blows, which, if they were to land anywhere on my head, could jar loose the fine surgical wiring that held a new plastic eye socket in place, and prevented those recently splintered bone fragments from penetrating in my brain.

Even before most of the stitching was removed from around my eye and on my forehead and along my upper jaw from my mouth back to my ear, I was aware that I had a delicate balance of cranial reconstruction to live with. One of the most eminent surgeons, the ophthalmic *ace*, had brought a group of medical students students to my bedside, and had told them that although my eye had been saved, that the positioning of the replacement (plastic) of the floor of my eye socket, would always deprive me of perfect vision, that I would have double vision in all quadrants (up, down, and sideways), but that this would not be so bothersome as I would most probably need to wear a protective patch over the eye, most of the time, as it would be virtually impossible for me to control the closing of the eye-lid. I was so certain that he was wrong, as was the prognosis of the plastic surgeon, that the right side of my face would remain immobile, frozen inactive because the major nerves had been severed, that I loudly protested and proclaimed to both groups that I would return in a year or so and *wink* at all of them, with the damaged eye, and that I would be able to smile with BOTH sides of my face, and that a dimple would re-appear on the scarred right side to dance in complementary tease with the one they could see on my left cheek.

It was actually more than *two years* later, before I was able to fulfill this prophecy, and it took well over five years before the dimple returned, and I regained full articulation of the right side. BUT, now, people have difficulty believing that there has ever been any injury to either side of my face, and they find it surprising that my nose has been broken six times, and that I set the bones in alignment that last time, in the hall mirror in the house in Fornalutx when the rest of the surface looked like a mushy hamburger patty, the "Moo" of that metaphoric cow still just eerily audible.

I was told to remain in London for at least three weeks after my final release from Kings College Hospital. Roberta Booth had arranged for me to stay in the single bedroom flat of her most gorgeous model friend, the one with the long platinum blond hair who had become the calendar for Michelin, and who best personified the purest organic food products for which she had become the symbolic, inimitable model, as she was in California for several photo assignments, and therefore, her flat was free. She was particularly sympathetic to my plight as she had been pushed in front of a subway train a few years before, and had not been expected to survive, and especially to regain her phenomenal special beauty. Her room was on the ground floor with a large picture window looking out toward Downing Street, within walking distance to the Houses of Parliament. The walls were plastered with enlarged photographic studies of her ...

many in the nude. But her figure was so perfectly formed and her entire aspect so pristine, that the effect was anything but erotic, and I was never aroused sexually by lying on the large bed which was the center-piece of that room. I was, however, brought to full sexual readiness by the visits of Roberta who appeared to delight in my bruised and battered condition, my weight having decreased so much that I could barely wear any of the clothing I had traveled to London in. She always said, " I like my men thin, Ben," and laughed naughtily at the poetic ring to her phrasing. She said that my still horrific *mask* also elicited a sexual "turn-on," and I wondered if she would still desire me when my intentions to restore my features to normalcy were realized and completed.

I still frequented the 'Chelsea Arts Club' and 'Queen's Elm,' but as I had no automobile, and the walk from my neighborhood, The Strand and Westminster was a fairly long hike - a taxi was as costly as several rounds of drink - I began to spend more time reading and attempting to write poetry and sketching out an idea or two I had for screen-plays which Michael Syson and I discussed often. He had recently begun writing another film, 'Hoss and the Major,' which he asked me to contribute to collaboratively. 'The Eagle's Wing' was being considered for production in the near future - the sale was pending some final negotiations and discussion between Michael and the investors. He credited me with half the dialogue in that piece, and although I never saw any money from it, I did attend the premiere showing, in his stead at Prince Charles cinema off Leicester Square in London in 1975 - he refused to attend in protest over the choice of director, because that individual was homosexual (the same man who directed 'Lion in Winter'). Martin Sheen played the lead,and our reviews by the critics were outstanding; however, the film played for only a few weeks and has rarely been seen since. I assisted in proofreading and editing the novel Michael churned out for the after-market, but that book was remaindered only a month after the film disappeared.

I actually was feeling rather dopey during most of the time of my convalescence, and so I wandered often in the Tate and National Portrait galleries and attended several poetry readings in pubs and local libraries. Brian Patten took me to a reading that he and his closest friend, Roger McGough, presented. I was still in a virtually semi-conscious state from my bruised brain, and so I was subdued enough for Brian to trust me not to be too outrageous in my behaviors so that he was not frightened of presenting me to Roger. I had not realized that Brian, and many of my other friends, had considered my personality so unpredictably explosive that I was regarded as a *loose canon* in most social situations, and that the only venue where my behavior was acceptable was in the rough-and-tumble milieu of an Irish pub like the 'Queen's Elm' or the late-night, last-call-for-drinks sessions at the 'Chelsea Arts Club.' I did not seek out any more sedate environs, and if I had found myself in any, would have fled forthwith, or been asked to leave. My manner had become increasingly uncivilized in the months just prior to my accident, and I did not them realize or appreciate that I was becoming a virtual stereotype of a very badly behaved, acute, chronic alcoholic.

Roger and I seemed to get on well from our first meeting. He was accompanied by Hilary Clough, a young woman he was dating now as he had left his wife with whom he had two sons. It was not till almost nine years later, that Roger and Hilary would come to stay as my house-guests in Puigpunyent, Mallorca, when I had ended my alcoholic drinking and had become a person more worthy of trusting, for house-guests to visit.. At the time of my first encounter with Roger, in 1973, I was still a barely functioning sociopath and would spend most of my later hours in pubs where I was not known and my behaviors might be forgotten, and I would not frequent the same places more than once in a month's period, to insure I might not be remembered, and perhaps *barred* from entry. And I was ready to leave London in just over a month's time as my health condition appeared to be considerably improved.

Upon take-off on the airplane from Gatwick, the pain in my head was blinding and severe from the shift in atmospheric pressure which the blockage in my sinuses could not mediate, and I asked the flight attendant for an ice-pack to staunch a similar cranial assault when we began our descent into Palma airport. Janet met me and had good news for both of us regarding our new place of residence. It was to be a two story house in the center of Fornalutx which Paul Arnaboldi offered us for free while he was traveling to the United States and Bali, that special site in Indonesia where many of those who had made Deya their home away from their American origins, to become another outpost of the rare breed of artist, addict, dilettante, *bon-vivant* who also claimed Key West, and Big Sur as their chosen turf. There was indeed a group who followed these migrational sorties and appeared as an interchangeable assembly in all of these locales throughout the year. Seminyak, Bali, and Key West, Florida connected then with Taos, New Mexico, the Big Sur, just south of San Francisco, California, and Chelsea, in London, England and in the section by that same name in New York City, and sometimes, Tangiers where Paul Bowles was the powerful artistic presence who had drawn most of the Kerouac and Ginsberg and Burroughs *gurus* of the earlier Beatnik movement. Mason Hoffenberg whose novel, *Candy* (written in collaboration with Terry Southern), had been the more degenerate version of Nabokov's, *Lolita*, had been the equivalent New York writer and Mati Klarwein, whose album cover for the musical group, Santanna's 'Abraxis' depicted the fishing port of Deya in surreal splendor, had drawn many like-minded painters and musicians, such as Kevin Ayers and his ilk of 'Soft Machine' [that group of musicians named by William Burroughs] as well. Deya had shared the elemental subterranean and subconscious (but on a *racial subconscious*, or *group unconscious* level, Jungians would contend) magnetic drawing force with these focal points along the specially constellated *ley lines*, which the indigenous inhabitants of Deya, Soller and Fornalutx had identified within the latter half of the twentieth century. The more accepted theory had been that Robert Graves attracted these particular soul-mates, but Gertrude Stein and Alice B Toklas, not to mention, Chopin and George Sand, had preceded these, and before that, the island had always been considered to possess primordial, preternatural, magical qualities.

Paul Arnaboldi had told Janet that he admired my distinct individuality and that he felt that we had been grievously and most uncharitably treated by our previous landlord, Harrop. Also, he said that the French Canadian writer, Robert Goulet [his only novel, *Violent Season* had become required reading in the secondary schools of his region of Canada, and this along with his marriage to an English chocolate manufacturing heiress, had allowed him to renovate and live sumptuously in the most magnificent house in the town] was a sometimes enemy of Paul's, and Goulet had become worried sick, tormented by the idea that I might bring a law-suit against him because the road on which I had been riding the Vespa when I skidded off and was thrown into a ravine, was one he had commissioned to be constructed to connect to another property he owned. This was a preposterous idea, but Paul had teased Goulet with the notion, suggesting that as I was an American of some means, and that as most of our countrymen (Paul was from Florida, by way of New York) were litigious by nature, that I might bring a financially crippling law-suit against the architects and builders, and especially the owner (Goulet) of the road that had been responsible for my great suffering and costly hospitalization [my treatment in a British charity ward by doctors working for National Health Services had not been common knowledge, and the gossip mill had made much of the operations and specialists consulted to save my life and restore my sight and ability to even walk again – in other words there had been enormous exaggeration and confabulation, which Paul Arnaboldi used to fuel Goulet's deep-seated and seething paranoia].

I was deeply touched by Arnaboldi's compassion and generosity, although he wanted me to believe that the gift of his house was motivated by his mischievous desire to torment Goulet. I had known Paul only slightly before this time, and that had been as a friend of Jackie, Bill Waldren's wife, whom many suspected of having borne him a child, conceived while Bill was in the United States, which Bill loudly proclaimed was really his, although it looked exactly – although a girl – like Paul. Arnaboldi claimed to be a sculptor, but his production was limited to some rough drawings and only a few clay pieces that stood in the back room of his house, and these were amateurish and unremarkable. He had joined the U.S. Army at the end of World War Two and had been stationed in Japan during the American Occupation, after which he volunteered to serve with the hospital ship, *Hope*, in the Philippine Islands. It was here that he worked with Robert Sherwood who invented and patented the *sea container*, making him one of the richest men in the world: as he was the sole owner of not only of Sea Container, whose central offices were based on the south Bank of the Thames in London, he also bought and directed the *Orient Express* in addition to many five-star hotels throughout the world. Later, when Paul was evading Interpol and Scotland Yard, pursued as a notorious drug czar, he used Sherwood's exclusive Paris home as a hide-out, a place in which criminal investigators would never have dreamed of searching.

While employed by *USS Hope* [charitable international hospital ship], Paul received an injury to his spine which granted him Workmen's Compensation and then a Social Security disability payment of a few hundred dollars a month which he claimed supported him in Spain, having purchased his Mallorcan houses for only a few hundred dollars and then received a few thousand when he improved them and sold them to other foreigners. He picked up odd jobs as we all did, and seemed to live comfortably on very little. Only a few years later, we were all astounded to discover that he had been manufacturing most of the world's supply of the drug, L.S.D., and had master-minded the ring which had distributed it internationally in the scandal that became known as "Operation Julie," so named for the Scotland Yard undercover agent who infiltrated the organization in 1977 in Wales. The "bust" sent all members of the outfit – except, most notably, Paul Arnaboldi – to prison for virtual life sentences in the United Kingdom. Curiously, the only photos which Interpol had of Paul derived from an amateur film directed by Mati Klarwein in which Paul appears as King Lear, and then there was also a photo in profile, wearing a Greek fisherman's cap which appeared as a promotional image of a figure called Captain Bounty, on billboards [*hoardings,* in the British idiom] throughout England, selling that chocolate candy bar, 'Bounty.' I appeared to be a virtual identical twin to this face in these representations. Chilling coincidence?

One person who received one of these stiff sentences was the Adelphi University professor, Dr. David Solomon, who had been intimately involved in the drug ring since he had first used L.S.D. with Paul and other Deya residents ten years before. He had proclaimed to all, that this mind-altering substance would change the history of Western Civilization as it was transforming the consciousness of all those who used it. His was a fervent and missionary zeal. He had given it to all his children and promoted it among his students. His best-selling books, *The Marijuana Papers, The Cocaine Papers*, and *The LSD Papers* became texts referred to as some of the leading authorities on the use and distribution of these drugs in the twentieth century. What a shock for many to learn that he was also a prominent dealer of that drug (L. S. D.) which his cartel distributed more widely than any other gang in the world! John St. Jorre and Brian Shakespeare, the two authors [both of whom had worked in military intelligence units (M.I. 6) for the British government) who collaborated in writing *The Brothers War* about the armed conflicts in Biafra, had also written a few international spy thrillers as novels and were amazed to later discover that Paul Arnaboldi, who had supplied them with some stories which they had considered ficitional inventions, had basis in the facts surrounding the actual bizarre, criminal life of this otherwise seemingly naive and innocent fabulist (Paul, himself), who claimed to live on a disability check and dabble in clay sculpture in that small, rustic, mountain village of Fornalutx, Mallorca.

Although I was somewhat suspicious of the motive behind our benefactor's generosity, I accepted the house, rent-free, and decided that as soon as we moved in, that I would inform Robert Goulet that his fear of a law-suit was groundless, that I was focusing my full energy on recuperating and gaining enough strength to rebuild my yacht, *Tsunami,* in order to set forth on the cruise that I hoped would be the maiden voyage of the Corporation Not For Profit foundation (the American Institute for Mythographic Studies) which Sam Coffing and I had envisioned as the charity into which to spill all profits from his enterprise, International Resources Management, whose processes for recycling waste from factories and even homes which we fully expected would bring us hundreds of millions of dollars. Sam Coffing had already received a several thousand dollar grant from the government to build the pilot model of his design for percolating the waste water from disposals and sewage into chemicals pumped up on to roof-tops to feed organic hydroponic gardens in individual homes, and his electro-flotation system for skimming off waste effluents from most factories, then provided fuel to drive the engines used in that very process; and the remaining outflow, was water so pure it could be sold for drinking.

I was intent on realigning my concentration on writing a constitution for the foundation devoted to the study of mythography, a field of research based on my understanding of the principles, not only of Robert Graves, but of Egerton Sykes, and Joseph Campbell, and many other writers who had attempted to penetrate the rich hidden treasure troves which most notably had first been revealed by the work of Heinrich Schliemann in his discovery and subsequent excavation of the several levels of the actual city of Troy, and the recovery of Priam's treasure, from the last days of the war with Greece chronicled by Homer in the *Iliad*, but considered to be merely a fanciful fairy tale since 800 B.C., or thereabouts – judged as fiction for roughly three thousand years. Machu Pichu had not even been known to exist until Hiram Bingham's accidental discovery in 1911. What other cities and civilizations lay hidden and forgotten? What did we really know about the Inca, Aztec, Toltec, Olmec, and Maya cultures? How many Native American nations disappeared before and after the arrival of the *conquistadors*?

I had offered to sell to Jim Peck and his associates, all my holdings in American Electric and Ben Wright Incorporated, the real estate holding company for all my deceased father's businesses. I had begun negotiations on this sale while I was at Eckerd College, and now, just as I had returned from my hospitalization, Phil Daugherty and his assistant, Kent Frates (Rodman's brother and my old antagonist colleague from Casady schoolboy days) informed me that we were indeed ready to close the deal, paying equally to me and my sister, roughly $500,000, for this company and assets worth probably two to four times that ... if we were a truly "going concern," but in the crippled state of my present physical condition, I deemed that the price was fair. I agreed, and prepared to return to America immediately to consult with Sam Coffing, who would represent my interest in this transaction, with no fee for his financial advisory services. I offered him $50,000 which was the fee my sister and I had agreed to pay Kent Frates; however, Sam declined. This was ironic, because several years later, it was on a defaulted loan of $50,000 I had made to Sam to save his company, 'International Resources Management,' that our friendship was severed, and in the subsequent legal proceedings against Sam Coffing, that he claimed that I drove him into bankruptcy. In this rupture of my oldest friendship and loss of my most trusted friend, and as a result of the bad debt of $50,000, I had to seek employment on a full-time basis for the first time in sixteen years; this was the year I began teaching for University of Maryland, European Division, in England and remained in their employ, till 2004, for the next eighteen years.

The state of the art in telephone service was nothing like it is today. In order to speak with Sam or Phil or Jim, I had to either arrange a conference-call at the telephone center in Palma, just off the Borne Boulevard, next to the Central Post Office, or I could struggle with the service provided in *cabines* (literally telephone booths which were called *cabins*) located in most town squares such as Soller. There were open pay telephone stands in the centers of the towns of Deya and Fornalutx. How I was able to arrange for the conferences to settle the sale and purchase of my holdings in my father's estate and to set up the establishment of the 'Institute for Mythographic Studies, A Corporation Not for Profit,' in Coconut Grove, Florida, using the available communications system and what people now call the "snail mail," is a tribute to my powers of concentration and the ingenuity of my associates – Jim Peck, Phil Daugherty, Kent Frates, Sam Coffing – and the patience of my sister, whose alcoholism at times caused her to panic or dive into emotionally depressive states which only the saintly attentions of her husband, Dr. Sam Cheesman, could alleviate.

So, in a matter of only a month from the time of my return from King's College Hospital in London, I was packed and ready to fly to meet Sam and the others in Oklahoma to make the final arrangements in the sale of my stocks and the receipt of the money which was then to be extended to a pay-out for the next several years. With some hefty cash payments, some for amounts as great as $20,000, my sister and I agreed to accept a sum of $2,500 each month. I had been living comfortably on no more than $500 each month in the prevailing British and European economies, so that this bounty would allow me to even set some money aside for extras. The expenses in the renovations and repairs to the boat had not been exorbitant. The largest bill I ever received was for the overhaul of the twin six-cylinder engines: $700 in total. My legal bill, which the Spanish lawyer's secretary, curiously enough, an English woman named Jessie James, the widow of a rich British yachtsman, was almost reluctant to present me, was for only a few hundred dollars, and she told me that it was rare for an English gentlemen to ask for a bill more than annually. However, I had also just constructed a holding company to protect my ownership of the large tract of land above Puigpunyent which I had bought with the idea of building a house some day. This was called a *Sociedad Anonima* (literally, Anonymous Society – the term for *corporation* in Spanish) and I was required by law to give one half of the shares of stock to a Spanish citizen. Perico Villaescusa had agreed to be my partner, and the lawyer, Luis Alarcon, and his assistant, Antonio Ferrer, were rather startled to have someone with the surname Villaescusa – my friend's famed uncle, who was the Chief Justice of the Supreme Court of Military Justice for the entire country – to be co-signer to my contract.

When I returned to Spain and told Janet of my new financial *profile*, she tried hard not to appear hungry to spend all the money at once, but she did begin looking at houses for sale at that time in our village and locations nearby. Instead of improving our relationship, the influx of ready funds seemed to arouse in Janet a new sense of insecurity. She reminded me that we were not married and that she had a small child for whom she felt the entire burden of parenthood, although I was willing to pay for any costs in his rearing, and I acted as a surrogate father in every way. Nevertheless, I had not given him my surname, thereby assuring him a *bona-fide* legal identity - he had been born out of wedlock, but Janet had since employed the last name Michaelis-Nicholson, combining her own maiden name and that of the biological father of Alaric, Eric Michaelis, a man who had been her lover when they both worked as apprentice croupiers in Las Vegas, but he was a person who had been flighty and addicted to drugs, and had never even known that she had given birth to his son, as he had abandoned her and literally disappeared long before she discovered she was pregnant. She claimed that he came from a prominent Austrian family and fantasized often about taking Alaric to their supposed elegant estate somewhere in that country. She had not, as yet, contacted them, so they could not have known of their grandchild and possible heir to the fortune she imagined ... rather, *insisted*, that they must possess.

When she gave up in trying to persuade me to actually marry her, or to legally adopt Alaric, Janet then began to talk of my creating a trust fund for her son's continued maintenance and education. I was seriously considering doing just that when circumstances, a few weeks later, demanded that I remove both Janet and Alaric from our village ... and Spain, entirely. We both drank heavily, and unknown to me, Janet had begun a heavy dependence on the tranquilizer, Valium, which, like any drug controlled by prescription elsewhere, could be bought in any quantities by anyone, whether medically authorized or not, from Spanish pharmacies. When large doses of Valium are combined with a steady intake of wine, cognac, and gin, the results can be fatal, or more often, can render one totally insane. I know personally, as I often combined the chemicals in an attempt to achieve hallucinogenic effects which I had enjoyed with smoking *cannabis* where it was available and did not risk such punishing prison sentences as were in effect in Spain during this epoch.

I surely would never have confronted the latest terror to arrive in Fornalutx, the Canadian giant named Dale, had I not been thoroughly intoxicated. Ishmael, the owner of the 'Bellavista Bar and Restaurant' where we had our melodramatic encounter told all his clients that there was no need ever for the Circus to come to our village as long as we had residents like Ben Wright to perform antics there.

I had heard vague rumblings about a newly arrived character in our small town, and most people who told me anything about him, related such bigger-than-life actual physical proportions when they described this man, that I discounted most of what was told me as a desperate need to confabulate and fabricate in order to take the edge off the continuously dull slate gray skies of our early winter days that

November provides in the Balearics, a time when semi-annual reports from the Bureau of Weights and Measures would be consumed voraciously as entertaining, and even exciting news..

So I was actually pleasantly surprised at what I found, upon entering the Bellavista one night toward the end of an otherwise enervating week which I had spent with Janet, playing in front of our home's fireplace with Alaric's favorite toy race-cars. There was a giant – *sans* bean-stalk. And it possessed a grotesquely over-stated physiognomy with long, lank, blonde hair cascading onto wide shoulders and dropping to the beer-stained bar's surface was producing yowls demanding more bottles of beer, and the eyes, a purplish corn-flower blue, shot sparks of iridescence into the smoke-filled restaurant which opened out on to a terrace on the roadside winding up from Soller around and up behind the Bellavista in to our town square beneath the ancient cobbled steps leading up to the church. I had taken the narrow street that led from our house in to the town square, and had wound back down the Soller Road and entered from the terrace through several tables, empty this night, as was the interior portion allocated to serve meals at three other tables, unoccupied as well, stretching to the end of the bar, nearest the opposite outside door and the entry in to Ishmael's living quarters behind and upstairs. Ishmael was hunched in this corner, not exactly cowering, but he had assumed a stance that was at once protective, as if readied for flight back in to his home where the telephone hung on the wall, which he could use to ring for the police, as he had been forced to do on some other occasions when trouble erupted and became too much for him to subdue with his usually forceful and formidable presence. He had been in the Merchant Marine for over twenty years, was a native of Andalusia, and possessed that gritty peasant bearing, married to a sailor's wily resilience, and an international background of broad experience from travel, so that he was equal to almost any challenge presented him as restaurateur and bar-tender in this mountain village milieu. However, tonight, when we greeted one another, he warned me with his hooded eyes and his curt aside - "Teng cuidao con este tio" - abbreviated Andaluz patois for, "Watch out for this *lad*" [Tenga cuidado (be careful - Take Care - literally) con este (with this) *tio* (guy, lad, bum, jerk - all equally applicable in translation for the slang word meaning *uncle*).

This *tio* was sprawled over almost the entire bar, a space covering that entire end of the restaurant. He was wearing a fringed buckskin leather coat, identical to one displayed in the surviving photos of the famed Buffalo Bill and also worn by Dennis Hopper in his blockbuster film, 'Easy Rider.' On his head was a planter's broad-brimmed palm leaf hat with peacock feathers sticking up out of the brim so as to exaggerate his height by at least ten more inches. He was a *monster*, as in the original definition of that word which means *gigantic*. Later, I learned that his actual height was seven feet and three inches - with the head-gear, that projected an impression of perhaps a good eight feet in height, and with his theatrical bombast and ear-shattering vocal delivery, he was, in actual fact, a *public health hazard.* ... especially in our drowsy little village of retired foreigners and a few aging Mallorquin peasants.

I was startled by the state of virtual terror my friend Ishmael had been reduced to. The *giant* was shouting at him to bring more bottles of San Miguel - the most popular of Spanish beers - and Ishmael was frozen in place, his eyes now darting to mine and back toward his doorway and the telephone. I watched in disbelief as the monster lifted two bottles in each hand, their necks looped between his fingers, and he poured the contents into his gaping mouth and guzzled almost their entire contents in that quaff – a practiced piece, obviously, but nonetheless, formidable and impressive.

I remembered my first encounter at 'Mam's Bar' in Terreno with Thord Sundquist, who was also well over seven feet tall, with long, lanky, blond hair past his shoulders ... and mad fire-cracker Nordic blue eyes ... this man's Viking or *Valkyrie* twin. Thord had theatrically poised his pet, white duck on the bar and then slammed his fist down demanding to be served a "fuck-driver", intentionally meaning to mispronounce the term for vodka and orange juice: *screw-driver.* I also recalled that this demented, overgrown specimen, Thord, had subsequently become my close friend, and I had then discovered him to actually be a shy and talented artist who had contrived his public *persona* to overcome his severe social ineptitude.

As I looked once more at the fiasco before me, I was not so sure that I was observing an introvert over-compensating for his lack of social skills, as I was seeing a dangerous psychopath landed by cruel fate on my turf when I most needed quiet convalescence from my recent severe invasive surgery at King's College Hospital. Actually, it was my still grotesquely damaged features and the prominent welted scars rippling across and up and down my face that probably saved me, on this day. It certainly got this man's attention, as I threw back my shoulders, braced myself and literally tipped up on my toes to project my full height ... then lifted my arms and clapped my hands in exaggerated applause.

"You can leave now. We've seen your trick, and we are amused. Thank you," I announced solemnly. "You know the way out. The same way you came in. That is the road down to Soller. From there, you go to Palma and will still be in time to catch the midnight ferry to Barcelona. Just do not come back. You will not be welcome again."

"And just who do you think you are, little man," he blasted in retort, glaring a ferocious challenge, with a curl to his upper lip that told of the great relish this character took in any conflict, the nastier the better, and bespoke a will to injure and dis-able and even dis-figure ... that bordered on a *gluttony for punishment*. ... the inflicting of it *upon others*, with fiendish delight [or, with *extreme prejudice* - that hackneyed term used in the Vietnam conflict to denote the most vicious extreme of physical damage, or, *death*, slithered into my consciousness].

I answered with alacrity and bravado and, I now consider, perversely pretentious authority, "My name is Ben. My fellow villagers call me El Benjamin, and I speak for them all in telling you to get out, leave, and do not come back. I repeat, 'You are not welcome here!' and we do not want you to stay one moment longer."

The ogre's lips drew back to reveal a full mouth of large white teeth - the canines alarmingly prominent - as the man threw his head back and the full assemblage of straw and feathers, brushed the ceiling, only inches above his upper-most, cranial decoration, and he roared in laughter, from his belly to his lips which slobbered and spit out a raucous braying like a burro gone hysterical, and he then delivered his response and made clear that he would have none of my advice, nor would he heed my orders to depart.

"I am Dale, and I just spent the last fourteen years in a Canadian prison for manslaughter ... Vancouver, British Columbia, to be exact.

I am staying here with my wife, till she gives birth to our baby ... any day now, and as soon as that happens, and my Rolls Royse Silver Cloud arrives by boat from France, I will gladly be on my way. But nobody, especially some Raggedy Andy patchwork pecker – and he pointed to his own cheeks and forehead to trace out the lines of my most prominent scars which had *remodeled* my face – like you – telling me where to go or when to do anything. So you just buy me and my friend some beers and go home and count yourself lucky you didn't get the other side of your head mashed."

It was only then that I noticed a figure hunched beside him at the bar, whose head reached barely to Dale's shoulder, a darkly clad rodent-like man, almost crushed against the far wall, who piped up, and then flung out a further gibe, "Tell him to fuck off, Dale. He don't know what kind of trouble he's messin' with. We would have his kind for breakfast back in the joint."

"Oh, I see you brought your punk along to back you up," I taunted. "Do you let him drink with you in public, or is he just for your idle moments of play..."

And the wounded minion howled with the insult, which sank that much deeper, because I had employed the term *punk*, which, in penitentiaries, was a synonym for *bitch*, which of course, was what one had as one's object for play and sexual enjoyment, a homosexual substitute for female companionship ... in the "joint." So much for the insider knowledge I had gleaned from my experiences working as an educational volunteer with Synanon in California and other prison facilities in America.

"I ain't nobody's punk. Tell him that, Dale. I ain't no punk ... "

But Dale had now focused on me in a new manner, before telling his pal to be quiet ... to not interrupt. He actually turned to look down on the smitten creature and wagged his finger in its mousy face, saying just the simple word, "Hush!"

I picked up on the shift in mood and interjected, "I really must apologize, Dale. I would never have considered that one beside you as your sweetheart. Your bitch would be light-years ahead in elegance on the evolutionary scale to that troglodytic trole.," I added, feeling most pleased with my *ad hoc,* alliterative, jingling gibe.

However, Dale's companion looked as if he was about to leap up on to the bar as he had begun screaming with his now inarticulate curses of outrage at me. Dale held him in place, as if restraining a rabid Yorkshire terrier, which, indeed he did somewhat resemble, as his face was covered with matted hair that did not quite constitute a beard, and looked more like the unkempt muzzle on a canine species. As he *yapped* on, Dale began to laugh, and turning his attention then back to me, he invited me to share in his amusement at the expense of the *ferocious* creature he now held aloft by the scruff of the neck , like some spasming specimen on display in a biology laboratory experiment.

"He will carry on so, when his little pride has been piqued," Dale remarked, and then looked at me with arched eyebrows and added with a sincere entreaty, "Would you mind, terribly, old chap, telling him that you did not consider him a *punk?* It is rather a trigger word for him. Definitely a deep insult in his lexicon, if you catch my drift. A definite slur of the vilest sort in prison."

I was also now smiling, and on the very verge of laughing at this new twist of action in what Ishmael would later call the "three-ring-circus" we had just performed that night at 'Bellavista.' Some byzantine bond beyond the usually surreal swirl in my Mallorquin world had been annealed tonight, so I said simply, "Sure."

I then adopted an avuncular tone, but with no tincture of oppositional patronizing, to carry on and state, " I did not mean to use that term, *punk*. You are certainly not that, or you would never be chosen as a boon companion and comrade of such a fine gentleman as Dale. Please accept my apology for an ill-considered word," and I waited to see if this could subdue the still raging vituperation of the small creature. He was visibly calmed then, but asked Dale a question that amused us both.

"What does he mean by 'boon', Dale? I don't look like no nigger, do I? I'm as white as you, ain't I?" he gibbered.

With benign condescension, a paternal, but not altogether patronizing, yet clearly in command, obviously accustomed to explaining the obvious and even the glaringly apparent to his dim little friend, Dale put his arm around the obsequious creature by his side and explained. "The man meant to say 'special friend.' That is what the term *boon companion* means. He is obviously a person who possesses an education above the average, so some of the words he uses will not be familiar to you, or for that matter, to most people who have not read extensively as I have. Remember my quarters at the penitentiary? My bookshelves and all the volumes that were stacked there. I did not have a television. I was too busy with my reading, and was *loath to consider such trivia*. That is, I could not be bothered with such crap."

"But you still love Rock and Roll, don't ya, Dale? Huh? And that cat, Muller? The church music he wrote with a bunch of singers and big bands?"

That *cat* was named Mahler, and yes, he did compose symphonies with huge orchestras and sometimes enormous choirs. Rock and Roll? You know that Little Richard will always be my man. And so are you, Clarence. Now you go on back to the house and tell my wife that I will be home soon. I have some things I want to talk about here. Now, scat!"

Dale wheeled the man about in his tracks and sent him scurrying for the doorway, and then he, himself, turned to address me. "Thanks for the humble apology. We need to make life easier for our lessers, at times. You are a good man. And we are neighbors, and we may even come to like one another."

Actually Dale and I stayed on in the bar for another hour, drinking and exchanging information. I was willing to accept him now, and was even aware of something kindred between us; *madness*, perhaps. There would be few dull moments in our village, for sure, as long as he resided there. He was a braggadocio, but I have always found that men who have been incarcerated for long periods, make up stories to fill in the years they lost, and yet sometimes, the reasons for their convictions and lengths of sentences derive from the extreme behaviors which serve to create their histories and color their biographies to such startling shades beyond the ken of the average *citizen*. Thoreau's remark that the average person leads a life of *quiet desperation*, and this appraisal definitely does not apply to a sociopath such as Dale ... *or, myself.*

We did not walk out of 'Bellavista' exactly arm-in-arm, but we did swagger together up the cobbled narrow road to our retrospective dwellings in concert. Dale was residing only about a hundred yards away, up the road which ran above my house toward the cemetery.

He invited me to come meet his wife, but I demurred, especially as I knew that Clarence would be hovering about inside, and I had no desire to encounter this bloke again. Dale assured me that his guest was leaving the next day, so I considered passing by then. I actually felt as if I had made a new friend, and perhaps this larger-than-life specimen would prove to become an amusing and lively variation of my two other out-sized pals, Thord Sundquist, the painter, and Christopher Wright, the British poet (although Kit Wright was only six feet eleven, with the flair of his prematurely gray hair worn in an Afro hair-do, he appeared to be seven and a half feet tall [actually he had inscribed himself in the *Guiness Book of Records* as the largest poet in the world ... but who was the *best?*]. Dale was certainly articulate and seemed intellectually well-developed for an auto-didact, as some long-term convicts do become as well educated as most career academics.

My next encounter with him was only a few days later, and that was late at night. I had been commuting to Palma daily to work on *Tsunami* with Karen as my help-mate and after-lunch sexual frolic pet [what the Spanish working-class call the post-prandial *cafe* - a relaxing fuck after lunch and before siesta] and had not been returning to Fornalutx till well after Janet had fed Alaric and put him to bed, when we had a light evening meal of soup or Tortilla Espanol with perhaps some Serrano ham and a bottle of wine, after which I would stay up for an hour or so reading in front of the fire-place and then climb in to bed with Janet for another sexual engagement. I was a hearty lad in these days, and I would be amazed at my lack of sexual activity that I now consider common-place: months without any sexual partner, and then only the minimum of fulfillment when only now rarely possible - three or four times weekly.

I was just about to lay down my book – I do *remember* savoring Pyncheon's *Gravity's Rainbow* and *Zen and the Art of Motorcycle Maintenance* at this time. The latter, I particularly enjoyed, as it seemed to be addressed to my sense of challenge in adapting my skill in poetics and philosophy to the practical application of this same mental discipline in becoming master of the mechanical issues confronting me in making *Tsunami* seaworthy and comfortable for going to live aboard. I had set myself the date of only two more months before I intended to get underway for the mainland of Spain, to follow that coast to France, and enter the canals there and travel up through that region to meet the English Channel and make the crossing to this vessel's original home, Port Hamble, Isle of Wight, in Great Britain, where the boat would, by maritime law, then be officially mine, as I would have passed through two separate Customs services (French and English), and that was the magic number to qualify for undeniable ownership certification under international law.

Suddenly one night, the tumultuous knock on the front gate, large wrought iron fabrication, meant to serve against any onslaught, was thunderous, and I feared that their hinges might come tearing out of their sockets on the stone of the front garden walls. The voice that accompanied this clamor was a scream of desperation, and my name was the primary word I heard above the shouted words of *Life* and *Death* and *Wife* and *Baby!*

I ran outside into the front garden to find Dale flailing his arms and tossing his head with the long mop of hair swinging wildly about the archway of the gate. He sputtered out that his wife was in the midst of delivering their baby and that he was desperate and terrified and needed help. I took him immediately to Robert Goulet who had a telephone in his house. Robert was able to contact his friend, the doctor in Soller, who promised to come directly to Dale's, and that is where we went to await him.

We climbed the stairway to the bedroom where Dale's wife was howling with the agonies of her labor, and as we entered, there she was, with her legs spread wide, and Dale attempted to provide an introduction, which caused Robert to make a remark which he repeated often in the future.

"I have never had the pleasure of meeting a woman in the exact position as you have introduced your wife, but I am sure that I shall never forget her face."

Under any other circumstances, this might have provoked a violent physical response in Dale, but on this occasion, we all were laughing heartily, the tension and terror of the situation having been removed by the most bizarre humorous offering, a quality of Robert's which had once placed him in a most unpleasant situation with the Guardia Civil, when he had referred to their organization as the "cajones of Franco" (Franco's testicles), and they had arrested him and placed him in the Palma Insane Asylum where he remained confined for two weeks till Robert Graves was able to effect his release with appeal to the highest levels of the legal establishment on the island and in Madrid. His most recent book, a novella entitled, *Manicomio* (Spanish, for madhouse or sanitarium) told of this horrifying ordeal. It was an indication of the waning of Franco's reign of terror that Robert Goulet was allowed to remain in Spain after its publication, although the book was not translated into Spanish, but remained a popular publication in English and in the French version published in his Canadian homeland

When the doctor arrived, after only a thirty minute wait, the heaving of the woman in delivery had reached the optimal stage, and the child was born with no further problems; so the three of us decided to walk down to 'Bellavista' to buy a few bottles of Spanish *cava* (champagne). Ishmael was pleased to receive the news of the birth and treated us all to some of his finest Havana cigars. This was to be the last time I would be celebrating anything in his bar, but I had no idea what was in store for me in the next few days, nor that I should have to be moving from this village on such short notice.

The next Monday evening, when I arrived in the village from Palma somewhat later than usual, at almost 10 P.M., I decided to stop off at the bar for a beer before walking up to my house, reckoning that Janet would already have put Alaric to bed and would most likely have gone to bed, herself. When I entered the bar, Ishmael gestured for me to come outside onto the terrace with him, out of hearing of the one family who were still seated in the restaurant having a late dinner.

He told me that Janet had been in the bar much earlier, and that he had been forced to take some extreme measures to deal with her. When I asked what this could all possibly mean, the key expressions being *extreme measures* and *deal with her*, he assumed a deeply grieved look, and said that he found it difficult to tell me what he must report. He said that the situation was so unusual that he had been unable to handle it by himself and had been forced to call upon the services of both his wife and daughter to assist in a matter which only women could properly deal with.

According to Ishmael, there had been only a few of the local men in the bar at the time, just after sunset, when many of the usual patrons came in for an aperitif before going home to supper. There had been no foreigners, and that was particularly fortunate, because their reactions to unusual incidents could be most unpredictable and might have brought in the Guardia Civil, as these people often believed in utilizing services of local constabulary as they did in their own countries with none of the disastrous results which could occur in Franco's Spain. Ishmael was about to regale me with some trivia about such incidents as a way of avoiding the topic that was most essential for me now to hear, really as a way of leavening the treat he was compelled now to deliver, and trying to soften the blow to come ... but I knew him well enough to tell him to stop worrying about my feelings, but to get right to the point. Some would say, "Let's cut to the chase."

The *juicy morsel*, the less than appetizing treat he then served up, was the image of Janet, stark naked, prancing in to the 'Bellavista' bar and asking if anyone there was man enough to come back to our home and give her a good fuck, or if necessary, she could bend over the wall outside and receive the cocks of all the men assembled, one at a time, or in any combinations that could be devised among them. She declared that Ben did not have the man-hood to serve a deserving, needy, sex-starved woman. She laughed hysterically, tossing her long, blond hair about her shoulders, cupping her full ripe breasts up in her hands, and then turned to bend over and wiggle her pear-shaped pink bottom at the crowd, while snorting and grunting as if in the throes of an intense orgasm. Ishmael left out no detail. I was particularly impressed by his own *snorting, grunting* imitation of Janet's simulation of the vocal representation of an intense orgasm.

He had rushed back into his living quarters and ordered his wife to come through with a blanket thrown over Janet's naked form, and they both shouted to his daughter who lived next-door to assist them as they escorted her outside and began walking her up to our house, where she probably was at this very time, still under guard by Ishmael's wife and daughter who had been relieved to find Alaric sound asleep in his own bedroom, unaware of his mother's *maenad* [those sexual ravaging drunken disciples of Dionysius] meandering that evening.

There was an empty plastic container with the farmacia's type-written script for Valium Ten's alongside a drained bottle of 'Fundador' brandy next to the bed in which Janet thrashed about, twisted in soaking wet sheets, gibbering curses which fortunately Ishmael's women could not understand except for the word *fuck*, with which she punctuated much of her diatribe. Her face looked purplish, and when I felt her pulse, there was not any regular beat that I could discern. If she had ingested the entire contents of the Valium dose and then the bottle of brandy, she might be in danger of losing her life. She did not respond to any of my questions as I knelt down on the bed and held her by the shoulders, trying to make her focus her attention on me, but her eyes appeared to be rolled back in their sockets, and her head lolled back and forth, and she could not keep it erect.

With a plea to remain with her, but to run for Ishmael if there might be a turn for the worse, I told the women that I would be gone for only a matter of minutes, while I ran to Robert Goulet's house, closer than 'Bellavista' by half the distance, and hoping that Robert could be of more assistance as a fellow English-speaking foreign resident, than Ishmael could be. I was right, but perhaps another course of action would have prevented what happened in the next few hours which removed us from Fornalutx forever and separated me from Janet and Alaric from that time on, as well.

The Soller doctor whom Robert contacted, arrived as promptly as he had for Dale's child-birth only a few days before. He assured us both that Janet had been on the brink of dying from the combination of drugs and alcohol. He had induced vomiting and then gave her a sedative injection. However, what was more alarming, was what Robert told me that the doctor had confided in him when I was out of the room. Because Alaric had awakened while all this commotion was occurring in saving his mother's life, he had wandered in to the bedroom bawling for his mother's solace and expecting her immediate cuddling embrace and kisses. What he encountered instead was a scene that was directly from a Casualty Ward where a drunk was being revived from a possible overdose of drugs and booze. Thus, the doctor considered this house to be unfit for the continued rearing and nurturing of such a fine young male specimen. He told Robert, that in good conscience, he must report Janet to the Social Services as an unfit mother and that he would personally set about the placing of Alaric in a suitable facility for endangered youngsters and that Janet herself should be sent to the 'Manicomio' (insane asylum) for observation and confinement as being a person in danger of committing suicide, and perhaps harming or killing her own child. The doctor told Robert that he was fed up with the irresponsible behaviors he had observed for the past several years when he had answered emergency medical calls within the foreign community in Mallorca. Often these careless, sybaritic ex-patriots succeeded in butchering and maiming themselves and innocent others and constituted a virtual public health hazard for everyone residing on his blessed island.

Robert told me that I had only a few hours in which to act, to escape such a certain fate for Janet and her child and perhaps some criminal *denuncio* for myself as well, as I would be considered to be a sort of accessory-after-the-fact as the financial support of this wanton woman and responsible for aiding and abetting her profligacy in perversity and degeneracy ... and ... I bade him cease and desist in his vituperation and relish for this sickening situation; and so I readily agreed that we must get out of town, off the island, and allow matters to cool considerably before considering our return, if that were to ever be an option. Frankly, I was more than ready to be rid of Janet, and I was anxious to take up residence with Karen in her village of Esporles, which was only ten kilometers from the marina berth at 'Real Club Nautico' in Palma where we were working on *Tsunami*.

Therefore, after some telephone calls, reserving seats on an early morning 'Iberia' flight to London, I returned home to pack up all our most necessary kit and the local taxi drove us to the airport in Palma at 1:30 A.M. Janet was like a zombie, but was cajoled into regarding this jaunt to London as a surprise treat, as was Alaric, who always found any travel an adventure [today, as a United States Air Force fighter air-craft pilot with the rank of lieutenant -colonel, he is still engaged in adrenaline-stress activities – perhaps my mentorship at his most impressionable age contributed to his career choice and success]. By 0600 we were winging over Barcelona and making our way northward to England, and well out of the clutches of the Spanish Social Services and whatever *sanity* commissions might put both Janet *and* myself in the *MANICOMIO*!

I had no trouble finding a studio apartment flat at a reasonable price for lease in Notting Hill Gate with the help of Michael Kenny, who was especially delighted that his daughter Camilla would have her ideal playmate, Alaric, back in town *for the duration* – whatever that should prove to be. I told him that once Janet was sufficiently recovered from the depressive episode she had experienced in Mallorca, that I would be flying back down to Palma to look after my boat's refurbishment. Actually, as soon as I was able, I established a bank account in Janet's name for a thousand Pounds Sterling, and then I paid the apartment's year's lease in full. I told Janet that I would be in touch with her as soon as we could arrange to return to Mallorca, but I left her, knowing that I would try to avoid being in her company for the rest of my days. I regretted leaving Alaric, but I knew that he was a sturdy lad and more devoted to his mother than to any surrogate father figure such as me.

Immediately upon my return to Mallorca, I moved in with Karen in the village of Esportles where she lived alone with her two small daughters, aged ten and seven. She claimed that she was deeply in love with me, and I found her sexy in the extreme. I playfully called her "Super Kraut" because she possessed most of the stereotype features of that nationality, and I was later to discover, when I met her family, that her father had been a dedicated member of Hitler's SS-Stormtroopers. And that was a curious ... and chilling ... encounter, indeed.

Karen's father and mother came to Spain on a package tour from Hamburg, Germany, and stayed in a beach hotel in Magaluf, Mallorca, renting a car from Hasso, the favored German agency. We met them in their hotel and I was relieved that they chose not to try to stay with us, as there was only one other bedroom for the two daughters. The father, Hans, was immediately abusive to his daughter, Karen, saying to all in earshot, in German, and then, in remarkably clear, unaccented English, "Karen is an ass-hole, an incompetent numb-skull." He went on to say that because she had allowed her husband to leave her and did not have even a minimum child-support payment from him, that she was therefore an unfit mother.

What a way to begin an introduction to the family! I was considered to be a rich find, and the father acted as if I were one of his former Nazi commanding officers. He was enormously pleased that my hair was virtually blond as a result of being exposed to the daily sun working on the boat, and my eyes have always possessed such a startling color of blue, that I remember when I first met Paul Newman on a film he was shooting in Miami when I was a professor at the university there and visiting the set between takes, the famous actor was amazed at how our eyes reflected each other's. These ice-blue eyes pleased Karen's father and confirmed for him my pure Aryan blood-lines - little did he know what an actual "dog's breakfast" my pedigree [Eliza Rogers Wright's creole quotient as a mixed blood would have horrified Herr Hans] consisted of in ethnic and racial conglomeration.

However, the former Stormtrooper was intrigued by *Tsunami*, with the Norwegian steel-reinforced fiber-glass rescue-vessel hull, designed to lift onto the plane with the two powerful six-cylinder Perkins diesel engines with Z-drive, inboard/outboard propeller shafts and all the special features of bullet-proof glass and salt-water conversion and auto-pilot and sailing rig as well - a boat designed for combat operations, if need be. Thus, he began to recall with relish his war-time experience in the early 1940s with a P.T. (Patrol Torpedo) craft he had served aboard which entered the Irish Sea and had contact with some of the Irish forces who chose to use this liaison with the enemy, to provide revolutionary thrust to the I.R.A. (Irish Republican Army) battle against Great Britain. I had read about several attacks by submarines on the coast of Virginia, sinking many thousands of tons of American shipping, virtually at the entrance to Chesapeake Bay in that period. Hans claimed that his small crew were all Stormtroopers, the elite of all German armed forces, with primary, personal loyalty to the Fuhrer, pledged in allegiance above that sworn to the Army or even to the nation. He was a rabid little bugger, and I could see much of Karen in his temperament.

I had once asked her what in the German language was equivalent to the word for *fair*. Her answer was that this did not exist in German, but that after the *last movement*, her designation for the Second World War, that our Allied Forces, the conquerors, had imposed *this word* on the German people, but that after the *next movement,*, that word would be removed from their vocabulary. As victors this next time, they would have no need for such words or such useless concepts. I hoped that she was teasing me, but I recalled a friend's jest about a German doctoral dissertation on humor entitled, 'No Laughing Matter.' Neither Karen, nor any other member of her family had a sense of humor, and I reckon that no intimate relationship, not even a friendship, can survive without laughter or whimsy ... in my life.

There was another apocryphal remark I had heard about Germans, those same lovely folks that brought us the Holocaust ... that they were either at your throat or at your knees. And when Karen was tired of begging for anything, she had a tendency to demand, and then threaten, if her desires were not fulfilled. I once observed her attempting to repair a small mechanical item. She carefully explored all possible solutions to make the mechanism function, and when she finally realized that she could not discover what would repair it, she smashed the piece to bits and walked away. Our relationship and its end could best be compared to this foreboding template scenario.

When it became clear that beyond the working together on the boat in Palma, that our days together would go no further, that we would not be compatible traveling companions – there were her two daughters in school who needed their mother's daily attention – it was obvious that our relationship must end. I moved the boat to a mooring in Puerto Andraitx, enjoying the company of my old friends there, especially that of John Stevens, yacht-delivery skipper and restauranteur, who was nicknamed Captain San Miguel, since that was the brand of beer always clutched in his hand. I then cruised farther around the island to place *Tsunami* on the quay in Puerto Soller, whence I could catch the trolley in to Soller and board the train to ride over the Teix into Palma whenever I needed to do business there.

I had met and employed two people who came to live aboard *Tsunami* and to serve as crew for me: Nick Johnson and Maya Anderson. The man was an English able seaman who had many years of experience in his country's Merchant Marine service, and the woman was a sleek, blond Finnish Swede who could cook and also handle any gritty deck job as she had spent several months working on yachts in Palm harbor. She had been residing with a wild novelist called Peter the Finn from Stockholm, a friend of Thord Sundquist. I had encountered these new ship-mates in 'Mam's Bar' in Terreno, and I felt comfortable that one - Nick - drank much more than I, and the other - Maya - appeared to be temperate and moderate in all her ways. Nick proved to be a great asset in any nautical endeavor, but when ashore, he was a decided liability, as he would begin his day by upending a full bottle of cognac, and displayed the most severe symptoms of acute chronic alcoholism I had ever encountered. I had to pay him off and send him on his way when we reached Barcelona where an encounter he had with one of the more degenerate trans-sexuals in the back streets there almost brought the local police down on us. However, by that time Maya and I had bonded in a relationship that became my third marriage which we legalized in her home town of Stockholm, Sweden, later that year of 1975.

My own drinking habits at this time were also moderate, and I was amazed at how easily Maya and I seemed to meld together, as if we had been programmed as a single interactive unit.. I do not embrace the notion of "soul-mates" or any other such romantic nonsense; yet,

473

we did find one another compatible and then, sexually united. However, there was one last incident with Janet - the word *scene* would be more appropriate to describe this final encounter - that took place in Puerto Soller.

Maya and I had been soundly asleep in one another's embrace in the forward converted V-bunk in the bow, when the hatch which was just above us was suddenly snatched open, it had been left unlocked, as we were in port and both aboard, and therefore not expecting any intruding company. As daylight poured in upon us, Maya sleepily turned on her side, a sound sleeper always, and content in her dreams. I looked up into the glaring face of Janet, wreathed with wild blond matted hair, and she remained crouched there above, as if ready to pounce and savage us both in our rapture and languor. I grabbed a pair of khaki shorts from beside me on the bed and pulled my legs in, hitching the top button into place before mumbling , "I'll be right back," to Maya's still recumbent form in the bed, and then pulled myself up out of the hatch, setting it down gently behind me, as Janet stepped back on to the deck of the bow to allow me to stand and address her.

The conversation began with her remark that my new whore was a pretty one and then moved into the realm of accusation and condemnation and curses which I invited her to elaborate over a cup of coffee, or a drink of alcohol at the bar and restaurant which stood along the quay over the docks, as I led the way there in bare feet off the boat and along the water-front. She followed, keeping pace, and swinging and flailing her arms in exaggerations of threats. We found a table at the edge of the water, where we were some few yards distance from the other people already gathered for breakfast, at the very edge of the ramp leading back down to several of the smaller fishing and pleasure craft assembled: European style motor-boats and the Mallorquin double-ended ancient *yauda* fishermen with

Arab-rig sailing masts.

I ordered two jiggers of 'Fernet Branca', that lethal kill-or-cure combination of herbs and strong liqueur, to accompany Cafe Americano, the Spanish name for the largest dose of black coffee, accompanied by a full liter bottle of sparkling mineral water, with two large glasses filled with ice, along with a couple of croissants and the local specialty, the flat Mediterranean breakfast roll, *ensaimada*. Tossing back our liqueurs, a grim toast followed by winces as the potent liquid hit our stomachs, followed by deep drafts of the mineral water as chaser, and then a few nibbles of our pastries and sips of the bracing coffee which served to slow down Janet's delivery of fiery invective for a few moments.

Nonetheless, she was steamed up and primed to deliver her punishing message. She told me she had arrived in Palma airport at dawn, rented a motorbike, and ridden straight over the Teix, all switch-backs, at full power, so she could awaken me on my yacht, hopefully in the arms of my latest paramour – her rather literary word choice, she being always the one to affect fancy dress in language whenever possible, one most charming trait I would indeed miss. Maya's vocabulary was limited, as English was her second language, learned from the sailors in Palma's bars, whose second language also was English, even though many had been born in English-speaking nations, the Cockneys and cowboys from the rural parts of Southern America such as Alabama being somehow swept on to the docks of Spain and able to secure jobs on the decks of even the most luxurious yachts there and on the French Riviera.

Janet had been taken in to the home of minor aristocracy, a lord and his wife, [he may have been a baronet or merely a knight], when she first arrived in England, pregnant with Alaric, and somehow, she had inveigled this family into caring for her through her ordeal with giving birth and the early post-natal days, and she had highjacked many of their manners, and more particularly, the skein of the upper class accent, but only to such a degree, that only those unfamiliar with the British class system would mistake her for one of that privileged order. Still, her vocal flavor was more delicious than what she had been born to, in Sacramento, California, and her voracious reading habits had provided her a vocabulary which would have been appropriate in a Jane Austen novel, and might even have pretended to belong to some of Henry James's major characters, some of whom, were, like her, and the author himself, *innocents abroad* - Americans living in a European setting and adapting to the local milieu so that they did not stand out as yokels (Henry James's own childhood neighborhood was Brooklyn, New York, but he was loath to claim it , or return there gladly, one of his famous remarks being, "When good Americans die, their souls go to Paris. The bad go to Boston" [this locale perhaps selected as his brother, William James, the Harvard professor of Psychology, resided there]). Janet subsequently married an Englishman whom she took back to America and then divorced. She somehow reunited with Alaric's biological father for a year or so, and then moved aboard a 36 foot yacht in Los Angeles and spent many of her years later cruising back and forth to Baja California and the Hawaiian Islands.

On this day in Puerto Soller, however, as we sat facing one another across a small table in the outdoor bar overlooking the harbor, she was building her frenzy to a severe, homicidal pitch and had just reached out to grasp the long-necked bottle of sparkling mineral bottle whose contents we had almost depleted, when I noticed something alarming just along the ramp to which boats were moored end-on, only a few yards away from where we were sitting. A small boy had been wandering along, peering into the spaces between the boats which swayed and sometimes slammed together, avoiding damage only because some had large oblong rubber buffers which were hung from their gunwales. Perhaps he had lost a ball he had been playing with? For whatever reason, he was now down on his hands and knees, his head stretched out from his shoulders as he reached out in to the murky water beneath the dock ... and at that moment, I realized I must act fast or he might fall and be crushed between the boats crashing against one another in the erratic swells. I turned back to Janet, just as she lifted the bottle above her shoulder and readied herself for a swing at my head, shouting, "You insensitive, selfish bastard!"

I held up my hand, almost sticking my fingers in her perky distended nose and said, "Hold it right there. I'll get back to you!"

I leapt out on to the dock and swept down toward the boats and knelt at the place where the boy had just toppled over into the water. Just as I looked down, he was coming back to the surface, his arms outstretched, and I grabbed him and jerked him bodily back out of harms' way. He was screaming with fright as I held him and I said, "Calmete [Calm Yourself]. Tranquilo [Easy]. You're all right now."

His parents, a young couple who had just rushed up, took him from me, thanking me effusively, and I sauntered back to Janet, who still held the bottle in her hand, but at an angle not for striking any telling blows. She looked at me with disbelief and said, "You staged all that, just to make me look foolish. I know you."

I offered to get her another drink and then proffered what I knew would settle her down: *money*. I had several hundred dollar bills,

Ben Franklins, aboard *Tsunami*, and my (English) Barclays Bank check-book in the same safe place hidden in a wallet in the bilges. I convinced her that for Alaric's sake it would be best to accept this pay-off and then return to London - no need for her to meet Maya or to attempt to undermine my intention to remain with her. Janet's fury had been dissipated by the rescue of the boy and the subsequent celebration of his survival by his parents and the onlookers who were applauding me as a minor hero. When I had returned to our table, she was still holding the bottle limply in her hand and only after I mentioned her awkward pose, did she seat herself and place the bottle upright beside our glasses and dishes. But now she eagerly rose to accompany me back to the boat, and I was then on and off the vessel in a matter of only minutes to retrieve my cache of funds so that she was meandering along the dock as I joined her to fetch her motor-bike and enact our last financial transaction by the curb of the Puerto Soller road leading back to Palma … and away to London.

In the following years, I heard through mutual friends such as the Kennys, that the ever-resourceful Janet bought herself an automobile and set up as a jitney mini-cab driver and then to insure that she could stay in England and provide more stability for Alaric, she had married a man named Kevin who worked as a sometimes hair-dresser, used-car salesman, and real estate agent. Alaric became a jet fighter pilot reaching the rank of lieutenant-colonel in the United States Air Force. All's well that ends well, but we have not ended our stories, yet.

Maya and I cruised up the coast of Spain to Barcelona and then placed *Tsunami* in the most hospitable port of Cap D'Agde, France, where we left her so that Maya and I could fly to Stockholm to be married. My closest friends in Cap D'Agde were Vernon Sewell, a film-maker who claimed to have made over forty movies (he referred to them all as merely "B" grade) as director and producer, and he was still a close friend of Blake Edwards, and reveled in the fact that he had employed Boris Karloff in his last job as an actor in Vernon's last cinematic production, 'Blood Altar.' Derrick Wright was our other fellow captain, and his credentials as a skipper were formidable indeed, as he had commanded the Royal Navy's Patrol Torpedo Boat fleet at the end of the Second World War as a youthful but thoroughly combat-trained officer - promotion was swift in those days as naval officers were killed off rather rapidly in the conflicts of such close engagements with the German navy's best.

As soon as we were settled back in Cap D'Agde as a honeymoon couple, the winter had begun, and I decided to move us to London where we stayed in Putney for a few weeks in the home of Jan Lynton, chair-person of Art History at Goldsmiths College, who offered me a lectureship in her department. Michael Kenny, coincidentally, was the chair of the Art Department at this same institution, so I felt delighted to accept the position which paid just enough to cover my travel expenses to and fro in London. I followed a lead to call on Rchard Saddleton, owner of the 'Madingley Club,' an actual yacht club whose dock held only two thirty-foot craft on Duck's Walk, East Twickenham, Middlesex, just below Richmond Bridge, the quay which lay on the river Thames in front of his large home which was provided a bar and restaurant on the ground floor, managed by his mother and wife.

Richard had once held the title of British kayak champion and also had placed high in sports car racing and rallies in his Triumph automobile, and he had been host to many a celebrity in the lush gardens and sumptuous dining facility of the Madingley Club which lay just across a wide stretch of the Thames from Richmond where Queen Elizabeth had kept her favorite residence and, some alleged, had actually been born there. The man who had given me that letter to present to Richard, I then discovered was the most famous race-car driver of his time in England, who had left and moved to Spain, vowing never to return as his car had caromed off the track and over the barricades into a crowd of people, killing and mutilating a sizable number. I had encountered the man as I saved his yacht in a flash storm that had struck us in Santa Eulalia, Ibiza, Spain, when I had been able to start my engines and pull this man's vessel, and then several others which were likewise imperiled, to safety, away from the wreckage and havoc being wreaked within the small yacht harbor. He had proclaimed me a hero, and I did humbly accept a few glasses of champagne, but my *heroic* feat had merely derived from the good fortune to be alert and actually at the wheel of my boat when the disaster had struck, so that I was able to save as many vessels as I did. I considered the man rather a melodramatic sort for declaring to the other boat owners and sailors that I had saved their lives. I considered my actions to merely be derivative of my rapid reflex actions when in crisis situations, what had characterized my military career as well as other life endangering challenges throughout my life.

When I arrived in London and telephoned Richard at his club and told him the name of the man who had recommended I do so, he asked, without further ado, if he could do anything for me, and he stressed the word *anything*. I told him simply that I owned a motor-sailor, a yacht measuring approximately nine meters and that I was looking for a mooring afloat somewhere in London, on the river if possible. He told me that the one other berth on his dock was free, and it was mine for as long as I should care to remain. I accepted and then informed Maya that I should have to find a truck transport to carry me and our boat from France to our new home, Madingley Club, and I immediately set about undertaking this project.

In the meantime, my new wife and I had been attending London based classes in the Silva Mind Control Program, conducted by my former instructor from Miami, Florida, in that process of self-hypnosis and guided visualization for healing of self and others, the very method I had used so well in eliminating the paralysis in the right side of my face, removing the disfiguring scars and rendering my vision perfect in both eyes. Paul Fransella, my teacher, had also taught Dr. Carl Simonton this healing technique which that doctor, a member in good standing of the American Medical Association, had used to establish the Bristol Cancer Clinic, in that city in western England; and then he had returned with his wife, a skilful psychotherapist, who had been likewise trained, and they established the center for curing cancer patients in Fort Worth, Texas, where they had been successful in effecting total remissions of the terminal cancer fates of well over 70% of those victims sent them by medical doctors who had diagnosed them as hopeless and *incurable*. I wanted Maya to know the methods I had employed to restore the feeling in my face and to remove the deep scars which had virtually rendered my facial features as grotesque. I was still struggling to wink my right eye, and Dr. David MacSweeney had nicknamed me Cyclops when we encountered him at the 'Queen's Elm' pub and at 'Chelsea Arts Club' where we drank together. The eye did have a certain prominence in that it appeared to be enlarged in the re-constructed socket and because the eye-lid was not so flexible. It appeared to be staring - merely an optical illusion, and that could be a joke, except that Cyclops was not an altogether inaccurate description of my facial appearance. My teacher, Paul Fransella, was amazed at the progress I had made in this recovery, as he had seen me when I first left 'King's College Hospital' in the post-operative condition, only two years before. Ironically, Roberta Booth was also enrolled in the course being taught, as was her partner, the musical producer, Jeff Dexter (he had first presented Jimi Hendricks in England, at the Glastonbury Festival, and had discovered and promoted 'America' whose song, 'Horse with No Name' had become such a pop hit). Roberta was delighted to see me happily married, and she and Maya became fast friends, virtual sisters [they must have been bound by some strong chemical connections as both had received my sperm in their vaginal tracts and might still be harboring some of my D.N.A. in their deep cell structures]. Maya bonded even more with another woman, Jill Gabriel, the wife of the musician, Peter Gabriel, who had just separated from his famous group, 'Genesis,' and now, at the urging of his old, boyhood friend, from 'Charterhouse School,' Richard Branson, who owned 'Virgin Records,' was preparing to launch a new career as a single performer. Another famed musician in this course was Steve Wynnewood who was also at a cross-roads in his life and was seeking new direction and some deeper understanding of his psychic and spiritual potential – and this reawakening of personal awareness was just what Silva Mind Control's founder, Jose Silva, and his primary instructor, Paul Fransella promised to deliver.

Because I had studied with Paul since we first met in 1972 when I was Poet-in-Residence at Eckerd College in Florida and I had already demonstrated in my recovery from the crippling rheumatoid arthritis which I had suffered from at that time, and most recently was in dazzling recovery from such severe injuries and surgery which had almost cost me my life and my vision, and still showed in the receding scars on my face, I was asked to assist in directing many of the relaxation and guided visualization drills conducted during the two week-end course. Peter and Jill, and Maya, requested that I conduct their Past-Life Regression session during which I read to them the carefully worded hypnotic entry script, and then gently led them into discovery of where they may have lived before now and who they had possibly been. A potentially dangerous exercise, especially with anyone who might be border-line psychotic or incipient schizophrenic – why Dr. Carl Jung refused to take certain patients of his into the deeper realms of self-discovery, and why this particular experiment was abandoned and removed from the Silva curriculum only a few months later – it had only been tried for half a year when we attempted it. I had already experienced something in my first encounter with Maya in Mallorca, long before she became my ship-mate, only some months later, when I had a *recognition* of her from some former existence of mine in her mother's home city Abu, [named Turku, in modern times] Finland, when I discovered that I may have been some sort of renegade errant warrior broken away from one of Attila's hordes ... *perhaps*!

As Jill and Maya welded their friendship, Peter and I became fond of discussing out favorite topic, the pre-history of man as recorded in the myths and legends that survived and then were written as history, when enough evidence corroborated what was still extant in song or fairy-tale or fable. Egerton Sykes, from Brighton, England, the noted mythographer, and I had recently become friends, and when I had accompanied Paul Fransella to visit Findhorn in Scotland, the burgeoning commune that was gaining world fame as a *Center of Light*, I had met one of the founders, Peter Caddy [dare I mention that this particular *enlightened* figurehead of this community offered me a T-bone steak and a tumbler full of malt whiskey in his private quarters? My spiritual mentor, Kalu Rinpoche, abbot of the Tibetan Buddhist Vajrana Monastery in Darjeeling, told me that even the most spiritually advanced mortal, even on the very brink of *bodhisattvahood* may eat meat if it is offered – one must always accept gifts of food with graciousness – the humble mendicant monk must therefore devour the finger of a leper dropped in his simple wooden begging bowl – Oh Dear!] and Ogilvie Crombie, a resident guru who claimed to have a conversational connection to the god Pan. Peter Gabriel had been working with many of these characters when he was developing his former musical group, 'Genesis', when he first left his preparatory academy, Charterhouse in Godalming, England , only shortly after Richard Branson [a close friend of Peter's when Branson left that school at fifteen] had blazed the trail with his establishment of a literary journal to which Robert Graves had contributed and then Branson had founded Virgin Records [Peter Gabriel's initial recording label], the flag-ship for the airline and all his multiplicitous successes from sodas to insurance and annuity retirement schemes by the same name. Peter and I seemed to have concordant and complementary collection of mythographic resource authorities, especially in the United Kingdom. He shared with me that the idea behind the wording and tonal construction of one of his most famous songs, 'Solisbury Hill,' had been his attempt to ratify, corroborate and reiterate the legend of Joseph of Arimathea bringing a piece of the wood from the cross of Jesus's crucifixion to plant at Glastonbury Abbey Cathedral to grow to the huge tree that stands there today - beneath which lay the supposed remains of King Arthur in a coffin whose lid holds the inscription, *Haec Jacit Arturus.*

Maya and I were invited to visit the Gabriels in their home in Somerset, on the old Roman Road ridge above Bath, after the completion of our Silva Mind Control course. It was in a small pond fed by a mountain steam, just below this house, said Peter, that King Bladud, the father of the actual historical figure named King Lear, had been cured of his leprous sores while rescuing a pig trapped in the muddy mire of the pond, and thus the waters which flowed down in to the town of Bath were declared miraculous, and the baths were established there and later used by Romans and English as healing cures, and are considered remarkably sanative and healing, even to this day. Unfortunately, this same King Bladud, when he arrived to rule in London, experimented with some novel ideas in experimental flight, and was killed as he attempted to soar out a high tower with some leather-winged construction strapped to his body. Curiously, there was a pub just two miles below the Gabriel's home, on the London Road, named 'The Flying Monk.' The actual village to which the Gabriel's home legally belonged was situated a half mile above them on the very crest of the hill, and although it consisted of no more than three houses, it was named Wooley, and it appears on large scale ordnance maps as an actual village. Peter confided in me that whenever he stayed in any hotel on tour in any country round the world, he always registered as Mr. Wooley – on one occasion, seven years later, when I heard that he was appearing in Frankfurt, Germany, and I happened to be in that city for the night, I did indeed locate him in the major five star hotel there registered under that name.

When Peter and Jill planned an extended trip to the United States and then a swing over to Switzerland to ski with Richard Branson, they invited Maya and me to be caretakers of their quaint cottage for that period of six weeks. I was relieved to leave London, especially Putney where we had been living in a cramped room in Jan Lynton's house which had no central heating and with her habit of flinging all the windows open for health purposes, Maya and I were both miserable and ready to move anywhere, before I could arrange for the delivery of *Tsunami* to 'Madingley Club' in East Twickenham. Our "gifted" residence in this location below Wooley above the Old Roman Road and adjoining the magical spring-fed pond which was supposedly the origin of the entire legend of King Bladud and the restorative waters of the city of Bath itself was idyllic. Maya and I were never so happy again. We took long walks in the lush countryside and visited many of the local pubs, especially 'The Flying Monk', whose owner maintained that its name had nothing to do with the legend of the winged King Bladud.

We entertained John Michelle with an intimate dinner party in this residence. His most famous mythographic text, *View Over Atlantis*, was, at that time, and for several years later, a best-seller among New Age students who were becoming even more obsessed with such subjects as dowsing - Tom Graves' books in the practice of this craft were also popular - and Theo Gimbel, a friend of Peter Gabriel's, whose studies of the resonances of colors had influenced most of that musician's light-shows for his major concerts. I was putting the final touches to the writing of the principles of the founding of the 'American Mythographic Society' which Sam Coffing was establishing as a Corporation Not For Profit in Coconut Grove, Florida, with his sister, Freda Tschumy, as Secretary-Treasurer [this dream project did receive licensing from the state and federal government and lasted until Sam and I became ensnarled in a law-suit ten years later to recover $50,000 he was in default of repaying me on a personal loan I made to his bankrupted 'International Resources Management Corporation,' whose bad debts may have inspired his own mother to put a bullet through her head, and whose collapse tore to shreds our friendship of over a quarter of a century. When I taught the course of my own design, and title, 'The Poetics of Megalithic Sites,' that same year at Goldsmiths College to art students, I camped out with my class in the field surrounding this pond at Peter's cottage, after we toured and examined Avebury, the village enclosed by a veritable megalithic ring, and then we finished our pilgrimage by sampling the healing waters in the ancient Roman baths of Bath, the city below.

After our sojourn in the Gabriels' cottage, I had arranged a contract for fetching my boat with a trucker, an International Routier, a fractious Welshman who invited me to ride with him into Provence, France, where he dropped a load before driving over to Cap d'Agde to lift my vessel on to a cradle on his truck. We drove up through France and crossed by ferry from Calais into England with no problems in either of the port authorities or customs agencies with *Tsunami*'s paperwork.

Vernon Sewell arrived to meet us at the point of launching into the Thames at Richmond Bridge on the East Twickenham side of the river. With his brutish but nautically savvy efficiency [I turned the throttles and the helm over to his command], we slid in snugly to the one available thirty foot mooring [my vessel's water-line length was twety-eight feet]. Before we had even placed the boat at the pier on Duck's Walk in front of Madingley Club, I had changed the name of vessel to *Merddin,* which was the Medieval spelling of the name, Merlin (that blessed old necromancer, wizard, sorcerer, *magus,* and mentor to the young King Arthur). I had found a local artist to inscribe the name in Gothic green letters on a plaque which I now hung on the stern of the boat just in the after cockpit where all who approached, cruising up the Thames approaching Richmond Bridge, would see this name as they neared. I was able to install a telephone line to our mooring, and my address was officially, Madingley Club, Duck's Walk, East Twickenham, Middlesex, England. It was at this same time that I was also officially elected as a member of the Chelesa Arts Club, so I had two legitimate London addresses. My closest friends were Laury Brough who owned the Dawes Press, and Brian Patten, the poet. These were probably the only people who regularly visited us on the boat; and even in the coldest bites of winter, we were comfortable in our floating redoubt.

Once we had settled in, and began taking meals and drinks in the club restaurant, it became apparent that Richard Saddleton, the owner, was afflicted with an incurable ailment. He had been surgically relieved of a deadly brain tumor, but his mental condition varied from day to day, and his levels of operational sanity were unpredictably erratic. Once, I had to *relieve* him of a long-barreled .45 caliber revolver which he carried in to the yard and down to the quay where he began plopping shots into the small uninhabited plot of land, named 'Corporation Island,' that lay in the Thames just in front of the pier and only some hundred yards downstream of Richmond Bridge. He was highly amused that I should ask him to give me his gun, as he had decided in his fantasy *script* that he was the sheriff of our "town' and that I was just a roving cow-poke passing through on the Old Chisholm Trail. I convinced him that I was, in actual fact, a Texas Ranger, and by some good fortune, I happened to be wearing my authentic high-topped cowboy boots and Madrid cape that chilly day, so he became convinced that my pose was for real, and followed my lead back in to the club-house where his mother and wife took him back to bed with a powerful sedating drug. Curiously, when I had lived in Galilea, Mallorca, and the old demented veteran of the Spanish Foreign Legion who lived in the house at the entrance to the village, had donned his combat uniform and posted himself at that turn in the road, blocking it and preventing all traffic from passing, as he imagined he had been placed there in sentry duty, I had been called upon by our local priest, Father Antonio, to dress in my Madrid cape, and high boots and my black Basque (*boina*) beret, to pretend to be this grizzly old soldier's commanding officer, to order him to leave his post. And he had accepted my charade, snapped to attention, saluted, and responded, "A sus ordenes , mi capitan!" (At your orders, my captain), then he had marched back to his home and did not repeat this stunt again in the village. Perhaps this explains how I was cast as the colonel in pursuit of Quantrill's Raiders in that film 'The Desperados' and also was cast as the ranking officer, Aide to Czar Nicholas in 'Nicholas and Alexandra,' and that in real life, as a young U.S. Navy lieutenant, I had become a battalion commander of 1200 sailors in recruit training at United States Naval Training Center, July, 1963.

Later that same year in Galilea, where I had moved to write my novel, *Ghost Dance,* by bizarre coincidence, Richard Saddleton mailed me my wrist-watch, a 'Bucherer' which I had purchased in Geneva, Switzerland, and then had lost in the Thames, just on the lower reach of the bank of Corporation Island which lay just alongside the Madingley Club pier, some hundred yards downstream from

Richmond Bridge. While still moored at Madingley Club, in the summer, I had taken my rubber dinghy, powered by my Seagull outboard engine to pull a boat which had run aground off the bank on Corporation Island one dark night, and was just pulling her free so that she would not be run down by one of the large pleasure dining-and-dancing summer barges steaming full throttle down from Richmond Bridge. The barge would have crushed the small craft I had just pulled free; however, my wrist had become entangled in the tow-line I had used to pull the grounded boat off the bank, and as I was being pulled into the water toward my own thrashing propeller, I bit through the wrist-band of my watch, severing it, and its bind to the line, and was thus able – just barely – to escape – but my watch sank and was lost in the river – *until Richard discovered it*, the following winter, when the water was drained and he located it with his metal detector; *and it was still ticking*! I should have sent the watch and this story to 'Bucherer' in Geneva as a publicity gimmick, but I just wore it as my time-piece.

When I completed my novel, *Ghost Dance* that April and prepared to return to Windsor, Canada. to retrieve my boat, *Merddin*, I bid farewell to Dr. Perico Villaescusa in his Galilea residence and Surgery where he was entertaining a group with champagne and a rich banquet of Spanish and Mallorquin food. A guest named Trover admired my watch, and when I gave it to him [following that old American Indian custom – if someone really admires some possession, one must give it to that person]; he therefore insisted that I accept his own wrist-watch in exchange. Several months later, when Maya and I were living in La Jolla, California, I received my old 'Bucherer' wrist-watch by post – with a shattered face, no longer ticking. Trover's wife had sent me the watch asking that I return to her the one I had taken in exchange, because it was a gift she had given her husband ... who had been killed in a motorcycle crash on that day of our meeting, and my watch had stopped on the moment of his death. I returned

Trover's watch ... *and I disposed of my 'Bucherer.'* I bought another 'Bucherer' the last time I visited Geneva, with my nephew, Allen Cheesman, for whom I purchased a wrist-watch. Allen was killed on his racing bicycle in a road accident in Arkansas. So it goes. I buy only cheap 'Timex' watches from 'Walmart,' now. Superstition is bad luck. Goya's painting of Kronos (the Titan god of Time) devouring his son hangs over my breakfast and dining table. Is there any meaning in any of this? Should I have sent the watch, instead, to 'Bucherer'? Why did I refuse publication offered *Ghost Dance*? That is why I write. So that we may discover *meaning*.

Then, three years later, when I telephoned 'Madingley Club' to ask after Richard's health, I learned of his final confinement for his affliction, and so I went to visit at 'Charing Cross Hospital' where his mother told me that he was expecting to have surgery soon, an operation which was only expected to relieve some of the more severe symptoms and was extremely life-endangering. I bought a fine Havana cigar and a collection of Zane Grey stories - Richard loved tales of the Wild West - and chatted with him for a short while and told him that the cigar was to celebrate *after* the operation. I had to fly out the next day, and it was only several months later, when I again telephoned the club, that his mother told me that she still had the cigar and that I was welcome to it. I never went to collect that Havana, and have never smoked one since. But I have fond memories of my pal, Richard Saddleton, one -time kayak champion of England and gracious Commodore of the 'Madingley Yacht Club,' Ducks Walk, East Twickenham, Middlesex. When I visited this locale recently, I discovered that all this has been replaced by high-rent housing and luxurious homes.

Another fond memory of that period was my acquaintance with Arthur Calder-Marshall, a writer with whom I shared some afternoons in the Madingley Club bar where he would drink only one half-pint of bitter and then walk home to dinner, after regaling me with vignettes about our mutual friend Ruthven Todd and their Fitzrovian (the neighborhood surrounding the Fitzroy Public House in Soho, London before, during, and after World War Two) artistic pals: Stephen Spender, Dylan and Caitlin Thomas, Thomas Sternes Eliot, Augustus John, and several of his models and paramours, of whom Caitlin Thomas had been one. Arthur had also known Malcom Lowry, whose best known novel, a chronicle of this writer's struggle with alcoholic madness, *Under the Volcano*, had been written at a time when Arthur and his wife were sharing a house in Mexico with Lowry and his wife. Arthur related an incident in which Lowry's wife had asked him to go into the nearest town and search all of the bars to find Malcolm and try to dissuade him from trading or selling their alarm clock for booze, as he had sold just about everything else that was easily portable to feed his insatiable alcoholic thirst. Arthur had found Malcolm Lowry sitting in a bar, absorbed in writing, scribbling away furiously on a tablet of paper, with several bottles of beer and the alarm clock all sitting together on a table beside him. When Arthur asked about the clock, Lowry nodded and set down his manuscript and said that he needed it to let him know when he should stop writing, on any normal day, but that Arthur's arrival was reason enough, then, to finish that day's work, and get down to some serious drinking. Arthur said that Lowry never sold that clock, although he did dispose of many other household items to pay for his drink, but he continued to use this method to time his regimen of writing. Lowry was able to sober up for certain periods as the novel was edited and finally published. Ironically, one physician who treated him was Natalie Drache's father in their hometown in Vancouver, British Columbia. Natalie wrote a screen-play adaptation of *Under the Volcano* which was never produced, although another version, directed by John Huston in 1984, starred Albert Finney, himself a man crippled by the disease of alcoholism. *Dark as the Grave Wherein My Friend Is Laid* is the only other significant prose work completed by this benighted writer, Lowry. I have some of Arthur Calder Marshall's short stories, but only his book, *Two of a Kind,* ever received any favorable notice.

Arthur encouraged me to attempt to begin writing seriously. I told Maya that I believed that I had a novel in me, and after arranging for transport of *Merddin* to America, as cargo on one of the ships owned by someone we met in the 'Queen's Elm,' I was ready to return to Galilea, where I meant to spend the next winter writing *Ghost Dance,* , a novel about a disillusioned American political radical university professor and his association with some equally outcast Mallorquin *suetas* (Jews who had been forcibly converted to Christianity in the time of the Spanish Inquisition).   Most of the professional class of the island were of that identity. *Sueta* is the Catalan word for pig fat – rather like our English word *suet.* Supposedly, the forced Jewish converts would make a display of eating pork to show their devout Christian neighbors that they had abjured their faith and no longer obeyed the Mosaic Law which forbids the consumption of swine.

I flew to Detroit where the boat was unloaded, and I placed it in a boatyard across the river in Windsor, Canada, for the winter. I had been convinced that my British Customs period of permission for remaining in England was to expire in the one year I had kept *Merddin* in the country. I had also conceived a plan for leaving the boat in Canada, till I finished my novel in Mallorca, and then to return here, before getting underway, cruising across the Great Lakes to Buffalo, New York and on to the Hudson River to proceed down through New York City to connect to the Inland Waterways and then drop on down to Florida to moor at Sam Coffing's dock in Coconut Grove. Maya, in the meantime, had found the ideal home for us in Galilea, a sprawling affair at the top of the village, just across a ridge from Nora's cluster of bungalows, 'S'Esbart.' Our main house consisted of three bedrooms, and there were two other guest houses attached in the courtyard. Virtually every large room had its own wood-burning fireplace, so the winter was bearable and we remained cozy. For my writing studio, I took the guest-house which had a view out over the steep roadway which climbed to the village, and I could see far out to sea, over toward the island of Ibiza. In my evenings during that winter, I visited with Ruthven Todd and Michelle Tripier. Every other Saturday, I drove Ruthven to Palma where we met Mark McShane and other writers for our *tertulia* (the old tradition amongst artists in Spain to bond as a dining club to help one another enriching a particular craft or art form: painting or writing), during these sessions we all generously assisted each other in every way necessary to surviving as serious writers, from finding an agent, to consulting a lawyer, if and when a contract were to be signed with a publisher, to how to handle punctuation of dialogue, or abbreviate an action or love scene in narrative style.

I also continued to indulge in some rather wild drinking scenes, carousing around the island with Perico Villaescusa. Michael Syson decided to come to work on his new novel, *The Breeders*, and I was able to convince Nora that he was such a refined and talented film-maker and writer, that she presented him with one of her bungalows, at no cost, and after meeting him, she prepared meals for him on any of those days he did not dine with us. Laurie Lee, whose novels, *As I Walked Out One Mid-Summer Morning* and *Cider with Rosie*, had been best sellers with Penguin books (the first of these became the very best-seller in their history of publishing) had been advising Michael to take more time with the selection of every word, and my already anal compulsive pal, Michael, had reached a point of writer's block that was totally paralyzing. I had convinced him to break away from the depressing weather of Chelsea and the oppressive influence of Laurie Lee, and promised that with the influence of Ruthven Todd and Mark McShane, that we would have his words flowing onto the page again and that his work would be of a publishable quality, albeit not as perfectly honed and ponderously *precious* as Laurie Lee's might seem in comparison. Ruthven's bibliography of published works was 34 pages long (single spaced) and Mark had published over 45 novels at this time in his career. When I had first met Laurie Lee one Sunday afternoon in 'The Queen's Elm' pub five years before, I had succeeded in offending his enormous pride by not at first recognizing who he was in the literary world. We had been discussing favorite first and last liners in literature and theatre. I had mentioned the translation of the line "...the dark root of a scream" from Garcia Lorca's play, 'Yerma,' which he claimed to know and appreciate, and then I said that there was a novel I once had read in which the title was the first line as well as the last line, but I could not remember the name of its author, and it had reminded me of William Carlos Williams collection of essays on poetry, entitled, *I Wanted to Write a Poem*, which was the same in construction – the title is the opening line as well as the last – but that the other book was a different genre – a novel – an entire narration of the travels and adventures of a young man who wanders of to travel throughout Spain, like a modern *picaro* [derivation of the term *picaresque* for this sort of novelistic thematic] at the beginning of the Spanish Civil War. When I gave the title, *As I Walked Out One Mid-Summer Morning*, Lee calmly proclaimed that the book was his; and I laughed as I told him that was impossible. We set of wager of a bottle of whiskey and left the bar to go across the road to the home of a friend of his, and Laurie Lee pulled a copy of the book from a shelf and showed up my ignorance and won the bottle and my undying admiration. Many times in the future, this same writer would arrive at 'The Queen's Elm' with at least two or more paperback copies of the book in his possession and would sign them and sell them to admirers for the price of the book and the purchase of a bottle of whiskey. Somehow, we were never as cordial with one another after that afternoon, but when my friend Brian Patten accompanied me once to the Chelsea Arts Club for lunch, Laurie Lee came to our table and said that he wanted Brian to know that he considered him one of the greatest poets in the land and expressed his admiration for all his published work. I introduced both Brian and Roger McGough to the club, and was able to find others to second my recommendations for their election to membership. Roger was later elected president of Chelsea Arts Club and held this office for three terms and was responsible for producing the last truly grand gala 1983 New Year's Eve Ball at Albert Hall, London.

Michael Syson had just undertaken the writing of another film which he had entitled 'Hoss and the Major,' and he was developing the major character to befit the personality of Charles Coburn with whom he had become close friends in his last visit in Hollywood, staying in the home of his former fiancee, Dana Winter, now married to a retired attorney who had represented countless successful actors there. David Munro, who had been his assistant in filming 'Conquista,' the fantasy about the oriiginal encounter of a Native American with the first horses to arrive on that continent, belonging to the Spanish *conquistadores*, titled now, 'Gift from the Gods', when viewed on British television, had been with him in California working on a documentary film. David had visited a bizarre experimental project in Berkeley which was purporting to be a Rape Crisis Center for dogs, but he had lost interest in this and had begun to plan those films in Southeast Asia with John Pilger which became famous: 'Do You Remember Vietnam?'; 'Year Zero'; 'Year One' [chronicles of the Khmer Rouge invasion and massive slaughter in Cambodia]. There were also films of American veterans returning to those Southeast Asia war-zones in the company of Captain Bobby Muller, founder of the 'Viet Nam Veterans Associastion' with whom he established the 'International Campaign to Ban Landmines' which enlisted the concern and photographic appeals of Princes Diana for the mutilated children victims, and inspired the Ottawa Treaty signed by 122 governments [with the exception of the United States refusing to sign] to ban landmine production and proliferation. Muller was awarded the Nobel Peace Prize in 1997 for his efforts, but David had died by that time. Before his alliance with Pilger, David had written and directed and produced the television drama, 'Knots,' a dramatic representation of the poems written by the psychiatrist R. D. Laing expressing in poetic forms the dilemma of people ensnarled in schizophrenogenic "knots" of their personal relations. He won an award for this film, as well as for the first Viet Nam film ('Do You Rmember Viet Nam?') in which the entire network of tunnels lying beneath Saigon - now Ho Chi Minh City - were at last openly revealed to enemy eyes and were discussed by their inhabitants, some of whom had lived in them for over twenty years in their combat operations against the American invaders and occupiers of their country. David also had written a screenplay adaptation of Roger McGough's epic poem,'Summer with Monika,' but many of David's typescripts have never been recovered from his archives after his demise.

In the early 1980s, when David Munro came to visit Michael Syson in Mallorca, he was often accompanied by Brian Wharton [although he had been a combat photographer in the Middle East and Southeast Asia, particularly Cambodia, Laos, and Viet Nam, Brian was now living more sedately and safely as the photographic editor of the *London Sunday Times*]. Michael referred to our assemblage as the "Galilea Light Horse." We combined some of our meetings with the crew of a large boat named *Berta of Ibiza*, an antique sailing cargo ship, twin-masted with an overall length of 120 feet, of a type referred to sometimes as *tall ship*, which was being outfitted in Puerto Andraitx, and preparing to sail across the Atlantic with her crew of dedicated men, all of whom owned a portion of the vessel as a sort of floating commune. Actually, each of the crew had been qualified yacht delivery skippers, or had been self-supporting mercenary soldiers and adventurers in some foreign war or investment enterprise. The ship had two enormous masts which had to be climbed to set the rigging as the old ships which feature in such films as 'Master and Commander' or 'Captain Blood.' Michael was able to arrange a lucrative contract for the ship and crew on a pirate adventure television film in production off the coast of France.

Although all of the crew had former careers as virtual soldiers of fortune – Nigel Palmer, for example, was a helicopter pilot as well as a former mercenary combatant who had seen action in Biafra and other unsavory conflicts in Africa – and all were able seamen, having also held commands of small cargo ships and large luxury yachts – perhaps the most intriguing of all in the group was Lindsay Decker claimed that his last exhibit of sculpture in resin and glass and plastic had been the Art feature in the final issue of *Life* magazine. Lindsay had sustained head injuries in an assault with a hammer by his son who had left him for dead in his New York City loft studio. In his slow recovery from this traumatic event, Lindsay decided to leave the art world and New York and took the job as chef on Errol Flynn's yacht which cruised the Caribbean and then crossed the Atlantic to arrive in Spain where it was later sold when its owner died of a heart attack – some said, while laughing at an off-color joke – how fitting for the *In-Like-Flynn*, rambunctious rascal. When I saw copies of photographs of Lindsay's work, I realized that he may have been considered one of America's leading sculptor's – not an Alexander Calder, but certainly as provocative and of the caliber of Edward Ruscha and David Hockney. I recognized some of the avant garde challenges that I had also observed in Michael Kenny's work.

Why was a major artist now working as a deck-hand and cook on the *Berta*? To answer that question would perhaps become an answer to why I, myself, have spent my life in the company of enormously talented but eccentric people. Robert Graves is reported as having remarked to a friend once, when he was to meet both Ava Gardner and J.R. Tolkien at a restaurant, how he could explain to either of these notable people, just how he had become acquainted with either: a Hollywood movie star and an eminent Oxford university Anglo-Saxon scholar and Philology professor. My associates in my saunter across this globe are as extraordinary and unusual. Like bright meteors, some burning out in their fall to earth, others still tearing a bright path across the horizon, but apparently heading for a crash, and burning disintegration, and leaving no memory, other than that incandescent momentary radiance. Slim Gaillard is remembered by a few, perhaps only for his hit song, 'Cement Mixer, Putty Putty,' or Rick Cluchy for 'The Cage Theatre' of San Quentin Penitentiary, or Paul Krassner for *The Realist*, and there are so many others of this ilk whom I have known only briefly, yet whose works of art have contributed so enormously to who I am. 'The Galilea Light Horse' celebrated with sumptuous feasts in my Galilea residence with *Berta*'s crew and their favorite Ibizenco [term used for those from the island of Ibiza – the Ibizenco or Ibizan Hound is also a registered breed of dog, similar to those canines owned by the Pharoahs of ancient Egypt] sweetheart, a Jewess from New York City called "Big Tits Renee" whose claim was that when captured by North African white-slavers and placed in an Arab sheik's harem, that she had so radicalized the other women with her American ideals of Women's Rights that she was given an airplane ticket home where she negotiated a contract with Hugh Hefner for her story to be featured in *Playboy* [it never appeared, and all of this story may have been her confabulation, as well, but her breasts were of an extraordinary amplitude, and were not implants].

Thirty years later, Renee, looking more like a re-tread model of the Venus of Willendorff, was operating as a pay-as-you-go seance organizer and fortune-teller and marital aids distributor in several night-clubs in London; the *Berta* was traveling the Caribbean as a cargo ship, the crew all gone their various ways, except that Lindsay Decker was serving out a long term in a French prison for drug trafficking. When the ship had sailed across the Atlantic, in 1978, it joined a gathering of tall-ships in New York, but was boarded by Customs authorities who had been alerted to the possibility that the antique cargo might include some *imported* drugs from North Africa and elsewhere in the Mediterranean where heroin was processed and available for distribution in America. There was even the suspicion that the L.S.D. manufactured by the 'Operation Julie' cartel might also be secreted in the ship's manifest

I next encountered the *Berta* dock-side in Miami, Florida, where I was teaching English at the University of Miami, in 1981, at the same time as I encountered Donald Embinder, the owner of *Blue-Boy* magazine and associated enterprises. He had become the Hugh Hefner of the homosexual alternative to *Playboy*, with clubs and film-making studios throughout the world. As I had known Don when he was having a love affair with the gorgeous [male] cousin of Grace Kelly at the University of Pennsylvania, and I had been privy to this hot relationship, long before *gay* men had revealed themselves – at that time, Don still swaggered about pretending to be a rough and tumble football player, his gladiator appearance enhanced by a broken nose and a broad set of wrestler's shoulders. When I visited with him in his *Blue-Boy* main office near that same Miami dock where the *Berta* was moored, he offered me a job as editor-in-chief of a new magazine he was launching to compete with *Gentleman's Quarterly*, a most appealing masculine flagship for an endeavor to lure closet gays into finally declaring themselves in a presumptively super-masculine venue ... or so Don presumed he would be able to achieve. I did not accept the job, and to the best of my knowledge, his enterprise never made any headway [curious metaphor for the failure of such a *flag-ship* ... to not make *head* - way]. After my visit with

Embinder, I strolled over to the brow of the *Berta* and left word for the captain, whoever that may have been, but never heard from him, and the boat had slipped its mooring, the day after, when I drove by. The *Berta* and her voyagers and Donald Embinder's *Blue-Boy* voyeurs have nothing to do with each other, but what can one ever make of the coincidence that Carl Jung labeled synchronicity? I met Erica Jong, Sloan Wilson, and G. Gordon Liddy in the very same week follow this chance encounter with this ship and that publisher.

I had been invited to meet Erica at the home of a television producer who was developing a feature which was to combine Erica and Sloan Wilson, the author of *The Man in the Grey Flannel Suit.* I was invited to the producer's home as he was also considering my screenplay, 'Ms. Machinegun Kelly,' to attract some venture capital to promote as a feature film. Somehow or other, he reckoned that I might have something in common with these other two writers. Ironically enough, Erica and I had both worked for University of Maryland, European Division [she had been in Germany; I worked in England]. A famous scene from her first best-selling novel, *Fear of Flying* had derived from her reveries while she was traveling on a train, commuting between campuses from the headquarters in Heidelberg, Germany, when she had projected her fantasy about a fellow passenger, an attractive man, in which she had coined the phrase, the "zipless fuck," in undressing him in her lustful mind. We somehow arrived at this reference in our conversation after a few cocktails, and then found ourselves roiling about the carpet of our host's living room howling with laughter as we teased each other and tickled and grappled in a childish tumble and began to plot the incorporating of her fantasy with an assault on the man whose *gray flannel suit* had become an icon of the entire repressive mind-set of the 1950's. Wilson's book, published in 1955 had become a popular film starring Gregory Peck in 1956. Sloan Wilson looked every inch the protagonist of his novel, and we felt that if we could drag him down to our level – literally tackle him and dog-pile him into a *naked* surrender to our *menage a trois* on the floor – that we would have accomplished a landmark in the sexual revolution of our own age and would have accomplished a significant breach of generational ideals of libidinal liberation. We became so absorbed in our plotting and ecstatic exchange in what could have become an actual coital coupling there on the carpet, but our host interrupted us to announce that Wilson had to leave and that we might wish to tell him goodbye. We somehow were able to re-arrange our rumpled and unbuttoned and disheveled clothing and actually did make a decorous attempt to bid farewell to this refined and polite writer, a gentlemen who registered no notice of our disarray and blushing distemper. Erica and I also felt somewhat embarrassed, and as we took leave of one another, exchanging telephone numbers and addresses, promising to stay in touch, we both realized that we would not really care to recall what we had so lavishly enjoyed for some intensely tender moments in Dionysian abandon in a Miami suburban living room floor moment of abandon.

My attempt at writing a novel, while residing in Galilea in 1976, assisted only by very general advice from Ruthven Todd and encouraged by fortnightly chats over cocktails with Michelle Trippier, lasted till I had a typescript of 380 pages which I entitled *Ghost Dance*. I had some idea that my orchestration was similar to the misunderstood convocation of most of the plains tribes which eventuated in their massacre at Wounded Knee, inspired by Wovoka, that demented shaman who convinced his Indian brothers that his shirt was impenetrable by U.S Army bullets. My saga portrayed some angry political discontents in the Mallorquin *sueta* community, and my protagonist, a disillusioned and slightly brain-damaged (with actual physical head injuries and a dreadful amount of admixtures of psychedelic drugs) former American literature professor, who believed that his own braggadocio and Marxist jabbering could topple

Franco's regime and that he could become impervious to the torture methods of the Guardia Civil. Although a literary agent named Halsey in Hollywood, who had represented Gabriel Jackson the eminent Spanish Civil War scholar and my former professr at U.C.S.D., had placed the book favorably with McMillan and a couple of other publishers, I withdrew the book from the market when Maya and I returned to live in La Jolla, and it has never been promoted since. However, there has recently been some renewed interest in the *suetas*, and especially after Franco's death when all the most radical elements in the Spanish political landscape were revealed. I never cared to revive my novel and did not seek another agent when Halsey died at the same time as I settled in to La Jolla and I had begun playing with the idea of writing a doctoral dissertation about Richard Brautigan to achieve a doctorate in Literature from U.C.S.D.

BOOK FOUR

America, Europe, Pacific Islands, Southeast Asia – homeward bound to Mallorca

After flying from Mallorca to Canada to move back aboard my yacht, Maya and I spent a month preparing our vessel for the journey we planned would take us from Detroit, to New York City and then through the Inland Waterway all the way down south to join Sam

Coffing and moor in Coconut Grove on Key Biscayne, in Miami, Florida. The voyage on *Merddin* through the Great Lakes from Windsor, Canada, to Buffalo and along the Erie Canal, was an adventure that nearly cost me my life, especially as I was caught on Lake Erie at the entry into Buffalo harbor in a tornado which the U. S. Coast Guard themselves were reluctant in leaving the safety of the port in order to brave the huge waves and high winds in assisting me to save my boat ... *and my life*. The deck-hand I had aboard with me at the time proved to be absolutely worthless in the emergency. He rolled up into a foetal position in a corner and moaned and yowled in terror as the waves came crashing over the boat. I had picked up this character in the yacht club in Conneaut, Ohio when the First Mate I had hired in Windsor, a man called Rasputin, had left to meet with his friends in New York. The young man from Ohio had been in the Army, but was surveyed out for disciplinary reasons, and his father had implored me to employ him for my continued voyage to Buffalo and through the Erie Canal and on the Hudson river to New York City. Without any competent aid or assistance from this disintegrated shipmate, I was somehow able to tie myself to the wrenching wheel with several yards of spare hemp deck lines and to hold the radio microphone to my chest as I shouted to the Coast Guard and received instructions as to how to find my way toward the harbor where all the lights had been extinguished by the tornado's impact.

I had sent Maya ahead from our last port, by bus, to visit in the home of Carl Gay, Robert Graves' former *amanuensis*, who was now in charge of the manuscript and holographic Special Collections division of the library of the University of New York at Buffalo. I had spoken to her and to Carl by radio-telephone before leaving the coast-line onto Lake Eire, that morning - he had graciously invited us to dinner that evening when I was expected to dock my boat at Buffalo - and I had also called to tell her, as I saw the fierce storm approaching, that we might be delayed in arriving in Buffalo harbor ... [*if at all*, I wanted to tell her, as the storm did look like the tornadoes I had grown up with in Oklahoma, and I was not sure that there was much chance of survival in my small boat on this treacherous lake]. In my passage from Windsor over the lake to Cedar Point, Ohio, I had employed a reckless, but courageous Canadian as First Mate on the boat. He called himself Rasputin and claimed to be part Algonquin Indian. He was six feet four inches, possessed massive shoulders and muscular arms, and long black hair which hung to his waist. He had a degree in Art History, but had worked as a garbage collector in the city of Windsor, Canada, for the past two years and that accounted for his impressive physique - he had hung from the back of trucks flinging bags about and had developed a truly formidable upper body in the Schwartzeneggar mode. The man I hired in Ohio to replace him was a youth who seemed to be in a depressive state, but could perform all the essential duties required on a boat as he had been helping his father on their family's boats since early childhood. There is no way to predict how a person will react in a life-endangering situation. This fellow had completed U.S. Army recruit training and had lasted two years in the military, but had seen no combat, nor had he experienced any endangering situations. He was able to help me to wrap myself in the coils of the rope which I secured to the wheel as I steered a course in this torrential onslaught, but as the large waves began to thunder down upon us, and to literally toss us about like a cork in a whirlpool, he fell to the deck, rolled into a foetal ball and began whimpering in abject surrender to what he reckoned to be imminent death.

I was blinded to all but the waves crashing on to the revolving windscreen tossing water-spray away, but to no avail, in clearing my line of sight farther than a mere few feet ahead of me. I was held fast to the wheel by the ropes tied about my chest and stomach, and my feet held firmly to the deck rising and falling and tilting beneath. I was able to tune the radio to access the Emergency Channel to Buffalo

Harbor and was informed by the Coast Guard on duty that I was now in the very crotch of a tornado and that it would be impossible for any boat to leave the break-water to come out to attempt to rescue me ... but that they would attempt to guide me with compass bearings toward the port entrance, whose lights had been smashed out by the storm.

"What's the good news?" I shouted into the microphone. I had always to salt my experiences, however grave, with some tincture of humor. Only Davey Jones was giggling. The Coast Guard told me that they were all praying for me. *Good news?* Praying to whom? Anyone I know? Would He or She care to remember me? Oh Dear ...

The next half hour, which I could say seemed like hours, but did not, although my only other similar challenge in such a torrential onslaught, that twelve hours, which did seem like a full day's work, with Sam Coffing and our *Nachen II* crew which had survived the Buford Force Eleven to Twelve [winds gusting from 100 to 110 miles per hour, with seas, forty feet in height from trough to crest] in the North Sea mine-fields battling to reach the refuge harbor of the Frisian island of Borkum that day in 1966, when some twenty other boats went down with all hands lost, I had to calculate my timing rather exactly as my approach to the Buffalo harbor entrance, flying blind, *on instruments,* as it were, had to be "dead-reckoning" at its most definitive, with the radio voice telling me my progress which they calculated to the *very foot,* not fathom, from their clear-sighted vantage point.

At last, I knew I had entered the harbor, only because at first the deck leveled out under my feet and then as if a panoramic opening scene of a film featuring the touristic delights of Buffalo Harbor were being screened before my hitherto beclouded eyes, I saw that I was safely in a calm dish of water about whose edges other boats were moored and rocked gently to the surge from outside the break-water. I made way, motoring slowly down the center, and almost immediately, a Zodiac pulled up alongside my starboard quarter and a loud hailer replicated the congratulations flooding in over my radio from my Coast Guard mentors and "wannabe" rescuers. A uniformed arm reached over the railings with a foaming bottle of champagne which I struggled to unwind from my ropes to grab and was able lift to my lips and pour over my mouth, startled by how dry it had become in the last hour of excitement and peak experience. These moments of intense living are deeply etched in my trove of special memories. The liquor I gulped down when we reached Borkum Island, a decade earlier, was Johnnie Walker Black Label which I drank in huge slugs from the upended bottle which Sam and I and David and Marian and Susie swung around among us like a pagan censor or a *not-so-lazy* Susan. My thirst then was easily comparable to what I quenched now, and I kicked at the still prostate form of my *ersatz ship-mate* and spat some of the frothy liquid on his forehead. I felt more like pissing on him, but restrained my impulse and just told him to pull himself together and help me make the boat ready for mooring.

I then telephoned Maya at Carl Gay's home, using the radio-telephone. She had arrived the night before by bus as I was not wanting to expose her to what I had supposed would be nasty weather and a tricky approach into Buffalo Harbor, never imagining that I would be cruising into the very heart of a tornado churning Lake Erie into a maelstrom of disaster. She had not been aware of the danger until Carl had informed her, and they had watched the exaggerated reportage on television ... and Carl told me later that he had not reckoned that I would survive the calamity. Maya calmly said that she expected me in time for cocktails and that she would be aboard in a few minutes, as soon as the taxi could pick her up and deliver her to the waterfront. She had complied with my request to contact Bob Creeley who was a visiting professor at the university where Carl supervised the Rare Books collection, then the best repository for hologram manuscripts of Twentieth Century authors in the world. Bob would arrive about sundown with his new wife, the one he had met in New Zealand – she was actually not much older than Maya – for whom he had divorced his former wife, Bobbie, who still resided in New Mexico where they had been involved with University of New Mexico for so many years before, where Bob had actually completed his Master's Degree in English while serving as an adjunct professor of poetry. No sooner had I made fast our mooring, connected all electric cables and the fresh water hose, than Maya stepped aboard carrying two huge brown paper bags of groceries to begin preparing one of her Swedish/Finnish feasts for a celebratory banquet. What a reversal of conditions in only a few short hours! Thus was our life ever so on *Merddin*, with my magical best ship and bed-mate, Maya.

Bob Creeley arrived carrying a couple of sacks filled with beverages. Bottles of wine, two six packs of beer and a quart of fine Scotch whiskey. His wife, a slim slip of a girl stood behind him as he attempted to step aboard over the gunwale just as the hull tossed upward and then leaped away from the pier as the surge from the storm still rocked and rolled our vessel. The bags came flying into the cockpit, but he fell back into the water. I dove to reach over and grabbed the collar of his jacket just as his feet and knees sank into the space between the stone wall and our *nine tons* of heaving hull stretched against the spring line and aft stanchion, just about to return, about to slam against the fenders and the solid rock of the quay. I jerked him up on to the lip of the gunwale, just as *Merddin*'s stern kissed that solid wall with a resounding wallop. Had anything or anyone been caught in that vise, there would have been only pulp and splintered bones remaining, and that poetic genius would have been recycled and flattened to a waffled waste.

Bob and I looked at one another, his one good eye riveted to mine. I had saved his life! I remembered my last rescue of a poet from death, Alastair Reid in Galilea, only five years before, and as I poured Bob a straight whiskey on the rocks and toasted him with the same for myself, I told him I hoped he wouldn't hold this against me and refuse to speak to me from that moment on, as Alastair had, perhaps fearful I might consider he owed me something special for the life-saving. I did reconcile with Alastair in 1997, only twenty-five years after the event, but *never did with Bob*. This evening was to be our last together, although I did not know this at the time

After dinner, Bob's wife, Jill, suggested that we all go to a bar in town where there was a band playing, and so we left the boat and soon were in the sort of place where we had to virtually scream at one another to be heard when the music was blaring out over the largely student-body crowd. I thought that Maya and Jill were bonding well until my wife grabbed the floppy campaign hat from the poet's head and pulled it down on her shaggy blonde crown, and this caused a screaming tirade and an attempt to snatch the hat away in such a fashion that the two women appeared to be savagely wrestling one another. Bob, himself, grabbed the hat and jammed it firmly back on his head. He then declared that since the moment he met Jill in New Zealand, that he had worn this hat, a symbol of their epiphantic encounter on the road where he had been hitch-hiking, and she had stopped to pick him up and place the hat on his head that had been sun-burned by exposure to the outdoors in her country on that road where he had stood for so long waiting for a lift. The hat, it seemed, had become the *emblemata* of their love-at-first-sight. He claimed that he had worn it even in their civil service wedding ceremony only a few months before. Maya's behavior was considered a sacrilegious act; and the entire tenor of the evening had turned sour. Bob demanded that we should leave.

As we drove through the streets of the city, there was hardly a word spoken in the car. I was startled however, when Jill suddenly grabbed the hat from Bob's head and tossed it out the window as she drove. Bob looked as if he had been slapped in the face. I demanded that she stop and after another block, when I threw my back door open and threatened to jump out, Jill finally did pull over. The rain was still pouring down, and I found my legs soaked as I ran back through the streets to at last come upon that benighted cap which I snatched up and sprinted back to the car to return to its owner. Bob silently accepted it, offering thanks to me for my gesture, and we then drove silently on to the dockside, where we said goodbye with hardly any thanks or indication we might ever meet again. And indeed, we did not ... ever ... meet again.

I telephoned the next day and was told by Jill when she answered that neither of the Creeleys would ever want to see us again. Perversely, or rather, not wanting to believe that my friendship with Bob of almost a decade could be destroyed by a silly incident during an evening of heavy drinking, I called the house later, and the telephone was answered by Bob. He assured me that the women had misunderstood each other and that our friendship remained firm and solid. He offered to mail his latest publications to me and asked more about my proposed visit to Richard Brautigan's literary agent, Helen Brann, in New York City. I reminded him that his only novel, *Island*, had been written when he lived in Banyalbufar, Mallorca, where, with Alastair Reid's assistance, he had launched the first publication of *Black Mountain Review* in Palma with a printer whom Reid had introduced him to, that my first novel, *Ghost Dance*, which I had just completed writing in Galilea, Mallorca, under the advice and counsel of Ruthven Todd, Alastair's mentor from his own youth in Edinburgh, feeling that all this bound us together in a sort of bizarre cabal of poetic brotherhood. He agreed, and we expressed the desire to meetin again, hopefully with Reid and Brautigan, so that I might then also introduce him to Ruthven Todd, Dylan Thomas's old drinking pal.

I really believed this might come to pass, but Ruthven would die in this year, Brautigan would abjure our friendship and Creeley would never send me any more correspondence or make contact with me again; and then Richard would suicide only a few years thereafter, in Bolinas, California (but ... after visiting with me in Palma, Mallorca).

When I was appointed Professor of Poetry at UCSD as a visiting lecturer six years later, Bobbie, Creeley's divorced wife had a financial grant for the same term, teaching Creative Writing, the academic award deriving from her success with a few books of poetry she had published while she and Bob had resided in New Mexico where he had completed his Master's degree while teaching there. I told Bobbie about the strange incident in Buffalo, the example of the supposedly, *sacrosanct* hat and the outrage of Bob's young wife at the prank my wife [then, my divorced wife – for the past four years – now residing in Stockholm with the man she had left me for, whom she married]. Bobbie told me that she had not had more than minimal contact with Bob since his marriage to Jill, that this young woman had become obsessively dismissive of any approaches by any and all of Bob's former friends and associates. This was lamentable, as Bob was a man with many close friends, who thrived on personal interaction and social interplay. Although he had been blinded in one eye at the age of seven, he had always led an active life, undaunted by what many would consider a handicap. In World War Two, he had volunteered to serve as an ambulance driver and had seen action in Burma in some devastating combat conditions, and after the war he still enjoyed carousing with some of the roughest crowds of drinkers and seemed to gravitate toward the sort of low-life bars that his pals Richard Brautigan and Charles Bukowski frequented. I well remember his story about being led outside one of these taverns into an alley where his antagonist was just about to start swinging his fists , intent on knocking Creeley senseless, when Bob happened to ask how his assailant had ever gotten into this mode of behavior – was it something imposed on him by his father or some other parent figure abusive in a violent physical manner ... and according to Bob, the man interrupted his swing, let his arms fall to his side, and began telling his life-story, which the two continued to examine with shared drinks back inside the bar, and they parted company after many more beverages and several hours of exchanging reminiscences, in a bonding that Bob considered an essentially important and vital learning experience. That he should now be protected by his young wife and not allowed to wander and roam and entertain himself as before was a matter which Bobbie and I found inexplicably sad and regrettable. Later that year, 1985, after our terms at UCSD, Bobbie traveled to London where I loaned her my river boat, *Moonbeaver*, moored in the Grand Union Canal at the entrance to Regents Park, just next to the aviary section there, and only a few hundred yards away from Camden Lock. I was residing at Eaton Square in the home of the Earl Cowley, Lord and Lady Wellesley, Garret and Paige, whom I had escorted on their honeymoon in Mallorca with their four children three years before. I took Bobbie to Chelsea Arts Club, and she seemed to become more at home in London by making some friends there with women her age who were also artists. However, she seemed to not really like such a foreign climate and returned to America after only a few weeks. I never heard from her again, either.

In London, I occupied a large (2,000 square feet) docklands studio and I continued my relationship with Anna Llewellyn, whose brother Robbie was still having a love affair with Princess Margaret. His fondness for me was because I had diverted his sister's attention from her former lover, called simply Henry of the Castle, who was expected to be heir to a small medieval redoubt along with a baronetcy in Wales near the Llewellyn family estate ... if Henry could ever prove to the trustees of his estate to be cured of his heroin addiction. My connection to Anna and her family had begun when I left Maya subsequent to our divorce in La Jolla. shortly after we left *Merddin* in

Florida.

Only a few days after the tornado and fracas with the Creeleys, I motored *Merddin* down the Hudson River. Except for avoiding what the local boatmen called "Hudson River alligators" (floating logs which could tear a crippling hole in a hull to sink a moving craft) the cruise was languorous and lovely. When I carefully drove in to the mooring at Seventy-Ninth Street Pier in New York City, I was run aground on a sandbar in the harbor which I had to await a tidal change to allow me to lift off and slip into a reserved place on the dock. We were allowed to stay in this inimitable and privileged Manhattan dwelling for a short while, but I had arranged with Steve Kopper to join me in delivering the boat to dry-dock in Stamford, Connecticut, the very next week. I had decided to have *Merddin* transported by truck down to Coconut Grove, Florida, where she would be docked behind Sam Coffing's home there on the slip where *Nachen II* had once lain. I was intending to submit my novel, *Ghost Dance*, to Helen Brann, Richard Brautigan's literary agent, whose office was in Sutton Place in Manhattan. He had told me that his introduction to her would insure that my book would be published and all the film rights sold to the highest bidder, as had all of his eminently successful books.

As soon as I was confident that the boat was secure, and after taking some days recreational relaxation up on the streets of New York, I made contact with Steve Kopper who was teaching Anthropology at Adelphi College and living in Brooklyn with his son, Stever. He was still separated from his legal wife, Gail, a brilliant woman who had been one of the first students to attend the famed Black Mountain College which had attracted so many prominent members of the *avant garde* in poetry under the guidance of Charles Olson. Even the musicologist, John Cage, had joined such verbal artists as Robert Duncan, Robert Creeley, and Edward Dorn. Gail's mother had bought the original house in Deya, Mallorca, where Robert Graves had lived with Laura Riding when he first established 'Siezin Press' and was writing the two *Claudius* novels and had just begun his monumental compendium, *The White Goddess*. Gail's mother was the person who had directed Steve Kopper to undertake the original excavation and exploration of the Muleta cave on the road to Soller where the remains of *myotragus balearicus*, the antelope/gazelle, which became extinct by 1,550 B.C. But it had been in a form of domesticated vitality as it was found with the skeletal remains of what must have been a shepherd boy, *in situ*, and subsequently to be carbon-dated, 5,000 B.C., and this miraculous find would thereby lay the foundation for establishing the Deya Archaeological Museum and become the corner-stone of Bill Waldren's claim to fame, garnering his grants of money to begin his career as doctoral candidate at Oxford University, while Steve Kopper was overseas attending University of Pennsylvania Museum School acquiring his doctorate, and missing out on the lime-light attention paid Waldren for this major archaeological discovery which the two men would have shared credit for, had their wives, Jackie and Gail, not quarreled so fiercely and jealously, dividing the two partners in this endeavor, and divorcing the two men, friends as closely bonded as brothers, from any contact with one another ... till death.

In my first foray up the stairway from our dock, into the Manhattan streets, *Merddin* snugly secure at 79th Street Pier, I found a local bar where I could play the pool-table game, Eight Ball, and was able to win a few rounds, some dollars, and many beers. My most fiercest competitor told me that my manner, my mode, my gait, my *panache* [his expression, not one of my favorite words for "flashy style"], reminded him of the man whose career he managed, a professional tennis player named Illie (Nasty) Nastasi, who at that time was out of the country on tour. I was told that if Maya and I wanted to stay in his apartment, and did not mind the clutter of many tennis racquets, that we were welcome to have the place for the next few days. Any time one has been living on a boat for extended periods, a hiatus on dry land, with a solid floor rather than a moving deck beneath one's feet, is enormously appreciated, sweetly savored, and will be leapt at instantly.

Maya and I did not accept the invitation to move in to that apartment till after I had driven *Merddin* around Manhattan, past the neighborhood known as 'Hell's Kitchen' and along the Long Island estuary up to the harbor at Stamford, Connecticut, where we installed the boat in a dry-dock and prepared her for transport by truck to Florida. Then we moved into the tennis star's apartment, and when we did encounter the supposedly dangerously ill-tempered *prima donna* of Wimbeldon and other sedate tennis venues, we found ourselves immediately at ease with the man who, if anything, was just another alpha male sort of hyper-thyroid, steroid-stressed version of Roman Polanski. A bright, witty and altogether charming Eastern European refugee making huge financial scores in the decadent West with an enormous talent and the Tartar brush that tinctured the blood of my own wife whose genes derived from Finland by way of Russia by way of those ancient Mongol pillagers and rapists of yore ... and so was my grandmother, whose long black hair still rustled in my subconscious in deep valence urgings..

We then began exploring New York City and located and invited some of our Mallorca friends who lived in there and directed them to gather for drinks and a a dinner in Greenwich Village: John St. Jorre and his most recent wife (an African-American woman); and the man we called "Black" George Campbell, primarily because it was always difficult to realize that he was actually African American, especially when he spoke of his Parisian French or Uxbridge-accented British governesses. We were surprisingly then joined by the wife of Michelle Decker, next door neighbor of Michelle Trippier of Galilea, Mallorca. Decker had been in both the French and Spanish Foreign

Legions and then had fought for the Republic against Franco in the Spanish Civil War, then joined a Free French Command unit in north Africa and finally drove on into Germany with Allied Forces and was shot and gravely wounded after all those previous years unscathed, by a fourteen year-old boy just then placed in uniform and given a rifle in Stuttgart. John St. Jorre who had written the book, *The Brothers' War*, when he was a British war correspondent with Brian Shakespeare, a former member of MI-5, was now a senior analyst with the Carnegie Institute, and he made the remark that our table in the bar we took over there in Greenwich Village that night could have become an international organization which could challenge both the U.N. and his own foundation for some truly vital world-changing proposals. As it was, we settled into getting convivially inebriated and lovingly familial. The Mallorca bunch were truly a *moveable feast*, in Key West, Florida, Denpasar, Bali, Bangkok, San Francisco, or Chelsea (New York or London). Three days were all Maya and I were to spend in Natasi's residence, as he returned and needed his space to himself. In the meantime, I had made my call on Helen Brann's office, having left the typescript of my novel, *Ghost Dance*, at the ground floor office of the building manager. When I telephoned to ask when my appointment for an interview was to be scheduled, I was abruptly informed that my *package* had been returned to the office of the manager on that ground floor, and that I could fetch it if I wanted it back. I was also informed - in harsh, no uncertain terms - I was to understand that I was to never attempt to make contact with Helen Brann and that my visits to her office would be considered as criminal trespass and that I would be expelled by law enforcement officers. Whoof! I was *astounded* –and I reflected on the Anglo Saxon origin of this word which meant to be struck in the head by a stone. *Astonished* would mean to be struck in the head with several stones, as in a *stoning* ... to the death.

I telephoned Richard Brautigan who told me that he was also shocked by his agent's reaction; however, it was Maya who pointed out to me that his latest novel, *Dreaming of Babylon*, prominently displayed in one of the major bookstores we had visited earlier in the week, might provide us a clue as to what was happening. It was a revelation which I denied being what was most likely the reason for the harsh and vicious dismissal by the literary agent, Helen Brann, who might have presumed that I had attempted to plagiarize her client's novel or would attempt to claim that Brautigan had stolen my idea and storyline. Richard's book told of a man who had suffered a severe head injury which caused him to imagine that he was suddenly living in Babylon, several thousand years before the twentieth century American baseball game in which he had been hit in the head by a pitched baseball and transported to another time, and even place, for the narrative by the author to project in this not very entertaining *tour de force* prose. The last book Brautigan had written, *The Hawkline Monster*, for which I had edited the galley proofs when I visited him in Key West, had been fraught with a multitude of grievous grammatical, logical and even basic spelling errors, so that I had wondered if Richard's heavy, alcoholic drinking was not beginning to erode his basic intellect.

Richard's brain seemed already to be so addled by booze, that the characterization of brain damage in his protagonist in *Dreaming of Babylon* had become readily accessible to him; however, the idea must have derived from my novel as I had told him when I sustained my head injuries, the severe concussion and the skull fracture that placed me in King's College Hospital in London and the months after when I reconstructed my consciousness. I had spoken to him in several of our long-winded telephone chats about how I sometimes felt as if I were drifting backwards and forward in time and space, that at last I could begin to grasp the weird time-warp projections and claims that Robert Graves made about having lived in Rome during the time of the emperor, Claudius, and then, even to claim to have been that ruler. Graves had been so severely wounded in action that his body had been thrown on to a heap with other corpses trucked away from the battlefield and later on, when that load of lifeless bodies were dumped, only revived to discover that he had been considered deceased; there had been a dispatch sent back to England to this effect which had to later be corrected. However, Graves believed that this near-death experience had enabled him to break through what he called the *fifth dimension* and to play with time like an elastic band, to his own demands and desires of consciousness. Obviously, Richard had exploited and expropriated my comments and remarks about this phenomenon to construct the thesis of his novel.

Fred Wolf, the physicist, whose book, *Taking the Quantum Leap,* won the National Book Award in 1983, had designed and constructed a best-selling cartoon version of an explanation of Einstein's general field theory and relativity hypotheses with Jack Sarfat in the La Jolla beach home of Lynda Brent for whose son, Boden Robitaille, I had dared the two scientists, one lazy Sunday afternoon to provide a simple explanation of general field theory and quantum physics for Boden's education, when we had been doping and drinking together. That experiment in visual goofiness became a text, which appeared in more than eight sold-out editions by E. P. Dutton, and the royalties from this book financed Fred's later work which has become seminal in most of the parallel-universe discussions among serious astrophysicists from Stephen Hawking to Frijof Capra, and although one of my poems from my last book of poetry, *Runey Tunes,* was selected for examination of the *elasticity of time* factor of the $E=mc$ squared formula, as the finagler's quotient or square root of $-n$ is regarded in the proposition, I have yet to understand why this has been construed from my poem, even though I am the author of that work, selected and considered to be quintessential by that group meeting in 1978 at the Berkeley Cyclotron Laboratories.

Regardless of all the peripheral connotations and implications, it would seem that Richard himself believed that he had stolen my idea and thus had instructed his literary agent to have a look at my book and if she considered it similar to his own, which had just been published, then he urged her to brush me off and discourage any further effort I might make to seek her assistance or representation as literary agent. Perversely, my poet friend, Brautigan, did greet Maya and me at the San Francisco airport and accompanied us to a hotel where the room he had reserved cost three times what we had ever been accustomed to paying, and then he told us that he was too occupied with some important work to be with us in the next few days which we had planned to spend in that city. Michael McClure was also stand-offish, but he had been cutting off his friendship with Richard for over two years now and flatly declared that any friend of Richard's was not a friend of his. Fickle poets. Bitchy would be a more appropriate term.

After Maya and I settled in La Jolla and I had purchased a condominium unit there, any attempt to make contact with Richard was rebuffed by him. Once, when a young woman answered at his home, she said that Mr. Brautigan was currently in Rio de Janeiro and would not be back in the Bay area for many months to come, and I heard his raucous laughter in the background. The next time I saw my friend was six years later in the Bar Bosch in Palma, Mallorca, only a month before he returned to America to commit suicide in his Bolinas home. At that time he was almost grovelling to regain my friendship, and one of the first things he said was that he wanted me to have the movie rights to *Dreaming of Babylon*. I reminded him that after I had edited his inchoate galley proofs for *The Hawkline Monster* in Key West a decade before and he had promised me the movie rights for that book as well, but that I had never heard another thing about such a gift, and as a matter of fact, he had strenuously denied me any personal contact and had repelled me for the entire six years before his arrival in Mallorca. He then pleaded that his affairs were in utter turmoil, that he had fired his literary agent and his accounting firm, and now had one lawyer who was setting about reorganizing his entire personal portfolio and financial estate, that only Jack Nicholson and his pal, Roman Polanski, could begin to understand how everyone had taken advantage of him. Francis Coppola was also still his ally, and he had told off Natasha Kinski, publicly, in Lorraine's Discotheque in New York City for her ingratitude toward that great film-maker, and then he railed against Michael McClure and Larry Ferlinghetti, who had attempted to launch a virtual conspiracy against him in North Beach, that even in Enrico's Restaurant he was not served as graciously as he deserved, and that in both Smiley's and Snarly's bars in Bolinas, he would no longer set foot because ... and I began to realize that this most light-hearted poet of the Sixties had become as much of a reactionary and bitter boozer as our other symbol of free thinking and saintly redemptive visions of youth and freedom in the decade before, Jack Kerouac.

Richard had not arrived in Mallorca to seek me out, but he had come to stay with the daughter of the Korean composer and conductor who had established the symphony orchestra of Palma and had inspired the city fathers to construct the magnificent Performing Arts auditorium on Paseo Maritimo where all the finest orchestral concerts and musical theatrical performances had been presented since the late 1950s. This young Asian woman had recognized Richard from photographs on the covers of his books when they were both in Amsterdam, and she had invited him to visit her in Mallorca where she resided with her widowed mother and a baby son in the outskirts of Palma in San Augustin, just beyond Terreno. For the entire month that Richard was in Mallorca, she never allowed him to stay overnight in her home as he became aggressively drunk and belligerent every afternoon. He telephoned me frequently begging to stay in my house in the village of Puigpunyent just twelve kilometers away, but I was newly sober and could not abide his drunken vulgarity either. I presumed that this incurable insomniac would wander from bar to bar throughout Palma and then nap on various park benches in several of the plazas, or along the waterfront by the yacht moorings. I was not feeling particularly resentful for his rejection of me and Maya in California; I just never again considered him to be as close a friend as he once had been. At this point in his life, he was fast becoming a stumble-bum and a dead-beat tramp. There was very little of the former glitter of the poetic or lyrical about the hulking figure that spent much of his time regaling those at his table in the open air Palma bars with gossip about his *glitterati* pals in Hollywood.

Gabriel Jackson, former U.C.S.D. chair-person of History, a professor for whom I had served as a teaching assistant in Humanities, whose books about the Spanish Civil War are still considered the most authoritative records of that epoch, introduced me to his agent, a man named Hulsey, an actual cousin of the famed admiral, who had Alfred Knopf interested in publishing my book, *Ghost Dance*, and then McMillan offered to take up the product, but when Hulsey died suddenly, and I left Maya, began a divorce, and returned to Mallorca, I never again tried to promote its publication again. Ironically, fifteen years later in Madrid, I introduced Jackson to Milton Wolff, commandant of the Lincoln Battalion in the Spanish Civil War, at an international reunion and convocation of all the *brigadistas* and their supporters, probably the last time in history that so many of the survivors of this moment in history would come together. Both men had always wanted to meet, and I was their point of first contact. *Ghost Dance* tells the story of a disillusioned political radical student instructor from the New Left university movement of the late Sixties, who leaves California and intends never to return to America till all the oppressive Right Wing Republican government is removed from power, and as he swears to never become involved in political causes, he is unwittingly drawn into the underground radical extremist cadre that has sworn to depose Franco and the Falangist dictatorship in Spain. The novel is decidedly autobiographical, and even though the protagonist, Zeke, is suffering from head injuries that often render him uncertain of the exact century or country in which he now resides, there is a definite late Twentieth century ambience and a a clearly defined Marxist sentiment that would convince any reader that this book does not resemble Brautigan's *Dreaming of Babylon*, although Zeke sometimes refers to the government of Richard Nixon as being a kingdom by that name [Babylon]. Nevertheless, Brautigan must have believed that I reckoned him to be a literary poacher, a plagiarist, a rustler, and thus, our close friendship ended. However, I am told that the poem, 'Ben,' included in hs collection *Loading Mercury with a Pitchfork* could only have been in reference to me, as it deals with Brautigan ringing the telephone in the trailer by the frog-pond in Oklahoma again and again, in a desperate attempt to connect with his pal there. If this is to be my place in literary history, I am pleased to note that Brautigan's writing has long been out of fashion, and I have my own literary product to present in order to memorialize me.

I had joined Michael Syson in Mallorca just after leaving La Jolla, California in 1978, where he and I began work on a new film script, 'Hoof and the Major', never completed because a key scene, in which the character Hoof, presumed dead and being carried to the graveyard in his coffin on a horse-drawn wagon, breaks out of the wooden container and begins *raising living hell* in the streets of town; and this was shared with the actor friend of Mike's, James Coburn, who gave it to the director of the film he was currently working in, and it was used in that film, and thus the scene was eliminated from our script. So, when we began to write again, our temperaments were never to coincide again harmoniously, as they had in co-writing

'Eagle's Wing,' which was produced with Martin Sheen playing the lead, premiered in London, but lasted for only two weeks in cinemas around the world, and then, as the Irish say, "It died a death". Also, at this time, Michael claimed to have fallen in love hopelssly – *helplessly* would better define the situation – with a beautiful woman named Pia, the present wife of the actor, producer, director, Gosta Ekman, a person described by his fellow Swede and distant cousin in that royal family, Christer Morner, as being the man in Scandinavia most like a dynamic combination of Clint Eastwood, Woody Allen, Brad Pitt and Paul Newman, even Alfred Hitchcock, he was so multi-talented and formidable in the Swedish film world. His father had been an acclaimed actor and film producer. His mother was the famed beauty and painter, Agneta Wrangle, whose ancestor Count Wrangle, two centuries before, had raided and pillaged all the greatest art treasures from their aristocratic owners throughout Europe on a latter-day Viking raid over several years, so that the present Wrangle Castle holds the finest collection of that Medieval surrealist,Archimboldi's *vegetative portraits,* whose descendant may be that scoundrel from Deya and Fornalutx, Mallorca, Paul Arnaboldi, a.k.a. Mr. Crow, who evaded and escaped Scotland Yard and Interpol for his masterminding of Operation Julie, the international L.S.D. manufacturing and international distribution in 1976.

I spent the next few months with Michael in attempting to resuscitate the film script, but much of my time was devoted to listening to Mike's laments for his obsession with Pia who had only left her husband, Gosta, for one week while he was away doing business in Stockholm. Those few days had constellated a love affair on the order of of Antony and Cleopatra – in Michael's imagination – and he had thus dedicated all his attention to his campaign to retrieve every smidgin of love-lorn solace he could recall from those moments he had spent with her. Pia, in the meantime, was devoting her attention to caring for an Indonesian orphan child whom she and Gosta had adopted in

Jakarta. On several dark evenings, Mike had visited the Ekman home, located above the village of Fornalutx, hiding in the shrubbery outside their illuminated living-room window, voyeuristicly peeking in on the domestic activity ... and bliss ... of the married couple. He told me that Gosta had used the child to enact emotional blackmail on Pia, that she would have returned to Mike if there had not been this maternal obligation. I suggested that perhaps she had decided to accept the family identity, that had lifted her to the highest social eyrie in Scandinavia, endowing her with a diadem greater than any royal heritage could bestow.

I also was tempted to say, 'Why would she want a crotchety old English bachelor, more than twice her age, with no definite income, and only a lyric imagination to recommend him as a mate and guardian, when she already has a man twice her age, but one who is considered the richest and sexiest movie star in all of Scandinavia, and who adores her and satisfies her every whim, with slavish devotion.'

Michael had always been involved with the glamor-girl types. The mother of his only child, Joanna, now lived in Norway with her movie-star mother, Julie Egge, one of those sex symbols who played opposite Sean Connery in the 'James Bond' films; and there was Slavitza, who lived with him on occasion, a tall brunette with enormous swollen breasts who had been Miss Yugoslavia - and when Robert Redford met her while he was strolling down Kings Road in Chelsea on one of his London visits and invited her out on a date, Michael was more than encouraging in delivering her to Redford's hotel, in order to promote her possible Hollywood career - gracious and generous; but Michael was not in love with Slavitza ... nothing like the desperate passion he claimed to have for Pia. It was patently obvious that this young bride had indulged in a wanton, but probably delicious, few moments with Mike, and then had scampered back to her lord and master and devoted true-love.

I had become acquainted with Gosta Ekman when visiting at the Terreno residence of his mother, Agneta Wrangle, who had established an amorous liaison with my sailing pal, the adventurer and explorer, Christer Morner. Christer and his brother, Stellar, had produced, directed, and starred in a television documentary series focused on the quest for the lost Inca treasure of gold and jewels [El Dorado] for which they claimed to have discovered an authentic map belonging to one of the earliest Spanish *conquistadores* to visit South America. The Morner brothers had sold shares in a corporation founded on the notion that they would indeed locate this bounty hidden in the Andes. Several years of trudging through jungle and climbing steep mountain ranges with teams of stock-holders and supposed experts in archaeologicaand mythographic studies had yielded nothing more than huge revenues of money for the Swedish brothers and exciting film footage for television broadcasts throughout. Scandinavia. After all this extravagant expenditure of energy and financial resources, Christer had landed in Mallorca, almost bankrupt, and had then moved in with Agneta after another failed marriage and subsequently established the Swediish Radio Service for the Balearic Islands, broadcasting from the studio apartment on the top of the building whose ground floor Agneta had leased for the past decades in Terreno. While visiting Agneta and Christer there, I came to know Gosta Ekman during his frequent visits staying over with his mother. I esteemed him as a humble, reasonable, sensitive person who had endured extreme bouts with depression which had brought him to the very brink of suicide, usually as a result of his passionate love affairs, none of which seemed to have ever been a stabilizing influence in his life ... quite the contrary. As a co-star with any of the most desirable actresses in the pantheon of feminine leading ladies in the entire world of cinema, he had nevertheless always chosen as conjugal partners, those females most likely to betray him and wound him so deeply that he would be driven to contemplating self-destruction. Agneta, his mother, asked me if I could be the sort of friend to help him in this dilemma; however, as I had dived into just such a relationship with Maya, a Swedish-Finn, the personality type notorious for such torrential relationships, who was I to be as an adviser? Agneta, herself, had only recently taken as a partner, Christer Morner, her distant cousin, already married three times, and an alcoholic of a decidedly amoral stamp, but he had an irresistible charm and gallant swashbuckling demeanor fitting for any pirate in history.

Paradoxically, or perhaps, reasonably, I was enormously sympathetic to both my close friend and writing partner, Michael Syson, and to Gosta Ekman, the son of my friend, Agneta Wrangle, friend of all my many years in Mallorca. Both men were virtual caricatures of that benighted elderly German professor in the film, 'The Blue Angel,' who falls in love with the young wanton cabaret star (Marlene Dietrich in her sexy, sultry prime), and both my friends (Michael and Gosta) would probably end up performing some silly imitation of a rooster crowing "cock-a-doodle-doo" as tragic cuckolds for all to pity or scorn. Michael finally was able to release his obsessional grip on his infatuation with Pia, and Gosta eventually had to divorce her for her scandalous behaviors in seducing teen-age school-boys whom she had lured off the streets of Soller, an activity so outrageous that few could bring themselves to believe it had actually happened, except that the *denuncios* with the Guardia Civil by the parents of so many of these young men and these documented charges defied any sane denial of her sexual predatory proclivity. I had left the island to spend time in London in the next few months while this was playing out, and Michael and Gosta were reeling from the shock, comforted by family and friends more readily available on site.

When I returned to London in 1978, I went to stay in the dockside artist's studio of my sculptor friend, Maurice Agis, whose enormous walk-through displays of multi-colored inflatable exhibits I had helped him to promote at the San Diego Zoo, but with never any definite exhibit being launched, as we could not find financial backing to offset the cost of transportation and insurance [in 2005 one of these inflatables was lifted by a strong wind, and several of the people trapped inside were dashed to their death when the exhibits crashed to earth - Maurice was tried and convicted of Manslaughter, but died of a heart attack before he could begin to serve a prison sentence]. Maurice found me a 2,000 square foot studio to lease across the Thames river from his residence, and we could literally wave to one another from our huge windowed perches [both on the fifth floor] just south of Tower Bridge, a location which today would cost millions to own and thousands to rent by the week. My rent was the Pound Sterling equivalent of $150 per month, and I immediately sublet studio space to two female artists so that I was left paying only $50 monthly. However, there were challenges in settling in. There was no furniture nor any heating, and the toilet was one shared by all occupants of this entire floor. I had a wash basin and a telephone which had a lock on the dial, placed there by the owner of the lease from whom I sublet. With great ingenuity, cunning, and virtual criminal wile, I was able to find an abandoned electric storage heater, some devious electricians working on another floor of the building taught me how to jimmy the electric meter to effect delivery of free electric power, and I used a tapping method to dial almost any numbers in England, Spain, or to America, and no charges for telephone calls could ever be levied against me, as the telephone was officially out-of-order.

I spent many of my afternoons and evenings consorting with the rambunctious drinking crowd at 'The Queen's Elm' pub on Fulham Road and 'Chelsea Arts Club,' which was just down the street, another hundred yards along Old Church Street. Laurie Brough, was the owner of Dawes Press, located at World's End and Fulham Road, on Dawes Road, and he was the original publisher of *Private Eye* and the designer and printer for the Henry Moore Trust and Bernard Stone's 'Turret Books,' and the only printer whom Ralph Steadman trusted to reproduce his finest artistic cartoons. Laurie wanted to print a new book of my poetry, but I was not as yet, ready for such an undertaking, as I had decided to focus my attention of the re-writing of my *Beowulf* film treatment and was adapting the treatment for *Ms. Machinegun Kelly* to a screen-play. As I had recently read some of the poetry of Dr. David McSweeney, whose text, *The Crazy Ape*, on neuro-surgery and psychiatry, I had been invited to edit for 'Peter Jones Press', his publishers, I decided to launch this pysician's career as a poet. He had a contract pending at the time with 'Alfred Knopf' in America to publish his first novel, *Jesus Delahunty*, a wild narrative of a psychiatrist and brain-surgeon who runs amok and becomes a serial killer in both England and the United States and eludes the elite of Scotland Yard and Interpol until a street-wise Manhattan cop finally snares him.

His poetry was also bizarre, as it was grounded in his experience in the several medical fields he had been certified to practice: Pediatrics, Ophthalmic and Brain Surgery, and Psychiatry. He also recalled his years as one of the most infamous rugby players in the United Kingdom, whom Richard Harris has made his model for his starring role in the film, 'The Sporting Life.' David had captained the Cambridge University and Irish International teams, the latter so savagely marshaled on the field that he was threatened with losing his Irish citizenship. While Chief Psychiatrist at 'Middlesex Hospital,' London, and while on Emergency .Room duty one night, he had taken off to have several drinks at a nearby public house in Soho, and upon staggering back to the hospital, he had encountered some police who considered his behavior anti-social and therefore had attempted to restrain him, and in the ensuing melee, he was beaten into manacled custody by the combined efforts of three of the Bobbies and was dragged to the local drunk tank where he pleaded with the unconvinced jailers to return him to his post as guardian angel at 'Middlesex Hospital Emergency Ward.' I used the police blotter photograph for the back page of the collection of poems entitled *So Why do You Kill Me?* which Nobel Laureate, Seamus Heaney esteemed as an outstanding example of modern poetry by a fellow Gaelic artist. Ralph Steadman provided a caricature portrait, entitled 'Portrait of the Irishman as Poet,' as illustration for the front cover, partially in return for psychological counseling that David had given him after his return from the trauma of his first meeting with Hunter Thompson to collaborate, as the *Gonzo* cartoonist, on drawing the illustrations used in the production of *Fear and Loathing in Las Vegas.*

Ralph shared with me an apocryphal tale about being on a drinking binge with McSweeney which well illuminates the ordeal of spending any leisure time with this doctor, as I endured and relished, over a period of several years, even being his host as house-guest in Mallorca until his behavior began to verge on the actually criminal in its gratuitous violent outbreaks, for many of which he was banned at 'Chelsea Arts Club,' so often that he was, on several occasions, threatened with being removed as a member, permanently.

On one summer day, Ralph and David had purchased a mini-keg of beer which held several gallons, to carry to a home in Fulham where they planned to continue to drink on a Sunday afternoon after normal licensing hours prohibited frequenting any bar for service. The home where they arrived had an outdoor terrace on the second floor overlooking the street, and some other friends joined them to drink in the open air there. When the contents of the mini-keg had been exhausted, even though there were still several bottles of wine and spirits to consume, David cursed the paucity of the container, picked it up in one hand and hurled it like an out-sized hand-grenade, over his head, out into the street. The keg flew straight into the front wind-shield of an automobile that was driving toward the house, and the occupants were crushed back against their seats, the car caroming off onto the sidewalk. David, ever the alert Emergency Ward Attendant, ran downstairs through the house, and was out onto the street in less than a minute, pulling the injured bodies of the man and his wife from the car, settling them on the pavement against a garage wall where he examined them and began First Aid treatment for their lacerations and bruises, and fortunately, no fractures, to their skulls. An ambulance arrived shortly, and David rode with them to the nearest hospital at Charing Cross where he offered his refined services, if needed, although he stank of alcohol and his clothing was in tatters from a pugilistic fracas he had been involved in during the party just before he shot-put the mini-keg. Brendan Behan, another Irish writer renowned for his alcoholic escapades had once been a drinking pal of David's at 'Finch's' and 'Queen's Elm' pubs on Fulham Road, but had strategically moved his scene to the 'Star' pub in Belgravia to avoid such physically over-active members of his carousing countrymen ... like David MacSweeney.

David's poetry addressed a wide spectrum of the activities of the medical professional life, and the inter-personal relationships of his drinking club and race-course indulgences. His friendship was freighted with surprising happen-stance. He told our companions that I was the only man whom he relied upon to control him when his behaviors went out of bounds, as I had more than once had to perform an *ad hoc* hip-throw and pound his skull into a stone floor to relieve him of his consciousness, and then bind his arms and hands tightly to insure that when he awoke he would be virtually strait-jacketed, or as a Swedish friend of Maya called it, "strict-shirted." So along with my attention to adapting the film treatment of 'Ms. Machinegun Kelly' to a screenplay, which my friend and lover, Charlotte Byng, said she had introduced to the film director, Michael Winner, I began spending much time with Laurie Brough of 'Dawes

Press' in the production of MacSweeney's book of poetry, to publish a first run of 2,000 copies in paperback under the imprint of my 'Eotensic Press' [*eoten* from Anglo Saxon in the Henry Sweet standard Glossary of that ancient Old English, as meaning the work of elves, gnomes and fairy folk, those creatures who had been cast into the Land Of Nod, East of Eden, and survived the Flood, became amphibian and were therefore more highly survival-prone than most humanoids].

I had given up spending much time at the docks and was living in a row-house in Notting Hill with Charlotte most of the time, now. She had become pregnant from our affair and consented to an abortion – at my insistence – as the entire history of her blood-line was rife with certifiable madness [she was the direct lineal descendant of all the Royal Stuarts (she was an exact look alike for Charles the First, and her temperament was often akin to Bloody Mary, Queen of Scots)] and her grandfather from Moldavia, on the other [non-blue blood] side had founded General Electric; yet, all his spawn had become suicidal [her own father's demise], and Charlotte's brothers had attempted homicide within the family, and had spent as many months and years in mental hospitals as she had – her pathological impulses had always been suicidal. She sometimes cajoled me with the notion that if I were to consent to her giving birth to our child, that my name would thereby have to appear in the pages of DeBrett and Burke's Peerage, and I would thenceforward be, *prima facie*, a *Roya*l. I, not so politely, demurred.

I had brought a Volkswagen back from Spain which I had acquired from an encounter with Thord Sundquist whom I discovered to have been living in a camper on the beach just north of Barcelona. I had not seen this merry prankster giant Viking painter since my student days in Madrid when I had provided him shelter at the time he was expelled from the country as *persona non grata*, as a result of his many alcoholic misdemeanors. I had arrived at his beach-front doorstep with another part-time lover, Diana Gay, the daughter of Carl Gay, a talented woman who had become involved with Bill Matthewson when he was resident editor-in-chief of all the English pornography in Europe [rumored to be an international Mafia enterprise], living at the Miramar Palace outside Valldemossa. The two had been in a high speed head-on collision with a bus: Bill was killed, and Diana had survived and mended slowly and painfully after being "splattered on the wind-shield like a bug" [her poignantly imagistic description of the crash]. Ironically, the automobile was one I had sold to Bill only a month before, a tangerine colored Fiat sports car which I had warned him would tempt one to drive at dangerously high speeds. Diana considered that my connection to the vehicle in which she had lost her lover and transformed her body and face most radically, somehow qualified me to become her next lover. I accepted her offer. She was one of the sexiest and most brilliant individuals I have ever had the good fortune to engage with.

She engaged instantaneously with Thord, having heard of him from the Terreno days, and he found her jaunty manner a lively relish in comparison with his current lover, a rather drab, aging hippie female beginning to run to fat who moved less than gracefully in her scuffed boots and shapeless smock. In stark and delectable contrast, the slender, sleek Diana wore tee-shirts that clung to her form like paint, highlighting her nipples which seemed to be always standing erect ... virtually inviting one to nibble. Thord remarked on the prominent nipples almost before we sat down to take a glass of wine, and we all shared a hearty laugh at his disarming, but undeniably engaging candor. As Thord's reputation in illustration of magazines had been largely derivative of his appreciation of the female body and exotic and even fettishistic variations, his admiration of Diana was like praise from Caesar, or so I interpreted it for our small gathering.

Because I had employed public transportation – the train from Barcelona and a taxi from the station – to arrive at his beach-side residence, Thord suggested an alternative for our continued journey into France and onward to England. He had left an automobile in the Barcelona airport parking lot several months before and because the price of the ticket for removing it would now be astronomical, he offered to give me the car for the nominal price of $100 if I could employ my wiles to retrieve it. I saw a solution immediately, and suggested that we give it a try, if for no other reason than that it was criminal, but not outrageously so, and would be like some of the shenanigans we had gotten up to on my former street in Madrid, Lope de Vega, especially when Thord had confused the Casanova Pension bordello with the Carmelite Convent located on the other side of my apartment block – the nuns had never forgotten the enormous Swede who had begged to paint one of them in the nude, and he had even attempted to remove the habit of one *sister* before the outraged Mother Superior arrived and telephoned the Guardia Civil after screaming for the drunk and, therefore, totally incapacitated Sereno (local street constable) to come to the rescue.

We put the plan into operation the very next morning. Thord and I and Diana arrived in Barcelona where I rented an automobile across from the railway station, and we proceeded to the airport. We all drove into the main parking lot, located Thord's car, a Volkswagen painted with a bow in bright yellow encircling the blue body, not exactly a low profile vehicle – typical of something belonging to this flamboyant artist; he remarked that he had also replaced the engine with a motor of 1,500 cubit centimeters. One tire was flat, but the battery, miraculously was live – Thord had fortuitously disconnected one of the terminal connectors when he had left the car there, months before, so the engine started after only a couple of revs. We sent Diana on to check out of the parking lot in the rental car, claiming she had lost her ticket, so she would willingly pay for a full day's parking, and then she would await us just outside the main exit gate. We would place the rental car's spare tire on Thord's car, and leave with the ticket stamped for only one half an hour before, the one we had collected on entry, with the rental vehicle. It all should have gone smoothly; however, we had not reckoned on police surveillance by a camera which had monitored our work on the Volkswagen, as we had been busy replacing that flat tire.

A special squad of Guardia Civil were on duty in all airports, a sort of S.W.A.T. team trained for quashing any international terrorist groups, or more particularly, the most troublesome on Spanish soil, the E.T.A. para-military Basque separatists who had wreaked so much havoc in the past few years with setting off bombs in densely packed civilian gatherings throughout the country. This team at Barcelona Airport were a Guardia Civil branch of the elite, and most brutal, in law enforcement. As we paid our meager parking fee and drove over to join Diana, whose rental sedan was parked on the verge just beyond the exit gate, we were met by two armored vehicles, pulling up directly in front of our parked cars, sirens blaring, lights blazing blue and red, roaring down on us from the highway ahead, which now was blocked to any and all other vehicular movement. We were frozen with fear, stopped dead in our tracks, but Thord was quick to grab the two joints of hashish from his shirt pocket and swallow both in an instant. He also began blathering and waving his gargantuan arms as he climbed from our car, but was slammed back against the door-frame, and then twisted about to be handcuffed, in a swoop, by two of the officers who had piled out of the police vans. I carefully bowed out of the driver's seat, with my hands lifted in the universal salute of surrender, and was not treated in like manner. Diana slithered from her car and slunk up to the ranking cop, the man most obviously in charge, set apart by his jaunty hip cocked and his hand raised to order the assemblage to attentive obedience. He spoke only to tell Diana to stop ... as it appeared she was about to press her luscious body into the buckles and straps and medals of his official uniform.

In her most elevated, socially privileged, formal Castillian Spanish, she protested that there must be some mistake, for she had been waiting for her friends who had been busy replacing the tire of their automobile parked in the airport lot, and she wished to be of any assistance to the most gracious gentleman officer of the highly esteemed branch of law enforcement, the glorious Guardia Civil, proud protectors of her beloved nation. And then she was interrupted by the officer who informed her that the surveillance cameras had projected what had appeared to be the transfer of some objects in and out of the Volkswagen that were of a suspicious nature. Upon this suggestion, Diana took the elbow of this Guardia and led him to the car, and she then opened all the doors and the hood and the cover over the engine in the rear, bobbing and dipping and performing what would have passed for *lap-dancing* under any other circumstances, so that after she had stepped back to ask that the car could be seen as not containing any bombs or weapons, the officer actually bowed to her, ordering Thord's release and then herded his men back to their vehicles, and we were left to do the same. However, we did stay for a few moments to gather our wits, catch our breath, and ask Diana what kind of a spell she had just cast, how she had so enthralled this *Gestapo* commander. I was reminded of similar instances in which those being interrogated had been brutalized or even killed in the process, for which this branch of law enforcement, although patently guilty, were never held accountable.

"The nipples," she said softly. "My precious pert nipples. Always erect and inviting. Irresistible. No man can think clearly once he focuses on them. And he was focused. Of that I can assure you. Then I delivered my little dip and dandle, as I showed him the Volkswagen, and he is probably even now, trying to find some place to get off by himself and have a hefty jerk-off before his balls turn blue and he chokes on his own tongue."

I could not resist embracing my darling and squeezing these precious *pert* ones till she screamed with pleasure. We then decided to stop at the first place where we could have a drink and cool off before driving back to the beach. Diana and I declined Thord's invitation to spend more time at his place; I paid him the $100 in two American fifties, the image of U.S. Grant on those bills being favorites of mine as the film director, Henry Levin, had cast me in the role of the general pursuing Jack Palance as Colonel Quantrill in the Columbia Pictures production originally called 'The Marauders' [now renamed, 'The Desperados'], saying that I looked just like that president ... with the make-up department graying my hair and providing wrinkles to my then 29 year-old face. [Today, I probably look more like Grant's elder brother].

As we headed that gaudy Volkswagen toward the French border, Diana told me that she would travel only so far as Paris. She had decided to fly from there to New York, and as she had some old friends who lived in a farm-house near Versailles, she wanted to visit with them for a few days before her flight to the States. She made it clear that I would not need to accompany her and that she would be uncomfortable with any intrusion on what she planned to be an intense interaction with these pals. She assured me that she would always feel a romantic and intellectual bond with me, but that she needed to sort out some of her still painful memories of her love for Bill Matthewson before she could be a suitable partner for anyone else, even someone as special as she considered me to be. Our sexual activity had been most satisfying, she assured me, but there was that lingering memory of Bill that denied her full access to her entire libidinal and spiritual reservoir. She was tearful and yet grim. She wanted to love me, but Bill's energies still haunted her. I could well imagine that he had left a lasting impression on Diana, as I had known the man, and had not liked him particularly, but could never deny the power of his presence, the harsh flavor of his character. His virtually institutionalized personality deriving from several years at Folsm and San Quentin prisons had left a distinct signature. I would not care to compete with his ghost, in bed, or anywhere else. I bade Diana my fondest farewell on the outskirts of Paris, and was never to see her again.

It was not far from this city that I encountered a hitch-hiker dressed in denim and wearing a red bandanna around her head who smiled so brightly as I approached that the car slowed down to offer her whatever she desired, without my conscious consent, or perhaps with all my volition and delight. She had a rucksack and a guitar which she swung easily into the backseat, and she fit herself into the the passenger seat, reaching toward me with a browned forearm and a strong handshake saying, " Lightfoot's my name. Call me Annie or Lightfoot. Whatever. Been picking strawberries, and I'm ready to go home now. You heading for London? That's where I'll get my flight home to New Zealand."

"Yes, Lightfoot. London it is. I'm Ben Welcome aboard. Can you play that? I can sing. We'll have fun," and we did, from then till she did fly away. And so I pulled back on the road toward Calais and our boat across to the White Cliffs of Dover.

Just before we caught the earliest boat in a the morning to cross over the English Channel, we stopped off at a roadside Bed and Breakfast where we shared a double bed heaped with piles of duvets and pillows, and we sat up till quite late sharing a bottle of wine and the guitar which we chorded to serenade each other, there being no attempt at sexual foreplay, nor even serious cuddling, especially as Lightfoot had chattered about her lover from the moment she entered the car, another woman who had been her "Row-Dog" [well-established prison term from the farms where convicts bonded with the fellow felon who worked the same *row*, picking or weeding, under the gun-boss's supervision]. Her "Row-Dog Sweetie" had flown out of Paris to return early to New Zealand where she had to re-enroll in classes at the university there. Lightfoot had a job which she had leave-of-absence from till the next month, so she had decided to visit London and see some museums and *take in* some theatre.

I invited her to stay with me because she could cook some simple meals, and then she would not have to worry about the high cost of even the youth hostels in that magical but expensive city. We got on like brother and sister. She reminded me of one of my favorite literary characters, Scout [just as Roberta Booth had been for me – but without the dazzling beauty of that Princess L'Oreal, whose commercial image had been her identity for so many years], the androgynous girl in Harper Lee's novel, *To Kill a Mockingbird.* And also with Anna Llewellyn had I felt so at ease with a female, and yet Anna and I had become lovers, and then, realizing our mistake, had avoided the activity thenceforward. With Roberta Booth, there was also only minimal sexual interaction. If I ever do meet Scout, I shall *must needs* [I adore that anachronistic literary affectation] scrupulously avoid any physical contact.

I was meeting David MacSweeney at the Chelsea Arts Club to work on editing his book of poetry on those occasions when we did not consult together with Laurie Brough at his print shop on Dawes Road. Lightfoot accompanied me and soon came to be accepted by the members of the club, especially the men who found her attractive, and as she did not feel a need to inform them of her *special* sexual persuasion, she was the recipient of many free drinks and some excellent meals from the dining room whose gourmet food was being offered up by our acclaimed chef, Tony, a Basque who had decided to abandon his beloved country till they should achieve independence from Spain - [he retired after thirty years at the club in 2009, and Viscaya still is ruled, to this day, by King Don Juan Carlos, Spain's monarch]. Lightfoot was quite open about her sexuality with Dale, MacSweeney's current wife, who was herself a lesbian.

Many evenings, as we left for our residence, Lightfoot freighted home enough scraps from her sumptuous meals to provide a lovely feast in our kitchen which she even was able to carry forward into breakfast as well as some lunches the following day when we stayed in till afternoon, as I was occupied with the editing and proofing of not only the book of poetry, but my adaptation of the film treatment of 'Ms. Machine-gun Kelly' to package in the format of a screen-play. In early evenings I would take Lightfoot to the West End to score some inexpensive student tickets at the theatres there. Some mornings, we also would visit the museums as well; and one fine afternoon we took the boat from Westminster to Greenwich and back. We also walked in most of the parks throughout the town and I was particularly delighted to escort her along the Serpentine Lake in Kensington Park to show her the bronze statue of Peter Pan with all the small animals that so delight children that most of the figures shine brightly from their continual touching. We even hired a row-boat and floated on those lovely waters and stripped off our shirts to take a blast of sunlight. Lightfoot was not at all shy about exposing herself bare-breasted to me, and as we had stretched ourselves out in the boat, our bodies were not so visible from the shore-line as to cause any scandal. Our behaviors were fraternal, familial, non-erotic, and so, when Lightfoot sprang her surprise in the last days of her stay, I was, at first, startled, then amused, and after only a few hours, utterly delighted. The reader probably has guessed, and was already prepared for what occurred, long before I would have been.

I was sitting back in a comfortable easy chair when she hoisted her leg up on its arm and pulled her skirt up to her hip and asked me what I thought of it.

What?   It?   I thought?

She then told me that she had shaved both her legs, all the way to the top. How about that?

I thought, 'What could that mean?' So I asked her.

"What does it mean?"

She answered, "Rather, what do I mean? You might well ask. Or should."

So I did, and she explained to me that the meal she was preparing that evening was to be special, accompanied with candles, and the flowers I had not as yet noticed ... in a vase, were roses – red. All of this was meant to provide a romantic *milieu* [I had taught her that word and yet was not sure its use was appropriate to this occasion]. Or was this appropriate ... to us? Or, what was happening might make everything somehow inappropriate ... or ... ?

Lightfoot told me that she had decided to try the heterosexual *alternative* ... with me ... because I had become the best friend she had ever had, and that the only other person she had ever felt so close to and had trusted so, was her lover, and so, she had decided that I could be her lover, too, that is, if I wanted to be, and if it worked the way it was supposed to, with the heterosexual couples she knew about, then this would be *appropriate*.

Sensing her embarrassment, I assured her that she was most attractive, that the shaven legs were a sexy touch, and that I had not had the accompaniment of flowers and candles to a love-making proposition in ever so long, that I was thrilled by what lay before us in this evening interlude, that, in a word (a clichéd phrse), I was *turned on*.

Although I had made love with two other lesbians, both of them had been married [Rhonda, in La Jolla was the former wife of the San Diego State College Biology professor who became a window-washer, naming himself Butt-Man, after he had experienced a bad acid trip] and they had been sexually active with their male partners for a few years, so that the experience was not totally foreign to them, but with Lightfoot, the challenge of her very first heterosexual union was to prove rather formidable. So, even though we felt like re-united brother and sister, perhaps *because* we felt that filial bond, the sexual act was not the most satisfying I have ever experienced. As a matter of fact, it had such a distinct flavor of incest, that neither one of us achieved anything like orgasm. I was able to ejaculate at last, but I felt as if I had completed a bowel movement of no particularly memorable sensation, and Lightfoot appeared to be immediately ready to re-confirm her allegiance to Lesbos ... forever. We did indeed try again once or twice in the few remaining days, but we told each other some ridiculously humorous jokes, such as, "What did one abominable snow-person say to the other, after? Abominable for you, too?" And so forth, till we admitted that our friendship was of a definitively *filia, agape, caritas* stamp, and that any more sexual experimentations would probably render us blind and insensate to a relationship that must really be treasured, especially as we were about to bid a fond farewell and might never see each other again. And, indeed, we never have, although sometimes, in my more ludicrously imaginative moments, I wonder if I impregnated my pal. Surely I would have heard from her if this were so. But maybe not.

After Lightfoot flew away, I began consorting with Anna Llewellyn, and was spending more time with Garret Wellesley , whose son needed my tutoring, which I generously provided, so that he could remain in the American Community School in London. I had escorted Garret on his honeymoon with Paige, the third Countess Cowley, that being the title for his earldom, in addition to Lady for his lordship, and Marquesa for his title of Marquis. He also had a baronetcy and knighthood, but the highest of all these was as the Earl Cowley, the position which made his ancestor the uncle of Arthur Wellesley, who, when ennobled with the title of Duke, for his winning the Napoleonic Wars, provided him with the title-name Wellington, deriving from Garret's family name of Wellesley. When I guided the family about in Mallorca, where I had placed them in houses in the cluster named 'S'Esbart' belonging to Nora Constens in Galilea, young Grahame, the Viscount, whose title as Lord Dangham had already been bestowed, was loath to use this appellation, so I rented the motor-scooter in my name. I had been unaware of Garret's grand aristocratic pedigrees before he had asked me to *vet* him as my candidate for membership at Chelsea Arts Club, and when I told him that the process would take weeks or months, he chuckled and told me to introduce him to Dudley Winterbottom, the manager, whose own father was a lord, having been ennobled for his British Army generalship in the Second World War. When I did so, Garret flashed his passport and check book which were in the name of Earl Cowley, and Dudley assured him that he would be a member by the following Monday, as soon as he had time to inform the board that one of the highest ranking peers [Garret was also an hereditary holder of the Order of the Garter – an honor bestowed on Winston Churchill *only after* defending England, as Commander -in-Chief of her armed forces, during World War Two] in the United Kingdom had made application for membership.

When Anna Llewellyn invited me to spend a weekend with her family in Wales, I was, at first, shy about going to stay in such a renowned estate with famous folk I considered might make me feel out of my depth, and a presumptuous social climber, but Garret pointed out to me that I already had been residing, as family, in his home at Eaton Place, the neighborhood of ambassadors and shipping magnates and even one or two embassies. He escorted me to the family library on the fifth floor of that home and took down the Burke's and Debrett's Peerage volumes, and gave me a quick course in assaying the aristocracy of his country. He showed me that his own titles were so close to royal that the minor knighthood of Sir Harry Llewellyn - also, coincidentally a retired colonel in Her Majesty's cavalry - were almost unworthy of notice, except by some untutored Okie like myself who had no notion of what the word *peer* meant, except as that venal perversion of the voyeauristic – as in *peeping*. That I had not only spent many weeks on end living in the ground floor of his Eaton Square home, but in that time had met and dined with some of the most notable and highly esteemed titles in England without ever having batted an eye or doffed my cap nor dug my toe in the sand to kow-tow in obeisance to these friends of the Wellesleys, and this experience should assure me that I would feel perfectly at home in Wales with Anna's kin.

Anna was most eager to show me off to her family, perhaps because she considered me either a rare bird, a bandit, or she truly may have been fond of me. Probably a combination of all three. I did feel comfortable in the rambling old ruin of her home, especially at ease walking the barn-yard and strolling through the stables where Sir Harry, the world -famous Colonel Llewellyn, still kept horses trained to the Hunt, great jumpers who shared bloodlines with "Fox-Hunter," whose huge body was buried beneath a mound on the front lawn with a monument which commemorated the winning of the Gold Medal in the Olympics in 1952, the first such award won for Great Britain since World War Two which had so devastated the entire kingdom. Although the colonel already had inherited a a baronetcy a few centuries old, he was knighted, and thereby doubly ennobled, by

Queen Elizabeth, for this proud achievement which lifted the spirits of all who had survived the horrors of not only the London Blitz, but all the losses of young men and women throughout the world in that war. Harry Llewellyn was a hero to many of the British public, and the man was a worthy figure to wear such a mantle. He and I stood toe-to-toe looking eye-to-eye upon introduction, and I had not felt such a consonant physical (perhaps primeval) energy exchange since meeting John F. Kennedy at the University of Pennsylvania in 1959. Yet Sir Harry's features put me in mind more of Robert Graves - a Roman consul, or Cherokee chief's demeanor – than of that young Irish senator from Massachusetts.

Llewellyn's first declaration following his *pro forma* welcome was to inform me that the only telephone operative in the entire house, other than the private line in his office, was a pay telephone which was hung on the wall in the hall between the dining room and the kitchen; and then, with a sly *moue*, he told me. "We dress for dinner." I was shown to my room and Anna was amused that I had been given the special guest accommodation [curiously, I noticed that the box containing Kleenex actually held folds of toilet tissue; I wonder if the last occupant, a Royal, noticed this economy as well?] as Princess Margaret, her brother's not-so-secret lover, who really could not have been bunked down in Roddie's quarters, as that would have been an open admission of the extra-marital dalliance, and that former Nursery where he and his brother Di had lived was little changed from the time of his youth.

Anna said that her mother was asleep that afternoon, as she was, most of the day, but that I would meet her at dinner, later, and she assured me I need not worry about her father's remarks - regarding the telephone or dressing for dinner ... I was not sure which to ignore. When I did enter the dining room and was introduced to Lady Llewellyn, Sir Harry made his entrance with a huge guffaw, as he

considered his choice of costume, a bright red and chartreuse gym
suit, to be a hilarious spoof of the usual *county* affectation of formal
wear - black tie and smoking jacket, or the next step up in formal
attire, a white bow-tie, starched shirt and cutaway dinner jacket with
tails. I had donned a fringed leather jacket of the Buffalo Bill stamp,
and wore an ascot of rich colored silk with a lavender flowered shirt.
Lady Llewellyn claimed to be fascinated by my hands, and she held
mine so that the thumbs were pressed backward so far that I felt the
pain. "Impulsive," she said with a chortle. "Like mine. See?" she said,
pressing the thumb of her hand back with the other.

"We are impulsive people. Can't help it," and I noticed that she
slurred some of her words and that her eyes sparkled with a radiance
not altogether natural ... or healthy Lady Llewellyn was a chronic
acute alcoholic, a hopeless dipsomaniac, as her kind was called in her
day; she had been a sloppy drunk for as long as she had been allowed
to drink, and nobody had ever been successful in showing her how to
stop. She was considered too *impulsive* ... she was virtually a *Royal*,
that segment of the British ruling class is the upper end that are the
ones who make the rules ... or break them ... if they so desire. Her
pedigree was close to that of my pal, Garret Wellesley. Her father was
an Earl, and her most notable ancestor had been the admiral who took
over command of the entire British fleet when Lord Nelson fell in his
last combat. I found it ironically amusing that the press should refer
to her son Roddie as a "commoner," when his affair with Princess
Margaret was publicized. The Hanoverian upstarts - Queen
Elizabeth's family - who resided in Buckingham Palace at that time,
had much to envy in the blood-lines of the Llewellyn family, a name
which might have been derivative of *Arturus Rex* (King Arthur)
himself, the wild Welsh guerrilla warrior who confronted and
subdued the Viking intruders who had invaded Britain from the
Northeast when the Romans pulled out in the early Fifth Century.
And Roddie's brother, Di, the heir by primogeniture, to the baronetcy,

would be ennobled with the baronet title when his father was deceased. So, where was the basis for calling Roddie a *commoner?* He would himself have been a lord - Sir Roderick [as he is , indeed, today since di's death only a few years ago, now] - had he merely been born before Di. And Di had married the daughter of the Duke of Essex, so his progeny would leap from the pages of the lower nobility in *Burke's Peerage* to the pages of his mother's ancestors and Garret's, in *DeBrett's*, the catalog of the uppermost echelon of the peers, who, themselves, were close to being Royals [Garret loved the written invitations to Buckingham Palace that opened with the appellation, "Dear Cousin." Funny old class system. Befuddling to most Americans, and British, as well. However, it took only a few *plummy* vowels to be uttered by these members of the privileged class, for almost all Brits in earshot to decide to *kow-tow*, grovel, or grit teeth in snarling servile reaction, seated deep in a memory of the most oppressive system of rule, the feudal order, deriving from the Holy Roman Empire, the Divine Right of Kings, that Caesaro-Papacy that maintained their *Dark Ages* and a *Great Chain of Being* [Johns Hopkins University's Professor Lovejoy's coined term from his definitive 1936 textbook by that title on this subject] privileged class, well beyond merely the Medieval period.

When Anna and I returned to London, she took me to the flat that her brother Roddie occupied in Fulham, and just as we were introduced, he raved about how I had received treatment by his family in Wales which only a member of the Royal Family closest to the throne - Princess Margaret, rather obviously - had received. He then stepped back and with his chin cradled in the fingers of one hand, fanned to provide a pedestal, declared that he could not imagine how a face like mine had ever developed, implying that he considered me strikingly handsome and appealing. I replied that it was merely the result of prayer and meditation, extreme self-denial, intense study; and severe brain damage. And I could see that I had made quite a hit with him.

He then begged to know if there was any favor he could do for me, and I just as readily admitted that because my loft at the Docklands had still not been provided with a shower or bath, and as I had been availing myself of the most Spartan regimen, washing myself in a bowl from a small vanity sink in that spacious but uncomfortable sprawling studio spread out 2,000 square feet above the Thames, I would be delighted to use his bathroom for that purpose, while he and his sister caught up on nursery gossip and family affairs.

He would have none of it – my bathing myself – and insisted that he would draw my tub, give me a thorough scrub, and even a shampoo, and with no more ado, he took us directly to that special room and turned the taps full on. I casually disrobed in front of both my *friends* and did climb in to the water which he had sprinkled with what he called *fairy powder*, a fragrant, balsamic bubble-bath concoction with upper tones of honeysuckle and lime-blossom which he confided that he had invented for his *friend* at Kensington Palace [another thinly veiled reference to Margaret]. As I slid down into the exquisite embrace of this tub, and he asked if there was anything else I might desire, probably hoping I would request a lathering lower down in my frame, I told him that I would love a pint of chilled lager and a cigar. He bolted from the flat, and within less than a quarter of an hour, he was back at my side with a frothy, chilled pint of beer and a six inch Havana cigar, both of which he had run to the corner public house to fetch for me, as he kept no such items in his home.

Anna later told me that she had never seen anyone whom Roddie had so taken to, and only her brother Di was ever able to inspire in him such a glowing camaraderie and playful gratuity. Curiously, that very same year, Di sold a scandalous newspaper series of stories about Roddie's love affair with Margaret to one of the daily tabloids, whose *yellow press* reputation was just a notch above *The National Inquirer* and whose policies were as low-down and cut-throat as *Private Eye*. I went to console Roddie one afternoon, and he was able to shrug off the brotherly betrayal with a line I have treasured ever since, almost as comforting as, "And aside from all that, Mrs. Lincoln, how did you enjoy the play?" which was this reminder of the relative insignificance of what we may now consider vitally important today with a perspective which history lends us: "Thus was it ever so in ancient Rome."

In the few other visits with the Llwellyn family, both in London and in Wales, I was also reminded of just how goofy and whimsical the members of those British upper-classes could become, and yet also, how senseless it would be to consider their privilege worthy of any esteem or respect as a model for behavior by any others in society. I particularly enjoyed my encounters with one of the Llewellyn's house-guests, Maggie, Duchess of Argyle, the woman who had shocked her generation with a divorce trial which had been so comic that it would have easily qualified for a spot on our modern 'Jerry Springer Show' with images of the lady and her lovers presented as evidence, cropped in the photos from the waist down, and the primary lover, whose genitalia were supposed to be of the most desirable in the kingdom and were not discovered to belong to an actual person [the actor, Douglass Fairbanks] till many years after her death. I also encountered Maggie in Galilea where she was occasionally the house guest of Michelle Trippier who was also carrying on an affair with Lord Beaverbrook's daughter, Janet Kidd, about whom Michael Syson later wrote a *London Times*, Sunday edition series entitled simply, 'Beaverbrook's Daughter.' Somehow, in one of m first meetings with the former Duchess Argyle, there had been a guitar available, and I was pressed into musically proving that I was indeed an authentic Oklahoma native with verifiable artistic roots in the arcane, rural and remote regions of that Indian Territory which had become so famous with the hit musical 'Oklahoma' which had been performed to sell-out audiences in London's West End since just after the Second World

War. I strummed some chords of one of the best known cowboy ballads, 'Give Me Land, Lots of Land, Under Starry Skies Above .... Don't Fence Me In,' swinging into the phrasing of Gene Autry's , "Way Down Yonder in the Indian Nation, Oklahoma Reservation ... in Them Oklahoma Hills Where I Was Born,' and after that, "They Call it That Good Old Mountain Dew ... and Them That Refuse It Are Few." I further wet and whet the assembled *whistle* with, "Your Love's Like a Faucet, You Just Turn It Off and On ... Everybody's Gettin' Wet, But Me Not Yet ... I Just Pay the Bills and Moan," and this last one proved to trigger something in Maggie that would elicit a rhapsodic howl from her any time whenever I came into her presence again, always demanding that I sing her that ballad, with or without accompaniment, and so I did, even in a neighboring grand estate in the sedate living room of a Dowager Countess in Somerset.

Ray Charles dedicated the second half of his concert to me in Palma, Mallorca, in July 1983. calling me his pal, Ben, after our backstage interview for my radio program at that time, 'B.B.& C.' [Big Ben and Company], and he then delivered an improvised yodeling version of 'Oh What a Beautiful Morning' from that musical, 'Oklahoma.' I was likewise flattered that Maggie, Duchess of Argyle, declared to many at that house party in Somerset, that the rendition of 'Your Love's Like a Faucet', sung by Ben Wright, was her ideal love song. Yikes! I did once serenade the North Carolina wife of Lord Brain with my own yodeling version of Hank Williams's, 'Lovesick Blues, ' in the rotunda dome of the House of Lords, London, after I had coached Lord Longford who had invited me to be his close adviser in this undertaking in their combined debate on behalf of the Tibetan refugees in that parliamentary forum in 1993. Penny Spencer, my fiancee at that time, told me that this moment would probably never be replicated in this hallowed hall, and that my high-pitched yodel would reverberate in that dome till perhaps the Tibetans were again allowed to return to their kingdom with their Dalai Lama

My radio program 'B. B. & C.' (Big Ben and Company: Everything Sometimes, broadcasting from Palma , Mallorca in 1983) was short-lived, but it was an amusing pastime and allowed me to indulge in most of my fantasies about perverting the progress of popular culture, at least in the Balearic Islands and Catalonia. I was unrestricted in playing Randy Newman's hilarious song, 'Short People,' as the ridiculing of any physically or intellectually *challenged* did not evoke the ire of the politically correcting monitors of public taste as in the United States where the song had been banned from play on all radio stations. When I met Randy Newman at a concert he gave at UCSD where I was Professor of Poetry for one semester in 1984, he told me that he was pleased to learn that this song of his had become a hit on all radio stations in our Spanish region as a result of my promotion. Because other broadcasters listened to my show and considered that I was better informed than most other Mallorcan radio producers in the realm of what was the *pointy* end of the latest in music, I played a practical joke on those who were blindly following my lead *anywhere* by promoting the music of a gangrenous unknown Country Western singer whose only album I had encountered once in the bus station in Mexicali: 'Sleepy Le Boef.' The man must have been overwhelmed when his agents received an invitation for him to perform later that year to a sell-out audience of his new admirers at the Barcelona football stadium. Tra La! Fickle fame! Especially so, if tickled by the devious digitals of 'Big Ben and Company.'   My creation of astrology readings every day was even more demented: "Come on, Scorpio, surely you can handle one more vicious grudge"; "And Pisces, that perfect love you encountered on the beach at Cala D'Or and later spent such a passionate weekend with, has at last found a cure for that disease that you both have been suffering from ever since, but the address you gave was a dead-letter box, so ... it is terminal, and its progress increases at an incremental rate ... so."

You get the idea. My predictions and prognoses were grim, at the very least, and terrifying, on average. That is why I told my listeners that it would be impossible to recognize me, or to attempt to find me outside the studio, where there were strict orders for me never to be disturbed with inquiries of any kind, and that in physical appearance I was not unlike a cross between Whoopy Goldberg, Woody Allen, and Godzilla. In fact, I was identified only once at the Palma airport boarding a flight as I asked the attendant at the gate a question, but I told my inquirer that I was actually the voice-over for the American National Public Radio program's narrator of , 'Prairie Home Companion,' Garrison Keillor, whose voice is eerily a duplicate of mine [who is the *doppelganger?*], and that I was just passing through Mallorca from an over-night lay-over on my way back to the United States from Sardinia. So much for my radio days. And the last time I ever sang for Maggie Campbell, Duchess of Argyle, was in Michelle Trippier's home in Galilea, just before he died.

Michelle Trippier's demise was an *event* which he and I shared as we had passed so many evenings like those spent with Maggie, and with our various lady friends who visited us on the island. In World War Two, Michelle had commanded a *corsair* (small combatant frigate), then gone on to lead a company of Free French Commandos in North Africa, and eventually had liberated a Nazi concentration camp whose population consisted primarily of only a desperate few Jews and Gypsies who had miraculously survived these death-camp horrors. Michelle had spent the following years directing major centers of Shell Oil in North Africa. He held the highest order of the Croix de Guerre, presented him personally by General Charles DeGaulle. I felt we had been comrades somehow, yet our age difference was four decades. As he lay dying in a hospital in Palma, Mallorca, I arrived to deliver a poem – 'Beau Geste' - which I had written for him to commemorate this *event*.

His two daughters, his most current visiting lady friend, Janet Kidd, famous socialite daughter of the newspaper, magnate, Lord Beaverbrook, and his two live-in servants, a Spanish man and his wife, were in attendance in the Intensive Care suite quietly and respectfully attending what everyone presumed to be his last day alive. I respectfully asked permission of my friend, and those present, to read my poem of tribute. The theme of this writing was that because Michelle Trippier was noted as being the finest host to any guests who ever visited him, and that in the realm where he was now going, it would be certain that he would also prepare the best possible festivity to greet those of us who were to follow him there. His trademark had always been that he made the *grand gesture,* translated in French: *beau geste.* I could see that my friend was not altogether satisfied with my performance, but what he said was that the poem was not as good as it might be, albeit the thought was appreciated, and he told me to go home, rewrite it, that he would hang on to life for twenty-four more hours, and that I should return the next day to give him the edited version. I did so.

The next morning, I arrived with a re-written text and the death-watch assembly appeared incredulous, but willing to let the two of us play out our game. We did. As I read the last words, which were also the title, I waited silently at *parade-rest,* quasi-military attention, for the last words of my auditor, my commandant, my comrade.

"It is good. I am pleased," he proclaimed, and then with a slight wave of his hand, he beckoned me to come to the head of the bed, to kiss him farewell.

I did so. On both cheeks, and we both were tearful and filled with the fondness that had always graced our friendship, now to be severed ... but only by the temporary measure of death. Michelle died only a few hours after I left that room.

In the following year, I had occasion to visit in the new home of one of his daughters in Greenwich, Connecticut, on my way to stay with Albrecht and Aggie Saalfield where, my old college pal, Brec, was then serving as headmaster of Greenwich Country Day School, having had to leave his post as a headmaster in a similar school in Quaker Heights, Cleveland, Ohio, to escape threats made against his family after they had endowed the presidential campaign of George McGovern. This daughter of Michelle's was married to the owner and publisher of *The International Herald Tribune* and her husband had just sold out his newspaper and moved to America from Paris, France. She told me that the family was deeply moved by the poetic *event* at the death-bed of her father, and that all had kept copies of the poem and cherished memories of the moment of benedictory farewell between these two unusual men (Michelle and me).

The *unusual* men I had known in Galilea would have been considered prominent in any setting, but were a treasure beyond compare for me at the time of my life when I was most impressionable and finally forging what would remain as my artistic temper and vector of intentional thrust for the remainder of my life: John Ulbricht, the painter whose portrait of Robert Graves rivals that of T.E. Lawrence by Augustus John; Michelle Decker, the Spanish and French Foreign Legion officer who later fought with the French Resistance against Hitler and with the Free French to finally liberate his country from the Vichy collaborationist oppression combined with the Nazi occupation forces there; Ruthven Todd, whose milestone studies of William Blake as an artist, and multiplicitous literary critical essays which comprised a single spaced bibliography of thirty pages; Doctor Pedro Garcia Villaescusa, nephew of the most powerful man in Francisco Franco's Fascist government, next to the Generalissimo himself: commandant of the military judicial system of Spain, chief justice of that supreme court under martial law – and Perico, whose family had left him an orphan reared as a son by that formidable general, had become a revolutionary radical who indulged in every illegal drug he could find, consorted with the known criminal element of the Gypsies in the *barrio chino* [the nickname for the red-light district, literally translating to China Town], he had printed and distributed Angela Davis tee-shirts, one of which he wore till it was reduced to tatters; and, Michelle Trippier, that aristocratic, Second World War hero commander of a combat frigate, then a North African Commando company and at the end of the war, was the liberator of a Nazi death camp, to be decorated with his nation's highest military order by De Gaulle who begged him to help reconstruct France, but was denied this service as Michelle felt he must build a sufficient fortune with Shell Oil to leave as inheritance to his daughters, and he confided once that he had smoked opium and hashish with Andre Gide, and he introduced me to both Janet Kidd and Margaret Campbell, two of the most famous and beautiful socialites in the world, and he told me that I was probably his dearest dinner partner and drinking pal in the declining years of his life in that *genius loci.* of Galilea which Alastair Reid, sometimes poetry editor of *The New Yorker* made famous as the locale of his most popular series of short stories, 'Notes From a Spanish Village.' *Unusual Men*, indeed!

After returning to the United States and settling in to a house next door to Sam Coffing in Coconut Grove, Florida, on the dock-side where several yachts were moored on Biscayne Bay, I accepted an English Composition instructor's post at University of Miami. My weekends were spent in fishing and sailing trips that launched from our back-door and often became virtual bacchanals at the small fishing house clusters called 'Stilts-ville' which were positioned out in the middle of the bay. Charlotte Byng and Muffie Hiss [grand-niece of Alger Hiss - so what?] came to stay with me for a few weeks at a time, but their tastes were too international to abide our slow tropical languor for long. Charlotte had to return to manage the Advertising Film Festival in Cannes, France, and then attend to her art gallery in Venice, Italy. Muffie was engaged in establishing a sculptor's studio and foundry in London which she had named 'Forge Ahead.' She suffered from an eating disorder, bulimia, which Anna Freud had not detected in her previous fifteen years of intensive psycho-analysis. I was irritated that regardless of how delicious – or expensive – some of our meals at Sam's [he had become a virtual *cordon bleu* chef since learning to provide food for his crew on *Nachen II* while crossing the Atlantic in 1966] or in the best restaurants in Coconut Grove or Coral Gables, it would end up filling the bath-tub or spewed all over the bathroom tile floor. Anna Llewellyn passed through town on a weekend in the first leg of her trip round the world. She had at last been able to retrieve one of her mother's be-jeweled necklaces from Princess Margaret and had sold it immediately to finance her lengthy global journey..

Even Del Negro arrived at one point, begging to stay over for a couple of weeks to prepare himself for the starring role in Werner Herzog's film, 'Fitzcarraldo,' to be shot in Peru, where Claus Kinski became so deranged that the Indians almost mutinied, and it was rumored that Herzog tried to bribe some of them to murder his fickle star, Kinski. Mick Jagger was also to have a significant acting role in the production, but he fled before any footage was expended in his behalf. Del Negro was fired at about the same time as Jagger left, and yet he had already endured another South American cinematic saga by Herzog, 'Aguirre, Wrath of God,' in which he had co-starred with Kinski, virtually upstaging that actor in his role as the mad monk whose written transcription of the ill-fated Amazon river adventure was the basis of the screenplay, a turbulent, chaotic maelstrom which seemed to be the only kind of subject that appealed to Herzog and Kinski. Natasha Kinski shared the *prima-donna* personality with her father.

Whenever in the company of Del Negro, I was, myself, often within inches of disaster, primarily because he would tease me into situations that were fraught with danger. Once, when at a local (Coconut Grove) drinks party, he lured me into a bedroom scene with a woman who told him she was sure that we both were movie stars, and I then began to make love to her as soon as Del left us alone. It was only moments thereafter that her husband began banging his fists on the door which I had closed and dragged a bed in front of, and as she screamed into my ear that he was an FBI Special Agent who had sworn to shoot and kill the next man he ever found her having sex with, I dived through an open window and was performing a modified *paratrooper roll* through the low shrubbery as he broke in to the room and opened fire out that window, the .45 hollow-point slugs slamming into one of the trees just above my head. I knew the neighborhood well enough to creep my way back to my house on the bay, and Del arrived shortly thereafter and told me that the man's friends had subsequently restrained him and convinced him to take his wife home and to try to forgive her this *slip* occasioned by her drinking excessive amounts of alcohol following her last unsuccessful try with the Alcoholics Anonymous program. The next day, Del and I listened to the answer-machine recording of a gruff male voice telling me that he was "Gonna choke your chicken," which we could only interpret as a sort of threat of his intention to render [with his bare hands] my penis, inactive, or at the very least, unattractive. Del protested that he had not set me up to seduce the wife, but it was always in his company that I engaged with unsavory women. It was his conversation with a woman on the beach that involved me with one of them, Beverly Walker, former lover of Clint Eastwood, and Publicity Manager for a film being shot in Miami starring Paul Newman. She had worked with Werner Herzog and had become a close friend of Claus Kinski on a film ('Nosferatu') the two had completed in Poland a few years before. She convinced me that I was wasting my time as an English instructor at University of Miami, that I would be able to sell both my 'Beowulf' treatment and my screenplay, 'Ms. Machine-gun Kelly,' by simply accompanying her back to Hollywood.

We became passionate lovers in the meantime, and so I decided to make the move. I stayed with her for only a week after arriving in California, finding her ideas about co-habitation to be on the order of the regimen in a Hitler Jungend training camp. I later learned from Paul Schrader, whose film idea for 'Taxi Driver' derived from living for several weeks in his automobile on Sunset Strip after also being tossed out of Beverly's apartment, that many other writers had arrived in Tinsel Town in similar relationships with Beverly Walker. He had also been an English Composition instructor, and had sold the screenplay, 'Blue Collar,' the only slightly edited writing assignment of one of his students in a class Schrader taught at UCLA night-school. I was always careful to copyright my writing, but I was not able to sell anything until the ABC mini-series offer on 'Beowulf' in 1983, which I turned down. Gray Frederickson, who had just left as director for 'Miramar' film studios and had set Francis Coppola up at Omni Zoetrope, asked my advice about a film titled 'Onan, the Barbarian' that his pal, John Milius, wanted to produce, starring the muscle-man, Arnold Scwhartzennegger, whose only prior film had been 'Pumping Iron,' produced, in part, by another pal from Deya, Mallorca, David Gamble.

Gray had never been any sort of intellectual at Casady School, nor had Jay Bernstein, who also went to Hollywood where both men became enormously successful in the film industry, or as Gray succinctly put it, the world of "make believe." Jay, who had grown up in Crown Heights, on Northwest Fortieth Street, just two doors away from my home, had become agent for Sammy Davis Junior and Farah Fawcett – the female star was a replication of Sandra Smith, the *Tomboy* softball player turned debutante who lived in the house between us, whom Jay had always been infatuated with, but who never paid him the least bit of attention. So, it was as if he created his own substitute feminine idol to anneal that adolescent injury to his pride, in the poster icon star - Farah Fawcett - of 'Charlie's Angels' television series. Jay represented many other mega-stars and then produced a television series of his own based on the Sam Spade character from the *only book*, a detective crime novel, he had ever read at Casady.

Gray was equally dim in terms of literature and asked me what I thought of the comic-strip novel, *Conan*. I told him that it was a piece of jerk-off twawdle for the soft-core pornographic market which also appealed to the body-builders and professional wrestling closet-queens and under-developed teen-aged fantasizers and masturbators who had made a cult piece of 'Pumping Iron,' and that this *beef-cake* muscle-man Schwartzenegger would draw a sizable audience and most likely offset the costs of production, regardless of how weak or moronic the screenplay employed to present this gargantuan hulk, huffing and puffing and stomping across the screen. At that same time, Gray had told me that as the head of 'Miramar,' he could have employed me at $20,000 a week as a script repair-writer, if only I had not been away from America for so long - only fifteen years at that time - and had lost out on what was *current* in our culture. I had responded by saying I had a half-hour to spare and would be grateful for him to catch me up. He replied that this dismissive attitude was what would disqualify me for any such salary. I was still an insouciant snob [although Gray would never have used such a modifier as *insouciant*. Smart Aleck would have been his chosen term]. But John Milius had taken some community college evening courses in literature, and his screenplays had become hit films. 'Dirty Harry' had firmly established him as a money-maker. Gray respected his minimal education, the kind of knowledge that would pay off at the box-office, and so he decided to do the *Conan* film. It was a box-office success! What a catapult to land Arnie in the California governor's office and marry into the Kennedy clan! Am I owed a commission of sorts? Yikes!

Milius also convinced Gray that he should produce the film which Gray came to regard as his most significant achievement in all his years in Hollywood: 'Apocalypse Now.' The snippets of dialogue by Marlon Brando from Jessie L. Weston's, *From Ritual to Romance: An Account of the Holy Grail from Ancient Ritual to Christian Symbol* and T.S. Eliot's poetic works were directly derivative of one of Milius's more memorable night classes in poetry, particularly a study of the mythographic elements in the inspiration for Eliot's epic poem, *The Wasteland*. [Weston's book is shown lying on a table by Brando in one scene, and the title is clearly in focus in print on the spine]. The basic thematic tenor deriving from Conrad's *Heart of Darkness*, from the characterization of Kurtz embodied in the Green Beret renegade colonel portrayed by Brando, and the journey up the Mekong River, was meant to correspond to Conrad's protagonist's journey deep into the Belgian Congo, played as a captain in Special Forces, also a Green Beret, which Martin Sheen enacted, and this was Milius's syncretism of what he had been taught were the quintessential elements comprising twentieth century Realism in literature. Perhaps so. But nobody yet has attempted to artistically sublimate the greatest nineteenth century genocide in that Congo region; one must read *Leopold's Ghost* for a bitter foretaste of what might thereby become a film of that heinous historical HORROR.

'Apocalypse Now' was a courageous attempt to fix some metaphysical meaning to the debacle of the Viet Nam experience. Directed by Francis Coppola, who himself had served in Viet Nam, the cost exceeding sixty million dollars, was the most expensive production in the history of film-making, until the one hundred million also spent by Coppola, on *Godfather Three*, in 1991. I was staying at Gray's house in Beverly Hills a few years after the release of *Apocalypse Now* and had used the downstairs bathroom where I noticed an odd painting on the wall there. It was a tropical scene with the figure of a man wearing a beret, beneath which his eyes glowered at the otherwise pacific milieu surrounding him. When I asked Gray what this could possibly represent, he told me that Milius had given him the picture when he had pitched his idea originally for the Viet Nam film which he had wanted Marlon Brando to star in as Mr. Kurtz in the character of a rogue Green Beret colonel. As Brando was someone whom Gray had used so effectively in his 'Godfather' films, both he and Milius reckoned his portrayal of the demented Special Forces fighter "gone native" would be an Oscar winner. It was only when Brando arrived from his indulgent Tahitian retreat where he had over-indulged in South Pacific *luaus* and weighed in at close to four hundred pounds of elephantine, grotesque obesity, that the genius of Coppola's filmic technique and shadow oblique ocllusionary camera work was called into play to render the star employable in this crucial role.

My own film projects were never to come to fruition with Gray's promotion. Although I told him that my 'Beowulf' was actually the archetypal origin of such comic book representations as a Conan [when John Milius asked Gray to produce the film, 'Conan,' with the body-builder, Schwartzennegger playing the lead, I told him that my pal, David Gamble, from Deya, had produced 'Pumping Iron,' and made a profit, because it appealed to an entire sub-culture of closet queers who loved exhibitions of over-developed masculine forms, he decided to take on the 'Conan' project] he did not really understand what I was talking about. I gave him my 'Beowulf' synopsis and treatment for feature film adaptation, and he had one of the so-called *readers* at Omni Zoetrope Studios look at it and present Coppola with her analysis of it. That particular assistant to the director was so witless as to describe me as a former "navel officer" who had a tale of sea-going adventure with a Viking called Beowulf, missing the entire thrust and thematic import of my writing. I was amazed at being called a *navel officer*. I was told by Gray that this particular *reader* was one of Coppola's favorites because she had once crawled under a conference table while a boring discussion was in session and had given blow-jobs to the director and several of his staff. Gray reckoned that I should be grateful that he had given my project to such a favored one of the boss's minions. Obviously, nothing ever came of any of this.

However, my former girl-friend, Robert Booth, from Fornalutx, Mallorca, whose Vespa had spilled me over the road-side cliff off a rain-slick road so that I had my head re-fabricated in King's College Hospital, Denmark Hill, London, invited me to a photo session at a wedding of a starlet from a television series, and as we chatted at the reception, Roberta told me that another aspiring starlet had told her that the producer of an epic about to be launched, 'Beowulf,' to be produced by a family friend living in the Beverly Hills home of Gray Frederickson, had told her that she had been selected as the royal consort of King Hrothgar, into whose mead-hall the young warrior, Beowulf, is invited to battle the monster Grendel. I was astounded at the accuracy of the casting-call details which this young woman had remembered from what was really no more than a casual remark by me that she would be ideal as the wife of Hrothgar ... if I were ever to be in a position to produce the film of my dreams, 'Beowulf.' How does the rumor-mill whirl in Holly-w*eird*? Yet I was sorry that this young woman should have had such a mistaken illusion, and I told Roberta that I hoped it had done her no harm. She assured me that it had cost her no more than an expensive permanent to model her hair to what she imagined would have been high-fashion coiffure for the late Eighth Century for Northern Denmark, and Roberta said that the appearance might be a definite improvement on the current Gidget surfer androgynous sun-bleached chop so prevalent lately on Sunset

Strip.

That same day, I was chatting idly with a rather dour looking, dumpy fellow who told me his name was Lee Majors, and that he was Fara Fawcett's husband. He told me that he was famous for his role as Bionic Man. I vaguely recalled the television series about a man reconstructed with several components as a high-tech Frankenstein, and as I looked him over again, and assayed him, I said that I could see where every little bit would help, and that he probably needed all the bionic replacements he could get to become a complete man. This was not particularly appreciated as a witty remark. It was not meant to be, and he moved out of range of my banter as quickly as he could. Roberta told me that I would not last long in Hollywood with such an attitude, but that she loved my candor and ascerbidity.

Fortunately, before I had to stand any longer in the California unemployment lines, as I did need to find some work to pay for food and rent, my former professor from UCSD, David Crowne, told me about the U.S. Navy P.A.C.E. college programs-afloat and I was accepted to teach English Composition and Public Speaking on the *USS Coral Sea*, an aircraft carrier sailing from San Francisco to Singapore for the equivalent of a two-month college term. I was berthed in a compartment with a lieutenant in E.O.D. (Explosive Ordnance Disposal), an expert swimmer with U.D.T. (Underwater Demolition Team) training, whose job was to disarm and deactivate any bombs or missiles attached to fighter aircraft we might lose overboard during combat operations while cruising across the Pacific. Our mission was to perform combat readiness exercises, wenty-four hours a day. We were to launch and retrieve combat jet aircraft round the clock as we crossed the ocean. The Russians, who were still considered our enemy in that epoch, would be conducting war-game operations much of the time that we were active, and so we were to be engaged in a mock conflict for a majority of our days and nights. My classes met in the forecastle just below the bow of the ship where the catapult crashed against its final blocks and the jets would cut in their after-burners for maximum thrust as they left that final portion of the deck over the sea to leap onto their trajectory of flight away from "mother ship." The entire classroom shook as the walls [bulkheads] reverberated in resonance to this incident every few minutes as an airplane was hurled into the air. My students had to plan their speeches to allow for silent hiatus as we heard the catapult beginning its wind-up run down the flight deck above us. My writing classes were apparently unperturbed by the continual thunder-claps. Some of my classes had to be re-scheduled at odd hours, such at 2 or 3 in the morning to accommodate special war-game surprises in calls to battle-stations. My own assigned General Quarters station was in the Training Officer's office on the 03 level above the hanger deck, but just below the flight deck.

There was a "dirty shirt" wardroom mess [dining room] for pilots and their navigators dressed in flight suits, and a formal wardroom dining area for officers not on deck assisting flights or in the aircraft themselves, and as my rank was equal to that of a lieutenant commander, and my duties were considered extraordinary, I could dine in either space, or in any of the galleys serving the enlisted men or chief petty officers elsewhere. I was accepted readily by all as an old Navy hand, more than ready to share my former active duty experience whenever able to offer it, eager to become part of the dynamic of this exciting tour at sea. A few days were spent as a port "liberty" call for the crew in Hawaii, where I met and became amorously involved with a Jungian psychotherapist named Janet Andrews, a woman who had been referred to me by friends of mine in San Diego; we agreed to meet at the Raffles Hotel in Singapore at the end of my cruise. We had agreed on "love at first sight" - neither of us had cared to weigh the implications of such a hasty decision, juices flowing freely and indiscreetly. As my ship pulled out of Pearl

Harbor, I believed that at last I had met someone worthy of me, and that we would have a relationship which would last. I knew very little about Janet, except that she was recently widowed in a SCUBA diving accident in which she stated that it was possible that she might have saved her husband's life, but was not well enough trained to help him when his re-breathing gear became jammed when they were at a critical depth. Her childhood had been one of social and developmental repression by a Fundamentalist Christian sect her parents belonged to. She had not been allowed to watch television, listen to the radio, nor was she allowed to go to movies, and dating was forbidden; even newspapers were not received in her household. So when she left home and attended college in California, it was as if she were reborn, and predictably, her libido and imagination ran riot for awhile, and she experienced not only a couple of abortions, two failed marriages, but even sessions in a venereal disease clinic in the Bay area. This was a set of experiences that I could relate to, and we had a hilarious time comparing "social disease" vignettes. It was gratifying to meet someone of the opposite sex who was so "laid back,' so sophisticated, especially so that I could tell my anecdote about being interviewed by one of the doctors in the Mission venereal clinic who suspected me of being a stock-boy working at Sears who had somehow seduced almost their entire female staff and thereby had spread a virtually incurable variety of sub-clinical gonorrhea to a major portion of the younger workers around the Market Street area of San Francisco. The *sub-clinical* signature of this form of "the clap" was what had caused it to spread like wild-fire; it often only showed up as the usual blockage of the urethra after about two weeks ... not in the normal time for incubation and painful urination after only forty-eight hours, or barely two days. Since my own variety had taken almost a week to become full-blown in the Petree dish, I was suspected of being the carrier, that infamous, but theretofore *masked bandit,* Sears stock-boy. I was able to escape the noose because I could prove with a canceled airplane ticket from Florida and some other evidence to certify that I had arrived in the city only a few days before this visit to the clinic.

Although I felt completely relaxed with Janet, I did not however, tell her of another time, a few years before, when I had been involved with Patty Ward, a transplanted Oklahoma girl, whose body was a wonder of perfect corn-fed proportion, whose long blond hair fell well before her divine, apple-shaped buttocks, who had been working as a massage therapist in downtown San Francisco and lived in a hippie commune in Haight Ashbury. I had been staying in that neighborhood on Downey Street in Michael McClure's house when I met her and was immediately sexually bonded and would have remained so except that I contracted venereal warts as well as herpes simplex genitalis from her and had no choice but to cease enfolding my penis in her pestilential vaginal tract. I found an aged medical practitioner to treat me who described himself as a syphlologist, and it was he who burned away every one of the multitude of warts lining the entire length of my penile shaft and told me that I had arrested the disease just in time, for if it had entered my urethra, the only remedy was a penectomy - surgical removal of the entire penis, so that urine could pass through that channel to void the kidneys and not develop into potentially fatal renal failure.

After cruising for many weeks, criss-crossing the Pacific, sometimes back-tracking, as we continued playing war-games with the Soviet fighter pilots [our pilots would sometimes hold up center-fold nude photos in their cockpits from *Playboy* and *Penthouse* for the passing Russian pilots to ogle, as their government forbade such salacious publications, and it was a good-natured and comradely gesture for our fellows in Yankee defiance of the strict Puritanical regime of the USSR. I was always amused at the adolescent attitude of our jet-jockeys, but was reminded that the personality type attracted to carrier landings and close-in combat flying, and dog-fights, was one which could not think in classic middle-minded suburban conservative ideational processes. These were the types who rode "chopper" style motorcycles and had re-designed their automobiles to become drag-racers. When the epic World War Two film, 'Tora, Tora, Tora,' was played in the officers' wardroom mess, it was received with raucous applause for the enemies' (Japanese) devastating blows to American forces at Pearl Harbor - fighter pilots, regardless of nationality, relate to each other on a warrior-soul level. The urinals in the head (toilet) adjoining that dining area compartment had red concentric circles as targets in the porcelain receptacles. Even jet-jockey urination was considered as a symbolic enactment of assault with weaponry.

We had just crossed the International Date Line at Bora Bora, and then had turned around and headed back East, as one evening I was walking forward to my class in the ship's bow from Officers' country, aft of the hanger deck, when the announcement was made following a trill of the boatswain's pipe over the 1MC (loud-hailer system throughout the ship) that as we were now back on the other side of the International Date Line, that it was *once again yesterday*, and that as soon as we turned around and headed far enough West for it to be *tomorrow again ... today ...* that we would be so informed. So I turned on my heel, and went back aft to bed down till it became tomorrow again, *that day.*

So, when we arrived in Subic Bay, in the Philippine Islands, and I went down the brow (Navy term for the gang-plank from ship to dock) to discover the delights of Olongapo City, I was ready for a few chilled beers, and although I had professed to be deeply in love with Janet, I was ready to taste the delights of the the sensual angelic beings that this tropical Archipelago has provided for sailors throughout history. I negotiated with a mature woman whose breasts hung lower than most of the nubile younger creatures who solicited my attentions, and for only a five dollar fee, we adjourned to a room behind one of the street bars, and I coupled with her on a narrow cot which appeared to have remarkably clean, starched sheets – a rare offering - in such bed-linen - for the so-called "hot-pillow" trade. I liked her so much that I invited her to join me for dinner afterward, and she agreed to the request without demanding pay for her usual hourly rate of personal attention. We could talk in a moderately fluent manner, and I learned from her that she had once studied English in order to teach school and had only entered her current profession to support a child she had borne out of wedlock, who now was completing high-school in a town some miles north of here. We made a date for lunch the following afternoon, and afterward went to a small studio apartment she rented on one of the back streets which all Navy personnel had been warned to avoid traversing as the local gangs preyed on servicemen who got drunk and wandered down these treacherous byways in error. I was made to feel secure in her presence, as I could see her nod to several of her neighbors to assure them that I was not some drunk *john*, but on the contrary, a friend. We made love that evening, and I stayed the night. As we talked and she told me more about her country, I became intrigued with traveling north, to a place called Baguio, where there was a U.S. Air Force base, Clark Field, and I had been told on the ship that the officers' club provided luxurious houses for people of my rank (lieutenant commander). After taking brunch together the next morning, I bought a ticket on the Baguio bus and after a journey of over six hours, I arrived in early evening, took a taxi to Clark, and before the sun had finally gone down behind a huge pine forest, I had moved into a sprawling two-bedroom house with a view of the golf course from my large picture glass window. I lazed about my first morning at the resort housing and after a walk thorough the touristic offering of the town and a brief visit to the Igorote Tribe (the reservation for these original *aboriginal* inhabitants of the Philippine Islands, as much displaced in their own land as the Hairy Ainu of Japan in their islands), I indulged in a huge Texas steak dinner at one of the restaurants catering to the appetites of American servicemen homesick for those sumptuous meals.

Strolling the twilight street afterward, I was approached by a man who told me he could take me in his taxi to meet the most beautiful women in town. He drove me through the local hills to a club which contained a a restaurant and dance-floor and active bar, with prostitutes well above average in appearance and attire and manner to those I had first encountered in Olongapo City. The establishment was a cross between an old time road-house and a modern city's country club, with bedrooms upstairs and cabanas strewn throughout the ample gardens for private dalliance with the ladies. I had begun speaking with a refined woman in her mid-twenties named Victoria who told me she was Chinese and Filipina, and she almost immediately informed me that this was not her usual line of work and that she would appreciate it if I were to rescue her, to take her away from this place, to escape the clutches of her *Mama-san* [Asian *patois* for a brothel's proprietary Madam] and the pimp who was keeping her here against her will. The taxi-driver who had brought me here was having a drink with some of his cronies at the bar, having been tipped by the management for bringing me, a new client to the *bordello*, and I told him what Victoria had just revealed to me. He would not discuss the matter in the hearing of anyone inside, so we walked outdoors, and he told me that he would be willing to contrive and execute an escape and a run-away, back to my quarters at Clark, where, once inside that virtual military fortress, I would be safe from any pursuit by gangsters who operated this particular enterprise, which he told me that he himself was willing to sabotage, as so often he had heard of other women held here against their will, and he had decided that he was no longer willing to work with these criminals. He was ready to help me save this *damsel-in-distress*, and was willing to take the necessary risks to enact the rescue and indulge in such an adventure. One of the most prudent strategies was for him to ask a male member of staff, a well-dressed, but burly body-guard of the Madame who owned the establishment what the "bar-fine" (the term used to pay for the sexual services when the lady-of -the night was absented to deliver her delights) might be in the case of our Victoria. When it was determined that her price for an outside over-night tour was the Philippine Peso equivalent of forty dollars, I told my taxi driver to give our accomplice a hundred dollar bill, and to not only make sure that the bar-fine was rung up with the cashier in the central office for the next two nights, but for him to arrange for Victoria's bag to be packed and for her to be escorted to the large picture-window overlooking the back garden, and to open it to allow her to climb out into one of the shrubs where I would await her for delivery to the taxi stationed, in waiting for our getaway, on a pathway by that garden.

All of this maneuver was accomplished with alacrity and smooth rhythm, and my driver drove me back down the hills and delivered us to the gate of Clark Air Foce Base where I paid him a hundred and another fifty as a tip [I had not used money for several weeks at sea and was lavish to the point of profligacy, in all my monetary transactions, spending like the proverbial *drunken sailor*]. The next few days with Victoria were calm to the point of numbing hum-drum – no matter how perfect or supple a female body, or willing, its owner to please, sexual arousal for me lasts only a finite matter of time, and so, after merely two days, I decided to take her to re-unite with her family in Manila, and that was a revelation in socio-economic deprivation and hardship I have rarely ever encountered again, except in the back streets of Delhi, India, or Kathmandu, Nepal, or Adana, Turkey.

Victoria was proud of her mother, a self-contained, tough creature of indeterminate age who claimed to be Chinese, but was acting the role a parent to at least four small Philippine children, orphans whom she had collected and protected in this tiny hovel of a single card-board and ply-wood hut of ten feet by ten feet, with communal access to a local water spigot which stood beside a shallow runnel of sewage forming the pathway separating a long column of other lean-to shelters comprising several hundred similar huts in the most poverty-stricken section of this part of Manila that most foreigners would never have believed existed and might not have survived penetrating and exploring as I did. For some reason, I was not afraid, and I was intrigued by the courageous survivalist fiber of Victoria's mother. After deciding to take them all on a recreational *outing* - out of this grim environment - I guided the entire *family* assemblage back through the labyrinthine circuit which had led me in, hailed a taxi, and crammed them in to drive to one of the main streets of the city so that we could all have a meal together at a restaurant. They had never been in such a place. The waiters appeared, at first, to be shocked by this motley crew and then in the wonderful fun-loving manner of most people of these islands, they accepted my proposal and seated us at a large round table where I ordered meals that could be served to each without the challenge or embarrassment of bothering with menus. Two of the children wiped their forks and spoons on the napkins, a habit learned from many other meals in their living conditions, when that sanitary measure was an absolute necessity.

After our *feast*, I then suggested what became a delight beyond measure. I carefully divided wads of the Philippine currency of Pesos among all our group and had us directed to the nearest department store where everyone was encouraged to buy whatever was possible with each gift packet of money I had divided up between them . It was a Christmas and Birthday and Saints' Day celebration for each person, which had probably never happened before, and might not ever occur again in any foreseeable future. For this reason, it was a pleasure for me, beyond any experience I have ever been privileged to bestow. After returning the children and their "mother" to the entry to their neighborhood, Victoria and I proceeded to the luxury of a down-town hotel which seemed - after the slums of her family - to be something closer to heaven than we at first were able to embrace without feeling guilty for our splendiferous accommodation. She told me that she loved me and that I was an angel for her family and that they all wanted me to return to live with them forever. What a thought? I must admit that I have often considered going back to live in that country, and every time I have visited, I have had the great fortune to encounter a passionate and lovely female like Victoria. They all seem to look alike, and in my photo collection I have to severely focus my attention to remember which one was named what: Victoria, Vanessa, Teresa, Cecilia – all such mellifluous feminine sounds; and what lingering dreams of solace and solicitude and sweetness. In my waning years, I wend my way to those Philippine Islands, and Bali, and Thailand, and Laos. Having taken the "Vow of Refuge" in Buddhism and being a member of that faith for over a quarter of a century now, I even more appreciate that gentle, compassionate *soul-set that* I first encountered with these children of the Orient.

I bade good-bye to Victoria in a bus station, and I regard the farewells one flings from the seat of this mode of transport as it pulls out onto a road to then roar off over the road, to be the most romantically satisfactory method of leave-taking I know. The ceremony of twisting withies with Anna Mahler on her back street in Belgravia, honoring a Li Po poem which had so influenced her father's [Gustav Mahler] last symphonies, is probably the most exquisitely poignant ceremony for farewell, otherwise. My last night in Olongapo, back on the dockside, only about one hundred feet away from the mooring of the *U.S.S. Coral Sea,* I spent drinking till almost passed out, paying a prostitute I went to bed with, to wake me the next morning when the ship was to get underway. The girl slipped away in the night, and I overslept and *missed ship's movement* [had I been on active duty as an actual member of the U.S. Navy, this would have constituted an infraction of the Uniform Code of Military Justice and would have constituted grounds for punishment by court-martial]. I felt panic-stricken and rushed out into the garbage-strewn streets of the neighborhood, through a deluge of rain, several city blocks to the Officers' Club on the Subic Bay Naval Base, and when I told my sad story in the bar there [it was 9 A.M. and only one drinker was present – a helicopter pilot who had seen action in Viet Nam, so he explained as his reason for early morning drinking, he offered me a ride in his helicopter to dash across the sea to my ship. My half-drunk Viet Nam veteran pilot drove us through hail and gusts of wind which I later discovered were the skirts of a devastating monsoon, and when we landed on *USS Coral Sea*, we were greeted with a huge fanfare of welcome by the men on deck. All air-craft had been grounded by this storm. I had been presumed lost at sea, as the search which had been conducted for me after I turned up as missing at quarters that morning, had now presumed that I had fallen over-board and drowned. The commanding officer considered punishing me by requesting Chapman College, my employer to dock my salary, but he relented, because I had become something of a heroic figure for the ship's company. Actually, some of the story of my rescue of Victoria from her *bordello* entrapment had leaked out and become a wild tale of me "stealing a hooker from a Filipino Mafia whore-house" with a wild chase by gangsters through the mountains of Baguio. Thus do legends accrue and confabulate. So many incidents in my life have taken on fantasmagoric coloration and exaggeration in the telling and fictionalizing by others. Tra! La!

My welcoming of Janet in Singapore, after leaving Subic Bay, roiling through the South China Sea, coming out of the Luzon Straits, was at the famed 'Raffles Hotel' where I took the 'Somerset Maugham Suite' in the gardens, at an exorbitant price. After leaving the Philippines, my accountant had contacted me while we were still operating under full combat conditions by "Mars Patch" telephone to inform me that I had an oil-well gusher that had just come in from my land near Woodward, Oklahoma, and that I was rich. I only vaguely remembered signing a lease several months before this time, with a drilling company exploring the possibility of oil and gas reserves on this property for which I owned only royalties. So I was really startled to learn that the well which had been dug was bringing in several thousand dollars in revenue every week. When we docked in Singapore, I telephoned Janet and arranged for a flight from Hawaii to join me there, and I then invited as many of my ship-mates as well as the officers from the wardroom and all my students from the P.A.C.E. (Navy Programs Afloat) courses in English and Public Speaking – to be my guests at the longest bar in the world, the home of the original "Singapore Sling" cocktail, at the most exclusive and expensive hotel in the country, 'Raffles.' The bill for that afternoon of hearty imbibing was extraordinary, but so was my tab for several days, with most meals delivered to Janet and me, lounging naked in the king-size bed in satin sheets, out in our garden abode, the 'Maugham Suite.'

Before another week went by, I bought tickets to visit the island of Bali, where Del Negro had built a home after his fiasco with the Werner Herzog film 'Fitzcarraldo.' He was living in a village in Seminyak, where the chief, Agum Boss, had arranged a long term lease with the government enabling him to buy a house which Agum's men constructed of coconut trees and bamboo, with two full bathrooms with toilets and even bidets [Del demanded that this French luxury be included], which my friend was entitled to lease at a nominal rate for a twenty year span. Janet and I were provided a single bedroom dwelling which also had completely modern bathroom and kitchen. Our first morning, we were awakened by a lovely teenage girl, bare from the waist up, wearing the sarong tied at her hip, as did both sexes in this country. Her breasts were as full and luscious as those on a much more mature woman, and her rich black hair hung well below her hips. She brought into our bedroom a huge bouquet of flowers and a large banquet tray of assorted peeled fruits; papaya, mango, cantalope, watermelon, grapes, orange and tangerine sections. The gorgeous young tropical maiden wanted us to know how delighted she and all her people were to welcome us to *Paradise*, for it is the belief of the Balinese that they actually live in *Heaven* and have been selected to reside on this island because they are receiving a reward from the gods for their special worthiness; in a word , they are angelic beings, living in a garden of delights, and are expected to celebrate their state of bliss and be aware that they are truly the elect, the select, the chosen ones; the favorites of all the gods. Rather a reassuring belief system. All that was required to continue in this blessed state and to remain in ecstasy was to maintain an attitude of gratitude, and to give thanks and express appreciation for this divine endowment. To further demonstrate her sincere dedication to her devotion, the girl asked us to sit up in our bed and she crawled in behind us, propped up by our pillows and began to apply her hands to our bare backs administering a massage that caused us to giggle with appreciation, as she covered both of us with stroking and caressing from our necks to the base of our spines and all over the shoulders and upper arms, her long coconut scented hair laving and lashing our skin with an additional sensuous stimulation and soothing embrace.

What a way to start our day! I only barely restrained myself from inviting her to slither between us to complete a more sensual commingling, and Janet and I did discuss the possibility with barely veiled descriptive phrasing before she rose from her ministrations and asked if she could bring us coffee or tea, and we sensuously nodded our heads in reply as she then left the room to go fetch our beverages. Janet and I reached for one another and were about to engage in the sexual coupling we had just then been describing, when the Balinese girl returned with a tray which she knelt to place at our bedside and then turned to leave as it was apparent that we were at the point of joining our bodies in an amorous clinch and would not to be able to converse any longer. Our pots of coffee and tea were no longer piping hot as we finished our mutual orgasm and felt the desire to now fill our upper orifices as well.

After breakfast, we showered together and wrapped our sarongs around our waists and ambled down by the rice paddies toward the beach. Del Negro was sitting by the bamboo bar where the specialty was Magic Mushroom omelet served with rice wine and guava jelly syrup. He was smoking a joint of hashish which he claimed was Black Afghani rolled in Maui Wowie Marijuana leaves. I elected to drink some pineapple juice and nibbled at some French toast smothered in the guava elixir. Janet ordered another coffee, a strong espresso which the barman was especially proud to produce from an Italian machine only very recently imported to the island. The primitive innocence of this Eden was fast being submerged by sophistication, and civilization's tendrils would, within a couple of years, jade, and then obliterate the vitality that we were now imbibing. When I recently visited the island (thirty years later), it was as if I were in a Southern California beach resort stretched out for too many miles over terrain that still held rice paddies, clusters of temples, jumbled statues to every god and goddess ever imagined in any of several cultures, none of them particularly appealing, except as surreal fantasies from some Hollywood drug-wrecked Special Effects design team. The thrill was gone ... and everyone was wearing 'Gap' and 'Ralph Lauren' and 'Calvin Klein' fashions. The sarongs were sold at the beach-wear shops with bikinis and surfer swim trunks, and every man and woman covered the upper torso with some article of clothing. I did spy one or two old men and women off the side-roads in some of the more remote villages, topless in a sarong, but they were old and wrinkled and obviously in some advanced tropical form of 'Alzheimer's,' or they would have noticed that they were *off the page*, marginal beings at best, the original Balinese shadows of my fondest nostalgic memories.

Janet and I somehow found ourselves squabbling. I had become irate at the advances of a drunk Australian man sitting at the round table in a local native restaurant eating Reis-taffel, the smorgasbord feasts that became communal free-for-all's, often in the "frenzied-feeding" assaults by foreign tourists like the Australians, and sadly, many of our drunk American countrymen, as well. Reaching for a morsel of food, this one rude Aussie had grabbed Janet's bare nipple and tweaked it so that she screamed, and I, without any hesitation, grabbed his wrist, twisting him sideways, and smashed his face into the food and the the solid table beneath, dragging him bodily over the side and on to the floor where I stomped his neck and scraped the side of his face raw with my leathery heel. He howled like an injured child and scrambling to his feet, fled the establishment yowling with outrage and pain. Janet was so upset with my behavior that she demanded we leave as well. Our scene in the bedroom was a high-pitched screaming indictment of my savage, militaristic, murderous, borderline psychotic behaviors - rem she was, after all, a trained psychotherapist, and had all the most punitive language skills at her beck and call. I begged off by claiming that my passion for her was verging on the psychopathic and was exacerbated by my intake of the alcohol which had been denied me on the long Pacific crossing on the U.S. Navy cruise; I therefore pledged to cut back to drinking only wine spritzers or watered-down beer in a quantity that would not inebriate me so unduly, and swore that I would never again resort to any physical act against anyone ... unless she should call upon me to do so in her actual self-defense.

Having reluctantly accepted my apology and promise to reform and to severely mend my ways, we decided to join Del in a touristic excursion inland to a remote village where he had been informed there was to be a ceremonial cremation of a village elder whose position was equal to a high chief. In such ceremonies, the mummified body of the deceased was encased in a huge, ornate *papier mache* model of a bull– over ten feet to the tip of the bull's head and at least twelve from his nose to tail - with bright red eyes and golden horns; the elaborate sacred construction of this inflammable sarcophagus having taken several weeks to fabricate. Several villages attended the event, and there was a sort of trance-dancing of all the brightly clad people around the site. The women, as well as the men, wore only the single sarong wrapped around their waists and tied in the so-called *royal* knot on the left hip. We were attired in the same fashion, and I was rather proud of Janet's full breasts, now as tan as her entire upper torso, although I saw several young women with equally appealing bosoms jouncing in the the rhythmic motion of the people chanting and dancing to drums and horns and cymbals orchestrating this funeral festivity in that jungle paradise. I became so enthralled with the event, that as the flames consumed the cardboard beast and the shrouded form of the corpse fell into the burning coals below the belly, I leapt forward to grab a long pole, poking and turning the *remains* with several other men. The smell was not unlike those one encounters at a huge barbecue where several pieces of meat and sausage sputter and crackle in cooking. Some greasy substances did indeed pop out on to my shoulders, upper arms and chest, and when I returned to join my friends, I offered free licks to all of them before Del wiped my upper body down with a wet cloth, telling me that even he was disgusted by my cannibalistic behavior and warned me that Janet was becoming horrified by my demeanor and that he had been entreating her not to abandon me then and there.

It was later in our bedroom that Janet unleashed her full range of emotional reaction. She exclaimed that she was horrified, disgusted, and even with her extensive study and training as a psychologist, she claimed to be dumbfounded that I had reverted to such an animalistic, atavistic, primeval state. She had never encountered such an unpredictable aberrant personality disorder such as mine; not even in the farthest reaches of Kraft-Ebbing could she recall observing anything so perverse as my temperament. That I should have suggested that she lick the still hot, greasy substance that had burst on to my body from the explosive combustion of the incinerating corpse at the funeral ceremony was not only indication of a pathology beyond necrophilia and cannibalism, but so sexually questionable that she could imagine me only capable of achieving orgasm in a mass-burial plot of a sanitarium for the criminally insane and she was convinced that the Marquis de Sade himself would have found cause to avoid my company. In a word, *or several*, delivered with spittle flying from her mouth and veins standing out so prominently in her throat and on her forehead that they bore striking resemblance to varicose veins, Janet appeared to be losing her temper and in the full grip of a mega-tantrum. I made the suggestion that perhaps a fruit drink with rum, a swim in the ocean and a massage on the beach might be appropriate recuperative therapy, and her response was to "fling away with high disdain" as one of the first novelists of the eighteenth century described his female characters's reactions when equally distressed.

On the following day, Janet demanded that we leave the island, to return to Singapore, and to plan our journey northward to Thailand. We stayed again at 'Raffles' and then flew 'Garuda' airline to Kuala Lumpur in Malaysia. While I was out of our hotel in that Malaysian city, investigating some resorts in Phuket, Janet changed her own airplane tickets and fled to the airport. I discovered the betrayal only upon my return to the hotel's Reception where the clerk told me she had done this. I hired a taxi to pursue her and did reach her as she was checking in to the International gate. She was willing to approach the cordoned off access, and spoke over that boundary, to tell me that she was unable to remain with me, that I was an alcoholic and probably would never recover but would damage everyone who might encounter me. I actually wept upon receiving this damning denunciation, suspecting that she was perhaps correct. She finished her *counsel* by stating that as she was a trained Jungian, that her ideal in psychotherapeutic practice, the Swiss doctor, Carl Jung, himself, had declared unequivocally, that there was no cure for any chronic acute alcoholic, that these lost souls should be locked away to prevent their harming others, and that the only remedy for me would be to cease *to be*.

Some prescription? *Cease to be?*

So often when dismissed, or abandoned, or, rejected, by some female companion, I had felt bereft, stricken, confused, bewildered, but never had I felt so deeply hurt and truly punished as by this separation. Perhaps it was that I had granted so much respect to Janet's opinion and judgment because she was a licensed psycho-therapeutic counselor, and held a position of trust in the medical community which was equal to that of some medical doctors. In our society, the role of psychologist had assumed the mantle of authority, usually reserved for medical practitioners, and as if we lived in a Third World village community, her identity would have been equal to the *shaman*, or witch-doctor. Albeit, I had good reason to not be worshipful of any of these offices in the civilized world, and had known some fraudulent members in those hallowed ranks, from General Practitioner, to such specialists as Neurologist to Internist, or Psycho-Therapist to Psychiatrist to Neuro-surgeon. However, Janet's remarks had struck deep in my consciousness. Was I indeed a hopeless alcoholic, the type described by the World Health Organization as "chronic acute alcoholic"? I had heard something about Dr. Carl Jung's reputed opinion that there was no known cure for people afflicted with this disease; but I had also heard his further opinion that in some rare instances there might be a conditional remission of the compulsion to drink if the subject experienced a psychic transformation, but that this was so rare indeed as to be almost impossible.

With this in mind, with this exacerbating and tormenting fear rasping at my tranquility and self-esteem, I bought a ticket to Penang, an island where the mother of one of my favorite Casady students had been born; it was her strict diet and vitamin supplement bombardment, I had credited with much of my recovery from Crippling Rheumatoid Arthritis when I had been told only ten years before in Oklahoma that I was dying of some irreversible liver ailment, and had then been stricken with the concomitant arthritic pains that restricted most of my physical activities for several months. I was imagining that somehow, my visit to the island of her birth might enact a cure to my present soul-wrenching suffering inflicted by Janet. I checked into a hotel, 'The Pines,' supposed to be the best in the capital city of Georgetown, and had just settled in for an afternoon on the veranda, had ordered a rum and fruit juice from the head-waiter dressed in starched white uniform, and then he asked me a question that shocked me.

"Would there be anything else, Mr. Crow?"

I recalled in a flash that the name Paul Arnaboldi had used in all his criminal maneuvers throughout Asia had been "Crow." In the European arena, as well, the name, Crow, was synonymous with this anonymous master-mind of what later came to be known as 'Operation Julie,' so named for the Scotland Yard under-cover agent who infiltrated the organization whose manufacture and distribution of the illegal drug called L.S.D., Paul Arnaboldi's cabal, the gang who all were sentenced to the maximum prison terms of confinement [life] when prosecuted in the United Kingdom – except for Paul, who escaped and even today lives luxuriously off his profits in Mexico, Rio de Janeiro, San Francisco and even holds title to, and sometimes resides in, a castle in Spain.

I also recalled that Arnaboldi was wanted in several of the locales in Southeast Asia for offenses that carried the death penalty, whether or not his activities had been involved with capital offenses as we know them in the West, or not, the penalties were severe. In Thailand and several other countries, death was the swift retribution for dealing drugs. China had long ago rid itself of a massive population of opium addicts simply by decapitating them. Regardless of any academic survey of Oriental Penology, the fact remained, for this particular moment, that I had been recognized as "Crow," a fugitive from the law, and the burden of proof more likely than not, would be on my head to disprove this identity mistake. Without finishing my drink, I left a substantial amount from the local currency – the tip being thus, 200% – thereby warping whatever legend was attached to "Crow," who actually was the meanest skin-flint I have ever known, notwithstanding the millions he reaped in profits from his international sales of L.S.D. I packed so rapidly that I forgot to check the bathroom and therefore left behind my favorite shampoo, but better a disheveled hairdo than no head at all, I thought, when I arrived at my next hotel in Bangkok, grabbing the first flight available out of Penang's airport.

I felt relatively safe arriving in this enormous metropolis, and stayed at 'Hotel Nana,' on Nana Square, off Sukumvit Boulevard, in an area famous for the loveliest and most readily available prostitutes in the world. I had complimentary shampoo as well as two different soaps for face or body, and after a deep massage, delivered in my room by a gorgeous lady I paid extra to deliver this service with herself naked, and to finish by covering her entire body with oil and using that for the finale known as the "Happy Ending," my ejaculation lasting so long I thought I might lose consciousness, I was ready to go out on the town and indulge in the many other fleshly delights of this Siamese center of sybaritic sensuality. *What Next: what next*, the title of the first publication of the collection of my poetry sprang to my lips, and rather than indulge in the ample offerings of Nana Square, just across from the hotel, which contained a variety of girlie bars where the available women for hire paraded virtually naked, string-bottomed, and topless, gyrating on poles on small stages, or simply performing sexually explicit calisthenics on the bars, approaching so close to the customers that "lap-dancing" would seem Puritanical in comparison; instead, I told the taxi driver to take me to 'Soi Cowboy,' the most notorious red-light district in town, originally established by an American serviceman who had arrived on R. and R. (Rest and Rehabilitation) from Viet Nam, and after leaving the Armed Forces, retired here as a millionaire, a grandiose pimp with all the rewards of a royal emperor.

The hottest bar on this strip drew me in like a Krypton magnet and as I found myself a small table in the farthest corner away from the entrance, I was swamped with luscious young maidens begging me to pay their "bar-fine," that fee paid the Mama-san (Madame) for the prostitute to be absent from her primary task of allurement and enchantment, and in many instances, at least in the Philippines, this same amount paid for her sexual performance [a tip was expected the next morning, and often the Filipina received half of the fee from her Mama-san that next day as well] however, so , at least for the achievement of the first ejaculation of her client. Some were so bold as to caress my crotch and whisper sibilantly in my ear, others offered to perform *fellatio* at that very table and they knelt down to grapple at my flies making lubricious smackings of their lips to further entice. I had just experienced a full ejaculation before my arrival here, and my body had been lavishly caressed in my room at the hotel, so I requested that I be provided a sort of chaperone to shoo away any bothersome sexual invitations and innuendos while I concentrated on merely observing the ambiance, and perhaps finding some inspiration for writing a poem. Yes, I actually reckoned that something like what I had experienced all those years before at the 'Cerveceria Alemania' in Madrid might inspire that sort of scribbling that had become one of my most satisfying personal achievements in poetry.

"Bring me the biggest whore in Bangkok, and I'll use her as my body-guard ... and *amanuensis*," I instructed the Mama-san whose name was Yoko.

She nodded compliantly as if she understood not only the words *body-guard* but *amanuensis*, as well. Perhaps she did. There might be other aspiring poets in her clientele. Bangkok attracts all sorts.

What arrived, in only a matter of a quarter hour or so, was a huge hulk in a a large silk kimono, or *inverted pup-tent*, who spoke in passable English and appeared grateful in the extreme for this employment. Her face was like a doll's with a mouth that could best be described as cupidic. However, the rest of her features were foreboding in their gargantuan dimensions. She was six and a half feet tall, and must have weighed one hundred and fifty kilos, or well over three hundred pounds. She might have had a promising future as a Sumo Wrestler if such an occupation were to open for women. I shuddered to imagine her mud-wrestling in some Hillbilly beer hall competitions in the Deep South of my country. Perhaps I should become her impresario, and we could amass wealth and fame in that milieu. I was always considering new career opportunities; for the moment, however, I bade her merely stand beside me and provide a protective umbrella so that my Poetic Muses might assemble in our makeshift Bangkok bower and hopefully guide my literary creativity for the next hour or so.

Whatever I wrote that night has disappeared, or perhaps I did nothing more than sketch some images on the bar napkins and then crumpled them and threw them on the floor. In any case, I paid her bar-fine, double the usual fee – she was, after all, double the volume, or more, of any other creature for hire in the house – and on the way back to 'Nana Hotel,' I bought her at least ten dozen bouquets of flowers: from gladiolas to roses to orchids. I had decided to perform a sort of *potlatch* disposal of the rest of my cash, and then I would have only the last of financial reserve to provide payment for my taxi to the airport and my air-plane ticket to Paris, France.

When she entered my bedroom, I could see that she was wondering what sort of perverse deeds I had in mind for her to enact. I avoided imagining what others might have requested of such an overly endowed performer, but I did not really care to know, so I simply told her to disrobe, not to bother with the usual cleansing shower, and just lie down on the bed with her face up, looking at the ceiling. I then undressed, myself, after laying the bouquets of flowers in heaps around the bed. I extracted all the American dollars from my wallet; I had been in the habit of accumulating masses of small bills – ones and fives – which I had used for tips throughout travels from Bali to Singapore and along the Malaysian peninsula.

I sang my yodeling version of Hank Williams' "Lovesick Blues" as I danced around the bed, tossing flowers and dollars on my "beached whale," this South Pacific *floating* object of beauty and delight [she did, indeed, appear to be a *float* from some festive street parade, under the heap of floral blossoms]. She giggled tumultuously as the stems and blossoms and green-backs wafted above and cascaded down on her glistening, suppliant body. I then fell onto my backside in a corner of the room and laughed till my sides ached, and I experienced momentary difficulty in catching my breath. I had once heard that Errol Flynn died in this manner, having a fatal heart attack as he was reacting to a joke he had just heard. What a way to go, I thought ... *and still do.*

I told her to go; and paid her a tip, a couple of twenty dollar bills and a couple of Thai Thousand Baht notes (each worth approximately forty American dollars at that time) from the small reserve of larger denominations I had kept for my final accountings with the hotel, the taxi and airline. I believe I still had one Franklin – a hundred – and some other Jeffersons (twenties). I had a credit card or two to *kite* [used to draw cash from foreign banks, while being actually overextended at one's own home bank in America – some wily stratagems I had learned with paper checks endorsed against those plastic cards, which would send the *paper* flying aloft into the sky, and, then *away*, without any actual financial anchor on the ground – like *kites*, virtually impossible in today's economy with instant internet connections which prove one *instantly* to be insolvent]. These should waft me back to Mallorca where I could be fairly certain of finding residence and sustenance for a minimal fee [this was still in the epoch when one could live well in the Balearics for less than $1,000 per month, and often for less than half that amount].

When I arrived in Paris, I took a train to the village in Provence where I had left my Spanish Seat Berliner, the 600 c.c. indestructible *tanque* (the Spanish had nicknamed this vehicle, *the tank*) which I had transported from Mallorca to England and then had driven from my last residence in London to join Charlotte Byng when she was managing the British Advertising Film Festival in Cannes, on the French Riviera, several months before. I had left it wrapped in a tarpaulin on the vineyard of her close friend, the second son of a baron whose closest friend was Krov Menuhin, son of Yehudi Menuhin, the famed violinist. I had not gotten on well with the British wine producer, but Krov, who had been SCUBA Harassment officer on a SEAL Team One in Coronado Beach, California, was someone I immediately related to, especially as his passion in documentary film-making was derivative of much of my own research in mythography. He had used a musical composition of Debussy as background to a film, 'The Mayan Connection,' a study of the relationship of the flying goddess, Tara, founder of Tibetan Buddhism in Bhutan [because these original monasteries were perched precariously on virtually inaccessible steep, high Himalayan cliffs, it was believed only a flying diety could have planted them there; Tara was believed to have possessed wings; thus the attribution of her endowment of this religion to Bhutan (and ironically, the daredevil, heroic U.S. Army Air Corps unit called 'The Flying Tigers,' derived their name from the garbled mispronunciation of "The Flying Taras," some muddled philologist/etymologist presumed). Krov had compared this legend with that of the one belonging to the Garuda, also a flying female goddess, which became the name of the national airline of Malaysia, and he interwove this with the Quetzalcoatl, plumed serpent/flying dragon of Mexico's Yucatan Penuinsula, which could have sprung from the Mayan *arcana*. Thus, his film's title, 'The Mayan Connection.' I was able to spend an evening with him, discussing what I had observed in my whirlwind sortie up the Malaysian peninsula and while penetrating the more remote regions of the island of Bali where I had actually shared a special, sacredotal meal with an isolated tribe who practiced a subversive form of cannibalism, using the blood of their departed elders to produce a paste used as a garnishment for meals served to a few select *chosen* [perhaps *closet cannibals* such as myself].

Only a few weeks before, how I had been one of these *elect* on this Island of the Gods, as Bali is sometimes called, I can only relate to my having been *selected* in that other village to be one of the few participants in poking the roasting corpse at that ceremonial cremation, the only non-native to be invited, and encouraged, to do so. Why Me? This has been a question I have been asking all my life. It is why I am writing this recollection, this memoir, these 'flamenco fugues.' I had sent a book to Krov from Florida, with extensive studies of the various locations of temples and relics of the Mother Goddess throughout Southern France, and particularly in Provence. This text had been given me by my French student in the English-as-a-Second-Language courses I had taught at University of Miami, and it had proven to be of some substantial historical importance to my friend, Krov, and I was pleased because I had not been able to read the material as it was written in French, and my fluency in that tongue was limited to ordering meals, and very little else. That student had been in love with me, and we had indulged in sexual unions at my house in Coconut Grove on many occasions, even in the week before she was married and went to Haiti on her honeymoon; she telephoned me from the airport as she and her groom boarded the air-plane to tell me that she would love me forever, regardless of wherever she might be ... or with whomever. All the French women I have been *coupled* with have demonstrated the quint-essentials of romantic passion, sometimes in an amusing manner, but always unforgettable in bed. Once when she had arrived for an afternoon tryst and came to my bed and disrobed herself, and then began weeping, I was eager to relieve her suffering and was told that because she was in the midst of her menstrual flow, she believed that she could not satisfy me properly, and so I suggested that we do it "in the French way," presuming that she would understand that this meant to perform *fellatio*. She responded in a manner I shall cherish forever, "Do you mean that you want me to talk dirty?"

Was that not surrealistically analogous to some dialogue from the film, 'A Fish Called Wanda,' with John Cleaves and Jamie Lee Curtis, the female lead always asking the male to speak Italian or French to arouse her in fore-play before sexual intercourse? I made my French student a pot of tea, and some toast and jam, which I served her on my terrace that afternoon, watching the sun slowly sink into Biscay Bay, instead, as my gallant gesture of gentilesse, more appropriate, at that juncture, than any grappling *en camara*, telling her that I had never enjoyed such a rejoinder as that in my entire life, and that the solace I was thereby deriving and savoring was directly from the Courts of Love of her own French medieval female ideal, Eleanor of Aquitaine.

When I recounted that tale with Krov, he said that the woman who gave us that book, obviously was one of the finest disciples of The Mother (Oethra/Oestra), and we laughed heartily and both sent her our blessings from that vineyard in Provence to shores of Haiti, or wherever this blessed damsel might now be. After only one day more, I was able to start my Seat Berliner with no trouble and drove on to Barcelona to take the ferry to Palma, Mallorca.

When I arrived on the island, I found lodging in the spare room of several friends in Fornalutx, Soller, Deia, and by serendipity, discovered that acquaintances whom I had met while living in Galilea [that year I was writing my first novel, *Ghostdance*], Renee and David Hart, wanted to rent their home in the village of Puigpunyent for only $100 per month, as they had relocated on a farm in the center of the island and were focusing all their attention on this new project of establishing themselves there. I decided to contract with the Harts to rent their house. It had a telephone – most rare in that period – was endowed with an upstairs bathroom as well as one, with shower, attached to the garden, and had two large bedrooms and an ample large spare upstairs room I could transform into an office. The location of the village was sufficiently secluded so that few of my former associates from Deya or Soller or even Palma would be tempted to drop in for visits. I had decided that I would attempt to rewrite my screenplay, 'Ms. Machinegun Kelly,' as a novel, in the first person voice, from the point of view of the adolescent Kate, maturing into the gangster's *moll* who actually was the intellect and coach of her bank-robber husband whom she had even taught to handle his famous Thompson .45 caliber weapon, and it was she who engineered the final kidnapping of the rich Oklahoma City oilman Erschel, which eventuated in their capture at the 101 Ranch and subsequent imprisonment for life.

I delighted in the challenge of telling a story through the voice and eyes of a woman of her amazing talent and courage. I had also decided to investigate the charges of Janet that I was a hopelessly acute chronic alcoholic, and so I went to my first Alcoholics Anonymous meeting in Palma, and I have not had a drink of alcohol since. What, at the time seemed almost haphazard in the introduction to this group's ideology, may indeed have been, in the terminology of some members – coincidence, as Providence (God) being anonymous – because I attended my first meeting on a dare. I had already considered the notion of using this means to control my drinking after a dreary Christmas Eve with John Stevens, A.K.A. Captain San Miguel – a phenomenal consumer of the Spanish beer by that brand name – in a restaurant in Puerto Andraitx, where we were the only customers as midnight approached, staring at one another in the murky, sooty mirror behind the bottles in that bar where we sat, keeping the waiter from going home to his family. I had asked John why we were stuck with each other on such a *sacred* night, when others were with loved ones, and he answered, "Because we're both alcoholics, and those who have loved us have been sensible to escape our company ... forever." John had actually held the official title of captain, as an Ocean Yacht Master and qualified yacht delivery skipper with certification from the Royal Yachting Association of England and similar boards of authority in the United States. He had also owned a restaurant where his meals were compared to those of a *cordon bleu* chef, and he had lived on a large estate with a home of several bedrooms to house his wife and several children. When I sat with him on that Christmas Eve, he was virtually homeless, occupying a spare bedroom in the apartment of his mother who had retired on a meager pension. His wife had taken the *finca* (the huge home and its entire farm estate), all the children, and what money was left in the bank, and had remarried.

John mentioned that there was a group of ex-drunks like us, some of whom we both knew from the bar life on the island, who had quit drinking and were, supposedly, enjoying sobriety. 'Alcoholics Anonymous'. I had heard about them all my life. My first girl-friend's father told his daughter that I belonged in this program of rehabilitation when I was dating her at seventeen years of age. He had been a member, but had found a way to go without drink by injecting morphine in a totally addictive manner. Most of those I knew who had joined this recovery program had relapsed and been institutionalized, usually only months before dying from complications resulting from the disease of alcoholism. I could not believe that anyone could quit drinking, and found it even more incredible that there could be any joy in life in total abstinence from alcohol.

"Of course, most of them are devout Christians," he added. "They say they have found a power greater than themselves, and for many of them, the Holy Bible is the key."

"Shit. At this point, I would swear undying allegiance to Beelzebub himself to avoid having to sit with you again in a bar on Christmas Eve and look at your ugly mug in that mirror," I snarled, defiantly [but wondering if this might, indeed, be my only hope].

"That's your own face you're looking at there," he replied, spluttering a guffaw. "And I agree it's an ugly mug. You're looking straight ahead. I'm over here and you can't see my face because of the bottles stacked behind the bar counter."

He was right. I was looking at myself, and the reflection told me that I did not have an appealing image. But I was also right, because I was ready to swear allegiance to any power other than alcohol, Beelzebub, Satan, or perhaps even Billy Graham, if I could be relieved of my overpowering addiction to booze. I reckoned once I was free of that demon, then I could choose a diety for myself, perhaps even *myself* as diety ... or the *inimitable, quintessential* self I was meant to be, before I had begun altering my states of consciousness with chemicals.

When I left John that night, an idea had been planted in my deeper consciousness, and when I swaggered into 'Christian's Bar and Restaurant' in Deya, two weeks later, the next catalytic agent was about to be propelled into my now vulnerable being.

Before I could even order my drink, a muscular blonde, blue-eyed man about my own age positioned himself behind the bar immediately in front of me and swung a baseball bat down on its flat surface with a resounding slam.

"You can just turn around and go back out. I will not serve you here."

"I'm the only person in this bar. You need my business. Give me half a dozen San Miguels," I ordered. "And if you hit me in the mouth with that bat, I'll spit toothpicks back in your face. So set em up, *Wolfgang*."

The line about being hit in the mouth with a baseball bat and spitting back toothpicks, I had heard from some Hell's Angels in California. I called the hostile barman Wolfgang, because it was one of my favorite names for German males who "get in your face," as they also say in California. Somewhere else, perhaps in England, I had heard the expression, "Germans are either at your throat, or at your knees." It took merely some return confrontational tactics to drop them down to the submissive stance after they played the initial aggressive gambit.

But this one was an enigma. He did roll the bat away, down to the end of the bar, and what he then told me was to change my life.

"I know who you are. You are me only a few years ago. When I was drinking I was like walking vomit. Everyone avoided me. I was sickening. And everywhere I went, others were made sick because of me. I am an alcoholic, but I do not drink now. It helps me to remember just how much of a disease I was when I look at you. So have all you want to drink here in my bar tonight. Free. You do not pay now. But you come with me to the Alcoholics Anonymous meeting day after tomorrow in Palma. That is how you pay. But maybe you do not have the balls to go there. If not, goo now. Leave my bar. And no drinks here. But, if you are such a brave man, drink up. No charge. And here is the address. That is my challenge to you."

Whoof! He wrote out an address for the Anglican Church in Terreno. I knew where it was. I had attended funerals there for my deceased drinking pals from 'Mam's Bar'. What did I have to lose? Free drinks? I could put back many more than the six beers I had first ordered. Might as well mix some tequila and rum in for chasers, and I had an ample stock of all varieties back at the place I had rented from the Harts in Puigpunyent. So I drank myself into an operative inebriation and then tooled back to my new village when he closed the bar at about 2 A.M. He did remind me that we would meet in Terreno. I told him I would change his *Temperance Club* forever, and then he might be able to drink again without any problems. I decided I rather liked the snotty little Hitler Jugend, although he had not dropped to his knees. But he had provided all I could drink ... for FREE! Or was it?

Although I drank just as heavily the next day and night, I decided that on the following morning, and during the day of that scheduled meeting at the church, I would not drink. I had enough alcohol in me to provide a stabilizing buzz all through the day, and was just beginning to feel the first jagged edges of a fierce hang-over, something Richard Brautigan had named the "Whips and the Jingles." I felt that just such an *edge* could endow a feriocity not otherwise available to me when I decided to go into oppositional hostile attack mode. Thus was I preparing myself to wreak havoc. After I parked on the curb by the Anglican Church, I met an American sitting on the front steps there. He told me he was a sailor whose ship, an aircraft carrier, was moored on a buoy in the harbor, and we discussed "bird-farms," and the U.S. Navy, till he said he had to go inside to the A.A. Meeting. I said I might as well join him, and we walked down the stairs into a room where my life was about to change forever.

I did not stop at 'Mam's Bar' on my way home, although it was just down the street, and when I reached home, I pulled a large (liter) bottle of beer from the refrigerator and telephoned a man who had given me his number because I remembered him from 'Mam's' and several other places I had drunk for the past few years on the island. He told me he did know me and asked why I called. I told him I wanted to drink a toast to him, my first of the day, and I poured the bottle into a large glass on the shelf by the phone. He said he would not talk to me if I were drinking. He asked if I could go to bed and sleep without a drink. Did I need to anesthetize myself in order to sleep?

I was rather offended. I told him I could surely get to bed without using booze. I did not have to drink all the time. I had not had a drink all day, and I almost blasted him with rebuke for insinuating that I might be an alcoholic, and could not live without a constant intake of alcohol. It was then he challenged me to try to go to bed without a drink and told me that if I had difficulty doing so, to call him back to chat. I slammed down the phone, offended, enraged ... wondering.

Fifteen minutes later, I called him back, and I asked him to define the condition known as alcoholism. We talked. I then bid him, "Good night".

Every half hour till 4 A.M. I continued to call him back, and I did not drink the beer I had poured upon arriving home, flat now, and no longer appealing, in any fashion .... and I went to bed without a drink and have not felt the desire or need to drink alcohol again since.

The next morning I called him upon awakening, and after walking in my garden where I noticed a lovely white blossom on the tree. I plucked it and placed it in a saucer of water. When I told him about my flower display, he told me that this was the season for the almond blossoms, a tourist attraction on the island like the cherry blossoms in Washington, D.C. I said I had never heard of that in my entire fifteen years in Mallorca, and I was being honest. He told me I would begin to notice all sorts of natural beauty, now that I was sober. Welcome to the world. *I did ... I have ... I am.* And every day, now, I find some new delight which I ignored in all those years of chemical benumbing and blinding to reality.

Art Director: Michael Offenberg

Made in United States
Orlando, FL
07 December 2023